AF712992

ARTIFICIAL INTELLIGENCE AND THE LEGAL PROFESSION

How are new technologies changing the practice of law?

With examples and explanations drawn from the UK, US, Canada, Australia and other common law countries, as well as from China and Europe, this book considers the opportunities and implications for lawyers as artificial intelligence systems become commonplace in legal service delivery. It examines what lawyers do in the practice of law and where AI will impact this work. It also explains the important continuing role of the lawyer in an AI world.

This book is divided into three parts:

Part A provides an accessible explanation of AI, including diagrams, and contrasts this with the role and work of lawyers.

Part B focuses on six different aspects of legal work (litigation, transactional, dispute resolution, regulation and compliance, criminal law, and legal advice and strategy) where AI is making a considerable impact and looks at how this is occurring.

Part C discusses how lawyers and law firms can best utilise the promise of AI, while acknowledging its limitations. It also discusses ethical and regulatory issues, including the lawyer's role in upholding the rule of law.

Artificial Intelligence and the Legal Profession

Michael Legg
and
Felicity Bell

•HART•
OXFORD • LONDON • NEW YORK • NEW DELHI • SYDNEY

HART PUBLISHING

Bloomsbury Publishing Plc

Kemp House, Chawley Park, Cumnor Hill, Oxford, OX2 9PH, UK

1385 Broadway, New York, NY 10018, USA

HART PUBLISHING, the Hart/Stag logo, BLOOMSBURY and the Diana logo are trademarks of Bloomsbury Publishing Plc

First published in Great Britain 2020

Copyright © Michael Legg and Felicity Bell, 2020

Michael Legg and Felicity Bell have asserted their right under the Copyright, Designs and Patents Act 1988 to be identified as Authors of this work.

All rights reserved. No part of this publication may be reproduced or transmitted in any form or by any means, electronic or mechanical, including photocopying, recording, or any information storage or retrieval system, without prior permission in writing from the publishers.

While every care has been taken to ensure the accuracy of this work, no responsibility for loss or damage occasioned to any person acting or refraining from action as a result of any statement in it can be accepted by the authors, editors or publishers.

All UK Government legislation and other public sector information used in the work is Crown Copyright ©. All House of Lords and House of Commons information used in the work is Parliamentary Copyright ©. This information is reused under the terms of the Open Government Licence v3.0 (http://www.nationalarchives.gov.uk/doc/open-government-licence/version/3) except where otherwise stated.

All Eur-lex material used in the work is © European Union, http://eur-lex.europa.eu/, 1998–2020.

A catalogue record for this book is available from the British Library.

Library of Congress Cataloging-in-Publication data

Names: Legg, Michael, author. | Bell, Felicity (Writer of Artificial intelligence), author.

Title: Artificial intelligence and the legal profession / Michael Legg and Felicity Bell.

Description: Oxford, UK ; New York, NY : Hart Publishing, an imprint of Bloomsbury Publishing, 2020. | Includes bibliographical references and index.

Identifiers: LCCN 2020026181 (print) | LCCN 2020026182 (ebook) | ISBN 9781509931811 (hardback) | ISBN 9781509931835 (ePDF) | ISBN 9781509931828 (Epub)

Subjects: LCSH: Artificial intelligence—Law and legislation. | Technology and law. | Practice of law.

Classification: LCC K564.C6 L455 2020 (print) | LCC K564.C6 (ebook) | DDC 340.0285/63—dc23

LC record available at https://lccn.loc.gov/2020026181

LC ebook record available at https://lccn.loc.gov/2020026182

ISBN: HB: 978-1-50993-181-1
ePDF: 978-1-50993-183-5
ePub: 978-1-50993-182-8

Typeset by Compuscript Ltd, Shannon

To find out more about our authors and books visit www.hartpublishing.co.uk. Here you will find extracts, author information, details of forthcoming events and the option to sign up for our newsletters.

Michael dedicates this book to Laetitia, Maxime and Alexandre.

Felicity dedicates this book to Joe and Ash.

PREFACE

Artificial Intelligence has been around for decades with interest waxing and waning. But by 2018 AI was being featured in major newspapers and other media around the world as having the capacity to fundamentally change human existence. Some saw enormous possibility while others worried about what might lie ahead. It was not just computer engineers and scientists who were actively debating a host of issues, but the humanities also took notice and weighed in. Government and not-for-profits started commissioning or producing reports. There was a cacophony of voices. Indeed, like many issues in the age of social media, multiple opinions were voiced, not all of them well informed.

A subset of this debate involved law and lawyers. Traditionally, lawyers are perceived as conservative and at the tail, rather than the forefront, of technology or change. The revamped focus on AI in law was greeted with a mixture of enthusiasm, hesitancy and even disengagement by the legal profession. It was in this atmosphere that we commenced the first of a series of annual research topics – Artificial Intelligence and the Legal Profession.

Two years earlier, in 2016, the Law Society of New South Wales (the professional body for solicitors in the state of New South Wales, Australia) established a Future Committee. This led, in turn, to the Future of Law and Innovation in the Profession (FLIP) Commission of Inquiry, which produced the FLIP Report in March 2017. The Report drew on the testimony of 103 witnesses who gave evidence at the Inquiry, on interviews and submissions, and on the diverse expertise of the Future Committee. The Report recognised the legal profession was undergoing change at a pace never before experienced and in unforeseen ways.

In November 2017 the Law Society entered into a strategic alliance with University of New South Wales (UNSW) Law to generate a stream of research to consider and respond to the issues raised by the FLIP Report. This collaboration established the Law Society of NSW Future of Law and Innovation in the Profession research stream at UNSW Law, or FLIP Stream.

Professor Michael Legg, a member of the Future Committee and participant in the Commission of Inquiry, was appointed as FLIP Stream's Director. The FLIP stream is comprised of the Director, Deputy Director Dr Justine Rogers, a senior lecturer at UNSW Law, and Research Fellow Dr Felicity Bell. UNSW Law students assist as interns and research assistants.

The goal of the research was to inform the profession, focussing on concrete examples of AI in legal practice so as to dispel the idea that all of AI and law was hype or puff. It meant avoiding hysterical headlines. As academics we did not have a legal AI product to sell. Rather our role was to listen, critique and put forward a balanced view as to what AI meant for legal practice.

Further, we wanted to consider the ramifications of AI for lawyers from the perspective of a detailed understanding of what the legal profession is and the diverse roles that lawyers play; in other words, to avoid sweeping generalisations and to try and factor in how AI would operate for different forms of lawyering.

Equally though, while recognising difference, all lawyers are members of a profession and share core understandings as to their role vis-à-vis society, the court system and clients. These ethical/professional requirements struck us as crucial to how lawyers would be impacted by AI. Much of the media commentary we were reading seemed to completely disregard the fact that law remains a profession, treating it solely as a business. Consequently we actively sought to bring ethical requirements to the forefront of the discussion about AI and the legal profession. Perhaps only humans would expect, and could adhere to, the potentially conflicting requirements of a duty to the administration of justice, which is community or public oriented and embodies supporting the rule of law, with a duty to the client which is private and individualistic, not to mention supported by obligations of confidentiality and legal professional privilege. However, adherence comes from the development, through study and experience, of professional skills such as judgement and integrity. Professionalism and ethics differentiate lawyers from business, and if adhered to, demonstrate both why and how lawyers will continue to be needed even with the adoption of AI.

As we put the finishing touches to this book, we are in lockdown. This inconvenience is minor when compared with the pandemic-induced challenges which people all around the world are facing. Yet it puts things in a new light. Technology, in particular communications technology, has been adopted in many jurisdictions as a way to allow courts to continue functioning. However, courts must deliver justice in accordance with the rule of law and its prescriptions have shaped how technology can be used. The COVID-19 experience has shown that courts and lawyers are capable of change, but they also are cognisant of the need to ensure the protection of key values such as procedural fairness. We hope that this experience of learning new skills and overcoming challenges will carry over to the way in which lawyers engage with AI. Lawyers as a whole need to be more receptive to using technology to deliver legal services. AI can promote access to justice and equality before the law. Lawyers also need to guard against core values of lawyering being lost through the adoption of technology. It is not an easy journey to navigate. We hope that this book will be of assistance along the way.

MJL
FB

ACKNOWLEDGEMENTS

The authors would like to thank:

The Law Society of New South Wales and University of New South Wales (UNSW) Law School who collaborated to create the Future of Law and Innovation in the Profession research stream (FLIP Stream), which provided funding to assist in the research that underlies this book.

The many officers and employees of the of the Law Society of New South Wales who had the foresight to address innovation and change, but also to recognise that independent research was required and that University academics who were engaged with the practice of law were ideal candidates to undertake that research. Special thanks go to Michael Tidball, Chief Executive Officer of the Law Society from 2006 to 2020; Gary Ulman, President of the Law Society and Chair of the Future Committee in 2016; 2017 President, Pauline Wright; 2018 President, Doug Humphreys; and 2019 President, Elizabeth Espinosa. All were very supportive of the FLIP stream and its mission.

Professor George Williams, Dean UNSW Law, for his support of the FLIP Stream and its research.

Dr Justine Rogers, Deputy Director of FLIP Stream, who shared her expertise in ethics and professions with the authors.

Nicholas Turner, Senior Software Engineer, Uber (and UNSW Law alumnus), who provided valuable expert comments on the operation of AI.

Anthony Song, UNSW Law student, who interned with the FLIP Stream for Term 2, 2019 and continued on as a research assistant in relation to the book.

Lauren Pavli and Carolyn Fox, for invaluable proof-reading.

Kate Whetter and Rosemarie Mearns at Hart Publishing, Bloomsbury Academic who guided the book through the publication process.

TABLE OF CONTENTS

Preface .... *vii*
Acknowledgements .... *ix*

1. Introduction **1**
Disruption 2
The Advent of AI and Lawyers – Into the Unknown? 5
The Lawyer's Value 8
Overview of Chapters 9

PART I
LAWYERS AND THE EVOLUTION
OF ARTIFICIAL INTELLIGENCE

2. Artificial Intelligence: What It Is and Why It Matters **13**
Introduction 13
History of AI and Law 17
Machine Learning and Natural Language Processing 28
Where Next? 36

3. The Practice of Law – What Do Lawyers Do? **39**
Introduction 39
Who are Lawyers? 43
The Work of Lawyers (What Do Lawyers Do?) 46
Organisational Forms (Where Do Lawyers Work?) 54
How are Lawyers Regulated? 64
Who (or What) Will Lawyers Become? 69

PART II
THE USE OF ARTIFICIAL INTELLIGENCE
IN LEGAL PRACTICE

4. AI and Outcome Prediction **75**
Introduction 75
Application of AI to Legal Outcome Prediction 78
Role of the Lawyer 94
Future Developments 101

5. AI, Pre-Trial Information Gathering (Discovery and Disclosure) and Litigation Lawyers **104**
Introduction 104
Litigation Lawyers – Gathering Information and Evidence 104
Application of AI to Pre-trial Processes 109
Role of the Lawyer 121
Future Developments 127

6. AI, Online Courts and Alternative Dispute Resolution **131**
Introduction 131
Advocates and Dispute Resolution Lawyers 133
Application of AI to Online Courts and ADR 137
Role of the Lawyer after ODR 149
Future Developments 160

7. AI and Transactional Lawyers **165**
Introduction 165
Transactional Law, Contract Commoditisation and Lawyers 166
Application of AI to Transactional Law 172
Role of the Transactional Lawyer 180
Future Developments 189

8. AI and Regulatory Lawyers **191**
Introduction 191
Regulatory Lawyers 192
Application of AI to Regulation 195
Role of the Lawyer in RegTech 210
Future Developments 217

9. AI and Criminal Lawyers **220**
Introduction 220
Criminal Law and Lawyers 221
Application of AI in the Criminal Justice System 226
Role of the Lawyer 237
Future Developments 255

PART III
THE FUTURE OF LAWYERS AND THE LEGAL PROFESSION

10. Limitations of AI **261**
Introduction 261
Data and Design 263
Can Data and Design Problems be Overcome? 271
Cost and Sustainability 281
Not being Human 285
Conclusion 287

11. Legal Ethics, Liability and Regulation in an AI World **289**
Introduction 289
Legal Ethics in an AI World 290
Liability for AI 308
Regulation 311
Legal Practice by Non-Lawyers 320
Conclusion 324

12. Future of the Legal Profession **325**
Introduction 325
Threats and Opportunities in the Use of AI for Lawyers 325
The Expertise Value 327
The Ethics Value 329
The Human Value 333
Education 339
Supporting AI-Enabled Legal Practice 346
Conclusion 348

Index *351*

1

Introduction

Law is one of the learned ancient professions dating back to ancient Greece and Rome. The origins of the legal profession may be linked to Cicero and Quintilian, who were to lay the foundations of legal education and the legal profession.[1] The profession disappeared in the Dark Ages, a period marked by repression and lawlessness, but reappeared in the Middle Ages to assist individuals with the procedures and complexities of a developing justice system.[2] The lawyer has been with us ever since. Yet, throughout history lawyers have been the subject of criticism,[3] often due to cost and delay. Equally, every society which has achieved a stable, organised form of government has had a legal profession.[4] Without law, life is 'nasty, brutish, and short'.[5]

The need for lawyers is manifold. They are essential to social ordering. Lawyers play critical roles in the administration of justice and in the maintenance of a free and democratic society. The lawyer enables the protection of human rights and facilitation of commerce. The lawyer is there for the client in times of trouble: 'Interests of vast magnitude – property, liberty, character, and even life itself – are entrusted to [them]'.[6] Lawyers combine extensive learning with ethical obligation. They strive to protect and advance their clients' interests, while also promoting the rule of law.

In this context of both essential service and critique comes the rise of artificial intelligence, or AI for short. In contrast to lawyers, there is significant praise, or at least expectation, for AI.[7] AI is described as 'the new electricity' because not only

[1] R Pound, 'What is a Profession – The Rise of the Legal Profession in Antiquity' (1944) 19 *Notre Dame Law Review* 203; J Ahern, *An Historical Study of the Professions and Professional Education in the United States* (Dissertation Submitted to the Faculty of the Graduate School of Loyola University in Partial Fulfilment of the Requirements for the Degree of Doctor of Philosophy, 1971) 84–85.

[2] P Brand, 'The Origins of the English Legal Profession' (1987) 5 *Law and History Review* 31; JA Brundage, 'The Medieval Advocate's Profession' (1988) 6 *Law and History Review* 439.

[3] J Rose, 'The Legal Profession in Medieval England: A History of Regulation' (1998) 48 *Syracuse Law Review* 1, 5; J Brundage, 'Vultures, Whores, and Hypocrites: Images of Lawyers in Medieval Literature' (2002) 1 *Roman Legal Tradition* 56.

[4] J Brundage, 'The Ethics of the Legal Profession: Medieval Canonists and Their Clients' (1973) 33 *Jurist* 237, 237.

[5] T Hobbes, *Leviathan* (1651).

[6] O Carter, *Ethics of the Legal Profession* (Northwestern University Press, 1915) 13.

[7] J Anderson and L Rainie, 'Artificial Intelligence and the Future of Humans', Pew Research Centre, 10 August 2018 (reporting on 979 technology pioneers, innovators, developers, business and policy leaders, researchers and activists addressing the question of whether people will be better off than they are today as a result of AI).

will it transform every sector of the economy, it will be an essential input for any activity that wants to remain relevant.[8] Law is seen as being a candidate for an AI transformation. *Forbes* magazine predicts that AI 'will unlock massive opportunities to transform and revitalize the field of law'.[9]

AI and the legal profession represent the intersection of the new and the old. They are depicted as representing a contrast between innovation and progress, others might say hype – with stability and tradition, some may say inertia. However, the new is not necessarily good and the old does not equate with bad. The advent of operational AI represents both a challenge and an opportunity for the legal profession, with the conclusion not yet written.

Disruption

Disruption used to mean an interruption to an event, activity or process. It was frequently annoying or unwelcome. Usually you could ignore it or wait for normal service to be restored. Today disruption refers to the displacement of an existing market, industry or technology with something new and more efficient. It is both destructive and creative. It cannot be ignored and there is no going back to what was 'normal'. Disruption is theorised to begin at the bottom of the legal market, which is under-served, but as AI improves it is adopted in other, more high-value, segments of the market.[10] Consequently, the incumbent must continuously innovate to maintain and protect their position. It has been observed that the incumbent may also be institutions, with the 'justice system … no exception' and disruption through technology altering the practice of law.[11]

AI is enjoying a renaissance due to increased computing power, growth in the availability of data and improvements in algorithms.[12] AI has existed as a concept since the 1950s and the idea that AI could be applied to the law has been explored since the 1980s. However, over the years, progress in the development of AI has been cyclical, and interest in and funding of AI research has fluctuated, with a number of 'AI winters' in which progress stagnated.[13] More recently AI has

[8] A Ng, Keynote Speech, *AI Frontiers Conference – Applied Deep Learning*, Santa Clara Convention Centre, 3 November 2017.

[9] R Toews, 'AI Will Transform the Field of Law', *Forbes*, 19 December 2019.

[10] CM Christensen, *The Innovator's Dilemma: When New Technologies Cause Great Firms to Fail* (Harvard Business School Press, 1997); CM Christensen, M Raynor and R McDonald, 'What Is Disruptive Innovation?' (2015) 93(12) *Harvard Business Review* 46.

[11] The Utah Work Group on Regulatory Reform, 'Narrowing the Access-to-Justice Gap by Reimagining Regulation' (August 2019) 8.

[12] See, eg, J Kaplan, *Artificial Intelligence, What Everyone Needs to Know* (Oxford University Press, 2016); Financial Stability Board, *Artificial Intelligence and Machine Learning in Financial Services* (1 November 2017) 6.

[13] S Russell, *Human Compatible: Artificial Intelligence and the Problem of Control* (Viking, 2019) 5 (at the time of writing, Professor Russell's AI classes at the University of California, Berkeley have over 900 students but in 1990 there were 25 students).

experienced a new spring, with significant leaps forward due to developments such as deep learning.[14] These advances have begun to carry over to the legal profession and legal practice, although mainly through more traditional AI such as expert systems and the recent advances through machine learning.[15]

This revival has heightened expectations as to what AI is capable of achieving and has led to doomsday predictions where humans are redundant and there is mass unemployment.[16] John Maynard Keynes' 'technological unemployment' has been revisited but without Keynes' optimism that society is dealing with 'a temporary phase of maladjustment'.[17] As AI is increasingly used in traditionally white-collar occupations such as law, this fetish for prophesising the end of humanity has also afflicted predictions for the future of the legal profession, with the mass media speculating that lawyers will be replaced by robots.[18]

Around the world the legal profession has started to focus on the forces of 'disruption' and what they mean for lawyers in their various roles; and for the users of law: corporations, government and individuals but especially the disadvantaged. For example, in June 2013 the German Bar Association contracted with consulting firm PROGNOS to produce 'Der Rechtsdienstleistungsmarkt 2030' ('The Legal Services Market 2030'), which outlines how the legal services market is expected to function in 2030.[19] The Canadian Bar Association established a Legal Futures Initiative which reported in August 2014 with the publication *Futures: Transforming the Delivery of Legal Services in Canada*.[20] The Law Society of England and Wales published its *Future of Legal Services Report* in January 2016.[21] The American Bar Association established a Commission on the Future of Legal Services, which reported in August 2016 and has continued providing resources for the profession.[22] In Australia the lead in seeking to understand these

[14] ibid 6.

[15] Types of AI and how they function are dealt with in Chapter 2.

[16] M Ford, *Rise of the Robots: Technology and the Threat of a Jobless Future* (Oneworld, 2015); J Kaplan, *Humans Need Not Apply: A Guide to Wealth and Work in the Age of Artificial Intelligence* (Yale University Press, 2015); D Susskind, *A World Without Work* (Allen Lane, 2020).

[17] J Maynard Keynes, 'Economic Possibilities for our Grandchildren' in J Maynard Keynes, *Essays in Persuasion* (WW Norton & Co, 1930) 358–73. See also R Campa, 'Technological Unemployment. A Brief History of an Idea' (2018) 6 *Orbis Idearum* 57.

[18] See, eg, GE Marchant, 'Artificial Intelligence and the Future of Legal Practice' (2017) 14(1) *ABA SciTech Lawyer* 20, 21, providing the following sample of media headlines: 'Rise of the Robolawyers', 'Here Come the Robot Lawyers', 'Why Hire a Lawyer? Machines are Cheaper', 'Armies of Expensive Lawyers, Replaced by Cheaper Software', 'Law Firm Bosses Envision Watson-Type Computers Replacing Young Lawyers' and 'Why Lawyers and Other Industries Will Become Obsolete. You Should Stop Practicing Law Now and Find Another Profession'.

[19] Deutscher Anwaltverein, *Der Rechtsdienstleistungsmarkt 2030* (PROGNOS, 2013).

[20] CBA Legal Futures Initiative, *Futures: Transforming the Delivery of Legal Services in Canada* (Canadian Bar Association, 2014).

[21] Law Society of England and Wales, *Future of Legal Services Report* (2016).

[22] American Bar Association, Commission on the Future of Legal Services, *Report on the Future of Legal Services in the United States* (2016). Numerous State bar associations in the US have also conducted inquiries and produced reports: www.americanbar.org/groups/bar_services/resources/resourcepages/future/.

developments and formulate responses has been taken by the Law Society of New South Wales and its report *The Future of Law and Innovation in the Profession*.[23] Much of this inquiring about the future is driven by the recognition that technology, particularly AI, is promising not just to automate past approaches but to reformulate how law is practised.

Academic research, as well as the media and various consultant-commentators, have also focussed attention on these changes. A significant literature has developed on the changing legal profession and the impact of the various changes.[24] One leading commentator, Professor Richard Susskind, has made the following predictions:

> Tomorrow's legal world … bears little resemblance to that of the past. Legal institutions and lawyers are at a crossroads, I claim, and will change more radically in less than two decades than they have over the last two centuries.[25]

Further, in relation to AI in particular and the claims of the media about AI and legal practice:

> In my view many of the current claims overstate the likely impact of AI over the next few years. On the other hand, extravagant though they are, I believe they understate the probable influence of technology in the very long term. Our machines and systems are becoming increasingly capable, and, over time, they will take on more and more legal tasks that we have historically regarded as the unique preserve of legal practitioners.[26]

This mirrors statements by Bill Gates[27] and Roy Amara.[28] This is a crucial argument but it cannot be disproved, at least not in the near term. Essentially, it says that if AI has not taken over a legal task it is because we have overstated its capabilities in the short term and not waited long enough for the prediction to come true. Others, though, argue that there has been widespread misreporting of AI's

[23] The Law Society of New South Wales, *The Future of Law and Innovation in the Profession* (2017).

[24] It is not possible to cover this whole literature but see, eg, L Terry, S Mark and T Gordon, 'Trends and Challenges in Lawyer Regulation: The Impact of Globalisation and Technology' (2012) 80 *Fordham Law Review* 2661; B Simpson, 'Algorithm and Advocacy: Does The Legal Profession Have a Future in a Digital World?' (2016) 25(1) *Information and Communications Technology Law* 50; V Waye, ML Verreynne and J Knowler, 'Innovation in the Australian Legal Profession' (2018) 25(2) *International Journal of the Legal Profession* 213; Symposium, 'Artificial Intelligence, Technology, and the Law' (2018) 69 *University of Toronto Law Journal* (Supplemental Issue); Symposium, 'Rise of the Machines: Artificial Intelligence, Robotics, and the Reprogramming of Law' (2019) 88 *Fordham Law Review*; Symposium: 'Lawyering in the Age of Artificial Intelligence' (2019) 72 *Oklahoma Law Review*; M Legg, P Vines and J Chan (eds), *The Impact of Technology and Innovation on the Wellbeing of the Legal Profession* (Intersentia, 2020).

[25] R Susskind, *Tomorrow's Lawyers – An Introduction to Your Future* (2nd edn, Oxford University Press, 2017) xvii.

[26] ibid 185.

[27] B Gates, *The Road Ahead* (Penguin Books, 1996) 316 ('People often overestimate what will happen in the next two years and underestimate what will happen in ten').

[28] S Ratcliffe (ed), *Oxford Essential Quotations* (4th edn, Oxford University Press, 2016) (Roy Amara: 'We tend to overestimate the effect of a technology in the short run and underestimate the effect in the long run' attributed in *The Age*, 31 October 2006).

achievements and what it will achieve in the future.[29] Indeed it has been observed that '[t]he last few years have seen an incredible amount of hype surrounding these technologies in the legal world, and it has become somewhat difficult to separate fact from fiction, and more often than not, heavy-handed marketing'.[30] Consequently, the lawyer must prepare for AI but without knowing when or how it will make a human undertaking that legal task redundant.

The Advent of AI and Lawyers – Into the Unknown?

Technology has augmented human activity for hundreds of years, from the wheel to the steam engine to the computer. Those technological advances changed the roles that humans played and enhanced what they could achieve. Humans needed to learn how to use those technologies, which required reskilling. Some roles disappeared and new roles were created.[31] Historically, in many cultures lawyers were revered for their oral advocacy but the role of the lawyer altered with technology, needing to move from advocacy to embrace the written word as printing became more widespread. Lawyers can, and have, adapted in the past. But there are those who argue that AI is not simply another technological development (like computerised word-processing, or e-conveyancing) which changes the process by which lawyers do their work.[32] Rather, it is claimed, it signifies a more fundamental transformation which will require significant shifts on the part of the profession.[33]

Predicting what will, or will not, be susceptible to automation in the future is risky. Thus, while most elements of what lawyers do are not under precipitate threat of automation by AI, this is unlikely to remain so. Indeed one academic posits that 'There will come a time when these automated systems' superior reliability extends to *all* of the work associated with a particular profession'.[34] Others deny that this will occur and point to the limitations of AI when it comes to many

[29] See, eg, G Marcus, 'An Epidemic of AI Misinformation' *The Gradient*, 30 November 2019; M Grupp, '25 Facts about AI & Law You Always Wanted to Know (But Were Afraid to Ask)', *Medium*, 7 April 2019, www.medium.com/@Grupp/25-facts-about-ai-law-you-always-wanted-to-know-but-were-afraid-to-ask-a43fd9568d6d.

[30] TF Bathurst, Chief Justice's Opening Remarks, *Law Society of New South Wales FLIP Stream Seminar*, Sydney, 10 April 2019, 2.

[31] United Nations Department of Economic and Social Affairs, *The Impact of the Technological Revolution on Labour Markets and Income Distribution* (31 July 2017) www.un.org/development/desa/dpad/wp–content/uploads/sites/45/publication/2017_Aug_Frontier–Issues–1.pdf.

[32] DM Katz, 'Quantitative Legal Prediction – Or – How I Learned to Stop Worrying and Start Preparing for the Data-Driven Future of the Legal Services Industry' (2013) 62(4) *Emory Law Journal* 909, 910–12.

[33] JO McGinnis and RG Pearce, 'The Great Disruption: How Machine Intelligence Will Transform the Role of Lawyers in the Delivery of Legal Services' (2014) 82(6) *Fordham Law Review* 3041.

[34] S Delacroix, 'Drawing a Non-Consequentialist Line: Augmenting v Replacing the Professions with Computer Systems', SSRN, https://ssrn.com/abstract=2840864.

aspects of legal work.[35] Nonetheless, consultants McKinsey project that nearly one-quarter of a lawyer's role could be automated.[36]

Transformation also brings opportunity.[37] One legal academic suggests that we think about 'intelligence augmentation' – 'a symbiotic relationship between humans and technology'.[38] In this prognosis, people continue to work, but 'do so interactively with technology in order to do it better'.[39] Another prediction is that two kinds of lawyers will benefit from the changes wrought by AI: 'superstars', who will become even more well known for their expertise; and those who can adapt to changing circumstances by using technology to work more efficiently and taking advantage of new markets for legal services.[40] Meanwhile Deloitte suggests that there will be a need for 'high-skilled roles' to innovate and manage automated processes but there is no suggestion that these roles will necessarily require lawyers to fill them.[41]

The rosiest views of AI and the legal profession focus on the efficiency which AI can engender if deployed well. Ideally, lawyers will eliminate dull, repetitive and routine tasks and be able to focus almost exclusively on higher-order and more interesting work. As we discuss in Part II of this book, the most developed applications of AI in law are in the 'mechanisation' of routine kinds of work, notably through technology assisted review, due diligence and document automation. At present, lawyers are still needed to supervise and direct these tasks, even if automation is involved,[42] but arguably work can be completed more quickly and at lower cost.

It is argued that automating these tasks will then enable lawyers to focus on 'core activities', such as giving legal advice.[43] Monotonous tasks will be performed by machine.[44] As Frank Pasquale comments, 'Many of the new software-driven

[35] A Sadauskas, 'Allens CIO Bets on Legal Sector AI Boom', itnews, 31 May 2016; A Paliwala, 'Rediscovering Artificial Intelligence and Law: An Inadequate Jurisprudence?' (2016) 30(3) *International Review of Law, Computers & Technology* 107.

[36] McKinsey, www.mckinsey.com/~/media/McKinsey/Global%20Themes/Digital%20Disruption/Harnessing%20automation%20for%20a%20future%20that%20works/MGI-A-future-that-works_Full-report.ashx.

[37] Katz (n 32) 913.

[38] AH Yoon, 'The Post-Modern Lawyer: Technology and the Democratization of Legal Representation' (2016) 66(4) *University of Toronto Law Journal* 456, 466.

[39] ibid 466.

[40] McGinnis and Pearce (n 33) 3042; Susskind (n 25) 133–34.

[41] *Developing Legal Talent: Stepping into the future law firm* (Deloitte, February 2016) 4–5.

[42] D Remus and F Levy, 'Can Robots Be Lawyers: Computers, Lawyers, and the Practice of Law' (2017) 30(3) *Georgetown Journal of Legal Ethics* 501.

[43] OECD Directorate for Financial and Enterprise Affairs Competition Committee, Working Party No 2 on Competition and Regulation, *Protecting and Promoting Competition in Response to 'Disruptive' Innovations in Legal Services* (13 June 2016) [68]; M Chui, J Manyika and M Miremadi, 'Four Fundamentals of Workplace Automation', *McKinsey Quarterly* (November 2015) www.mckinsey.com/Insights/Business_Technology/Four_fundamentals_of_workplace_automation.

[44] S Semmler and Z Rose, 'Artificial Intelligence: Application Today and Implications Tomorrow' (2017–18) 16(1) *Duke Law & Technology Review* 85, 90.

"legal services" take on low-value tasks that were either rarely performed by lawyers or rarely generated much revenue for them (like uncomplicated contract drafting)'.[45] Ideally, this work being done by AI would create a kind of trickle-down effect, where junior lawyers no longer undertake such tasks and are able to do 'higher-level' work earlier in their careers: 'Rather than handling the typical mundane tasks, associates are now supervising the information being fed to the systems, and are often tasked with managing the programming teams'.[46] Expertise can be directed towards work that requires uniquely human and professional skills such as judgement, creativity, empathy and advocacy: 'Lawyers will be increasingly able to engage in the analytical, creative, and strategic parts of legal practice, ie the work of the intellect'.[47]

It is also argued that efficiency gains will enable lawyers to take on more clients and that smaller firms and conglomerations of lawyers at online sites will be able to make use of technology to deliver 'leaner', more competitive services, challenging large firms for certain work.[48] The counter-argument is that large firms are, so far, better placed to acquire and make use of the technology that is currently available. The cost of AI is a substantial barrier. Lawyer respondents to surveys in both the UK and Australia have reported that 'lack of finance, lack of skilled expertise, and regulatory factors' were the main barriers to innovation.[49]

As well as efficiencies, it is claimed that firms utilising AI can also provide better services for clients.[50] McKinsey suggests that expertise will be 'amplified'.[51] Especially when it comes to prediction, it is claimed that data-driven approaches can balance out or improve lawyers' decision making. On the other hand, there are warnings about automation bias among people – a penchant for giving too much weight to the perceived accuracy of machines:

> [A]n increasing body of evidence shows that humans suffer from automation bias and automation-induced complacency. Humans have a tendency to rely too much on the machine's decision, lowering their own vigilance and critical analysis … This leads to errors, including situations where the human decision would have been correct

[45] F Pasquale, 'Automating the Professions: Utopian Pipe Dream or Dystopian Nightmare?' *Los Angeles Review of Books* (15 March 2016) https://lareviewofbooks.org/article/automating-the-professions-utopian-pipe-dream-or-dystopian-nightmare/.

[46] N Ismail, 'Artificial Intelligence in the Legal Industry: Adoption and Strategy – Part 1', *Information Age*, 6 August 2018, www.information-age.com/artificial-intelligence-in-the-legal-industry-123473948/.

[47] MM Bues and E Matthaei, 'LegalTech on the Rise: Technology Changes Legal Work Behaviours, But Does Not Replace Its Profession' in K Jacob, D Schindler and R Strathausen (eds), *Liquid Legal* (Springer, 2017) 105.

[48] B Rubin, 'Big Law, Big Problems: The Bright Future For Small Firms', *Forbes*, 7 July 2014, www.forbes.com/sites/basharubin/2014/07/07/big-law-big-problems-2/#238547a96a3e; Semmler and Rose (n 44) 90. Similar arguments are made for small businesses in general, eg, A Cain, 'AI Levels the Playing Field for Small Business', *Sydney Morning Herald*, 9 May 2018.

[49] Waye, Verreynne and Knowler (n 24) 231.

[50] JA Sherer and E Walters, 'Transitioning from Consumer Tech to Legal Intelligence Engineering' (2018) *Law Practice* 33, 34.

[51] Chui, Manyika and Miremadi (n 43).

> at the outset but was reversed by the human to align with the computer's erroneous recommendation.[52]

Importantly, the diversity of the profession in terms of sector, areas of practice and firm structures means that it is not useful to generalise about the impact of AI on lawyers or legal practice as a whole. Rather, what is required is a closer look at the role of the lawyer in each particular area, and the AI technologies being used, grounded in the specificities of legal practice.[53] Through this analysis, we can see commonalities across what lawyers will continue to be uniquely placed to do, and the skills that they will need to do it.

While technology promises much, lawyers must be wary of technology's siren song and understand what it delivers. In Greek mythology the Sirens were enchantresses whose beautiful song would lure sailors to rocky islands and their ensuing shipwreck. Lawyers need a clear-eyed view of what technology offers and how it functions so as to avoid being seduced by technology that is inappropriate or impermissible. Lawyers need to understand how AI functions so that they are able to adhere to their professional obligations such as competence, independence and protecting client confidentiality.

The Lawyer's Value

Professions continue while they are valuable to, and serve, society. Lawyers need to focus on what they can provide that a machine cannot. Previously this was expertise. Expertise is still important but technology will allow machines to become competent in more and more areas. Initially this will be the more straightforward and repetitive interactions with law, but it will increasingly reach into more complicated areas. The human expert lawyer may maintain an edge in dealing with novel issues and developing creative solutions. Law and society exist in a constant feedback loop – law changes. Technology may also have difficulty in replicating that aspect of legal decision making that requires judgement and discretion. This is not to say that technology cannot provide tools to assist the lawyer.

The second aspect is what may be called humanity or human skills, such as empathy, understanding and trust. These human characteristics are essential to legal practice. While crucial to assisting the client who has been injured or wronged, they apply to any human interaction where one person seeks to assist another, as a lawyer does. They are the bedrock of representation, collaboration and providing solutions to client problems.

[52] JD Lohr, WJ Maxwell and P Watts, 'Legal Practitioners' Approach to Regulating AI Risks' in K Yeung and M Lodge (eds), *Algorithmic Regulation* (Oxford University Press, 2019) 224, 228, citing K Goddard, A Roudsary and J Wyatt, 'Automation Bias: A Systematic Review of Frequency, Effect Mediators, and Mitigators' (2012) 19 *Journal of the American Medical Informatics Association* 121.

[53] Pasquale (n 45) ('Only specific, situated, technical, and sociological analyses of particular areas of law are truly valuable [in understanding the impact of AI]').

Third are the lawyer's ethical obligations. Ethics rules require a lawyer to 'act in the best interests of a client'. As a fiduciary, the lawyer is held to the highest standards of honour and must avoid conflicts of interest. The lawyer must maintain the client's confidences and their communications are protected by legal professional privilege, also called attorney–client privilege. But the ethics rules also impose a duty to the court and the administration of justice. Lawyers play a societal or structural role in upholding the rule of law.[54] As Robert Bolt pointed out through the voice of Thomas More in *A Man For All Seasons*, if you cut down all the laws 'd'you really think you could stand upright in the winds that would blow?'[55] These obligations are crucial to what makes law a profession and to trust between the lawyer and client, but also the lawyer and society.

Lawyers of the future need expertise and they need to embrace technology to assist them in performing their role as lawyers. But lawyers also need strong client-focussed skills combined with the highest integrity and comprehension of their ethical responsibilities.

The lawyer and the legal profession must strike the balance between adaptation and maintenance. Lawyers must adapt to be able to utilise AI. Lawyers must also ensure they maintain and uphold the ethical values of the legal profession.

Overview of Chapters

The aim of this monograph is twofold. First it aims to inform the legal profession about what AI is and how it is being used in specific areas of legal practice. Knowledge among the legal profession of AI is uneven and that needs to be addressed so that all lawyers can engage with AI. The text seeks to walk the line between how AI is actually being used, such as for technology assisted review in discovery and due diligence, and probable future applications. The discussion of the former is critically important because for those persons, particularly lawyers, who believe that law is immune from AI or argue that the use of AI is for the future, the current uses clearly rebut that viewpoint. AI is here and is being used. AI does have limitations, and lawyers must understand these too. Its role in the law is currently circumscribed. In relation to predicting future applications, it is readily accepted that this is a difficult task. However, the legal profession must prepare for the future now.

The second objective is to consider the role of the lawyer in an AI world. To do this the text examines what lawyers do now and what they do when AI is part of legal practice, highlighting the continuing role of the lawyer in serving the client

[54] T Bingham, *The Rule of Law* (Penguin Books, 2011) 92–93; American Bar Association, Model Rules of Professional Conduct: Preamble, [6] ('a lawyer should further the public's understanding of and confidence in the rule of law and the justice system because legal institutions in a constitutional democracy depend on popular participation and support to maintain their authority').

[55] R Bolt, *A Man for All Seasons* (Vintage, 1990) 66.

and in the justice system. This role may be seen as technical or practice oriented as the lawyer performs various steps in providing a legal service. Yet, though it is often underestimated by many writers in the area, law is a profession. The lawyer is bound by ethical requirements that protect the client and, through the duty to the administration of justice, the rule of law and society more generally. We examine how the use of AI and lawyers' ethical obligations interact.

While there is no doubt that technology will change many legal roles, just as it has impacted other occupations, the need for lawyers will continue. Central to this continuing role are expertise, humanity and ethics.

This book has three parts. Part I: Lawyers and the Evolution of Artificial Intelligence provides an accessible but rigorous explanation of AI, including development of the 'AI and Law' field of research, and early systems up to recent developments in machine learning. Part I also explains the role and work of lawyers. Lawyers are not the same around the world, nor do all lawyers in a single jurisdiction work in the same way or in the same areas of law, but there are commonalities in what makes a legal profession. This part forms a backdrop for Part II.

Change will affect all areas of legal practice, and lawyers and firms of all kinds, but in different ways. For this reason, Part II: The Use of Artificial Intelligence in Legal Practice is structured to focus on the use of AI in six different areas of legal work or practice, namely: advice, especially on prospects of success (Chapter 4); information gathering, also called discovery or disclosure, in the pre-trial stage of civil litigation or arbitration (Chapter 5); civil dispute resolution (Chapter 6); transactional practice (Chapter 7); regulatory practice, including in-house or corporate lawyers (Chapter 8); and criminal law (Chapter 9). Each of these chapters explains lawyers' function in each area, describes how AI is being utilised through specific examples and then considers the role of the lawyer after the adoption of AI.

Having seen the successes of AI and its actual use in practice, Part III: The Future of Lawyers and the Legal Profession then turns to consider the ramifications of these developments for lawyers. It does this by first discussing the limitations of AI and the various factors that prevent AI from usurping the lawyer. Part III then examines the ethical, legal and regulatory frameworks in which lawyers operate. Lawyers who face this strict scrutiny sometimes bemoan these, but here they are seen as enhancing the lawyer's offering vis-à-vis AI. Attention is also drawn to the regulation, or lack thereof in relation to AI and how that impacts the protections available for client-consumers. Part III concludes with some thoughts on the future of the legal profession. This is a future in which lawyers remain important servants of the public interest but through embracing AI and the necessary learning that goes with being able to capably employ and question AI.

PART I

Lawyers and the Evolution of Artificial Intelligence

2

Artificial Intelligence: What It Is and Why It Matters

Introduction

Interest in AI and its use in the legal sector has been growing rapidly. While there is a long history of attempts to combine law and AI, this chapter explains the recent upsurge in interest in the legal sector and why so many developments seem to have taken place, at speed, in the last few years.[1] Largely, this is to do with improvements in the capabilities of AI which have enabled the development of more sophisticated legal tools, within a general digital transformation of society.

AI is not new. The term itself has been in use for over 60 years.[2] It was 1950 when Alan Turing published 'Computing Machinery and Intelligence', in which he propounded the 'Turing Test' of whether machines could be said to be intelligent.[3] Yet, AI's development has been cyclical rather than linear,[4] with profound periods of dormancy. Now, though, AI seems to be on 'an upswing'.[5]

There are many books giving comprehensive histories of AI and its development,[6] and it is not our intention to repeat those. Our interest is, rather, in the present-day use of AI in legal services and the corresponding impact on the profession of law. Lawyers need to understand various aspects of how AI functions in order to comprehend its applications and outputs – but do not themselves need to become computer scientists, knowledge engineers or data analysts. This chapter

[1] T Walsh, *It's Alive! Artificial Intelligence from the Logic Piano to Killer Robots* (LaTrobe University Press, 2017) 51; 'Why Artificial Intelligence is Enjoying a Renaissance', *The Economist*, 15 July 2016, www.economist.com/the-economist-explains/2016/07/15/why-artificial-intelligence-is-enjoying-a-renaissance.

[2] Ascribed to John McCarthy at the Dartmouth Conference of 1956: he later published *Ascribing Mental Qualities to Machines* (Stanford University, Department of Computer Science, 1979). See J Kaplan, *Artificial Intelligence, What Everyone Needs to Know* (Oxford University Press, 2016) ch 2 'The Intellectual History of Artificial Intelligence' for an accessible and informative history.

[3] AM Turing, 'Computing Machinery and Intelligence' (1950) 49 *Mind* 433. In this paper, Turing also 'introduced … machine learning, genetic algorithms, and reinforcement learning': SJ Russell and P Norvig, *Artificial Intelligence: A Modern Approach* (3rd edn, Pearson, 2016) 17; and see also L Dormehl, *Thinking Machines: The Quest for Artificial Intelligence and Where It's Taking Us Next* (TarcherPerigee, 2017) 10–11.

[4] Walsh (n 1) 49; Kaplan (n 2); and V Dhar, 'The Future of Artificial Intelligence' (2016) 4(1) *Big Data* 5, 5.

[5] Walsh (n 1) 51.

[6] See, eg, Dormehl (n 3); A Husain, *The Sentient Machine: The Coming Age of Artificial Intelligence* (Scribner, 2017); Kaplan (n 2); and Walsh (n 1).

gives a background on AI, including a short history of 'AI and Law', the branch of computer science research concerned with AI's legal applications.

The concept of intelligence is generally thought by humans to be almost uniquely human and is therefore usually measured by reference to human traits and achievements.[7] Definitions of intelligence vary widely and involve myriad interconnected human characteristics that are themselves complex to define, including language use, the ability to learn, the ability to adapt, the ability to abstract, consciousness, self-awareness and the ability to reason.[8] It was originally thought that AI would have to reason in the same way as a person in order to be considered intelligent.[9] The test described by Turing and given his name hinges on whether human judges could be fooled into thinking that a machine was a person.[10] Stuart Russell and Peter Norvig identify four different tests or requirements that have been applied to define AI or determine what it is: thinking humanly, acting humanly, thinking rationally and acting rationally.[11] They explain that each has been followed, and each entails different methods of evaluating AI.[12] Another definition of AI centres on its capacity to carry out tasks which, if performed by a human, would be taken as evidence of intelligence.[13] Here, we use 'AI' as an umbrella term to capture a number of different technologies. Other familiar terms that are sometimes used for AI are non-biological intelligence, robots, cognitive technologies, machine learning or algorithms. Pedro Domingos describes an algorithm simply as 'a sequence of instructions telling a computer what to do'.[14]

Chess grandmaster Garry Kasparov was defeated by IBM's Deep Blue in 1997,[15] another IBM program called Watson prevailed on the TV quiz *Jeopardy!* in 2011,[16] and in 2016 DeepMind's AlphaGo outplayed champion Lee Sedol at the ancient Chinese game of Go.[17] This last exemplifies the novel ways that machine

[7] MU Scherer, 'Regulating Artificial Intelligence Systems: Risks, Challenges, Competencies, and Strategies' (2016) 29(2) *Harvard Journal of Law and Technology* 353, 359.

[8] ibid 360.

[9] SD Becerra, 'The Rise of Artificial Intelligence in the Legal Field: Where We Are and Where We Are Going' (2018) 11 *Journal of Business, Entrepreneurship & Law* 27, 34.

[10] D Ben-Ari, Y Frish, A Lazovski, U Eldan and D Greenbaum, 'Artificial Intelligence in the Practice of Law: An Analysis and Proof of Concept Experiment' (2017) 23(2) *Richmond Journal of Law & Technology* 2, 15–16; Walsh (n 1) 62–67.

[11] Russell and Norvig (n 3) 2.

[12] ibid 1.

[13] Kaplan (n 2) 1.

[14] P Domingos, *The Master Algorithm: How the Quest for the Ultimate Learning Machine Will Remake Our World* (Basic Books, 2015) 24.

[15] B Weber, 'Swift and Slashing, Computer Topples Kasparov', *The New York Times*, 12 May 1997, 1.

[16] S Borenstein and J Robertson, 'Oh, the Humanity: Computers Whip Us at "Jeopardy!" But There's Still a Place for People', *Associated Press Newswires*, 17 February 2011; M Ford, 'Artificial Intelligence Is the Next Killer App', www.Atlantic.com, 16 February 2011.

[17] 'The Latest AI Can Work Things Out Without Being Taught', *The Economist*, 21 October 2017, www.economist.com/science-and-technology/2017/10/21/the-latest-ai-can-work-things-out-without-being-taught. Previously, it was thought that Go was too complex a game for a computer to excel at because there are too many possible moves: 'Google Achieves AI "Breakthrough" by Beating Go Champion', *BBC News Online*, 27 January 2016. DeepMind Technologies was acquired by Alphabet Inc, a Google subsidiary, in 2014.

learning has recently developed, as explained below. As AI has achieved more and more milestones in areas such as these, once thought to be the sole province of humans, the definition of what constitutes intelligence in terms of AI has continued to shift.[18] Yet, it is also said that 'intelligence' is not the correct word for AI and what it does, as it lacks self-awareness: it does not know what it is doing, or why it is doing it.[19]

What is sometimes referred to as 'soft AI' tries to emulate human intelligence in terms of outcomes but not in terms of processes.[20] To take the example of playing chess, an AI system does not play chess the same way as a person. A person cannot calculate every possible chess move and work out which would be optimum – but this is what Deep Blue could do. The system is not really 'thinking' but is mathematically analysing a huge amount of data to infer a probability.[21] This power is often described as 'brute computational force'.[22]

Harking back to Domingos' description, AI systems function by '[breaking] down a complex human intellectual task … into a set of computational steps or algorithm'.[23] Having said this, programs can also act autonomously, 'much as Kasparov is autonomous of his coaches … [the program] responds and adapts its game plan in response to the moves that its opponents make, thereby being situated in and interacting with its environment'.[24] In the case of AlphaGo's successor, AlphaGo Zero, the program was provided only with the rules of Go and taught itself to play using reinforcement learning (and playing against the original AlphaGo). It went on to learn to play chess the same way. Bradley Wendel has eloquently explained:

> Unlike Deep Blue and other systems that used brute force to out-compute human players, the AlphaZero chess system 'played like no computer ever has, intuitively and beautifully, with a romantic, attacking style.' Garry Kasparov wrote that the computer had developed its own style, not that of its human programmers, and it was one that 'reflects the truth' about chess.[25]

[18] Scherer (n 7).

[19] M Mills, 'Siri, Esq – The AI Robots Are (Not) Coming', 14 May 2018, *Law Practice Today* (ABA Law Practice Division), www.lawpracticetoday.org/article/3417/.

[20] DM Katz, 'Quantitative Legal Prediction – Or – How I Learned to Stop Worrying and Start Preparing for the Data-Driven Future of the Legal Services Industry' (2013) 62(4) *Emory Law Journal* 909, 918.

[21] V Mayer-Schonberger and K Cukier, *Big Data* (First Mariner Books, 2014) 12; B Barton, 'The Lawyer's Monopoly: What Goes and What Stays' (2014) 82(6) *Fordham Law Review* 3068, 3070–71.

[22] See Husain (n 6) 24; Walsh (n 1) 57; Kaplan (n 2); Barton (n 21).

[23] KD Ashley, *Artificial Intelligence and Legal Analytics: New Tools for Law Practice in the Digital Age* (Cambridge University Press, 2017) 4.

[24] B Allgrove, *Legal Personality for Artificial Intellects: Pragmatic Solution or Science Fiction?* (Dissertation Submitted for Master of Philosophy, University of Oxford, 2015) 7.

[25] WB Wendel, 'The Promise and Limitations of Artificial Intelligence in the Practice of Law' (2019) 72(1) *Oklahoma Law Review* 21, 22 citing S Strogatz, 'One Giant Step for a Chess-Playing Machine', *New York Times*, 26 December 2018.

While AI software does not legally reason the way that people do, arguably it does not need to. Therefore, it is argued, just because computers cannot yet 'think', that does not mean they cannot perform some tasks better than humans can.[26]

There are different ways of classifying AI. 'Strong AI' refers to AI which can reason in an independent manner; 'weak AI' (like soft AI) refers to a program that mimics human thinking without actually being able to reason similarly to a human.[27] We can also distinguish between 'general' and 'narrow' AI.[28] At present, AI works best with narrowly defined tasks, and most current applications of AI, including legal uses, fall into this category.[29] Within specific parameters, some AI programs can outclass humans, and the list of well-known examples, such as those mentioned above, is ever growing. Finally, 'general' AI, or Artificial General Intelligence, refers to the creation of systems which can perform many and varied human activities. Taken to its extreme, this is referred to as 'the singularity' – the term given to the concept of machine superintelligence.[30] But we are not at this point yet, and currently, 'machines are still hopeless at many basic unsupervised learning tasks that humans accomplish with ease or those where we use common-sense knowledge'.[31] In terms of physical movement, Moravec's Paradox describes the fact that while computers excel at high-level reasoning, they are generally still poor at 'low-level sensorimotor tasks'.[32] Nor does AI have emotional intelligence or empathy[33] – though machines are becoming increasingly sophisticated at 'reading' human emotions.[34]

AI is an umbrella term.[35] There are different branches of AI, including robotics, computer vision and speech functions (see Figure 2.1). Substantial gains have

[26] R Susskind and D Susskind, *The Future of the Professions: How Technology Will Transform the Work of Human Experts* (Oxford University Press, 2015) 159–60.

[27] Ben-Ari et al (n 10) 6; Allgrove (n 24) 3.

[28] S Semmler and Z Rose, 'Artificial Intelligence: Application Today and Implications Tomorrow' (2017–18) 16(1) *Duke Law & Technology Review* 85, 86.

[29] Ben-Ari et al (n 10) 8.

[30] V Vinge, 'The Coming Technological Singularity: How to Survive in the Post-Human Era', Vision-21: Interdisciplinary Science and Engineering in the Era of Cyberspace (Symposium held at NASA Lewis Research Center, 30–31 March 1993); R Kurzweil, *The Singularity Is Near: When Humans Transcend Biology* (Viking, 2005); Dormehl (n 3) 216–17; T Walsh, *2062: The World that AI Made* (La Trobe University Press, 2018) 37–39.

[31] Dhar (n 4) 8–9; see also GK Hadfield, *Rules for a Flat World: Why Humans Invented Law and How to Reinvent It for a Complex Global Economy* (Oxford University Press, 2017) 25.

[32] M McKamey, 'Legal Technology: Artificial Intelligence and the Future of Law Practice' (2017) 22 *Appeal: Review of Current Law and Law Reform* 45, citing H Moravec, *Mind Children: The Future of Robot and Human Intelligence* (Harvard University Press, 1988) 15; see also Dormehl (n 3) 20.

[33] See, eg, D Remus and F Levy, 'Can Robots Be Lawyers: Computers, Lawyers, and the Practice of Law' (2017) 30(3) *Georgetown Journal of Legal Ethics* 501, 512. On the value of empathy in legal practice, see DO Linder and N Levit, *The Good Lawyer: Seeking Quality in the Practice of Law* (Oxford University Press, 2014) ch 1 'The Good Lawyer is Empathetic'.

[34] See, eg, Affectiva: www.affectiva.com/; Z Wu, B Singh, LS Davis and VS Subrahmanian, 'Deception Detection in Videos', Cornell University Library, 12 December 2017, Paper arXiv:1712.04415v1.

[35] JA Sherer and E Walters, 'Transitioning from Consumer Tech to Legal Intelligence Engineering' (2018) *Law Practice* 33.

been made in these areas in recent years, for example in object recognition and computer speech functions.[36] Not all branches of AI, however, have any present application to the law or legal services. Here, we focus on those that do – expert systems, machine learning and Natural Language Processing (NLP). A key focus in recent years has been on machine learning, though it encompasses many different techniques,[37] as we explore further in Part II of this book.

Figure 2.1

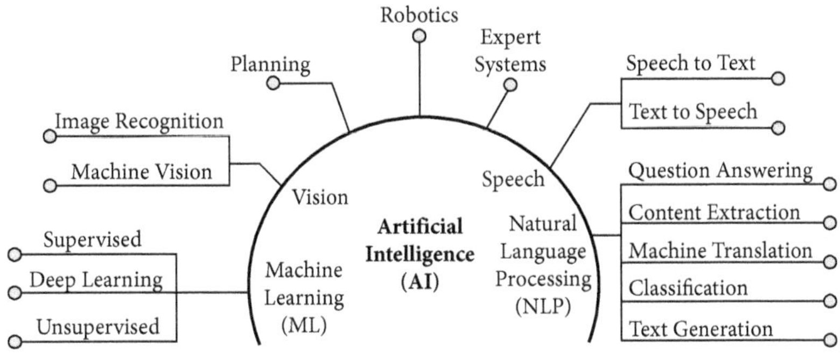

While our focus is on current applications, many of these have their roots in earlier (and continuing) efforts by the AI and Law research community. Accordingly, we traverse some of this history for a more complete understanding of current research and commercialisation in legal AI. After discussing some of these earlier applications we turn to recent developments in machine learning.

History of AI and Law

As a research field, 'AI and Law' stretches back to the 1970s.[38] It is a branch of AI research focused 'on designing computer programs – computational models –

[36] J Schmidhuber, 'Deep Learning in Neural Networks: An Overview' (2015) 61 *Neural Networks* 85; Y LeCun, Y Bengio and G Hinton, 'Deep Learning' (2015) 521 *Nature* 436; C Metz, 'A New Way for Machines to See, Taking Shape in Toronto', *New York Times*, 28 November 2017.

[37] Domingos (n 14) 51–55; Walsh (n 1) ch 3 'The State of AI Today'.

[38] Generally attributed to the paper of BG Buchanan and TE Headrick 'Some Speculation about Artificial Intelligence and Legal Reasoning' (1970) 23 *Stanford Law Review* 40: see RE Susskind 'Expert Systems in Law: Jurisprudential Approach to Artificial Intelligence and Legal Reasoning' (1986) 49(2) *Modern Law Review* 168, 178; PN Gray, *Artificial Legal Intelligence* (Dartmouth, 1997) 23. See also EL Rissland, KD Ashley and RP Loui, 'AI and Law: A Fruitful Synergy' (2003) 150 *Artificial Intelligence* 1, 6–13.

that perform legal reasoning'.[39] An overview of the field lists many sub-categories, including computational legal logic, legal argumentation systems and machine learning in the law.[40] We do not examine all these sub-categories in detail but give a background on some early systems and approaches.

In an early paper, Richard Susskind argued that AI and Law endeavours can be categorised as either 'pragmatic' (systems which can be operationalised, and indeed, commercialised) or 'purist' (where the research goal is 'to clarify the nature of legal reasoning, of human and artificial intelligence, and of computational models of law').[41] A number of past projects in the AI and Law domain addressed such 'purist' goals rather than necessarily generating practical applications, though some did have a practical side.[42]

One area of general importance has been the extent to which a system can produce an explanation for its outputs.[43] Traditionally, explanation is important to law: beyond a correct answer, a justificatory reasoning process as to why that answer is correct is expected.[44] This has driven the pursuit of systems which can 'explain' their outputs, particularly when it comes to generating reasons for a prediction.[45] More recently, the volume of available data and increased computer processing power has spurred interest in data-driven techniques. Such programs can often generate quite accurate results but cannot provide an explanation for their outputs. Indeed, even a human expert may not be able to understand how the system arrived at its own particular conclusions. The University of Melbourne's Networked Society Institute has suggested that a useful means of classifying the types of systems which might be used for automated legal advice is around two axes – whether they use statistical or causal reasoning, and whether they are 'hand-coded' or programmed by people, or are 'data-driven' (Figure 2.2).[46]

[39] KD Ashley, 'Teaching Law and Digital Age Legal Practice with an AI and Law Seminar' (2013) 88(3) *Chicago-Kent Law Review* 783.

[40] G Sartor and A Rotolo, 'AI and Law' in S Ossowski (ed), *Agreement Technologies* (Springer, 2012) 199, 199–200.

[41] R Susskind, 'Pragmatism and Purism in Artificial Intelligence and Legal Reasoning' in A Narayanan and M Bennun (eds), *Law, Computer Science and Artificial Intelligence* (Ablex, 1991) 33.

[42] M Grupp and MM Bues, 'The Status Quo in Legal Automation' in M DeStefano and G Dobrauz (eds), *New Suits: Appetite for Disruption in the Legal World* (Staempfli Verlag, 2019) 227, 230.

[43] Ashley (n 39) 786.

[44] G Greenleaf, A Mowbray and P Chung, 'Building Sustainable Free Legal Advisory Systems: Experiences from the History of AI & Law' (2018) 34 *Computer Law & Security Review* 314, citing Ashley (n 23) 17.

[45] A Adadi and M Berrada, 'Peeking Inside the Black Box: A Survey on Explainable Artificial Intelligence (XAI)' (2018) 6 *IEEE Access* 52138.

[46] J Bennett et al, *Current State of Automated Legal Advice Tools: Discussion Paper 1* (Networked Society Institute, University of Melbourne, April 2018) 13.

Figure 2.2 Rating system

	Statistical Reasoning	Causal Reasoning
Hand-coded Knowledge Hand-coded by people	Reasoning is by association only, and knowledge is limited to what the human can encode	Reasoning is reasonably sophisticated in that the intelligence reasons about cause and effect between variables to derive outcomes and can answer questions about interventions and counterfactuals.
Data-learnt Knowledge Learnt from data	Reasoning is by association only; predictions are based on patterns found in data. May extract relationships seen by human encoder	Combines the power of causal reasoning with ability to learn from data

Source: J Bennett, T Miller, J Webb, R Bosua, A Lodders and S Chamberlain, *Current State of Automated Legal Advice Tools: Discussion Paper 1* (Networked Society Institute, University of Melbourne, April 2018) 24, Figure 4.

Absence of explanation or interpretability has caused consternation in legal AI and has significance for policy questions.[47]

Rule-based Reasoning and Logic

Early forays into computational modelling of law conceptualised the law as a programmed system of rules. When presented with a set of facts, the system could apply these rules, resulting in a 'legal' conclusion. Knowledge systems, also referred to as symbolic reasoning systems,[48] were early designs for applying this type of rule-based reasoning. As these names indicate, the goal of such systems was to represent knowledge and rules symbolically and use computerised logic to solve problems. Thus, the system's logic 'is to find relevant rules on [the] basis of the available information, operate them, and continue to search for a rule until a result has been obtained.'[49] This type of system can be contrasted to the data-driven systems discussed below.

[47] R Calo, 'Artificial Intelligence Policy: A Primer and a Roadmap' (2017) 51(2) *UC Davis Law Review* 399, 405.

[48] See Kaplan (n 2) 23; R Gruner, 'Thinking Like a Lawyer: Expert Systems for Legal Analysis' (1986) 1(2) *Berkeley Technology Law Journal* 259. This is referred to as 'Good Old-Fashioned AI': J Haugeland, *Artificial Intelligence: The Very Idea* (MIT Press, 1985).

[49] M Bal et al, 'Performance Evaluation of the Machine Learning Algorithms Used in Inference Mechanism of a Medical Decision Support System' (2014) *Scientific World Journal* DOI: 10.1155/2014/137896.

Expert systems are a type of knowledge-based system.[50] An expert system seeks to mimic human expertise by combining a knowledge base ('a collection of facts, rules and relationships about a specific domain of interest represented in symbolic form') and an 'inference engine', which is programmed to manipulate the knowledge base material.[51] The system uses conditional statement rules (if this, then that) to move through a legal problem. This is an example of deductive reasoning – following the reasoning process logically results in the programmed answer. A human with expertise in the relevant domain must be involved in crafting the questions, creating a network of queries and answers to 'generate a scripted output'.[52] This is accordingly sometimes referred to as knowledge engineering or 'expertise modelling'.[53] For relatively simple legal problems, the program can guide users by asking a set of questions.[54]

By the 1980s, some expert systems could replicate a degree of 'legal' reasoning around simple problems.[55] Famous early examples, using deductive reasoning, include the TAXMAN system,[56] the system developed by Marek Sergot and Robert Kowalski at Imperial College London which used PROLOG (programming in logic) to support immigration officials' work;[57] and the program designed by Donald Waterman and Mark Peterson (of RAND Corporation's Center for Civil Justice) to recommend settlements in product liability disputes.[58] Waterman and Peterson's system was programmed with general rules about the nature of a plaintiff's loss based on the applicable product liability law (that of California). Presented with facts, the 'inference engine cycled through the rules', checking to see if any were applicable.[59] An example is: 'IF victim's use of product was foreseeable and reasonable, AND victim was injured by product, AND product was defective, AND defendant manufactured product, THEN consider a strict liability claim'.[60]

[50] Susskind (n 38) 172–73; Gruner (n 48) 261–62; AR Lodder and JJ Zeleznikow, 'Developing an Online Dispute Resolution Environment' (2005) 10 *Harvard Negotiation Law Review* 287, 293.

[51] Kaplan (n 2) 23.

[52] CEA Karnow, 'The Opinion of Machines' (2017) 19 *Columbia Science and Technology Law Review* 136, 142–43.

[53] EA Feigenbaum, 'Knowledge Engineering' (1984) 426(1) *Annals of the New York Academy of Sciences* 91, 91.

[54] Remus and Levy (n 33) 31.

[55] See Ashley (n 23) 8–9; DA Waterman, J Paul and M Peterson, 'Expert Systems for Legal Decision Making' (1986) 3(4) *Expert Systems* 212, 213 (Table 1); DA Waterman and MA Peterson, 'Evaluating Civil Claims: An Expert Systems Approach' (1984) *Expert Systems* 1.

[56] L Thorne McCarty, 'Reflections on TAXMAN: An Experiment in Artificial Intelligence and Legal Reasoning' (1977) 90 *Harvard Law Review* 837.

[57] MJ Sergot, F Sadri, RA Kowalski, F Kriwaczek, P Hammond and HT Cory, 'The British Nationality Act as a Logic Program' (1986) 29 *Communications of the ACM* 370–86 (described as the seminal work on logical representation of legislation); see also Susskind (n 38) 180.

[58] See the summary of Ashley (n 23) 8–10, citing DA Waterman and MA Peterson, *Models of Legal Decision Making: Research Design and Methods* (Rand Corporation, Institute for Civil Justice, 1981).

[59] Ashley (n 23) 9.

[60] Gruner (n 48) 277.

This type of rule-based or knowledge-based system continued to be explored in various ways in the 1980s and 1990s.[61] The functioning of a legal expert system is not dissimilar to the way that a lawyer might use an instructions sheet to guide their questioning of a client – moving through a sequence of queries. One key difference, though, lies in the ability of the lawyer to revisit earlier conclusions in light of new information. In contrast, what is termed a classical model of logic is 'monotonic' or 'monological'. In other words, 'once a conclusion is drawn, it cannot be "taken back" even in the light of new information'.[62] This 'traditional approach' is 'concentrated on a single inference, where the premises and conclusion are designated in advance, and applied formal models like propositional calculus and quantification theory determine whether the conclusion conclusively follows from the premises'.[63] Such an approach does not sit well with legal reasoning. Accordingly, law has been a site for the exploration of non-monotonic (or defeasible) logic in computing.[64] Under this approach, rather than focusing on a single inference, a dialectical mode is employed. Two sides of an argument are examined, with the goal of determining which is the stronger and therefore most likely to prevail. Also described as an argumentation approach,[65] it was widely explored in the 1990s.[66]

Case-Based Reasoning

While research into rule-based reasoning systems continued in the 1980s, another branch of AI and Law research was examining 'reasoning with cases and analogies'.[67] Case-Based Reasoning (CBR) is a general programming method for the creation of knowledge-based systems 'where the central issue is past cases or experiences'.[68] In other words, the reference to 'case-based' need not refer specifically to legal cases or decisions, though in AI and Law it likely does. Kevin Ashley, a pioneer of legal CBR, explains that its goal is to determine whether fact patterns are legally similar to existing precedents. In order to achieve this, a CBR system

[61] Sartor and Rotolo (n 40) citing Sergot et al (n 57).

[62] Ashley (n 39) 793, citing D Berman and C Hafner, 'Obstacles to the Development of Logic-Based Models of Legal Reasoning' in C Walter (ed), *Computer Power and Legal Language: The Use of Computational Linguistics, Artificial Intelligence, and Expert Systems in the Law* (Quorum, 1988) 183.

[63] D Walton, 'Argumentation Theory: A Very Short Introduction' in GR Simari and I Rahwan (eds), *Argumentation in Artificial Intelligence* (Springer, 2009) 1, 4.

[64] eg, H Prakken and G Sartor, 'Argument-Based Logic Programming with Defeasible Priorities' (1997) 7 *Journal of Applied Non-Classical Logics* 25–75.

[65] See generally Walton (n 63); H Prakken and G Sartor, 'A Dialectical Model of Assessing Conflicting Arguments in Legal Reasoning' (1996) 4 *Artificial Intelligence and Law* 331.

[66] H Prakken and G Sartor (eds), *Logical Models of Legal Argumentation* (Kluwer, 1997); M Araszkiewicz, 'Haijme Yoshino (1995) "The Systematization of Legal Meta-Inference"' in T Bench-Capon et al (eds), 'A History of AI and Law in 50 Papers: 25 Years of the International Conference on AI and Law' (2012) 20 *Artificial Intelligence & Law* 215–319 [6.1].

[67] Rissland, Ashley and Loui (n 38) 8.

[68] B López, *Case-based Reasoning: A Concise Introduction* (Morgan & Claypool, 2013) 1.

must represent legally relevant factors, thus seeking to approximate legal reasoning, including reasoning by analogy.[69]

Often the two approaches – case-based and rule-based – were presented as antipathetic to one another. As Trevor Bench-Capon explained: 'Proponents of case-based reasoning would argue that [logical tools] neglected the adversarial nature of legal reasoning, and that it was unable to handle indeterminacy and conflict'.[70] A considerable amount of work was also devoted to attempts to variously bridge, reconcile or hybridise these two approaches.[71]

The CBR system developed by Ashley in the 1980s, Hypo (a reference to 'hypothetical'),[72] seeded the development of various subsequent systems.[73] Hypo dealt with trade secret misappropriation, using various legal factors to model existing trade secret cases.[74] Within Hypo, though legal factors were given weight, that weight was not expressed quantitatively. This is because the factors are context dependent.[75] Ashley explains: 'Given an input fact situation, Hypo retrieved all cases in its database that shared a dimension with the case factors'.[76] It attempted to model legal reasoning by finding relevant precedents and comparing those which are the most similar (and therefore likely most persuasive) to the facts at hand. This was later labelled 'factor based reasoning'.[77]

Another well-known system, CABARET, was the first system to integrate a rule-based and a case-based approach as it could switch between them as required.[78] Specifically, when the rules ran out (for instance, there were no further criteria specified in a statute), the program could switch over to CBR. In terms of unifying logic-based approaches and CBR, Prakken and Sartor wrote in 1997:

> The separation between logic and dialectic seems to be coming to an end … CBR researchers have acknowledged the use of rules, and of theory formation, in legal argumentation, while logically inclined researchers have developed logical models of defeasible legal argumentation.[79]

In the early 1990s, the path of CBR development was altered by the work of Donald Berman and Carole Hafner, who published three papers in which they considered

[69] Ashley (n 23) 77.

[70] T Bench-Capon, 'From Logic to Dialectics in Legal Argument' in Bench-Capon et al (eds) (n 66) 215–319.

[71] Rissland, Ashley and Loui (n 38) 8, citations omitted.

[72] KD Ashley, *Modeling Legal Argument: Reasoning with Cases and Hypotheticals* (MIT Press, 1990).

[73] eg, CABARET, CATO, IBP.

[74] KD Ashley, 'Reasoning with Cases and Hypotheticals in HYPO' (1991) 34 *International Journal of Machine-Man Studies* 753, 763–64.

[75] Ashley (n 23) 81–82.

[76] ibid 86.

[77] T Bench-Capon, 'Special Issue in Memory of Carole Hafner: Editor's Introduction' (2016) 24(4) *Artificial Intelligence and Law* 325.

[78] Using an agenda mechanism – Ashley (n 23) 88. See also Rissland, Ashley and Loui (n 38) 10–11. CABARET concerned US tax law related to home office deduction.

[79] H Prakken and G Sartor, 'Editors' Introduction' in H Prakken and G Sartor (eds), *Logical Models of Legal Argumentation* (Kluwer, 1997) 1, 1.

how different elements of legal reasoning might be lost or not considered when using factor-based reasoning.[80] In one paper, they addressed the absence of consideration of 'underlying purpose or values'.[81] Besides being fundamental to the law, this is highly relevant when there are *no* applicable precedents. Thus, it is relevant to the law's temporal development, or the way the law changes over time.[82] This line of thinking led to exploration of the possibility of incorporating 'values' into CBR.[83] Ashley notes that reasoning with values (teleological reasoning) is central to the law, so as well as incorporating legal rules, it was seen as important that values be represented computationally and incorporated into the reasoning process.[84]

Some Australian academics recently commented:

> Despite nearly 40 years of research into case-based legal reasoning, there is probably not much role for AI representations of case law … The theoretical basis of case-based reasoning is still too much in dispute, and the identification of attributes in reported cases is still too time consuming and requires too much expertise to represent (and therefore is too costly).[85]

Ashley is more optimistic, focusing on the interaction between CBR models and programs which can extract factors automatically from text.[86]

Limitations of Expert Systems

In 2017, academics Remus and Levy argued that expert systems 'can only be constructed for repetitive and fairly narrow tasks under specific bodies of law'.[87] Ashley has commented likewise that while they still have application, this is not the 'paradigm' that will fundamentally revolutionise the practice of law.[88] The limitations of expert systems can be summed up as existing on two levels – one

[80] D Berman and C Hafner, 'Incorporating Procedural Context into a Model of Case-Based Legal Reasoning', *Proceedings of the 3rd International Conference on Artificial Intelligence and Law* (ACM Press, 1991) 12 (exploring the effect of procedural context); D Berman and C Hafner, 'Representing Teleological Structure in Case-Based Legal Reasoning: The Missing Link', *Proceedings of the 4th International Conference on Artificial Intelligence and Law* (ACM Press, 1993) 50 (teleological context); and D Berman and C Hafner, 'Understanding Precedents in a Temporal Context of Evolving Legal Doctrine', *Proceedings of the 5th International Conference on Artificial Intelligence and Law* (ACM Press, 1995) 42 (temporal context).

[81] Ashley (n 39) 795, citing Berman and Hafner, 'Representing Teleological Structure' (n 80).

[82] See, eg, B Verheij, 'Formalizing Value-Guided Argumentation for Ethical Systems Design' (2016) 24(4) *Artificial Intelligence and Law* 387.

[83] T Bench-Capon, 'Persuasion in Practical Argument Using Value-Based Argumentation Frameworks' (2003) 13(3) *Journal of Logic and Computation* 429; see also T Bench-Capon and G Sartor, 'A Model of Legal Reasoning With Cases Incorporating Theories and Values' (2003) 150 (1–2) *Artificial Intelligence* 97–143; and T Bench-Capon, 'Relating Values in a Series of Supreme Court Decisions' in K Atkinson (ed), *Legal Knowledge-Based Systems* (IOS Press, 2011) 13–22.

[84] Ashley (n 23) 73–74.

[85] Greenleaf, Mowbray and Chung (n 44) [3.4].

[86] Ashley (n 23) 105. See further Chapter 4.

[87] Remus and Levy (n 33) 31.

[88] Ashley (n 23) 11.

technical, the other (more fundamental) related to the ways these systems are able to represent legal knowledge.[89] To put it another way, Susskind described those problems related primarily to law (being jurisprudential) and those related to AI (being 'computational and cognitive').[90] These categories largely remain relevant.

In the category of technical limitations, three are generally agreed upon: knowledge acquisition; knowledge representation; and knowledge utilisation.[91]

In terms of 'knowledge acquisition', expert systems run up against problems when they encounter incomplete information and, because they must be programmed manually, the process is not especially efficient. As science and technology author Luke Dormehl explains, 'knowledge had to be programmed, one piece at a time. In many scenarios this could be done well enough to perform limited tasks at an acceptable level. The problem came with scaling'.[92] Maintaining such a system is time consuming. This is sometimes referred to as the 'knowledge acquisition bottleneck' as all the rules, and relations between them, must be coded manually or 'hand-coded'.[93] Any change to the system, whether this is altering something or increasing the knowledge base, must be made via the same cumbersome process.[94] As currency is highly important in the law, this is a significant drawback.

The second issue, 'knowledge representation', describes the fact that not all knowledge is able to be represented symbolically. Turning legal knowledge into formalised terms is challenging.[95] Law is described as 'open textured' in nature, meaning that its terms are often conceptually loose.[96] Fuzzy concepts which are familiar to the law, such as 'reasonable foreseeability', confound simple logic systems. Even statutes cannot simply be interpreted as logical rules.[97] For CBR systems, teleological considerations are relevant to the definition of legal concepts, yet incorporating values into their programming has been challenging.[98] 'Hard cases' are also confounding as they are by nature exceptional and indeterminate.

Finally, as regards 'knowledge utilisation', deductive reasoning systems are also limited[99] due to the need for agreed facts, or the challenge of reasoning with

[89] See P Leith, 'The Rise and Fall of the Legal Expert System' (2016) 30(3) *International Review of Law, Computers & Technology* 94.

[90] Susskind (n 41) 34–35.

[91] Susskind (n 38) 173; U Schild, *Expert Systems and Case Law* (Ellis Horwood, 1992) also adopts these categories.

[92] Dormehl (n 3) 31.

[93] See A Greinke, 'Legal Expert Systems – A Humanistic Critique of Mechanical Legal Inference' (1994) 1(4) *Murdoch University Electronic Journal of Law*; and Russell and Norvig (n 3) 28.

[94] M Aikenhead, 'The Uses and Abuses of Neural Networks in Law' (1996) 12(1) *Santa Clara Computer and High-Technology Law Journal* 31.

[95] Russell and Norvig (n 3) 4.

[96] See Schild (n 91) 25–27, attributing 'open texture' to F Waismann, 'Verifiability' in A Flew (ed), *Logic and Language* (Anchor Books, 1965) 122; but noting it was applied to the law, famously, by HLA Hart, *The Concept of Law* (Oxford University Press, 1961).

[97] Ashley, 'Digital Age Legal Practice' (n 39) 793.

[98] T Bench-Capon and K Atkinson, 'Abstract Argumentation and Values' in G Simari and I Rahwan (eds), *Argumentation in Artificial Intelligence* (Springer, 2009) 45, 47–50.

[99] Susskind (n 38) 188–91.

contested or not-yet-determined facts; and the problem of an absence of explanation. Susskind said:

> We have already noted that the systems do not reason with heuristic, judgmental knowledge. Moreover, not all the systems are transparent, and even those that do offer explanations of their lines of reasoning, do so simply by regurgitating the rules that were fired. If a system is to replicate a human expert in law, it ought to provide more penetrating explanations.[100]

Exploration in the areas of CBR, neural networks and NLP show that there is interest in overcoming these limitations. However, using inductive reasoning systems to ascertain legal rules is also fraught with difficulty.[101] These systems are not scalable, as Grupp and Bues explain: 'Programs perform well in a circumscribed problem area [but] once they are asked to perform outside their limited domain, there is not a graceful decline but rather a sudden and dramatic drop in performance'.[102]

Ironically, the opprobrium directed towards a lack of explanation for outputs continues to be raised in recent critiques of machine learning as applied to the law, yet seemingly with less impact. On the other hand, as we consider below, perhaps machine learning techniques, especially deep learning, will be able to recognise trends in case law which CBR could not.

Legal Information Retrieval

Alongside developments in logical reasoning and CBR a parallel exploration of legal information retrieval was taking place. The general idea of information retrieval (IR) is how to most effectively search for 'words phrases and sentences … so as to get a perfect match and retrieve only a very small number of documents from a huge text corpus'.[103] As a field of study, IR has also existed since the 1970s.[104] Within this discipline, *legal* IR has focused on locating or 'retrieving' similar cases from computerised databases in order to analyse whether the case in question is sufficiently similar to those other cases to match the outcome.[105] As well as legal search, legal text summarisation functions have also been investigated for the

[100] ibid 191. See also Susskind (n 41) 35.

[101] D Hunter and J Zeleznikow, 'Reasoning Paradigms in Legal Decision Support Systems' (1995) 9 *Artificial Intelligence Review* 361, 367.

[102] M Grupp and MM Bues, 'The Status Quo in Legal Automation' in M DeStefano and G Dobrauz (eds), *New Suits: Appetite for Disruption in the Legal World* (Staempfli Verlag, 2019) 231.

[103] E Schweighofer, 'Commentary on J Bing (1987) "Designing Text Retrieval Systems for Conceptual Searching"' in Bench-Capon et al (eds) (n 66) 215.

[104] The Inaugural Research and Development in Information Retrieval International Conference was held in 1978.

[105] See, eg, J Bing, *Handbook of Legal Information Retrieval* (Elsevier Science, 1984); M van Opijnen and C Santos, 'On the Concept of Relevance in Legal Information Retrieval' (2017) 25(1) *Artificial Intelligence and Law* 65–87.

pragmatic reason that 'lawyers need to find precedent cases quickly',[106] for example by reading case summaries instead of whole cases.

The priority for early IR systems was to overcome the technical challenge of searching large volumes of documents based on specific rules. Boolean keywords were used to perform searches: the search retrieves documents which contain the combination of keywords specified by the searcher. This makes Boolean searching relatively simple but it also has drawbacks: degree of relevance is based only on the number of search terms ('hits') present within a document, so results are not ordered meaningfully; and the process of constructing search terms is not intuitive for a user and it can accordingly be difficult to formulate or refine the search terms.[107] Language is contextual, but while humans are adept at discerning the particular meaning of a word (which likely has multiple meanings) from its context, this is challenging for computers.

'Syntax' refers to the structure or grammatical arrangement of words in a sentence. Syntactic analysis therefore includes techniques like parsing, segmentation and stemming for grammatical simplification. 'Semantics' refers to the meaning conveyed by words such as sense, implication and presupposition. Semantic analysis of text involves computer analysis with the goal of understanding meaning and interpretation of words.[108] Using a word's context to establish its meaning is referred to as 'semantic analysis' or 'latent semantic analysis' (and also latent semantic indexing).[109] Semantic analysis moves away from counts of word frequency as a guide to relevance, using more sophisticated patterns of word use. This is a technique used in NLP, discussed in the final section of this chapter.

Early work in legal IR was geared towards moving beyond keyword searching. The use of 'fuzzy' concepts in law means that it is important to be able to search beyond words and phrases to look for concepts – ie, to do semantic analysis. On this basis, some distinguished between IR and document retrieval, saying that the former should be about capturing pure information (concepts) rather than simply text (documents).[110] Hafner's doctoral research in the 1970s likewise attempted to do 'conceptual retrieval' and she used what are referred to as semantic net representations for this purpose.[111] By constructing a set of relationships among words, the legal IR system would extend the search to include terms which were conceptually related to the search term, or similar, even if those terms had not been specified by the user. Early legal IR systems were not regarded as 'intelligent' but could form a part of intelligent systems.[112] Interest in legal IR was reinvigorated

[106] F Schilder, 'Ben Hachey and Claire Grover (2005) "Automatic Legal Text Summarisation: Experiments with Summary Structuring"' in Bench-Capon et al (eds) (n 66).

[107] Russell and Norvig (n 3) 868.

[108] A Arruda, 'An Ethical Obligation to Use Artificial Intelligence: An Examination of the Use of Artificial Intelligence in Law and the Model Rules of Professional Responsibility' (2017) 40(3) *American Journal of Trial Advocacy* 443, 447.

[109] Remus and Levy (n 33) 510.

[110] Susskind (n 38) 168, 176, citing B Niblett, *Expert Systems for Lawyers* (1981) 29 *Computers and Law* 2.

[111] Rissland, Ashley and Loui (n 38) 7; the system was known as LIRS: see Gray (n 38) 32.

[112] Gray (n 38) 13.

in the 1990s with the advent of 'improved retrieval engines, new learning-based information extraction techniques, and the dramatic rise of the World Wide Web'.[113] From this point on, there was interest in combining IR with CBR,[114] with rule-based systems, and with argument retrieval.[115] Now, advances in NLP and the use of machine learning to analyse texts are also being incorporated.[116] Modern approaches focus less on technical search, and more on the automatic detection of relevance between concepts.

Decision Trees

Broadly, a decision tree is just a structure setting out different possible choices (Figure 2.3). Decision trees can be used for decision support systems (expert systems), but also for statistical modelling and in machine learning,[117] though they are used in quite different ways.

Figure 2.3 Decision tree on Titanic survival data

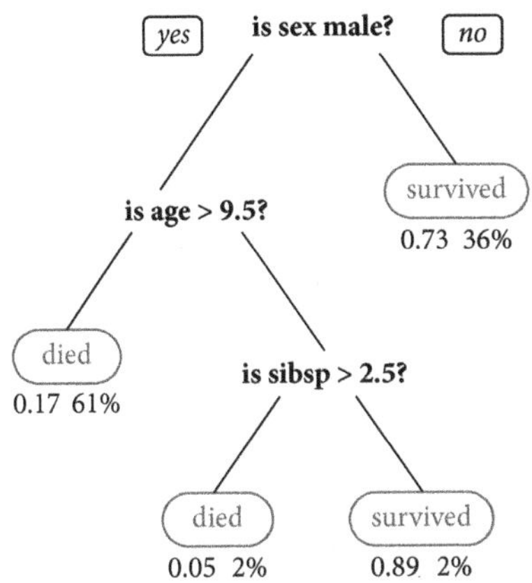

Source: JJ Hox, 'Computational Social Science Methodology, Anyone?' (2017) 13(Supplement) *Methodology* 3, 9, Figure 2

[113] Rissland, Ashley and Loui (n 38) 12 (discussing a number of examples, including AustLII, and SMILE); Russell and Norvig (n 3) 884.

[114] AZ Wyner, 'Edwina L Rissland and Jody J Daniels (1995). "A Hybrid CBR-IR Approach to Legal Information Retrieval"' in Bench-Capon et al (eds) (n 66).

[115] H Yamada, S Teufel and T Tokunaga, 'Building a Corpus of Legal Argumentation in Japanese Judgement Documents: Towards Structure-Based Summarisation' (2019) 27(2) *Artificial Intelligence and Law* 141.

[116] eg, S El Jelali, 'Legal Retrieval as Support to EMediation: Matching Disputant's Case and Court Decisions' (2015) 23 *Artificial Intelligence & Law* 1; T Maxwell and B Schafer, 'Natural Language Processing and Query Expansion in Legal Information Retrieval: Challenges and a Response' (2010) 24(1) *International Review of Law, Computers & Technology* 63–72 ('NLP and IR have traditionally been viewed as incompatible because of the lack of results showing how incorporation of NLP into IR substantially improves performance compared to "bag-of-words techniques" where terms are viewed just as independent space-separated tokens').

[117] B de Ville, 'Decision Trees' (2013) 5 *WIREs Computational Statistics* 448, 448.

The choices are shown as nodes in a hierarchical structure, beginning with a root node, and branching out into further nodes. Nodes which have no 'children' are called leaves, and these leaves represent the answers – all the possible solutions which could be derived from the tree:

> Every tree is comprised of nodes. Each node is associated with one of the input variables. The edges coming from that node are the total possible values of that node. A leaf represents the value based on the values given from the input variable in the path running from the root node to the leaf.[118]

Decision trees may be binary – where every node has no more than two children, or two possible choices (such as Figure 2.3) or they may have multiple branches.

A rule-based or expert system decision tree has facts as its nodes, and rules for how the tree should be traversed. A user can be stepped through a series of questions to classify a problem and generate a pre-scripted solution.[119] In this instance, the programmer or creator defines the branching of the decision tree. In machine learning, algorithms determine the branching or the best place to split data, based on the dataset itself.

Machine Learning and Natural Language Processing

The present upsurge of interest in AI has been largely fuelled by developments in machine learning, a term which is becoming nearly as well known. Indeed, Domingos suggests that, although a subfield of AI, machine learning 'now eclipses its proud parent'.[120] What is revolutionary about machine learning is that systems can adapt themselves as they encounter new data and continually enhance their own performance.[121] Unlike most software development, where programmers tell the software a set of rules for it to follow (a manual process),[122] a machine learning system can produce its own computational model and apply it to new and not previously seen data. Rather than a person inputting a large number of rules, the system can 'learn' the rules by analysing examples. This is why Domingos describes machine learning as 'the inverse of programming'.[123]

A prerequisite for machine learning is sufficient data. There is now vastly more electronic data in existence in the world than ever before, and its volume is multiplying at speed.[124] The amount of data available means less reliance on humans to

[118] ibid 48.
[119] DR Mountain, 'Could New Technologies Cause Great Law Firms to Fail?' (2002) 52 *Syracuse Law Review* 1065, 1067.
[120] Domingos (n 14) 8.
[121] H Surden 'Machine Learning and Law' (2014) 89(1) *Washington Law Review* 87, 89.
[122] ibid 93.
[123] Domingos (n 14) 30.
[124] Mayer-Schonberger and Cukier (n 21) 8; B Alarie, A Niblett and H Yoon, 'How Artificial Intelligence Will Affect the Practice of Law' (2018) 68 Suppl 1 *University of Toronto Law Journal* 106, 124.

'painstakingly encode' knowledge.[125] It is important to note, however, that data quantity and quality impact on the functioning of machine learning systems. Poor-quality and 'messy' data is a substantial impediment to obtaining useful results from a machine learning system, hence the expression 'garbage in, garbage out'.[126] Organisations may have volumes of data but not in useable form, or it may be corrupt, badly labelled or contain many irrelevancies.[127] To an extent, this can be overcome by 'cleaning' data, which means ensuring that missing or wrong data is corrected either by deleting the subjects with missing data or making a guess as to what the missing data would be by comparing other, complete, data in the set. Yet, as we discuss in later chapters, this can be a complex task in itself.

Machine learning programs excel at finding statistical patterns in data.[128] The model developed is a pattern of statistical relationships that exist between different features of the data in the dataset.[129] Typically, the more data analysed, the greater the accuracy of the model. The dynamism of machine learning comes from the ability of the program to refine itself as it encounters even more new data, and its capacity to scale to huge amounts of data. Unsurprisingly, machine learning is therefore much better at managing complex, changing situations where it would not be possible for a human programmer to predict the best rule to apply.[130] As explained at the beginning of this chapter, the ability to perform many calculations at speed is also one way of distinguishing computational and human intelligence.

Machine learning can be discussed by reference to 'learning style', which may be 'supervised', 'unsupervised' or a mixture of both. The difference lies in the data with which the system is presented in order to learn. In supervised learning, the data is already labelled (for example, an image is labelled as depicting a dog or a cat), and the program can therefore identify 'associations between the data and the labelled outcome, or classification'.[131]

Another way of classifying kinds of machine learning is to group the type of algorithm used in terms of its function. In his 2015 book, Domingos prophesises the development of a 'master algorithm' or the superlative form of machine learning which will eclipse all others.[132] Yet there are many kinds of algorithm, and little overarching consensus on classifications. Some popular types are regression

[125] Kaplan (n 2) 24.

[126] TC Redman 'If Your Data is Bad, Your Machine Learning Tools Are Useless', *Harvard Business Review*, 2 April 2018, https://hbr.org/2018/04/if-your-data-is-bad-your-machine-learning-tools-are-useless?autocomplete=true; T Redman 'Data's Credibility Problem' (2013) 91(12) *Harvard Business Review* 84.

[127] See D Shapiro, 'Artificial Intelligence and Bad Data', *Towards Data Science*, 6 November 2017, www.towardsdatascience.com/artificial-intelligence-and-bad-data-fbf2564c541a.

[128] Kaplan (n 2) 27; see also Husain (n 6) 21.

[129] S Barocas and AD Selbst, 'Big Data's Disparate Impact' (2016) 104 *California Law Review* 671, 677.

[130] Surden (n 121) 93.

[131] Husain (n 6) 21.

[132] Domingos (n 14).

algorithms, decision trees,[133] Bayesian algorithms (which apply Bayes' Theorem for classification and regression problems),[134] clustering algorithms and ensemble algorithms (composed of various other models).

Several writers, however, posit that it is Artificial Neural Networks (or Computational Neural Networks, or simply neural nets) and their descendants, Deep Learning algorithms, that are making the most significant advances in machine learning at the moment.[135] Walsh explains that 'previously research in machine learning focused on probabilistic techniques … Deep Learning builds neural networks somewhat like that of our own brains'.[136] Yet neural networks are not new – these techniques have existed for decades.

Neural Networks

The year 1987 is described as a significant year for AI and Law but in the general world of AI research it marked the start of the second 'AI winter', when funding dried up and once-successful commercial entities floundered.[137] The limitations of expert systems were being felt, yet there was pessimism around exploring other approaches, such as neural nets.[138] Researchers using neural nets called themselves 'connectionists' as they tried to replicate the connections between synapses in the human brain.[139] This stood in contradistinction to previous work focused on logic and symbolic reasoning systems, whose proponents have been termed 'symbolists'.[140]

Neural networks (also referred to as perceptrons) are a key part of machine learning today. Though they have a long history, Dormehl suggests that for decades 'they were largely ignored' in favour of logical reasoning models.[141] Neural nets are so named because they seek to emulate the architecture of the human brain: neuroscience hypothesises that the brain functions via 'electrochemical activity in networks of brain cells called neurons'.[142] In simple terms, it is posited that within the brain

> biological neurons are cells that send and receive electrical impulses from other neurons that they are connected to. A neuron will only fire an electrical impulse when it receives impulses from other neurons that together are stronger than a certain threshold.

[133] Attributed to the work of J Ross Quinlan: see de Ville (n 117) 452–53.
[134] R Matthews, 'Bayes's Theorem' (2010) 207(2777) *New Scientist* 35.
[135] Dormehl (n 3) 53–56; 'Why Artificial Intelligence is Enjoying a Renaissance' (n 1).
[136] Walsh (n 1) 51.
[137] Bench-Capon (n 70); Dormehl (n 3) 27.
[138] See Leith (n 89).
[139] Dormehl (n 3) 46; Russell and Norvig (n 3) 24.
[140] Domingos (n 14) refers to five different groups – symbolists, connectionists, evolutionaries, Bayesians and analogizers: at 51–55.
[141] Dormehl (n 3) 32 and ch 2, 'Another Way to Build AI'.
[142] Russell and Norvig (n 3) 727.

> Anything lower than that threshold and the neuron won't do anything. Just what that threshold is depends on the chemical properties of the neuron in question and varies from neuron to neuron. Upon firing, an electrical impulse shoots out of the neuron and into more neurons downstream and the process continues. In the brain, billions of these interconnected neurons communicating with each other form the basis for consciousness.[143]

Computational neural networks seek to replicate this structure, as nodes or processors called neurons (see Figure 2.4) are linked together in layers, with input and output layers. The neural network functions by layers of neurons working in connection with one another. Each individual neuron takes in 'any number' of inputs and generates a single output. As biological neurons are posited to do, it is the weighting of different inputs which determines whether the neuron is activated: 'A neuron weights its inputs and then sums them up with a bias. An activation function is then applied, which produces the output for the neuron'.[144]

Figure 2.4 An individual neuron

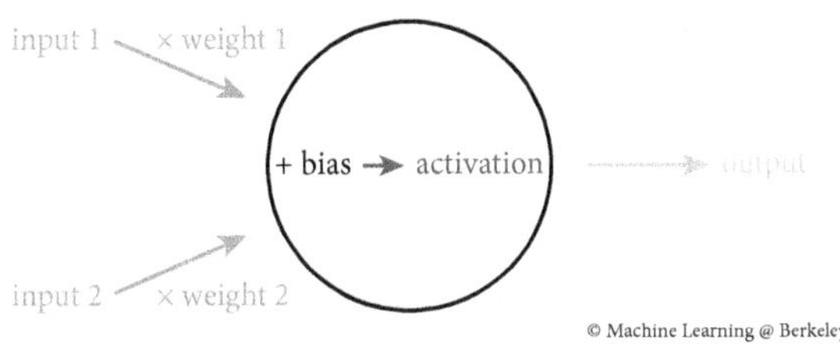

Source: D Geng and S Shih, 'Machine Learning Crash Course: Part 3', *Machine Learning @Berkeley*, 4 February 2017, medium.com/@ml.at.berkeley/machine-learning-crash-course-part-3-4a5bfd72294a.

The activation function is the 'firing' which is described in reference to biological neurons. The activation function determines whether the neuron is triggered to 'fire', that is, whether the information received in terms of outputs is over the threshold, or relevant. An important characteristic of the activation function is that it can be differentiable or smooth – representing all values from 0 to 100 per cent probability that the neuron should be triggered.[145] If the function is not differentiable, for example, if it is a step function, only specific levels of probability can be represented.

The output of one neuron then becomes input for another, so they work together – again, similarly to the way the human brain is thought to process data, by clustering neurons into groups.[146] In neural networks the neurons are grouped into layers. As we explain below, a deep neural network has many hidden layers.

[143] D Geng and S Shih, 'Machine Learning Crash Course: Part 3', *Machine Learning @Berkeley*, 4 February 2017, medium.com/@ml.at.berkeley/machine-learning-crash-course-part-3-4a5bfd72294a.

[144] ibid.

[145] For a clear explanation of this, see ibid 'The Model (Details)'; Russell and Norvig (n 3) 728–29.

[146] Geng and Shih (n 143).

The significance of neural networks to law and legal reasoning is that, unlike the maintenance of a database wherein the relationships between rules and information is specified, the relationship between pieces of information need not be explicitly stated. Neural nets are therefore 'subsymbolic reasoners'.[147] In contrast to the 'if this, then that' models described earlier in relation to rule-based reasoning – stepping from a to b to c; or working backwards from c to a – a neural network's operation is described as follows:

> The case knowledge base is learned by the network at a subsymbolic level, and recorded as [synaptic] connection weights. Put simply, where 'if a then b' occurs sixty times, and 'if c then a' occurs four times, the system will calculate the relative weights of the two rules.[148]

Importantly, neural nets could also 'learn' – for example by using backpropagation, a method by which, when told its outputs are erroneous, a system can work back through the layers, adjusting the 'weights', until a better answer is reached.[149] Russell and Norvig have explained the 'reinvention' of backpropagation in the mid-1980s.[150] Further terminology used in reference to neural networks relates to the direction of the neurons in the network, or its topology. Russell and Norvig explain:

> A *feed-forward* network has connections only in one direction … Every node receives input from 'upstream' nodes and delivers output to 'downstream' nodes; there are no loops … A *recurrent* network, on the other hand, feeds its outputs back into its own inputs. This means that the activation levels of the network form a dynamical system.[151]

There was a resurgence of interest in neural nets within AI and Law in the 1990s as they were seen as a viable way of automatically generalising from many examples. Pamela Gray noted contemporaneously that neural nets 'are particularly useful in distilling all the rules from a large body of cases'[152] which assisted in overcoming the problem of the symbolic representation of legal knowledge. It was surmised, therefore, that neural networks might be able to overcome some of the issues stemming from the open-textured nature of law[153] – that is, the complex, multi-layered and sometimes contradictory nature of legal reasoning. While a logic system flounders with too many exceptions – requiring the creation of new rules – neural nets are good at reasoning around oddities. One early application of neural nets to law was described in Bench-Capon's article 'Neural Networks and Open Texture', published in 1993.[154] Bench-Capon 'tested a number of alter-

[147] Aikenhead (n 94) 34.

[148] Gray (n 38) 67.

[149] Dormehl (n 3) 44–46; D Hunter, 'Out of Their Minds: Legal Theory in Neural Networks' (1999) 7(2–3) *Artificial Intelligence and Law* 129, 130.

[150] Russell and Norvig (n 3) 24.

[151] ibid 729 (emphasis in original). See also I Goodfellow, Y Bengio and A Courville, *Deep Learning* (MIT Press, 2016) 197–216 for an explanation of backpropagation.

[152] Gray (n 38) 67.

[153] B Verheij, 'Commentary: Trevor Bench-Capon (1993) Neural Networks and Open Texture' in Bench-Capon et al (eds) (n 66).

[154] T Bench-Capon, 'Neural Networks and Open Texture', Proceedings of the Fourth International Conference on Artificial Intelligence and the Law (ACM Press, 292).

nate network architectures, all of which were feed-forward networks, trained using backpropagation'.[155] Hunter later called this 'methodologically the most sound implementation of any neural network we have seen', as it used both a large number of cases as training data, and trialled different architectures.[156]

Yet the exploration of neural nets in the 1990s did not lead to the hoped-for breakthroughs, due in part to limited or inappropriate data, and also to the absence of explanatory functions.[157] These problems arguably reflect current criticisms about the use of machine learning to 'predict' legal decisions.

Deep Learning

Perhaps the most widely hyped term currently used in relation to machine learning at present is 'deep learning', typically (but not necessarily) using neural nets.[158] The Organisation for Economic Co-operation and Development (OECD) has explained:

> Neural networks involve repeatedly interconnecting thousands or millions of simple transformations into a larger statistical machine that can learn sophisticated relationships between inputs and outputs. In other words, neural networks modify their own code to find and optimise links between inputs and outputs. Finally, deep learning is a phrase that refers to particularly large neural networks; there is no defined threshold as to when a neural net becomes 'deep'.[159]

Martin Heller notes that deep learning may 'produce useful results where other methods fail', but it is often not very interpretable.[160] Deep learning is credited with rapid improvements in NLP and image recognition.[161] As Heller explains, however, it also requires significant computing power, and interpretation can be challenging.[162]

While 'shallow' neural networks have been around for a long time, 'deep' neural networks are a more recent phenomenon.[163] 'Deep' refers to having more than one

[155] Hunter (n 149) 137.

[156] ibid.

[157] Hunter (n 149); Sartor and Rotolo (n 40) 204 ('The application of neural networks to model legal decisionmaking has been subject to some criticisms, focusing in particular on the lack of explanations').

[158] Dhar (n 4) 8; Russell and Norvig (n 3) 728; Goodfellow, Bengio and Courville (n 151) 13–14. Random Forests are also examples of deep learning algorithms.

[159] OECD, *Artificial Intelligence in Society* (OECD Publishing, 2019) ch 1: 'The Technical Landscape'.

[160] M Heller, 'What is Deep Learning?', 24 May 2019, *Info World*, www.infoworld.com/article/3397142/what-is-deep-learning-algorithms-that-mimic-the-human-brain.html.

[161] eg, A Krizhevsky, I Sutskever and GE Hinton, 'Imagenet Classification with Deep Convolutional Neural Networks' (2012) *Advances in Neural Information Processing Systems*, 26th Annual Conference on Neural Information Processing Systems 2012, Volume 2, 1097–105; D Silver et al, 'Mastering the Game of Go with Deep Neural Networks and Tree Search' (2016) 529 *Nature* 484.

[162] Heller (n 160).

[163] Schmidhuber (n 36) 4.

'hidden' layer (in between input and output layers).[164] There may be many hidden layers:

> [E]ach layer is fully connected to the one before it and after it. This means the output of a single neuron in a layer connects to (or is the input of) every neuron in the next layer, because the information that a neuron provides in one layer could be useful to any neuron in the next layer.[165]

A group of data scientists based at UC Berkeley have illustrated the operation of a (deep) neural network using the example of how a system might identify a picture of a dog (see Figure 2.5). They explain that this is (conceptually) how a neural network functions, once it has been trained with voluminous data.[166]

Figure 2.5 How a neural network identifies a picture of a dog

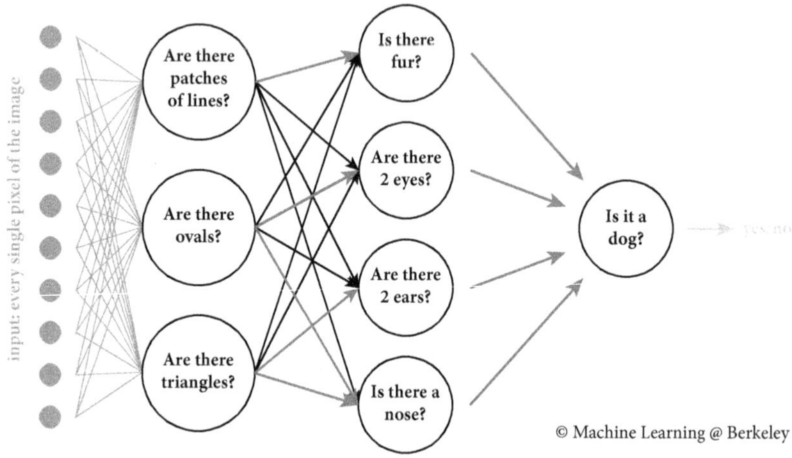

Source: D Geng and S Shih, 'Machine Learning Crash Course: Part 3', *Machine Learning @Berkeley*, 4 February 2017, medium.com/@ml.at.berkeley/machine-learning-crash-course-part-3-4a5bfd72294a.

Deep learning can be used for supervised or unsupervised learning. In unsupervised learning the data is not labelled and the software searches for patterns in the data. Thus, rather than tell the software which pictures depict cats and which do not, until it learns the difference, it is provided with sufficient pictures that it can detect the pattern for itself.[167] This may, or may not, have anything to do with how humans recognise a picture of a cat – but it indisputably works.[168] Thus,

[164] Kaplan (n 2) 34.

[165] Geng and Shih (n 143).

[166] ibid. See also MD Zeiler and R Fergus, *Visualizing and Understanding Convolutional Networks* (2013) arXiv:1311.2901.

[167] Kaplan (n 2) 30; Silver et al (n 161); Karnow (n 52) 146–47; J Markoff, 'How Many Computers to Identify a Cat? 16,000', *New York Times*, 25 June 2012.

[168] Kaplan (n 2) 30.

supervised learning can be described as an exercise in classification; while unsupervised learning is about identifying patterns in data. So far, most of the benefits of deep learning have involved supervised learning, but it also has enormous potential for unsupervised learning.[169]

Natural Language Processing

Prakash Nadkarni, Lucila Ohno-Machado and Wendy Chapman explain that NLP 'began in the 1950s at the intersection of artificial intelligence and linguistics', and was originally distinct from text IR, though over time the fields have focalised somewhat.[170] Now, most NLP techniques apply machine learning.[171] Very broadly speaking, since language is contextual, statistics are used to work out the probability of words appearing near one another in a text.[172] NLP breaks sentences down and examines individual words and how they relate to one another. NLP usually involves both syntactic and semantic analysis.[173] Techniques for semantic analysis include[174] word sense disambiguation – using the context of a word to work out its meaning – and named entity recognition – for example identifying words which are names of people and places.

NLP includes 'question answering, machine translation, text summarisation and speech recognition'.[175] It enables humans to communicate with computers using natural language but also for computers to obtain knowledge from large collections of messy and unstructured text – such as found on the internet.[176] Another important use is for text classification functions, for example identifying spam email,[177] or Technology Assisted Review, as discussed in Chapter 5. As explained above, a focus for law and legal research has been on legal IR. Most legal repositories have now moved from simple Boolean searching to more sophisticated methods which are able to score or rank documents according to relevance. In addition to legal IR, areas of interest for law include question answering, text classification, summarisation and argument retrieval. NLP is also important for regulatory technology (RegTech) as it permits analyses of large volumes of textual data, including 'unstructured' data such as social network sites, in order to monitor human behaviour. It can also be used as a means of rendering data accessible

[169] A Ng, Presentation at Stanford University, 16 July 2014, www.youtube.com/watch?v=W15K9PegQt0.

[170] PM Nadkarni, L Ohno-Machado and WW Chapman, 'Natural Language Processing: An Introduction' (2011) 18 *Journal of the American Medical Information Association* 544, 544.

[171] Ben-Ari et al (n 10) 29.

[172] See Walsh (n 1) 43–44.

[173] Nadkarni, Ohno-Machado and Chapman (n 170) describe these as 'lower-level' and 'higher-level' forms of analysis, respectively.

[174] See ibid 545–56 for a complete list.

[175] Walsh (n 1) 110.

[176] Russell and Norvig (n 3) 860.

[177] ibid 865–66.

for processing by another AI system: NLP might be better at extracting the context of a word which can be an input into another system.

A well-known current example of using NLP in a legal context is ROSS Intelligence, described as a legal application of IBM's Watson.[178] ROSS is intended to enable a user to ask a natural language legal question and receive 'contextualized answers with snippets from the document in question'.[179] ROSS thus promises improved and more user-friendly legal searching; it also has a memo-writing function. Ashley suggests that this approach will lead to the development of programs which can 'extract relevant information automatically from legal decision texts'.[180] The capacity to do so will overcome the problem of either manually inputting information to a system (the knowledge acquisition bottleneck) but also the need for data labelling.[181] It can also make use of the large corpora of legal texts in existence. Floris Bex has suggested that in the area of argumentation mining, programs may be able to 'automatically detect the structure of … arguments in legal texts'.[182] Ashley has also argued that while AI programs cannot engage in legal reasoning (as they cannot explain their answers), they will be able to do 'argument retrieval': in other words, 'generate arguments for and against particular outcomes in problems input as texts, predict a problem's outcome, and explain their predictions with reasons that legal professionals will recognise'.[183]

Where Next?

Many current projects in legal applications of AI are combining or incorporating various of the methods described above.[184] Livio Robaldo and colleagues, for instance, have written that

> [r]ecent research has highlighted the need to create a bridge between conceptual questions, such as the role of legal interpretation in mining and reasoning, as well as

[178] ROSS Intelligence: www.rossintelligence.com; Kaplan (n 2) 42–43.

[179] KM Cutler, 'YC's ROSS Intelligence Leverages IBM's Watson to Make Sense of Legal Knowledge', 28 July 2015, www.techcrunch.com/2015/07/27/ross-intelligence (quoting Andrew Arruda); K Van Paassen, 'University of Toronto's Next Lawyer: A Computer Program Named Ross', *The Globe and Mail*, 11 December 2014, updated 25 March 2017.

[180] Ashley (n 39) 800; citing D Ferrucci et al, 'Building Watson: An Overview of the DeepQA Project' (2010) 31(3) *AI Magazine*.

[181] Ashley (n 23) 11.

[182] F Bex, 'Raquel Mochales and Marie-Francine Moens (2009) "Automatic Detection of Arguments in Legal Texts"' in Bench-Capon et al (eds) (n 66).

[183] Ashley (n 23) 3.

[184] Ashley says current research is integrating logic-based, case-based and value-based approaches: 'Digital Age Legal Practice' (n 39) 796; and at 800 citing Ferrucci et al (n 180). See also L Robaldo et al, 'Introduction for Artificial Intelligence and Law: Special Issue "Natural Language Processing for Legal Texts"' (2019) 27(2) *Artificial Intelligence and Law* 113.

computational and engineering challenges, such as the handling of big legal data and the complexity of regulatory compliance.[185]

Differing approaches have their own strengths and weaknesses. Speaking in general terms, Domingos commented that 'there's no sign that knowledge engineering will ever be able to compete with machine learning outside of a few niche areas'.[186] However, one strength of expert systems lies in platforms which can guide many users through simple legal problems and thereby provide legal assistance at scale. Importantly, expert systems are also far more transparent and interpretable than machine learning systems.

A well-known example is the free DoNotPay chatbot that was created in 2015 by Joshua Browder.[187] Having himself accumulated many parking infringement notices, Browder became aware of the similarities in the letters he was writing as he attempted to dispute his fines.[188] He created the app as a means to assist many users to also draft a similar letter, automatically generated after the user answered a series of simple questions. DoNotPay is credited with being the first 'legal chatbot'. By 2017 it had reportedly been used to overturn more than 375,000 parking tickets,[189] and Browder had turned his attention to other areas where it was perceived the cost of legal advice was deterring people who required assistance.[190] More specifically, the Networked Society Institute has identified different kinds of 'automated legal advice tools', including:

- Specialised standalone technologies, such as legal chatbots, apps and virtual assistants;
- Enablers of legal advice such as legal automated drafting, legal document review and legal algorithms;
- Further enablers of legal advice such as legal data analytics and predictors, and legal artificial intelligence.[191]

There are a growing number of applications of legal expert systems that are being utilised to increase accessibility to legal information.[192] Increasingly, for instance, universities are offering law students courses in building simple apps with access

[185] Robaldo et al (n 184): 'To facilitate progress towards integrating the efforts on these two objectives, the EU has recently funded several research projects, [including] "MIREL: Mining and Reasoning with Legal texts", www.mirelproject.eu'.

[186] Domingos (n 14) 36.

[187] A Sehmer, 'Teenager's Parking Appeals Website Saves Motorists £2m after Overturning Thousands of Fines', *Independent Online*, 30 December 2015; P Olson, 'This Teen's Lawyer-Bot is Busting Thousands of Parking Tickets', www.Forbes.com, 28 June 2016; J Lee-Young, 'Entrepreneur Launches Robot Lawyer Chatbot in Four Canadian Cities', *Postmedia*, 1 November 2017.

[188] V Li, 'Joshua Browder: His "Chat" Is Not Just Talk', *ABA Journal*, 14 September 2017.

[189] ibid.

[190] E Krause, 'This Robot Will Handle Your Divorce Free of Charge', *Wall Street Journal Online*, 27 October 2017.

[191] Bennett et al (n 46) 22.

[192] LR Lupica, RA Franklin and SM Friedman, 'The Apps for Justice Project: Employing Design Thinking to Narrow the Access to Justice Gap' (2017) 44(5) *Fordham Urban Law Journal* 1363, 1368–69; Bennett et al (n 46) 5.

to justice aims. Greenleaf, Mowbray and Chung have argued that the true goal of expert systems is to support human decision making, rather than entirely replace humans in the legal advice-giving process.[193] They also point out that in smaller jurisdictions there may be insufficient relevant cases to render a machine learning system any more accurate or viable than 'a formal statute-based expert system' which may assist to identify relevant legislation, for instance.[194]

Domingos says that the move to machine learning requires letting go of deterministic thinking and shifting to statistical thinking.[195] But such a shift has its own challenges for law. In particular, the tension between approaches which attempt to model human legal reasoning, and those which may be described as purely 'data-driven', continues. Ronald Loui has written:

> There have been many important competing approaches in the history of AI, and representationalists and algorithmists are often in discord. In AI generally, the ebb of domain-based ontologies and the whitecap crest of abstract machine learning might currently be at its greatest discordance.[196]

The rise of deep learning techniques, in particular, exemplifies systems whose outputs cannot be intelligibly explained to people. Meanwhile other types of system – certainly more basic expert systems, but also other statistical approaches – have much greater explanatory potential. In the case of deep learning, unlike other machine learning approaches, even those who built the system are unlikely to be able to explain its outputs.

For lawyers and the legal profession the potential of machine learning is debated – for some it spells the end of lawyers; others say that it is largely over-hyped. In response, we make two claims: first, that the effects of AI on law will not be unitary, and we therefore need to consider individual applications in much more detail; second, that it is most likely human lawyers will be augmented by machine intelligence. The use of AI in legal services shows no signs of halting or reversing. Lawyers will need to become familiar with these applications as their use becomes increasingly common – whether due to being mandated by courts or governments, demanded by clients or simply through the need to remain competitive. The application of AI to aspects of legal service delivery has profound implications for individual lawyers and for the legal profession. Yet grasping the impact of AI on legal practice is complicated by the fact that lawyers are a diverse group who will be affected differently by different developments and applications. The next chapter turns to consider what it is that lawyers do, in order to better understand the changes AI is bringing.

[193] Greenleaf, Mowbray and Chung (n 44). See also Leith (n 89).

[194] Greenleaf, Mowbray and Chung (n 44) citing Ashley (n 23) 13.

[195] Domingos (n 14) 9.

[196] RP Loui, 'From Berman and Hafner's Teleological Context to Baude and Sachs' Interpretive Defaults: An Ontological Challenge for the Next Decades of AI and Law' (2016) 24(4) *Artificial Intelligence and Law* 371, 374.

3

The Practice of Law – What Do Lawyers Do?

Introduction

In some cultures, lawyers have existed for centuries – legal scholar Roscoe Pound dated advocates back to antiquity, and suggested that thirteenth-century England saw a recognisably similar legal profession.[1] By the nineteenth century, the profession of law was well established in Western Europe and the US.[2] By contrast, in China, lawyers were not traditionally recognised as an occupational group, with civil disputes typically being resolved informally by local leaders or respected elders.[3] The professionalisation of lawyers there began in the twentieth century and developed rapidly in the 1970s and 1980s with the modernisation of the legal system.[4] Likewise, in India, law was historically a profession of pleaders (*vakils*) until the first law firms emerged to serve British clients in the colonial era.[5]

Despite the long history of the profession, and a voluminous scholarship on legal ethics,[6] the role of the lawyer remains hard to define. As Robert Mnookin and Lewis Kornhauser observed in their classic 1979 essay 'Bargaining in the Shadow of the Law', 'In view of the critical role of lawyers and the disparate functions they may perform, it is startling how little we know about how lawyers actually behave'.[7] This is especially so when adopting a global view as 'different varieties of professionalism

[1] R Pound, *The Lawyer from Antiquity to Modern Times* (West Publishing, 1953) ch 2 'Origins: The Lawyer in Antiquity' and ch 5 'The Organization of Lawyers in Medieval England'.

[2] GC Hazard Jr and T Schneyer, 'Regulatory Controls on Large Law Firms: A Comparative Perspective' (2002) 44 *Arizona Law Review* 593, 594; see also NG Foster and S Sule, *German Legal System and Laws* (Oxford University Press, 2010).

[3] AHY Chen, *An Introduction to the Legal System of the People's Republic of China* (3rd edn, LexisNexis, 1993) 128 cited by MC Szto, 'Towards a Global Bar: A Look at China, Germany, England, and the United States' (2004) 14 *Indiana International Comparative Law Review* 585, 587.

[4] Szto (n 3) 586–87.

[5] A Gupta, VS Khanna and DB Wilkins, 'Overview of Legal Practice in India and the Indian Legal Profession' in DB Wilkins, V Khanna and D Trubek (eds), *The Indian Legal Profession in the Age of Globalization: The Rise of the Corporate Legal Sector and Its Impact on Lawyers and Society* (Cambridge University Press, 2017) 40–41.

[6] See the summary of BA Green, 'The Role of Personal Values in Professional Decisionmaking' (1997) 11(1) *Georgetown Journal of Legal Ethics* 19, 22–23, and the references cited at fnn 11–13.

[7] R Mnookin and L Kornhauser, 'Bargaining in the Shadow of the Law: The Case of Divorce' (1979) 88 *Yale Law Journal* 950; see also J Flood, 'Doing Business: The Management of Uncertainty in Lawyers' Work' (1991) 25(1) *Law & Society Review* 41.

can be expected in different jurisdictions' and are shaped by 'nationally contingent behaviours, beliefs and ideals'.[8] In the broader context of legal professionalism, artificial intelligence and the future of work, it is important to think about what lawyers do in order to gauge the impact of automation, not just on tasks undertaken or skills needed, but for the meaning of professionalism and expertise, and the role of ethics and values. This chapter gives a broad overview of the profession in order to better consider what it is that lawyers do. This provides a basis for the consideration, in Part II of this book, of how that work may be affected by AI.

A widely promoted theory of the future of law and the legal profession concerns the use of technology in furtherance of the 'commoditisation' of law. Richard Susskind described this process in *The Future of Law*, pursuing it further in *Transforming the Law*[9] and later works.[10] Legal work is seen as readily capable of being broken down into discrete parts,[11] some of which may be performed by non-lawyers, or by technology. Of course, legal roles may be more or less susceptible to such decomposition. Some argue that certain types of lawyer or legal work are not capable of being done by an automated system, especially work requiring qualities which are still seen as inescapably human, such as empathy.[12] For those who emphasise the relationships between professionals and their clients, disaggregation strikes a jarring note:

> If legal services … can be stripped down to their component parts and tasked to the lowest cost provider, is relational trust still part of the equation? Are attorneys selling a product, or are they selling, in a very real sense, a relationship? Put simply, can relationships be disaggregated?[13]

Others identify negative consequences, particularly for individualised justice and the rule of law,[14] which concerns we discuss in Chapter 12. In like vein, it is argued both that commoditisation and technology can solve the access-to-justice crisis, and that (conversely) they can provide neither true access nor 'justice'.[15]

[8] A Babacan, A Di Iorio and A Meade, 'The (In)Effective Regulation of Incorporated Legal Practices: An Australian Case Study' (2013) 20(3) *International Journal of the Legal Profession* 315, 317 (citations omitted).

[9] R Susskind, *The Future of Law: Facing the Challenges of Information Technology* (Oxford University Press, 1996); R Susskind, *Transforming the Law: Essays on Technology, Justice and the Legal Marketplace* (Oxford University Press, 2000).

[10] eg, R Susskind, *Tomorrow's Lawyers: An Introduction to Your Future* (2nd edn, Oxford University Press, 2017); R Susskind and D Susskind, *The Future of the Professions: How Technology Will Transform the Work of Human Experts* (Oxford University Press, 2015).

[11] LE Ribstein, 'The Death of Big Law' (2010) (3) *Wisconsin Law Review* 749, 771.

[12] N Semple, 'Personal Plight Legal Practice and Tomorrow's Lawyers' (2014) 39(1) *Journal of the Legal Profession* 25.

[13] RK Vischer, 'Big Law and the Marginalization of Trust' (2012) 25(1) *Georgetown Journal of Legal Ethics* 165, 177.

[14] F Pasquale and G Cashwell, 'Prediction, Persuasion, and the Jurisprudence of Behaviourism' (2018) 68 (Supplement 1) *University of Toronto Law Review* 63; S Delacroix, 'Computer Systems Fit for the Legal Profession? (2018) 21(2) *Legal Ethics* 119.

[15] N Robinson, 'When Lawyers Don't Get All the Profits: Non-Lawyer Ownership, Access, and Professionalism' (2016) 29(1) *Georgetown Journal of Legal Ethics* 1; EST Poppe, 'The Future is ~~Bright~~ Complicated: AI, Apps & Access to Justice' (2019) 72(1) *Oklahoma Law Review* 185.

In many ways, this discussion is about professionalism and its meaning for lawyers and clients but also its place among social structures and foundational concepts. Howard Gardner and Lee Shulman wrote of professions generally:

> In our view, six commonplaces are characteristic of all professions, properly construed: a commitment to serve in the interests of clients in particular and the welfare of society in general; a body of theory or special knowledge with its own principles of growth and reorganization; a specialized set of professional skills, practices, and performances unique to the profession; the developed capacity to render judgments with integrity under conditions of both technical and ethical uncertainty; an organized approach to learning from experience both individually and collectively and, thus, of growing new knowledge from the contexts of practice; and the development of a professional community responsible for the oversight and monitoring of quality in both practice and professional education.[16]

These indicia resonate with the traditional conception of a lawyer, seen as a 'trusted advisor'. David Maister, Charles Green and Robert Galford argued that this role should be aspired to by all lawyers.[17] They note, however, that lawyer–client relationships develop over time and likely begin at the 'vendor' level: 'performing a specific task or "one-off" service, employing our technical skills'.[18] They suggest that the lawyer–client relationship can move beyond this, to where lawyers 'are seen in terms of our ability to put issues in context and to provide perspective', and finally to the role of 'trusted advisor'.[19] Maister, Green and Galford do not counsel lawyers against working at the vendor level.[20] Indeed, they posit that most lawyer–client relationships begin there. Yet their description of it – task based, technical, limited in scope – aligns with the type of work more susceptible to automation. Meanwhile, the trusted advisor role, or even the intermediate stages, are not as susceptible. This suggests that there are elements of most lawyers' work which could be automated but also that the pinnacle or idealised form of lawyering cannot be. One question for the future is how lawyers become the 'trusted advisor' without beginning at the bottom of the ascent as the vendor performing a one-off technical task. If expert lawyers remain in demand in the future, the path to attaining their expertise will likely be different.[21]

Likewise, Bradley Wendel identifies a question as to the character of law and lawyering, namely

> whether lawyers provide only information and technical expertise, or whether there is a thicker conception of professionalism that is bound up with the exercise of judgment

[16] H Gardner and LS Shulman, 'The Professions in America Today: Crucial but Fragile', *Dædalus* (Summer 2005) 13, 14.

[17] DH Maister, CH Green and RM Galford, *The Trusted Advisor* (Free Press, 2000) 7.

[18] ibid.

[19] ibid 8.

[20] ibid.

[21] Jordan Furlong, *Do Law Differently – Futures for Young Lawyers* (The Canada Bar Association, 2016).

> about morality, relational interests, the public good, or the substance beyond the form (or the spirit beyond the letter) of the law.[22]

Wendel argues that the formulation of lawyers as 'legal service providers' flattens out this thick concept, skimming off in the process a layer crucial to professionalism.[23]

At the same time, however, the role of lawyer has continued to change, and conceptions of professionalism frequently manifest as strained. In many jurisdictions, traditional hierarchies between lawyers and clients have shifted; lawyers are increasingly turning to new methods of delivering services and new structures from which to do so; and the demographics of the profession have radically altered. Finally, lawyers are also adopting altogether new means of working, including through the use of AI technologies.

Though a popular exercise, estimating what proportion of legal work (in terms of tasks) could be undertaken by AI is complex. Various predictions have been made, ranging from 10 per cent, to 40 per cent, to over 80 per cent.[24] The variation in perspectives stems from two elements: the fact that 'hard data' about what lawyers actually do is hard to come by;[25] and that the profession is highly diverse.[26] Even within jurisdictions, lawyers' work is varied:

> Lawyers advise clients in a wide variety of contexts, with respect to, *inter alia*, past, present, or future conduct; criminal and quasi-criminal public law regimes, or private interactions such as contracts or corporate structures; clients who are sophisticated or who have never previously dealt with a complex legal problem; clients who are organizations that employ the lawyer or for clients who are individuals barely able to afford the lawyer's fees.[27]

This diversity manifests itself in numerous ways, some of which are charted in this chapter – what kinds of work are 'legal' work in a given jurisdiction, the lawyer's practice area, the organisation in which the lawyer works and the type of clients they serve.

[22] WB Wendel, 'The Rule of Law and Legal-Process Reasons in Attorney Advising' (2019) 99(1) *Boston University Law Review* 107, 111.

[23] See also F Pasquale, 'Automating the Professions: Utopian Pipe Dream or Dystopian Nightmare?', *Los Angeles Review of Books* (15 March 2016) https://lareviewofbooks.org/article/automating-the-professions-utopian-pipe-dream-or-dystopian-nightmare/; and J Flood, 'Legal Professionals of the Future' in M DeStefano and G Dobrauz (eds), *New Suits: Appetite for Disruption in the Legal World* (Staempfli Verlag, 2019) 115.

[24] eg, McKinsey Global Institute estimates that 23 per cent of a lawyer's job could be automated: www.public.tableau.com/profile/mckinsey.analytics#!/vizhome/AutomationandUSjobs/Technicalpotentialforautomation; Deloitte predicts that up to 39 per cent of legal jobs could be automated: Deloitte, *Developing Legal Talent: Stepping into the Future Law Firm* (Report, 2016); D Remus and F Levy, 'Can Robots Be Lawyers? Computers, Lawyers, and the Practice of Law' (2017) 30(3) *Georgetown Journal of Legal Ethics* 501.

[25] FA Pasquale and G Cashwell, 'Four Futures of Legal Automation' (2015) 63 *UCLA Law Review Discourse* 26, 35.

[26] J Wade, 'Expanding the Concept of Legal Knowledge (Yet Again): Some Strategies for Reopening Deadlocked Negotiations' (2000) 11 *Australian Dispute Resolution Journal* 25, 25.

[27] A Woolley, 'The Lawyer as Advisor and the Practice of the Rule of Law' (2014) 47(2) *UBC Law Review* 743, 763.

Here, we first sketch a picture of the legal profession – a challenging exercise, given its scope. A prevailing distinction in terms of legal systems is that between common law and civil law countries, encapsulating a distinct history and development. We might also distinguish between Global North and Global South, or emerging economies (such as the BRICs – Brazil, Russia, India and China) and developed. Other distinctions can be drawn between public and private law, or domestic and international legal orders. Rather than adopting a particular typology, we here draw on a range of different jurisdictions and illustrations. This is the approach we use throughout this book, in our search for the most pertinent examples. We do, however, focus predominantly on common law systems such as those of the UK, the US, Australia and Canada.

We then turn to look at the work which lawyers perform and adopt five categories to encapsulate this work: transacting, advising, negotiating, representing and structuring. We examine the various organisations in which lawyers work, and the professional controls and regulatory structures under which they do so. We conclude the chapter by flagging some key sites of change.

Who are Lawyers?

Problems of nomenclature arise when discussing the legal profession in a global sense. Michael Burrage has proffered the following broad definition:

> Wherever full-time legal practitioners have come to recognize that they have certain common interests based on the work they perform, or on the knowledge and skills they share, have taken collective to defend these interests, and in so doing have received some recognition or privileges from the state that set them apart from other occupations, they will be taken to be a profession.[28]

This points to some of the traditional indicia of a profession: special skill and knowledge, a method of accrediting or admitting those who possess it, and recognition from the state.[29] There are jurisdictional differences as to precisely who is included within the profession of lawyer,[30] meaning that it is difficult to make international comparisons of (for instance) what proportion of the population are lawyers.[31] Noting the variability in terms of what elements of legal work are regulated or

[28] M Burrage, *Revolution and the Making of the Contemporary Legal Profession: England, France, and the United States* (Oxford University Press, 2006) 9.

[29] A nuanced overview is given by A Boon, 'Professionalism under the Legal Services Act 2007' (2010) 17(3) *International Journal of the Legal Profession* 195.

[30] D Rueschemeyer, 'The Legal Profession in Comparative Perspective' (1977) 47(3–4) *Sociological Inquiry* 97, 105.

[31] ibid 99.

controlled (or indeed, what constitutes legal work), Julian Webb draws attention specifically to the following:

- Representation of a party to court proceedings;
- The protection of specific legal professional titles (such as attorney, notary, or solicitor);
- The provision of specific categories of legal advice for financial reward.[32]

In many countries, there is not a single occupation of lawyer and the profession is instead divided into two or more branches which have different functions and fulfil different roles. This may devolve around those who speak in court (eg barrister, advocate, *advokat*,[33] *avocat*, *abogado*, *advocatura*[34]) and those who advise and draft documents (eg solicitor, *procuradore*, *notaire*) but the distinction is typically not so clear cut. As a result, 'countries differ markedly in the degree to which they restrict who can perform various [legal] tasks'.[35] Other related professions, which may be separate or included in the definition of lawyer, are those of notary, prosecutor, judge, and patent lawyer or patent attorney.[36] Matthias Kilian writes of Germany: 'In 2016, there were approximately 164,000 members of the bar (*Rechtsanwälte*), 1,500 notaries (*Notare*), 250 registered legal advisers (*Rechtsbeistände*), 83,000 tax advisers (*Steuerberater*), 3,500 patent attorneys (*Patentanwälte*), 20,000 judges (*Richter*) and 5,000 public prosecutors (*Staatsanwälte*)'.[37]

In many European countries, notaries are a separate, additional profession – these persons hold public office, yet are paid by their clients rather than the state, and their role involves authenticating transactional documents and ensuring the legal validity of transactions. They operate in the areas of property conveyancing, succession, marriage and corporate services (for instance, incorporating companies),[38] where they may hold a monopoly. In Spain, for example, notaries sit outside the 'legal profession' per se, which is divided into advocates (*abogados*) and

[32] J Webb, 'Regulating Lawyers in a Liberalized Legal Services Market: The Role of Education and Training' (2013) 24(2) *Stanford Law and Policy Review* 533, 535.

[33] In Denmark the Danish Bar and Law Society is called 'Advokatsamfundet'.

[34] In Russia: S Carle, G Davidson, T Mcdonald, and D Nougayrede, 'The Reform of the Russian Legal Profession: Three Varying Perspectives' (2018) 42(2) *Fordham International Law Journal* 271.

[35] '… such as representation in court, representation before administrative bodies, conveyancing of property, preparation of various kinds of legal documents and providing advice on legal matters': HM Kritzer, 'Lawyers' Professional Liability: Comparative Perspectives' (2017) 24(2) *International Journal of the Legal Profession* 73, 76, citing PSC Lewis (1989) 'Comparison and Change in the Study of Legal Professions' in RL Abel and PSC Lewis (eds), *Lawyers in Society: Comparative Theories* (University of California Press, 1996) 51–56.

[36] For example, Slovenia has four 'legal professions', judge, prosecutor, notary and lawyer: M Kilian, 'German Chocolates, Austrian Trainees, Swiss In-House Counsel and More: Correspondent's Report from Europe' (2010) 13(2) *Legal Ethics* 220, 222.

[37] M Kilian, 'Germany: The Constitutional Court as the Driver of Change in the Regulation of Legal Professions' in A Boon (ed), *International Perspectives on the Regulation of Lawyers and Legal Services* (Hart Publishing, 2017) 185, 185 fn 1.

[38] R Van den Bergh and Y Montagnie, 'Competition in Professional Service Markets: Are Latin Notaries Different?' (2007) 2(2) *Journal of Competition Law and Economics* 189, 200.

solicitors (*procuradores*).[39] Russia has around 8,000 *notaryusi* who handle conveyancing matters.[40] In other jurisdictions, however, solicitors may undertake some or all notarial tasks.

The work conducted by lawyers depends on context, context which is fleshed out to varying degrees in the sections which follow. This includes the role of lawyers (what kind of legal work); the jurisdiction in which they work and the professional strictures imposed on lawyers in that jurisdiction; and the kind of organisation they work within. Lawyers' work is also mediated by two additional key factors – the area of law in which they practise, and the clients for whom they work. These are synergistic: a lawyer practising in family law inevitably works for individuals; a lawyer who specialises in large-scale construction projects likely works for companies. North American academics have long suggested that the distinction between lawyers who work for individuals and those who work for corporate entities is the most significant in the legal services market.[41] In the 1980s John Heinz and Edward Laumann put forward the theory of the 'two hemispheres' of legal work: 'In the "personal-plight" hemisphere, lawyers … provided legal services to individuals and small businesses. In the "corporate hemisphere," … elite law school graduates and members of influential law firms represented corporations, labor unions, and other complex organizational clients'.[42]

Gillian Hadfield has commented that '"Hemi" is no longer even close to accurate', as much more time is now spent serving corporate clients, but notes that who a lawyer's clients are is still a fundamental indicator of all other attributes of the legal practitioner.[43] Meanwhile, William Henderson recently used the same typology to draw a picture of the economics of legal practice in the US.[44] Henderson further classified 'organisational clients' into six types – essentially ranging from individuals conducting businesses as companies through to very large entities with layers of management and in-house legal departments.[45] The theory of hemispheres has also been adopted to analyse developments in India.[46]

[39] FH Stephen, *Lawyers, Markets and Regulation* (Edward Elgar, 2013) 78.

[40] Carle et al (n 34).

[41] T Rostain, 'Robots versus Lawyers: A User-Centered Approach' (2017) 30(3) *Georgetown Journal of Legal Ethics* 559; GK Hadfield, 'The Price of Law: How the Market for Lawyers Distorts the Justice System' (2000) 98 *Michigan Law Review* 953; BH Barton, *Glass Half Full: The Decline and Rebirth of the Legal Profession* (Oxford University Press, 2015); WD Henderson, *Legal Market Landscape Report, Commissioned by the State Bar of California* (July 2018) 12–17.

[42] DA Remus, 'Out of Practice: The Twenty-First Century Legal Profession' (2014) 63(6) *Duke Law Journal* 1243, citing, inter alia, JP Heinz and EO Laumann, *Chicago Lawyers: The Social Structure of the Bar* 1 (revised edn, Northwestern University Press, 1994) 1, 330, 328.

[43] GK Hadfield, *Rules for a Flat World* (Oxford University Press, 2016) 124–25; see also Henderson (n 41) 12.

[44] Henderson (n 41) 12–17.

[45] ibid 16 (Figure 6).

[46] DB Wilkins, V Khanna and D Trubek, 'An Introduction to Globalization, Lawyers, and Emerging Economies: The Case of India' in Wilkins, Khanna and Trubek (eds) (n 5) 5–6.

The Work of Lawyers (What Do Lawyers Do?)

All the divisions described above make it difficult to reach overarching conclusions about the work of lawyers. In turn, estimating the effect of automation or AI on the legal profession is similarly complex. The challenges are illustrated by an exercise undertaken by two US academics, Dana Remus and Frank Levy, who attempted to quantify such an estimate.[47] Remus and Levy used empirical data from a billing software company to gain a clearer picture of the proportions of time which American lawyers, at top-tier and lower-tier firms, spent (at least as so far as billing reflects this) on different tasks.[48] By considering which of the tasks could be readily automated, they paint a picture of how lawyers will be impacted. In the resulting typology, lawyers' tasks were grouped into 13 categories: 'Advising Clients; Other Communications/Interactions; Case Administration and Management; Court Appearances; Document Drafting; Document Management; Document Review; Due Diligence; Fact Investigation; Legal Analysis and Strategy; Legal Research; Legal Writing; and Negotiation'.[49]

Remus and Levy used this data to argue that lawyers were unlikely to feel significant employment effects from AI as those tasks which are susceptible to automation presently constitute only a small portion of lawyers' work.[50] A critique of their exercise is that data about sole practitioners or those in small firms was omitted, even though they comprise a large portion of the industry.[51] (Indeed, this is also the case globally, as discussed below.) Tanina Rostain has argued that this omission is a crucial one for Remus and Levy's conclusions, essentially because the two hemispheres are overlooked, and lawyers serving individuals will be quite differently affected by automation.[52]

In an early attempt to evaluate the impacts of computerisation on legal practice, academics Andrew Clark and Kim Economides proposed, in the early 1990s, an 'object-oriented typology of legal work'.[53] Unlike Remus and Levy, Clark and Economides had no data to draw upon – 'object-oriented' indicated rather that the *purpose* of the work is the classifier.[54] There is nonetheless overlap with Remus and Levy's tasks.

Under this purpose-driven approach five facets of legal practice are identified: transacting, advising, negotiating, representing and structuring (this last intended to capture lawyers' broader influence on the development of the law).[55] Clark and

[47] Remus and Levy (n 24).
[48] ibid.
[49] ibid 506, fn 16.
[50] *cf* Pasquale and Cashwell (n 25) 39, who state that 'lawyers spend significant amounts of time doing repetitive work'.
[51] Rostain (n 41) 565.
[52] ibid 565.
[53] A Clark and K Economides, 'Computers, Expert Systems and Legal Processes' in A Narayanan and M Bennun (eds), *Law, Computer Science and Artificial Intelligence* (Ablex, 1991) 3, 13.
[54] ibid 13.
[55] ibid 3, 13.

Economides noted that lawyers were increasingly a heterogeneous group and further that their work typically cut across these categories.[56] Still, the categories have resonance, and we adopt them here in order to consider in more detail what it is that lawyers do.

Transacting

Transacting, or facilitating deals, is likely how most lawyers spend most of their time. As others have commented, this does not readily fit with popular perceptions of what lawyers do, as there is likely no dispute between the parties.[57] Rather, the lawyer's efforts are usually geared toward avoiding or controlling for any future disputes (including setting the parameters of dispute resolution processes).[58] Thus:

> The functions of an attorney in a transactional context are fundamentally different from those in a litigation context. A transactional attorney advises and negotiates on the client's behalf, seeking to effectuate a beneficial transaction for the client while minimizing the prospect of litigation. Within the scope of the engagement, she uses her practical and legal acumen, knowledge of applicable legal principles, and understanding of customary practices to draft requisite transactional documents.[59]

In addition to conveyancing, transactional work includes associated real estate transactions, the drafting of contracts and wills, procuring licences, 'enterprise formation and operations, mergers and acquisitions, securities, tax, oil and gas'[60] as well as financing. Arguably transactional work also includes work done for individuals, such as probate, and separation or divorce matters, as these are usually non-contentious.[61] David Howarth describes the transactional lawyer's task as 'translation': 'taking the clients' business agreements as the starting point and translating them into legal form',[62] and we return to the idea of translation in Chapter 7.

International transactional work is prevalent among large and very large firms, which 'are even more oriented to deals than the profession as a whole'.[63] Fleur Johns evokes the role of lawyers involved in large-scale transnational deals as follows:

> Documenting all of the arrangements among the parties involved in a deal, and their authority to enter into those arrangements, is the responsibility of lawyers. For the lawyers concerned, 'getting the deal done' will mean, at a minimum, getting those

[56] ibid 12–13.

[57] D Howarth, Law as Engineering: Thinking About What Lawyers Do (Edward Elgar, 2014) 22.

[58] Very few contracts become subject to court proceedings: see SL Schwarcz, 'Explaining the Value of Transactional Lawyering' (2007) 12(2) *Stanford Journal of Law, Business and Finance* 486.

[59] MI Steinberg and LJ Weissler, 'The Litigation Privilege as a Shelter for Miscreant Legal Counsel' (2018) 97(1) *Oregon Law Review* 1, 27.

[60] ibid.

[61] Howarth (n 57) 27.

[62] ibid 30.

[63] ibid 24.

> documents prepared, negotiated, and signed, so that money (debt and equity) may start to move. Included in that task will be the satisfaction of a litany of legal and nonlegal conditions precedent to financing. The issues to be negotiated to that end are numerous and often fraught. In the project-finance context, for example, they typically revolve around the entitlement of foreign lenders to oversee a project's day-to-day financial and technical management and, should problems arise, to step in and take over. This is the sort of scene being evoked here: a complex transaction, presenting an array of multijurisdictional, multidisciplinary issues for negotiation, in which sizeable amounts of money and the provision of basic services (via energy infrastructure, for example) are at issue.[64]

Henderson notes that 'the sheer complexity of a highly regulated and interconnected global economy' has vastly increased the complexity of much transactional law.[65] Further, he connects this complexity to the 'front line' of costs pressures that strain, in particular, corporate or in-house legal departments.[66] Lori Johnson described the work of 'today's sophisticated transactional lawyers' as 'structuring, drafting, conceptualizing, negotiating, and executing the complex, risky, and often cutting-edge transactions their clients bring to the table'.[67] As can be seen from this description, transacting bleeds into other categories such as *advising*, *negotiating* and *structuring*.

Transactional work may often be routine but is not necessarily straightforward or uncomplicated. Clark and Economides give the example of conveyancing (transfer of real property).[68] While the procedures of conveyancing are typically standardised, they note that 'high levels of expertise may be required to identify and act in circumstances where standard procedures prove to be inadequate'.[69] As discussed in Chapter 7, the combination of complexity and routinisation, volume and profit, means that AI has a number of applications to transactional work (as did computerisation in the 1990s[70]).

Advising

The paradigmatic role of a lawyer is as an expert advisor.[71] Remus and Levy found that 'advising' took up only between 3 and 9 per cent of lawyers' time.[72] Yet 'advising' may involve many elements. It is likened to a diagnostic process of

[64] F Johns, 'Performing Party Autonomy' (2008) 71(3) *Law and Contemporary Problems* 243, 257.
[65] Henderson (n 41) 15.
[66] ibid 25.
[67] LD Johnson, 'Redefining Roles and Duties of the Transactional Lawyer: A Narrative Approach' (2017) 91(4) *St John's Law Review* 845, 846–47.
[68] Clark and Economides (n 53) 13.
[69] ibid 13.
[70] ibid 13–14.
[71] Maister, Green and Galford (n 17); HM Kritzer, *The Justice Broker: Lawyers and Ordinary Litigation* (Oxford University Press, 1990).
[72] Remus and Levy (n 24).

gathering information and considering the means of resolution;[73] and to a series of steps: identifying the legal issue, collecting salient facts in a given case, locating relevant legal references, situating the specific situation among them, and supporting clients.[74] Clark and Economides thought that advising goes beyond the law to 'detailed consideration of how the client's "legal position" relates to his or her particular situation and objectives'.[75] This likely includes both legal and non-legal considerations. Clients' interests should be understood holistically and from the client's point of view, rather than being imposed or projected onto the client.[76]

Traditionally, advising was more directive of the client, and more paternalistic.[77] This was the case with other professions too – particularly medicine, where the development of informed consent practices is (in historical context) relatively recent. The lawyer's privileged position, often in terms of social status and education as well as subject-matter knowledge, resulted in generalised expectations that the lawyer would make decisions rather than seeking the client's input or giving the client choice. This may be contrasted with a newer conception – while both the traditional and the new envisage the lawyer as problem solver,[78] the newer paradigm has a different understanding of how problems are solved. The lawyer is less directive and more 'facilitative, collaborative and evaluative',[79] with problem solving focused on generating options for the client, rather than telling the client what to do. Increasingly, there is also a blurring of legal and business elements in terms of what lawyers, particularly in-house lawyers, are called upon to advise.

A broad formulation of the contemporary lawyer role is 'to help clients solve complex problems and make appropriate choices'.[80] The meaning of *appropriate* in this context is fluid but must include a balancing of different duties and obligations. Lawyers typically have a multiplicity of obligations: to clients, courts and the administration of justice. They are encapsulated in more or less stringent 'laws of lawyering', which might encompass formal legislation but also rules, ethical codes or guidelines, or simply conventions of practice. These considerations are bound up in advice giving, too. Alice Woolley says that 'The lawyer's opinion must provide an objectively reasonable assessment of the law while tailoring that

[73] FH Stephen, 'Regulation of the Legal Professions or Regulation of Markets for Legal Services: Potential Implications of the *Legal Services Act 2007*' (2008) 19(6) *European Business Law Review* 1129, 1130.

[74] AH Yoon, 'The Post-Modern Lawyer: Technology and the Democratization of Legal Representation' (2016) 66(4) *University of Toronto Law Journal* 456, 459.

[75] Clark and Economides (n 53) 15.

[76] KR Kruse, 'Beyond Cardboard Clients in Legal Ethics' (2010) 23(1) *Georgetown Journal of Legal Ethics* 103, 104.

[77] P Baron and L Corbin, *Ethics and Legal Professionalism in Australia* (Oxford University Press, 2014) 3.

[78] P Brest and L Hamilton Krieger, 'Lawyers as Problem Solvers' (1999) 72(4) *Temple Law Review* 811.

[79] Baron and Corbin (n 77) 4.

[80] LA Kloppenberg, 'Lawyer as Problem Solver: Curricular Innovation at Dayton' (2007) 38 *University of Toledo Law Review* 547, 550. Problem solving itself is complex and can be further broken down into subtasks: Wade (n 26) 25.

assessment towards accomplishment of the client's goals'.[81] She elaborates on the complexity of this exercise by noting that the laws of lawyering cannot govern every detail of advice giving, leaving open questions

> with respect to whether legal advice must be objectively reasonable in all circumstances; the balance between advice being objectively reasonable and advancing client goals; what is meant by the requirement that advice must not facilitate unlawful conduct; and the propriety of advice addressing moral concerns as well as legal ones.[82]

For these and other reasons, Remus and Levy conclude that 'most client advising remains outside the current domain of automation'.[83] There are also, however, questions as to whether machine learning can be used to generate predictions about case outcome, thus feeding into the advice-giving process.

Negotiating

Separate, yet integral to all the other categories, is the category of negotiation: it heavily informs (for instance) the work comprising *transacting* and *advising* but also that of *representing*. Andrew Boon has explained that, largely because negotiation takes place in private, 'In no other area of legal representation is the conduct of lawyers as important to clients or the ethics of lawyers more tested and difficult to verify'.[84]

There is a large body of literature on negotiating and negotiation theory.[85] There are also lawyer roles which are primarily focused on negotiation and dispute resolution.[86] Negotiation ranges from the informal to the formal: forms of negotiation procedure are required in many jurisdictions and span civil and criminal, international and domestic law. Citing studies undertaken in the US, Britain, Indonesia, Japan, Korea and Ethiopia, Stewart Macauley explained that despite differences 'in social structure, culture, and political and economic ideology', all found a unifying preference for negotiated resolutions to disputes.[87]

Clark and Economides used the term negotiation loosely, to capture a range of interpersonal interactions. For them, negotiating 'plays a central role in legal

[81] Woolley (n 27) 746.

[82] ibid.

[83] Remus and Levy (n 24) 526.

[84] A Boon, The Ethics and Conduct of Lawyers in England and Wales (3rd edn, Bloomsbury, 2015) 649; see also J Rogers, 'The Lying Lawyer and the Ethics of Negotiation' in M Legg (ed), *Resolving Civil Disputes* (LexisNexis, 2016) 197.

[85] C Menkel-Meadow, AK Schneider and LP Love, *Negotiation: Processes for Problem Solving* (2nd edn, Wolters Kluwer, 2014).

[86] M Keet, 'Settlement Counsel: An Innovative Strategy for the Management and Resolution of Commercial Litigation Files' (2017) 95(2) *Canadian Bar Review* 357. J Macfarlane argued that negotiation was an essential lawyer skill: *The New Lawyer: How Settlement is Transforming the Practice of Law* (UBC, 2008) 23; and negotiation may form part of law students' core courses: M Kumar, M Legg, I Vickovich and J Metzger, *Civil Procedure in New South Wales* (4th edn, Thomson Reuters, 2020) ch 4.

[87] S Macaulay, 'Elegant Models, Empirical Pictures, and the Complexities of Contract' (1977) 11(3) *Law & Society Review* 507, 507.

work and takes a variety of different forms; lawyers negotiate with clients, other lawyers, officials, and other parties'.[88] Thus, writing in the 1980s, John Griffiths described divorce lawyers' tactics in negotiating with their own clients, explaining: 'The lawyer seeks to do this with a varied mix of practical advice, social norms, authoritative legal pronouncements and technical legal advice, control over the client's access to legal information, and procedural and formal control of the case'.[89] Negotiating can therefore also fit within the function of advising, and as with other components of the work which lawyers do, involves non-legal (or not strictly legal) skills to a large degree, such as communication (including non-verbal communication), empathy and being attuned to non-legal considerations. Remus and Levy considered that automation will have only 'weak' impacts on this particular activity. They do note, however, the challenge of online dispute resolution,[90] which we address in Chapter 6.

Representing

'The popular image of lawyers is all about litigation', Howarth observed.[91] In Anglo-American culture, this plays out through the courtroom drama; French legal drama tends to focus on investigation rather than trial, with the *juge d'instruction* in the lead role.[92] The focus on such roles is unsurprising: litigation lends itself to storytelling and performance. Though contentious (and often criminal) processes are emphasised, as these dramatic depictions attest, representation entails more than simply 'speaking' or 'advocating' in court – it is the cultural embodiment of the law. In the common law tradition particularly, oral advocacy is fundamental to the process and the development of the law, as Boon explained: 'Specialisation in advocacy not only ensures greater efficiency in the court system, but may also contribute to higher quality decision making, and therefore precedents, through the sophistication of argument and the ability of judges who were themselves expert advocates'.[93] Despite the prominence of in-court work, the transactional activity discussed above is far more prevalent, yet also more hidden.[94]

In many jurisdictions (whether common law or civil law), the branches of the legal profession are divided according to whether the lawyer is active in court or not – the distinction between court representation and out-of-court activities.

[88] Clark and Economides (n 53) 16.

[89] J Griffiths, 'What Do Dutch Lawyers Actually Do in Divorce Cases?' (1986) 20(1) *Law & Society Review* 135, 171.

[90] Remus and Levy (n 24) 527–28.

[91] Howarth (n 57) 22.

[92] The investigating judge: ibid; see also B McKillop, *Anatomy of a French Murder Case* (Hawkins, 1997).

[93] Boon (n 84) 204.

[94] Howarth (n 57) 22–28; Wendel (n 22) 109; Woolley (n 27).

Integral differences between the two branches in the common law system, historically, related to work structures, with barristers working as sole practitioners and solicitors with the choice of forming partnerships; the requirement for solicitors to instruct barristers; and associated rights of appearance in higher courts. These types of restrictions persist: in Germany, for instance, only attorneys with special admission may appear in the Federal Court of Justice (Bundesgerichtshof);[95] while in Japan, only one segment of legal professionals, the *bengoshi* (a translation of barrister)[96] are permitted to undertake representation in higher courts.[97] Yet they have also been abolished or relaxed in other jurisdictions.

The role of advocate is typically focused on in-court work, or representation in formalised dispute resolution processes such as arbitration. In Spain, the advocate role involves 'legal defence of clients before courts' (meanwhile, solicitors represent clients in court but without legal defence).[98] Likewise, in Finland, only advocates (*asianjaja*) undertake criminal defence representation, while persons qualified with a Masters-level law degree (*lakimes*) may undertake solicitors' work and representation in civil matters.[99]

In other countries, the lines of demarcation have blurred somewhat with the relaxation of many of the rules previously delineating these roles. For example, solicitor-advocates – solicitors who have had some additional training in advocacy but are not barristers – may perform the work of a solicitor yet also routinely act in an advocacy role, such as in Scotland.[100] Canada has a 'fused' profession in which lawyers are admitted as both barrister and solicitor; so too do the Netherlands,[101] New Zealand and some States of Australia. The US makes no distinction: all lawyers pass a bar exam and are referred to as 'attorneys', with those specialising in trial or court work described as trial attorneys.

Nevertheless, the distinction between in-court advocacy and out-of-court activities is highly important in terms of daily work. In many jurisdictions, the separation of the profession into those who undertake primarily in-court

[95] President of the Federal Court of Justice, *The Federal Court of Justice* (Karlsruhe, 2014) 17 and 24, www.bundesgerichtshof.de/EN/TheCourt/Brochure/brochure.html.

[96] Kritzer (n 35) 76, citing KR Minami, 'Japanese Thought and Western Law: A Tangential View of Japanese Bengoshi and the Japanese-American Attorney' (1986) 8 *Loyola of Los Angeles International and Comparative Law Review* 301, 315–16.

[97] Kritzer (n 35) 76, citing Japanese Federation of Bar Associations, *White Paper on Attorneys* (2014).

[98] Stephen (n 39) 78, citing Organisation for Economic Co-operation and Development, *Competitive Restrictions in Legal Professions*, OECD Roundtables on Competition, DAF/COMP (2007) 39, 225.

[99] Stephen (n 39) 78–79, citing SEO Economic Research, *Regulation of the Legal Profession and Access to Law: An Economic Perspective*, SEO Report No. 2008-1 (SEO Economic Research, 2008) 58. See also H Rosti, J Niemi and M Lasola, 'Legal Aid and Legal Services in Finland', National Research Institute No. 237 2008 (reporting that from 2013, law graduates (*lakimes*) will require training supervised by the Finnish Bar Association before they will be permitted to represent clients in contentious civil cases).

[100] *Law Reform (Miscellaneous Provisions) Scotland Act 1990*, s 25A, came into force 1993 (providing for solicitor-advocates).

[101] The separate strand of *procureur* (akin to barrister) was abolished in 2008: 'Afschaffing procuraat per 1 September 2008 definitief', *Nederlandse Orde van Advocaten*, 22 August 2008.

representation, and those who do not, is the primary determinant of how a lawyer spends their time. On the other hand, with the relaxation of strict rights of appearance, and dependent on area of law, non-advocates might undertake in-court work other than trials or appeals in higher courts.

As Remus and Levy's main task items for 'non-top tier firms' indicate, representation likely also includes legal analysis and strategy, legal writing and fact investigation.[102] As we examine in Chapters 4 and 5, AI is primarily impacting the work of litigation lawyers in these areas – those encompassing strategy and preparation.

Structuring

The final category devised by Clark and Economides is the somewhat opaque 'ordering or structuring of law itself'.[103] Here, they are referring both to the activities of legislative or public service lawyers to implement policy[104] and those trying to influence the law in furtherance of the interests of private clients – in other words, 'structuring' encapsulates policy goals. Structuring may also capture broader law reform efforts via 'public interest litigation, class actions and test cases',[105] all of which may have impact beyond individual clients. In some ways structuring can be seen as a scale effect of the work which lawyers do, rather than a separate category of activity.

In terms of the corporate sphere, Clark and Economides explained that such work 'ranges from activities like corporate reorganisation and tax planning to assisting clients in their efforts to secure specific legislative change'.[106] Howarth describes similar activity in what he terms 'regulatory smoothing':

> [E]nsuring that the deal will not fall foul of action by regulatory agencies or become commercially unattractive because of the costs of regulatory compliance or taxation … often the task will not be confined to designing compliant structures but might also include persuading regulators that the proposed structures are indeed compliant.[107]

Structuring, then, might also incorporate work involving regulatory compliance, a significant area for AI, as we discuss in Chapter 8.

These categories, then, give us a sense of how lawyers predominantly spend their time. We now turn to consider the organisations in which they work.

[102] Remus and Levy (n 24) 508, Table 1 (figures are for 'Tiers Two-Five Firms'). Lawyers' time spent on these tasks (as a percentage of total time) was: legal analysis and strategy: 27 per cent; legal writing: 18 per cent; court appearances and preparation: 14.5 per cent; fact investigation: 10 per cent.

[103] Clark and Economides (n 53) 20.

[104] Howarth (n 57) 40–49.

[105] Clark and Economides (n 53) 20.

[106] ibid.

[107] Howarth (n 57) 32.

Organisational Forms (Where Do Lawyers Work?)

Among the most significant changes to the legal profession in recent decades have been changes in the organisational or workplace context in which lawyers are situated. The profession has witnessed the development of firms, large firms, global firms, corporate legal departments and new types of business structure for legal practice, all against a backdrop of general growth in the number of lawyers. Hadfield charted the surges and plateaus of the American profession, commenting: 'By the end of the [twentieth] century there were almost 400 lawyers per 100,000 Americans. Other Anglo-American jurisdictions saw similar growth, although the number of lawyers in Canada, the UK, and Australia topped out below the US high'.[108]

The rise of the global law firm should not obscure the fact that many lawyers continue to work in small firms or as sole practitioners, which is the case even in developed nations such as the US, Australia and France.[109] In Australia, for example, approximately 70 per cent of practising lawyers are in private practice and nearly 80 per cent of private law firms are sole practitioners or firms with one partner.[110] Small or solo practice is also the norm in countries such as India and Brazil, where the split between smaller practices serving local clients and large practices serving foreign or international clients is arguably even more pronounced. Gilles Muller has explained of the legal profession in India:

> Originally the principal role of the lawyer was that of representation before the local court. However, economic development has seen the emergence of new fields of law, such as business and trade law, which in most cases require legal counselling in matters involving transactions, relationships and disputes outside court proceedings. This evolution has resulted in the coexistence of two types of lawyers: the traditional lawyers whose main role is representation before a court and lawyers involved in counselling in sophisticated business matters.[111]

The professional divisions described above have also influenced, and continue to influence, the business structures in which lawyers work. Barristers practise and run their businesses independently, though they may group together in chambers or stables with shared office facilities and clerks. Other key groups of lawyers are those employed within government bureaucracies – which may include instruments of state justice such as prosecutors and court staff, but also legal departments within branches of government or ministries of justice – and those employed

[108] Hadfield (n 43) 122.

[109] ibid 176 ('About a third of all [US] lawyers are solo practitioners'); L Lark Hill, 'Alternative Business Structures for Lawyers and Law Firms: A View from the Global Legal Services Market' (2017) 18 *Oregon Review of International Law* 135, 180, citing A-C Monkam, 'France Says "Non" to ABS', *The Journal of the Law Society of Scotland* (11 July 2012).

[110] Law Society of NSW, *National Profile of Solicitors 2018* (Urbis, 17 July 2019) www.lawsociety.com.au/sites/default/files/2019-07/2018%20National%20Profile%20of%20Solicitors.pdf at 22 and 26.

[111] G Muller, 'Liberalization of Legal Services in India: The Role and Consequences of the Free Trade Agreements *EU-India*' (2012) 7(11/12) *Global Trade and Customs Journal* 493, 493.

'in-house' within corporations or public entities. Dietrich Rueschemeyer observed in the 1970s that some jurisdictions – such as the (then) Soviet Union and West Germany – had many more lawyers employed within government (close to 50 per cent) than, for example, England and Wales, and the US.[112] This reflects political transitions: following the Russian Revolution (1917), for instance, the legal profession 'was radically transformed and at various times in the ensuing decades, it entirely disappeared as an institution independent from the state'.[113]

Partnership

Up until roughly the beginning of the twentieth century, solo legal practice (with apprentices) was the norm for Anglo-American lawyers[114] and firms tended to be family affairs.[115] In England, lawyers worked proximate to one another at the Inns of Court[116] but the concept of the firm did not arise until the nineteenth century.[117] Similar developments took place within the American legal profession[118] and the French and German professions, too.[119]

Once lawyers had moved from solo practice to firm structures, partnership with other lawyers was viewed as the only appropriate way to ensure the profession's independence and promote adherence to ethical values. Partnership is 'the ultimate cooperative organization, a marriage of equals', embodying 'collegiality and equality'.[120] In a traditional partnership, partners share equally in profits, but the partnership also has unlimited liability and all partners are jointly and severally liable for the actions of other partners.[121] In many countries, lawyers were prohibited from sharing fees with non-lawyers: in some jurisdictions, they continue to be so prevented.

[112] Rueschemeyer (n 30) 111.

[113] Carle et al (n 34) 271; Kilian (n 37) 193 ('When in 1878 the first law regulating the lawyers' profession (*Rechtsanwaltsordnung*) for the German empire was passed, members of the bar were for the first time seen as an entity separate from the state').

[114] Hazard and Schneyer (n 2) 594–95.

[115] O Mendelsohn and M Lippman, 'The Emergence of the Corporate Law Firm in Australia' (1979) 3 *UNSW Law Journal* 78, 79.

[116] Burrage (n 28) ch 4 'Learned Friends and Gentlemen in England – Beneficiaries of the Glorious Revolution'. See also RL Abel, *The Making of the English Legal Profession: 1800–1988* (Ringgold, 1998); D Lemmings, *Gentlemen and Barristers: The Inns of Court and the English Bar, 1680–1730* (Clarendon Press, 1990).

[117] J Rogers, D Kingsford-Smith and J Chellew, 'The Large Professional Service Firm: A New Force in the Regulative Bargain' (2017) 40(1) *UNSW Law Journal* 218.

[118] LM Friedman, *A History of American Law* (3rd edn, Oxford University Press, 2005) 489.

[119] 'Small firms and sole practitioners dominated the *Rechtsanwälte*, the segment of the German legal profession comprised of litigators and transactional lawyers. The average large German firm had just twenty-one lawyers in early 1989': EL Martin, 'Liberalization and Cravathism: How Liberalization Triggered the Reorganization of the Legal Profession in Germany and Japan' (2007) 43(1) *Stanford Journal of International Law* 169, 180.

[120] SS Samuelson, 'The Organizational Structure of Law Firms: Lessons from Management Theory' (1990) 51(3) *Ohio State Law Journal* 643, 650.

[121] S Fortney and T Gordon, 'Adopting Law Firm Management System to Survive and Thrive: A Study of the Australian Approach to Management-Based Regulation' (2012) 10 *University of St. Thomas Law Journal* 152, 156; Stephen (n 39) 102.

Until the 1950s, law firms in Britain, the US, and other common law countries retained this same 'basic shape' of small partnerships.[122] For instance, by the early 1980s, virtually all advocates in Paris were still either in sole practice or members of very small (two- to three-person) partnerships;[123] this was also the case in Brazil until the 1990s.[124]

Growth in firm size began in the 1950s but increased considerably in the 1970s and 1980s: in the US, the size of the legal profession as a whole more than doubled between 1960 and 1985.[125] In China, there were reportedly only around 200 lawyers, working in fewer than 80 firms, in the late 1970s.[126] Only 20 years later, in 1999, there were an astonishing 110,000 lawyers working in close to 9,000 firms.[127] This exceptional growth rate has continued: there are now over 400,000 lawyers in 30,000 firms.[128]

Meanwhile, India today reportedly has over a million lawyers, though most are sole practitioners who undertake in-court work.[129] Having to date resisted allowing foreign lawyers or firms to practise within its jurisdiction,[130] there are few 'elite' law firms in India: a 2010 estimate put the number at fewer than 50.[131] India is, however, a major supplier of legal process outsourcing to developed countries.[132]

In jurisdictions such as the US, Australia and the UK, the 1970s saw growth in the number of lawyers and large firms, and the development of so-called corporate 'mega firms'.[133] Two American academics explain:

> [O]nly thirty-eight American law firms had more than fifty lawyers in the late 1950s … by 1986 over 500 firms were that large and about half of them had more than 100 lawyers. By the 1990s, as a result of internal growth and mergers, the largest 100 law firms accounted for 20% of all legal fees. Several firms now have over 1000 lawyers.[134]

[122] M Galanter and S Roberts, 'From Kinship to Magic Circle: The London Commercial Law Firm in the Twentieth Century' (2008) 15(3) *International Journal of the Legal Profession* 143, 144.

[123] Burrage (n 28) 190 (citations omitted).

[124] M Da Gloria Bonelli, 'Gender and Difference Among Brazilian Lawyers and Judges: Public and Private Practice in the Global Periphery' (2013) 20(2) *Indiana Journal of Global Legal Studies* 1291, 1293.

[125] Samuelson (n 120) 653.

[126] Szto (n 3) 586, citing S Zongwei, 'Lawyers Urged to Improve Ethics', *China Daily*, 29 April 1999, www.chinadaily.com.cncndydb/1999/04/d2-81aw.d29.html.

[127] ibid.

[128] Notary Law Department of Ministry of Justice, www.en.moj.gov.cn/.

[129] Muller (n 111) 494.

[130] This was confirmed by the Indian Supreme Court in 2018.

[131] Muller (n 111) 494, citing J Krishnan, 'Globetrotting Law Firms' (2010) 23(1) *Georgetown Journal of Legal Ethics* 57, 61–65.

[132] See, eg, E Noronha, P D'Cruz and S Kuruvilla, 'Globalisation of Commodification: Legal Process Outsourcing and Indian Lawyers' (2016) 46(4) *Journal of Contemporary Asia* 614 ('In 2011, LPO firms in India employed more than 10,000 lawyers').

[133] D Weisbrot, 'The Changing Face of Australian Legal Practice' (1986) 58(4) *The Australian Quarterly* 426, 427; see also M Galanter, 'Mega-Law and Mega-Lawyering in the Contemporary United States' in R Dingwall and P Lewis (eds), *The Sociology of the Professions: Lawyers, Doctors and Others* (Palgrave Macmillan, 1983).

[134] Hazard and Schneyer (n 2) 596–97.

Marc Galanter and Simon Roberts sketch out the growth of commercial firms in the city of London, long recognised as a global hub for legal services:

> [F]or the first sixty years of the century [they retained] a sharply stratified aggregation, with a small, typically kin-based, partnership and a patriarch at the apex. This formation was succeeded by the 'modern' firm, the 'professional' partnership, lasting, at most, for a thirty-year period. In the last decade of the century, firms came to look and behave much more like international businesses.[135]

As these authors note, much discussion in the latter part of the twentieth century concerned the rise of large, very large and/or global law firms. In Australia, while small and solo firms still predominated (as they do today) in terms of numbers, it was argued that professional power 'clearly shifted from the far more numerous small firms to the large corporate firms'.[136] Another major growth area was in the largest global accounting firms, with their substantial legal departments.[137] Indeed, growth in 'global professional services firms' is described as 'perhaps one of the most significant changes of the past 20 years within the realm of professional work',[138] and elemental to the contemporary global economy:

> A significant and profitable portion of these firms' work involves helping transnational clients to develop complex cross-border projects, structures and systems of production; something which requires the seamless delivery of integrated advisory services across all the different jurisdictions in which transnational clients operate.[139]

The rise in transnational legal practice[140] has impacted the legal profession, especially in countries such as Brazil, China and South Korea, where there are distinct local and foreign legal services markets. In Brazil, economic globalisation and the privatisation of public enterprise led to increased demand for lawyers and corporate specialisation from the mid-1990s onwards.[141] In Germany, despite initial resistance, growth in the legal sector has occurred primarily via mergers between local firms and large Anglo-American firms.[142] By 2001, reportedly 'all of the most

[135] Galanter and Roberts (n 122) 168.

[136] Weisbrot (n 133) 433. Before the 1970s, partnership law prevented more than 20 principals, thereby constraining growth: A Lamb and J Littrich, *Lawyers in Australia* (2nd edn, Federation Press, 2011) 67.

[137] Originally the 'Big 8', these firms are now referred to as the 'Big Four' following a series of mergers and the collapse of Arthur Andersen.

[138] D Muzio and J Faulconbridge, 'The Global Professional Service Firm: "One Firm" Models versus (Italian) Distant Institutionalised Practices' (2013) 34(7) *Organization Studies* 897 (citations omitted).

[139] ibid, citing J Faulconbridge, JV Beaverstock, D Muzio and PJ Taylor, 'Globalizing Law Firms and the Expansion of the US and English Legal Profession' (2008) 28(3) *Northwestern Journal of International Law and Business* 455.

[140] Martin (n 119); Trubek et al (n 137) 433.

[141] Da Gloria Bonelli (n 124) 1293.

[142] Stephen (n 39) 74, citing U Schultz, 'Regulated Deregulation: The Case of the German Legal Profession' in WLF Felstiner (ed), *Reorganisation and Resistance: Legal Professions Confront a Changing World* (Hart Publishing, 2005) 93; M Henssler and L Terry, 'Lawyers without Frontiers – A View from Germany' (2000/01) 19 *Dickinson Journal of International Law* 269; and FH Stephen, 'The European Single Market and the Regulation of the Legal Profession: An Economic Analysis' (2002) 23 *Managerial and Decision Economics* 115.

highly regarded German firms were linked in some way with English firms'[143] and, together with large accounting firms, they comprised the biggest players in the German legal services market.[144] John Flood has noted, generally, the significant implications for professional regulation of this growth and internationalisation, as the sheer scale of global firms tends to place them beyond a single jurisdiction.[145]

In the US, the expansion of the largest firms was often described as 'Cravathist' after the venerable firm of Cravath, Swaine & Moore – referencing a leveraged model of partnership, in which new lawyers are drawn straight from law school and receive rigorous training within the firm, and 'lateral hires' (recruiting more senior lawyers or partners from other firms) are discouraged.[146] The concept of the 'tournament of influence' – a phrase coined by Galanter and Thomas Palay in the early 1990s[147] – references the intense competition of the path to partnership, in a model which also requires growth, as partners must have associates working under them.[148] Massive expansion of firms around this time also fuelled lawyers' increasing specialisation into discrete areas of legal practice.[149] Remus has argued that the unitary presentation of 'the bar' in the twentieth century was never completely accurate, in that already, lawyers' work was quite varied.[150] During the 1980s and 1990s, however, the profession became further segmented and specialised.[151] In turn, it is argued, the meaning of professionalism has altered.[152]

The large firm group was 'the fastest-growing, most prosperous and most dynamic sector of the [American] profession' in 2000[153] and their lawyers comprised over 10 per cent of the total attorney population.[154] For several decades, from the 1980s until 2011, firms grew rapidly and average profits per partner

[143] S Lace, 'Mergers, Mergers Everywhere: Constructing the Global Law Firm in Germany' in J Van Hoy (ed), *Legal Professions: Work, Structure and Organization* (Emerald Group Publishing, 2001) 51, 52.

[144] Stephen (n 39) 74.

[145] J Flood, 'The Re-landscaping of the Legal Profession: Large Law Firms and Professional Re-Regulation' (2011) 59(4) *Current Sociology* 507. E Wald made a similar point about US national firms transcending state-based regulation: 'Federalizing Legal Ethics, Nationalizing Law Practice, and the Future of the American Legal Profession in a Global Age' (2011) 48(1) *San Diego Law Review* 489.

[146] Martin (n 119) 173–75; DB Wilkins and M José Esteban Ferrer, 'Taking the "Alternative" out of Alternative Legal Service Providers' in DeStefano and Dobrauz (eds) (n 23) 32–33.

[147] M Galanter and TM Palay, *Tournament of Lawyers: The Transformation of the Big Law Firm* (University of Chicago Press, 1991).

[148] An updated version is discussed in M Galanter and WD Henderson, 'The Elastic Tournament: A Second Transformation of the Big Law Firm' (2008) 60 *Stanford Law Review* 1867.

[149] Martin (n 119) 173–74, citing RT Swaine, *The Cravath Firm and Its Predecessors 1918–1948* (The Ad Press, 1946–48) 4; see also Clark and Economides (n 53) 12; Da Gloria Bonelli (n 124) 1293; Hadfield (n 43)123.

[150] Remus (n 42).

[151] ibid, citing Heinz and Laumann (n 42) and JP Heinz, RL Nelson, RL Sandefur and EO Laumann, *Urban Lawyers: The New Social Structure of the Bar* (University of Chicago Press, 2005) 7–8.

[152] MS Ariens, 'Sorting: Legal Specialization and the Privatization of the American Legal Profession' (2016) 29(3) *Georgetown Journal of Legal Ethics* 579. Further, the theory of the Cravath Model has undergone various changes: see 'An Introduction' in Wilkins, Khanna and Trubek (eds) (n 5) 6–7.

[153] Galanter and Henderson (n 148) 1868–69.

[154] ibid.

increased massively.[155] Per lawyer profits began to stagnate around 2007, when a flattening of demand for corporate legal services became apparent. Henderson posits that this flattening could be due to the fact that in-house teams took up more of the corporate sector's work; outsourcing became more prevalent; work was moved to cheaper, regional firms; reliance on expensive associates declined (shifting to staff or contract lawyers); and large firms were offering volume discounts to retain market share (while losing profits).[156] The seeming decline led some – such as Larry Ribstein, in the 'Death of Big Law' – to foretell the demise of the very large firms.[157] Ribstein's predictions rested primarily on the decline of reputational capital (a means of describing the value that lawyers offer – as reputation is enabling of client trust). Ribstein said that structural and competitive pressures risked destroying firms' ability to preserve these reputations as individual lawyers were incentivised to prefer their own income and reputation to the firm's. He also referenced external factors such as the increased capacities of in-house teams.

Contrary to Ribstein's predictions, American firms continued to grow. Differences are instead found in *how* growth is occurring. Rather than hiring entry-level lawyers (which fewer and fewer firms are doing, or doing at the scale they had previously) more lawyers move between firms.[158] Firms hire 'non-partner track' lawyers, and grow through mergers with other firms.[159] Henderson finds that, rather than dying, Big Law is significantly restructuring in the face of disruptive innovation.

Though Henderson challenges some aspects of Ribstein's predictions (especially in that there has, in fact, been a continued growth in large firm size[160]), he does note significant changes to the 'traditional' partnership model. As well as structural changes, there have also been changes in perceptions and goals around partnership, with non-equity partners, lawyers who are not seeking partnership,[161] and firms or legal service providers which lack a partnership structure altogether.[162] Yet almost one-quarter of the 'Am Law 100' – the 100 most profitable law firms in the US, as reported by *American Lawyer* – have over 1,000 lawyers, and six have more than 2,000.[163] Law firms, particularly big law firms, have shown remarkable stability and longevity, given they have been critiqued on many fronts, including

[155] WD Henderson, 'From Big Law to Lean Law' (2014) 38 *International Review of Law and Economics* 5, 7–8 (relatively more than Consumer Price Index and Gross Domestic Product increases).

[156] ibid 8.

[157] LE Ribstein, 'The Death of Big Law' [2010] (3) *Wisconsin Law Review* 749 (making economic arguments, based on observation of large firm and market practices, for the decline of 'Big Law').

[158] Henderson (n 155) 8 (lateral movement grew 60 per cent in each of 2010 and 2011).

[159] ibid.

[160] ibid 7.

[161] Samuelson (n 120).

[162] JS Dzienkowski, 'The Future of Big Law: Alternative Legal Service Providers to Corporate Clients' (2014) 82(6) *Fordham Law Review* 2995, 3005.

[163] AJB Cable, 'When Does Big Law Work?' (2019) 102(3) *Marquette Law Review* 875, 876–77.

managerialism, sexism, unhealthy and even discriminatory hierarchies and competition, deleterious leverage and billing methods, and unethical practices.[164]

In-House Counsel

Another major change, along with growth and internationalisation, has been the rise of in-house lawyers or corporate counsel, in the form of globally increasing numbers but also status gains. In 2017 the Law Society of England and Wales reported that 'the in-house sector is now home to 22.2% of working solicitors (those attached to organisations) across 4,500 commercial and 1,000 not-for-profit organisations'.[165] In Australia, in-house lawyers comprise 35 per cent of all commercial lawyers; in emerging economies such as India, their increased importance both within corporate entities, and the legal profession itself, has also been noted.[166] This is a distinct change from the historically somewhat devalued and powerless position of in-house lawyers, an ascension termed the 'in-house counsel movement' in the US.[167] It has been spurred predominantly by three factors: saving costs by making rather than buying; superior advice giving, as in-house counsel are more familiar with the business; and finally in-house counsel can be anticipated to have more interest in the company's long-term prospects.[168] This latter might lead to prioritising long-term strategy over short-term gains, including when it comes to risk assessment. The increased prominence of in-house counsel has arguably spread to other jurisdictions too, such as the UK and Europe.[169]

Another major driver of the rise of in-house counsel is the need to manage risk and compliance. Mari Sako suggests that this is the key reason for increased prominence of German in-house counsel, following a series of corporate scandals in the 2010s.[170] She explains:

> In-house lawyers have always had responsibilities to ensure legal compliance with respect to anti-trust, anti-corruption, data protection, export control, and technical standards. But … risk is increasingly not just legal or financial, but also a matter of corporate reputation. The multi-disciplinary nature of risk control poses an extra challenge.[171]

[164] See, eg, PJ Schiltz, 'On Being a Happy, Healthy, and Ethical Member of an Unhappy, Unhealthy, and Unethical Profession' (1999) 52 *Vanderbilt Law Review* 871; H Sommerlad, 'Women Solicitors in a Fractured Profession: Intersections of Gender and Professionalism in England and Wales' (2002) 9(3) *International Journal of the Legal Profession* 213.

[165] The Law Society, Trends in the Solicitors' Profession: Annual Statistics Report 2017 – Executive Summary (June 2018) 3.

[166] Gupta, Khanna and Wilkins (n 5) 115.

[167] RE Rosen, 'The Inside Counsel Movement, Professional Judgment and Organizational Representation' (1989) 64(3) *Indiana Law Journal* 479; DB Wilkins, 'Is the In-House Counsel Movement Going Global? A Preliminary Assessment of the Role of Internal Counsel in Emerging Economies' (2012) (2) *Wisconsin Law Review* 251.

[168] Wilkins, Khanna and Trubek (n 152) 7.

[169] Wilkins (n 167) 258.

[170] M Sako, 'The Changing Role of General Counsel' in DeStefano and Dobrauz (eds) (n 23) 69.

[171] ibid.

When it comes to thinking about AI in the legal profession, the role of in-house counsel is very significant as often in-house counsel control how legal services are performed within the company and also have input into the 'make or buy' decision. Hence, decisions made by large corporate legal departments, such as choosing to invest in AI products to increase efficiency, or to send work to law firms or alternative legal service providers who are using such products, affect the legal services market more widely. Referring to the Corporate Legal Operations Consortium,[172] Henderson explains that its thousand-plus members 'tend to be influential in how their organizations buy legal services, often demanding better use of data, process, and technology'.[173]

Alternative Business Structures

Historic prohibitions on lawyers sharing fees or profits with non-lawyers prevented lawyers from engaging in partnership with non-lawyers; non-lawyers having ownership stakes in a law firm; and external investment in legal practices. This 'is supposed to ensure that … legal practitioners' ethical responsibilities are not adulterated by the competing interests of non-lawyer investors or partners who are not bound by the [same] ethical obligations'.[174] The US, with the exception of the District of Colombia (and foreshadowed changes in California[175]), has continued to prohibit 'fee sharing' between lawyers and non-lawyers in order to preserve the independence of the profession. Many Latin American jurisdictions also impose such restrictions.[176] This manifests as prohibitions on business arrangements involving non-lawyers and lawyers, and non-lawyer ownership of legal services organisations.

Early relaxation around some of these rules did not travel far: forms of incorporation for law firms were permitted but without offering significant differences or benefits when compared with the traditional partnership.[177] For example in the Australian State of New South Wales, law practices were permitted to incorporate from the early 1990s but in such a restricted way that this structure did not present

[172] https://cloc.org/.
[173] Henderson (n 41) 6.
[174] C Parker, 'Law Firms Incorporated: How Incorporation Could and Should Make Firms More Ethically Responsible' (2004) 23(2) *University of Queensland Law Journal* 347, 349–50.
[175] 'California Opens Door to More Legal Tech, Non-Lawyer Roles', www.news.bloomberglaw.com/us-law-week/california-opens-door-to-more-non-lawyer-roles-tech-solutions; R Ambrogi, 'California Task Force to Vote This Week On Sweeping Changes To Legal Services Delivery', *Above the Law*, 24 June 2019, www.abovethelaw.com/2019/06/california-task-force-to-vote-this-week-on-sweeping-changes-to-legal-services-delivery/.
[176] eg, Brazil: M Gómez and R Pérez-Perdomo, 'Introduction' in M Gómez and R Pérez-Perdomo (eds), *Big Law in Latin America and Spain: Globalization and Adjustments in the Provision of High-End Legal Services* (Palgrave Macmillan, 2018) 3, 64.
[177] Parker (n 174) termed this 'phoney' incorporation. In the US, UK and Singapore: Babacan, Di Iorio and Meade (n 8) 315–16.

a generally attractive option.[178] In North America, the limited liability partnership is widely used to reduce the vicarious liability burden on partners but has no other features of incorporation.

The 1990s saw growing interest in the multi-disciplinary partnership (MDP), within which lawyers may practise in partnership with professional non-lawyers – such as accountants. There were widespread inquiries (eg, in the US, Canada, Britain, Australia and New Zealand) into the possibilities, and potential drawbacks, of permitting MDPs.[179] The results and recommendations, however, reflected 'a serious lack of consensus' about whether or not MDPs could be appropriate for lawyers and how they ought to be regulated.[180] Initially, MDPs were particularly associated with the rise of global firms: in some jurisdictions they were a means of circumventing otherwise strict rules about non-local lawyers or firms engaging in legal practice.[181] John Coffee attributes their decline to the role of Arthur Andersen in the Enron scandal, which came to light in 2001.[182] Yet around the world, their numbers increased in the 2000s;[183] Francisco Marcos, for instance, discussed the inroads that the legal arms of multi-national audit firms made in the Spanish market at this time.[184] Meanwhile, one of China's Special Economic Zones, the province of Hainan, permitted non-lawyers to become partners in law firms as recently as October 2019.[185]

The 2000s, too, saw further moves to allow lawyers to set up 'alternative' business structures beyond MDPs. States of Australia were the first jurisdictions to permit incorporated legal practices, a form of corporate structure. Such regimes allow external investment in law firms and non-lawyer ownership but subject to restrictions – for example, there must be at least one legal practitioner director, and the interests of shareholders are secondary to legal professional responsibilities. New South Wales was also the first jurisdiction to allow an incorporated law firm to list publicly on the stock exchange, and the first to do so listed in 2007.[186]

[178] Babacan, Di Iorio and Meade (n 8). See also Parker (n 174).

[179] M Trebilcock and L Csorgo, 'Multi-Disciplinary Professional Practices: A Consumer Welfare Perspective' (2001) 24(2) *Dalhousie Law Journal* 1, 3, citing K Roach and E Iacobucci, 'Multi-Disciplinary Practices and Partnerships: Prospects, Problems and Policy Options' (2000) 79 *Canadian Bar Review* 37.

[180] Trebilcock and Csorgo (n 179) 3.

[181] Stephen (n 39) 76 (citations omitted).

[182] JC Coffee, *Gatekeepers: The Professions and Corporate Governance* (Oxford University Press, 2006) 196, citing RA Prentice, 'The SEC and MDP: The Implications of the Self-Serving Bias for Independent Auditing' (2000) 61 *Ohio State Law Journal* 1597.

[183] Ontario, British Columbia and Quebec permit MDPs: Lark Hill (n 109) 154, citing R Mullerat, 'The Multidisciplinary Practice of Law in Europe' in SJ McGarry (ed), *Multidisciplinary Practices and Partnerships: Lawyers, Consultants and Clients* (Law Journal Seminars Press, 2002) 4–28; Stephen (n 39) 78, citing F Marcos, 'The Storm Over Our Heads' (2000) 7(1) *International Journal of the Legal Profession* 7.

[184] Stephen (n 39) 78, citing Marcos (n 183).

[185] www.economists-pick-research.hktdc.com/business-news/article/Regulatory-Alert-China/Hainan-Special-Economic-Zone-Liberalises-the-Legal-Service-Sector/bacn/en/1/1X000000/1X0AIRJ8.htm.

[186] A Grech and K Morrison, 'Slater & Gordon: The Listing Experience' (2009) 22(2) *Georgetown Journal of Legal Ethics* 535.

This year also saw the passage of the *Legal Services Act 2007* (LSA) in England and Wales, which, among many changes aimed at deregulation of the legal services market, permitted 'alternative business structures' (ABSs), though none were authorised until 2011. Non-lawyers may own 100 per cent of an ABS. The LSA also changed the scope of activities reserved solely to lawyers.[187]

There is an ongoing debate about the appropriateness of 'alternative' structures for lawyers. Hadfield attributes lack of innovation in the provision of legal services directly to restrictions on organisational form.[188] A particular issue has been the inability of law firms to raise capital via external investment. Prior to the LSA's enactment, it had been argued that lawyers should be given greater freedom in their choice of business structure. However, there are also concerns around the professional ethical ramifications of lawyers working in alternate structures (as indeed, there are about in-house lawyers).

The response to the concept of ABSs in other jurisdictions has been mixed. In 2010 Scotland made the move to permit them but restricted non-lawyer ownership to 49 per cent.[189] In 2011 Italy introduced ABSs which give lawyers their choice of corporate structure and permit external (non-lawyer) shareholders.[190] The Canadian Bar Association recommended permitting ABSs in a 2014 report[191] but this has not been taken up. The US permits neither ABSs nor MDPs.

France and Germany have also to date resisted ABSs.[192] Europe's Council of Bars and Law Societies opposes outside investment in law firms.[193] This may also in some circumstances restrict local lawyers whose jurisdictions prohibit ABSs from working in international firms operating in multiple jurisdictions.[194] In a 2014 article, Jakob Weberstaedt wrote that 'the German Federal Bar was the earliest and loudest European critic of the English reforms and continues to be one of the main drivers behind efforts to organise a united Continental defence against [ABSs operating in the Continent]'.[195]

[187] Legal Services Act 2007 (UK).

[188] GK Hadfield, 'Legal Barriers to Innovation' (2008) 60 *Stanford Law Review* 1689.

[189] Legal Services (Scotland) Act 2010 (UK).

[190] www.ccbe.eu/fileadmin/user_upload/NTCdocument/newsletter_29_enpdf1_1327503311.pdf.

[191] Canadian Bar Association, Final Report, CBA Legal Futures Initiative, 'Futures: Transforming the Delivery of Legal Services in Canada' (August 2014).

[192] Lark Hill (n 109) citing Conseil National des Barreaux, 'Les Alternatives Business Structures (ABS) mettent en danger les principes essentiels de la profession d'avocat et les intirets du public' (22 June 2012) www.cnb.avocat.fr/Les-Alternatives-Business-Structures-ABS-mettent-en-danger-les-al290.html.

[193] LS Terry, C Silver and ES Rosen, 'Transnational Legal Practice 2009' (2010) 44(1) *International Lawyer* 563, 567, citing Council of the Bars and Law Societies of Europe, 'Response to the Solicitors Regulation Authority Consultation Concerning the Amendment of Rules 3 (Conflicts of Interest) and 4 (Duty of Confidentiality) of the Solicitors' Code of Conduct 2007' (2009); and 'Response to the Solicitors Regulation Authority's Consultation on New Forms of Practice and Regulation for Alternative Business Structures' (2009).

[194] Boon (n 84) 203 noted that 'Legal professions, even in Europe, are resisting multi-disciplinary practice and … the European Court held that, while European Community competition laws apply, they may reasonably restrict new business forms considered incompatible with the proper practice of law' (citations omitted).

[195] J Weberstaedt, 'English Alternative Business Structures and the European Single Market' (2014) 21(1) *International Journal of the Legal Profession* 103, 104.

Organisational form is, therefore, closely connected to the ways that lawyers are regulated, to which we now turn.

How are Lawyers Regulated?

How professionals are regulated is a fundamental aspect of professionalism, as is the character of the regulatory regime. A unifying idea is that professions have a particular role to play in society, founded upon putting the interests of others before self-interest. Regulation is necessary to guarantee standards, and professionals agree to this regulation in return for the privileges which acceptance as a professional confers. In terms of the legal profession, regulation typically encompasses whether or not certain activities are reserved exclusively to lawyers (in other words, whether a state-sanctioned monopoly exists) and the nature and extent of those activities. It extends also to who enforces the monopoly and who controls admission to, discipline within, and exclusion from, the profession. Self-regulation is one of the traditional indicia of a profession, often comprising restrictions around entry, requirements for ongoing adherence to professional standards, and mechanisms for discipline or expulsion if such adherence is lacking.

In return for the onus of professional duties, lawyers have received recognition from the state. Primarily, this has meant protection of professional status by permitting self-regulation and in ensuring a monopoly over legal work. Yet the story of the legal profession has over many years been one of competition policies, loss of exclusive self-regulation and the erosion of monopolies or areas of work reserved exclusively to lawyers, though these do continue to exist. The legal profession has been influenced in the last few decades especially by economic liberalisation and globalisation. In many countries, the trajectory has involved relinquishment of pure self-regulation in favour of independent regulators or co-regulatory arrangements,[196] often following the reports of competition inquiries.[197] This is sometimes referred to as 're-regulation' rather than 'deregulation'. There are exceptions to this trend: of the common law world, Noel Semple says that regulatory regimes can be bisected, describing 'a *competitive-consumerist* paradigm' which can be contrasted with 'a *professionalist-independent* mode which

[196] See the summary of N Semple, RG Pearce and R Newman Knake, 'A Taxonomy of Lawyer Regulation: How Contrasting Theories of Regulation Explain the Divergent Regulatory Regimes in Australia, England and Wales, and North America' (2013) 16(2) *Legal Ethics* 258.

[197] Webb (n 32) citing D Clementi, *Report of the Review of the Regulatory Framework for Legal Services In England and Wales* (2004); Law Council of Australia, *Blueprint for the Structure of the Legal Profession: A National Market for Legal Services* (1994); Scottish Executive, *Report by the Research Working Group on the Legal Services Market in Scotland* (2006); J Darrois, 'Rapport sur les professions du droit' (2009) available at www.http://www.justice.gouv.fr/art_pix/rap_com_darrois_20090408.pdf; and Koh Y, Kim D, Yoon K, Lee S and Chung W, 'Improving the Regulatory Framework of Professional Services in Korea' (Korea Development Institute, Report No 800, 2009).

survives [primarily] in the United States'.[198] Semple's bifurcation is marked out by attributes such as the extent of monopoly, permissible business structures, and regulatory approach, including whether self- or state regulated.[199]

Traditionally, the legal profession was self-regulating, including the promotion and enforcement of rules around entry and ongoing standards, though there might also be sharing of this responsibility 'with the state, the judiciary, or some other – usually state-sponsored – entity'.[200] Certainly, in many European jurisdictions, and in common law countries, the profession was regulated by its own representative associations such as bar associations and law societies, but with oversight from the courts, which typically retained inherent disciplinary functions over lawyers, as officers of the court.[201] Hadfield describes the rise of the American Bar Association from the nineteenth century on, especially the invocation of the courts' authority to regulate lawyers, as fundamentally shaping the nature of 'legal infrastructure' in the US, in part by the strict exclusion of non-lawyers.[202] The establishment of representative associations thus gives some guidance in classifying legal practitioners, too. They may be local, with state or national-level bodies comprised of representatives from the local organisations.[203] France has nearly 180 local bar associations, for example, with the largest being in Paris, and all represented at a national level by the Conseil National des Barreaux.[204] Meanwhile, in China, the All China Lawyers Association (founded in 1986) is the official, and sole, bar association. In Russia, private sector lawyers are unregulated, lacking an advocacy body or rules of professional conduct.[205]

In terms of controlling entry to the profession, jurisdictional differences are evident in the qualifications (education and training) necessary to become a lawyer, such as whether a national or regional bar exam must be passed; and further in additional, 'character-based' requirements, such as the requirement to be a 'fit and proper' person. Justine Rogers et al explain: '"Fit and proper" has tended to mean honest, trustworthy, courteous and traditionally "gentlemanly", and has come to explicitly include competence … However, it is this test of character that has exemplified the focus on the individual professional in the self-regulatory model'.[206]

Historically, entry to the legal profession was restricted to privileged groups, and it was exclusionary of women and ethnic minorities. Time has seen enormous demographic changes in many jurisdictions: for instance, half of practising lawyers

[198] N Semple, 'Canada: Legal Services Regulation in Canada: *Plus Ça Change*?' in Boon (ed) *International Perspectives* (n 37) 95, citing N Semple, *Legal Services Regulation at the Crossroads: Justitia's Legions* (Edward Elgar, 2015).

[199] ibid 96.

[200] Webb (n 32) 535.

[201] Webb (n 32); see generally Rogers, Kingsford-Smith and Chellew (n 117); and Kilian (n 37) (on the power of the German Constitutional Court in legal regulation).

[202] Hadfield 114–20.

[203] eg the German Federal Bar, the Japanese Federation of Bar Associations.

[204] Lark Hill (n 109) 178.

[205] Carle et al (n 34) 277 (discussing the 2002 Law on Advokatura and 2003 Code of Ethics).

[206] Rogers, Kingsford-Smith and Chellew (n 117) 226.

in England and Wales in 2014 were the first generation in their families to attend university, a marker of socio-economic background.[207] Yet vestigial hierarchies and status remain important. Manuel Gómez and Rogelio Pérez-Perdomo identify *grand advocates*—the most influential lawyers working in Latin America, who are esteemed not only for technical skill but 'because of their ability to navigate the legal system, and more importantly because of their influence and political connections'.[208] Even in jurisdictions which have long abolished any discriminatory restrictions on entry, lack of diversity persists. Where women comprise half of all lawyers,[209] continuing disadvantages are still documented, from harassment to slower or derailed career progression.[210] In Australia, women have been called '"fringe dwellers" in the upper echelons of the profession, vastly underrepresented at the Bar generally and in particular in its senior ranks, or as partners in law firms'.[211] In the US, women comprise less than 40 per cent of lawyers, and just over 20 per cent of law firm partners.[212] Emily Carroll and Steven Vaughan have summarised:

> While the profession opens up to the many, only the few (white men from privileged backgrounds) make it to the top: this leaves those outsiders as 'flatliners', undertaking lesser work and unable to ever join the ranks of (equity) partnership and the 'fraternity of peers'.[213]

In common law jurisdictions, this flows on to the composition of the judiciary as judges are usually appointed from the ranks of senior practising lawyers, typically though not exclusively barristers (in those jurisdictions which have a separate advocacy speciality). In civil law countries the judiciary is treated in a manner more akin to the civil service, and hence law graduates choose to enter the judiciary rather than practising as lawyers first. In some instances, such as in Switzerland, a degree or qualification in law might not even be a prerequisite.[214] The 'civil service model' may be used for all but the higher constitutional courts, whose work tends to be more politicised: thus there might be a civil service system for appointment

[207] Law Society of England and Wales, 'Diversity Profile of the Profession 2014: A Short Synopsis' (June 2015) 13.

[208] Gómez and Pérez-Perdomo (n 176) 12.

[209] Law Society of England and Wales (n 207) 7.

[210] S Embry, 'ABA Profile Reveals a Profession in Crisis', *TechLaw Crossroads*, 10 August 2019, www.techlawcrossroads.com/2019/08/aba-profile-reveals-a-profession-in-crisis/; A Wallace and I D'Souza, 'Stress, Bullying and Harassment in the Legal Profession: A Risky Business' in M Legg, P Vines and J Chan (eds), *The Impact of Technology and Innovation on the Wellbeing of the Legal Profession* (Intersentia, 2020) ch 4.

[211] F Bartlett and L Haller 'Australia: Legal Services Regulation in Australia – Innovative Co-regulation' in Boon (ed) (n 37) 161, 163.

[212] Though only 19 per cent of equity partners: American Bar Association, '2019 Profile of the Legal Profession' Report, 47.

[213] E Carroll and S Vaughan, 'Matter Mills and London-Lite Offices: Exploring Forms of the Onshoring of Legal Services in an Age of Globalisation' (2019) 22(1–2) *Legal Ethics* 3, 6–7 (citations omitted).

[214] See B Abel-Smith and R Stevens, *Lawyers and the Courts: A Sociological Study of the English Legal System, 1750–1965* (Heinemann, 1967) 464.

to ordinary courts and a different process for constitutional courts.[215] There may be traditions of a lay magistracy or lay judges.[216] In specialised areas – such as family proceedings or building disputes – people without legal training may sit on benches or panels along with judicial members.

The extent and erosion of monopoly protections, tempered by the degree to which these historically existed, has been a significant change for the profession in many countries.[217] The precise areas of work reserved exclusively to lawyers varies between jurisdictions and have not remained constant. On the one hand, the monopoly may be restricted or has narrowed over time. Russian advocates are subjected to some regulation but have a monopoly extending only to representation of clients in criminal matters;[218] in many common law countries, lawyers lost the right to exclusivity in conveyancing (transferring legal title to real property) in the 1980s and 1990s. On the other, the monopoly may remain more extensive. Kilian explains that under the previous German law, the RBerG, 'legal services remained a reserved activity for members of the bar, notaries and tax advisers; licences for non-lawyers were rarely granted'.[219] He notes, though, that the RBerG was replaced effective from 2008, and the new law[220]

> takes a slightly more liberal approach and allows alternative service providers to offer legal services on the fringes of the legal services market. In principle, however, the provision of legal services, both in court and out of court, is still subject to licensing of individuals or groups of certain professionals … As a result, the provision of legal services has remained the domain of jurists with a law degree, who have passed two state exams (*Juristische Prüfung*) and undertaken a two-year, state-organised clerkship (*Referendariat*) resulting in a universal qualification to become a judge (*Richter*), prosecutor (*Staatsanwalt*), notary (*Notar*) or a member of the bar (*Rechtsanwalt*).[221]

Growing interconnectedness and globalisation in the 1980s and 1990s prompted regulatory changes and growth in legal services but also often provoked resistance from bar associations, which (for example) resisted the loss of the conveyancing monopoly in many jurisdictions. In Germany, even the merging of local firms into national firms was initially controversial,[222] let alone international firms. Firms based

[215] ML Volcansek, 'Appointing Judges the European Way' (2007) 34(1) *Fordham Urban Law Journal* 363 (discussing Italy, France and Germany).

[216] See Abel-Smith and Stevens (n 214) 464; JC Donoghue, 'Reforming the Role of Magistrates: Implications for Summary Justice in England and Wales' (2014) 77(6) *Modern Law Review* 928; A Watson, *Popular Participation in Japanese Criminal Justice: From Jurors to Lay Judges* (SpringerLink, 2016); DT Johnson, 'Japan's Lay Judge System' in JE Ross and SC Thaman (eds), *Comparative Criminal Procedure* (Edward Elgar, 2016) 396.

[217] D Hartstein and J Rogers, 'Professional Associations as Regulators: An Interview Study of the Law Society of New South Wales' (2019) 22(1–2) *Legal Ethics* 49, 50.

[218] Carle et al (n 34) 277.

[219] *Gesetz zur Verhütung von Mißbräuchen auf dem Gebiete der Rechtsberatung* or 'Law to Prevent Malpractice in the Provision of Legal Services': Kilian (n 37) 189.

[220] *Rechtsdienstleistungsgesetz* ('Legal Services Act') or RDG.

[221] Kilian (n 37) 190–91.

[222] Martin (n 119) 183.

abroad were frequently seen as a competitive threat in the market for corporate legal services.[223] The deregulation ultimately compelled by European Union competition policies[224] was resisted by the bar associations of France, Germany and Italy;[225] the opening up of the South Korean legal services sector resisted by the Korean Bar Association;[226] and India's continuing bar on foreign law firms attributed to 'very restrictive Indian regulation on the legal profession combined with fierce resistance of a significant portion of domestic lawyers against the presence of foreign lawyers'.[227] Such insularity remains prevalent, and jurisdictions such as Malaysia, Egypt and Barbados continue to bar foreigners from practising law entirely.[228] On the other hand, since 2015, Singapore (promoted as a global legal services hub) has had a unified regime for the discipline of both domestic and foreign lawyers.[229]

Reservation of legal work itself continues to be a dominant concern in the face of new technologies and business models. A long-standing issue is whether automation in legal applications may breach prohibitions on non-lawyers engaging in legal practice. Such prohibitions exist in many jurisdictions though in others they have been somewhat relaxed, as noted above.[230] Unauthorised practice of law may be a criminal offence. The purpose is generally twofold: to enable the administration of justice, and to protect the clients of lawyers and law practices.[231] The OECD has argued that 'The exclusivity enjoyed by legal professionals, and the precise scope of activities to which it applies, is becoming unclear as unlicensed entrants offer a widening range of services'.[232] Often the target of unauthorised practice of law claims have been services which assist clients to prepare legal documents; the same claims can also be directed at any form of tailored advice, for example via a chatbot or online expert system.

[223] Burrage (n 28) 150–51, citing 'La Réforme des Professions Juridiques et Judiciaires: Vingt Propositions', Rapport de M Daniel Soulez-Larivière à M Phillippe Lafarge, bâtonnier de l'Ordre des avocats à la cour de Paris, June 1988.

[224] Prior to this, it was the policy of the European Economic Community (the precursor to the EU): see DM Venezia, 'An EU Lawyer's Right to Practice Throughout the European Union' (1995) 3 *Cardozo Journal of International and Comparative Law* 427.

[225] See Stephen (n 39) 83; Burrage (n 28) 13; G Alpa, 'Lawyers' Ethics in Italy' (2010) 17 *International Journal of the Legal Profession* 309. Along with Austria, these countries are identified as the most regulated in terms of legal services: Stephen (n 39) 79 (citations omitted).

[226] H Kim, 'Legal Market Liberalization in South Korea: Preparations for Change' (2006) 1591) *Pacific Rim Law and Policy Journal* 199.

[227] Muller (n 111) 494.

[228] A Omran, 'The Appearance of Foreign Counsel in International Arbitration: The Case of Egypt' (2017) 34(5) *Journal of International Arbitration* 901.

[229] A Chen and H Whalen-Bridge, 'Singapore: Regulating Domestic and Foreign Lawyers – Singapore's Unified Approach' in Boon (ed) (n 37) 45.

[230] See LS Terry, S Mark and T Gordon, 'Trends and Challenges in Lawyer Regulation: The Impact of Globalization and Technology' (2012) 80 *Fordham Law Review* 2661, 2676; J Bennett, T Miller, J Webb, R Bosua, A Lodders and S Chamberlain, *Current State of Automated Legal Advice Tools – Discussion Paper 1* (Networked Society Institute, University of Melbourne, 2018) 19.

[231] See, eg, Legal Profession Uniform Law (NSW) s 9.

[232] OECD Directorate for Financial and Enterprise Affairs Competition Committee, Working Party No 2 on Competition and Regulation, *Protecting and Promoting Competition in Response to 'Disruptive' Innovations in Legal Services* (13 June 2016).

An important distinction is that made between 'legal advice' and 'legal information'; the provision of the former is reserved for lawyers, while the latter is not. However, as one commentator noted drily in the early days of the internet: 'Non-lawyers are … providing legal advice on the Internet, although they characterize their service as providing "legal information" in order to avoid admitting that they are engaged in the unauthorized practice of law'.[233] Low-cost legal drafting websites have existed since at least the early 2000s, and the questions arising about whether these services are providing legal advice or not have been in play ever since. Although this question seems straightforward, it in fact raises a significant policy question about whether the profession should try to stop such activities or rather view them as a means of increasing the availability of legal services to people who might otherwise not have access to them.[234] In the US, 'unauthorised practice of law' charges have been used by state bar associations to attempt to curtail the activities of providers of such websites or software.[235] Prosecution of unauthorised legal practice has to some degree been complicated by the widespread acceptance of new kinds of business structures for lawyers.

The distinction between legal and non-legal work, along with other regulatory features, is especially salient when it comes to new technologies. As we see in Chapter 11, the way that lawyers are regulated impacts the way that they can or should use AI; while the way that AI is regulated or not regulated impacts how lawyers may use it, too.

Who (or What) Will Lawyers Become?

The rise of global firms, and new structures for legal practices, should not distract from the fact that the majority of lawyers continue work in sole practice or small firms. Having said this, though, the last decade has seen growing numbers of 'alternative' firms, also referred to as 'New Law'. These may or may not adopt different business structures, but include virtual firms[236] and 'innovative' firms, which omit some key aspects of the traditional law firm model.[237] Some may use marketplace or platform models, wherein lawyers bid or are allocated work online. The use of

[233] CJ Lanctot, 'Regulating Legal Advice in Cyberspace' (2002) 16 *St. John's Journal of Legal Commentary* 569, 572.

[234] ibid 579.

[235] eg, *Unauthorized Practice of Law Committee v Parsons Technology* 1999 US Dist LEXIS 813 (ND Tex Jan 22, 1999) (after a backlash, the law was changed and the decision vacated on appeal); Barton (n 41) discusses this at pp 3081 et seq; C Blades, 'Crying Over Spilt Milk: Why the Legal Community Is Ethically Obligated to Ensure LegalZoom's Survival in the Legal Services Marketplace' (2015) 38(1) *Hamline Law Review* 31, 34–37; www.abajournal.com/news/article/legalzoom_hits_a_hurdle_in_north_carolina.

[236] See R Susskind, *The End of Lawyers? Rethinking the Nature of Legal Services* (Oxford University Press, 2010).

[237] JC Williams, A Platt and J Lee, 'Disruptive Innovation: New Models of Legal Practice' (2015) 67(1) *Hastings Law Journal* 1, 2.

technology to achieve significant changes to the ways that lawyers deliver legal services has been widely remarked.[238] On the other hand, Henderson argues that for many large law firms, 'the emphasis on large, short-term, distributed profits has placed a substantial stranglehold on innovation'.[239] He predicts that 'many Big Law brand names will survive' but foresees internal changes: fewer owners/partners who are more financially invested, or 'an employee-owned company in which each lawyer is carefully vetted at hiring and is expected to think and behave like an owner'.[240] Similarly, Deloitte predicts that UK law firms will become organisations with a small number of equity partners and much larger groups of long- and short-term employees.[241] Ultimately, Henderson thinks, 'we will witness a new era in which reputational capital – based on some variation of better, faster, cheaper – is built up rather than spent down'.[242] Yet Big Law will likely continue to excel in particular areas.[243]

The lawyer workforce is also much changed and changing, though still an imperfect reflection of the diversity of the public it serves. Latterly, there has been speculation as to how younger generations of lawyers – such as millennials, the generation born between 1981 and 1996 – will differ from their predecessors. Some suggest that millennials are more focused on work–life balance, have high expectations of their work, and place a premium on flexibility, collaboration, relationships and innovation.[244]

Aside from this structural picture, though, impacts on lawyers' professionalism more generally are hard to estimate. In the context of deregulatory changes allowing more non-lawyers into the legal services sector, Boon noted the assumption that 'non-lawyer capital will be more motivated to build technological infrastructure and less inhibited by the professional assumptions of lawyers'.[245] Webb has claimed that deregulation has already had multiple impacts, including at an ideological level:

> [It has] led to new forms of external regulation of legal practice, to the dismantling of some of the demarcations between legal and non-legal services, and, at a more ideological level, to the treatment of lawyers as just another category of 'service provider', rather than an ethically and constitutionally distinct profession.[246]

It is difficult to separate out the considerable changes already impacting lawyers' sense of who they are as professionals from the impact of AI technologies. Some

[238] eg, Dzienkowski (n 162); Williams, Platt and Lee (n 237); Susskind and Susskind (n 10).
[239] Henderson, 'From Big Law to Lean Law' (n 155) 11.
[240] ibid 16.
[241] Deloitte (n 24).
[242] Henderson (n 155) 16.
[243] Williams, Platt and Lee (n 237) 6.
[244] See J Rogers and F Bell, *Change Leadership for Lawyers* (Law Society of NSW, 2019) 15 (citations omitted).
[245] Boon (n 84) 204.
[246] Webb (n 32) 538–39.

writers have suggested lawyers can be automated out of existence; some predict a range of new types of quasi-legal role; others see a heightened need for lawyers in a complex legal and regulatory environment. The approach taken here begins from the premise that we need look closely at both the different roles, functions and ethos of lawyers, and the current applications of AI technology in legal work, to begin to answer these questions. This we turn to do in Part II.

PART II

The Use of Artificial Intelligence in Legal Practice

4

AI and Outcome Prediction

Introduction

In 2019 it was reported that a litigation finance company, Legalist, had raised US$100 million in capital to put towards financing lawsuits.[1] The cases to be funded are determined by application of a machine learning system which scrapes data from case law databases and uses its analysis to predict the chances of success of a given case. This chapter focuses on the use of AI systems like this to make predictions in a civil (as opposed to criminal) context. In law, this has unsurprisingly centred on predicting the outcomes of – or ancillary decisions made in – litigated cases.[2] Using machine learning to 'predict' the outcomes of legal cases is one of the most-hyped applications of AI to law to date. The use of statistical methods in this area is not especially new but the popularity of machine learning, the availability of data, and readily identified commercial applications are driving an abundance of innovation. Thus, 'Predicting court behavior is arguably the fastest growing sector of the legal-analytic marketplace'.[3]

The next chapter, Chapter 5, focuses on Technology Assisted Review, primarily an exercise in classification. There is also a body of research work concerned with description – notably, identifying patterns in judicial decision making – though this still, typically, is for normative purposes. For example, authors working in jurimetrics (application of quantitative methods to law) and in the broad space of empirical legal studies (ELS) have argued that having an accurate picture of cases, case outcomes and judicial tendencies is important for a number of different reasons. Frank Fagan argues that it can enable the development of consensus positions, commenting that 'big data methods can provide greater comprehensiveness and less subjectivity than traditional approaches'.[4] In other words, quantitative

[1] R Ambrogi, 'Litigation Finance Startup Legalist Raises $100 Million to Fund Lawsuits' LexBlog, 19 September 2019, www.lexblog.com/2019/09/19/litigation-finance-startup-legalist-raises-100-million-to-fund-lawsuits/.

[2] KD Ashley, *Artificial Intelligence and Legal Analytics: New Tools for Law Practice in the Digital Age* (Cambridge University Press, 2017) 108 ('Predicting courts' decisions has long been a goal of AI & Law research').

[3] P Flanagan and M Hook Dewey, 'Where Do We Go from Here: Transformation and Acceleration of Legal Analytics in Practice' (2019) 35(4) *Georgia State University Law Review* 1245, 1253.

[4] F Fagan, 'Big Data Legal Scholarship: Toward A Research Program and Practitioner's Guide' (2016) 20(1) *Virginia Journal of Law and Technology* 1, 2.

methods provide an empirical foundation to ground the development of theory – rather than unsubstantiated assertion. Fagan suggests that this can clarify rule application and produce thorough and wide-ranging description.[5] Likewise, academics Gabriel Rauterberg and Eric Talley describe their machine learning analysis of US Securities and Exchange Commission (SEC) filings as establishing key 'empirical facts' about the prevalence of corporate opportunity waivers.[6] Typically, company officers and directors may not personally benefit from opportunities belonging to the corporation: the waiver is a means by which the corporation can 'give up' an opportunity and in turn enable an individual to benefit. Rauterberg and Talley argue that having an accurate picture of the use of such waivers provides an important counterpoint to conventional understandings of their use.

Statistical and computational modelling of legal cases has a relatively long history and many early systems aimed to predict case outcomes, though in a different way to machine learning systems. Both Case-Based Reasoning (CBR) and machine learning, and sometimes a combination of both, can be employed to undertake prediction.[7] Yet while CBR is 'focused … on case comparison' and identifying the strength of legal arguments to make predictions (in other words, seeking to emulate a human reasoning process), machine learning methods are statistical in nature.[8]

Earlier variants of expert systems that sought either to apply legislative rules or to mimic human reasoning about case law encountered sticking points around fuzzy or indeterminate rules, 'hard cases', and the role of values and policy in legal decision making. These issues are not exclusive to expert systems: the body of work concerned with statistical mapping or analysis of legal issues (described below) also runs up against criticisms about values, ideology and reductionism in the face of the complexity of legal reasoning.[9]

Machine learning systems utilise statistical modelling somewhat differently in order to find patterns so as to enable prediction, hence the widely used expression 'predictive analytics'. Statistics is generally more concerned with building a model and describing the relations between data, while machine learning is geared towards outcomes. The model used in machine learning may not be especially interpretable. Machine learning systems are also much more scalable and indeed may require vast amounts of data to achieve accurate results. Interestingly, early concerns about using neural nets (for example) for predictive purposes within law

[5] ibid 2.

[6] G Rauterberg and E Talley, 'Contracting Out of the Fiduciary Duty of Loyalty: An Empirical Analysis of Corporate Opportunity Waivers' (2017) 117(5) *Colombia Law Review* 1075.

[7] Ashley (n 2) 108.

[8] ibid 107.

[9] See, eg, C Shapiro, 'Numbers, Motivated Reasoning, and Empirical Legal Scholarship' (2015) 63(2) *Buffalo Law Review* 385; C Shapiro, 'The Context of Ideology: Law, Politics, and Empirical Legal Scholarship' (2010) 75(1) *Missouri Law Review* 79.

centred on the inability of the program to provide reasons for its prediction.[10] While this concern remains, and presents problems for lawyers as regards how they use such systems, it appears to have been overshadowed by the vast quantities of data that can be processed, and the relatively good accuracy which can be attained.

How such programs could or *should* be used is another question. Christine Goodman writes that 'machines may be very good at telling the human lawyers what to do and when to do it, but not necessarily how to do it (strategy) or why (ethics)'.[11] But this technology might be used to augment human decision making in a number of ways – through support, structuring or guidance, by enhancing and even possibly replacing or replicating humans. The application of predictive analytics is therefore a theme running through several chapters of this book: in this chapter we discuss multiple examples, first in order to explain the use of machine learning (in particular) in this area, and secondly to illustrate current usage in the civil (as opposed to criminal) law, including in administrative decision making and litigation funding. We then discuss the use of machine learning in Technology Assisted Review of documents in Chapter 5; and touch on prediction again in Chapter 6, in relation to online dispute resolution – though, as explained there, its use is less prevalent than might be assumed. Chapter 7 discusses the use of machine learning in transactional law, and Chapter 8 in relation to regulatory strategies. Perhaps the most notorious application of predictive analytics at present is its controversial use in the criminal justice system, especially to assess the 'risk' presented by applicants for bail or parole, or even in sentencing persons who have been convicted of an offence, themes which are discussed in Chapter 9.

It has been claimed that using predictive analytics to predict the outcome of legal cases is a new form of legal realism.[12] The aspect which resounds most strongly with the claims of the Legal Realists is the statistical modelling of decisions to identify possible biases in human (judge) decision making. But this is a controversial exercise in the legal sphere, evidenced by the reporting of an amendment to French law prohibiting 'judge analytics'.[13] Article 33 of the *Justice*

[10] Ergo, as noted in Chapter 2, attempts to build reason-giving into CBR systems.

[11] C Goodman, 'AI/Esq: Impacts of Artificial Intelligence in Lawyer–Client Relationships' (2019) 72(1) *Oklahoma Law Review* 149, 160.

[12] N Aletras, D Tsarapatsanis, D Preoţiuc-Pietro, V Lampos, 'Predicting Judicial Decisions of the European Court of Human Rights: A Natural Language Processing Perspective' (2016) 2 *PeerJ Computer Science*, www.doi.org/10.7717/peerj-cs.93, 11; *cf* F Pasquale and G Cashwell, 'Prediction, Persuasion, and the Jurisprudence of Behaviourism' (2018) 68(Supp 1) *University of Toronto Law Journal* 63; see also MC Suchman and E Mertz, 'Toward a New Legal Empiricism: Empirical Legal Studies and New Legal Realism' (2010) 6 *Annual Review of Law and Social Science* 555.

[13] See, eg, 'France Bans Judge Analytics, 5 Years in Prison for Rule Breakers', *Artificial Lawyer*, 4 June 2019, www.artificiallawyer.com/2019/06/04/france-bans-judge-analytics-5-years-in-prison-for-rule-breakers/.

Reform Act bans the publication of statistical information about judges' decisions, punishable by a maximum of five years' incarceration.[14] A translation of part of the section reads:

> The identity data of magistrates and members of the judiciary cannot be reused with the purpose or effect of evaluating, analysing, comparing or predicting their actual or alleged professional practices.[15]

This change to the law appeared to be a reaction to a burgeoning legal analytics sector in Europe, exemplifying an attempt to regulate legal technology. Of course, whether such attempts will succeed is another matter.

After discussing some current examples of outcome prediction in the civil law, this chapter turns to the role of the lawyer, and some of the critiques of predictive systems. It considers in some detail both the shortcomings and utility of such applications, including some of the criticism made of both human prediction and human decision making. Finally, it discusses the role of the lawyer in utilising outcome prediction in law.

Application of AI to Legal Outcome Prediction

There is imprecision, overlap and intersection in the terminology used to describe the use of AI for outcome prediction. As Viktor Mayer-Schönberger and Kenneth Cukier explain in their book *Big Data*, that term became synonymous (around 2010) with data analytics using machine learning.[16] In *Predictive Analytics*, Eric Siegel said that what is significant about 'big data' is its rate of growth, not how much there is.[17] In 2012 *New York Times* journalist Steve Lohr described it as 'a shorthand label that typically means applying the tools of artificial intelligence,

[14] *Justice Reform Act* art 33 (loi n° 2019-222 du 23 mars 2019 de programmation 2018–2022 et de réforme pour la justice (1)) www.legifrance.gouv.fr/eli/loi/2019/3/23/2019-222/jo/article_33.

[15] *Justice Reform Act* art 33: 'Les données d'identité des magistrats et des membres du greffe ne peuvent faire l'objet d'une réutilisation ayant pour objet ou pour effet d'évaluer, d'analyser, de comparer ou de prédire leurs pratiques professionnelles réelles ou supposées'. The section continues: 'La violation de cette interdiction est punie des peines prévues aux articles 226-18, 226-24 et 226-31 du code pénal, sans préjudice des mesures et sanctions prévues par la loi n° 78-17 du 6 janvier 1978 relative à l'informatique, aux fichiers et aux libertés'.

[16] V Mayer-Schönberger and K Cukier, *Big Data: A Revolution That Will Transform How We Live, Work, and Think* (Houghton Mifflin Harcourt, 2013). See also S Lohr, 'Amid the Flood, A Catchphrase Is Born', *New York Times*, 12 August 2012, BU3.

[17] E Siegel, *Predictive Analytics: The Power to Predict Who Will Click, Buy, Lie, or Die* (John Wiley & Sons, 2013) 113–14 (he also notes that '"Big data" is … grammatically incorrect … it should be "a lot of data" or "plenty of data"').

like machine learning, to vast new troves of data beyond that captured in standard databases'.[18]

Machine learning refers to 'an automated process of discovering correlations (sometimes alternatively referred to as relationships or patterns) between variables in a dataset, often to make predictions or estimates of some outcome'.[19] Academic Harry Surden explains: 'Machine learning is closely associated with the larger enterprise of "predictive analytics" as researchers often employ machine learning methods to analyze existing data to predict the likelihood of uncertain outcomes'.[20] More specifically, big data enables legal outcome prediction 'in the mould of machine learning but using deep learning techniques' such as recursive neural networks.[21]

The methods used have several things in common. They require inputs in order to generate their outputs (in this chapter, our focus is on outputs which constitute a prediction). Usually, the output will be the predicted outcome of the case, such as whether the application will succeed or fail. As explained below, though, the generation of an output is only the final stage in a long process, where human designers have many choices to make. This series of stages is described below in greater detail, beginning at the first step of collecting and cleaning data, up to the point of 'real world' or actual deployment on new and not previously seen data.

Machine learning is not the same as statistical modelling but there are similarities, and there is a body of earlier, and contemporaneous, work in the area of legal prediction which utilises statistical modelling of case decisions. Accordingly, we turn to first consider the use of statistical modelling in relation to legal cases.

Statistical Modelling

Statistical modelling of legal cases has a relatively long history. The discipline of jurimetrics, and later ELS, use data, including statistical data, to illuminate legal issues or assist in the study of the law.[22] This includes applying research methodologies hailing from the behavioural sciences to different aspects of the study of law. North American scholarship, in particular, has examined areas such as

[18] S Lohr, 'How Big Data Became So Big', *New York Times*, 11 August 2012, www.nytimes.com/2012/08/12/business/how-big-data-became-so-big-unboxed.html.

[19] D Lehr and P Ohm, 'Playing with the Data: What Legal Scholars Should Learn About Machine Learning' (2017) 51(2) *UC Davis Law Review* 653, 671, citing KP Murphy, *Machine Learning: A Probabilistic Perspective* (MIT Press, 2012) 1.

[20] H Surden, 'Machine Learning and Law' (2014) 89(1) *Washington Law Review* 87, 90.

[21] F Coenen and T Bench-Capon, 'A Brief History of AI and Law' (AI & Law Workshop, University of Liverpool, 12 December 2017).

[22] See, eg, W Anderson and MT Wells, 'A Bayesian Hierarchical Regression Approach to Clustered and Longitudinal Data in Empirical Legal Studies' (2010) 7(4) *Journal of Empirical Legal Studies* 634.

patterns of judicial decision making[23] and success rates of particular kinds of court applications.[24]

Machine learning has its roots in statistical modelling but differs in key respects. One distinction is the emphasis on inference ('a mathematical model of the data-generation process') in statistics, as opposed to prediction or forecasting.[25] Statistical modelling is a means of characterising the relationships in data. This may include mapping data to an outcome variable in an inferential process. However, evaluating the model occurs via evaluating its parameters (rather than focusing only on outcomes). Usually, the robustness of the measures used, such as whether the relationship between variables is statistically significant, is important. The concept of statistical significance is described as follows:

> [It] refers to the probability that the association between two or more variables in a sample has occurred by chance. The commonly cited probability level of $p < .05$ means that there is less than a 1 in 20 probability that such an association would occur in the population by chance alone; it also means that if 100 tests are conducted, then 5 are likely to be significant by chance alone.[26]

Machine learning, on the other hand, typically involves 'training' a model on a subset of data, and then evaluating its performance by comparing how it works on a test set. Interpretability, as discussed below, is not necessarily important in machine learning, provided that the system can be shown to produce accurate results. Writing in the journal *Nature*, Danilo Bzdok, Naomi Altman and Martin Krzywinski describe machine learning as '[concentrating] on prediction by using general-purpose learning algorithms to find patterns in often rich and unwieldy data'.[27] They explain further: 'as the numbers of input variables and possible associations among them increase, the model that captures these relationships becomes more complex. Consequently, statistical inferences become less precise and the boundary between statistical and ML [machine learning] approaches becomes hazier'.[28]

[23] CL Boyd, L Epstein and AD Martin, 'Untangling the Causal Effects of Sex on Judging' (2010) 54(2) *American Journal of Political Science* 389.

[24] This has been applied in other jurisdictions too: eg, M Medvedeva, M Vols and M Wieling, 'Using Machine Learning to Predict Decisions of the European Court of Human Rights' (2019) *Artificial Intelligence and Law*, https://doi.org/10.1007/s10506-019-09255-y.

[25] See generally D Bzdok, N Altman and M Krzywinski, 'Statistics versus Machine Learning' (2018) 15(4) *Nature Methods* 233.

[26] J Cashmore and P Parkinson, 'The Use and Abuse of Social Science Research Evidence in Children's Cases' (2014) 20(3) *Psychology, Public Policy, and Law* 239.

[27] Bzdok, Krzywinski and Altman (n 25), citing D Bzdok, 'Classical Statistics and Statistical Learning in Imaging Neuroscience' (2017) 11 *Frontiers in Neuroscience* 543 and D Bzdok, M Krzywinski and N Altman, 'Machine Learning: A Primer' (2017) 14 *Nature Methods* 1119.

[28] Bzdok, Krzywinski and Altman (n 25).

For a number of years, databases of US decisions have been available to researchers and others wishing to use them for modelling,[29] and some of these statistical analyses look quite similar to later machine learning approaches. The Supreme Court Database, for instance, has been used for many different projects.[30] In 2004 Theodore Ruger, Pauline Kim, Andrew Martin and Kevin Quinn published the results of a study called the Supreme Court Forecasting Project.[31] These authors took 628 past decisions of the Supreme Court as training data, using the results to build simple classification trees in order to predict whether the Court would affirm or reverse future decisions. With only six variables based on 'general case characteristics', the model achieved accuracy of 75 per cent as to this binary outcome.[32] The variables were:

(1) circuit of origin;
(2) issue area of the case;
(3) type of petitioner (eg, the United States, an employer, etc);
(4) type of respondent;
(5) ideological direction (liberal or conservative) of the lower court ruling; and
(6) whether the petitioner argued that a law or practice is unconstitutional.[33]

Ruger et al's model easily outperformed the human experts, who were asked to make forecasts about the Court's decisions over a year-long period, and who achieved just under 60 per cent accuracy.[34] These experts (numbering 83) were predominantly academics and some appellate attorneys, who were asked to make predictions on cases 'within their areas of substantive expertise'.[35]

The model developed by Ruger et al was trained using judgments of the Court during a stable period in terms of its membership – the same bench had decided nearly 10 years' worth of cases together.[36] Ruger et al created 11 decision trees, nine of which represented the way which each individual Supreme Court Justice would decide, and one each to predict whether there would be a unanimous reversal or a unanimous affirmation.[37] Figure 4.1 shows the classification tree for Justice Sandra Day O'Connor.

[29] CL Boyd, 'In Defense of Empirical Legal Studies' (2015) 63(2) *Buffalo Law Review* 363, 372–74 (listing 21 databases).

[30] HJ Spaeth et al, '2019 Supreme Court Database, Version 2019 Release 1', www.supremecourtdatabase.org.

[31] T Ruger, P Kim, A Martin and K Quinn, 'The Supreme Court Forecasting Project: Legal and Political Science Approaches to Predicting Supreme Court Decisionmaking' (2004) 104(4) *Columbia Law Review* 1150; AD Martin, K Quinn, T Ruger and P Kim, 'Competing Approaches to Predicting Supreme Court Decision Making' (2004) 2(4) *Perspectives on Politics* 761.

[32] Ruger et al (n 31) 1151.

[33] ibid 1163; Martin et al (n 31) 762.

[34] The human experts were not asked to predict the outcome of every case but only a few selected cases.

[35] Ruger et al (n 31) 1168.

[36] ibid 1160–61.

[37] ibid 1164–65.

Figure 4.1 Example of decision tree

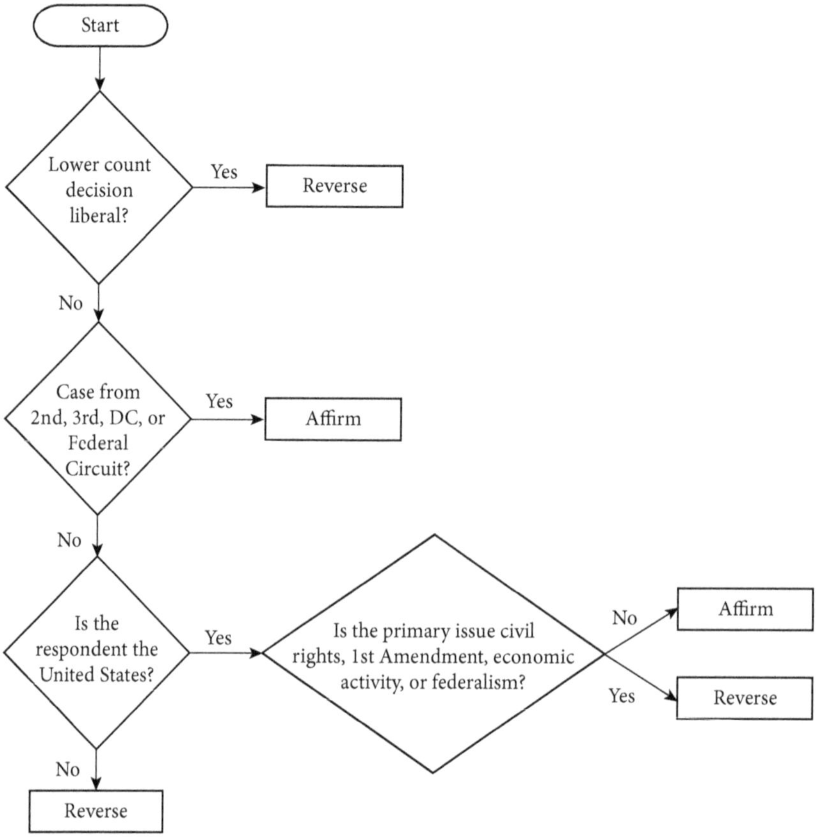

Source: AD Martin, K Quinn, T Ruger and P Kim, 'Competing Approaches to Predicting Supreme Court Decision Making' (2004) 2(4) *Perspectives on Politics* 761.

In the decision tree shown in Figure 4.1 all the questions are posed as binaries (yes or no). They may also be represented as other values, for example 'Age' could be split into 'Under 55' and '55 and above'; or more categories.

Machine Learning

Over a decade after the Ruger et al study, Daniel Katz, Michael Bommarito and Josh Blackman published the results of their predictive model for Supreme Court decision making.[38] The ultimate goal of the study was the same as that of Ruger

[38] D Katz, M Bommarito II and J Blackman, 'A General Approach for Predicting the Behavior of the Supreme Court of the United States' (2017) 12(4) *PLoS ONE* e0174698.

et al, but instead of a single classification tree model, Katz et al built a machine learning program which used ensembles or random forests of decision trees.[39] Katz et al also had more variables and vastly more data: the study utilised over 200 years' worth of Supreme Court decisions, with each decision having up to 240 variables. As a result, the study was not confined, as Ruger et al's was, to predicting decisions only of the Supreme Court bench in question. Katz et al's study could predict cases from any time period in the Court's history, though interestingly it was less accurate for very early cases and for recent cases (those determined by the Court under Chief Justice John Roberts).[40]

Machine learning has been applied to predict other, discrete legal issues, too. For example, Blakeley McShane and colleagues built a model to make predictions about US securities fraud class actions.[41] Using a dataset of 1,200 cases, their model could predict both the likelihood that the class action would settle as opposed to being dismissed and also the amount for which settled cases would resolve.[42] Likewise, in 2010, Mihai Surdeanu et al built a model for intellectual property lawsuits that used existing factors such as judges and originating districts, and predicted outcomes with 64 per cent accuracy.[43] The relevance of using only information which would be available at the time of filing one's court application is to enable true prediction and give such models practical utility.[44] Jack Conrad wrote of Surdeanu et al's paper: 'it represents an early and encouraging investigation into the prospects of using available evidence to predict key outcomes in one sub-domain of the legal field'.[45] These, and other examples, are discussed in the following sections.

The Machine Learning Process

David Lehr and Paul Ohm have emphasised the need for legal scholars to understand all the steps or stages in the development of a machine learning program.[46]

[39] Attributed to L Breiman, 'Random Forests' (2001) 45(1) *Machine Learning* 5.

[40] Katz, Bommarito and Blackman (n 38) 13 ('it does appear that the Roberts Court is less predictable than its immediate predecessors').

[41] BB McShane, OP Watson, T Baker and SJ Griffith, 'Predicting Securities Fraud Settlements and Amounts: A Hierarchical Bayesian Model of Federal Securities Class Action Lawsuits' (2012) 9(3) *Journal of Empirical Legal Studies* 482.

[42] ibid 484.

[43] M Surdeanu, R Nallapati, G Gregory, J Walker and CD Manning, 'Risk Analysis for Intellectual Property Litigation' (2011) *Proceedings of the 13th International Conference on Artificial Intelligence and Law* 116.

[44] Katz, Bommarito and Blackman (n 38) describe this quality as 'out-of-sample applicability'. They note that Supreme Court decisions, as well as obviously impacting the immediate participants in the case, have wide-ranging effects, including on financial markets.

[45] JG Conrad, 'Commentary: Mihai Surdeanu, Ramesh Nallapati, George Gregory, Joshua Walker and Christopher D Manning (2011) "Risk Analysis for Intellectual Property Litigation"' in T Bench-Capon et al, 'A History of AI and Law in 50 papers: 25 Years of the International Conference on AI and Law' (2012) 20 *Artificial Intelligence and Law* 215.

[46] Lehr and Ohm (n 19).

This is important, too, for lawyers, whether their clients are seeking to use machine learning to enhance or quantify decision making, or being subjected to it in some form, such as during the criminal justice process.

Lehr and Ohm therefore break the process down into stages, summarised in Table 4.1. They argue that most legal critics have focused on only the final stage, when the machine learning system is deployed in the 'real world', at the expense of comprehending the significance of the earlier steps – especially as these stages typically demand considerable human involvement in design choices.

Table 4.1 Lehr and Ohm's machine learning stages

	Stage	
1	Problem definition	'Playing with the data'
2	Data collection	
3	Data cleaning	
4	Summary statistics review	
5	Data partitioning	
6	Model selection	
7	Model training	
8	Model deployment	Real-world deployment

We adopt these stages here, though with less detail than the explication of Lehr and Ohm, to further explain the complexity of the process. It should also be noted, as other authors have discussed, that the choices that must be made – such as in problem definition, data collection, and how features are measured – are also potential sources of bias.[47] We briefly consider issues of bias and fairness below, and discuss them more extensively in Chapter 9 (in relation to criminal justice) and Chapter 10 (on AI's limitations).

Problem Definition

As a starting point, an abstract, 'real world' goal must be translated into a predictive goal.[48] This predictive goal must then be linked to a specific 'outcome variable' – what measures will likely be most accurate in making the prediction? In a legal context, that predictive goal is likely what a court's decision will be. In the case of the US Supreme Court, that would be to affirm the decision of the court below, to reverse it, or another decision (for instance, if the court is exercising its original jurisdiction).

[47] S Barocas and AD Selbst, 'Big Data's Disparate Impact' (2016) 104(3) *California Law Review* 671; J Kleinberg, H Lakkaraju, J Leskovec, J Ludwig and S Mullainathan, 'Human Decisions and Machine Predictions' (2017) 133(1) *The Quarterly Journal of Economics* 237; J Kleinberg, J Ludwig, S Mullainathan and CR Sunstein, 'Discrimination in the Age of Algorithms' (2018) 10 *Journal of Legal Analysis* 113.

[48] See Lehr and Ohm (n 19), who give the goal of reducing violence between prison inmates.

Whether or not the outcome variable or output is specified is a key difference between supervised and unsupervised learning. In unsupervised learning, there is only input data and no corresponding output variables. In other words, the program is not being directed to measure or classify any particular thing but is left to identify patterns itself. In supervised learning, there are both input and output variables, and the goal is to use an algorithm to model, and adjust, how the inputs are mapped to the outputs. This can be used, correspondingly, to predict the outputs which will result from the inputs.

Of course, as soon as the predictive goal or outcome variable involves something about which reasonable human minds might differ – such as what qualities are desirable in a future employee – the variable itself cannot be measured, and a proxy must be chosen instead.[49] Accordingly, determining the outcome variable/s depends both on knowledge of the subject matter of what is to be measured, and technical aspects. As explained below, there are different types of algorithm, and they have different capabilities, which may be more or less suited to the different types of outcome variable that are sought.[50]

Data Collection and Cleaning

The data itself must be collected, and there must be enough of it. Running a machine learning algorithm on a small dataset is described, succinctly, as 'pointless'.[51] Lehr and Ohm also explain the need to be certain that variables do actually measure what they are supposed to measure. This requires paying attention to latent as well as surface characteristics.[52] In other words, how accurate is the chosen input variable as a potential predictor of the outcome variable? In the criminal justice context, this becomes particularly fraught and often relies on assumptions about the soundness of certain measures. For example, using past arrests as a variable relevant to future criminality cannot take into account the fact that many people may commit offences but are not arrested, while others are arrested but not charged or convicted – or were not guilty.[53] In terms of legal case outcomes, even a comprehensive database does not take into account cases which settled (even at a late stage) or where participants withdrew. In still other machine learning applications, the data is based on assumed facts rather than those established at a trial.

In addition, generalisability must be possible. Usually, this is achieved by using a random sample, which in turn ensures that it is representative of the real-world data on which the algorithm will be used.[54] True randomness is hard to come by. But without it, something which is true for the training dataset may not be

[49] ibid 675.
[50] ibid.
[51] ibid 678.
[52] ibid 679.
[53] ibid.
[54] ibid 680.

true of the data which the model will be processing. On the other hand, Mayer-Schönberger and Cukier note that it is possible to avoid sampling (and therefore the need to take a random sample) altogether by using *all* the data that is available. Increased computer processing power means that this is now possible.[55] As noted above, while Ruger et al's Supreme Court decision analysis used judgments from a particular period and six data points for each, Katz et al's program used all the available judgments from 200 years of the Court's history, and up to 240 data points.

As well as simply being accumulated, data must also be 'cleaned'. Cleaning refers to correcting errors or dealing with missing data. Usually there will be at least some data missing and there may be incorrect values. Cleaning the data means that this missing or wrong data is corrected either by deleting the subjects with missing data or making a guess as to what the missing data would be by comparing other, complete, data in the set.[56]

Machine learning can itself be used to classify data, as explained further in the next chapter dealing with Technology Assisted Review. Rauterberg and Talley described their use of a machine learning system to classify instances of corporate opportunity waivers found in SEC filings.[57] They explain that the first step was to sample, in a deliberately over-inclusive manner, 'textual snippets' which potentially contained corporate opportunity waivers. They then employed human coders to create a set of training data for supervised machine learning:

> From a data set of 10,682 snippets that included candidate waivers, the authors and a team of research assistants manually coded 1,000 randomly selected snippets along over 40 dichotomous dimensions, including not only the presence/absence of a waiver disclosure (our primary topic of interest), but also the scope, reach, and location of such disclosures when they occurred. The most significant variable, of course, is whether the candidate disclosure was a bona fide disclosure of a waiver (in whatever form). They find approximately 62% of the hand-classified sample fits this description. The hand-coding of this sample, in turn, creates a 'training' data set for a machine learning *perceptron* – an algorithm for predicting the presence or absence of a genuine disclosure in a given document.[58]

This illustrates the role of humans in preparing and labelling data.

Statistics Review and Data Partitioning

A summary statistics review must be conducted. This means, essentially, eliminating outliers from the dataset. Outlier is a term for an aberrant data point in a dataset, one which is significantly 'outside' the parameters of the rest of the data.

[55] Mayer-Schönberger and Cukier (n 16) 26–31.

[56] Lehr and Ohm (n 19) 682.

[57] The SEC maintains a large database for research purposes: see G Rauterberg and E Talley, 'A Machine Learning Classifier for Corporate Opportunity Waivers' (2016) Colombia Law & Economics Working Paper No. 553, www.scholarship.law.columbia.edu/faculty_scholarship/2008; Rauterberg and Talley (n 6).

[58] Rauterberg and Talley (n 57) 7; see also Rauterberg and Talley (n 6) 1122–23.

Data partitioning is a method for using some data to train a model and some to test the model. This enables the program to be trained on one set, and then tested on new and unfamiliar data, to evaluate its performance.[59] Rauterberg and Talley explain their use of Monte Carlo simulations to investigate how well their model would work on new data. A Monte Carlo simulation (named for the casinos of Monte Carlo, Monaco) is a means of seeing a range of possible outcomes by performing a calculation over and over in different iterations, but substituting different probability distributions for uncertain factors:

> Within each iteration of the simulation, the hand-coded data were randomly segregated into two groups: A provisional 'training' dataset, consisting of roughly 75% of our observations, and a provisional 'testing' dataset, consisting of the remaining 25% of the data. We then fit equation (2) to the training data, marshalling the resulting coefficient estimates to generate predictions of the presence/absence of the waiver in the testing data, and generating predictive metrics similar to those discussed above. We repeated the Monte Carlo simulation for 1,000 iterations, which produced empirical distributions for each of these metrics.[60]

An issue for some machine learning programs, though, is the phenomenon of 'overfitting'.[61] Lehr and Ohm explain that 'many (but, arguably, not all) machine-learning algorithms suffer from a phenomenon called "overfitting." … if a statistical method is particularly adept at finding correlations in data, it risks identifying as legitimate correlations [which are] due to randomness, including outliers'.[62] In other words, the program is so proficient at finding patterns in data that it may identify random noise as part of a pattern. This is problematic because the pattern will not be present in any other data, namely the data on which it is to be deployed.

Model Selection and Model Training

In the penultimate stages, the algorithmic model must be chosen. As explained in Chapter 5, this might be a Bayesian analysis, a 'near neighbour' approach or a regression analysis, for example. Within this discussion, Lehr and Ohm identify six considerations arising when it comes to choosing the model, including the nature of the outcome variable that is sought, the degree of explainability required, and the likelihood of getting false positives or false negatives (as discussed in Chapter 9, this is of especial significance in criminal justice applications).[63] As they describe:

> Which class of model performs best is often a function of peculiarities of a given data set. Therefore, it is common for this model selection step to result not in the selection of just one kind of algorithm, but in the narrowing-down of an analyst's choices to a

[59] Lehr and Ohm (n 19) 686.
[60] Rauterberg and Talley (n 57) 8–9.
[61] Siegel (n 17) 168–69.
[62] Lehr and Ohm (n 19) 684.
[63] ibid 690.

> few candidates. These candidates would then be taken through the next step – model training – to determine which performs optimally and, thus, should be deployed.[64]

The model is then trained using the training set data.[65]

Deployment

The final stage is the deployment of the algorithm on real-world data, or as Lehr and Ohm describe it, 'converting … into a "running model"'.[66] Lehr and Ohm explain some final challenges here: ensuring that the model can run 'at scale' or even in real time (for example, suggesting other products to an online shopper as they browse); and making the model user-friendly to the person who is its ultimate consumer – which requires an interface that can be used by a non-expert.[67] Their main point is that human decisions are required throughout the process – and these decisions all carry their own particular implications.

Text Analysis and Natural Language Processing

When it comes to legal outcome prediction, the input data can be thought of as containing different 'features' – different elements of the data which the program may factor into its analysis. In Ruger et al's Supreme Court Forecasting Project, the features were the six variables mentioned – things like where the case had originated, and the status of the petitioner (applicant). By connecting features to outcomes, a program can identify a pattern and use it to make predictions about the outcome of cases with similar features.[68] How the features are used depends on the type of analysis or algorithm selected but also on how the machine learning program 'learns' – ie, refines its parameters.

Features might include any number of things. One way to think about features in legal outcome prediction is to consider whether they are external things which are technically legally irrelevant to the merits of the case (though may act as proxies for things which go to merit), or whether they are internal, case-specific factors (which might be more readily recognised as going to the merits). Examples of the former would include who the judge was, who the lawyers were, whether the plaintiff/applicant was a natural person or a company, the location where the application was filed, and so on. Internal features could be factual information about the events which have generated the claim. Another approach might be to

[64] ibid 695.
[65] ibid 696.
[66] ibid 701.
[67] ibid 702.
[68] Ashley (n 2) 107.

use text itself – for instance, the text of judgments. Fagan has described the process of doing regression analysis with the text of decided cases:

> All of the words in a given [judicial] opinion are assumed to potentially relate to the judicial outcome. The analyst determines a relationship between the words and outcome by regressing the words as independent variables against the dependent variable of judicial outcome. The results are then interpreted to support a given theory. The key difference between big data regression and traditional regression is the sheer number of covariates. A dataset consisting of a 20,000-word vocabulary will consist of 20,000 covariates.[69]

Fagan argues that words may also 'function as surrogates' for the facts of a case, as determined by the judge.[70] Whether this is a meaningful way to analyse a case, however, is open to question. Referring to the Surdeanu and Katz studies mentioned above, Kevin Ashley has noted that the features used

> do not capture the particular substantive factual features of a case. The closest they come are issue and issue area. This means that neither … prediction program can explain their predictions in terms of the substantive legal merits of a case. Presumably, either program could provide information on the weightiest features underlying a prediction, but those features do not correspond to substantive factual features of the case.[71]

How the relevant 'features' are arrived at (or extracted from data) has also changed over time; as has the volume of data (such as existing case law or data about decisions) which is subjected to analysis. A facet of many studies is that human experts originally identified the features considered likely to be relevant to outcome, although algorithmic models then 'learned' how to weight these features.[72] An important differentiator of programs is the extent to which the program must be told by humans about which features to use.[73] Early programs required the relevant features to be identified, which involved humans determining those features which seemed to be important, either based on analysis of key cases, or from research.[74] The program would then use the features as input variables and map them against outcomes, developing a model to apply to new, or future, cases. For instance, one early program used a database of 64 tax cases and mapped their features. The features were those elements of cases which earlier studies had suggested were important.[75] Forty-six features were addressed in a binary manner (answered

[69] Fagan (n 4) 20–21.

[70] ibid 19.

[71] K Ashley, 'Automatically Extracting Meaning from Legal Texts: Opportunities and Challenges' (2019) 35(4) *Georgia State University Law Review* 1117, 1125, citing Surdeanu et al (n 43) and Katz, Bommarito and Blackman (n 38).

[72] Ashley (n 2) 125.

[73] ibid.

[74] E Ejan Mackaay and P Robillard, 'Predicting Judicial Decisions: The Nearest Neighbour Rule and Visual Representation of Case Patterns' (1974) 3 *Datenverarbeitung im Recht* 302, 306, cited by KD Ashley and S Brüninghaus, 'Automatically Classifying Case Texts and Predicting Outcomes' (2009) 17(2) *Artificial Intelligence and Law* 125, 129; and by Ashley (n 2) 108–109.

[75] Mackaay and Robillard (n 74).

yes or no) for each case, and all the cases were then plotted.[76] A 'near neighbour' approach was used. This assumes that the outcome of a new case will be the same as its closest neighbours – in this instance, of three of the five nearest.[77]

Meanwhile, a key element of both the Ruger et al and the Katz et al models described above is the capacity to forecast the outcome of the case using only information which would be available at the time of filing of the application.[78] In other words, these studies sought to replicate as far as possible the 'real life' prediction of lawyers. In the Ruger et al study, the predictions of both the statistical model and the human experts whose views formed a counterpoint were published online before the Court delivered its judgments.[79] However, the Supreme Court studies do not rely on extracting features automatically from the text of judgments; rather, the features are determined by humans.[80]

Labelling factors is often a laborious process. A key issue, then, is whether relevant features can be identified from the text of cases by the program (or another program) itself. Here, machine learning intersects with topic modelling and regression analysis in the broader field of computational linguistics.[81] At present, as might be expected, it is more straightforward to automatically extract 'external' features from cases or case-related documents, capturing information such as the identity of judges and area of law.[82] The fact that programs using such information can generate results with quite good predictive accuracy suggests that these factors can act as proxies for features which go more directly to merit.[83]

Now, the hope is that by using capabilities in reading text, a program will be able to analyse a mass or corpus of documents to *itself* identify (and weight) the relevant features.[84] Instead of relying solely on a human to identify and program the features needed, they will be extracted automatically from the textual data using machine learning. In 2009 Kevin Ashley and Stefanie Brüninghaus reported on a program which did this: automated analysis of textual description of the facts of a case was used to identify features.[85] A program described as a 'natural language interface' or 'bridge' identified the features after being trained on example data.[86] It then passed these lists of features to the Issue-based Prediction program, which built the predictive model using the features.[87] Ashley and Brüninghaus'

[76] As Ashley explains, the two-dimensional plotting was a simplification down from the original, multidimensional vector space representation: Ashley (n 2) 108.
[77] Ashley (n 2) 109.
[78] Ruger et al (n 31) 1164.
[79] ibid 1163.
[80] Ashley (n 71) 1125.
[81] Fagan (n 4) 34–52.
[82] As described by Ashley (n 2) 123.
[83] ibid 124.
[84] ibid 13.
[85] Ashley and Brüninghaus (n 74).
[86] The SMart Index Learner (SMILE) program: see Ashley (n 2) 294–98.
[87] Ashley (n 2) 125.

bridging program was trained using case notes which had been coded (annotated) by law students.

Further Examples

As well as researchers, many commercial providers now purport to offer some form of legal predictive analytics within subject-specific domains.[88] Some of these products were born out of research and are the creation of different research groups at different institutions.

Nikolaos Aletras et al, a group of researchers from the University of Pennsylvania and the University of Sheffield, sought to build a program that could predict the outcomes of cases heard by the European Court of Human Rights (ECtHR) based on the text of cases alone.[89] Their dataset was relatively small, comprising fewer than 600 cases. Many applications filed with the ECtHR are dismissed at an early point for failure to meet admissibility criteria (such as having exhausted all rights and remedies in the domestic courts of one's home jurisdiction). In 2015 approximately 83,000 cases were declared inadmissible and therefore did not proceed to any form of merits hearing, as opposed to approximately 900 decisions on the merits.[90] Aletras et al's analysis also excluded these inadmissible cases.[91]

Aletras et al did not have access to any materials (such as materials filed by the applicants in proceedings) other than the text of judgments. ECtHR judgments are somewhat unusual (at least when compared to judgments in the common law world) in that they must be structured in a certain way, using particular subheadings. Decisions are therefore 'clearly divided into different sections'.[92] This fixed structure was utilised by Aletras et al, who used the published judgments of the Court, specifically the 'Circumstances' section of judgments, as 'proxies' for case materials.[93] This Circumstances section contains the facts of a case and its history in domestic courts.

Aletras et al's conclusions rest on the assumption that using the Court's judgments in this way – as proxies for external materials – is satisfactory and accurate. Yet, as Frank Pasquale and Glynn Cashwell observed in a critical article, there is nothing to indicate whether the recitation of facts in the Circumstances section is actually a neutral rendering.[94] Indeed, Aletras et al, given their inability to access any other materials, could have no way of estimating that it was. As Pasquale and

[88] eg, Fastcase, Ravel Law (including Judge Analytics), Lex Machina, CARA.

[89] Aletras et al (n 12); see also University College London 'AI Predicts Outcomes of Human Rights Trials', *UCL News*, 24 October 2016, www.ucl.ac.uk/news/news-articles/1016/241016-AI-predicts-outcomes-human-rights-trials.

[90] Aletras et al (n 12) 3.

[91] ibid.

[92] ibid 4.

[93] ibid 5.

[94] Pasquale and Cashwell (n 12) 69–70.

Cashwell point out, 'almost any court writing an opinion to justify a judgment is going to develop a facts section in ways that reflect its outcome'.[95] The finding that this section was most determinative of outcome should come as no surprise, given the justificatory process of how judges construct and explain the facts of a case.

Aletras et al explain that they utilised decisions of the ECtHR for their analysis in part because of the 'distinctive structure' of judgments.[96] In many jurisdictions, however, legal judgments lack the structure which would presently allow AI software to identify patterns from which to learn effectively.[97] The judge may discuss the issues, the facts and the law, to a degree and in any order they see fit; headings may or may not be used; and alternative arguments may or may not be discussed extensively before being rejected. It has been argued that AI software also works better with subject-specific cases, as it is 'very difficult for an algorithm to get a database of many different kinds of cases (eg, workplace, traffic, divorce) and then somehow glean rules that could make sense out of any possible new case'.[98]

The study of intellectual property actions by Surdeanu et al,[99] mentioned above, was presented when most of the authors worked at Lex Machina. Originally a research project at Stanford University (the IP Litigation Clearinghouse), Lex Machina launched as a for-profit company in 2009,[100] and was acquired by LexisNexis in 2015. Lex Machina was created to analyse decisions on patents. A feature called 'Motion Chains' predicts whether particular motions (court applications) are likely to succeed, based on past data.[101] Lex Machina has made its collection available for free to academics and US federal judges, who can use it to investigate different aspects of patent decisions, and Lex Machina itself produces reports of trends in patent law. Among the data available are law firm 'handicaps' – so potential clients, or in-house lawyers, can use Lex Machina's information to find out which firms perform best before particular judges or for particular motions.[102] Lex Machina can, for example, identify what proportion of cases a particular judge will summarily dismiss. A user can then see a sample of cases to try and identify the arguments which appear to have been the most effective.

Another start-up originating at Stanford is Ravel Law, which was also acquired by LexisNexis, in 2017. Initially, Ravel was best known for its graphics: it included

[95] ibid 70.

[96] Aletras et al (n 12).

[97] D Orr and C Rule, 'Artificial Intelligence and the Future of Online Dispute Resolution', *New Handshake*, www.newhandshake.org/SCU/ai.pdf.

[98] ibid.

[99] Surdeanu et al (n 43).

[100] Business Wire News, 'Stanford Law School Spins off New Venture, Offering Commercial Access to Intellectual Property Legal Data', *Business Wire*, 5 January 2010, www.businesswire.com/news/home/20100105006564/en/Stanford-Law-School-Spins-New-Venture-Offering; P Hoge, 'Lex Machina: "Moneyball" Meets Patent Lawsuits', *San Francisco Business Times*, 3 September 2013, www.bizjournals.com/sanfrancisco/blog/2013/09/lex-machina-mines-lawsuit-data.html?page=all.

[101] SD Nelson and JW Simek, 'Running with the Machines' (2017) 78(3) *Oregon State Bar Bulletin* 22, 24.

[102] D Fisher, 'Stanford-Bred Startup Uses Moneyball Stats to Handicap Judges, Lawyers', *Forbes*, 2 February 2015, www.forbes.com/sites/danielfisher/2015/02/02/stanford-bred-startup-uses-moneyball-stats-to-handicap-judges-lawyers/.

visual representations of case law.[103] In 2015 its 'Judge Analytics' tool became available. This ostensibly enables lawyers 'to see patterns in how a judge ruled on an issue'[104] by analysing data about courts and judges along with case law precedents. It has now been expanded to include data about law firms and motions. Ravel claims to 'surface' the most persuasive language dependent upon the judge and court, as well as 'uncover buried connections' between cases with its visualisation tools.[105] In 2018 Lexis launched 'Context', developed from its acquisition of Ravel. Context offers information such as the cases which judges are most likely to cite when deciding on motions. It also has data on 380,000 expert witnesses.[106] Other operators in this space include Gavelytics,[107] Premonition™[108] and Judicata,[109] which also reportedly analyse judicial decisions and the success rate of lawyers.

At present, Ravel and Lex Machina appear to be primarily engaged in presenting information, notably patterns in information, in the most useful way. Their claims about 'prediction' are less conspicuous. In contrast, some entities make more explicit claims about prediction. UK-based CaseCrunch reported that its software was more accurate than London lawyers in predicting the outcomes of complaints about payment protection insurance decisions made by the Financial Ombudsman.[110] Little detail is provided about this 'challenge' although one critique made of the process is that the lawyers pitted against the software were not experts in payment protection insurance, and indeed did not work in that area at all.[111] A similar criticism has been raised about the US Supreme Court studies – it is suggested that attorneys who actually work in the area of Supreme Court appeals would achieve more accurate results.[112] By their nature, Supreme Court appeals deal with a diverse range of factual and legal issues – so indeed, one might expect also that lawyers with specialist knowledge of the subject in question might be better placed to undertake prediction.

[103] M Gediman, 'Artificial Intelligence: Not Just Sci-Fi Anymore' (2015) 21(1) *AALL Spectrum* 34, 36.

[104] JP O'Grady, 'Analytics and Insights: It's All about Asking the Right Questions' (2017) 22(2) *AALL Spectrum* 40, 42.

[105] Florida International University College of Law, 'eResources Spotlight: Ravel Law', *FIU Law*, 10 June 2019, www.law.fiu.edu/2019/06/10/eresources-spotlight-ravel-law/.

[106] R Strom, 'New Data Analytics Tool Knows Every Federal Judge's Favorite Cases' (2018) 260(105) *New York Law Journal* 7.

[107] www.gavelytics.com/.

[108] premonition.ai/; and see further Chapter 10.

[109] www.judicata.com/.

[110] See Case Crunch, www.case-crunch.com; see also LawGeex, 'Comparing the Performance of Artificial Intelligence to Human Lawyers in the Review of Standard Business', February 2018, 19, www.ai.lawgeex.com/rs/345-WGV-842/images/LawGeex%20eBook%20Al%20vs%20Lawyers%202018.pdf; the CaseCrunch website claims that 'lawyers scored an accuracy of 62.3%' while the software scored 86.6 per cent. No detail as to how this was calculated is provided. See also R Cellan-Jones, 'The Robot Lawyers Are Here – And They're Winning', *BBC News Online*, 1 November 2017, www.bbc.com/news/technology-41829534.

[111] J Tashea, 'Artificial Intelligence Software Outperforms Lawyers (without Subject Matter Expertise) in Matchup', *ABA Journal*, 3 November 2017, www.abajournal.com/news/article/artificial_intelligence_software_outperforms_lawyers_without_subject_matter.

[112] R Moorhouse, 'Lawyers Learning About Prediction', *Lawyer Watch Blog*, 19 January 2017, https://lawyerwatch.blog/2017/01/19/lawyers-learning-about-prediction/.

Role of the Lawyer

Various scholars have argued that the type of prediction which is possible from machine learning algorithms can simply never replace legal reasoning.[113] Early headlines referencing machines taking over the function of lawyers seem to have given way to the premise that outcome prediction is a supplemental tool – one which enables more thorough case preparation, gives additional knowledge about courts, judges and different kinds of court application, and ostensibly grounds a lawyer's judgement in objectivity. The assumption that lawyers have a continuing role is highlighted in LexMachina's market pitch, which reads:

> For the first time, lawyers can combine insights gleaned from bottom-up data with traditional top-down controlling authority found in statutes, rules, and court opinions. It's new, it's unorthodox and it's extremely valuable. But Legal Analytics also brings lawyering back to its roots. It provides lawyers with facts on which to base opinions – the core element of good lawyering.[114]

Such programs might be used by lawyers to advise clients about the merits of their case. A UK insurance law firm has explained, of its data analytics tools: 'This is not about replacing lawyers. It's about giving them tools to help them make better predictions'.[115]

They might also be used by clients themselves; by litigation funders, to determine whether funding a particular lawsuit is a good investment;[116] or by legal aid bodies to determine whether a person should receive legal aid assistance.

Yet, this recasting of data analytics as an enhancer rather than replacer of lawyers still leaves unanswered questions. Such questions span the wider scale effects of using predictive analytics for legal cases and associated rule-of-law concerns. For example, in their study of ECtHR decision making, Aletras et al suggested that their predictive tool could be used to triage applications made to the Court, so that those most likely to succeed could be prioritised.[117] But to prioritise cases based on a prediction of success would be problematic in terms of fundamental rights to due process of law and the right to have one's case heard (especially in a court dealing exclusively with alleged human rights violations). Many cases now considered fundamental, such as civil rights litigation in the US, might never have been brought or permitted to proceed to a hearing if they were 'triaged' in this way. In other instances, success and failure have different and more

[113] CR Sunstein, 'Of Artificial Intelligence and Legal Reasoning' (2001) 8 *University of Chicago Law School Roundtable* 29, 32–34, suggesting that computer programs do not reason analogically the way humans do.

[114] LexMachina, www.lexmachina.com/what-we-do/.

[115] N Hilborne, 'Law Firm Launches Data Analytics Team to Help Lawyers Predict the Future', *LegalFutures*, 7 June 2017, www.legalfutures.co.uk/latest-news/law-firm-launches-data-analytics-team-help-lawyers-predict-future quoting Andrew Dunkley.

[116] See, eg, Ambrogi (n 1).

[117] Aletras et al (n 12).

complex meanings – viz 'winning' a case but being awarded 'one dollar damages'. There are also questions as to how any benefits generated from the use of legal predictive analytics are likely to be distributed as, to date, the industry seems to be geared towards wealthy and sophisticated clients, in areas such as patent law.[118] In addition, challenges arise for lawyers in balancing the use of machine learning tools with their professional responsibility obligations. Some such questions are investigated further in Chapters 10 and 11, where we consider the limitations of AI, and the role of lawyers' professional ethics, respectively.

Conversely, there is a substantial body of literature about the flaws of human decision making, including of course, that of lawyers and judges. Studies suggest that human prediction suffers from cognitive biases and heuristics, as Jon Kleinberg et al have explained:

> A large body of research from behavioral science … tells us that people themselves may not know why and how they are choosing – even (or perhaps especially) when they think that they do. Many choices happen automatically; the influences of choice can be subconscious; and the rationales we produce are constructed after the fact and on the fly.[119]

Experience as a lawyer does not necessarily improve predictive judgement and decision-making skills.[120] One academic has commented, for instance, that there are 'serious questions' to be asked about whether lawyers and clients actually make 'good decisions' in the midst of litigation.[121] LexMachina emphasises objectivity over anecdotalism, encapsulated by the claim that 'Objective data replaces subjective "anec-data"'.[122] But as noted, volume of data is also highly relevant: some areas, such as insurance, have much data already available to them, which dovetails with the desire to make decisions 'easier, quicker and with greater certainty'.[123] On the other hand, the past decisions comprising the data to be analysed were generated through the same imperfect process.[124]

[118] P Wongchaisuwat, D Klabjan and JO McGinnis, 'Predicting Litigation Likelihood and Time to Litigation for Patents' (*Proceedings of the 16th edition of the International Conference on Artificial Intelligence & Law*, London, 12–16 June 2017).

[119] Kleinberg et al (n 47) 116, citing RE Nisbett and TD Wilson, 'Telling More than We Can Know: Verbal Reports on Mental Processes' (1977) 84 *Psychological Review* 231–59; and T Wilson, *Strangers to Ourselves* (Harvard University Press, 2004).

[120] R Kiser, *Beyond Right and Wrong: The Power of Effective Decision Making for Attorneys and Clients* (Springer, 2010).

[121] M Keet, 'Litigation Risk Assessment: A Tool to Enhance Negotiation' (2017) 19 *Cardozo Journal of Conflict Resolution* 17, citing SR Gross and KD Syverud, 'Getting to No: A Study of Settlement Negotiations and the Selection of Cases for Trial' (1991) 90 *Michigan Law Review* 319; SR Gross and KD Syverud, 'Don't Try: Civil Jury Verdicts in a System Geared to Settlement' (1996) 44 *UCLA Law Review* 1; JJ Rachlinski, 'Gains, Losses, and the Psychology of Litigation' (1996) 70 *Southern California Law Review* 113; RL Kiser, MA Asher and BB McShane, 'Let's Not Make a Deal: An Empirical Study of Decision Making in Unsuccessful Settlement Negotiations' (2008) 5 *Journal of Empirical Legal Studies* 551; Kiser (n 120).

[122] LexMachina, 'What We Do', www.lexmachina.com/what-we-do/.

[123] Hilborne (n 115) (quoting Mike Brown).

[124] For a discussion of issues of fairness and bias in machine prediction, see further Chapter 9.

In this section we explore the role of the lawyer in using predictive analytics in civil settings, including providing context, human qualities, and taking on 'unpopular' cases. As a precursor, however, we consider some of the literature on the limitations of human prediction and decision making.

What the Judge Ate for Breakfast

Human thinking and decision making are often flawed. We tend to be overly optimistic about chances of success yet also susceptible to loss aversion: we are more concerned to avoid a loss than to achieve an equivalent gain. We also use heuristics when evaluating uncertainty, meaning that we are susceptible to particular biasing effects such as framing and anchoring.[125] However, there are studies that suggest humans are capable of overcoming or counteracting the effects of cognitive biases, too.[126]

One commonly raised response to concerns about predictive analytics in law, therefore, is to counter that humans, including human judges, are equally flawed and opaque decision makers.[127] This argument relies on a number of psychological studies that collectively suggest humans operate with various cognitive biases and shortcuts; and that judges (a particular focus of study, as professional decision makers) are not immune from their impacts.[128] In a now notorious study, Shai Danziger and colleagues found that judges in Israel were more likely to accede to a prisoner's request for parole (either by granting it, or varying the conditions of parole) immediately after a food break.[129] These researchers concluded that 'the caricature that justice is what the judge ate for breakfast might be an appropriate caricature for human decision-making in general'.[130] They attributed these patterns in judicial decision making to 'decision fatigue', which could be alleviated by (in this instance) taking a break and ingesting some food.[131]

[125] RJ Gilson and RH Mnookin, 'Foreword: Business Lawyers and Value Creation for Clients' (1995) 74(1) *Oregon Law Review* 1, 12–13.

[126] J Jung et al, 'Simple Rules for Complex Decisions', Stanford University Working Paper, 2017, https://arxiv.org/pdf/1702.04690.pdf; T McElroy and DL Dickinson, 'Thoughtful Days and Valenced Nights: How Much Will You Think About the Problem?' (2010) 5 *Judgment & Decision Making* 516, 519 (deliberative processing can overcome framing effects).

[127] AW Flores, K Bechtel and CT Lowenkamp, 'False Positives, False Negatives, and False Analyses: A Rejoinder to "Machine Bias"' (2016) 80(2) *Federal Probation* 38; J Zerilli, A Knott, J Maclaurin and C Gavaghan, 'Transparency in Algorithmic and Human Decision-Making: Is There a Double Standard?' (2019) 32(4) *Philosophy & Technology* 661.

[128] C Guthrie, JJ Rachlinski and AJ Wistrich, 'Blinking on the Bench: How Judges Decide Cases' (2007) 93 *Cornell Law Review* 1, 13–19, noting that judges are just as susceptible as other humans to relying on intuition rather than deliberative judgement.

[129] S Danziger, J Levav and L Avanim-Pesso, 'Extraneous Factors in Judicial Decisions' (2010) 108(17) *Proceedings of the National Academy of Sciences* 6889.

[130] ibid 6892.

[131] Responding to K Weinshall-Margel and J Shapard, 'Overlooked Factors in the Analysis of Parole Decisions' (2011) 108(42) *Proceedings of the National Academy of Sciences of the United States of*

In another, recent, study, Ozkan Eren and Naci Mocan looked at the impact of an unexpected loss suffered by the Louisiana State University (LSU) football team on judges' decision making in the US state of Louisiana.[132] These researchers found that in the week following an upset loss, judges handed down disproportionately longer sentences. This effect was most pronounced in the case of judges who had received their Bachelor's degree from LSU. In addition, Eren and Mocan found that 'an upset loss increases the disposition length by about 43 days for black defendants, which translates into an increase in sentence severity by almost 8 percent'.[133] The impact on white defendants (an additional five days) was statistically insignificant. The authors conclude, therefore, that 'the brunt of judges' emotional reaction is borne mostly by black defendants. This disparity in sentencing following an upset loss implies unequal treatment of black defendants, triggered by an outside event, unrelated to the merits of the case'.[134]

Absent 'the football effect', black defendants did not receive longer sentences in comparison to whites.[135] Eren and Mocan considered that these findings provide support for the hypothesis that emotional upset in one domain of life (one's football team unexpectedly losing) can affect decision making even in an entirely unrelated domain (one's sentencing of juvenile defendants).

The weaknesses which have been demonstrated in judicial reasoning[136] (though not without controversy, as these studies have not gone unchallenged) have also been investigated in relation to lawyers' advice. Some US studies have suggested that litigation lawyers tend to be overly optimistic about their clients' chances of success.[137] In 2008 Randall Kiser, Martin Asher and Blakeley McShane published the results of a study of over 2,000 Californian cases in which settlement negotiations were unsuccessful, resulting in a determination either at a trial or an arbitration.[138] They compared settlement offers which were rejected with the ultimate result, finding that while plaintiffs' rate of error was much higher than that of defendants (concluding that a trial was a better option in 61.2 and 24.3 per cent of cases, respectively), the monetary consequences of defendants' mistakes were considerably higher.[139] These findings lent support to those of

America E833, S Danziger, J Levav and L Avanim-Pesso confirmed the robustness of their findings: 'Reply to Weinshall-Margel and Shapard: Extraneous Factors in Judicial Decisions Persist' (2011) 108(42) *Proceedings of the National Academy of Sciences of the United States of America* E834.

[132] O Eren and N Mocan, 'Emotional Judges and Unlucky Juveniles' (2018) 10(3) *American Economics Journal: Applied Economics* 171 (using data from 1996 to 2012).

[133] ibid 191.

[134] ibid.

[135] ibid 193.

[136] eg, EG Thornburg, '(Un)Conscious Judging' (2019) 76 *Washington & Lee Law Review* 1567.

[137] EF Loftus and WA Wagenaar, 'Lawyers' Predictions of Success' (1988) 28 *Jurimetrics Journal* 437, 450; J Goodman-Delahunty, P Granhag, M Hartwig and EF Loftus, 'Insightful or Wishful: Lawyers' Ability to Predict Case Outcomes' (2010) 16 *Psychology, Public Policy, and Law* 133, 153; see also G Loewenstein, S Issacharoff, C Camerer and L Babcock, 'Self-Serving Assessments of Fairness and Pretrial Bargaining' (1993) *22 Journal of Legal Studies* 135, 145.

[138] Kiser, Asher and McShane (n 121).

[139] ibid 598-90.

three earlier studies from the 1980s and 1990s.[140] Some of the messages from this research (all of it undertaken in the US) were that there was not an even distribution of 'mistakes' among plaintiffs and defendants, as plaintiffs tended to make more: plaintiffs were more risk averse but generally benefited more from litigation.[141] In another study, Andrew Wistrich and Jeffrey Rachlinski suggested that lawyers' reliance on 'intuition' – beset by numerous cognitive 'illusions' or biases – may have the effect of delaying settlements which should have been reached earlier; or even excluding them altogether.[142] These failures may have serious consequences. Kiser, Asher and McShane found that what they termed 'superficial' similarities in cases ('story line, causes, context, and phrasing') led to extremely poor predictive capacity among defendants as to whether punitive damages would be awarded. In other words, defendants seemed to unwittingly analogise between their own case and others that appeared similar but where punitive damages were not an issue – resulting in costly errors.[143]

There is research suggesting that simple statistical formulas tend to be more accurate even than human experts.[144] Daniel Kahneman has explained that this is due to the fact that 'human predictions tend to be "noisy": given the same input, different people (or even the same person at different times) will make vastly different predictions'.[145] Using statistical formulas removes this 'noise' (or irrelevant, extraneous factors).

A key purported benefit of the use of predictive analytics in law is therefore as a guide or corrective to the flaws of human prediction. As Katz has argued, 'While an experienced lawyer might be familiar with hundreds, if not thousands, of prior events, he or she is unlikely to have observed tens of thousands, hundreds of thousands, or millions of prior events'.[146] Fagan has similarly suggested that the use of 'big data' in legal analytics can 'lower the costs of judging, litigating, and administrating law; increase comparative justice and predictability; and support the advocacy of better rules and policies'.[147] The adoption of big data in the Chinese court system might be a case in point.[148]

[140] ibid 553–54, citing S Gross and K Syverud (n 121); JJ Rachlinski, 'Gains, Losses and the Psychology of Litigation' (1996) 70(1) *Southern California Law Review* 113.

[141] Rachlinski (n 140) 160.

[142] AJ Wistrich and JJ Rachlinski, 'How Lawyers' Intuitions Prolong Litigation' (2013) 86(3) *Southern California Law Review* 571.

[143] Kiser, Asher and McShane (n 121) 586, citing M Bassok, 'Analogical Transfer in Problem Solving' in JE Davidson and RJ Sternberg (eds), *The Psychology of Problem Solving* (Cambridge University Press, 2003) 343.

[144] D Kahneman, AM Rosenfield, L Gandhi and T Blaser, 'Reducing Noise in Decision Making' (2016) 94(12) *Harvard Business Review* 18, 18.

[145] JN Matias 'Bias and Noise: Daniel Kahneman on Errors in Decision-Making', *Medium*, 18 October 2017, www.medium.com/@natematias/bias-and-noise-daniel-kahneman-onerrors-indecision-making-6bc844ff5194.

[146] DM Katz, 'Quantitative Legal Prediction – Or – How I Learned to Stop Worrying and Start Preparing for the Data-Driven Future of the Legal Services Industry' (2012) 62(4) *Emory Law Journal* 909, 928.

[147] Fagan (n 4) 2.

[148] Supreme People's Court, 'White Paper on Chinese Courts and Internet Judiciary' (5 December 2019).

Winning Isn't Everything

It is trite to say in law that winning isn't everything – or more pertinently perhaps, that exactly what 'winning' means is contextual and varies from individual to individual. If we accept a view of the lawyer's role as a problem-solving one, generating different options for their clients, then mathematical predictions of 'success' are only one facet of a many-sided inquiry. Clark and Economides wrote:

> Although legal rules play a very important part in legal advice work, decontextualised knowledge of legal rules is rarely sufficient and may even be counterproductive. If knowledge of a legal rule is not accompanied by knowledge of how the rule is applied in practice and how its application relates to the implementation of policies and the exercise of discretions, then the opportunity to challenge any particular application of the rule may be missed.[149]

This context might include many factors, both legal and non-legal. Frequently, law involves 'open-ended' problems which have no fixed or definitive answer, leaving space for creativity in problem solving.[150] Legal advice also requires consideration of whether legal rights should even be exercised, or fully exercised. Forgoing legal remedies may at times result in a better and more satisfactory outcome.[151]

This illustrates the difference between prediction and judgement. While somewhat ill-defined, legal judgement typically encapsulates a broader role – the holistic one of the lawyer as 'trusted advisor'. Bradley Wendel has referred to 'client counselling requiring emotional intelligence' and 'creative, strategic advising or that which requires assessing not only legal risks but also taking into account multifaceted, ambiguous, possibly conflicting client objectives and interests' as examples of such roles.[152]

Judgement has a moral and ethical quality. As a number of legal academics are now pointing out, while 'prediction' may be replicable by machines, judgement is not, including because of its moral aspects.[153] Mireille Hildebrandt argues that in our pursuit of machine prediction, we are confusing legal judgement with the 'mathematical simulation of legal judgment'.[154] Hildebrandt quotes Jeremy Waldron, who said:

> The institutionalized recognition of a distinctive set of norms may be an important feature [of legal advice]. But at least as important is what we do in law with the norms

[149] A Clark and K Economides, 'Computers, Expert Systems and Legal Processes' in A Narayanan and M Bennun (eds), *Law, Computer Science and Artificial Intelligence* (Ablex, 1991) 3, 15.

[150] K Rosenberry, 'Organizational Barriers to Creativity in Law Schools and the Legal Profession' (2005) 41(2) *California Western Law Review* 423, 425, citing TM Amabile, 'Entrepreneurial Creativity Through Motivational Synergy' (1997) 31 *Journal of Creative Behavior* 18, 18; see also R Florida, *The Rise of the Creative Class* (Basic Books, 2004) 69.

[151] Rosenberry (n 150) 424.

[152] WB Wendel, 'The Promise and Limitations of Artificial Intelligence in the Practice of Law' (2019) 72(1) *Oklahoma Law Review* 21, 25.

[153] ibid.

[154] M Hildebrandt, 'Law as Computation in the Era of Artificial Legal Intelligence: Speaking Law to the Power of Statistics' (2018) 68(1) *University of Toronto Law Journal* 12, 23.

> that we identify. We don't just obey them or apply the sanctions that they ordain; we argue over them adversarially, we use our sense of what is at stake in their application to license a continual process of argument back and forth, and we engage in elaborate interpretive exercises about what it means to apply them faithfully as a system to the cases that come before us.[155]

David Luban has described the lawyer's ability to reason with the client as the exercise of moral suasion, a process of dialogue which a machine cannot replicate.[156] This is not just explanation but something more – a normative, rule-of-law-supportive exercise.

Why is it So?

Linked closely to the role of contextualising is the role of explanation. Clearly, explanation is typically important for the judiciary, who must justify their decision making. It is significant, too, for lawyers. Under a 'client-centred' model of lawyer–client interactions, the lawyer must provide the client with sufficient information so as to enable the client to make an informed choice.[157] This enables the client to instruct the lawyer as to the course of action to be followed. Explaining why a particular result might follow (or why a decision has been reached) is fundamental to legal reasoning. It is also, arguably, important for engendering trust – it has been suggested that people are less likely to place trust in the outputs of a system that is not intelligible to them.[158] This can be contrasted, though, with an opposing tendency of humans to impute to sophisticated technological systems objectivity, accuracy and even infallibility.[159] It is not clear that lawyers' use of automated systems will necessarily erode client trust in the manner suggested may occur for medical professionals – trust could, paradoxically, be heightened, if the domain of the lawyer's expert knowledge is extended.

The importance accorded to explanation in legal reasoning meant that providing forms of explanation has long been a goal of AI and Law research. The idea of CBR was that it would be capable not just of reasoning analogically to identify competing arguments, but also of providing explanation through identifying

[155] J Waldron, 'The Rule of Law and the Importance of Procedure', New York University Public Law and Legal Theory Working Paper, 2010, 19, www.lsr.nellco.org/nyu_plltwp/ 234, quoted by Hildebrandt (n 154) 21–22.

[156] D Luban, 'Optimism, Skepticism, and Access to Justice' (2016) 3 *Texas A&M Law Review* 495, 507.

[157] See D Rosenthal, *Lawyer and Client: Who's in Charge?* (Russel Sage Foundation, 1974); *cf* D Binder and S Price, *Legal Interviewing and Counseling: A Client-Centered Approach* (West Publishing Company, 1977) cited by JW Collins, 'Improving the Relationship between Lawyers and Business Clients' (1983) 20(4) *American Business Law Journal* 525, 527. See also RD Dinerstein, 'Client-Centered Counseling: Reappraisal and Refinement' (1990) 32(3) *Arizona Law Review* 501.

[158] RC Feldman, E Aldana and K Stein, 'Artificial Intelligence in the Health Care Space: How We Can Trust What We Cannot Know' (2019) 30(2) *Stanford Law & Policy Review* 399, 407.

[159] I Bogost, 'The Cathedral of Computation', *The Atlantic*, 15 January 2015, www.theatlantic.com/technology/archive/2015/01/the-cathedral-of-computation/384300/.

superior arguments. Ashley surmises that in law, 'an ability to provide a meaningful explanation of the prediction'[160] is important, but 'most prediction approaches have not been able to explain predictions in terms of legal reasons that are meaningful to legal practitioners'.[161] The struggle to do so, however, is evidenced in Ashley and Brüninghaus's review of attempts to build computer models for legal prediction.[162] In contrast, as Dan Hunter has explained, neural networks may be able to generate quite accurate predictions, but are

> unable to explain the basis for the decision and certainly cannot do so by reference to 'rules'. The neural network's 'rule base' is simply the collection of statistical weights which it has learnt. This statistical information is of little use to the user asking why the network advises as it does.[163]

It is likely that the role of providing explanations, in both legal and lay-intelligible ways will remain with lawyers. Yet there is a growing discussion about whether there are ways of increasing the transparency and explainability of algorithmic systems in many different areas which may come to have application in law. We discuss these developments in Chapter 10.

Future Developments

At the broadest level, two major concerns around legal outcome prediction can be identified. The first is technical, the second can be described summarily as social, but really comprises social, legal and ethical concerns.

In terms of the technical, there are many hurdles and limitations to AI prediction using case law. These range from the very definition or framing of the problem, to the nature of the 'data' used to train a machine learning system, and applying the system to facts which are assumed, rather than established. Although AI seems to promise a more perfect application of a system of precedent by drawing on *all* past cases, statistical analysis of judgments is limited: it is necessarily based on past decisions; and settled cases are excluded, leading to datasets composed primarily of outliers. There are other problems with using legal case law as 'data' – related to the nature of legal reasoning and the difficulties of rendering it into a form useable by machine learning systems.

The CEO of one analytics company has acknowledged the uncertainty surrounding results from machine learning analyses, caused by 'small sample sizes

[160] Ashley (n 2) 120.

[161] KD Ashley and S Brüninghaus, 'Computer Models for Legal Prediction' (2006) 46(3) *Jurimetrics* 309, 310.

[162] ibid 311–26.

[163] D Hunter, 'Out of Their Minds: Legal Theory in Neural Networks' (1999) 7(2–3) *Artificial Intelligence & Law* 129.

after filtering, cognitive biases, the tendency to interpret random trends as valid patterns, and having a lot of data noise'.[164] He commented:

> Overall, the quantitative analysis of legal data is much more challenging and error-prone than is generally acknowledged. Although it is appealing to view data analytics as a simple tool, there is a danger of neglecting the science in what is basically data science. The consequences of this can be harmful to decision making.[165]

There are arguments that data analytics can make lawyers more accurate in the advice that they give to clients. Yet at present, there are only particular areas of law, and jurisdictions, where it can be applied in a meaningful way. In small jurisdictions, such as Australia, there would seem to be insufficient case law available on select issues to generate meaningful predictions. As Remus and Levy suggest,

> the model's predictive ability is restricted to cases that are generally similar to the judge's past cases on which the model was estimated … More generally, machine learning models – estimated statistical models – have difficulty processing contingencies that lie outside the data on which they were trained.[166]

Further, the way that courts and judges are allocated may mean that parties may have no choice about who the decision maker will be or ability to 'judge-shop'.

There is scepticism as to whether many AI projects in law can actually succeed, are as successful as promised, or are sustainable. In a 2019 post on *Medium*, lawyer and entrepreneur Micha Grupp commented: 'There were a number of projects that were successful in theory but failed in terms of scalability and practical adoption. Few products were successfully introduced to the market and close to no project has remained since'.[167] Indeed, Grupp described the research field of AI and Law (or 'legal informatics' in the European terminology) as having 'come to an end'.[168]

Social concerns are also plentiful. Hunter identified two concerns that lawyers might express about the use of statistical modelling in the law: the absence of normative reasons for decision making, and the inability of this method to 'capture any element of the abstract reasoning of judges'.[169] Hildebrandt has made a similar point when she notes that while legal prediction may be able to predict the content of positive law: 'judgment itself is predicated on the contestability of any specific interpretation of legal certainty in the light of the integrity of the legal system, which goes way beyond a quasi-mathematical consistency'.[170] And in

[164] EA Rayo 'AI in Law and Legal Practice – A Comprehensive View of 35 Current Applications', *Emerj*, 21 November 2019, www.emerj.com/ai-sector-overviews/ai-in-law-legal-practice-current-applications/.

[165] ibid.

[166] D Remus and F Levy, 'Can Robots Be Lawyers: Computers, Lawyers, and the Practice of Law' (2017) 30(3) *Georgetown Journal of Legal Ethics* 501, 511.

[167] M Grupp, '25 Facts about AI & Law You Always Wanted to Know (But Were Afraid to Ask)', *Medium*, 7 April 2019, www.medium.com/@Grupp/25-facts-about-ai-law-you-always-wanted-to-know-but-were-afraid-to-ask-a43fd9568d6d.

[168] ibid.

[169] Hunter (n 163) 130.

[170] Hildebrandt (n 154) 23.

like vein, Wendel has explained that 'legal advising is about reason giving, not hitting the target. When lawyers provide legal advice, they are … expressing commitment to a specific pattern of justification, in reliance on particular types of considerations'.[171]

By and large, these concerns speak to the need for lawyers' continued involvement. Yet there are open questions as to how lawyers will adapt to working with predictive analytics and what impacts (if any) this will have on their professionalism. Goodman has suggested that it is 'one thing for artificial intelligence to assist attorneys in making better, or fairer, or more efficient judgments, but it is a different situation where the human is simply ratifying what the computer has chosen to do'.[172] Yet the line between making 'better' decisions and ratifying the computer's outputs (noting that an automated system is not able to exercise a 'choice') would seem to be an indeterminate one. Largely, this boils down to whether the lawyer happens to agree with a system's outputs, or not. The lawyer's role in contextualising and explaining will take on even more importance. Likewise, it is suggested that lawyers have a role to play in keeping AI systems 'accountable': 'Smart lawyers will constantly question both the algorithms and the underlying data in order to avoid courts, or clients, from over-reliance on technically questionable platforms'.[173]

Pasquale and Cashwell have explained that 'these systems purport to predict how judges will decide cases, how individual judges will vote, and how to optimize submissions and arguments before them'.[174] This remark raises the spectre of precisely how lawyers might adjust their legal practice based on predictive analytics, and what wider ramifications this might have. Potentially, widespread use could generate feedback loops:[175]

> In full bloom, predictive analytics would not simply be a camera trained on the judicial system, reporting on it, but it would also be an engine of influence, shaping it. Attorneys may decide whether to pursue cases based on such systems; courts swamped by appeals or applications may be tempted to use [machine learning] models to triage or prioritize cases.[176]

We return to discuss these considerations, and their implications for legal professional ethics and the rule of law, in more detail in Chapter 11.

[171] WB Wendel, 'The Rule of Law and Legal-Process Reasons in Attorney Advising' (2019) 99(1) *Boston University Law Review* 107, 112.

[172] Goodman (n 11) 160.

[173] N Ismail, 'Artificial Intelligence in the Legal Industry: Adoption and Strategy – Part 1', *Information Age*, 6 August 2018, www.information-age.com/artificial-intelligence-in-the-legal-industry-123473948/ (quoting AF Lindsay).

[174] Pasquale and Cashwell (n 12) 64; Premonition™ makes similar claims: www.premonition.ai/law.

[175] J Chan and L Bennett Moses, 'Using Big Data for Legal and Law Enforcement Decisions: Testing the New Tools' (2014) 37(2) *University of New South Wales Law Journal* 643; Siegel (n 17).

[176] Pasquale and Cashwell (n 94) 67.

5

AI, Pre-Trial Information Gathering (Discovery and Disclosure) and Litigation Lawyers

Introduction

This chapter focuses on the use of AI in the procedural steps prior to a civil trial or evidential hearing. Of the numerous steps that form part of the pre-trial process, the use of AI has been most prevalent in relation to information gathering. In common law systems information gathering usually employs the civil procedure called discovery, or disclosure as it is referred to in some jurisdictions. The AI applications discussed may also be utilised for discovery processes in arbitration. Further, even in civil law jurisdictions where discovery may not be permitted, the need for a party to locate documents to support their own case may benefit from the use of AI.

Litigation Lawyers – Gathering Information and Evidence

A crucial role for the lawyer in the resolution of disputes is ascertaining the facts, or determining what happened. The factual compass may be limited and derived mainly from eye-witness accounts, such as in relation to a fall in a supermarket or motor vehicle accident. Alternatively the facts may be complex, highly contested and scattered across large collections of documents. Examples include securities law, competition law and product liability claims.[1] Indeed large amounts of documentary evidence are often a hallmark of complex civil litigation.[2]

[1] M Legg, *Case Management and Complex Civil Litigation* (Federation Press, 2011) 9–11.

[2] ibid 19; R Cranston, 'Complex Litigation: The Commercial Court' (2007) 26 *Civil Justice Quarterly* 190, 192–93; R Sackville, 'Mega-Litigation: Towards a New Approach' (2008) 27(2) *Civil Justice Quarterly* 244, 245–46.

Common Law Jurisdictions

In the common law world the gathering of information, and ultimately evidence for trial, involves searching the client's records, but also engaging in the process of discovery.

Discovery has a long history that dates back to the English Courts of Chancery.[3] Discovery provides a procedure that allows a party to obtain information about a claim or defence from an opponent. Discovery increases the likelihood that a judgment or settlement will be correct and fair by facilitating knowledge of the facts. The ability to inspect an opponent's documents places parties on an equal footing and avoids trial by ambush.[4]

Despite the compelling arguments for discovery it also necessitates cost and delay. In some cases, particularly large or complex disputes, approaches to discovery that leave 'no stone left unturned' in search of an informational advantage or employ discovery as a 'club' to batter the opposition with cost, undermine the advantages explained above.[5] In short, discovery has been problematic when it has been abused. In response courts have tended to curb the scope of discovery and exercise greater oversight of conduct related to the discovery process. Equally court rules have adopted requirements for the court's processes to be used in a manner that minimises cost and delay.[6] Further, reference is often made to the concept of proportionality: that the expense of procedural steps is warranted by what is at stake in the dispute.[7]

Consequently, while discovery was originally very permissive,[8] and in some jurisdictions even encouraged the metaphorical 'fishing expedition' for documents that could make a case,[9] this is no longer the approach. Court rules specify the scope of discovery which the court through its orders, and then the lawyers in complying with those orders, must operationalise. Generally speaking this is finding and producing documents that are responsive to the issues raised by the specific case, that is, identifying 'relevant' documents.

[3] P Matthews and H Malek, *Disclosure* (5th edn, Sweet & Maxwell, 2017) 8.

[4] D Bailey and E Evans (eds), *Discovery & Interrogatories in Australia* (LexisNexis Online) [1010]; A Zuckerman, *Zuckerman on Civil Procedure* (3rd edn, Sweet & Maxwell, 2013) [15.2].

[5] See, eg, R Kagan, *Adversarial Legalism* (Harvard University Press, 2001) 108; Zuckerman (n 4) [15.4], [15.6].

[6] M Legg and A Higgins, 'Responding to Cost and Delay Through Overriding Objectives – Successful Innovation?' in C Picker and G Seidman (eds), *The Dynamism of Civil Procedure – Global Trends and Developments* (Springer, 2015) ch 8.

[7] L Hunt, 'Trending: Proportionality in Electronic Discovery in Common Law Countries and the United States' Federal and State Courts' (2014) 43 *University of Baltimore Law Review* 279.

[8] *Compagnie Financiere v Peruvian Guano Co* (1882) 52 LJQB 181, 11 QBD 55 at 62; *Mulley v Manifold* (1959) 103 CLR 341: documents were discoverable if they might lead to a train of inquiry that might affect either party's case.

[9] *Hickman v Taylor* 329 US 495, 507–08 (1947) where the US Supreme Court held that 'No longer can the time-honored cry of "fishing expedition" serve to preclude a party from inquiring into the facts underlying his opponent's case'.

For example in the Federal Court of Australia the requirements for standard discovery under the Federal Court Rules 2011 (FCR) are that the party give discovery of documents[10]

(a) that are directly relevant to the issues raised by the pleadings or in the affidavits; and
(b) of which, after a reasonable search, the party is aware; and
(c) that are, or have been in the party's control.

For documents to be directly relevant the rules require that they must meet at least one of the following criteria:[11]

(a) the documents are those on which the party intends to rely;
(b) the documents adversely affect the party's own case;
(c) the documents support another party's case;
(d) the documents adversely affect another party's case.

The meaning of direct relevance has been interpreted as requiring that the document be directly on point, that it tends to prove or disprove the allegation in issue.[12] However, the FCR also define direct relevance by requiring that at least one of the above criteria be met. The criterion that 'the documents support another party's case' has also been considered and interpreted as meaning strengthening of a position, contributing to success, preventing failure or corroborating or substantiating a claim.[13]

In England and Wales there is also standard disclosure, which is expressed in similar terms.[14] However, in both jurisdictions an approach other than standard discovery is permissible.[15] This is illustrated by the England and Wales Civil Procedure Rules (CPR), which are said to adopt a 'menu' approach[16] in CPR 31.5(7), which provides:

> At the first or any subsequent case management conference, the court will decide, having regard to the overriding objective and the need to limit disclosure to that which is necessary to deal with the case justly, which of the following orders to make in relation to disclosure—
>
> (a) an order dispensing with disclosure;
> (b) an order that a party disclose the documents on which it relies, and at the same time request any specific disclosure it requires from any other party;
> (c) an order that directs, where practicable, the disclosure to be given by each party on an issue by issue basis;

[10] FCR r 20.14(1).
[11] FCR r 20.14(2).
[12] *Construction, Forestry, Mining and Energy Union v BHP Coal Pty Ltd (No 2)* [2011] FCA 1396, [33]–[37]; *Adelaide Brighton Cement Limited, in the matter of Concrete Supply Pty Ltd v Concrete Supply Pty Ltd (Subject to Deed of Company Arrangement) (No 3)* [2018] FCA 1058, [8].
[13] *Dennis v Chambers Investment Planners Pty Ltd* [2012] FCA 63, [34].
[14] CPR 31.6.
[15] See FCR 20.15, which allows for 'non-standard and more extensive discovery'.
[16] R Jackson, *Civil Litigation Costs Review – Final Report* (December 2009) 364–74.

(d) an order that each party disclose any documents which it is reasonable to suppose may contain information which enables that party to advance its own case or to damage that of any other party, or which leads to an enquiry which has either of those consequences;
(e) an order that a party give standard disclosure;
(f) any other order in relation to disclosure that the court considers appropriate.

In contrast the US Federal Rules of Civil Procedure (FRCP) deal with the scope of discovery in more general terms:

> Unless otherwise limited by court order, the scope of discovery is as follows: Parties may obtain discovery regarding any nonprivileged matter that is relevant to any party's claim or defense and proportional to the needs of the case, considering the importance of the issues at stake in the action, the amount in controversy, the parties' relative access to relevant information, the parties' resources, the importance of the discovery in resolving the issues, and whether the burden or expense of the proposed discovery outweighs its likely benefit. Information within this scope of discovery need not be admissible in evidence to be discoverable.[17]

The US rule in adopting the 'any party's claim or defense' wording introduced, on its face, a narrowing of discovery compared to the earlier wording of 'relevant to the subject matter involved in the pending action'. However, in practice a liberal approach to discovery prevails, subject to the increased emphasis on proportionality.[18] However, as with Australia and England the court may limit discovery.[19]

At a very general level, within the above framework the litigation lawyer is tasked with determining what information to seek from an opponent and what information to provide in response to an opponent's request. This role is explained in greater detail below in relation to electronic discovery by reference to the Electronic Discovery Reference Model (EDRM).

Civil Law Jurisdictions

In civil law countries the common law-style discovery described above is virtually unknown.[20] However, this does not mean that there is no provision of documents or a complete inability to seek the court's assistance in obtaining evidence.[21]

[17] FRCP r 26(b)(1).
[18] R Marcus, 8 *Federal Practice and Procedure* (3rd edn, Wright & Miller, 2018) §§ 2007–08.
[19] FRCP r 26(b)(2)(C); Marcus (n 18) § 2008.1.
[20] N Trocker and V Varano, 'Concluding Remarks' in N Trocker and V Varano (eds), *The Reforms of Civil Procedure in Comparative Perspective* (Giappichelli, 2005) 255–58; O Chase, H Hershkoff, L Silberman, Y Taniguchi, V Varano and A Zuckerman, *Civil Litigation in Comparative Context* (West Group, 2007) 222, 228.
[21] Matthews and Malek (n 3) 17.

In France the party alleging the facts has the burden of proving them, which is normally done by introducing written documents into evidence. However, prior to a hearing on the merits the parties must exchange the documents upon which they intend to rely. Parties may also ask the court to order the production of a document but the exercise of this discretion is limited.[22]

In Germany the taking of evidence usually occurs before the court. However, evidence is only to be taken 'if (i) a certain fact is disputed among the parties, (ii) such fact is of importance for the legal situation regarding the matter at dispute, and (iii) the party bearing the burden of proof requests the taking of the evidence'. A party may request that evidence be obtained but it has to identify the fact that shall be proven by the evidence and provide the evidence to the court. If the requesting party does not have the evidence then it may petition for a court order for another person (whether a party or not) to provide the evidence.[23]

Japanese attorneys prepare for trial by collecting as much evidence supporting their allegations as possible. Under the Japanese *Code of Civil Procedure* there are essentially four formal means commonly employed by Japanese attorneys for collecting evidence. They are: (1) a motion for the preservation of evidence; (2) an application for an evidentiary request through a lawyer association; (3) court ordered production of documents; and (4) an inquiry by a party.[24] However, requests for documents require that the document be described with specificity.[25]

While the scope of information or evidence gathering is much narrower in civil law jurisdictions, a party will still need to locate documents to support its own case, and possibly to respond to requests for documents.

Arbitration

Arbitrations 'take advantage of technology developed for litigation purposes'.[26] In an arbitration the parties or the arbitral tribunal may address whether documents need to be searched for and disclosed as part of the procedure in the arbitration.[27] The institutional rules for arbitration may specifically address the production of documents.[28]

[22] V Mercier and DD McKenney, 'Obtaining Evidence in France for Use in United States Litigation' (1994) 2 *Tulane Journal of International and Comparative Law* 91, 94; O de Courcel, 'France' in T Blair (ed), *The e-Discovery and Information Governance Law Review* (Law Business Research Ltd, 2019) 62.

[23] O Förster and O Almughrabi, 'Managing the Conflict Between U.S. E-Discovery and the German Data Protection Act' (2013) 36 *Hastings International and Comparative Law Review* 111, 116.

[24] CP Wagnild, 'Civil Law Discovery in Japan: A Comparison of Japanese and U.S. Methods of Evidence Collection in Civil Litigation' (2002) 3 *Asian-Pacific Law and Policy Journal* 1, 8.

[25] C Yakura, LC Stoupe and Y Teraguchi, *Litigation and Enforcement in Japan: Overview* (Thomson Reuters, 2019).

[26] M Moses, *International Commercial Arbitration* (2nd edn, Cambridge University Press, 2012) 170.

[27] S Blake, J Browne and S Sime, *The Jackson ADR Handbook* (2nd edn, Oxford University Press, 2016) [25.14].

[28] R Rana and M Sanson, *International Commercial Arbitration* (Thomson Reuters, 2011) 180–81; P Hibbert, *The Electronic Evidence and E-Disclosure Handbook* (Sweet & Maxwell, 2016) ch 16.

The International Bar Association Rules on the Taking Evidence in International Commercial Arbitrations (2010) (IBA Rules) are intended to provide an efficient, economical and fair process for the taking of evidence in international arbitrations, particularly those between parties from different legal traditions.[29] In relation to the gathering of information the IBA Rules employ a two-stage process of a party producing the documents it intends to rely upon and then giving the opposing parties the opportunity of submitting a request to produce. The request to produce must include a statement as to how the documents requested are relevant to the case and material to its outcome.[30]

More generally, the practice in international commercial arbitration is to limit discovery to those documents both relevant to the issues in dispute and necessary for the proper resolution of those issues.[31] Consequently, the disclosure of documents is likely to be part of international arbitrations, especially where the representation is provided by lawyers from both common law and civil law backgrounds.[32]

Regulatory Investigations

The need to review and produce large amounts of documentary information also arises in regulatory investigations and in subsequent regulatory litigation. This has been most clearly seen in the US, where there is a need to identify and review documents for production during large-scale antitrust and securities law investigations.[33] However, even in civil law countries such as France, regulators are empowered to require the disclosure of large amounts of data stored in various mediums.[34]

Application of AI to Pre-trial Processes

Perhaps the best-known and most long-standing use of AI in law is the application of machine learning called Technology Assisted Review (TAR) to documents

[29] IBA Rules Preamble.

[30] IBA Rules art 3.

[31] P Ashford, 'Documentary Discovery and International Commercial Arbitration' (2006) 17 *American Review of International Arbitration* 89, 93.

[32] R Trittmann and B Kasolowsky, 'Taking Evidence in Arbitration Proceedings Between Common Law and Civil Law Traditions – The Development of a European Hybrid Standard for Arbitration Proceedings' (2008) 31(1) *UNSW Law Journal* 330, 337.

[33] The Sedona Conference, 'The Sedona Conference TAR Case Law Primer' (2017) 18 *Sedona Conference Journal* 1, 42–44.

[34] de Courcel (n 22) 67.

for discovery.[35] Historically, documents to be produced or inspected as part of discovery were reviewed initially through a manual process undertaken by a junior lawyer or paralegal. Documents whose relevance was unclear or which involved issues of privilege or confidentiality would be escalated to a more senior lawyer for review.[36]

Advances in computing and communications technology resulted in the expansion in the information generated as part of the factual matrix that a dispute emanated from, which in turn meant an increase in the scope of potentially discoverable documents. Photocopiers started this trend but the development of computer programs such as Microsoft Word for creating documents and the prolific use of email to create and exchange documents has meant an enormous increase in electronically stored information (ESI).[37] To this may be added the rise of social media such as Facebook, Twitter, Instagram, LinkedIn and YouTube, which provide additional avenues for the creation of ESI. The advent of the 'Internet of Things' has created even more data that may be relevant to civil disputes.[38] Future technologies are likely to add to the data available for disputes.

Due to limitations in lawyer review capacity and client budgets the manual discovery process was not feasible for ESI.[39] Just as technology had created the problem of voluminous discovery, technology was resorted to as a solution. This was first addressed through keyword searches in a form of set-based searching using simple words or word combinations, with or without Boolean operators such as 'and', 'or' and 'not'. Keyword searches were a step forward from manual review but were frequently inaccurate and would miss synonyms, abbreviations and jargon. The substantial improvement came with the use of machine learning.

Supervised Machine Learning

Technology Assisted Review uses machine learning's capacity to identify patterns in textual data. The program is provided with a set of documents referred to as a 'training set' or 'seed set'. The training set may be randomly compiled from

[35] J McGinnis and R Pearce, 'The Great Disruption: How Machine Intelligence Will Transfer the Role of Lawyers in the Delivery of Legal Services' (2014) 82 *Fordham Law Review* 3041, 3047. Other terms include 'computer-aided review', 'content-based advanced analytics' and 'predictive coding': S Brown, 'Peeking Inside the Black Box: A Preliminary Survey of Technology Assisted Review (TAR) and Predictive Coding Algorithms for eDiscovery' (2016) 21 *Suffolk Journal of Trial & Appellate Advocacy* 221, 255.

[36] Legg (n 1) 84.

[37] *Goodale v The Ministry of Justice* [2009] EWHC B41 (QB), [1].

[38] M Legg, 'New Sources of Discovery and Evidence: Electronically Stored Information, Social Media and the Internet of Things' in M Legg (ed), *Resolving Civil Disputes* (Lexis Nexis, 2016) 355; D Caruso, M Legg and J Phoustanis, 'The Automation Paradox in Litigation: The Inadequacy of Procedure and Evidence Law to Manage Electronic Evidence Generated by the Internet of Things in Civil Disputes (2019) 19 *Macquarie Law Journal* 157.

[39] Australian Law Reform Commission, *Managing Discovery – Discovery of Documents in Federal Courts – Report 115* (2011) 13–14.

all the potentially discoverable documents, or documents may be selected for particular characteristics.[40] A reviewing lawyer then codes the documents in the training set, labelling them (for example) as 'relevant, not relevant, privileged, or not privileged'.[41] Using this information, the program applies this to other documents. Just as a machine learning program can eventually successfully label a not-previously seen picture of a cat as a cat, once trained it can also identify which documents in the discovery are relevant, and which are not.[42] Using the training set the software creates a model or classifier which 'can then predict the classifications of other documents'.[43]

This TAR process may be labelled as simple passive learning as the documents in the training set are chosen by a human and the software learns from those choices. This may be compared with simple active learning, where the software chooses some or most of the documents for training. The human still needs to code the documents but the software can identify the documents that will be most useful to it in developing its model or classifier. The software identifies documents for coding based on uncertainty sampling, ie the documents it is most uncertain about in relation to relevance. However both approaches aim to develop a model/classifier that meets agreed levels of recall and precision (discussed below) by comparison with the control set. The classifier is then applied to the entire collection of documents either to identify those that need to be manually reviewed for relevance or to be treated as relevant for discovery purposes.[44]

The TAR process described above, where there is a training set followed by a number of rounds of sampling and correction, may be contrasted with an alternative approach called continuous active learning:

> the human review and software training process are melded together; review and training occur simultaneously. From the outset, the software continuously analyzes the entire document collection and ranks the population based on relevancy. Human coding decisions are submitted to the software, the software re-ranks the documents, and then presents back to the human additional documents for review that it predicts as most likely relevant.[45]

This approach does not require a training set, rather coding begins and the software learns continuously from how the reviewed documents are coded. However, continuous active learning can also begin with a training set to try and lessen the

[40] Which method is preferable has given rise to debate in the US: see, eg, M Paulbeck, 'The Ethics of Predictive Coding: Transparency and Judgment-Formed Seed Sets' (2017) 30(4) *Georgetown Journal of Legal Ethics* 971.

[41] ibid.

[42] ibid.

[43] Brown (n 35) 237.

[44] G Cormack and M Grossman, 'Evaluation of Machine-Learning Protocols for Technology-Assisted Review in Electronic Discovery' in *Proceedings of the 37th International ACM SIGIR Conference on Research & Development in Information Retrieval* (2014) 153; *Technology Assisted Review Guidelines* (Bolch Judicial Institute, Duke Law, 2019) 23.

[45] *Technology Assisted Review Guidelines* (n 44) 5.

time taken to find the most relevant documents.[46] Continuous active learning also employs recall and precision but in each round of coding the software suggests the next most likely relevant documents for review. The rounds of coding continue until precision reduces dramatically or the predictions of relevance cease to change and become static or stable.[47]

All of the forms of TAR explained above, simple passive learning, simple active learning and continuous active learning, are examples of supervised machine learning as humans – preferably a lawyer familiar with the case – code documents and review (correcting where necessary) the software's categorisations. Human review is needed to 'teach' the software whether it has classified different documents correctly, and the method for teaching the software about which documents are relevant is referred to as a TAR 'protocol'.

Validation

Human review is also needed to create a control set or to perform random sampling as part of the validation requirements for TAR. Lawyers will manually code the control set or sample and record features such as recall (discussed below) so that the TAR results have a comparator to determine TAR's effectiveness or performance.

The size of the random sample is determined by statistical parameters such as richness, confidence level and confidence interval. The Bolch Judicial Institute's TAR guidelines define each as follows:

> CONFIDENCE INTERVAL (MARGIN OF ERROR) AND CONFIDENCE LEVEL. The confidence interval and confidence level characterize the certainty of the point estimate. For example, the recall point estimate of 80% can be combined with a margin of error of 5%, allowing for a confidence interval of 75% (5% below 80%) and 85% (5% above 80%). Moreover, a confidence interval is meaningful only if accompanied by a confidence level, which is a measure of how likely the sample is to represent the true set, within the confidence interval. Continuing the example used here, a confidence level of 95% means that 95 times out of 100, the result of the sample will include the actual recall within its confidence interval. Put another way, there is a 95% chance that the actual recall is between 75% and 85%.
>
> RICHNESS. Richness is the estimated proportion of documents in a data set that are relevant. For example, if a set of one million documents contains 100,000 relevant documents, it has 10% richness. Richness is also known as prevalence.[48]

The greater the richness of a data set the lower the number of randomly selected documents needed to establish a statistically valid sample.[49]

[46] Cormack and Grossman (n 44) 154.
[47] *Technology Assisted Review Guidelines* (n 44) 21–22.
[48] ibid 41, 43.
[49] Hibbert (n 28) 180.

Algorithms

A number of algorithms are able to be used in supervised machine learning forms of TAR, such as Support Vector Machines, Logistic Regression and Bayesian Classifiers, to infer relevance or non-relevance of documents based on the coding of documents by a human.

The above algorithms may be defined as follows:

- Logistic Regression: attempts to draw a 'best-fit line' separating distinct classes of points, or here documents. The algorithm defines a linear equation to describe the 'best-fit line.' Once the algorithm establishes the 'best-fit line', then the same equation can be used to predict the classification of new documents. To be more precise, logistic regression uses a sigmoid, step-function to classify items. The algorithm assigns documents with sigmoid computer values near 1.0 (the 'top') to one class and values near 0.0 (the 'bottom') to another class. The algorithm also commonly optimises the best-fit line by making slight changes to the model through multiple iterations until the classification errors are minimised.
- Support Vector Machine (SVM): an SVM also seeks to find a line that separates responsive from non-responsive documents so that, ideally, all of the responsive documents are on one side of the line and all of the non-responsive ones are on the other side. However, it also employ a 'soft margin hyperplane', which is a buffer either side of the line which aids in better fitting the line and reducing errors. An SVM's line and hyperplane may be non-linear. This is explained further below in the section providing examples.
- Naïve Bayesian Classifier: a system that examines the probability that each word in a new document came from the word distribution derived from a trained responsive document or trained non-responsive documents. The system is naïve in the sense that it assumes that all words are independent of one another. For example, a Bayesian algorithm might combine the evidence gleaned from the fact that a document contains the words 'credit', 'default' and 'swap' to indicate that there is a 99 per cent probability that the document concerns financial derivatives, but only a 40 per cent probability if the words 'credit' and 'default', but not 'swap' are present.[50]

Unsupervised machine learning methods may also be employed in relation to information gathering and discovery. Clustering is an example of such a method, in which documents are segregated into categories or groups so that the documents in any group are more similar to one another than to those in other groups. Clustering algorithms measure the similarity of documents by using a geometric distance calculation and then cluster documents that are of geometrically similar distance. The algorithm selects representative documents as the anchors for each

[50] H Roitblat, *Introduction to Predictive Coding* (OrcaTec, 2013); M Grossman and G Cormack, 'The Grossman-Cormack Glossary of Technology-Assisted Review' (2014) 7(1) *Federal Courts Law Review* 85; Brown (n 35) 260–77.

cluster and then measures the distance of all other documents to the representative documents so as to group documents with a similar distance measure in similar clusters. Clustering involves no human intervention. However, the resulting categories may or may not reflect distinctions that are valuable for the purpose of search and review, ie clustering may not produce relevant documents. Examples of clustering algorithms are k-Means and k-Nearest Neighbours.[51]

Precision and Recall

The field of information retrieval has defined two core metrics for assessing the effectiveness of a search or document categorisation tool. Precision is the fraction of retrieved documents that are relevant. Recall is the fraction of relevant documents that are retrieved.[52] These definitions can be expanded as follows:

$$\text{Precision} = \frac{\text{Total number of documents retrieved that are relevant}}{\text{Total number of documents that are retrieved}}$$

$$\text{Recall} = \frac{\text{Total number of documents retrieved that are relevant}}{\text{Total number of relevant documents in the database}}$$

To provide an example, suppose TAR software retrieves 300 pages from a collection of documents and that only 200 of those pages were relevant while failing to return 400 additional relevant pages, its precision is 200/300 = 2/3 while its recall is 200/600 = 1/3.

To illustrate precision and recall in a different setting, assume a computer program trained to recognise dogs in photographs identifies eight dogs in a picture containing 12 dogs and some cats. Of the eight identified as dogs, five actually are dogs (true positives), while the rest are cats (false positives). The program's precision is 5/8 while its recall is 5/12.

Precision and recall can also be depicted diagrammatically through Figure 5.1.

Precision is 'how useful the search results are', and recall is 'how complete the results are'. Precision is important because it means that only relevant documents are subject to manual review at the end of the TAR process and therefore costs are minimised. Recall is also important because it demonstrates compliance with the orders for discovery to find and produce the relevant documents.[53]

Precision and recall usually involve a trade-off, so that increasing one can lower the other. If only relevant documents are being retrieved so that precision is high, it is likely that other relevant documents are being missed. Similarly, every relevant document can be found (high recall) by including all documents (low precision).

[51] Ernst and Young, *Insiders' Guide to Technology-Assisted Review* (Wiley, 2015) 9; Brown (n 35) 277–81.

[52] Hibbert (n 28) 180. The two measures are sometimes used together in the F1 Score (or f-measure), the harmonic mean – a weighted average of precision and recall, to provide a single measurement for a system.

[53] B Dimm, 'Misleading Metrics and Irrelevant Research (Accuracy and F1)', Clustify Blog (12 December 2018) https://blog.cluster-text.com/2018/12/12/misleading-metrics-and-irrelevant-research-accuracy-and-f1/.

The aim of TAR is to maximise both measures through effective training of the software program.

As explained above, validation or testing of recall involves the use of a control set or random samples. In relation to simple passive learning and simple active learning the control set created at the outset allows for recall to be measured because it is a random sample and is reflective of the larger population of documents. For continuous active learning random samples are also employed but the sample does not need to occur at the beginning of the process.

Figure 5.1 Recall and precision

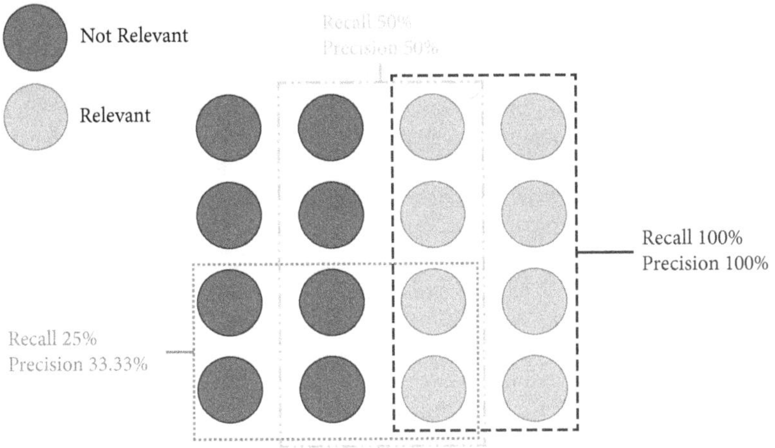

Source: T Davey.

Relevance

The aim or obligation in relation to discovery is to find and produce relevant documents. Some TAR systems produce a simple yes/no as to relevance, while others give a relevance score (say, on a 0 to 100 basis) that lawyers can use to prioritise review. Where a score is employed a 'cut-off' point is identified in the TAR set, with documents ranked at or above the cut-off point identified as the predicted relevant set, and documents below the cut-off point as the non-relevant set.

Decisions about relevance involve not only the use of metrics such as precision and recall, but also the requirements in court rules about cost, delay and proportionality. The metrics may be able to be improved but in some cases only though increasing the number of documents to be reviewed. More documents means greater cost and delay.

TAR can go beyond relevance to find particular categories of documents. The software is trained using exemplars of concepts, words or phrases so as to find documents responsive to the category.[54]

[54] See Brown (n 35) 262.

Examples

The first reported decision of a court accepting the use of TAR was from the United States District Court for the Southern District of New York: *Da Silva Moore v Publicis Groupe* 287 FRD 182 (SDNY 2012). The case dealt with allegations of gender discrimination, pregnancy discrimination and related violations. The Court's judgment annexed the parties' proposed protocol for the use of TAR. The protocol explained that the Plaintiffs would use the Axcelerate software by Recommind. The protocol then sets out the process for the use of Axcelerate. The overview of how TAR operated was as follows:

> The process begins with [the lawyers for the defendant] developing an understanding of the entire e-mail collection while identifying a small number of documents, the initial seed set, that is representative of the categories to be reviewed and coded (relevance, privilege, issue-relation). It is the step when the first seed sets are generated which is done by use of search and analytical tools, including keyword, Boolean and concept search, concept grouping, and, as needed, up to 40 other automatically populated filters available within the Axcelerate system. This assists in the attorneys' identification of probative documents for each category to be reviewed and coded.
>
> Plaintiffs' counsel will be provided with preliminary results of [the defendant's] hit counts using keyword searches to create a high priority relevant seed set, and will be invited to contribute their own proposed keywords. Thereafter, Plaintiffs' counsel will be provided with the non-privileged keyword hits – both from [the defendant's] keyword list and Plaintiffs' keyword list – which were reviewed and coded by the [defendant]. Plaintiffs' counsel will review the documents produced and promptly provide defense counsel with their own evaluation of the initial coding applied to the documents, including identification of any documents it believes were incorrectly coded. To the extent the parties disagree regarding the coding of a particular document, they will meet and confer in an effort to resolve the dispute prior to contacting the Court for resolution. The irrelevant documents so produced shall be promptly returned after review and analysis by Plaintiffs' counsel and/or resolution of any disputes by the Court.
>
> The seed sets are then used to begin the Predictive Coding process. Each seed set of documents is applied to its relevant category and starts the software 'training' process. The software uses each seed set to identify and prioritize all substantively similar documents over the complete corpus of the e-mail collection. The attorneys then review and code a judgmental sample of at least 500 of the 'computer suggested' documents to ensure their proper categorization and to further calibrate the system by recoding documents into their proper categories. Axcelerate learns from the new corrected coding and the Predictive Coding process is repeated.
>
> [The defendant attorneys] will have access to the entire e-mail collection to be searched and will lead the computer training, but they will obtain input from Plaintiffs' counsel during the iterative seed selection and quality control processes and will share the information used to craft the search protocol as further described herein. All non-privileged documents reviewed by [the defendant] during each round of the iterative process (i.e., both documents coded as relevant and irrelevant) will be produced to Plaintiffs' counsel during the iterative seed set selection process. Plaintiffs' counsel will review the documents produced and promptly provide defense counsel with its own evaluation of

> the initial coding applied to the documents, including identification of any documents it believes were incorrectly coded. To the extent the Parties disagree regarding the coding of a particular document, they will meet and confer in an effort to resolve the dispute prior to contacting the Court for resolution. Again, the irrelevant documents so produced shall be promptly returned after review and analysis by Plaintiffs' counsel and/or resolution of any disputes by the Court.
>
> At the conclusion of the iterative review process, all document predicted by Axcelerate to be relevant will be manually reviewed for production. However, depending on the number of documents returned, the relevancy rating of those documents, and the costs incurred during the development of the seed set and iterative reviews, [the defendant] reserves the right to seek appropriate relief from the Court prior to commencing the final manual review.
>
> The accuracy of the search processes, both the systems' functions and the attorney judgments to train the computer, will be tested and quality controlled by both judgmental and statistical sampling. In statistical sampling, a small set of documents is randomly selected from the total corpus of the documents to be tested. The small set is then reviewed and an error rate calculated therefrom. The error rates can then be reliably projected on the total corpus, having a margin of error directly related to the sample size.[55]

The protocol deals with each of the above steps in greater detail.

In 2016, Recommind was acquired by OpenText. Axcelerate is described as utilising continuous machine learning.[56]

In the *Actos (Pioglitazone) Products Liability* litigation, claims were made that the use of Actos, a prescription medication approved for use in the treatment of type 2 diabetes, created an increased risk of developing bladder cancer.[57] For the discovery process the defendant Takeda utilised Equivio's Relevance software provided by Epiq Systems to search and review ESI.[58]

The Court's judgment annexed the parties' proposed protocol for the use of TAR. The TAR software was to be trained by three individuals nominated by the defendants and three individuals nominated by the plaintiff. The nominated individuals reviewed 500 documents to create a control set for evaluating training progress and results.[59] The Equivio Relevance software then generates a random sample of 40 documents which are coded for relevance by the nominated persons. The software assesses the coded documents with a view to determining if 'Stability' has been achieved. If Stability has not been achieved the software selects further samples of 40 documents using 'Active Learning' for coding, ie:

> each training sample is selected based on what has been learned from previous samples. The object is to maximize the sample's contribution to the training process. Therefore, the system chooses samples that provide comprehensive coverage of the population

[55] *Da Silva Moore v Publicis Groupe* 287 FRD 182, 199–200 (SDNY 2012).

[56] OpenText Axcelerate Product Overview (2018) www.opentext.com.au/file_source/OpenText/en_US/PDF/opentext-po-axcelerate-en.pdf.

[57] *In re: Actos Products Liability Litigation*, 840 F Supp 2d 1356 (US Jud Pan Mult Lit 2011).

[58] *In re Actos (Pioglitazone) Product Liability Litigation*, 2012 WL 7861249, *4 (WD La July 27, 2012) (*In re Actos Products Liability Litigation* (2012)).

[59] ibid.

> (reducing under-inclusiveness), while fine-tuning the concept of relevance that the Classifier is developing (reducing over-inclusiveness). The system reaches Stability when the marginal contribution of additional samples to the enhancement of the Classifier approaches zero.[60]
>
> The Classifier is not defined in the protocol but it is the model that the algorithm or program is creating based on the trained received to code the documents as relevant or not.
>
> Once Stability is reached the software will calculate relevance scores for each document. The parties then meet and confer regarding which relevance score will provide a cut-off that will yield a proportionate set of documents. All of the documents above the agreed upon relevance score are reviewed by the defendant with the resulting relevant and non-privileged documents being produced.[61]

Equivio describes the operation of the Relevance software as follows:

> Relevance leverages predictive coding technology to organize a collection of documents by relevance. The application is 'trained' by one or more attorneys to find relevant and privileged documents. Following this initial training, Relevance uses statistical and self-learning techniques to calculate graduated relevance scores for each document in the data collection.

In 2015 Microsoft acquired Equivio.[62]

The Irish High Court in *Irish Bank Resolution Corporation Limited v Quinn* [2015] IEHC 175, a case dealing with the recovery of assets as part of a liquidation, considered whether TAR was permissible under the court rules and found that it was. Justice Fullam explained the process, which began with the creation of training and control sets. Once the system accurately predicted relevance over a series of consecutive samples the model was applied to the rest of the collection. The model graded the documents into bands of potential relevance. These bands were at 10 percentage point intervals. The model identified a cut-off point above which it predicted the bands would contain truly relevant documents. These were then manually reviewed and any false positives eliminated. The documents below the cut-off threshold were then randomly sampled to ascertain the presence of relevant documents (false negatives). The effectiveness of the model was assessed based on recall and precision.

An expert was retained to opine on the system reaching stabilisation, on the appropriate cut-off point and 'to produce an expert certificate confirming that the TAR was statistically valid and providing a detailed basis for drawing that conclusion'.[63]

[60] ibid.

[61] ibid.

[62] Microsoft, 'Microsoft Acquires Equivio', Microsoft Blog (20 January 2015) blogs.microsoft.com/blog/2015/01/20/microsoft-acquires-equivio-provider-machine-learning-powered-compliance-solutions/.

[63] *Irish Bank Resolution Corporation Limited v Quinn* [2015] IEHC 175, [43], [46].

The TAR employed was the Clearwell system provided by Symantec.[64] This system 'uses active learning technology to automatically determine each subsequent training set after the initial training set, selecting documents for training which result in the highest improvement in prediction accuracy'.[65]

In *Rio Tinto PLC v Vale SA*,[66] the plaintiff alleged fraudulent conspiracy and corruption in the granting of iron ore concessions in Guinea against its competitors.[67] In *Rio Tinto PLC v Vale SA*, Rio Tinto and its vendor, Precision Discovery, used Relativity Assisted Review ('RAR'). While the protocol used in this case is attached to the Court's reasons, a more detailed explanation of RAR is available in a Relativity white paper.[68] The white paper explains that RAR employs a binary supervised machine learning classifier called support vector machine. As reviewers code documents, SVM places the documents into one of two groups by determining if it belongs to a given class (eg X or not X). In the case of discovery the classes are relevant and not relevant.

Active learning means that a recommendation algorithm uses the SVM classification to retrieve specific data to be reviewed by the lawyers to further train and improve SVM. The reviewed data is sent back to the classifier and the recommendation algorithm suggests new data to be reviewed. This process repeats until a desired outcome is achieved.

Figure 5.2 Illustration of SVM classifier

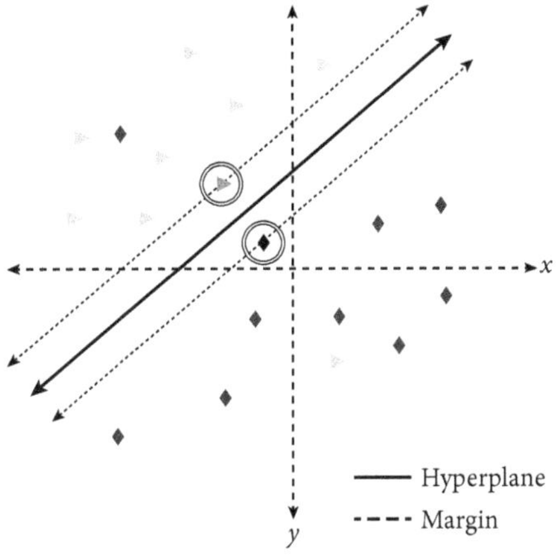

[64] ibid [29].

[65] Symantec™ eDiscovery Platform, powered by Clearwell Datasheet (2013).

[66] *Rio Tinto PLC v Vale SA* 306 FRD 125 (SDNY 2015).

[67] A Soto and B Pierson, 'U.S. Judge Dismisses Rio Tinto Lawsuit against Vale', *Reuters* (21 November 2015).

[68] J Borders, B Gauthier and E Tropiano, *White Paper – Active Learning in Technology-Assisted Review* (Relativity, 2018).

Support vector machine separates two classes of data into distinct categories with a mathematical divider called a hyperplane. The hyperplane is the decision boundary between the classes – relevant and not relevant. The operation of SVM is illustrated in Figure 5.2. To improve the classification through active learning data points on the edge of the hyperplane's margin (those circled in Figure 5.2) are selected by the recommendation algorithm and coded by the lawyers. SVM then adds the learning from the coding to its classifier.

Relativity is used by 198 of the Am Law 200 and 78 of Fortune 100 companies.[69]

In *Pyrrho Investments Ltd v MWB Property Ltd*,[70] a case dealing with breach of fiduciary duty by company directors, the English High Court addressed the use of TAR and described it, including that there would be a representative sample of documents that would be coded for relevance to act as the training set and based on that training the software would review and categorise every document in the set as either relevant or not. Further, samples of the TAR coded documents are reviewed by a human with the 'overturns' (the human disagreed with the program) being fed back to the program for further learning and recoding of documents. The sampling process continues until the overturns are brought within agreed tolerances, typically where the expense of further rounds of sampling are not justified due to the low chance of finding further errors.[71] The judgment did not refer to a particular TAR program.

In *McConnell Dowell Constructors v Santam*,[72] Justice Vickery of the Supreme Court of Victoria held that manual review of documents in a case alleging breach of a contract for the construction of a natural gas pipeline would be too time consuming and expensive so that TAR was warranted.[73] The operation of TAR was explained by reference to *Irish Bank Resolution* and *Pyrrho Investments Ltd*, discussed above.

Following *McConnell Dowell* the Supreme Court of Victoria introduced a new Practice Note dealing with technology in civil litigation, which clarified that 'In larger cases, [TAR] will ordinarily be an accepted method of conducting a reasonable search in accordance with the Rules of Court', and noting that the Court may order the use of TAR in large cases even if the parties do not consent.[74] The Practice Note added that the protocol should include:

> A general description of the system to be used … including, but not limited to:
>
> - A continuous active learning protocol (using a constantly changing body of documents which are used to train the technology assisted review algorithm);
> - A simple active learning protocol (using statistical samples, including control sets, or random samples and the like);
> - A simple passive learning protocol (using other recognised statistical methods); and
> - Any other appropriate system.[75]

[69] Relativity Information Sheet, www.relativity.com/ediscovery-software/.
[70] *Pyrrho Investments Ltd v MWB Property Ltd* [2016] EWHC 256 (Ch).
[71] ibid [19]–[23].
[72] *McConnell Dowell Constructors v Santam* [2016] VSC 734.
[73] ibid [5].
[74] Supreme Court of Victoria, SC GEN 5 Technology in Civil Litigation (29 June 2018) [8.7].
[75] ibid [8.9].

The above examples demonstrate that while there are common elements due to the use of supervised machine learning in each software program, the examples are not identical and each program has its own particular features. In a competitive marketplace it is not surprising that TAR providers compete based on functionality. However, for lawyers, this means that the details of how a particular TAR program operates are important in understanding how discovery is to be undertaken.

Role of the Lawyer

To understand the role of the lawyer and AI in the information-gathering or discovery process it is useful to examine discovery more broadly and then to focus on the operation of TAR.

EDRM

To situate AI in the discovery process reference may be made to EDRM. In May 2005 EDRM was founded by attorney George Socha and technologist Tom Gelbmann to address the perceived lack of standards and guidelines in the e-discovery industry. EDRM was acquired by Duke Law School in the US in 2016. Among EDRM's first projects was the creation of the EDRM diagram, which mapped the stages of e-discovery and has since become an industry-wide standard for managing the e-discovery process. The diagram is set out in Figure 5.3. The EDRM diagram provides visibility on how ESI in a party's possession, custody or power/control[76] is found and ultimately produced to an opponent or used by the party, including as evidence.

Figure 5.3 Electronic Discovery Reference Model

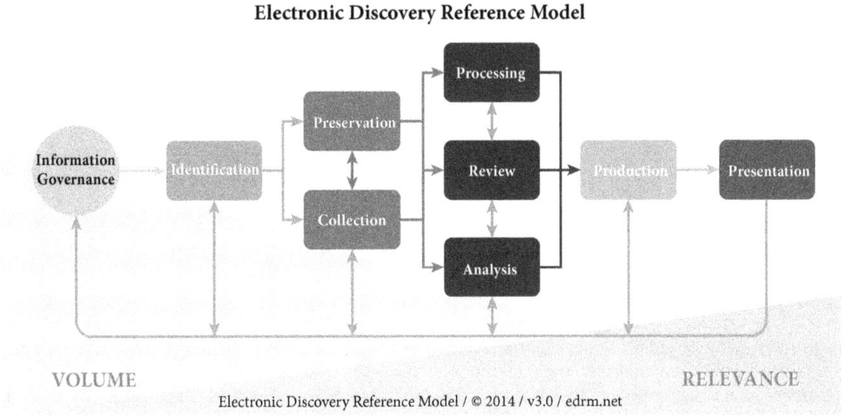

Source: EDRM Stages Diagram, www.edrm.net.

[76] This expression is a combination of English, Australian and US terminology for the ESI that a party is obligated to discover/disclose if relevant: Matthews and Malek (n 3) 178.

The content of each of the EDRM Stages may be summarised as follows:

- Information Governance – Getting your electronic house in order to mitigate risk and expenses should e-discovery become an issue, from initial creation of ESI (electronically stored information) through to its final disposition.
- Identification – Locating potential sources of ESI and determining its scope, breadth and depth.
- Preservation – Ensuring that ESI is protected against inappropriate alteration or destruction.
- Collection – Gathering ESI for further use in the e-discovery process (processing, review, etc.).
- Processing – Reducing the volume of ESI and converting it, if necessary, to forms more suitable for review and analysis.
- Review – Evaluating ESI for relevance and privilege.
- Analysis – Evaluating ESI for content & context, including key patterns, topics, people & discussion.
- Production – Delivering ESI to others in appropriate forms & using appropriate delivery mechanisms.
- Presentation – Displaying ESI before audiences (at depositions, hearings, trials, etc.), especially in native & near-native forms, to elicit further information, validate existing facts or positions, or persuade an audience.[77]

Artificial intelligence in the form of TAR has an important role to play in the review and analysis stages of voluminous discovery as the economic efficiency of the AI process is undeniable when compared to a 'manual' or human review of documents.[78] However, AI is not employed at every stage and therefore does not perform the entire process.[79]

The lawyers have important roles in relation to discovery and the EDRM in addition to the review and analysis stages where TAR is employed. For example, the duty to preserve evidence clearly extends to ESI.[80] In relation to preservation clients have responsibilities in relation to ensuring that documents are not lost or destroyed, either deliberately or inadvertently, which lawyers must explain. This is commonly achieved through the use of a 'litigation hold notice'.[81] In some

[77] The summary of EDRM stages is from www.edrm.net/resources/frameworks-and-standards/edrm-model/.

[78] MR Grossman and GV Cormack, 'Technology-Assisted Review in e-Discovery Can Be More Effective and More Efficient than Exhaustive Manual Review' (2011) 17 *Richmond Journal of Law & Technology* 1; Ernst and Young (n 51) ch 3.

[79] This is not to say that technology is not used in other stages. For example, de-duplication and de-NISTing technology is used in the processing stage. De-duplication technology eliminates duplicate documents, such as emails, letters or contracts, from a collection of potentially discoverable documents. De-duplication may use such methods as hash-based data de-duplication using a hashing algorithm such as Secure Hash Algorithm 1 or 256 (SHA-1 or SHA -256) or Message-Digest Algorithm 5 (MD5). De-NISTing is the removal of system files, program files, and other non-user-created data from ESI because these files are unlikely to contain relevant content. See *McConnell Dowell Constructors v Santam* [2016] VSC 734, [5] fn 1.

[80] 'The Sedona Principles, Third Edition' (2018) 19 *Sedona Conference Journal* 1, 93.

[81] ibid 104–08.

jurisdictions the duty to preserve material relevant to litigation may arise prior to litigation being commenced. In the US, for example, a duty to preserve material relevant to litigation arises when litigation is commenced or when there is a reasonable anticipation of litigation, ie there is a credible threat of litigation.[82] The scope of the litigation hold requires an understanding of the claims being made. Moreover, if the claims change during the duration of the dispute, for example where a pleading is amended to add claims or expand the time period in issue, then preservation obligations will need to be revisited. Preservation is of central concern because a failure to properly take steps to preserve relevant information that results in that information being destroyed may prejudice an opponent who is denied access to the documents and undermine the court's ability to determine the dispute on the facts. Consequently, this can lead to sanctions including adverse inferences, preclusion of evidence or the striking out of a claim or defence.[83] It is the lawyer who must advise on preservation obligations, how they can be met and the ramifications of non-compliance.[84]

EDRM is also accompanied by a project management model which explains the roles of the client, the lawyers and the e-discovery vendors (third parties who provide technology solutions, including TAR).[85] The need for project management highlights that planning, co-ordination and monitoring of the steps in the EDRM is required. The project management role will frequently be undertaken by the lawyers, possibly lawyers or paralegals with specialist skills in technology and project management.[86]

The identification and processing stage is likely to require the lawyer to liaise with the client so as to understand how the client's business functions, including the roles performed by personnel, and what IT systems exist. The lawyer will also need to exercise their judgement based on the allegations made and the information obtained from the client to determine matters such as the relevant time frame, the list of custodians of potentially relevant records, and the repositories of data to be examined. This information can be used to explain why certain sources of data will or will not contain relevant information.[87] The Australian Law Reform Commission in its review of discovery in the Federal Court noted that many organisations do not have systems for managing records and the lawyer will need to create such a system before a review can commence.[88] Other issues which may arise include the initial conversion of documents to a readable electronic format

[82] ibid 93.

[83] M Lange and K Nimsger, *Electronic Evidence and Discovery: What Every Lawyer Should Know* (2nd edn, American Bar Association, 2009) 91–94.

[84] See, eg, *Zubulake v UBS Warburg LLC*, 229 FRD 422 (SDNY 2004).

[85] EDRM, 'EDRM Model Project Management', www.edrm.net/frameworks-and-standards/edrm-model/project-management. See also Matthews and Malek (n 3) 228.

[86] Hibbert (n 28) 15.

[87] See *Zubulake v UBS Warburg LLC*, 229 FRD 422, 432 (SDNY 2004).

[88] Australian Law Reform Commission (n 39) 191–92.

and indexing of documents,[89] and the question of whether the entire cohort of documents should be processed by the software or whether some kind of 'cull' (generally by keyword searches) should be undertaken first.[90]

The conduct of a number of EDRM stages, such as identification and production, in addition to how review and analysis are to be undertaken (eg manual review or using TAR), may also be the result of negotiations with the opponent's legal representatives or argument before a judge. Much will depend on how a particular court approaches decisions about the discovery process.

In *Brown v BCA Trading Limited* in the English High Court,[91] Registrar Jones ordered the use of TAR, rather than keyword searches, for discovery. In doing so the Registrar noted that the successful use of TAR depended, at least to some extent, 'upon the success of the parties having been able first to narrow down the issues and therefore the categories/types of documents relevant to the disclosure process'.[92] The Registrar went on to indicate the role of the lawyers in this process:

> When the size of potential disclosure is significant both in terms of quantity of documents and the time required to be spent on the disclosure process, it is particularly important for the lawyers to identify by reference to the true issues, the anticipated categories of documents and to enter into discussions to seek to minimise the work required and therefore the costs.[93] …
>
> [T]hose discussions will be between experienced solicitors who can be relied upon to hold the reins within the context of them owing their duties as officers of the court, as well as their duties to their clients. I have absolutely no reason to have any doubt that the solicitors on both sides will do other than undertake their task in accordance with their duties and proceed properly and appropriately.[94]

Similarly in Australia it has been said:

> Unless there is a clear identification of what the relevant categories of documents are, and a clear appreciation of the extent of the scope of the issues in the case upon which they might be disclosable or discoverable, the process is still likely to miscarry, as much by capturing too many documents as by too few.[95]

More generally, the steps to be taken in discovery may be overlaid with a range of obligations necessitating legal and ethical judgements, such as proportionality,[96] conducting a 'reasonable search'[97] and compliance with an overarching or

[89] For more detail on these steps, see Brown (n 35) 239. Some documents are not amenable to a TAR process, such as spreadsheets: see *Money Max Int Pty Limited (Trustee) v QBE Insurance Group Limited* [2018] FCA 1030, [166].

[90] S Serhan, 'Calling an End to Culling: Predictive Coding and the New Federal Rules of Civil Procedure' (2016) 23(2) *Richmond Journal of Law & Technology* 1, 3.

[91] *Brown v BCA Trading Limited* [2016] EWHC 1464 (Ch).

[92] ibid [6].

[93] ibid [4].

[94] ibid [14].

[95] *Parbery v QNI Metals Pty Ltd* [2018] QSC 276, [19].

[96] See, eg, CPR (UK) r 1.1; FRCP (US) r 26(b)(1); *Federal Court of Australia Act 1976* (Cth) s 37M(2).

[97] See, eg, CPR (UK) r 31.7; FCR (Cth) r 20.14(1)(b), (3); *Irish Bank Resolution Corporation Limited v Quinn* [2015] IEHC 175, [55]–[56].

overriding purpose that requires the conduct of a proceeding in a manner which promotes efficiency.[98]

These roles for the lawyer are also found in relation to arbitration.[99] The IBA Rules provide that in the case of ESI, the requesting party (or the Arbitral Tribunal by order) should 'identify specific files, search terms, individuals or other means of searching' for documents in 'an efficient and economical manner'.[100]

Multiple government agencies in the US, including the Federal Trade Commission and the Department of Justice, have also approved the use of TAR coding to identify and review documents for production during investigations,[101] which again requires the input of legal expertise.

TAR Process

When TAR in the form of simple passive learning is considered as a series of steps, the need for a lawyer's input becomes apparent, as at each step, a lawyer must make important 'judgement calls':

1. Creation of training set based on lawyer decision making – the training set may be created using random sampling or judgemental sampling (eg, keyword searching and/or conceptual ranking).
2. Training set coded by lawyer.
3. Computer codes some or all documents.
4. Sample of computer coded documents reviewed by lawyer – errors identified and checked – 'overturns'.
5. Overturns fed back to computer and software learns from overturn to recode all documents.
6. Steps 4 and 5 are repeated until errors within acceptable tolerances or limits.
7. Documents coded as non-responsive by the computer sampled and coded by lawyer to ensure that the level of overturns is within acceptable tolerances or limits (validation set).

Lawyers continue to have a role within the TAR process in the training of the software, from the initial labelling of documents to subsequent training rounds. Even when simple active learning or continuous active learning versions of TAR are employed so that TAR selects documents for coding the lawyer is still training the software. It is the lawyer's knowledge or judgement of relevance (and other categories) that TAR seeks to model and then replicate. As Fulham J observed in *Irish Bank*, TAR 'combines man and machine'.[102]

[98] See, eg, CPR (UK) r 1.1; FRCP (US) r 1; *Federal Court of Australia Act 1976* (Cth) s 37M(1).

[99] See J Kwan, J Ng and B Kiu, 'The Use of Artificial Intelligence in International Arbitration: Where Are We Right Now?' (2019) 22(1) *International Arbitration Law Review* 19, 20.

[100] IBA Rules art 3.3(a)(ii).

[101] The Sedona Conference (n 33) 42–44.

[102] *Irish Bank Resolution Corporation Limited v Quinn* [2015] IEHC 175, [68].

It is important that lawyers who are deeply familiar with the case are involved in this training. If the task is delegated to someone without sufficient knowledge, then there is a risk that the software will either over- or under-identify documents.

In addition to the mechanics of training the TAR program there will be questions of strategy. Some courts may expect cooperation between the lawyers in determining the protocols to apply.[103] There may also be debate as to whether steps in the TAR process, discussed above, are confidential or should be conducted in a transparent manner.[104] In *McConnell Dowell*, the parties ended up in a dispute about TAR; specifically, whether additional rounds of training should be conducted.[105] Disputes around discovery and TAR are common in the US.[106] This suggests that there is a tactical issue as to whether to adopt the traditional approach of conducting discovery unilaterally in response to court orders as to the scope of discovery, or to engage with an opponent in relation to the search strategy, which means 'the parties work together to develop, test and agree upon the nature of the information being sought'.[107] Frank Pasquale and Glyn Cashwell have noted that TAR may in fact generate new issues and disputes around discovery, pointing to problems which arise when legal and technological departments or personnel fail to communicate effectively.[108] It is the lawyer, after advising and obtaining instructions from the client, who needs to determine what issues should be resolved through agreement and when a more adversarial approach is required.

Privilege

Privileged documents are exempt from disclosure but if disclosed the privilege may be lost or waived. The main focus is legal professional privilege[109] but other privileges such as public interest immunity, privilege against self-incrimination and without prejudice privilege may also need to be protected.[110] Confidential

[103] See, eg, *Mancia v Mayflower Textile Servs Co*, 253 FRD 354, 363 (D Md 2008) (endorsing The Sedona Conference Cooperation Proclamation and explaining how cooperation is consistent with the lawyer's obligation to the court).

[104] Ernst and Young (n 51) 16.

[105] *McConnell Dowell Constructors (Aust) Pty Ltd v Santam Ltd & Ors (No 2)* [2017] VSC 640 [10], [23].

[106] 'Discovery disputes concerning the collection, review and production of ESI "present[ ] special challenges" that standard discovery disputes do not': *Blackrock Allocation Target Shares: Series S Portfolio v Bank of New York Mellon*, 2018 WL 2215510, at *7 (SDNY May 15, 2018); *Winfield v City of New York*, 2017 WL 5664852 at *7 (SDNY Nov 27, 2017) quoting *William A Gross Construction Associates Inc v American Manufacturers Mutual Insurance Company* 256 FRD 134, 136 (SDNY 2009).

[107] The Sedona Conference, 'The Case for Cooperation' (2009 Supp) 10 *Sedona Conference Journal* 339, 342; see also M Legg and N Turner, 'When Discovery and Technology Meet: The Pre-Discovery Conference' (2011) 21(1) *Journal of Judicial Administration* 54.

[108] F Pasquale and G Cashwell, 'Four Futures of Legal Automation' (2015) 63 *UCLA Law Review Discourse* 26, 41.

[109] See Chapter 11.

[110] Matthews and Malek (n 3) 254.

documents may need to be identified and subject to regimes that limit disclosure so as to protect confidentiality.

Privileged documents may be found by using key word searches that focus on the word 'privilege' and the names of law firms or lawyers known to have advised the entity. Such a search can be incomplete and TAR may also be employed. However, TAR has a number of limitations in relation to privilege. These include that the indicia of privileged information may be difficult for an algorithm to discern as it cannot assess the purpose of a document's creation or the existence of confidentiality. Indeed the same content may be privileged in one document but not in another, such as the description of a factual scenario for which legal advice is sought, or copies of unprivileged documents provided to lawyers for advice.[111]

Lawyers may then determine to review all documents that are to be produced to an opponent for privilege. However, this may undermine the goal of reducing cost and delay through using technology. As a replacement, or adjunct, to complete review lawyers will need to combine available court rules, court orders, agreements with other parties, and the law on waiver to protect against loss of privilege.[112]

The US has attempted to address these issues, at a federal level, through the introduction of Rule 502 of the Federal Rules of Evidence, which was signed into law on 19 September 2008. Inadvertent disclosure is dealt with in Rule 502(b), while Rule 502(d) provides certainty that privilege will not be waived by the use of party-agreed procedures that are the subject of a court order to streamline privilege review.[113] While the Rule 502 regime was a major advance it still has various procedural potholes that the lawyer must avoid, including that much may turn on the agreements reached with opposing counsel and the terms of court orders.[114] Lawyer knowledge and judgement persists as a crucial requirement in the protection of clients' interests.

Future Developments

Better TAR

The competitive marketplace for TAR suggests that algorithms and computing power will improve its accuracy. It is likely to become less expensive as it becomes more widely adopted and will also be used for smaller collections of documents and for larger collections without culling as its effectiveness and efficiency improves.

[111] *Technology Assisted Review Guidelines* (n 44) 32.

[112] Legg (n 1) 88–90.

[113] J Redgrave and J Kehoe, 'New Federal Rule of Evidence 502: Privileges, Obligations, and Opportunities', *Federal Lawyer*, January 2009, 34.

[114] M Legg, 'Client Legal Privilege, Discovery and Expense Reduction in the Information Age' (2014) 3 *Journal of Civil Litigation and Practice* 78, 80–82.

There is also the possibility that as AI becomes more advanced it may be able to be used to assist the lawyer in more steps in the discovery process/EDRM stages and the pre-trial process more generally. For example, NLP may enable AI to review a new claim or pleading so as to use the learning from past cases (pleadings and relevant documents) to suggest what discovery would be relevant and then to look for that relevant discovery in a party's collection of documents. The TAR algorithm is trained based on past cases that it has been used for. The difficulty is being able to use the material from those past cases where there are confidentiality or Harman[115] undertakings (material produced in discovery can only be used for the specific case in which it is produced). It is not suggested that AI replaces the lawyer, but rather it could assist the lawyer in determining what is relevant or responsive to a claim. The reason for this position is that human oversight is necessitated not just because of the limitations of AI, which may reduce over time, but because a human – 'the lawyer on the record' – needs to take responsibility for the process.

Adding NLP

NLP is a form of machine learning that can analyse and process the human language, including language in a document. As explained in Chapter 2, NLP uses machine learning to use the context and relationship of words to find meaning. However, NLP may also be able to advance beyond finding the meaning of a sentence or question but to extract the content or meaning of a paragraph or collection of paragraphs, building up to determining the meaning of the entire document.[116]

The role of NLP in relation to information gathering or discovery may be that it provides a way in which to search a set of documents for particular information. TAR may be used to classify documents as relevant or not relevant and then NLP is used to request documents that are responsive to a particular issue in a dispute. Alternatively, TAR may cease to be used and rather than seeking to find relevant documents, the process may be reversed and NLP is used to find documents responsive to each issue in a case, and when all the issues are brought together then there is a collection of relevant documents.

While it is tempting to say that AI is reading the document for relevance, the discussion in Chapter 2 and this chapter makes clear that the AI is really building a mathematical model that statistically predicts the document is responsive.

[115] *Harman v Secretary of State for the Home Department* [1983] 1 AC 280; *Hearne v Street* (2008) 235 CLR 125.

[116] Brown (n 35) 285.

Fewer Lawyers More Legal Technologists

The discussion in this chapter has focussed on the role and knowledge of lawyers in a discovery process that employs TAR. However, consideration must also be given to what the ramifications of employing TAR are for the lawyer population more broadly.

Dana Remus and Frank Levy considered that TAR will have 'a strong employment effect on discovery practice',[117] but the lawyers whose work it is replacing will largely be junior lawyers and paralegals in large firms who would previously have undertaken the manual review step. Herbert Smith Freehills has pointed to discovery as illustrating the trend of tasks that once required huge teams of legal professionals being able to be undertaken by a smaller number of legal professionals using the latest technology.[118] There seems to be little doubt that lawyer work that involved lower-level skills (tagging documents as relevant or not relevant) will not be undertaken by lawyers.

However, there may also be a need for a position with a new skillset that still has a legal aspect. It has been recognised that 'ESI presents special challenges during the discovery process. Locating, collecting, producing and ultimately analyzing electronic data are more difficult than traditional paper discovery processes' and as a result an expert may be required.[119] Prior to the use of TAR, when search terms were being used, a US Court observed that whether keywords 'will yield the information sought is a complicated question involving the interplay, at least, of the sciences of computer technology, statistics and linguistics' which required the input of experts.[120] More generally, when a particular search or review methodology is employed, including TAR, lawyers need to be able to defend their approach if it is challenged by an opponent.[121] TAR's lack of easy intelligibility means that the process will require the use of experts or trust in a 'black-box' process.[122]

Consequently, legal technologists have become a core part of large law firms. They frequently have law degrees but may not be admitted to practice and have advanced proficiency in the technology they employ. Legal technologists assist the lawyers to work more efficiently and focus on higher-value legal activities through

[117] D Remus and F Levy, 'Can Robots be Lawyers? Computers, Lawyers, and the Practice of Law' (2017) 30 *Georgetown Journal of Legal Ethics* 501, 516. See also J McGinnis and R Pearce, 'The Great Disruption: How Machine Intelligence Will Transfer the Role of Lawyers in the Delivery of Legal Services' (2014) 82 *Fordham Law Review* 3041.

[118] L Langenhoven, 'The Symbiotic Relationship Between Lawyer and Legal Tech', Herbert Smith Freehills Latest Thinking Blog (8 October 2018).

[119] *Electronic Discovery* (Law Journal Press, 2019) §§9.01–9.02.

[120] *United States v O'Keefe*, 537 F.Supp.2d 14 (DDC 2008).

[121] D Waxse and B Yoakum-Kriz, 'Experts on Computer-Assisted Review: Why Federal Rule of Evidence 702 Should Apply to Their Use' (2012–13) 52 *Washburn Law Journal* 207, 218–19.

[122] S Katsuya Endo, 'Technological Opacity & Procedural Injustice' (2018) 59 *Boston College Law Review* 821, 826.

the technologist providing and guiding technology solutions such as TAR.[123] While ready access to inhouse TAR expertise is efficient it may not be sufficiently independent if evidence is required in an interlocutory dispute in litigation. It is also likely that smaller firms engaged in litigation may not be able to afford a full-time legal technologist. As a result, third-party legal technologists may also be needed. Third-party e-discovery vendors have existed for some time but rather than just selling their particular product they will offer independent review of a TAR process – proposed or completed. These third-party providers may also become competitors for lawyers and seek to have corporate clients unbundle their legal representation needs with a view to having discovery undertaken by an e-discovery vendor rather than a law firm. However, the main difficulty with this approach is that discovery is part of civil procedure and still very much a legal process. A legal technologist would have difficulty in dealing with all the steps in the EDRM model. As a result the future is more likely to involve a collaboration between lawyers and technologists.

Conclusion

A continuing theme through this book is that while AI can provide numerous advantages to law and the legal profession, lawyers are still critical to the functioning of the legal system. US Federal Magistrate Andrew Peck in *Da Silva Moore* observed that TAR 'is not a case of machine replacing humans', rather there must be interaction between man and machine.[124] As Vickery J noted extra-curially, 'discernment and judgment is called for'.[125] The human element remains important:

> [T]he technologies that exist cannot assemble theories of a case, sort documents based on varying grounds of liability, or even decide whether a document is helpful or hurts a particular side's case. The technology that exists is more accurately described as technology-assisted review, because all that computers are capable of right now is making human-conducted discovery more efficient and accurate.[126]

Technology Assisted Review will undoubtedly continue to improve but it will be most effective when combined with the judgement of a lawyer.

[123] Ashurst, Legal Technologist QA – Ashurst Advance (12 February 2019); V Pivovarov, '5 New Legal Professions Under the Impact of Legal Tech', *Medium* (11 May 2019).

[124] *Da Silva Moore v Publicis Groupe* 287 FRD 182, 189 (SDNY 2012).

[125] P Vickery, 'Managing the Paper: Taming the Leviathan' (2012) 22(2) *Journal of Judicial Administration* 51, 69.

[126] C Yablon and N Landsman-Roos, 'Predictive Coding: Emerging Questions and Concerns' (2013) 64 *South Carolina Law Review* 633, 637.

6

AI, Online Courts and Alternative Dispute Resolution

Introduction

Online dispute resolution (ODR) may refer both to alternative dispute resolution (ADR) which is conducted online (OADR), and to systems of online courts.[1] ODR may encompass the entire dispute resolution process, or it may refer to only some steps in the process, such as initiating the process or negotiating with an opponent. However, when technology is employed it has the ability to change, or diverge from, previously accepted approaches to ADR or litigation.[2] Indeed, in seeking to achieve cost reductions and efficiency and promote access, change is inevitable. The change may only be a digital version of a pre-existing analogue step, or it may fundamentally alter the pre-existing process.

The focus of this chapter is the employment of AI in ODR although the chapter also notes the use of other technology in ODR. The chapter sets out the traditional role of the lawyer in litigation and ADR. It explains and illustrates the use of AI in ODR. The chapter then brings the lawyer and AI together in the ODR setting by examining the role of the lawyer after ODR. The chapter concludes by discussing the future of ODR.

Technology, Courts and ADR

Information technology provides courts with the opportunity to streamline their operations and make justice more accessible. The combination of the internet, email and social media means that litigation steps such as filing and serving court documents can be done remotely.[3] Courts can also communicate with parties and

[1] M Legg, 'The Future of Dispute Resolution: Online ADR and Online Courts' (2016) 27 *Australasian Dispute Resolution Journal* 277.

[2] E Katsh and C Rule, 'What We Know and Need to Know about Online Dispute Resolution' (2016) 67 *South Carolina Law Review* 329, 330.

[3] See, eg, F Gascón Inchausti, 'Electronic Service of Documents National and International Aspects' in M Kengyel and Z Nemessányi (eds), *Electronic Technology and Civil Procedure* (Springer, 2012) 137; MJ Beazley, 'Social Media and the Courts: Service of Process' (Fourth Judicial Seminar on Commercial Litigation, Singapore, 16–18 May 2013); F Xuhui, 'Recent Development of Internet Courts in China' (2018) 5 *International Journal on Online Dispute Resolution* 49, 55.

the public with greater ease. To this can be added social media, with courts now providing official 'tweets' when judgments are handed down.[4] YouTube has been used to provide short videos explaining court processes.[5] Information technology also impacts on the traditional trial format with the use of real-time transcripts, telephone/video conferencing facilities to allow for witnesses to testify from remote locations and exhibits being shown to witnesses, lawyers and the public on screens. Trials and technology can be taken even further with a virtual hearing using email or instant messaging to create an online court.[6] The advent of services like Skype, WhatsApp and Zoom allow for visual as well as audio communications. Many of these developments are also able to be used in relation to ADR, such as arbitration and mediation, both by courts who build ADR into the process[7] and by non-court ADR service providers.[8]

Two important points about these developments should be noted. First, while these developments facilitate access to, and the dispensing of, dispute resolution or justice, they do not involve the use of AI. Second, these developments largely automate existing court or dispute resolution processes. This is not to say they are the same – indeed they can be qualitatively different, electronic service compared to personal service, or video testimony compared to live testimony. However, they do not seek to alter, replace or disrupt traditional processes.[9]

More recently, private developers have begun to create ODR platforms that seek to use blockchain technology to decentralise the delivery of dispute resolution to disputing parties in any location through a worldwide network of self-selecting juror-arbitrators, all of whom interact through decentralised apps built on top of the blockchain.[10] While highly novel and potentially very disruptive, this form of ODR does not use AI.

[4] See, eg, @UKSupremeCourt for the Supreme Court of the United Kingdom, @USSupremeCourt for the Supreme Court of the United States, @SCC_eng and @CSC_fra for the Supreme Court of Canada and @HighCourtofAus for the High Court of Australia.

[5] B Barton and S Bibas, *Rebooting Justice* (Encounter Books, 2017) 140.

[6] See, eg, New South Wales Department of Attorney General and Justice, *OnLine Court User Guide*, Version 0.4 (1 November 2010).

[7] See, eg, Matterhorn, available at getmatterhorn.com/, which has been employed in US courts such as Franklin County Municipal Court, Columbus; Ohio, available at sc.courtinnovations.com/OHFCMC; and Washtenaw County, 14A District Court Michigan, available at www.courtinnovations.com/MID14A.

[8] See, eg, M Piers and C Aschauer, 'Survey on the Present Use of ICT in International Arbitration' in M Piers and C Aschauer (eds), *Arbitration in the Digital Age: The Brave New World of Arbitration* (Cambridge University Press, 2018) 18–20.

[9] When ADR, particularly mediation in its various forms, received widespread adoption it may be argued that this was an example of the court system being subject to disruption. Today, ADR is often part of the court system or at least the broader civil justice system and no longer seen as disruptive.

[10] J Metzger, 'Decentralized Justice in the Era of Blockchain' (2018) 5(2) *International Journal of Online Dispute Resolution* 69; J Metzger, 'The Current Landscape of Blockchain-Based, Crowdsourced Arbitration' (2019) 19 *Macquarie Law Journal* 81.

Advocates and Dispute Resolution Lawyers

In popular culture's depiction of dispute resolution the lawyer is typically portrayed as the advocate or trial lawyer who through courtroom skills such as oral argument and cross-examination of witnesses advances or defends his/her client's interests. Advocacy is a core component of the culmination of litigation that plays out publicly in the court. Many books have been written on advocacy. However, only a couple will be drawn on here to illustrate the role of the lawyer. Francis Wellman, a practising attorney in New York who wrote one of the earliest texts on cross-examination, explained that the advocate requires rapidity of perception and sound and prompt judgement.[11] Wellman adds the power of imagination, sincerity, courage and clarity to take the fact finder to the events in question, to help them comprehend and to convince.[12] Richard Harris KC, who first wrote his text on advocacy in 1879, pointed out a number of requirements for good advocacy – common sense was the foundation, experience was needed but the advocate must always remember that they are dealing with human nature, and knowledge of human nature or human character was 'the key to success'.[13]

The advocate's role also has an institutional significance in the common law in that the outcome of a dispute is determined through the endeavours of competing lawyers subjecting 'each hypothesis, fact, analysis, reasoning, and conclusion … to interrogation'.[14] As Lord Eldon said, 'truth is best discovered by powerful statements on both sides of the question',[15] or as the former Chief Justice of Australia, Murray Gleeson, explained while a member of the Bar:

> The essential role of the advocate in an adversary system is to present the client's case to its best advantage, to cut down the opponent's case, and to endeavour by all legitimate means to persuade the tribunal to a view of the facts and the law most likely to result in a decision in favour of the client.[16]

However, behind this public face of the lawyer as advocate are a number of constituent roles, including ascertaining the facts (focussing on the helpful and diminishing the unhelpful),[17] determining how to prove the necessary facts by determining which witnesses to call and which documents to place into evidence, and applying the law[18] (bringing forward helpful, or ideally controlling, authority

[11] F Wellman, *Day in Court or The Subtle Arts of Great Advocates* (The Macmillan Company, 1910) 33–34.

[12] ibid 35–40.

[13] R Harris, *Harris' Hints on Advocacy* (17th edn, Stevens & Sons Ltd, 1937) 2–3.

[14] D Farrands, 'Artificial Intelligence and Litigation – Future Possibilities' (Victorian Bar CPD Programme, 22 December 2017) 31.

[15] *Ex parte Elsee* (1830) Mont 69 at 70n, 72, cited in JD Heydon, 'Reciprocal Duties of Bench and Bar' (2007) 81 *Australian Law Journal* 23, 25.

[16] AM Gleeson, 'Advocacy', The New South Wales Bar Association Bar Practice Course (November 2001) 1.

[17] This may include pre-trial steps such as document gathering, which are dealt with in Chapter 5.

[18] This will require legal research and views on prospects of success, which are dealt with in Chapter 4.

and distinguishing unhelpful authority).[19] It is often said that there must be a theory of the case, a version of events or story about what happened and what the consequences of that are as a matter of law. The theory then guides what has to be proved and how it can be proved.[20] The advocate embodies a skill set that combines knowledge of the law, procedure and evidence, but also judgement and discretion.

However, these skills or roles are also the subject of ethical and professional requirements, including that they are performed as part of a system of justice which must be administered according to law. Of central concern is the duty to the client, which incorporates duties of competence, loyalty (including avoiding conflicts of interest) and confidentiality (which is supported by legal professional privilege or attorney–client privilege in some jurisdictions), but also the duty to the court or the administration of justice.

In litigation the duty to the client is typified by zealous or resolute advocacy, at least in common law countries. However, that duty must also coexist with the duty to the court. In England, Lord Reid stated how the two duties operate in *Rondel v Worsley*:

> Every counsel has a duty to his client fearlessly to raise every issue, advance every argument, and ask every question, however distasteful, which he thinks will help his client's case. But, as an officer of the court concerned in the administration of justice, he has an overriding duty to the court, to the standards of his profession, and to the public, which may and often does lead to a conflict with his client's wishes or with what the client thinks are his personal interests. Counsel must not mislead the court, he must not lend himself to casting aspersions on the other party or witnesses for which there is no sufficient basis in the information in his possession, he must not withhold authorities or documents which may tell against his clients but which the law or the standards of his profession require him to produce.[21]

In the *Application of Griffiths*, Chief Justice Burger in dissent explained:

> The role of a lawyer as an officer of the court predates the Constitution; it was carried over from the English system and became firmly embedded in our tradition. It included the obligation of first duty to client. But that duty never was and is not today an absolute or unqualified duty. It is a first loyalty to serve the client's interest but always within – never outside – the law, thus placing a heavy personal and individual responsibility on the lawyer.[22]

[19] L Stuesser, *An Introduction to Advocacy* (2nd edn, Thomson Reuters, 2011) ch 1; A Palmer, *Proof* (3rd edn, Thomson Reuters, 2015).

[20] Stuesser (n 19) ch 1; Palmer (n 19) 44–47.

[21] *Rondel v Worsley* [1969] 1 AC 191, 227. See also A Boon, *The Ethics and Conduct of Lawyers in England and Wales* (3rd edn, Hart Publishing, 2015) 684.

[22] *In the Application of Griffiths* 413 US 717, 731–32 (1973).

In Australia the position was authoritatively stated in *Giannarelli v Wraith* by Chief Justice Mason:

> The peculiar feature of counsel's responsibility is that he owes a duty to the court as well as to his client. His duty to his client is subject to his overriding duty to the court. …
>
> It is not that a barrister's duty to the court creates such a conflict with his duty to his client that the dividing line between the two is unclear. The duty to the court is paramount and must be performed, even if the client gives instructions to the contrary.[23]

The duty to the administration of justice and to uphold the rule of law operates on lawyers generally not just in litigation.[24] However, it has particular resonance in relation to litigation and includes the following specific requirements:

- the lawyer must not knowingly or recklessly mislead or attempt to mislead the court;
- the lawyer must not abuse his or her role as an advocate;
- the lawyer must take reasonable steps to avoid wasting the court's time;
- the lawyer must take reasonable steps to ensure that the court has before it all relevant decisions and legislative provisions;
- the lawyer must ensure that his or her ability to act independently is not compromised.[25]

While the trial and courtroom advocacy is the role of the law and lawyers that the public is most familiar with, in fact the number of trials has been diminishing for some time,[26] and there has been an increase in ADR, in particular mediation.[27]

Role in Mediation

Although mediation provides for greater client involvement and introduces the mediator who has a role to play in facilitating resolution, the lawyer still has important functions to fulfil. For example a lawyer may advise if the dispute is suitable for mediation, advise on alternative options/outcomes, negotiate on the client's behalf, reduce power imbalances and seek to protect the client's interests, draft position papers and settlement agreements, and, if necessary, obtain the appropriate court order to put an end to court proceedings.[28]

[23] *Giannarelli v Wraith* (1988) 165 CLR 543, 555–56.

[24] See Chapter 11 for further discussion of this duty.

[25] *Halsbury's Laws of England* (LexisNexis Online) [884].

[26] J Langbein, 'The Disappearance of Civil Trial in the United States' (2012) 122 *Yale Law Journal* 522; K Hayne, 'The Vanishing Trial' (Supreme and Federal Courts Judges Conference, Sydney, 23 January 2008).

[27] E Katsh and O Rabinovich-Einy, *Digital Justice* (Oxford University Press, 2017) 14.

[28] M Kumar, M Legg, I Vickovich and J Metzger, *Civil Procedure in New South Wales* (4th edn, Thomson Reuters, 2020) 209.

The lawyer may also play a range of roles in the conduct of the actual mediation. Olivia Rundle devised a spectrum of roles that lawyers may play in mediation, differentiated by their levels of involvement (Table 6.1).[29]

Table 6.1 Lawyers' roles in mediation

Absent advisor	Advisor observer	Expert contributor	Supportive professional participant	Spokesperson
Less involvement				**More involvement**

The absent advisor assists the client to prepare for the mediation but does not attend the mediation session itself. The absent advisor's role is to support the client to participate effectively in the process. This is a cost-effective approach to mediation provided the client is able to adequately represent themselves. The advisor observer performs the same role as the absent advisor, but the lawyer attends the mediation. The lawyer observes but does not interact directly with the mediator, other party or other lawyer. The lawyer advises the client as requested during the mediation. The expert contributor performs all of the tasks of the advisor observer. In addition, the lawyers engage with one another during the mediation about the legal issues, ie views on the applicable law.

The supportive professional participant works with the client to prepare for the mediation and supports the client through the mediation process by working collaboratively towards an acceptable outcome. The lawyer and client work as a team. There is no clear partitioning of the roles of lawyer and client. The lawyer provides legal advice but may also assist in determining the client's interests and settlement offers.

The lawyer 'spokesperson' speaks on behalf of their client throughout the mediation. The client has a very limited role in the process. The parties merely observe rather than participate directly and obtain legal advice from and provide instructions to their lawyers outside the joint mediation sessions. This model may be appropriate when mediation would otherwise be inappropriate because of capacity or power imbalance issues.

As Rundle concludes, there is no correct model that lawyers must follow. Rather, the model will depend on the needs of the client, including their financial resources and abilities to negotiate effectively.

[29] O Rundle, 'A Spectrum of Contributions That Lawyers Can Make to Mediation' (2009) 20 *Australasian Dispute Resolution Journal* 220. See also R Angyal, 'Advocacy at Mediation: An Oxymoron or an Essential Skill for the Modern Lawyer' in M Legg (ed), *Resolving Civil Disputes* (LexisNexis, 2016) 185.

The ethics rules discussed above also apply to lawyers in negotiation and mediation.[30]

Application of AI to Online Courts and ADR

A key component of AI in ODR is the expert system, or decision tree analysis. Expert systems are explained in Chapter 2. To recap in the context of dispute resolution, human experts are utilised to determine the questions that a citizen/client needs be asked to generate the information to determine how to proceed when faced with a particular legal problem. The aim is to structure the learning from the experts in a logical and user-friendly manner using technology as a way to identify the problem and then posit next steps.

The operation of an expert system is well summarised by Darin Thomson, a lawyer with the Ministry of Justice in British Columbia, Canada, as follows:

> The basic structural components of an expert system are the knowledge base, inference engine and user interface.
>
> The knowledge base is the core of the system where domain-specific expert knowledge is stored. Expert content is structured in the knowledge base in the form of production rules. In general terms, a production is a condition, followed by an action, used to define a step in the reasoning process. The antecedent part of the rule is factual or 'real-world' in nature. The consequent part expresses the application of the rule to that condition once it is satisfied or asserted to be 'true'. The condition–action formulation permits the system to reason deductively, by way of conditional 'if … then …' statements written in the English language. In this formulation, the 'if …' represents the condition, while the 'then …' determines the action to be taken, resulting in 'if (condition), then (action)' statements. …
>
> The inference engine is the module that manipulates and interacts with the knowledge base to perform the system's reasoning. When the condition of a rule is satisfied, it 'fires' or executes a specific action. This action often involves setting a subsequent production rule into action. The inference engine thus interacts with the production rules, which form the structure of the knowledge base.
>
> Humans interact with the system through its user interface. This part of the expert system translates user inputs into a format that can be understood and computed by a computer. In turn, it also translates outputs into a format the user can understand.[31]

An ODR process typically has three steps: first, problem identification and provision of information; second, facilitation of voluntary forms of dispute resolution

[30] S Blake, J Browne and S Sime, *The Jackson ADR Handbook* (2nd edn, Oxford University Press, 2016) ch 6; J Rogers, 'The Lying Lawyer and the Ethics of Negotiation' in M Legg (ed), *Resolving Civil Disputes* (LexisNexis, 2016) 197.

[31] D Thomson, 'Creating New Pathways to Justice Using Simple Artificial Intelligence and Online Dispute Resolution' (2015) 1(2) *International Journal of Online Dispute Resolution* 4, 14.

such as negotiation between the parties and third-party-facilitated ADR such as mediation; and third, preparation for more formal dispute resolution through initiating the steps to commence court proceedings. The ODR system may be linked with the court/tribunal system in a particular jurisdiction so that there is a seamless progression into that system. Alternatively, the system may generate the forms and other documents (such as letter of demand, pleadings or affidavits) that the user can employ to commence legal proceedings.

The aim of the expert system is to resolve as many disputes as possible as early as possible. The more self-resolution that occurs the quicker and cheaper the process is for both user and provider.

The provision of information using an expert system can be a stand-alone system that educates the user about their legal issue. However, in relation to ODR it is a crucial first step for being able to identify, commence and resolve a dispute. Just as in a traditional trial, where the relevant facts need to be put before the judge, the necessary background to the dispute is needed for the AI. The first step seeks to diagnose the problem by asking a series of questions but also through providing information so as to educate the user. Information can be provided using text, videos, chatbots (which employ natural language processing) or through helplines. The information is mainly oriented to explaining why particular facts are relevant or helping in selecting the correct legal category, but it can also be aimed at skills such as communicating with another party or calculating losses. The provision of information aids in the user more accurately answering the questions posed by the expert system, which in turn facilitates the choice of the next question or option. AI may also be employed to create any documents necessary to support the dispute resolution process such as a letter of demand.

The second step of promoting voluntary resolution, with or without a third party, draws primarily on technology that facilitates communication between the parties (and third party) such as text messaging and telephone/video conferencing, depending on whether synchronous (continuous or real-time) or asynchronous negotiation is desired or chosen. However, AI utilising machine learning may also have a role to play in terms of suggesting possible resolutions based on the information provided by the parties and the AI's learning from past, similar disputes. Indeed, the AI's ability to generate options may see it become the third party.

The third step utilises AI to create the necessary forms or documents based on the information provided by the user to move into more formal dispute resolution. The dispute resolution process, like the second step, primarily draws on technology to facilitate communication, including traditional litigation steps such as service and hearings. The decision-making step remains with humans, namely tribunal members and judges. However, a possible future development is where the AI, having obtained the facts, then determines the relevant law and applies it. The outcome may be a recommendation for a human judicial officer, or an AI-generated determination that may be binding or non-binding.

The technology, highlighting AI, used in each of the above three steps is summarised in Table 6.2.

Table 6.2 Use of technology in ODR

Steps	Use of technology
1. **Online legal information/intake mechanism** (ascertain facts, help user comprehend their rights and determine if they have a claim/defence)	• Online portal using expert system (AI) to obtain facts • Document intake to support claim/defence • Online portal using expert system (AI) to communicate legal information/advice • Chatbots using NLP (AI) • Document creation using NLP (AI) (eg letter of demand, mediation position paper)
2. **Online ADR** (facilitate voluntary ADR methods such as negotiation and mediation)	• Online communication tools to facilitate interaction eg text and voice messaging, video conferencing, virtual meeting spaces • Online tools using machine learning and NLP (AI) to suggest or evaluate options for resolution.
3. **Online court/tribunal** (binding determinations)	• Document creation using NLP (AI) to complete forms and create pleadings • Filing and communication (service) of documents/originating process • Case management (timetabling) • Virtual courtroom using text messaging and video conferencing for directions hearings and trial • Observation of trial by public (internet) • Communication of judgments

Examples

To illustrate the operation of ODR five examples are explained below:

- e-commerce platforms such as eBay and Alibaba;
- the Netherland's platform called Rechtwijzer (Roadmap to Justice);
- the Canadian province of British Columbia's Civil Resolution Tribunal;
- the England and Wales online court; and
- China's internet courts.

As explained above, the technology used in each example is broader than AI and where AI is employed it is usually less advanced approaches such as expert systems. However, even without advanced forms of machine learning the progress in making justice accessible is substantial.

E-commerce

One of the best-known e-commerce platforms is the eBay Resolution Centre, which is generally cited as resolving at least 60 million disputes per year.[32] The average value of each dispute is between $70 and $100.[33] Many of the disputes addressed by eBay are a result of miscommunications or inadvertent errors that can readily be resolved if addressed quickly.[34] Further, the volume of disputes means that a private but formal dispute resolution system, such as arbitration, would be costly and time consuming. As a result eBay devised an online resolution system that facilitates identification of the particular problem and communication between buyers and sellers as to a preferred resolution.[35] If a negotiated outcome is not achieved then the dispute is resolved by eBay. Buyers and sellers agree when using eBay that they 'permit [eBay] to make final decisions about all cases, including appeals'.[36]

The eBay approach to disputes is set out in its 'Money Back Guarantee' policy available on its website.[37] Recovery is limited to the purchase price for the buyer, and full reimbursement for the seller. Indirect or consequential damages are excluded and cannot be claimed. Personal injury or property damage suffered by a buyer that resulted from a defective good cannot be pursued through the eBay dispute resolution system. The policy places certain procedural restrictions on claims, such as: (1) the case was opened within the required time frame, usually no later than 30 days after actual or latest estimated delivery date; (2) the buyer made the purchase on eBay.com via checkout or an eBay invoice with one of the following payment methods: PayPal, PayPal Credit, credit card or debit card, eBay gift cards, eBay bucks and eBay vouchers; and (3) the item was paid for in a single payment. The policy also sets out exclusions such as 'Buyer remorse or any reason other than not receiving an item or receiving an item that isn't as described in the

[32] See, eg, C Rule and C Nagarajan, 'Leveraging the Wisdom of Crowds: The eBay Community Court and the Future of Online Dispute Resolution' (Winter 2010) *ACResolution Magazine* 4, 5; C Rule, 'Designing a Global Online Dispute Resolution System: Lessons Learned from eBay' (2017) 13 *University of St. Thomas Law Journal* 354. See also A Sela, 'The Effect of Online Technologies on Dispute Resolution System Design: Antecedents, Current Trends, and Future Directions' (2017) 21(3) *Lewis & Clark Law Review* 633, 636.

[33] L Del Duca, C Rule and K Rimpfel, 'EBay's Defacto Low Value High Volume Resolution Process: Lessons and Best Practices for ODR System Designers' (2014) 6 *Yearbook on Arbitration and Mediation* 204, 205.

[34] Katsh and Rabinovich-Einy (n 27) 16.

[35] See resolutioncenter.ebay.com/.

[36] See www.ebay.com/help/policies/ebay-money-back-guarantee-policy/ebay-money-back-guarantee-policy?id=4210 under the heading 'Other Terms'.

[37] See www.ebay.com/help/policies/ebay-money-back-guarantee-policy/ebay-money-back-guarantee-policy?id=4210.

listing', duplicate claims through other resolution methods and items shipped to another address after original delivery.

The stages in the eBay system may be summarised as follows:

- Stage 1 – identification of problem through users selecting a pre-determined category ie non-delivery of goods, goods not matching description or non-payment for goods.
- Stage 2 – negotiation between buyer and seller of a resolution to the identified problem. This can include provision of information from the buyer and seller as to the problem, such as seller providing shipping and delivery information where a product was not received.
- Stage 3 – if the matter cannot be resolved through negotiation, the dispute can be escalated to the Resolution Services team within Customer Support. The Resolution Services team evaluates the buyer/seller claims and makes a decision about who is right and who is wrong.

eBay has also added resolution platforms dedicated specifically to several categories of purchases, including the Vehicle Purchase Protection (VPP) and Business Equipment Purchase Protection (BEPP) programmes, each with specific minimum and maximum price limitations.

The learning from eBay was made more broadly available through Modria (modular online dispute resolution implementation assistance), which is composed of four modules. The first of these is a diagnosis module that gathers and organises information with a view to identifying possible negotiated solutions and suggesting these to the disputants. If no agreement is reached the disputants enter the negotiation module and engage in direct negotiation. If that fails, then the next step is the mediation module, which engages a third party to facilitate negotiation. The final module is arbitration, which may be binding or non-binding.[38] While Modria was developed in an e-commerce environment, it has subsequently been employed for online divorce mediation, property tax disputes and no-fault motor vehicle insurance cases.[39]

Alibaba, a Chinese multinational technology company specialising in e-commerce, adopts a similar approach to resolving e-commerce disputes as eBay. The steps in the Alibaba process are summarised on its website as follows:[40]

> 1. After the buyer submits dispute, parties have 3 to 30 days to negotiate without the involvement of Alibaba. From the 4th day onward, the buyer can request Alibaba.com's assistance by clicking the 'Escalate Dispute' button, or may continue to negotiate with the seller.

[38] Barton and Bibas (n 5) 113–14; Tyler Technologies, *Online Dispute Resolution* (2017) 1.

[39] Barton and Bibas (n 5) 115.

[40] See service.alibaba.com/buyer/faq_detail/10609493.htm. See also Alibaba.com Transaction Dispute Rules (25 September 2018) rule.alibaba.com/rule/detail/8882.htm.

2. During the negotiation period, both parties need to respond each other's proposal within 7 days, otherwise the dispute will be escalated (no reply from supplier in due time) or cancelled (no reply from buyer in due time) automatically.
3. Alibaba.com will also act as a mediator for any disputes which remain unresolved after 30 days of initial opening. The reference to mediation would not appear to be mediation in the non-binding sense understood by ADR practice as the outcome does bind the parties.

The process when Alibaba is called on to resolve the dispute at stage 3 is also summarised on its website. It explains that the system determines whether evidence needs to be submitted and by whom – the buyer and/or the seller.

The provision and use of evidence is governed by Articles 20–22 of the Alibaba.com Transaction Dispute Rules:

- Article 20 The Buyer and the Seller shall provide evidence for their respective claim or defense no later than three working days after making application for dispute resolution or receiving the notice of dispute resolution from Alibaba.com, and shall undertakes that the evidence provided is authentic, complete, relevant and legitimate. Alibaba.com has the right to obtain evidence on its own or from a third party as it deems necessary, and determine the liability of the parties and the disputes based on the reasonable man standards and international trade practices.
- Article 21 If either party submits false, altered, or forged evidence, or fails to submit evidence that meets relevant requirements within the time limit set by Alibaba.com, Alibaba.com has the right to terminate the dispute resolution process or make a decision based on the evidence submitted.
- Article 22 The correspondences between the Buyer and the Seller via the Alibaba.com's official chat tool will serve as basis for dispute resolution, and correspondence between the parties through other means of communication (including but not limited to offline written contracts, telephone calls, e-mails, and third-party instant chat tools) will not be the basis for the dispute resolution, unless both the Buyer and the Seller agree that such correspondence are authentic and valid.

The way in which Alibaba determines the dispute is not set out on its website. Researchers have referred to the use of a jury system using Alibaba registered members, a customer representative and a panel of Alibaba's ODR team.[41]

It is worth noting that stage 3 in both eBay and Alibaba is not transparent and has caused some discontent amongst users, particularly sellers.

Other private forms of ODR can be found on platforms such as Smartsettle, VirtualCourthouse.com, net-arb.com and SettleToday.com.[42] The great advantage

[41] Katsh and Rabinovich-Einy (n 27) 65–66; D Becker and A Maia, 'ODR as an Effective Method to Ensure Access to Justice: The Worrying, But Promising Brazilian Case', Mediate.com (September 2018); A Schimtz, 'Building on OArb Attributes in Pursuit of Justice' in M Piers and C Aschauer (eds), *Arbitration in the Digital Age: The Brave New World of Arbitration* (Cambridge University Press, 2018) 196–97.

[42] See Sela (n 32) 651–52; Schimtz (n 41) 197–200.

of private ODR is that it can 'act as a kind of incubator, where ideas and methods can be explored and refined'.[43]

Rechtwijzer

One of the first ODR systems was provided by the Netherlands platform called Rechtwijzer (Roadmap to Justice) for couples who are separating or divorcing. Couples pay €100 for access to Rechtwijzer, which starts by asking each partner for their age, income, education and other information, such as whether they want the children to live with only one parent or part time with each, then guides them through questions about their preferences. The platform uses algorithms to find points of agreement and then proposes solutions. If the proposed solutions are not accepted then couples can employ the system to request a mediator for an additional €360 or a binding decision by an adjudicator.[44] The Legal Aid Board has explained the aim of Rechtwijzer as 'to empower citizens to solve their problems by themselves or together with his or her partner. If necessary, it refers people to the assistance of experts'.[45] Rechtwijzer is voluntary and non-binding up until the point where the parties seek a binding decision.

After three years funding for the website was discontinued as it was deemed financially unsustainable. The problem appears to have been that there was insufficient use by parties as it was voluntary and sat outside the state-provided court system.[46]

However, Rechtwijzer has been reincarnated as uitelkaar.nl and is operated by a tech start-up company, justice42. The basic cost became €425 euros per party with additional charges for mediation. As for Rechtwijzer, the website takes the user through the stages from free intake and assessment to the production of an agreement for lawyer approval and then forwarding to a judge for the final court consent. However, an important change is the incorporation of more human assistance to users, including call centre assistance and review by a manager of the final agreement before it goes to the lawyer for approval.[47]

[43] S Salter, 'Online Dispute Resolution and Justice System Integration: British Columbia's Civil Resolution Tribunal' (2017) 34(1) *Windsor Yearbook of Access To Justice* 112, 116.

[44] JH Verdonschot, 'In The Netherlands, Online Application Helps Divorcing Couples in Their Own Words, on Their Own Time' (2015) 21(2) *Dispute Resolution Magazine* 19; E Bickel, M van Dijk and E Giebels, 'Online Legal Advice and Conflict Support: A Dutch Experience' (University of Twente, March 2015) www.utwente.nl/igs/icrisp/news/content/online-legal-advice-and-conflict-support-utwente.pdf; C Matlack, 'Robots Are Taking Divorce Lawyers' Jobs, Too', *Bloomberg.com* (30 June 2016) www.bloomberg.com/news/articles/2016-06-30/robots-are-taking-divorce-lawyers-jobs-too.

[45] Legal Aid Board, 'Legal Aid in the Netherlands: A Broad Outline' (2015) 8, www.rvr.org/binaries/content/assets/rvrorg/informatie-over-de-raad/legalaid-brochure_online--2015.pdf.

[46] R Smith, 'Goodbye, Rechtwijzer: Hello, Justice42', *Law, Technology and Access to Justice Blog* (31 March 2017); T Etherton, 'The Civil Court of the Future' (Speech delivered at the The Lord Slynn Memorial Lecture, 14 June 2017) 16, www.judiciary.gov.uk/wp-content/uploads/2017/06/slynn-lecture-mr-civil-court-of-the-future-20170615.pdf.

[47] R Smith, 'The Rechtwijzer Rides Again', *Law, Technology and Access to Justice Blog*, 7 December 2017, https://law-tech-a2j.org/odr/the-rechtwijzer-rides-again/.

British Columbia Civil Resolution Tribunal

One of the most prominent and acclaimed examples of successful ODR is the British Columbia Civil Resolution Tribunal. In 2012 the British Columbia government passed the *Civil Resolution Tribunal Act* with the goal of using technology and ADR to increase access to justice for British Columbians with small claims and condominium property disputes. The Civil Resolution Tribunal started with strata property disputes and expanded to small claims under $5,000 and then to motor vehicle accident and injury claims below $50,000. The small claims jurisdiction is planned to be gradually increased to claims under $25,000.[48]

The Civil Resolution Tribunal involves four stages:[49]

Stage 1 – employs AI through an expert system called Solution Explorer that uses interactive questions and answers to give people tailored legal information as well as tools and resources, like template letters, to help them resolve their dispute consensually. For example, the expert system may ask questions to diagnose a person's problem as follows:

> Karin has a Small Claims problem
>> Karin's Small Claims problem relates to the purchase of a good or service
>>> Karin's purchase is a consumer (personal, family or household use) type
>>>> Karin is the consumer (purchaser)
>>>>> Karin's purchase is a service contract
>>>>>> Karin's service contract is a continuing service contract (eg a fitness club membership)
>>>>>>> Karin wants to cancel and is having a disagreement over the terms of cancellation.[50]

If no consensual resolution is achieved, then Solution Explorer provides an online intake process that commences a claim. The process seeks factual information and supporting evidence. The focus of the intake process is to avoid an adversarial approach and instead focus on collaboration.

Stage 2 – party-to-party negotiation is provided for to try and resolve the dispute without the Civil Resolution Tribunal becoming involved. The expectation is that 'the negotiation phase is unlikely to resolve a high percentage of disputes, but is consistent with the principle of empowering people with as many up-front opportunities to resolve a dispute as possible before imposing a resolution through adjudication.'[51]

[48] British Columbia Civil Resolution Tribunal website, civilresolutionbc.ca/resources/crt-jurisdiction/; S Salter and D Thompson, 'Public-Centred Civil Justice Redesign: A Case Study of the British Columbia Civil Resolution Tribunal' (2016–2017) 3 *McGill Journal of Dispute Resolution* 113; S Salter, 'Online Dispute Resolution and Justice System Integration: British Columbia's Civil Resolution Tribunal' (2017) 34(1) *Windsor Yearbook of Access To Justice* 112.

[49] M Barendrecht, JH Verdonschot, F Singleton-Clift, J Poeteray, G Petreikyte and F Braarud, 'Trend Report 4 – ODR and the Courts: The Promise of 100% Access to Justice? (The Hague Institute for Innovation of Law, 2016) 57.

[50] Salter and Thompson (n 48) 129.

[51] ibid 132.

Stage 3 – there is a further attempt to reach a resolution through a range of online and in-person ADR techniques employed by facilitators, who are Tribunal employees. The resolution of most disputes takes place online and asynchronously, within specified timelines set by the Tribunal's rules or directions from facilitators. It has been described as a 'mediation carried out remotely'.[52] However, facilitators may also provide a non-binding neutral evaluation of the parties' claims. Agreements can become orders of the Civil Resolution Tribunal. If the parties consent, and if the facilitator is also a Tribunal member, the facilitator can act as the Tribunal and issue a binding decision.

Stage 4 – if an agreement is not reached the dispute proceeds to adjudication, where a Tribunal member, who is a lawyer with relevant expertise, hears the parties' evidence and submissions and makes a binding decision. Hearings will generally take place through electronically submitted written documents, or through telephone or videoconferencing.

The expectation is that most parties will progress through the stages in the above sequence but the processes can be reordered, depending on the parties' requirements. Participants can seek legal assistance throughout the process, but if a hearing becomes necessary, a party will require permission to have a lawyer represent them.

England and Wales Online Court

The starting point for the England and Wales online court is Lord Justice Briggs' Civil Courts Structure Review reports, which recommend an online court for claims up to £25,000.[53] The online court as described in the reports would involve three stages:[54]

Stage 1 – a largely automated, interactive online process for the identification of the issues and the provision of documentary evidence. The online portal will guide the litigant through an analysis of their grievance so as to produce a document capable of being understood both by opponents and by the Court. It will in effect be a simplified pleading. This process would utilise an expert system similar to that used in the British Columbia Civil Resolution Tribunal described above. The Interim Report provides the following example:

> Suppose that A has a dispute with her builder B relating to works carried out at her house. After entering the common Court Service Portal and selecting the OC as the appropriate court (if necessary with online guidance), and after providing her name and contact details, A would be asked to identify the object of her grievance by reference to a series of tick boxes which might include her bank, her holiday company, her next

[52] ibid.

[53] M Briggs, *Civil Courts Structure Review – Interim Report* (December 2015) (Briggs – Interim Report) and M Briggs, *Civil Courts Structure Review – Final Report* (July 2016) (Briggs – Final Report).

[54] Briggs – Interim Report (n 53) [6.7]; Briggs – Final Report (n 53) [6.108]–[6.114].

door neighbour and her builder. Having ticked 'Builder' the software would present new questions designed to elicit the essential nature of the dispute, for example whether it was about the quality of the work, the amount charged or delays in completion. Ticking (or clicking) the appropriate box would reveal further successive pages, including a page requiring A to identify B and provide his (or if a company, its) contact details, to state whether the building works were covered by an agreement and, if in writing requiring A to attach any electronic copy, or scan or photograph with her smart phone any paper copy, so that the central document required by the court for determination of the dispute would be lodged electronically from the outset. Further automated pages would question A as to the details of the dispute.[55]

Stage 2 – conciliation and case management, by case officers. Once the claim and supporting information is extracted through stage 1 the aim is to then employ ADR where appropriate. Part of the purpose of stage 2 is to educate litigants of small claims about the existence of ADR.

Stage 3 – resolution by judges. There is no presumption that this requires the traditional trial. Rather, the court may choose to determine the matter on the documents, or by communicating with the parties through telephone or video. A face-to-face hearing, if employed, may only be used for resolving particular issues.

In the final report reference was also made to a stage 0 and stage 0.5 so as to acknowledge that there is a need for advice on the law and on alternatives to the online court. Further, it was recognised that some claims will not be disputed and the court is being engaged so as to access the state's enforcement mechanisms.[56]

To reduce costs the online court is to be designed for use by litigants without lawyers.[57] However, lawyers are not excluded. Rather, depending on the recovery-of-costs mechanism that is adopted, the result could be a lawyer-free online court 'by economic means'.[58] This is because individuals may be dissuaded from seeking legal assistance if those costs must be borne by the individual, even when they are successful.

The recommendations for an online court have been pursued through a number of pilots. The pilots operate within the existing court framework but subject to specific Practice Directions.[59] However, as Sir Terence Etherton, Master of the Rolls and Head of Civil Justice, explained:

> In an online environment the rules will to a significant extent be instantiated in the online court's operating code. As such, there will sometimes be no need to refer to rules. All that will be necessary will be to use the platform.[60]

[55] Briggs – Interim Report (n 53) [6.8].
[56] Briggs – Final Report (n 53) [6.108]–[6.109].
[57] Briggs – Interim Report (n 53) [6.5]; Briggs – Final Report (n 53) [6.22].
[58] Briggs – Final Report (n 53) [6.25].
[59] L Frazer, Parliamentary Under-Secretary of State for Justice, Letter to B Neill MP, Chair, Justice Select Committee, HM Courts & Tribunals Service New Online Civil Claims Pilot Rolled Out (April 2018). See also attached Fact Sheet.
[60] Etherton (n 46) 17.

The Online Civil Money Claims Pilot, which is set out in Practice Direction 51R, allowed persons who were not legally represented to file a claim for a specified amount of money not exceeding £10,000 including interest. There is to be only one claimant making the claim, and only one defendant, who the claimant believes will also not have legal representation. The Practice Direction then provides for a number of possible actions by the defendant, including defending the claim, indicating a willingness to negotiate, making payment, and proposing a repayment plan, which is followed by a number of possible actions by the claimant such as rejecting the defendant's offer and proposing alternative repayment plans. The response can be online or through traditional paper documents.[61] The Online Civil Money Claims Pilot was initially only available to users invited to adopt the new system but from March 2018 was available to all eligible users.[62]

The County Court Online Pilot is set out in Practice Direction 51S. The Practice Direction enables legal representatives to file claims online at the County Court Money Claims Centre (CCMCC), using the County Court Online website, and for the claims to be issued to those legal representatives online, for the claimant then to serve. The pilot is run on an invitation-only basis. In contrast to the Online Civil Money Claims Pilot, in addition to being available for lawyers rather than unrepresented persons, eligible claims may be for a specified or unspecified sum of money and a monetary cap is not specified.[63]

Other pilot online schemes have been adopted for probate claims, uncontested divorce claims and individual taxpayer appeals.[64] However, to date the pilots have moved the court processes online but not adopted any form of AI, such as the expert system envisaged by Lord Justice Briggs' Interim Report described above.

China's Internet Courts

The Supreme People's Court of the People's Republic of China (SPC) determined to make full use of technologies such as the internet, cloud computing, big data and artificial intelligence to modernise the court system through online or internet courts. Initially two People's High Courts, in the provinces of Jilin and Zhejiang respectively, were chosen to initiate the pilot programmes within their jurisdictions.[65]

[61] Practice Direction 51R – Online Civil Money Claims Pilot.

[62] Frazer (n 59).

[63] Practice Direction 51S – The County Court Online Pilot.

[64] T Etherton, 'Civil Justice After Jackson' (Speech delivered at the Conkerton Memorial Lecture 2018, 15 March 2018) 15–16.

[65] AL Xu, 'Chinese Judicial Justice on the Cloud: a Future Call or a Pandora's Box? An Analysis of the "Intelligent Court System" of China' (2017) 26(1) *Information & Communications Technology Law* 59, 62–63.

The procedure applicable in the pilot programmes was set out in the Provisions on Several Issues Concerning the Trial of Cases by the Internet Courts published by the SPC. As a general rule, the entire litigation process in the internet courts will be conducted online, including the service of legal documents, the presentation of evidence, and the actual trial itself. The Provisions also provide that the internet courts may consider electronic evidence provided by the parties that can be authenticated by electronic signatures, time stamps, hash value verification, blockchain and other tamper-proof verification methods.[66]

Jilin province adopted an approach familiar to many common law countries by putting traditional court processes online, although perhaps to a greater extent than previously attempted, so that commencing proceedings, service of documents, filing and exchange of evidence, hearings, mediation and enforcement could all be undertaken online.[67]

In the city of Hangzhou in Zhejiang province the approach was to address disputes arising from online shopping and other online activity. Chinese procedural law dictates that suits against companies must be filed in their principal place of business or in the place where they have their registered address. Hangzhou is the domicile of many Chinese e-commerce corporations.[68] Indeed the Zhejiang province approach owes much to a collaboration with Alibaba Group Holding Ltd.[69] The internet court was initially only open to individuals who held an account with Alipay (similar to PayPal), which is an Alibaba affiliate. The court only heard disputes involving online sales conducted on the Taobao or Tmall shopping platforms, both of which are subsidiary companies of Alibaba. Evidence was usually drawn from these shopping platforms. Court judgments could then be enforced immediately against a debtor's Alipay account.[70] The Zhejiang province has expanded the internet court to include divorce, road accident and contract cases.[71]

In both the Jilin and Zhejiang province High Courts, AI is employed in a number of ways. First, an online litigation platform may be used by a party to obtain a litigation risk assessment, a report that identifies risks by combining the litigant's case and the 'analysis of judicial data and similar cases'.[72] This appears to be a form of machine learning used for outcome prediction, similar to that discussed in Chapter 4. The aim of the risk assessment is to help litigants avoid common pitfalls, appreciate the uncertainty of litigation and promote the use of ADR.[73] Parties may also avail themselves of the Intelligent Complaint Machine,

[66] E Greenberg and N Ebner, 'What Dinosaurs Can Teach Lawyers About How to Avoid Extinction in the ODR Evolution' (St John's School of Law Legal Studies Research Paper Series, 17 January 2019) 15.
[67] Xu (n 65) 63.
[68] Greenberg and Ebner (n 66) 15.
[69] Xu (n 65) 66.
[70] ibid 67.
[71] ibid 67–68.
[72] Xuhui (n 3) 54.
[73] ibid 54.

which generates a 'complaint letter' by having the person select answer choices that align with a cause of action. However, the complaint letter can be used to initiate court proceedings, suggesting that it may also function as a form of originating process.[74] AI, through speech recognition, is also used to generate a transcript or trial record and to draft simple judgments.[75]

Hangzhou was also the first court to introduce a litigation guiding robot in October 2016 which was then adopted throughout China. The robot, called Hubao, is able to answer legal questions, suggest ways to resolve disputes and assist in selecting lawyers.[76] The first guiding robot in Beijing First Intermediate People's Court has been described as having the capacity to

> answer about 40,000 litigation questions and 30,000 legal issues. It knows more than 7,000 laws and regulations and can assist the parties in searching laws and procedures as well as the trial situation of similar cases according to the requirements of the parties.[77]

Role of the Lawyer after ODR

The role of the lawyer after AI is deployed in ODR is determined by citizen/client need and the cost and value provided by the lawyer. This is the same equation as existed prior to ODR, but ODR shifts what the citizen/client needs from a lawyer and what the lawyer must provide to continue to be relevant and then retained.

Citizen Expectations and Types of Disputes

The citizen's concept of justice in many developed countries has been defined by reference to courts – the independent, state-provided form of dispute resolution that is characterised by procedural fairness and open justice. The citizen sought to have their rights vindicated through their 'day in court'.[78] It was the court which offered the historical protections of due process that can be traced back to Magna Carta and which are enshrined in the Fifth Amendment of the US Constitution.[79]

[74] ibid.

[75] ibid 34.

[76] ibid 53. See also J Kang and A Zhang, 'Need Legal Advice in China? Ask a Robot' (2018) 260(23) *New York Law Journal* 2 (Chinese province of Qinghai made robots capable of answering 50,000 legal questions available to the public).

[77] Xuhui (n 3) 53.

[78] See B Garner (ed), *Black's Law Dictionary* (10th edn, Thomson Reuters, 2014) 481 'Day in Court' – '1. The right and opportunity, in a judicial tribunal, to litigate a claim, seek relief, or defend one's rights. 2. The right to be notified and given an opportunity to appear and he heard when one's case is called'.

[79] *R (on the application of UNISON) v Lord Chancellor* [2017] UKSC 51, [74]; *Constitution of the United States of America: Analysis, and Interpretation* (Congressional Research Service, Library of Congress, 2017) 1556–58.

Indeed, access to justice is a human right and is equated with 'a fair and public hearing by a competent, independent and impartial tribunal established by law'.[80]

The main obstacle to the 'day in court' or access to justice is cost. The legal fees to litigate a claim are unaffordable or greater than what is at stake.[81] Consequently the court system is only accessible by the wealthy (typically corporations and government) or those able to obtain legal aid or pro bono legal assistance.[82]

Applying theories of disruptive innovation, it has been said that there appears to be an incumbent collection of lawyers who are providing a range of high-priced services that a large segment of the population does not want or cannot afford, giving rise to a latent market for new entrants to serve.[83] The demand in that latent market is for cheap, and ideally quick, legal services, which can only be met through using technology.

At the same time citizen expectations are changing due to online experiences in other areas of life. Citizens now expect an online option including internet portals or smart phone apps.[84] Pressure to change may arise prior to direct competition because of 'liquid expectations', that is, consumer experiences from one industry create expectations in other industries.[85] For example, banking, ride-sharing and online marketplace apps or websites may influence citizens' views about how they should be able to access justice, or dispute resolution services.

However, to assume that every dispute can be addressed wholly online or with technology only would be to unduly homogenise citizen needs and/or types of dispute.

While cost will limit the legal services that a person can afford, it must be remembered that legal fees can be charged in a variety of ways depending on what is legal in a jurisdiction, so that contingency fees or conditional fees can alleviate cost pressures. Equally, litigation funding or insurance products may cover various legal costs. Of course the dispute must involve a quantum that renders these forms of funding economic.[86] Consequently, smaller-value claims (unless they can be grouped together for the purposes of litigation, eg as a class action) or non-monetary claims are unlikely to attract funding and online processes will be highly desirable.

[80] See *International Covenant on Civil and Political Rights*, opened for signature 16 December 1966, 99 UNTS 171 (entered into force 23 March 1976) art 14. See also *Universal Declaration of Human Rights*, GA Res. 217A (III), UN Doc A/810 at 71 (1948) art 8.

[81] R Brescia, 'What We Know and Need to Know about Disruptive Innovation' (2016) 67 *South Carolina Law Review* 203, 206; P Hodge, 'Law and Technological Change', *British Irish Commercial Bar Association*, Edinburgh, 4 April 2019) 8.

[82] Salter and Thompson (n 48) 118.

[83] Brescia (n 81) 206; R Susskind, *Tomorrow's Lawyers* (2nd edn, Oxford University Press, 2017) 128–29.

[84] American Bar Association, Commission on the Future of Legal Services, 'Report on the Future of Legal Services in the United States' (2016) 31.

[85] Katsh and Rabinovich-Einy (n 27) 150–54.

[86] S Yeazell, *Lawsuits in a Market Economy* (The University of Chicago Press, 2018) 33–55.

In addition to cost concerns the individual may desire or need legal assistance to understand their dispute and to choose and navigate a resolution process. An individual may desire the help of a lawyer to ensure their rights are protected[87] or to seek a solution that is not bounded by strict legal rights[88] – much depends on understanding what options (or strategies) are available. The individual may also seek understanding and trust from another person, the lawyer, to be able to confide in and know they have someone dedicated to protecting and advancing their interests – not the interests of the state or a commercial entity.

For 'important' disputes an internet portal or smart phone app may not meet the citizen's needs – too impersonal, too confidential, too quick – because the citizen wants to be heard, wants their dispute to be given due consideration, and/or wants a resolution according to law.

Delawyering

The role of the lawyer in dispute resolution described above, particularly in the trial setting, places the lawyer as a central actor. However, in contrast, in many of the examples of ODR described above the lawyer is eliminated from the process.

More and more commentators speak of law without lawyers.[89] In some instances legal representation may be precluded, while in others the ODR is thought to be sufficiently user-friendly that legal representation is no longer needed.[90] The desire for delawyering is straightforward – lawyers are too expensive, especially for smaller claims, but often even for a claim of $1 million, because the legal fees to litigate the claim are greater than what is at stake.[91]

If legal representation is not permitted, then the system has determined to 'delawyer'. However, if lawyers are not excluded by the system, then the decision falls to the user, who must weigh the costs and benefits of legal representation. For example, in England and Wales, to reduce costs the online court was to be designed for use by litigants without lawyers.[92] However, lawyers were not to be expressly excluded.[93] Rather, depending on the recovery-of-costs mechanism that

[87] M Legg and S Mirzabegian, 'Appropriate Dispute Resolution and the Role of Litigation' (2013) 38 *Australian Bar Review* 55.

[88] J Macfarlane, *The New Lawyer* (2nd edn, University of British Columbia Press, 2017) 54.

[89] Barton and Bibas (n 5) 116; N James, K Galloway, J Walkden-Brown, M Guihot, M Burgess and A Perry-Peterson, The Implications and Consequences of Law without Lawyers (Law Without Lawyers: Centre for Professional Legal Education Symposium, Bond University, Gold Coast, Australia, 19 October 2017); R Susskind, *Online Courts and the Future of Justice* (Oxford University Press, 2019) 102.

[90] Greenberg and Ebner (n 66) 22.

[91] Brescia (n 81) 206.

[92] Briggs – Interim Report (n 53) [6.5]; Briggs – Final Report (n 53) [6.22].

[93] The above discussion of the England and Wales online court system demonstrates that the approach discussed by Lord Briggs does not appear to have been carried over to the pilot studies, where the Online Civil Money Claims Pilot excluded lawyers and the County Court Online Pilot necessitated the use of lawyers.

was adopted, the result may be a lawyer-free online court 'by economic means'.[94] The costs mechanisms that exist in common law jurisdictions usually have to deal with two sets of costs: the person's own legal costs and any liability for the opponent's legal costs if a claim/defence is unsuccessful. As explained above in relation to client expectations, there are mechanisms for payment of a person's own legal costs. In relation to an opponent's costs, in some jurisdictions a successful party cannot recover their costs from the unsuccessful party (each party bears their own costs), while others do allow for cost shifting. If an individual must bear their own costs, either because mechanisms for covering legal fees are not available, or because they cannot recover from an unsuccessful opponent, the individual may be dissuaded from seeking legal assistance.

If lawyers are excluded or not retained by the user, achieving effective dispute resolution then falls on the technology and on the user. Even if lawyers are removed from the day-to-day dispute resolution it is still necessary to ensure that the ODR system operates fairly, and if applying the law rather than being a form of ADR, it is consistent with the law. Lawyers are prime candidates for ensuring fairness, and possibly the only candidate for ensuring compliance with the law. Effective dispute resolution also needs effective communication and understanding. Clarity of expression is crucial. As a result the AI needs to be teamed with legal design – the application of human-centred design to law to make the law more accessible and understandable.[95] Legal design aims to create better interfaces and tools as part of the ODR process. Achieving human-centred design requires inter-disciplinary teams, especially because users are not lawyers and the aim is to assist the user.[96] However, recognising the need for a variety of viewpoints does not mean excluding lawyers; to the contrary, lawyers are part of the inter-disciplinary team – they know the law and procedure.

Without lawyers the user or disputant needs to be self-sufficient. Below, a middle ground called limited scope services is discussed, where lawyers may play a role in only some steps. However, assuming no lawyer there will need to be assistance for many users in understanding what the ODR platform is asking and the ramifications of particular choices.[97] The Briggs Interim Report on the England and Wales online court observed there will be a need for 'substantial assistance online, in the form of digital help, for the purpose of completing online forms' as well as a telephone helpline.[98] In the Final Report, Lord Briggs reported that one of the most widespread issues raised in response to the recommendations in the Interim Report was how to assist persons who would find using a computer (or paper) to resolve their dispute challenging.[99] The concern has continued as online

[94] Briggs – Final Report (n 53) [6.25].
[95] See M Hagan, *Law by Design*, www.lawbydesign.co/en/home/, ch 1.
[96] ibid ch 2.
[97] F Bell, 'Family Law, Access to Justice, and Automation' (2019) 19 *Macquarie Law Journal* 103, 124.
[98] Briggs – Interim Report (n 53) [6.54]–[6.55].
[99] Briggs – Final Report (n 53) [6.2], [6.11].

processes have been rolled out in the English court system.[100] Similarly, in British Columbia it has been reported that between 3 per cent and 5 per cent of people do not use the internet.[101] The answer to these concerns is that there will remain a need to provide an analogue or in-person service for those without access to the technology or an inability to use the technology. Alternatively, or in addition, state-provided or volunteer in-person advice and assistance will be needed. Often the assumption is that the people providing this advice and assistance will be non-lawyers.[102] However, the persons providing this service may be legally trained, which creates a further role for lawyers or paralegals in the legal aid or not-for-profit sector as legal service assistants who combine knowledge of technology, law and assisting disadvantaged persons.[103] Alternatively, government could reduce infrastructure costs and extend geographic reach by allowing law firms to provide legal service assistance through lawyers or paralegals but at fixed rates payable by users. Various approaches may be envisaged. Once again the lawyer may be removed from the front line due to the use of expert systems, but the safety net requires lawyers.

A further source of assistance where ODR is at the court stage is the judge. Richard Susskind argues that it is time to 'recalibrate the division of labour between judges and court users' whereby judges 'nudge' parties to be clearer in their arguments, and to identify when evidence or 'a point' is missing.[104] It has been accepted that in providing a fair trial it may be appropriate for the judge to give some assistance to unrepresented parties, however the judge cannot give assistance in such a way as to conflict with his/her role as an impartial adjudicator.[105]

Limited Scope Services – 'Unbundling'

Limited scope services, also called unbundling, à la carte legal services, discrete task representation or disaggregated legal services, is a form of delivering legal services that involves breaking down a legal matter into various tasks, with a lawyer only providing representation for some or one of those tasks.[106] The disputant accepts the responsibility for undertaking the remainder of the legal matter until reaching the desired resolution.

[100] House of Commons Justice Committee, 'Court and Tribunal Reforms – Second Report of Session 2019' (31 October 2019) 16. For a contrary view see Susskind (n 89) ch 21.

[101] Salter (n 48) 116.

[102] Susskind (n 83) 98–99. However, see Susskind (n 89) 136–37 (referring to case officers who may or may not be lawyers).

[103] M Legg, 'UNSW Law Mini-Curriculum Review Report on Technology and the Law School Curriculum' [2017] UNSW Law Research Series 90, 6.

[104] Susskind (n 89) 154, 158.

[105] The Judicial Commission of NSW, *Equality before the Law Bench Book* (September 2019) [10.1].

[106] S Kimbro, 'Law a la Carte: The Case for Unbundling Legal Services' (2012) 29(5) *GPSolo*; LC Levin, 'The Monopoly Myth and Other Tales About the Superiority of Lawyers' (2014) 82 *Fordham Law Review* 2611, 2616–17.

Unbundling has been used to assist with access to justice and the provision of legal services to disputants with limited economic resources for many years.[107] The disputant simply cannot afford to retain a lawyer for all steps in addressing their legal issue and therefore seeks assistance with only some of those steps. In that context the disputant acts for themselves on those parts of the legal matter for which the lawyer does not act. The suggestion here is that the disputant utilises ODR but at various junctures may seek legal assistance depending on their needs.[108]

To understand unbundling it is useful to look at the role of the barrister in countries such as England and Australia, and to further consider the role of the lawyer in mediation as developed above.

The barrister who only provides legal advice or advocacy is an obvious form of unbundling that has a long history in England and Australia. However, traditionally a client wishing to brief a barrister would first retain a solicitor, who would then brief the barrister.[109] Unbundling has taken on a new complexion in relation to barristers as it is now possible to directly brief a barrister. In England the public access scheme allows members of the public to instruct a barrister directly. The Public Access Guidelines explain to the public the steps that remain with them – being able to gather together the papers and the evidence in support of their case, to file documents at court (for example expert reports or witness statements) and write to the court and other parties.[110]

To draw on an example from Australia, the Bar Association of Queensland sets out the types of work that can be suitable for direct briefing:

- Legal advice – written or in conference;
- Provide advice on dispute resolution, including strategy and resourcing;
- Negotiate for a client to settle or compromise a case, or represent a client in mediation, arbitration or other form of dispute resolution; and
- Appearing in litigation – direct briefing is particularly suited to urgent applications and less complex matters.[111]

The range of roles that a lawyer may play in mediation as depicted above using Rundle's categories may also be seen as an example of unbundling. The lawyer can take a limited role and only assist in preparing for a mediation, or the lawyer can attend the mediation and advise, or the lawyer can negotiate on the client's behalf, having also performed the other roles, or only being involved in the actual mediation.

[107] See Australian Law Reform Commission, *Managing Justice: A Review of the Federal Civil Justice System, Report 89* (2000) [5.158]; A de Smidt and K Dodgson, 'Unbundling Our Way to Outcomes: QPILCH's Self Representation Service at QCAT, Two Years On' (2012) 21 *Journal of Judicial Administration* 246; The Law Society UK, 'Practice Note – Unbundling Civil Legal Services (19 March 2015) [1.2].

[108] Briggs – Final Report (n 53) [6.36]–[6.37]; Susskind (n 89) 237.

[109] GE Dal Pont, *Lawyers' Professional Responsibility* (5th edn, Thomson Reuters, 2013) [3.30].

[110] The Bar Standards Board, 'Public Access Guidance for Lay Clients' (October 2019).

[111] Bar Association of Queensland, 'Briefing Barristers Directly' (undated).

Unbundling allows for access to legal expertise at those points in the dispute resolution process where it is needed and affordable. However, as explained above in relation to delawyering, there will be situations where a person, due to their characteristics or the nature of the dispute, really should have legal assistance for all steps.

While unbundling can provide more tailored and cheaper legal assistance, it can create concerns for the lawyer. For the lawyer providing unbundled legal services the usual professional and ethics requirements still apply to the part of the matter being performed, such as competence, diligence, confidentiality and duties to the court. Consequently, while the scope of representation may be limited, the professional and ethics requirements apply in full. If unbundling is not supported by relevant court and ethics rules lawyers may be reluctant to take unbundled matters on.[112]

Defender of the Rule of Law and of the Client

Courts are 'not just another provider of dispute resolution services in a market of different providers' but rather are unique in that they 'carry out the adjudication function involving the exercise of judicial power'.[113] Moreover, the courts give effect to the rule of law by ensuring that all members of society, including government, are bound by, and act consistently with, the law.[114] Litigation is the practical way in which the rule of law is secured as it involves the application of the law and the vindication of rights.[115] Lawyers play an important part in facilitating the role of the courts and protecting the rule of law.[116] The litigation system proceeds on the basis that 'the skill and probity of specialist trial advocates is a vital element in protecting and advancing the rule of law'.[117] Moreover, as explained above:

> [J]ustice is most likely to be achieved as the outcome of a contest in which the case of each opposing party is presented by a professional advocate, learned in the law, and

[112] M Legg, 'Recognising a New Form of Legal Practice – Limited Scope Services' (2018) 50 *Law Society Journal* 74.

[113] R French, 'Perspectives on Court Annexed Alternative Dispute Resolution', Law Council of Australia – Multi-Door Symposium, Canberra, 27 July 2009. Judicial power may be defined 'as the power of a sovereign authority to decide controversies between its subjects or between itself and its subjects … by ascertainment of the facts, by application of the law and by exercise, where appropriate, of judicial discretion': *Fencott v Muller* (1983) 152 CLR 570, 608.

[114] AV Dicey, *Introduction to the Study of the Law of the Constitution* (10th edn, Macmillan & Co, 1960) 188–203; *R (on the application of UNISON) v Lord Chancellor* [2017] UKSC 51 [68].

[115] J Jacob, *The Hamlyn Lectures 1986 – The Fabric of English Civil Justice* (Stevens & Sons, 1987) 66; H Edwards, 'Alternative Dispute Resolution: Panacea or Anathema?' (1986) 99(3) *Harvard Law Review* 668, 671; G Brennan, 'The State of the Judicature' (1998) 72 *Australian Law Journal* 33, 35.

[116] T Bingham, *The Rule of Law* (Penguin Books, 2011) 92–93; American Bar Association, Model Rules of Professional Conduct: Preamble, [6] ('a lawyer should further the public's understanding of and confidence in the rule of law and the justice system because legal institutions in a constitutional democracy depend on popular participation and support to maintain their authority').

[117] Heydon (n 15) 23.

> operating within the constraints and disciplines of an organised profession whose members owe a duty not only to their clients but also to the court.[118]

The lawyer's duty to their client, which includes acting to protect and promote their client's interests within the bounds of the law, advances the individual's rights. Procedural fairness, which is a defining characteristic of courts and the rule of law, includes providing each party to proceedings 'with an opportunity to be heard, to advance its own case and to answer, by evidence and argument, the case put against it'.[119] Competent legal representation best allows for a client to secure the protections of procedural fairness. More generally, the lawyers' duties promote public confidence in the justice system.

A continuing role for lawyers may be argued to be necessary from an institutional perspective. The lawyer is crucial to the operation of the court system and to the maintenance of the rule of law in a democracy.

Even with the advent of AI, there remains a continuing role for the existing court system and it must be accessible, with legal representation, for individuals.[120] Technology, including AI, may assist in the provision of justice but the technology must uphold or be used in a manner that upholds the fundamental values that characterise the rule of law, such as procedural fairness.[121] Indeed the role of the lawyer will be to challenge the use of technology where it is not consistent with the rule of law, which is most likely to arise when it impinges on the client's rights.[122] Technology will provide the capacity to reconfigure the court and its processes as historically conceived. While it may be unnecessary 'to congregate physically in a court building to resolve [disputes]',[123] it is necessary to preserve fairness.[124]

However, the initiation of litigation is a voluntary act and a person does not have to commence litigation regardless of how important the issue to be determined is.[125] Choosing ADR or OADR may be preferred. Indeed scholars have challenged the idea that litigation is the only source of justice.[126] However, the rule of law still

[118] Gleeson (n 16) 1. See also A Lahav, *In Praise of Litigation* (Oxford University Press, 2017) 5 ('The central contribution of litigation is to promote reasoned discussion of competing values through the language of the law by allowing individuals to present their arguments on equal terms and with information that supports those arguments').

[119] *International Finance Trust Co Ltd v New South Wales Crime Commission* (2009) 240 CLR 319, 354 [54].

[120] See Lahav (n 118) 7–8.

[121] Legg (n 1) 229.

[122] See, eg, American Bar Association (n 84) 45–46.

[123] Online Dispute Resolution Advisory Group, *Online Dispute Resolution for Low Value Civil Claims* (Civil Justice Council, February 2015) [1.9]; R Susskind and D Susskind, *The Future of the Professions* (Oxford University Press, 2015) 70.

[124] Legg (n 1) 229; J Allsop, 'Technology and the Future of the Courts' (2019) 38(1) *University of Queensland Law Journal* 1, 3.

[125] JA Jolowicz, *On Civil Procedure* (Cambridge University Press, 2000) 21.

[126] C Menkel-Meadow, 'Whose Dispute Is It Anyway?: A Philosophical and Democratic Defense of Settlement (In Some Cases)' (1995) 83 *Georgetown Law Journal* 2663, 2669–70; Macfarlane (n 88).

looms large.[127] Consequently, even where a person may seek to resolve a dispute outside of the formal court system using OADR, fairness will still be crucial.[128] As discussed above, a person may desire the assistance of a lawyer to ensure their interests are protected. Society also has an interest in fair dispute resolution. Why a lawyer? Because of their duties to the administration of justice and to the client.

These concerns about the rule of law and fairness are reflected in the European Ethical Charter on the use of AI in judicial systems and their environment, which the European Commission for the Efficiency of Justice (CEPEJ) adopted at its 31st plenary meeting on 3–4 December 2018.[129] The CEPEJ identified five core principles to be respected in the field of AI and justice, including the first principle:[130] 'Principle of respect of fundamental rights: ensuring that the design and implementation of artificial intelligence tools and services are compatible with fundamental rights'. In relation to Principle 1 the CEPEJ draws on Article 6 of the European Convention on Human Rights[131] (ECHR) and explains that

> when artificial intelligence tools are used to resolve a dispute or as a tool to assist in judicial decision-making or to give guidance to the public, it is essential to ensure that they do not undermine … the right to a fair trial (equality of arms and respect for the adversarial process).
>
> They should also be used with due respect for the principles of the rule of law and judges' independence in their decision-making process.[132]

[127] C Parker, 'Access to Justice' in C Parker, *Just Lawyers: Regulation and Access to Justice* (Oxford University Press, 1999) 30, 47–54; M Moffitt, 'Which Is Better, Food or Water: The Rule of Law or ADR?' (2010) 4 *Dispute Resolution Magazine* 8, 14.

[128] See, eg, J Nolan-Haley, 'Informed Consent in Mediation: A Guiding Principle for Truly Educated Decisionmaking' (1999) 74 *Notre Dame Law Review* 775, 787 fn. 57 ('There is little dispute that fairness is the fundamental goal of any dispute resolution process including mediation'); S Elnegahy, 'Can Mediation Deliver Justice?' (2017) 18 *Cardozo Journal of Conflict Resolution* 759, 777; Sela (n 32) 680–81.

[129] European Commission for the Efficiency of Justice (CEPEJ), *European Ethical Charter on the Use of Artificial Intelligence (AI) in Judicial Systems and their Environment* (2018) rm.coe.int/ethical-charter-en-for-publication-4-december-2018/16808f699c.

[130] The other principles are:

2. Principle of non-discrimination: specifically preventing the development or intensification of any discrimination between individuals or groups of individuals;
3. Principle of quality and security: with regard to the processing of judicial decisions and data, using certified sources and intangible data with models conceived in a multi-disciplinary manner, in a secure technological environment;
4. Principle of transparency, impartiality and fairness: making data processing methods accessible and understandable, authorising external audits;
5. Principle 'under user control': precluding a prescriptive approach and ensuring that users are informed actors and in control of their choices.

[131] Article 6 provides: (1) In the determination of his civil rights and obligations or of any criminal charge against him, everyone is entitled to a fair and public hearing within a reasonable time by an independent and impartial tribunal established by law.

[132] CEPEJ (n 129) 8. In relation to Principle 4 it was also recognised that there was a need for 'fairness and intellectual integrity (prioritising the interests of justice)' 11. For an example of the interaction between technology and the rule of law see Salter (n 48) 117 ('administrative law requires that people have the right to be heard, even though it might be more efficient from a data processing and storage perspective for a software program to impose a character limit on submissions').

The lawyer is trained, practised and ethically obligated to uphold the rule of law and protect their client's interests. These skills and obligations transcend the method of dispute resolution. In particular, in an ODR world, they apply outside of the traditional trial in the physical court building.

Human Needs – Human Skills

AI will increase the relative value of exclusively 'human' skills, including emotional intelligence, empathy, trust, cooperation, creativity and wisdom.[133] These skills are of particular importance in dealing with a client engaged in a dispute and as part of the lawyer performing their role in the dispute resolution process.

Human skills such as trust, wisdom and empathy are core components of advocacy. The law depends on reasoning and logic but it is also very much a human endeavour. The advocate must present their case in a rational and logical way to allow the fact finder to follow and assess the argument. The lawyer uses inductive and deductive reasoning.[134] Moreover, reasoning by analogy or example is said to be 'The basic pattern of legal reasoning'.[135] However, as Wellman and Harris in their discussions of advocacy above indicate, advocacy is very much a human undertaking, involving the advocate using human skills to interact with other humans – judge, jury, witness, client. In more recent times, Chief Justice Allsop of the Federal Court of Australia, in reflecting on the meaning of independence for the advocate, observed:

> It involves being human and recognising the human elements at play in a dispute. It involves recognition and appreciation of the whole. It involves bringing wisdom to resolution of the dispute. It involves wisdom in presentation of the case. It involves integrity, respect and civility … Independence (and the degree of abstraction within it) involves the recognition of the significance of the dispute to the lives of the humans involved. Every advocate (and every judge) should be conscious that what might seem a routine or banal case may represent the most significant and potentially catastrophic event in the lives of the people involved.[136]

Human skills are also necessary for effective negotiation and mediation.[137] A central feature of interest-based negotiation and mediation as developed by the Harvard Negotiation Programme and the *Getting to Yes* text by Roger Fisher,

[133] This is discussed more generally in Chapter 12.

[134] See, eg, E Levi, *An Introduction to Legal Reasoning* (University of Chicago Press, 1949) 27.

[135] ibid 1–3.

[136] J Allsop, 'The Future of the Independent Bar in Australia' (Australian Bar Association and NSW Bar Association Biennial Conference, Sydney, 17 November 2018).

[137] D Remus and F Levy, 'Can Robots Be Lawyers: Computers, Lawyers, and the Practice of Law' (2017) 30(3) *Georgetown Journal of Legal Ethics* 501, 527; S Schoonmaker, 'Withstanding Disruptive Innovation: How Attorneys Will Adapt and Survive Impending Challenges from Automation and Nontraditional Legal Services Providers' (2017) 51 *Family Law Quarterly* 133, 146.

William Ury and Bruce Patton is the development of a range of options that satisfy the parties' interests.[138] As a result there is space for 'creative problem solving'.[139] Creativity can arise in varied circumstances and be applied in quite different ways. Rosenberry, in an essay extolling the importance of creative thinking in law, gives the following example of when a person failed to pay the 'assessments' (strata fees) to the owners association of an apartment block:

> Instead of immediately resorting to legal procedures, the association inquired and discovered that the owner had not paid his assessments because he had lost his job. So they loaned him money at market rate interest to pay the late assessments. The other owners then contacted their friends and relatives and found the person a job, making it possible for him to pay back the loan and pay assessments on time in the future.[140]

Rosenberry points out that while there was a clear 'legal' remedy available to the association to compel payment of the fees, the approach taken was more effective as it provided a long-term solution and engendered positive feelings between those involved.[141] The example demonstrates an understanding of when *not* to use a legal remedy and the generation of alternative options, which AI would not be capable of. AI cannot think outside the box.

A further example is family law, which suffers from significant access-to-justice problems.[142] However, ODR alone may not meet the needs of people undergoing a divorce, especially when children are involved. People needing to adapt to an altered but necessarily continuing relationship due to the presence of children may want options that work well for everyone involved rather than strict legal outcomes.[143] Moreover, as Julie Macfarlane found in her study of Canadian self-represented parties, 'Many … expressed the need for more than on-line resources, however good – a need for human contact and support as they navigate the justice system and prepare their case to the best of their ability'.[144] Humanity and empathy are needed in facing difficult times.

While human skills may become more valued, that does not mean they become more affordable. Consequently, there will still be disputes where a person foregoes access to human skills because the ODR can resolve the dispute more cheaply. ODR can replace or significantly reduce the role of humans and instead use AI

[138] R Fisher, W Ury and B Patton, *Getting to Yes* (2nd edn, Penguin Books, 1991) ch 4.
[139] K Rosenberry, 'Organizational Barriers to Creativity in Law Schools and the Legal Profession' (2005) 41(2) *California Western Law Review* 423, 425, citing TM Amabile, 'Entrepreneurial Creativity Through Motivational Synergy' (1997) 31 *Journal of Creative Behavior* 18, 18; see also R Florida, *The Rise of the Creative Class* (Basic Books, 2004) 69.
[140] ibid 424.
[141] ibid.
[142] Bell (n 97) 112.
[143] ibid.
[144] J Macfarlane, 'The National Self-Represented Litigants Project: Identifying and Meeting the Needs of Self-Represented Litigants' (Final Report, May 2013) 67.

to become the third party that performs the mediation or decision making.[145] An example is 'blind-bidding' systems which use multivariate algorithms to help parties arrive at the optimal outcome. The technology obtains information from the disputants as to how they rank or value issues within the dispute and then combines those outcomes to suggest solutions.[146] This type of ODR is not appropriate for every dispute, but where involving the human lawyer is not cost-effective it may present as the only viable option.

Future Developments

More Technology, but will it be AI?

As explained at the commencement of this chapter ODR may employ a range of technologies. It remains an open question as to which technologies will receive the greatest adoption. Many ODR projects, but especially those that are state run, may choose to focus on using more commonplace technology, such as internet portals, instant messaging and video conferencing, to reduce cost and increase convenience because major gains can be made without investing in expensive and still-developing AI technology. Indeed, the COVID-19 pandemic forced courts to more broadly adopt information and communications technology to be able to continue operating while also complying with health recommendations. This included using internet portals and email to facilitate access to court-related documents. The pandemic also necessitated quickly moving to online hearings, and trials in some cases, which saw the increased use of court-specific audio-visual technology or the adoption of other platforms such as Microsoft Teams or Cisco WebEx.[147] This experience is likely to make courts more open to the continued use of information and communications technology in appropriate circumstances. This may facilitate an acceptance of other technologies, such as AI. Alternatively, there may be a view that having modernised to a degree, and needing to more fully evaluate and, where appropriate, incorporate those technologies into court processes, there will be little enthusiasm for more change, at least in the short to medium term.

Equally, expert systems, which have a long history in law, have been successfully developed as shown by the Civil Resolution Tribunal in British Columbia

[145] S Shackelford and A Raymond, 'Building the Virtual Courthouse: Ethical Considerations for Design, Implementation, and Regulation in the World of ODR' (2014) *Wisconsin Law Review* 615, 628; S Van Arsdale, 'User Protections in Online Dispute Resolution' (2015) 21 *Harvard Negotiation Law Review* 107, 118–19.

[146] A Raymond and S Shackelford, 'Technology, Ethics, and Access to Justice: Should an Algorithm Be Deciding Your Case? (2014) 35 *Michigan Journal of International Law* 485, 514–15.

[147] M Legg and A Song, 'The Courts and the Pandemic: The Role and Limits of Technology' (2020) 66 *Law Society Journal* 65.

adopting the Solution Explorer. However, its success is not due wholly to AI, or to technology. Two of its architects have emphasised that it adopts a 'user-focussed justice design' and is a 'human-driven process'.[148] Much depends on adopting technology that the user can in fact understand and use – the user interface may be as, or more important, than the underlying technology. Further, users may need access to assistance. The later steps of online ADR and online hearings utilise information and communications technology. Employing expert systems in an end-to-end ODR system requires a holistic approach that goes beyond AI.

In the private sector, such as e-commerce platforms, the aim is to remove humans as much as possible because they are costly, and there is therefore a greater incentive to utilise effective AI, which has primarily been expert systems. E-commerce may be the main laboratory for AI-driven ODR although the Chinese experience where Zhejiang province collaborated with Alibaba may see e-commerce experiments impacting court systems.

However, expert systems have limitations – they are hard coded, drawing on human expertise, and may gain limited traction where the legal options multiply and standards are more abstract and open ended, such as reasonableness, unconscionability or good faith.[149] The programming required for an expert system is time consuming as all the rules (and any changes to the rules) must be expressly prescribed.[150] This is referred to as the 'knowledge acquisition bottleneck'[151] as the way the system acquires new knowledge is inefficient. As a result, expert systems are likely to be developed for more static and straightforward areas of law.

Accepting the factors against the adoption of expert systems, it still seems likely that given the need for access to justice for small and straightforward claims, the expert system's ability to provide tailored information and direction (or triage) at scale makes it a desirable option. However, careful planning and user interaction is needed. Much turns on the abilities of the human team designing the expert system.

Looking further into the future one may ask: could AI be designed to obtain the facts, determine the relevant law and apply it?[152] The outcome may be a recommendation for a human judicial officer, or an AI-generated determination that may be binding or non-binding. The current use of AI in this vein, ie outcome prediction, was discussed in Chapter 4. Here the suggestion is that the prediction *is* the result or outcome. AI provides an answer to a certain degree of statistical accuracy. The AI answer could be a further input into a judge's decision or it could be the final

[148] Salter and Thompson (n 48) 134–35.

[149] H Surden, 'Artificial Intelligence and Law: An Overview' (2019) 35(4) *Georgia State University Law Review* 1305, 1322, 1326.

[150] Susskind (n 83) 186.

[151] SJ Russell and P Norvig, *Artificial Intelligence: A Modern Approach* (3rd edn, Pearson, 2016) 28; M Aikenhead, 'The Uses and Abuses of Neural Networks in Law' (1996) 12 *Santa Clara Computer & High Technology Law Journal* 31.

[152] Susskind (n 89) ch 27.

outcome. However, for it to be either there would be an expectation that it would be accurate and fair. The limitations of AI are discussed in detail in Chapter 10.

Complex and High-stakes Disputes

The removal of lawyers from the dispute resolution process is most likely to occur where the type of dispute has a narrow range of variables and follows a known and limited number of paths to an outcome.[153] Lawyers may currently have little concern with, or more likely welcome, technology that services a market of great need but which they cannot profitably service. However, as the forms of ODR improve they may then move into areas where claim values are higher and/or the law and procedure is more complicated.[154] Sir Geoffrey Vos, Chancellor of the High Court of England and Wales, has observed:

> I hear many people in the Business and Property Courts saying that the online solutions court is not really their concern, because major litigation will carry on as before. I do not agree. I think that business lawyers need to look very closely at the developments in smaller litigation, because these are bound to be the blueprint for the roll-out of online dispute resolution to more significant and high value disputes.[155]

For high-value claims where the law is less complicated ODR may be able to gain traction as persons seek to minimise transaction costs. As more is at stake an individual may want legal expertise. Indeed the courts in their proportionality rules assume that it is permissible to expend more on legal costs when the stakes are higher.[156] However, value of a claim and complexity do not have to be aligned.

For ODR systems employing AI to move into the more complicated areas of law it would seem likely that some form of advanced AI will be necessary, and even then insufficient alone in many instances. For complex areas AI may only operate in relation to a subset of issues or steps, perhaps as an aid to decision making as is discussed in Chapter 4. The degree to which AI can be employed will depend on the degree and speed with which it advances. Expert systems may be able to model more complex environments, but greater advances may come from machine learning. In the immediate future it is more likely that non-AI technology, mainly in relation to online communication, will be deployed in complex cases.[157]

[153] Barton and Bibas (n 5) 154; D Farrands, 'Artificial Intelligence and Litigation – Future Possibilities' (Victorian Bar CPD Programme, 22 December 2017) 24.

[154] Schoonmaker (n 137) 141 (discussing the operation and critique of Clayton Christensen's theory of disruptive innovation).

[155] G Vos, 'The Law Society's Inaugural Lecture on the Future of Law' (speech delivered 8 May 2018) [22]–[23]. See also Remus and Levy (n 137) 528 (stating that Modria aims to expand into larger and more complicated disputes).

[156] See, eg, Civil Procedure Rules (England) r 1.1, Federal Rules of Civil Procedure (US) r 26(b)(1). Greater costs are also permitted for more complex litigation: M Legg, *Case Management and Complex Civil Litigation* (Federation Press, 2011) 43–46.

[157] See *Capic v Ford Motor Company of Australia Limited (Adjournment)* [2020] FCA 486 and *Australian Securities and Investments Commission v GetSwift Limited* [2020] FCA 504 where the Federal

Simplified Process – Simplified Law

Courts have been criticised for operating on the assumption that every litigant has a lawyer and court processes can proceed on the basis that users are legally trained. Indeed the self-represented or pro-se litigant is seen as an anomaly but in many areas of law this is the norm.[158] When an individual confronts a complex and inaccessible court process this undermines public confidence in the justice system.[159] As a result the question has been posed as to what a court would look like if it were designed for non-lawyers.[160] Processes would have to be simplified and expressed in plain language. Such a change could also assist ODR, including AI systems.

The question may be expressed more broadly as to what laws would look like if they had to be understood and applied by non-lawyers. One response is that laws may be simplified or redesigned so as to be more definitive. This is turn could make the interpretation and/or application of those laws by AI more of a possibility, although new laws would be more difficult to address through expert systems or machine learning as there would be a dearth of expert knowledge or data for design and training.

However, there are at least two possible drawbacks to simplification/definitiveness. First, complexity often comes from abstract or value-laden concepts which necessitate judgement. Do humans want a legal system that excludes discretion and humanity?[161] Second, is such simplification possible when the law must reflect the complexity and changing nature of the subject matter that it regulates to be effective? For example, principle-based regulation was designed to allow the law to adapt and prevent 'legal-engineering' aimed at evading rule-based regulation that can be under-inclusive.[162]

More Disputes

Much of the market for ODR is based on there being a latent legal market that is underserved. If that market is able to access ODR then instead of 'lumping it' when a dispute arises, they will instead be able to take action.[163] This is portrayed as a positive for access to justice. However, it must be remembered that when it is

Court of Australia determined that the trial of a class action and a regulatory suit (civil penalty), respectively, would be conducted using audio/video conferencing.

[158] Barton and Bibas (n 5) 145.

[159] American Bar Association (n 84) 33.

[160] Barton and Bibas (n 5) 146.

[161] See, eg, K Leetaru, 'Will AI-Powered Law Enforcement Force Us To Rewrite Our Laws?' *Forbes* (13 August 2018).

[162] D McBarnet and C Whelan, 'The Elusive Spirit of the Law: Formalism and the Struggle for Legal Control' (1991) 54 *Modern Law Review* 848; M Legg, 'Regulatory Theory, Litigation and Enforcement' in M Legg (ed), *Regulation, Litigation and Enforcement* (Thomson Reuters, 2011) 11.

[163] J Paquin, 'Avengers, Avoiders and Lumpers: The Incidence of Disputing Style on Litigiousness' (2001) 19 *Windsor Yearbook of Access to Justice* 3; D Coates and S Penrod, 'Social Psychology and the Emergence of Disputes' (1980–81) 15 *Law and Society Review* 655.

easier and cheaper to resort to a dispute resolution mechanism then people may do so more often. Frances McGovern, a class actions and ADR expert, explained that as courts became more efficient at achieving resolution of disputes, including through settlements, this resulted in more filings as plaintiffs were attracted by the quicker and cheaper process.[164] It is important to remember that facilitating the resolution of disputes may have some negative aspects, such as creating disputes.

Avoiding Disputes

The conduct of dispute resolution online and the existence of big data now mean that information about the source and types of disputes can be captured and employed to determine how disputes might be avoided. There is a secondary research function in addition to the conflict resolution function. For example, conflicts that arise because of a misunderstanding or lack of clarity around contractual requirements or consumer protection laws could signal a need to better explain those requirements/laws, or possibly suggest reform.[165] eBay and Alibaba have already started to use AI in this way so as to understand and respond to client expectations.[166]

Conclusion

The use of AI in ODR holds out the prospect of greater access to dispute resolution services, including access to justice. However, ADR and courts are not purely mechanical dispute resolvers. To a greater or lesser extent, depending on the particular process, they require procedures for ensuring fairness and justice, as well as extending humanity to the disputants, not just efficiency. The lawyer has both an institutional and humanitarian role in dispute resolution.

[164] See, eg, F McGovern, 'An Analysis of Mass Torts for Judges' (1994) 73 *Texas Law Review* 1821; F McGovern, 'Settlement of Mass Torts in a Federal System' (2001) 36 *Wake Forest Law Review* 871.

[165] See O Rabinovich-Einy and E Katsh, 'Lessons from Online Dispute Resolution for Dispute Systems Design' in M Abdel Wahab, E Katsh and D Rainey (eds), *Online Dispute Resolution: Theory and Practice* (Eleven International Publishing, 2012) 42 (discussing the approaches used by eBay and Wikipedia); Katsh and Rule (n 2) 330 ('a large amount of data on disputing patterns is now available, and algorithms can now analyze that data quickly and efficiently, gleaning patterns and lessons that a human would not be able to discern').

[166] Katsh and Rabinovich-Einy (n 27) 35, 66.

7

AI and Transactional Lawyers

Introduction

Of the many areas of practice and categories into which we might divide members of the legal profession, transactional lawyers are among those most affected by AI. Staples of transactional law such as contract review, contract creation and due diligence are all being impacted by AI.

'Transactional' law is typically contrasted with litigation. Rather than litigating, the archetypal transactional lawyer is focused on 'front-end' work or 'deal making'.[1] Ironically, despite the ubiquity of the lawyer-as-litigator image, transactional law is more pervasive: most lawyers spend their time facilitating transactions.[2] Transactional law is also often lucrative. In its transnational sphere it is significant to multinational companies, global law and professional services firms, and indeed the global economic order.[3] These underpinnings also give security: Elisabeth de Fontenay notes that the top-tier global law firms – engaged in high-stakes corporate transactions – retained their status even post the global financial crisis, when downturn and failure were affecting the market for legal services more generally.[4] The resources available to both firms and clients, and the fact that many companies themselves have large in-house legal departments, have spurred AI developments for transactional law. While various forms of automation are quite long-standing, there is increasing use of machine learning or 'big data' methods too. Noting that this field is 'a densely populated space', Robert Dale identifies especially the prevalence of LegalTech applications for contract review and document automation.[5]

In this chapter, we give an overview of the work of transactional lawyers, which spans work for individuals, work for corporations; contracts, financing and enterprise formation. Transactional law is enmeshed with the in-house lawyer role as

[1] RK Neumann Jr, *Transactional Lawyering Skills: Becoming a Deal Lawyer* (Wolters Kluwer, 2012).

[2] For instance, the Law Society of England and Wales reported that more solicitors reported practising in the area of 'business affairs' than any other category: *Categories of Work Undertaken by Solicitors 2015*, 7 December 2015, 1.

[3] See D McBarnet, 'Transnational Transactions: Legal Work, Crossborder Commerce and Global Regulation' in M Likosky (ed), *Transnational Legal Processes: Globalisation and Power Disparities* (Cambridge University Press, 2002) 98.

[4] E de Fontenay, 'Law Firm Selection and the Value of Transactional Lawyering' (2015) 41(2) *Journal of Corporation Law* 393.

[5] R Dale, 'Law and Word Order: NLP in Legal Tech' (2019) 25(1) *Natural Language Engineering* 211. The other categories Dale describes are legal research, electronic discovery and legal advice.

it comprises a substantial part of what most corporate counsel do, and they make up a large and often influential portion of transactional lawyers. Transactional lawyers may also advise on compliance in areas such as tax, banking and securities. These regulatory aspects we deal with comprehensively in the next chapter, Chapter 8, in light of AI's particular applications for regulation and compliance.

In this chapter we discuss where AI is being used in transactional law, adopting the categories of analysis, review, management and drafting to consider its different applications. We then analyse the role of the transactional lawyer in using AI applications. Finally, we consider future developments.

Transactional Law, Contract Commoditisation and Lawyers

A large body of scholarly work has investigated transactional law, especially contracting, and the associated role of transactional lawyers. Such studies traverse the economic and the sociological; the behavioural and the organisational. They may centre on lawyers or have a wider purview – like Ronald Coase's theory of the firm,[6] or relational theories of contract.[7] In many areas, transactional law has grown massively in complexity. Contracts tend to be much longer and more intricate than they historically were, increasing both transaction and enforcement costs.[8] One answer to this has been found in standardisation, referring to the use and re-use of the same or standard forms of terms, also termed 'boilerplate'. Some academic writing, particularly on contract law, has focussed on standardisation and customisation in drafting.[9] Standardisation is important for efficiency in negotiating agreements,[10] regardless of the nature or scale of the transaction. For simple consumer contracts, standardisation might simplify the process of contracting, though it may also skew against the consumer:

> Over time, certain types of contracts can become commoditized, by operation of the market or even by regulatory fiat. [Particular contracts] for example, may have terms that are substantively identical … and are never negotiated with the consumer.

[6] RH Coase, 'The Problem of Social Cost' (1960) 3 *Journal of Law and Economics* 1 (Coase's theory of the firm famously posited that transaction costs largely explain the emergence of vertically integrated firms. Where the transaction costs of market exchanges – including calculating prices, negotiating deals and accounting for future uncertainty – exceed those of coordinating production within hierarchical firms, vertical integration will prevail).

[7] I Macneil, 'Contracting Worlds and Essential Contract Theory' (2000) 9 *Social and Legal Studies* 431; S Macaulay, 'Non-Contractual Relations in Business: A Preliminary Study' (1963) 28 *American Sociological Review* 55.

[8] M Jennejohn, 'The Architecture of Contract Innovation' (2018) 59(1) *Boston College Law Review* 71, 74.

[9] M Kahan and M Klausner, 'Standardization and Innovation in Corporate Contracting (or "The Economics of Boilerplate")' (1997) 83 *Virginia Law Review* 713; M Klausner, 'Corporations, Corporate Law, and Networks of Contracts' (1995) 81 *Virginia Law Review* 757.

[10] MR Patterson, 'Standardization of Standard-Form Contracts: Competition and Contract Implications' (2010) 52 *William and Mary Law Review* 327.

> Uniform terms and the absence of bargaining make the contracting process a simple exercise: the consumer need only look up the going market price and decide whether or not to transact.[11]

The peculiarities of 'stickiness' in contract terms – the continual reusing of certain terms, even where those terms are imprecise or have been subjected to differing interpretation, rendering their effect uncertain – has also been investigated.[12] It is often thought that stickiness is a response to the transaction costs of changing clauses, when the market has adapted to certain standard terms, though this is not always necessarily the case.[13] In any event, the use of precedent agreements is widespread in transactional law, though 'major bilateral transactions' do continue to be marked by individually (and privately) negotiated terms.[14] The significance of the use of standard terms and precedents for AI is that, as one law firm data scientist has said, contracts are 'kind of neatly organised'[15] – making them easier to break down into component parts. Further, there are many similar examples available.

What, then, is the role of the transactional lawyer in this context? In the 1980s Ronald Gilson conceived of the transactional lawyer as 'cost engineer', one whose value to clients comes through devising transactional structures that reduce uncertainty costs.[16] Gilson explained:

> [T]he tie between legal skills and transaction value is the business lawyer's ability to create a transactional structure which reduces transaction costs and therefore results in more accurate asset pricing … My hypothesis about what business lawyers really do – their potential to create value – is simply this: Lawyers function as *transaction cost engineers*, devising efficient mechanisms which bridge the gap between capital asset pricing theory's hypothetical world of perfect markets and the less-than-perfect reality of effecting transactions in this world.[17]

In later work linking transactional law and negotiation, Gilson and Robert Mnookin had noted that both 'value creation and *value division* are central to what business lawyers do' (emphasis added).[18] In other words, transactional lawyers are concerned with maximising the value of transactions overall, but also in obtaining

[11] De Fontenay (n 4) 406.

[12] M Gulati and RE Scott, *The 3½ Minute Transaction: Boilerplate and the Limits of Contract Design* (University of Chicago Press, 2013); DG MacDiarmid, SJ Korney, M Teetaert, JJM Taylor, R Martz and RE Slaney, 'The Oil and Gas ROFR: Understanding Current ROFR Issues from the Point of View of the Transactional Lawyer, the Litigator, and In-House Counsel' (2017) 55(2) *Alberta Law Review* 253.

[13] Gulati and Scott (n 12).

[14] De Fontenay (n 4) 407.

[15] G Orum Hernandez, 'Artificial Intelligence Has Found a Home in Contract Management' (2016) 222(32) *New Jersey Law Journal* 30 (quoting B Borden).

[16] RJ Gilson, 'Value Creation by Business Lawyers: Legal Skills and Asset Pricing' (1984) 94(2) *Yale Law Journal* 239, 255.

[17] ibid 255.

[18] RJ Gilson and RH Mnookin, 'Foreword: Business Lawyers and Value Creation for Clients' (1995) 74(1) *Oregon Law Review* 1, 3.

the best deal for their client.[19] In a 2009 article, George Dent Jr argued that Gilson had framed his analysis too narrowly (and that the role of the 'business lawyer' had broadened in the two decades since Gilson was writing).[20] Dent characterised the role as one of 'enterprise architect' to reflect this broader outlook.

Transactional lawyers have also been conceived of as reputational intermediaries. The idea of a reputational intermediary comes from economic theory which posits that 'a firm selling quality products in a market plagued with asymmetric information will make investments in firm-specific assets such as a reputation for quality'.[21] In this paradigm, reputation has more value than the benefits of any one instance of dishonesty or poor quality. If such a reputation is not available, the transactional lawyer (or rather, their firm) may fill the role of 'reputational intermediary' or reputational gatekeeper – the means by which the entity borrows such a reputation. The assumption is that the intermediary receives little or substantially less financial gain from any one transaction but risks a decline in their reputational capital and is therefore incentivised to guard against any misdeeds.[22] Discussing relationships between bankers and their lawyers, John Flood described the reputational role as follows:

> Having established enduring relationships, the banks, working to tight deadlines, find it difficult to invest in a new set of relationships that would require an expenditure of resources and capital to discover whether a law firm meets their standards. Lawyers thus rent their reputation to transactions, as do investment bankers; and by virtue of being associated with particular transactions and banks, indirectly certify the business taking place.[23]

Whether or not the reputational value of lawyers, firms and in-house counsel is shifting has been debated. In 2008 Steven Schwarcz argued that the reputational value of external lawyers might be diminishing, just as that of in-house lawyers was increasing.[24] William Henderson has also discussed Big Law's declining reputational capital and noted growth in in-house and alternate legal service providers, against a general flattening of demand for corporate legal services, in the US market.[25] Henderson said:

> With improved ability to evaluate cost and value, legal departments can avoid the price premiums of Big Law by expanding their own in-house capacity. In-house lawyers also have a proliferating array of options to address their legal needs, including hiring of

[19] SL Schwarcz, 'Explaining the Value of Transactional Lawyering' (2007) 12(2) *Stanford Journal of Law, Business & Finance* 486.

[20] GW Dent Jr, 'Business Lawyers as Enterprise Architects' (2009) 64(2) *The Business Lawyer* 279.

[21] KS Okamoto, 'Reputation and the Value of Lawyers' (1995) 74 *Oregon Law Review* 15, 18–19, 22.

[22] MC Adams, 'Breaking Past the Parallax: Finding the True Place of Lawyers in Securities Fraud' (2010) 37(4) *Fordham Urban Law Journal* 953.

[23] J Flood, 'Corporate Lawyer-Client Relationships: Bankers, Lawyers, Clients and Enduring Connections' (2016) 19(1) *Legal Ethics* 76, 84.

[24] S Schwarcz, 'To Make or to Buy: In-House Lawyering and Value Creation' (2008) 33(2) *Journal of Corporation Law* 497, 510.

[25] WD Henderson, 'From Big Law to Lean Law' (2014) 38 *International Review of Law and Economics* 5.

> non-US global law firms, legal process outsourcers with operations in India and other lowcost countries, non-lawyer companies and consultants, and mechanized legal advice or products delivered through sophisticated software.[26]

As identified here, technology, along with myriad other factors, may be contributing to a reputational capital shift, and with it changing the role of the transactional lawyer.

The Work of Transactional Lawyers

The breadth of the category 'transactional lawyer' makes generalisations difficult. Transactional lawyers assist both businesses and individuals: their role involves facilitating deals, the allocation of risk between parties, and planning for contingencies.[27] In an ethnographic study of business lawyers in the 1990s, Flood suggested their work could be condensed to 'advising, negotiating, and drafting documents', noting that these activities were not undertaken linearly, but rather were intermingled.[28] Similarly, in a study of lawyers working for entrepreneurs and tech start-ups in Silicon Valley, Mark Suchman reported observing 'dealmaking' and 'counseling' ('in which law firms mediate flows of constitutive information'):[29] essentially Americanisms for negotiating and advising. Later, describing transactional lawyers as 'transactional engineers', John Coffee said: 'corporate lawyers have a skill set focused on negotiation, drafting, business planning, and the ability to maintain a comprehensive, almost encyclopaedic, understanding of extremely complex and integrated business transactions'.[30]

Here, we generally adapt these categories to capture different aspects of a transactional lawyer's work: advising, planning and structuring; negotiation and dealmaking; and drafting and disclosure. Coffee referred to the centrality of 'planning, structuring and negotiation of transactions for … largely corporate and institutional clientele'.[31] It is suggested that there are cultural differences in lawyers' appetites for providing advice that might be seen as more commercial than legal, with distinctions drawn between US and English lawyers, in particular.[32] The role of the transactional lawyer depends also on the point in a process at which they

[26] ibid 7.

[27] L Penland, 'What a Transactional Lawyer Needs to Know: Identifying and Implementing Competencies for Transactional Lawyers' (2008) 5 *Journal of the Association of Legal Writing Directors* 118, 122.

[28] J Flood, 'Doing Business: The Management of Uncertainty in Lawyers' Work' (1991) 25(1) *Law & Society Review* 41, 48; see also J Flood, *What Do Lawyers Do? An Ethnography of a Corporate Law Firm* (Quid Pro, 2013) 94–95.

[29] MC Suchman, *On Advice of Counsel: Law Firms and Venture Capital Funds as Information Intermediaries in the Structuration of Silicon Valley* (Stanford University, 1994).

[30] JC Coffee Jr, *Gatekeepers: The Professions and Corporate Governance* (Oxford University Press, 2006) 192–93.

[31] ibid 193.

[32] Flood (n 23) 89; see also D Howarth, *Law as Engineering: Thinking About What Lawyers Do* (Edward Elgar, 2014) 30.

become involved. Discussing Gilson's mergers and acquisitions examples, Dent notes that the external lawyers often involved in those kinds of transactions tend to become involved later.[33] On the other hand, in-house lawyers are likely involved earlier, 'not only before major issues are settled but often before many of them are identified'.[34] This means a different kind of involvement and scope of work. Dent argued that in-house lawyers, particularly, could be instrumental in 'ferreting out difficulties and finding solutions' at early stages.[35] Likewise Suchman referred to an activity he described as 'matchmaking' (a precursor to 'dealmaking') – where experienced lawyers were able to bring together potential business partners (in Silicon Valley, these were predominantly start-ups and investors) because of their inside knowledge of those players' businesses and behaviours.[36]

The use of the transactional lawyer's insider knowledge resonates with arguments later made by de Fontenay, who characterised the value added by large-firm transactional lawyers as their knowledge of the terms of private deals, which can be used to give otherwise unknowable insights to clients.[37] Advising the client requires predictions be made as to the likelihood of litigation, regulatory change or action or legislative reform, among many other contingencies.[38] Thus the basis for the advisor's predictions becomes relevant.

'Deal making' comprises the translation of a client's business goals into legal terms agreed by parties to the transaction.[39] Those goals could range from small and simple to vast and complex. Much has been written about the lawyer's role in transactional negotiations.[40] Research has suggested that transactional lawyers are influential as to whether legal agreements are successfully negotiated and in the time that negotiation takes.[41] Andrew Boon has explained:

> There is a voluminous literature on the theory of negotiation. Much of this is based on studies of lawyers. The research suggests that there are generalisations that can be made

[33] Dent (n 20).

[34] ibid 309.

[35] ibid 310.

[36] MC Suchman, 'Dealmakers and Counselors: Law Firms as Intermediaries in the Development of Silicon Valley' in M Kenney (ed), *Understanding Silicon Valley: The Anatomy of an Entrepreneurial Region* (Stanford University Press, 2000) 71.

[37] De Fontenay (n 4); see also S Williams, 'Predictive Contracting' (2019) 2 *Columbia Business Law Review* 621, 683.

[38] MK Osbeck, 'Lawyer as a Soothsayer: Exploring the Important Role of Outcome Prediction in the Practice of Law' (2018) 123(1) *Penn State Law Review* 41, 52–53.

[39] CS Harrison, *Make the Deal: Negotiating Mergers & Acquisitions* (John Wiley & Sons, 2016) (describing how deals are made combining both legal framework and business strategy).

[40] RK Neumann Jr, 'What We Don't Know About Deal Negotiation by Lawyers' (2011) 12 (Special Issue) *Transactions: The Tennessee Journal of Business Law* 153, 156, citing as key texts R Fisher and WL Ury, *Getting to Yes: Negotiating Agreement Without Giving In* (Penguin, 1981); JC Freund, *Smart Negotiating: How to Make Good Deals in the Real World* (Simon & Schuster, 1992); RH Mnookin, SR Peppet and AS Tulumeulo, *Beyond Winning: Negotiating to Create Value in Deals and Disputes* (Harvard University Press, 2000) and WJ Ury, *Getting Past No: Negotiating Your Way From Confrontation to Cooperation* (Bantam Books, 1991).

[41] RJ Gilson and B Black, *The Law and Finance of Corporate Acquisitions* (Foundation Press, 1996); CJ Karsten, U Malmendier and Z Sautner, 'M&A Negotiations and Lawyer Expertise' (Working paper 2014)

> about the process of negotiation and bargaining. These cover the orientation of negotiators, the importance of problem type and practices of bargaining in different contexts. Certain patterns tend to be universal in different cultures and cover both transactions and disputes.[42]

He notes further that negotiation styles may vary dependent on the nature of the problem and the negotiator, who may adopt a competitive or a cooperative approach: 'Many accounts of legal negotiation suggest that it often take the form of co-operative positional bargaining. Very few research studies have found evidence that lawyers make much use of problem-solving approaches to negotiation, such as principled negotiation'.[43]

A bigger-picture aspect of deal making is the 'structuring' component of transactional lawyering, capturing the idea of this area of law as malleable yet stable. As David Howarth explained, it is to the benefit of transactional lawyers to maintain a level of predictability in the law but their role is not merely 'static'.[44] Though they might wish to seek consensus and avoid 'the risk of destabilising litigation', transactional law is also 'dynamic' and adaptive.[45] Flood described the role of law firms in this mix as 'supporting structures' which assist in stabilising expectations among diverse actors within transactional law.[46] This stabilising role is closely linked to risk management.

Lastly, 'the special skill of the corporate lawyer has been drafting and disclosure, including the special verification skills – known as "due diligence" work within the profession – that accompany the preparation of disclosure documents'.[47] Due diligence is typically the review of a business's affairs undertaken prior to entering into a contractual arrangement. Prior to the transaction, the risks associated with the entity must be assessed, which generally entails a review of the companies' contracts, among other things. The International Bar Association explains that due diligence might be undertaken in various situations, such as corporate or asset transactions, in issuances of securities, or in an investigatory sense (eg in cases of improper corporate conduct, or health and safety concerns).[48] In the merger and acquisition context, they say:

> Legal due diligence carried out by potential acquirers in order to analyse the conditions of the businesses they intend to buy are standard and frequently involve not only various

ssrn.com/abstract=2576866; CNV Krishnan and RW Masulis, 'Law Firm Expertise and Merger and Acquisition Outcomes' (2013) 56 *Journal of Law and Economics* 189.

[42] A Boon, *The Ethics and Conduct of Lawyers in England and Wales* (3rd edn, Hart Publishing, 2014) 650 (citations omitted).

[43] ibid 659, citing M Heumann and JM Hyman, 'Negotiation Methods and Litigation Settlement in New Jersey': "You Can't Always Get What You Want" (1997) 12(2) *Ohio State Journal on Dispute Resolution* 253.

[44] Howarth (n 32) 286.

[45] ibid, citing G Hadfield, 'Don't Forget the Lawyers' (2007) 56 *DePaul Law Review* 401.

[46] Flood (n 23) 87, citing F Sosa, *Vertrag und Geschäftsbeziehung im Grenzüberschreitenden Wirtschaftsverkehr* (Nomos, 2007).

[47] Coffee (n 30) 192–93.

[48] International Bar Association, *IBA Corporate and M&A Law Committee Legal Due Diligence Guidelines* (IBA, 2019) 5.

legal practice areas but also professionals from various jurisdictions. Well-conducted due diligence processes tend to bring clarity to parties involved in transactions, thereby mitigating the risk of litigation post-closing between buyers and sellers, and contributing to successful post-closing integration of targets into acquirers.[49]

Drafting represents the finalisation of advice and negotiation: capturing the parties' agreement in legally enforceable form. As the earlier discussion of boilerplate indicates, drafting is not merely a technical exercise but invokes social and cultural, as well as legal, norms.

Application of AI to Transactional Law

The main areas of application where AI is impacting transactional law and the work of transactional lawyers we describe as analysis, review, management and drafting, but there is considerable overlap in these categories. Using machine learning to identify patterns in (for instance) contract terms has both academic and practical applications, which we discuss under the heading *analysis*. Analysis has implications for drafting, review functions are relevant for management, and management in turn enables information extraction or data collection for analysis (see Figure 7.1).

Figure 7.1 AI's transactional law applications

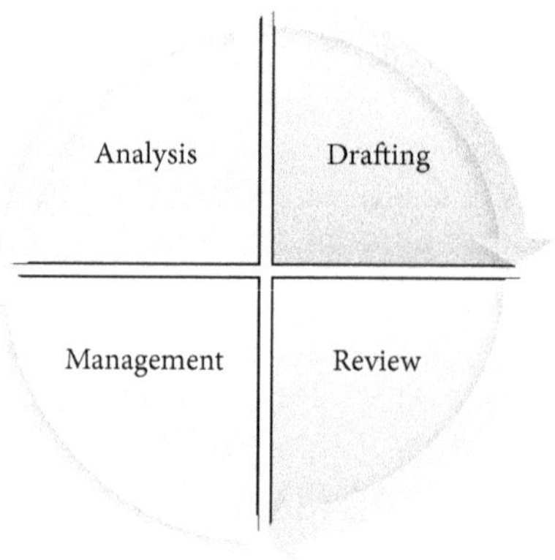

Document *review*, in this context, may refer to a review of thousands or even millions of documents as occurs in Technology Assisted Review[50] but also to

[49] ibid.
[50] See Chapter 5.

review of single documents. Aside from our discussion of due diligence, we focus primarily on review of single documents. Dale has said, of such individualised review:

> Automated contract review systems can be used to review documents which are relatively standardised and predictable in terms of the kinds of content they contain. The process involves decomposing the contract into its individual provisions or clauses, and then assessing each of these, either to extract key information or to compare against some standard (which might just be the set of other instances of such contracts held by a firm).[51]

Management we adopt as a term to discuss the extraction of information from corpora of legal documents and how this may be utilised for managerial functions – such as tracking parties, dates and forms of contractual clause. A quite different approach is then found in the use of software to undertake *drafting*. There has been interest in this for decades but recent years have seen huge growth in automated drafting software[52] – for use by lawyers but also directly by people or companies to prepare contracts or simple legal documents such as wills.

Analysis

Recently, academics have begun to investigate transactional law using machine learning methods to analyse many thousands of contracts. Some demonstrate a taxonomic approach – where, similarly to some of the work described in Chapter 4, volume of data is used to make empirical findings about transactional law issues. For instance, Lea-Rachel Kosnik undertook an empirical study of Coase's theory of transaction costs through a regression analysis of the text of hydroelectric licence contracts.[53]

In addition to illuminating patterns, Spencer Williams argues that machine analysis of contracts can be used to inform the drafting of clauses.[54] Specifically, he says that those who are drafting contracts are constrained in two keys ways: first, they have limited data about 'outcomes' such as whether terms have been the subject of litigation; and secondly, analytical tools have not been sufficiently sophisticated to enable in-depth analysis of contract data.[55] Williams argues that these limitations may be overcome by what he terms 'predictive contracting': using data analytics to generate insights into connections between contract terms and outcomes.[56] We discuss this further below in relation to drafting, but it indicates

[51] Dale (n 5) 214.
[52] See, eg, Stanford CodeX list, techindex.law.stanford.edu/.
[53] LR Kosnik, 'Determinants of Contract Completeness: An Environmental Regulatory Application' (2014) 37 *International Review of Law and Economics* 198.
[54] Williams (n 37) 621–95.
[55] ibid 627–28.
[56] ibid 629, 662.

that the use of machine learning for broad-scope analysis potentially has practical application – beyond the taxonomic or descriptive – which commercial providers are also exploring.

In 2017 Gabriel Rauterberg and Eric Talley published their machine learning study of 'corporate opportunity waivers' from publicly available US SEC data.[57] They utilised the same techniques that Talley and data scientist Drew O'Kane had deployed in an earlier analysis of merger agreements.[58] In another study published that year, Robert Anderson and Jeffrey Manns used a machine learning system to analyse 12,000 public company merger agreements spanning a 20-year period.[59] Merger agreements – the legal agreement by which one company is acquired by another – are also referred to as change of control transactions. The premise of Anderson and Manns' analysis is that while transactional law has enormous economic significance and is lucrative for the law firms involved, the process by which agreements are drafted is relatively under-studied. Among their findings were that inefficiencies in drafting were routinely present, with seemingly non-substantive, yet extensive, edits being made.[60] Anderson and Manns conclude that the drafting of merger agreements is both inefficient and leads to uncertainty in outcomes for clients. Many empirical studies of transactional lawyering have highlighted the weaknesses of human lawyer drafting, an issue we return to below when analysing the role of the transactional lawyer.

Studies of this kind may also highlight inconsistency in judicial doctrine, as Jonathan Macey and Joshua Mitts stress in their analysis of when courts will 'pierce the corporate veil' – ie, look behind a corporate structure to hold individuals liable for company actions.[61] Using a machine learning system to classify over 9,000 US decisions on corporate veil piercing, they argue that policy or remedial goals 'are a superior predictor of actual veil-piercing decisions than the largely incoherent doctrines espoused by the courts'.[62] These kinds of analysis rely on information extraction from large corpora of example documents such as specific types of agreements. In their study, Macey and Mitts describe using

> the common predictive coding algorithm for text classification known as the *naive Bayes* classifier. The naive Bayes algorithm reflects a *probabilistic* approach to classification whereby a probability is estimated for each document being of each type

[57] G Rauterberg and E Talley 'Contracting Out of the Fiduciary Duty of Loyalty: An Empirical Analysis of Corporate Opportunity Waivers' (2017) 111(5) *Columbia Law Review* 1075 (the EDGAR database). Corporate opportunity waivers refer to the corporation waiving an opportunity and thereby enabling an individual director or company officeholder to benefit.

[58] E Talley and D O'Kane, 'The Measure of a MAC: A Machine-Learning Protocol for Analyzing Force Majeure Clauses in M&A Agreements' (2012) 168(1) *Journal of Institutional & Theoretical Economics* 181.

[59] R Anderson IV and J Manns, 'The Inefficient Evolution of Merger Agreements' (2017) 85(1) *George Washington Law Review* 57.

[60] ibid 61.

[61] JR Macey and J Mitts, 'Finding Order in the Morass: The Three Real Justifications for Piercing the Corporate Veil' (2014) 100(1) *Cornell Law Review* 99.

[62] ibid 103.

(i.e., a veil-piercing decision, a denial of a veil-piercing claim, or an irrelevant decision), and each document is classified into the type with the highest probability.[63]

It is, therefore, primarily an exercise in classification, and using the resulting classification to identify correlations between patterns and outcomes.

Review and Management

In 2018 LawGeex, a provider of contract review software, published a report of its 'experiment' in automated review of non-disclosure agreements (NDAs). The LawGeex website explains that the software 'reads and analyzes incoming contracts, suggesting edits based on a company's pre-defined legal policies. Contracts that meet these policies can be automatically approved within an hour. Contracts that don't align … are escalated for guided editing and approval'.[64] LawGeex compared the efforts of 20 experienced lawyers in reviewing five different NDAs with those of its software.[65] The software outperformed nearly all the lawyers in terms of accuracy, but perhaps more importantly, it vastly outperformed them in terms of speed.[66] The lawyers took, on average, 92 minutes to review all five contracts, while the software took a mere 26 seconds.

A machine learning system must be trained to review particular types of documents.[67] The technology works by using a database of similar types of documents (usually, particular types of contracts) – as has been done for the analytical purposes described above. Then, when presented with a new contract, the system can compare that document with its existing database, identifying similarities and differences. Recognising certain kinds of clauses enables a program to spot issues. In other words, it can identify (typically in a matter of seconds) which clauses differ from the 'benchmarked' language in which it has been trained.[68] For instance, one company used 250,000 employment agreements to build a program that can, when presented with a new (not previously seen) employment contract, identify which clauses are non-standard by comparison with the database.[69] It is therefore contracts which are largely standardised that are susceptible to the automation of review – such as commercial leases or the NDAs utilised by LawGeex.

[63] ibid 143.

[64] www.lawgeex.com/features/.

[65] 'The study, a collaboration between US-based academic institutions Duke University School of Law and the University of Southern California, was overseen and administered by independent lawyer Christopher Ray and independent consultants from Stanford University's School of Law and the Department of Computer Science at Bar Ilan University': U Verma, 'Israeli AI Software Whips Expert Lawyers in Contract Analysis', *The Times of Israel*, 26 February 2018.

[66] LawGeex, *Comparing the Performance of Artificial Intelligence to Human Lawyers in the Review of Standard Business Contracts*, February 2018, 14–15.

[67] O Hanson, 'Product Review: Kira' (April 2018) 47 *Colorado Lawyer* 13; see also Osbeck (n 38).

[68] JA Sherer and E Walters, 'Transitioning from Consumer Tech to Legal Intelligence Engineering' (2018) *Law Practice* 33, 36.

[69] KM Standards, kmstandards.com/.

This technology uses both syntactic and semantic techniques to process the textual information in the document and then undertakes a comparison against the rest of the dataset. It is important to go beyond simply searching for keywords or terms because differing language may be used to express the same concepts or to cover the same clauses. Dan Yang et al give an example found in a specific type of service agreement:

> For example the term 'force majeure' stands for unavoidable events, while a 'force majeure' provision is the language that specifies the contractor and customer's rights and responsibilities when such an event occurs. Performing keyword search on 'force majeure' can be ineffective as the phrase … seldom appears explicitly.[70]

As Dana Remus and Frank Levy wrote in relation to large-scale review, reliance on specific word searching runs the risk of producing 'results that are both under-inclusive (risking that important documents were being overlooked) and over-inclusive (raising the costs of review by returning large quantities of non-responsive document)'.[71] They give an example of software

> that reviews all of a company's contracts in a particular area, extracts the common provisions, and creates a basic template. The software also highlights discrepancies between the template and contracts proposed by other parties. Both tasks involve identifying similar meaning between pieces of texts and are likely accomplished using [latent semantic analysis] or a probabilistic language model.[72]

Another application of this kind of technology is to the large-scale review undertaken for due diligence reasons. Much like document review for discovery, legal due diligence has traditionally been done by teams of lawyers reading large numbers of documents in a time-consuming and often expensive process:

> Manual due diligence is getting harder and harder; usually there is way too much data to review everything, so you do not know what you will find and what you miss; the sources can be geographically dispersed; and doing due diligence manually is prone to errors.[73]

It is claimed that AI systems can dramatically reduce the time taken for this review.[74] One lawyer explained of Kira Systems:[75]

> We used Kira recently for a very large contract analysis project for one of our clients. The project involved reviewing various agreements and documentation to assess the

[70] D Yang, C Leber, L Tari, A Chandramouli, A Crapo, R Messmer and S Gustafson, 'A Natural Language Processing and Semantic-Based System for Contract Analysis' in *2013 IEEE 25th International Conference on Tools with Artificial Intelligence*, (IEEE, 2013) 707.

[71] D Remus and F Levy, 'Can Robots Be Lawyers? Computers, Lawyers, and the Practice of Law' (2017) 30(3) *Georgetown Journal of Legal Ethics* 501, 515.

[72] ibid 514.

[73] International Bar Association (n 48) 38.

[74] ibid.

[75] A Kim, 'Kira Diligence Engine Named International M&A Technology Product of the Year by ACQ Global Awards 2015', *Kira Systems Latest News*, 21 October 2015, finance.yahoo.com/news/kira-diligence-engine-named-international-214900876.html.

> risk associated with various assets. Since Kira did not have built-in models for these types of documents, Kira was not immediately able to extract the required information automatically. But we were able to use the learning capabilities of Kira to teach it to identify the key clauses within the documentation that we were looking for. Kira learned these well and after the training, it was able to pull out the relevant clauses in various documents.[76]

A review of Kira explains that it 'has more than 430 provisions that it is already trained to look for', but as the lawyer described, it can also be trained to look for provisions 'specific to your deal type'.[77] Using machine learning, the software can continue to refine itself as it is exposed to more documents. A similar point about refining the software's performance is described in relation to RAVN System,[78] which also extracts specific information from large corpora of documents: 'RAVN made some mistakes, but it improved when lawyers added information to their queries. The platform also picked up some mistakes missed on a first review by lawyers'.[79]

Another program, Leverton,[80] can also be used for due diligence: 'information such as payable rent, maintenance costs and expiration dates [can be] extracted from thousands of documents and then organized on a spreadsheet'.[81] Remus and Levy argue, though, that review for due diligence differs from discovery in that it has what they term an 'unstructured' aspect.[82] That is, while in TAR the corpus of documents requires classification into pre-defined categories, due diligence has an exploratory element: it 'encompasses … an unstructured component (searching for unexpected or surprising information from a diverse set of documents)'.[83] These authors therefore caution that while technology can do a good job of the classification part, it is not good at identifying anomalous or unexpected information.[84]

In 2016 financial services firm JP Morgan Chase made headlines by reporting that it had

> recently introduced COIN, a contract intelligence platform that uses unsupervised machine learning to analyze legal documents and to extract important data points and clauses. In an initial implementation of this technology, we can extract 150 relevant attributes from 12,000 annual commercial credit agreements in seconds compared with as many as 360,000 hours per year under manual review.[85]

[76] RK Gowling, WLG National Director, Project Management and Legal Logistics, quoted by SD Nelson and JW Simek, 'Running with the Machines: Artificial Intelligence Advances Bring Benefits, Threats to Practice of Law' (2018) 43(8) *Montana Lawyer* 18, 19.

[77] Hanson (n 67) 13.

[78] imanage.com/product/ravn/.

[79] Nelson and Simek (n 76) 19.

[80] A spin-off from the Deutsches Forschungszentrum für Künstliche Intelligenz (DFKI), the German Institute for Artificial Intelligence.

[81] EA Rayo, 'AI in Law and Legal Practice – A Comprehensive View of 35 Current Applications', *TechEmergence*, 29 November 2017, www.techemergence.com/ai-in-law-legal-practice-current-applications/.

[82] Remus and Levy (n 71) 517.

[83] ibid 517.

[84] ibid 517–18.

[85] JP Morgan, 'JP Morgan 2016 Annual Report' 49, www.jpmorganchase.com/corporate/investor-relations/document/2016-annualreport.pdf. COIN refers to 'contract intelligence'.

In this instance, 'manual review' meant review by lawyers, generating headlines such as 'Are Robots Taking Over the World's Finance Jobs?'.[86] Note that JP Morgan's annual report figures would seem to be premised on each commercial credit agreement normally necessitating 30 hours of review. Nevertheless, the example demonstrates that the major saving available from automated information extraction is in lawyers' time, even if such time may have been overestimated.

Likewise, it is reported that legal services company Axiom uses automated contract management to 'collect over three hundred data points from each of its contracts'.[87] Data points refer to particular variables obtained from documents (eg contracts) in a dataset – which might include items such as parties' names, and so on.[88]

> A typical large organisation can have more than 100,000 live contracts across its suppliers, contractors and partner networks. It is impossible for any legal team or chief executive to have a complete birds eye view of the current state of play when it comes to contracts. The harsh reality is that an organisation only realises that there's a problem with a contract when something goes wrong. Our system allows a rapid and accurate assessment of contracts a company is processing and it quickly identifies which ones may need further review.[89]

The software thus has benefits in terms of organisation and search functions – the management side of things. It can, for example, flag all the contracts which are to expire within a certain time period or identify all of those which contain a certain clause. This kind of process could also be used by legal practices to streamline back office tasks: for example, by prompting staff to step through a process; or for client intake, as the potential client can provide key information prior to a first meeting. This ability to extract information also enables legal analytics based on the aggregated data, as discussed above.

Drafting

There is a debate as to whether much automated drafting software is, in fact, 'AI'. In the case of transactional lawyers, document automation or document assembly software has been used, in some jurisdictions, for 30 years or more.[90] Indeed, supporting lawyers' drafting with technology has been referred to as an 'ancient'

[86] N Alam and G Kendall, 'Are Robots Taking Over the World's Finance Jobs?', *The Guardian*, 11 July 2017.

[87] Williams (n 37) 650.

[88] B Rich, 'How AI Is Changing Contracts', *Harvard Business Review*, 12 February 2018, 3.

[89] M2 Presswire, 'ThoughtRiver's AI Contract Analysis Technology Aims to Disrupt How Business Contracts Are Reviewed', 18 September 2017, www.m2.com (Quoting Tim Pullan of ThoughtRiver).

[90] WE Foster and AL Lawson, 'When to Praise the Machine: The Promise and Perils of Automated Transactional Drafting' (2018) 69(3) *South Carolina Law Review* 597, 598.

pursuit within AI and Law research,[91] though one which lawyers have perhaps not adopted as extensively as they might.[92] We have already noted the widespread use of templates, especially in transactional work, and the adherence to certain terms even when the clauses or language of the template are demonstrably problematic.

Document assembly is described as a technique involving the use of templates into which specific information is entered. For example, Neota Logic self-describes as a 'no-code AI platform' which enables users to automate their own, existing document templates.[93] In 2006, Richard Susskind said:

> I cannot help but feel that document assembly technology is and will remain forever, as it were, a fundamental technology. If one looks at the heart of legal work, it's about the production of documents and document assembly is an enabling tool that automates and streamlines that process.[94]

There is overlap with 'advice-giving' or question-and-answer programs, as most document assembly involves the user responding to the program's queries, and the responses being used to create a document.[95] Dale notes this overlap, saying:

> There's a fuzzy boundary between document automation systems and legal advice applications … Legal advisors are interactive systems which, based on a set of questions posed by the system, produce advice tailored to the circumstances and requirements of the user. In many cases, the output is a legal document of some kind, so legal advice often amounts to document automation. Document automation systems, on the other hand, typically use some kind of fill-in-the-blanks templating mechanism that enables the creation of a legal document tailored to specific criteria. In some cases, the data required to generate the document is obtained via an iterative question-and-answer dialog … In such circumstances, the document automation system has the same kind of interface as that provided by a legal advice system.[96]

Programs have become more sophisticated, though the basic premise or way that the system operates remains essentially the same.[97] For lawyers, using document automation software is a step up from using templates or creating documents based on previous iterations. Most document automation software is centrally hosted and available to lawyers or legal practices on a subscription basis. Lawyers can choose whether to automate their own existing documents (the firm's existing precedents) or subscribe to a system which is pre-populated with documents designed by the

[91] M Lauritsen and TF Gordon, 'Toward a General Theory of Document Modeling' (2009) *Proceedings of the 12th International Conference on Artificial Intelligence and Law, Barcelona, Spain, 8–12 June 2009*, 202.

[92] KD Betts and KR Jaep, 'The Dawn of Fully Automated Contract Drafting: Machine Learning Breathes New Life into a Decades-Old Promise' (2015) 15 *Duke Law & Technology Review* 216, 216.

[93] Neota Logic, 'Perfect NDA', www.neotalogic.com/product/perfectnda/.

[94] R Susskind, 'The Next Ten Years' (speech delivered at Society for Computers and Law 2006 Annual Lecture, 6 March 2006) cited by DR Mountain, 'Disrupting Conventional Law Firm Business Models using Document Assembly' (2007) 15(2) *International Journal of Law and Information Technology* 170, 171.

[95] Foster and Lawson (n 90) 618.

[96] Dale (n 5) 215–16.

[97] Betts and Jaep (n 92) 219.

service. This type of automation works most effectively when contracts are largely standardised and few deviations from standard clauses are needed.[98]

It is argued that machine learning enables a fundamentally new approach to drafting, which Williams terms 'predictive contracting':

> A predictive contracting system can supply contract drafters with information on the statistical connections between contract terms and outcomes, including the likelihood of litigation and potential adverse judicial interpretation. Equipped with this information, contract drafters can make better-informed decisions about the inclusion of nonstandard terms.[99]

Williams says that such a system will make 'contracts substantively better'.[100] The limitations of the available data are important, however. For instance, given how many contracts are on foot at any point in time, likelihood of litigation is already inestimably small across the board. Hence, as Howarth explains: 'Transactions lawyers are not looking for arguments that might persuade a judge, they are looking for law solid enough in the minds of other lawyers that no one would even think about asking a court to reconsider it'.[101] It may also be the case, ironically, that uncertainty about the meaning of a term actually discourages litigation. On the other hand, as Richard Neumann has expressed:

> How much lawyering actually adds value and how much of it is just over-lawyering – lawyers trying to solve problems that may never matter by negotiating issues that are highly unlikely ever to blow up. From what I've been able to figure out, this is a continual issue in deal work … We could spend a lot of time ironing out the wording so that both your client and my client feel that our interests are protected … On the other hand, if this issue stands less than a one percent chance of blowing up and if it does, will it cause only minor dislocation for both parties, are we wasting our clients' time and money by doing so?[102]

Nevertheless some contract drafting technology companies have ostensibly begun to experiment with machine learning in this way. LexPredict and Bloomberg's Corporate Transactions tools use these algorithms to process publicly available contracts and suggest drafting language based on these contracts.

Role of the Transactional Lawyer

Two US writers have argued that AI is best positioned to do two things – take over repetitious tasks (such as document review) and produce 'commodity legal documents'.[103] Both are salient for transactional lawyers. Yet the nature of

[98] Williams (n 37) 662.
[99] ibid 667.
[100] ibid 662.
[101] D Howarth, 'Lawyers and the Rule of Law' in C May and A Winchester (eds), *Handbook on the Rule of Law* (Edward Elgar, 2018) 271.
[102] Neumann (n 40) 161.
[103] DM Horn and I Meislik, 'How to Ride the Coming Tidal Wave of Technology and Competition' (2018) 32(6) *Probate and Property* 9.

transactional law means that legal practitioners span a wide arc from those in specialised areas within multinational firms, those working in-house for a range of corporations, and those practitioners who assist small businesses and individuals at a local level. The use of AI for transactional legal work can be seen at both ends of the arc – or death from above, and death from below, in the rather more distinctive phrasing of Benjamin Barton.[104] Large firms are adopting one or many AI products in the hope of increasing their lawyers' efficiency and satisfying clients' demands for cost-effectiveness. It is claimed that Big Law is 'positive' about experiences with AI-based systems which can 'help the firms deliver greater value to their clients'.[105] Corporate legal departments are also making great use of AI to reduce costs and streamline processes. Meanwhile, as they are challenged by entities and software seeking to cut lawyers out from tasks such as will writing and simple drafting (Barton's 'death from below'), small and sole practitioners may also turn to automated options.

Arguments about the reduction of the lawyer role – even to the point of non-existence – are discussed in the final section below but many legal AI products are marketed to lawyers themselves, as is the case with those discussed in other chapters of this book. This is especially so for products designed for due diligence, or the type of contract management which would be done by the in-house counsel of large entities. The developers of these products accordingly tend to position them as either time-saving, enhancing or augmenting tools. Noah Waisberg, a founder of Kira Systems, has said 'A person using our system misses less than they would otherwise. It's an enhancement tool'.[106] Avoiding talk of lawyer replacement, their strategy is focused on reducing time spent on tasks which are either not strictly legal or do not require engaging in complex analytical processes; and perhaps in providing a safeguard against mistakes. As LawGeex observed, enabling an extremely fast 'initial review' of a document means that lawyers would be freed up to spend their time only on the clauses of the contract which are relevant, at least as determined by the system.[107] Another benefit lies in reducing human lawyer errors. Whether of commission or omission,[108] it is argued that automation can guard against them.[109]

The 'efficiency' line seems to have been largely accepted and adopted, by both legal commentators and firms themselves. Thus, AI is promoted as enabling a

[104] BH Barton, *Glass Half Full: The Decline and Rebirth of the Legal Profession* (Oxford University Press, 2015) ch 4: 'Death from Above: Big Law Stumbles' and ch 5: 'LegalZoom and Death from Below'.

[105] Betts and Jaep (n 92) 226.

[106] V Li, 'Technology Rewires the Drafting and Reviewing of Contracts', *ABA Journal*, November 2014, www.abajournal.com/magazine/article/contracts_2.0_technology_rewires_the_drafting_and_reviewing_of_contracts (quoting Noah Waisberg).

[107] LawGeex, *Comparing the Performance of Artificial Intelligence to Human Lawyers in the Review of Standard Business Contracts* (February 2018) 20.

[108] Betts and Jaep (n 92) 226.

[109] Foster and Lawson (n 90).

better use of lawyers' time rather than loss of lawyer jobs (though that is predicted by some).[110] Roles for lawyers remain because while a program may be able to 'flag' a non-standard clause in a previously unseen document, it cannot yet explain its meaning, or what, if any, action should be taken in response.

In this section, we consider the roles of the transactional lawyer: technically adept, but also playing important roles as intermediaries and as stewards of ethicality. We also consider, though, whether the lawyer's role can, indeed, be rendered superfluous by technology.

The Technical

While AI technologies can provide more efficient ways to manage and search voluminous legal documents, and to draft and review documents, they generally provide only a starting point. All other elements needed to bring deals to completion, as we discussed earlier, will typically still be undertaken by lawyers. Moreover, these activities are interlinked, as our discussion of the work of transactional lawyers above makes clear. It is the combination of advising, negotiating and ultimately drafting and facilitating agreements that makes a good transactional lawyer. While AI can supplement elements of this work, it will likely remain in lawyers' domain for the time being. In similar vein, de Fontenay argues that the value of experienced lawyers and prestigious firms will remain, as despite more standardisation, there is also increasing complexity.[111] She explains:

> Although many corporate transactions become standardized and even commoditized over time, others involve increasingly complex or rapidly changing terms for a sustained period of time. The latter type consists of heavily negotiated, bilateral transactions, characterized by variation in the market price of deal terms, the constant development of new terms, or both. Such transactions stray from the perfect-market ideal of transparent, uniform pricing. Rather, information about individual deal terms and their pricing remains largely private (and therefore scarce). For a given deal, the final set of negotiated terms will be determined by a combination of market forces and bargaining under incomplete information and will thus be heavily affected by the parties' respective information in the bargaining stages.[112]

[110] See, eg, J Kahn, 'Mike Lynch's Invoke Aims to Replace M&A Lawyers with Robots', *Bloomberg Law*, 14 September 2016, www.bloomberg.com/news/articles/2016-09-14/mike-lynch-s-invoke-aims-to-replace-m-a-lawyers-with-robots.

[111] De Fontenay (n 4) 396. Hadfield makes a similar argument about complexity and the need for lawyers: GK Hadfield, *Rules for a Flat World: Why Humans Invented Law and How to Reinvent It for a Complex Global Economy* (Oxford University Press, 2017) 124–26. Jennejohn (n 8) 74 ('a recent analysis of a large sample of merger agreements found that they have grown dramatically more complex over the last two decades'), citing JC Coates IV, 'Why Have M&A Contracts Grown? Evidence from Twenty Years of Deals' 14 (European Corporate Governance Institute, Working Paper No 333, 2016).

[112] De Fontenay (n 4) 396.

In other words, the only entities which can know how to value different terms (given terms are usually private) are those that regularly engage in similar large-scale transactions, and hence the largest firms retain their advantage. The value of the firm is scalar in being able to aggregate its knowledge of terms and deals across many. De Fontenay also notes that while 'third-party data providers have made substantial inroads in aggregating and comparing corporate deal terms, they are largely confined to reviewing publicly available documents ex post'.[113] Some types of deal have not yet evolved any standardised terms,[114] meaning that the creativity of lawyers will be needed to develop them. Moreover, as Tina Stark explains:

> Drafters are more than scriveners. They must understand the full implications of the deal to be able to implement it. Rarely can a lawyer simply take a term from the letter of intent and repeat it verbatim and be done with that business term. Generally, the term in the letter of intent is a bottom line statement of what the parties have agreed to. But in order to achieve the parties' expectations, the contract may need to address that term in multiple ways. The drafter must know how to use the law and her drafting skills to memorialize the business deal so that it provides for what the parties agreed to, but does so in a way that advantages the client. Choosing the wrong words or the wrong contract concept can increase risk, decrease a party's control, or lose the client a monetary advantage.[115]

The significance of accessible data cannot be overstated. As identified above, the central claims made about document automation and automated document review are that they enable greater efficiency and have been driven by client demands for lawyers to spend less time on tasks such as review. It is also suggested that they can reduce errors, though not, however, that such tools are themselves error free. Their accuracy likely depends on the data which they have to work with – was the software trained on a very large database of similar agreements (in terms of, for instance, jurisdiction, area of law, contemporaneity, clients)? Or was it developed using a database that was less similar, or less specific? For example, Bloomberg Law's tool, 'Draft Analyzer' uses the SEC's public database, EDGAR, as did some of the studies mentioned above.[116] 'Draft Analyzer' then identifies equivalent clauses which are alternatives to the agreement it has analysed. Yet, as William Foster and Andrew Lawson note:

> These suggestions can be highly useful to drafters who take the time to carefully evaluate each potential alteration. But the user must act cautiously in determining whether to change his or her language based on the system's proposed wording, especially when the user inputs a highly unique document such as a promissory note, as some recommendations are clearly inappropriate for the particular transaction.[117]

[113] ibid 397.
[114] Dent (n 20) 317.
[115] T Stark, 'Contract Drafting: A Prerequisite to Teaching Transactional Negotiation' (2011) 12 (Special Issue) *Transactions: The Tennessee Journal of Business Law* 162, 163.
[116] See, eg, at n 57.
[117] Foster and Lawson (n 90) 622–23.

Contractual terms may also be interrelated, meaning that substitution of one term may affect the choice of others.

Kathryn Betts and Kyle Jaep make a similar point in relation to drafting programs but rather more forcefully. They say that programs which are reliant on public databases such as EDGAR have no means of 'sorting' based on the quality of drafting, arguing that 'As a result, the contract provisions generated by these algorithms sometimes "parrot" confusing or poorly written language, in a sort of "garbage-in, garbage-out" cycle'.[118] This points to a broader issue about the intricacies of drafting and the concept of quality in drafting. Accordingly, Foster and Lawson argue:

> [T]he drafter can never be absolutely certain of the documents' sound nature without possessing adequate knowledge of the legal principles and scrutinizing the provisions. And drafters who simply rely on the assembly system documents face serious questions of whether they have satisfied their duty of competence.[119]

In other words, drafting software may speed things up, and may give the lawyer a wider and therefore better choice of options, but the lawyer's input remains an important safeguard. The counter-argument is, however, that legal drafting can be (as studies such as Mitu Gulati and Robert Scott's *The 3½ Minute Transaction*[120] or Anderson and Manns' 'The Inefficient Evolution of Merger Agreements'[121] indicate) a messy, at times counter-intuitive process fundamentally shaped by human concerns and culture, rather than a careful and technical exercise in pursuit of quality. Ironically, it is the imperfections of previous agreements which give rise to data quality concerns, as well as the volume of information which is not public and hence not accessible.[122]

It is argued that automation can also prevent lawyers from making errors. For drafting, this likely relates to protecting against 'the most egregious failures to customize'.[123] For review, it might increase the accuracy of the review process in terms of identifying issues. One firm partner gives an example of property due diligence:

> It takes a lawyer an average five to six hours to review one lease thoroughly and identify material issues that require further investigation. On a complex real estate transaction, there can be 200 or more leases for review. Traditionally, this work is done by junior lawyers and is a time-consuming process.[124]

[118] Betts and Jaep (n 92) 227.
[119] Foster and Lawson (n 90) 628.
[120] Gulati and Scott (n 12).
[121] Anderson and Manns (n 59).
[122] Osbeck (n 38) 99–100.
[123] Foster and Lawson (n 90) 626.
[124] Property Council of Australia, 'AI-Enabled App Removes Property Pain', 13 June 2018, www.propertycouncil.com.au/Web/Content/News/National/2018/AI-enabled_app_removes_property_pain.aspx (Victoria Holthouse) (Reporting on Allens' Real Estate Due Diligence App, REDDA).

In response, the firm designed an app to mimic 'the logic of a human lease review', which 'automatically detects key risks'.[125]

Likewise, eBrevia says that its software can analyse more than 50 documents in under a minute but is also more accurate than a manual review process.[126]

The software cannot, however, advise as to the meanings of the clauses, their relative importance, and where they fit into the negotiation of other terms in the process of risk allocation between the parties, though in giving this kind of advice, it is argued that transactional lawyers can make their approach more 'data-driven' by using the insights of large-scale analysis of types of documents and clauses.[127] One law firm partner has said:

> Transactional lawyers have, even before the computer age, relied upon their personal databases of 'form' contracts and clauses that they analyse and adapt for the 'next' deal. So as AI is able to handle more and more of that type of work autonomously, lawyers of the future are going to have to become more innovative in finding new ways to use all that data to provide clients better insights in an efficient way.[128]

The Relational, Reputational and Ethical

Stewart Macaulay observed the disjunct between a classical model of contract and the messiness of actual contracting and dispute resolution.[129] A relational theory of contract distinguishes between relational contracts, which are those between parties with ongoing relationships; and discrete, one-off or transactional contracts, between parties who lack such relations. It observes further that there is typically no single moment of consensus on the contract terms but rather a graduated process of negotiation.[130] It is likely, too, that wealth maximisation is not the parties' only goal, being tempered by other considerations pertaining to the ongoing nature of their relationship. Also in a sociological vein, Flood noted the importance of human interaction to what business lawyers do, observing that the activities in which they engaged 'were ultimately social constructions'.[131] By this he meant that human interactions were a central underpinning of all the lawyers'

[125] ibid.

[126] Rayo (n 81); eBrevia was acquired by Donnelley Financial Solutions' DFIN in December 2018. Note, it is not clear how 'accuracy' in this context is calculated.

[127] F Fagan, 'Big Data Legal Scholarship: Toward a Research Program and Practitioner's Guide' (2016) 20(1) *Virginia Journal of Law & Technology* 1.

[128] N Ismail, 'Artificial Intelligence in the Legal Industry: Adoption and Strategy – Part 1', 6 August 2018, *Information Age*, www.information-age.com/artificial-intelligence-in-the-legal-industry-123473948/ (quoting Alvin F Lindsay).

[129] S Macaulay, 'Elegant Models, Empirical Pictures, and the Complexities of Contract' (1977) 11(3) *Law & Society Review* 507, 508.

[130] Macneil (n 7); D Campbell, 'Ian Macneil and the Relational Theory of Contract' in D Campbell (ed), *The Relational Theory of Contract – Selected Works of Ian Macneil* (Sweet & Maxwell, 2001).

[131] Flood (n 28) 68.

tasks: 'Negotiating, drafting, and advising all depend on an interactional context for their fulfillment, no matter how mundane the matter may be'.[132] These specific, contextual, interactional features – which we summarise as the relational, reputational and ethical – are all salient for the role of the lawyer.

In terms of the relational, we can consider the 'messy' context alluded to above. Whether assisted by drafting software or analytic tools, the role of transactional lawyers remains to undertake the task of translating business agreements into legal ones: advising, negotiating, checking drafts; but perhaps more fundamentally, protecting their client's rights while making appropriate concessions and achieving the business outcomes which the client desires. There is also what Suchman and Mia Cahill identified as the technical and presentational aspects of the transactional lawyer's role: ensuring both that legal devices are effective, but also transmitting symbolic messages. There is overlap in these roles:

> In individual transactions, for example, 'due diligence' background investigations seem like reasonable technical efforts to substantive unpredictability; yet at a more macroscopic level, due diligence merely identifies and symbolically labels risk without eliminating it. Conversely, in individual transactions, standard-form contracting seems largely presentational, since it displays the symbols of certainty and formality without actually addressing the unique aspects of the deal at hand; yet, if standard contracts become sufficiently widely diffused within a larger business community, their ritual enactment can produce a kind of 'socially constructed' certainty, by reaffirming local expectations of good faith and fair dealing.[133]

This calls up (among other things) the role of trust between transactional lawyers and clients. Robert Vischer distinguishes between what he terms a 'cognitive' form of trust – which largely depends on it being in another party's interests to protect one's own interests[134] – and an 'affective' form of trust, which he terms relational:

> A cost-benefit reliance on market discipline or regulatory codes can only go so far. A trust that is grounded in the personal relationship between the attorney and client allows for a broader and deeper vulnerability than what is afforded by calculation … Is this sort of relational trust – by which I mean a client's trust in the relationship itself, as opposed to the client's trust in the market or regulatory safeguards in which the relationship is embedded – still relevant to a lawyer's work?[135]

Vischer's focus is on the place of lawyers in global law firms, operating in a corporate environment in which cost-benefit calculations loom and lawyers' work can be seen as increasingly fungible.[136] Many of these strains placed on a relational

[132] ibid 69; Johns wrote of the performativity of deal making: F Johns, 'Performing Party Autonomy' (2008) 71(3) *Law and Contemporary Problems* 243, 256.

[133] MC Suchman and ML Cahill, 'The Hired Gun as Facilitator: Lawyers and the Suppression of Business Disputes in Silicon Valley' (1996) 21(3) *Law & Social Inquiry* 679, 682, fn 17.

[134] RK Vischer, 'Big Law and the Marginalization of Trust' (2012) 25(1) *Georgetown Journal of Legal Ethics* 165, 168–70, citing R Hardin, *Trust and Trustworthiness* (Russell Sage, 2002) 1.

[135] ibid 173.

[136] ibid.

concept of trust, such as disaggregation and globalisation, are apposite to the impact of AI in transactional law.[137] However, the place of trust in the transactional lawyer–client relationship continues to be esteemed and is intertwined with reputational and ethical concerns. The reputation of individual lawyers is important. Boon wrote, of negotiation, 'In no other area of legal representation is the conduct of lawyers as important to clients or the ethics of lawyers more tested and difficult to verify'.[138] Unlike litigation, there is likely to never be any third-party scrutiny of a lawyer's negotiation practice: it lacks court or regulatory oversight.[139] For that reason:

> Negotiators are wise to cultivate good reputations for credibility and trustworthiness because one's reputation is a critical factor in their counterpart's negotiation tactics. Negotiators tend to use more competitive negotiation tactics with those who, through dishonest or overly competitive behavior, have a negative reputation and are more forthcoming with those who have good reputations.[140]

Beyond individual lawyers, reputation is important for firms too for engendering trust[141] and ethical credibility. As explained above, there is debate about whether law firms have maintained and can retain their reputational capital. Henderson suggests not, arguing that the way that Big Law is currently organised will continue to diminish its reputational capital, at the same time as new market entrants, many of them utilising technology, will offer better value to clients.[142] But when value is conceived of holistically, we see that law firm reputation, liability and ethical oversight remain important. For example, lawyers provide 'an insurance function': 'To put it simply, lawyers can be sued if something goes wrong'.[143]

No Role at All?

In 2016 it was reported that users could 'upload any type of contract to [the LawGeex] platform and receive, within 24 hours, an in-depth report of what's good, bad and even missing from their contract'.[144] This targeting of non-lawyer

[137] Vischer also identifies rapid growth and lateral hiring (as this prevents enculturation into firm values, or attenuation of those values) and use of contract attorneys: ibid 185.

[138] Boon (n 42) 649.

[139] GC Hazard Jr and T Schneyer, 'Regulatory Controls on Large Law Firms: A Comparative Perspective' (2002) 44 *Arizona Law Review* 593, 600–01.

[140] A Hinshaw 'Teaching Negotiation Ethics' (2013) 63(1) *Journal of Legal Education* 82, 94. Boon makes the same point (n 42), citing M Galanter 'Why the "Haves" Come Out Ahead: Speculations on the Limits of Legal Change' (1974) 9 *Law & Society Review* 95.

[141] GA Fine and L Holyfield, 'Secrecy, Trust, and Dangerous Leisure: Generating Group Cohesion in Voluntary Organizations' (1996) 59(1) *Social Psychology Quarterly* 22, 26 quoted by FM Kay and J Hagan, 'Building Trust: Social Capital, Distributive Justice, and Loyalty to the Firm' (2003) 28(2) *Law & Social Inquiry* 483, 484.

[142] Henderson (n 25) 11.

[143] Mountain (n 94) 183.

[144] 'Contract Review Platform Co LawGeex raises $2.5m', *Israel Business Arena*, 19 April 2016, Globes Publisher.

consumers appears to have later shifted. LawGeex's tagline is now 'contract review automation that lets your legal team pursue impactful work'.[145] Yet there are systems and entities which do seek to bypass lawyers, providing services that are marketed directly to the client/consumer.[146] Users upload agreements and the system reviews them by identifying clauses which differ from standard terms;[147] or complete questionnaires which result in a system generating a completed form or document.[148]

Omitting the use of lawyers and serving a previously disregarded market of consumers (people who would not have used a lawyer as they could not afford it) fits broadly within the theory of a disruptive innovation, as Michele Pistone and Michael Horn have noted:

> A disruptive innovation gains traction by initially offering simple, more affordable, or more convenient products or services to nonconsumers – people for whom the alternative is nothing. Individuals would rather have some service, which is infinitely better than their alternative – nothing at all – even if the service provided by the disruptive innovator appears initially to be of lesser quality than the dominant service, as judged by the historical measures of performance.[149]

Transactional law, certainly for individuals and small businesses, has already been affected by non-lawyer software providers, especially in the US.[150] In a chapter titled '*LegalZoom* and Death from Below', Barton characterises the titular enterprise as a disruptor, first serving the clients that lawyers were not interested in taking, but gradually gaining market share until it encroaches robustly on the space formerly occupied by small practitioners.[151] The story is more complex than this but takes in the transition from glorified form filling to those activities more closely resembling legal work. Nevertheless, lawyers remain in the picture Barton paints of the future, but perhaps with a reduced role – one confined to reviewing automatically generated drafts or answering questions. Indeed, the main competition to LegalZoom and like entities, Barton suggests, may well be those offering similar form completion services for free.

The provision of 'legal services' by non-lawyers is (as we flagged in Chapter 3) a regulatory issue in most jurisdictions, given restrictions on who may work as a lawyer. Restricting legal work to legal professionals is regarded as a means of

[145] LawGeex, 'Let Your Lawyers Be Lawstars', www.lawgeex.com/?utm_source=google&utm_medium=cpc&utm_campaign=Global_sch_brand&utm_adgroup=42250155000&device=c&placement=&utm_term=lawgeex&gclid=EAIaIQobChMIjb7l3-zc5wIViIqPCh1tqAWUEAAYAiAAEgLGgvD_BwE.

[146] See, eg, Beagle, www.beagle.ai/.

[147] S Semmler and Z Rose, 'Artificial Intelligence: Application Today and Implications Tomorrow' (2017–18) 16(1) *Duke Law & Technology Review* 85, 89.

[148] LegalZoom claimed to be responsible for one-fifth of all limited liability company incorporations in California in 2011: M Pistone and MB Horn, *Disrupting Law School: How Disruptive Innovation Will Revolutionize the Legal World* (Clayton Christensen Institute for Disruptive Innovation, 2016) 6.

[149] Pistone and Horn (n 148) 4.

[150] See, eg, Barton (n 104).

[151] ibid ch 4.

ensuring the protection of consumers of legal services. As well as quality control safeguards, clients typically have access to professional indemnity insurance in the event that loss flows from the improper actions of their lawyer. More holistically, as the concept of the trusted advisor suggests, it engenders a holistic, ongoing relationship, rather than one-off, decomposed services. In contrast, the idea of removing lawyers from the picture requires a different understanding of trust, which Vischer terms

> part of a broader, society-wide move (not just in law, but in medicine and securities, for example) from trust to verification – providing information to consumers, leaving it to them to engage in independent verification of the quality and veracity of the services in question. It is premised on a functioning market of information, rather than a set of relationships with trusted providers.[152]

It may be that developing and offering computer programs which can complete legal work breaches prohibitions on unauthorised practice of law. In terms of receiving legal advice from a non-lawyer or an automated system, the OECD Working Party on Competition and Regulation has noted that the absence of such a scheme may give rise to issues as

> without a fiduciary duty administered through a professional regulatory framework, it is not clear how online services, automated systems or non-lawyers providing legal services can be held accountable, through consumer protection laws, for their behaviour to the same standards as current legal professionals.[153]

The counter-argument is, though, that the goal of protecting clients is 'substantially weakened' if the work 'can be undertaken with the same degree of diligence and effectiveness but at lower cost by a non-lawyer or by an artificial intelligence'.[154] We return to these and other issues in Chapter 11, in terms of how, if at all, services of this kind ought be managed.

Future Developments

In many ways, this chapter demonstrates how transactional legal work can be successfully supported with AI technology but also that the technology is some way off replacing lawyers, at least for anything but the simplest form filling. The use of AI fits within a general concept of 'unbundling', or limited-scope services.[155] Many

[152] Vischer (n 134) 179.

[153] OECD Directorate for Financial and Enterprise Affairs Competition Committee, Working Party No 2 on Competition and Regulation, *Protecting and Promoting Competition in Response to 'Disruptive' Innovations in Legal Services* (13 June 2016) 25–26, [82].

[154] V Waye, ML Verreynne and J Knowler, 'Innovation in the Australian Legal Profession' (2018) 25(2) *International Journal of the Legal Profession* 213, 217.

[155] JS Dzienkowksi, 'The Future of Big Law: Alternative Legal Service Providers to Corporate Clients' (2014) 82(6) *Fordham Law Review* 2995, 3015.

aspects of transactional law can be 'unbundled', and some parts can be performed well by AI. Whether this is a useful and cost-effective means of doing the work will depend on the context, such as how much the technology will be used and reused, how much lawyer or other time is being saved, and whether there are other benefits such as enabling data collection for later analysis. Typically, investments need to work at scale:

> If an organization can continuously innovate and create systematized/packaged solutions to legal issues and problems that can be sold over and over again to a large base of clients, the organization can enjoy the prospect of 'making money while you sleep'.[156]

The main benefits to lawyers are efficiency gains through saving time. As LawGeex observed, enabling an extremely fast 'initial review' means that lawyers would be freed up to spend their time only on the relevant clauses or most important issues.[157]

Remus and Levy argue that the applications of AI that have had the most success within law are those involving language processing, specifically the comparison of textual extracts with other textual extracts.[158] Along with TAR, this encompasses the applications discussed in this chapter: analysis, review, management and drafting. Remus and Levy write that 'By focusing on comparisons between two documents, the software sidesteps problems in inferring meaning in less structured situations'.[159] For the moment, they posit, lawyers' work which requires 'unstructured communication' is not replicable by AI.

There are also possible strains on lawyers' ethicality arising from the use of AI. In the LawGeex example, the lawyer will save time only if they are able to rely on the software not to miss or misidentify issues. This is an issue for lawyers if their retainer is to review the whole contract as they will bear the burden of professional responsibility obligations if something is missed. Generally, Foster and Lawson suggest that ethical considerations have been largely overlooked when considering the use of technology in transactional law.[160] In part, this relates to taking responsibility for errors, or responding to the errors of others:

> Transactional lawyers relying on AI face several questions. Must they advise their client of their malpractice when using a new process? May they take advantage of counterparties' substantive mistakes? Similarly, may they take advantage of counterparties' scriveners' errors that may result from reliance on AI?[161]

With increasing use of automated options in transactional law, professional responsibility obligations and regulatory questions will likely become even more important.

[156] Henderson (n 25), 12 citing R Susskind, *The End of Lawyers? Rethinking the Nature of Legal Services* (Oxford University Press, 2008) 37.

[157] LawGeex, *Comparing the Performance of Artificial Intelligence to Human Lawyers in the Review of Standard Business Contracts* (February 2018) 20.

[158] Remus and Levy (n 71) 538.

[159] ibid.

[160] Foster and Lawson (n 90) 598.

[161] TE Spahn, 'Artificial Intelligence: Litigation-Specific Ethics Issues (Part 1)' (2018) 64(2) *Practical Lawyer* 43–62.

8

AI and Regulatory Lawyers

Introduction

RegTech, short for regulatory or regulation technology, refers to the use of technology by regulated entities to assist in achieving compliance with regulatory requirements, but also to reduce costs.[1] The need for RegTech has become clearer as the combination of more laws and larger, more complex business organisations gives rise to greater risk of non-compliance. Regulatory contraventions may lead to litigation, including fines and even criminal prosecutions, possibly civil claims by customers and shareholders, as well as reputational costs.[2]

The lawyer has a central role in achieving compliance within corporations. The Law Society of England and Wales has identified that 'Regulatory and compliance requirements have increased significantly, placing huge burdens on law firms and in-house lawyers'.[3] Examples of regulatory requirements are the reporting and compliance obligations mandated by the *Dodd-Frank Act* in the US, the Markets in Financial Instruments Directive (MiFID II) within the EU and anti-money laundering (AML) requirements globally. Technology, including AI, is a key response to meeting regulatory requirements.

RegTech may also cover the use of technology by regulators to fulfil their statutory obligations in a more thorough and efficient manner. In March 2017 Ravi Menon, Managing Director of the Monetary Authority of Singapore, coined the phrase 'supervisory technology', or SupTech.[4] As finance rapidly becomes automated and generates massive amounts of data, so too regulation needs to adopt technology to be able to keep up.[5] For example, the SEC's Market Abuse Unit

[1] S Griffith, 'The Question Concerning Technology in Compliance' (2016) 11 *Brooklyn Journal of Corporate, Financial & Commercial Law* 25, 29; 'Regtech 101: What It Is, Why Now, & Why It Matters', *CB Insights*, 2 November 2017; M Piwowar, 'Remarks at the 2018 RegTech Data Summit – Old Fields, New Corn: Innovation in Technology and Law' (speech delivered Washington DC, 7 March 2018); C Armour, 'ASIC Regtech Monitoring Financial Promotions: Demonstration and Symposium', 2 August 2019, asic.gov.au/about-asic/news-centre/speeches/asic-regtech-monitoring-financial-promotions-demonstration-and-symposium/.

[2] B Heineman Jr, *The Inside Counsel Revolution* (American Bar Association, 2016) 13, 131.

[3] The Law Society, *Lawtech Adoption Research* (February 2019) 19.

[4] R Menon, 'Financial Regulation – The Forward Agenda' (speech delivered at the Australian Securities and Investments Commission Annual Forum, Sydney, 28 March 2017).

[5] L Baxter, 'Adaptive Financial Regulation and Regtech: A Concept Article on Realistic Protection for Victims of Bank Failures' (2016) 66 *Duke Law Journal* 567, 598.

Analysis and Detection Center deploys technological tools to detect insider trading and market manipulation activities.[6] Regulators can also use technology as part of their investigation and litigation roles, which is typically similar to that used in the pre-trial procedures discussed in Chapter 5.

RegTech is often seen as being as a subcategory of FinTech. FinTech is the application of technology to the field of financial services. It can employ AI, but also distributed ledger technology (DLT).[7] It includes digital payments, robo-advice, platforms for investment, trading, peer-to-peer lending and equity crowdfunding.[8]

However, RegTech should be viewed as a separate phenomenon. In contrast to FinTech's inherently financial focus, RegTech has the potential to be applied in many regulatory contexts, such as compliance with environmental regulations or workplace safety requirements.[9] Nonetheless in the financial services sector, FinTech and RegTech are complementary because '[a]s Fintech firms automate the delivery of financial services, they need client onboarding, authentication and fraud control technologies that are more automated, yet equally or more secure'.[10]

Regulatory Lawyers

The regulatory lawyer is an omnibus term for in-house lawyers employed by banks and corporations (also called corporate counsel), lawyers in private practice and lawyers employed by government regulators who have a regulatory or compliance responsibility.

In-house Lawyers

In-house lawyers may work as part of a legal team in larger organisations or be the sole lawyer in smaller organisations. They will usually have a subject-matter specialisation linked to the industry in which they work. However, they will often be required to advise on a much broader range of areas, depending on the size of

[6] See discussion of SupTech below.

[7] DLT is a specific configuration of technology components that records and tracks information in a 'distributed' (as opposed to 'centralised') manner. This configuration enables participants of the network to have secure access to a consistent view of the information on the ledger at any point in time – with that view limited by their individual access privileges. See Australian Securities and Investment Commission, 'Evaluating Distributed Ledger Technology – Information Sheet 219' (March 2017) asic.gov.au/regulatory-resources/digital-transformation/evaluating-distributed-ledger-technology/.

[8] B Nolens, 'Fintech and Regtech: A Securities Regulator's Perspective' (speech delivered at Hong Kong Fintech Week 2016, 9 November 2016); International Organization of Securities Commissions, 'IOSCO Research Report on Financial Technologies' (February 2017).

[9] D Arner, J Barberis and R Buckley, *FinTech and RegTech in a Nutshell, and the Future in a Sandbox* (CFA Institute Research Foundation, 2017) 10.

[10] Nolens (n 8).

the corporation.[11] The general counsel may be a direct report to the chief executive officer, but even if not, they will be the chief source of legal advice for the corporation.[12] The in-house lawyer may also be found in positions outside the in-house legal team. For example, they may be a company secretary or part of a compliance or risk function within the corporation. The remit of the in-house lawyer can be broad or narrow. This chapter argues for a broad approach in relation to RegTech.

In-house lawyers are frequently given responsibility for dealing with compliance.[13] The Association of Corporate Counsel, a global bar association of more than 40,000 in-house counsel, employed by over 10,000 organisations in 85 countries, found in its *Skills for the 21st Century General Counsel* survey that 54 per cent of directors ranked 'ensuring a company's compliance with relevant regulations' as one of the top three ways general counsel provide value to the company.[14] Global law firm Allen & Overy has identified that in-house lawyers have been 'charged with managing their organisation's response to such global, cross-border compliance and implementation challenges' as AML and data privacy.[15]

The in-house counsel differs from the lawyer in private practice by having a single client, being close to management, having a detailed knowledge of that client and its business and legal objectives, and managing the acquisition of legal services.[16] The in-house counsel is thus responsible to, and shares the culture of, both the legal profession and the corporation that employs them.[17]

Private Practice

Herbert Smith Freehill's regional managing partner, Andrew Pike, said 'the rise of the regulatory lawyer' was one of the most significant recent developments in legal practice and described them as 'lawyers who are good at navigating that

[11] M Steinberg and S Yeager, *Inside Counsel – Practices, Strategies and Insights* (West, 2015) 50.

[12] ibid 16; V Richardson and M Blatch, *Leveraging Legal Leadership: The General Counsel as a Corporate Culture Influencer* (Association of Corporate Counsel, 2018) 8.

[13] SH Kim, 'The Ethics of In-House Practice' in L Levin and L Mather (eds), *Lawyers in Practice – Ethical Decision Making in Context* (University of Chicago Press, 2012) 198; Steinberg and Yeager (n 11) 14, 181–211; Heineman (n 2) 21.

[14] Richardson and Blatch (n 12) 3.

[15] J Brayne, *The Future of the In-House Legal Function* (Allen & Overy, 2019) 18. See also KPMG, *Restoring Corporate Trust: What It Means for the General Counsel* (2019) 9 (finding a consensus in survey responses that general counsel was in the best position to lead an assessment of the impact of regulatory change).

[16] C Day, 'Teaching Students How to Become In-House Counsel' (2001) 51 *Journal of Legal Education* 503, 505; J Coffee Jr, *Gatekeepers – The Professions and Corporate Governance* (Oxford University Press, 2006) 195, 223–26; Steinberg and Yeager (n 11) 17.

[17] American Bar Association, 'Section of Legal Education and Admissions to the Bar, Legal Education and Professional Development – An Educational Continuum, Report of the Task Force on Law Schools and the Profession: Narrowing the Gap' (1992) 135; R Moorhead, S Vaughan and C Godinho, *In-House Lawyers' Ethics* (Hart, 2019) 7, 132–34.

complex regulatory environment'.[18] The chief executive partner for King & Wood Mallesons, Berkeley Cox, and DLA Piper Australia managing partner, Amber Matthews, see law firms as having an important role in helping clients navigate complex regulation and the expectations of regulators.[19] Regulatory lawyers in private practice typically have expertise in a particular area of regulation and can apply it across firms and industries. The areas of regulation include environmental, securities, competition, anti-bribery, AML, healthcare, pharmaceuticals, gaming, education, transport and insurance. Some have broad application to a range of industries, while others are more focussed. Some are domestic in focus while others tend to apply across borders. The regulatory lawyer's practice can then be placed into one or more of the following three categories: (1) interpreting regulatory provisions and assisting a client to navigate and comply with those provisions; (2) dealing with regulatory agencies, including clarifying requirements, or responding to inquiries, and in some jurisdictions, such as the US, lobbying and participating in the rule-making process; and (3) challenging laws and regulations through administrative law and constitutional law. A fourth category, responding to regulatory litigation or enforcement is not discussed in this chapter as it is undertaken by litigation or white-collar crime specialists and does not involve RegTech.

Government/Regulator Lawyers

Lawyers employed by regulators may have a number of roles involving different expertise and knowledge. Often it is an enforcement role. They may be responsible for conducting investigations and, where wrongdoing is thought to have occurred, the filing and litigating of enforcement actions. However, it may also be an advisory role where the lawyer determines what laws require and the regulator's stance or policy on those laws. The lawyer may also assist in educating the regulated population as to what the regulator expects from them in relation to legal requirements.[20] It is the advisory role that is of main interest in this chapter.

The in-house government lawyer may also have a compliance role. This can involve 'regulatory smoothing' where they ensure the government actor complies with regulatory requirements, such as freedom of information. In this regard they are similar to the in-house corporate lawyer. However, they may also be required

[18] M Pelly, 'They Are Gold – The Rise of the Regulatory Lawyer', *Australian Financial Review*, 28 June 2019, 37.

[19] M Pelly and H Wootton, 'Hayne Fallout Yields Work in Difficult Times', *Australian Financial Review*, 6 December 2019, 31.

[20] 'Rethinking the Professional Responsibilities of Federal Agency Lawyers' (2002) 115 *Harvard Law Review* 1170, 1178–80; CJ Lanctot, 'The Duty of Zealous Advocacy and the Ethics of the Federal Government Lawyer: The Three Hardest Questions' (1991) 64 *Southern California Law Review* 951, 1012–17.

to ensure that the government actor acts in accordance with their legislative mandate.[21]

The government lawyer may also be seen as having a single client, namely the agency or regulator that employs the lawyer. However, the lawyer working for a regulator may also be seen to have obligations to act in the 'public interest', and serving the public interest is the lawyer's primary duty.[22]

Application of AI to Regulation

The global RegTech market is expected to grow from USD 4.3 billion in 2018 to USD 12.3 billion by 2023, at a Compound Annual Growth Rate of 23.5 per cent during the forecast period.[23] RegTech has expanded and matured more quickly than many other technology applications for law due to its adjacency to FinTech, which has expanded rapidly through a combination of both institutional and customer demand.[24] Equally the cost of compliance has increased.[25] It has been estimated that governance, risk and compliance (GRC) costs account for 15 to 20 per cent of the total 'run the bank' cost base of most major banks.[26] Unsurprisingly RegTech applications that can reduce cost but better achieve compliance have attracted considerable interest.

Deloitte has classified and listed entities that form part of the 'regtech universe' based on the following categories:[27]

- Regulatory Reporting – enables automated data distribution and regulatory reporting through big data analytics, real-time reporting and cloud.
- Risk Management – detects compliance and regulatory risks, assesses risk exposure and anticipates future threats.
- Identity Management & Control – facilitates counterparty due diligence and Know Your Customer (KYC) procedures. Also incorporates AML and anti-fraud screening and detection.
- Compliance – real-time monitoring and tracking of current state of compliance and upcoming regulations.

[21] D Howarth, *Law as Engineering* (Edward Elgar, 2013) 40–41.

[22] SK Berenson, 'Public Lawyers, Private Values: Can, Should, and Will Government Lawyers Serve the Public Interest?' (2000) 41 *Boston College Law Review* 789; 'Rethinking the Professional Responsibilities of Federal Agency Lawyers' (n 20).

[23] 'Global RegTech Market Forecast to 2023 – Application of Artificial Intelligence (AI), Machine Learning, and Blockchain to Offer New Efficiencies in Compliance', *Global Newswire*, 12 December 2018.

[24] The Law Society (n 3) 26.

[25] T Butler and L O'Brien, 'Understanding RegTech for Digital Regulatory Compliance' in T Lynn, JG Mooney, P Rosati and M Cummins, *Disrupting Finance* (Palgrave Macmillan, 2019) 87–88.

[26] M Memminger, M Baxter and E Lin, *Banking Regtechs to the Rescue?* (Bain & Co, 2016).

[27] Deloitte, 'RegTech Universe 2020: Take a Closer Look at Who Is Orbiting in the RegTech Space', www2.deloitte.com/lu/en/pages/technology/articles/regtech-companies-compliance.html.

- Transaction Monitoring – solutions for real-time transaction monitoring and auditing. Leverages the benefits of distributed ledger through Blockchain technology and cryptocurrency.

Meanwhile the 'Planet Compliance RegTech Directory' divides RegTech companies into their respective industry focus, creating eight broad categories:

1. Client and Counterparty Identification – focuses on the gathering and processing of the necessary information of a firm's clients and counterparties for KYC, AML and due diligence purposes.
2. Data Protection – focuses on protecting the privacy of individuals in data use especially in light of regulations like the General Data Protection Regulation (GDPR).[28]
3. Data Warehousing and Analytics – access, management and analytics of data, especially in relation to large amounts of data.
4. General Compliance – includes risk modelling, scenario analysis and forecasting and workflow management.
5. Legal and Regulatory Analysis – encompasses the identification and interpretation of laws and regulations, including identifying changes to the law and the ramifications for corporate policy and compliance.
6. Monitoring – checks to determine whether transactions breach AML, Market Abuse or Payments regulations as well as for the purpose of fraud prevention and detection.
7. Reporting – automates traditional transaction and regulatory reporting obligations, such as MiFID II.[29]
8. Training – products and services that educate staff on laws, regulations and internal policies, which apply to their day-to-day responsibilities. In addition to the above areas it can include conflicts of interest and market misconduct.[30]

These categories of RegTech employ many forms of technology, however, not just AI.[31] The examples provided below narrow the focus of RegTech to only AI applications. In general, RegTech employs machine learning techniques to find patterns in large amounts of data from diverse sources. These sources include relevant laws, regulations and policies, internally generated documentation to undertake a transaction, consumer apps such as for banking and securities trading, and the numerous forms of electronic communication ranging from email and telephone to instant messaging and chat rooms. NLP becomes a particularly important application of machine learning as the written and spoken word is a chief source of data

[28] The GDPR regulates how companies protect EU citizens' personal data.

[29] MiFID II is a regulatory framework of the EU for investment firms that provides certain services linked to 'financial instruments' (eg shares, bonds, derivatives).

[30] PlanetCompliance, 'PlanetCompliance RegTech Directory 2019' (2019) 4, www.planetcompliance.com/wp-content/uploads/2019/07/PlanetCompliance-RegTech-Directory-2019-v1_1.pdf.

[31] See World Economic Forum, 'The New Physics of Financial Services', August 2018, 12.

that needs to be classified.[32] While machine learning identifies correlation rather than causation it can identify complex relationships that a human would most likely miss, but which a human can then consider.[33]

Examples

Anti-Money Laundering and Know Your Customer

AI-powered RegTech has substantial utility in the AML, KYC and counter-terrorism financing (CTF) space, as well as requirements in other areas for background checks, as the laws necessitate verification of identity and monitoring of transactions.[34]

Money laundering has long been a challenging area for institutions to respond to. Money laundering is the attempted transformation of criminal assets into a more usable and legitimate form.[35] Traditional money laundering operates in three stages – placement (entry into system), layering (blurring of the audit trail) and integration (re-entry into system).[36] However 'cyber-laundering' has altered the process, facilitating the phenomenon of disintermediation, ie bypassing traditional financial intermediaries.[37] This makes it easier for criminals to go through the placement and layering stages as by using the internet a complex, multi-jurisdictional audit trail can be created almost instantly.

The last two decades have seen increasingly stringent regulatory responses, including enforcement actions worldwide. There is now an unprecedented volume and variety of regulation.[38] These include the US *Patriot Act*,[39] the Hong Kong *Anti-Money Laundering and Counter-Terrorist Financing Ordinance*, Australia's *Anti-Money Laundering and Counter-Terrorism Financing Act 2006* (Cth) and the UK's Money Laundering Regulations 2017,[40] which implements the EU's Fourth

[32] Financial Stability Board, *Artificial Intelligence and Machine Learning in Financial Services*, 1 November 2017, 20; S Aziz and M Dowling, 'Machine Learning and AI for Risk Management' in Lynn et al (eds) (n 25) 44–45.

[33] Financial Stability Board (n 32) 22.

[34] M Wright, 'Can AI Really Disrupt Monitoring for Suspicious Activity?' in J Barberis, D Arner and R Buckley (eds), *The RegTech Book* (Wiley, 2019) 231.

[35] DS Demetis, *Technology and Anti-Money Laundering: A Systems Theory and Risk-Based Approach* (Edward Elgar, 2010) 12.

[36] ibid.

[37] ibid 12–13.

[38] See generally M Bergström, 'Money Laundering' in V Mitsilegas, M Bergström and T Konstadinides (eds), *Research Handbook on EU Criminal Law* (Edward Elgar, 2016); C King, C Walker and J Gurulé (eds), *The Palgrave Handbook of Criminal and Terrorism Financing Law* (Palgrave Macmillan, 2018).

[39] *Uniting and Strengthening America by Providing Appropriate Tools Required to Intercept and Obstruct Terrorism Act of 2001*.

[40] Money Laundering, Terrorist Financing and Transfer of Funds (Information on the Payer) Regulations 2017 (MLR 2017).

Directive on Money Laundering (4MLD). The 4MLD requires screening against the Office of Foreign Assets Control (OFAC) and Financial Action Task Force (FATF) standardised AML watchlists, intending to restrict investors with a criminal or politically exposed person (PEP) status, requiring firms to employ software to conduct activities such as currency transaction reporting in relation to large cash transactions.

At a general level the requirements under AML/CTF regimes are for institutions to perform due diligence on their customers before they enter into a relationship, mostly establishing their identity and the ultimate beneficiary, ie KYC. Going forward the institution must monitor the relationship on a risk basis looking for concerning activity (red flags) and reporting those concerns to the relevant regulator.[41]

The AML/CTF regimes have led to a commercial desire to digitise and store data onto global online systems that can collect the necessary KYC information and be readily interrogated to identify concerning activity. However, current KYC processes are often 'costly, laborious and highly duplicative across many services and institutions'.[42] It is estimated that with traditional systems nine out of ten alerts are false alarms.[43] The result is that both regulated entities and regulators are 'drowning' in voluminous amounts of low-risk or irrelevant Suspicious Activity Reports (SARs).[44] High volume combined with human fatigue from performing a repetitive task can lead to errors and therefore risk of contraventions for the institution.[45]

AI is increasingly being adopted as a solution. Such software can trawl the vast data reserves and apply logical functions to maximise efficiency. AI is ripe for application to AML/KYC because of its ability to find commonalities and spot anomalies in large data sets. This holds the promise of improving risk profiling as rather than relying on static information, AI can create a real-time, event-driven process of onboarding and continuous review.[46] A number of examples are chosen to illustrate how AI-enabled RegTech works in this space.[47]

Merlon Intelligence employs AI for AML risk screening. The AI model collects and analyses risk-related information around each client by continually analysing relevant industry news and sanction lists, and collecting transactional activities and alert trending. The analysis undertaken by the AI can be used to onboard new clients and monitor transactions.[48]

[41] S Loesch, *A Guide to Financial Regulation for Fintech Entrepreneurs* (John Wiley & Sons, 2018) 131.
[42] Financial Stability Board (n 32) 20.
[43] S Netke, 'RegTech and the Science of Regulation' in Barberis et al (eds) (n 34) 60.
[44] S Kalyanam, '2019: An Artificial Intelligence-Enhanced AML Odyssey', *IBM RegTech Innovations Blog*, 9 January 2019.
[45] Netke (n 43) 60.
[46] Financial Stability Board (n 32) 20.
[47] For further examples see J Hanley-Giersch, 'RegTech and Financial Crime Prevention' in Barberis et al (eds) (n 34) 23.
[48] merlonintelligence.com/.

Quantexa's AI scans data to understand the flow of money, allowing it to flag potential money laundering activity. The AI first gathers all the raw data, combining a customer's transactional data with internal as well as external data from such places as credit reporting agencies and company information databases, but also more esoteric sources such as the Panama Papers. It then provides a visual representation of a network of entities and their relationships to each other.[49] This representation provides context to otherwise huge data volumes and helps professionals uncover hidden customer connections, criminal channels or suspicious links. Besides reducing false positives, the platform finds connections that might be missed such as records where names are slightly different. HSBC has integrated Quantexa technology into its systems[50] after a successful pilot project of its Global Social Network Analytics Platform, which used Quantexa's network analytical capabilities.[51] HSBC was able to analyse data from the 50 jurisdictions where it had a presence and provide a contextual view of customer profile connections. By operating on a single platform, it removed legacy tools and the need to transfer enterprise data, improving operational efficiency in identifying suspicious activity across its network.

In terms of KYC, various RegTechs around the world offer localised services to expedite the KYC process and facilitate digital contracting. Onfido, a UK RegTech start-up, uses machine learning and biometrics, working with digital banks such as Revolut to verify user's photo identifications for KYC compliance.[52] Similarly, Ecertic in Spain uses machine learning with face biometrics to 'face match' between the customer's real image and document photo. This is supported by video recording, proprietary optical character recognition (OCR) and a biometrics electronic signature.[53] Likewise, IDmission, based in the US, is a KYC platform that uses machine learning to automatically analyse documents over four kinds of biometrics (face, fingerprint, iris and voice).[54] More generally chatbots can be employed to assist both customers and compliance staff in completing online forms seeking information for the KYC process.

'Next generation' suspicious activity monitoring may include using AI to identify customers with similar characteristics, such as type of business, so as to compare transaction activity. This could be combined across financial institutions through a shared data lake so that the number of a particular type of businesses could be compared to identify similarities and differences. The AI could also be used to identify what customer behaviours led to an SAR and then use that learning to predict what customers with similar characteristics but no SAR may do.[55]

[49] Quantexa, 'Continuous KYC Whitepaper' (2017).

[50] www.quantexa.com/quantexa-technology-helps-hsbc-fight-financial-crime/.

[51] J McGowan, 'Case Study HSBC: Fighting Financial Crime with Big Data Analysis', *Celent*, 12 April 2019.

[52] 'Onfido Case Study: Revolut', *Onfido.Com*, 2017 hub.onfido.com/case-studies/ revolut-case-study.

[53] www.ecertic.com/#services.

[54] www.idmission.com/homepage-en/.

[55] Wright (n 34) 233.

Banking Requirements

Banks face numerous risks but traditionally the largest risk has been credit risk or the risk of loss if a borrower fails to meet their obligations of repaying interest and the principal.[56] Credit risk has involved estimating the probability of default (PD), loss given default (LGD) and exposure at default (EAD), ie Expected Loss = PD × LGD × EAD. The approach to making these estimates has been to apply a classification technique on past customer data, including those that defaulted, to determine the relationship between the characteristics of a customer and their potential failure to pay. Algorithms have been used to perform the classification previously, but various forms of machine learning have been adopted as it can process more data and greater varieties of data (eg social media) and performs better in identifying non-linear relationships.[57]

After the global financial crisis regulatory reporting requirements and risk management pressures significantly increased. BASEL III, an international regulatory accord, requires banks to meet minimum capital and liquidity regulations and provide stress test documentation for crises.[58] Regional laws such as the EU's European Market Infrastructure Regulation[59] and Capital Requirements Directive IV[60] or the US's *Dodd-Frank Act*[61] add an additional layer of regulation related to stress testing, capital adequacy and loan defaults. These are supplemented with further domestic rules – for example, in the US, since 2011, banks have had to submit to the Federal Reserve Comprehensive Capital Analysis and Review (CCAR), which reports their internal procedures for protecting capital or their ability to carry out stress test scenarios.

In this area, due to the sheer volume of data required, AI-driven RegTech has been applied as a promising solution.[62] The RegTech generally uses machine learning and natural language processing to interpret data inputs from numerous sources, such as emails, spoken word, instant messaging, documents and metadata. This can then be used for regulatory reporting, risk modelling, scenario analysis or forecasting.

[56] M Leo, S Sharma and K Maddulety, 'Machine Learning in Banking Risk Management: A Literature Review' (2019) 7(1) *Risks* 1, 2–3.

[57] Financial Stability Board (n 32) 12; Leo, Sharma and Maddulety (n 56) 7–10.

[58] Basel Committee on Banking Supervision, *The Basel Framework* (Bank for International Settlements, 2019) www.bis.org/basel_framework/index.htm?export=pdf&pdfid=15683490022431591.

[59] Regulation (EU) No 648/2012 of the European Parliament and of the Council of 4 July 2012 on OTC derivatives, central counterparties and trade repositories.

[60] Directive 2013/36/EU of the European Parliament and of the Council of 26 June 2013 on access to the activity of credit institutions and the prudential supervision of credit institutions and investment firms.

[61] *Dodd-Frank Wall Street Reform and Consumer Protection Act*, Public Law No 111-203, § 929-Z, 124 Statute 1376, 1871 (2010) (codified at 15 USC § 78o).

[62] See E Hill, 'Is RegTech the Answer to the Rising Cost of Compliance?', *FX-MM*, 13 June 2016; A Cornell, 'AgTech, ResTech, RegTech, FinTech – Actual Solutions or Techno-Babble?', *ANZ Blue Notes*, 23 February 2016; J Eyers, 'Welcome to the New World of RegTech', *Australian Financial Review*, 20 June 2016.

Theta Lake[63] uses machine learning to supervise video, audio and chat communications, amplifying compliance coverage to large volumes of atypical data which would otherwise require manual review. Specifically, the technology streamlines finding relevance in transcription, extracts important content, performs OCR and then detects compliance risks which are then fed into the AI-assisted workflow.

Ayasdi[64] finds hidden patterns in historical financial data using a machine intelligence platform that has built in unsupervised learning capabilities. In contrast to supervised learning, which generally requires expert data scientists to manually 'label' the data, Ayasdi allows firms' domain experts to input any 'unlabelled' data which it then uses to design contextual solutions. It does so by 'clustering' similar data together, using algorithms to continually test different iterations of calculations until it finds the best results. This has powerful applications in regulatory risk modelling or predicting regulatory risk for problems such as LGD and PD. It is particularly useful for high-dimensional modelling problems where the goal is to cut down the number of variables being used.

A case study from 2017 with Citigroup demonstrates Ayasdi's success in creating justifiable models of Citigroup's revenue and capital reserve forecast which passed the Federal Reserve's CCAR process. Citigroup had previously failed two out of three annual CCAR stress tests. Ayasdi first used subject matter from Citi's business units to review its macroeconomic variables for the forecast. The machine learning platform then correlated the impact of these variables on each business unit's monthly revenue performance over a six-month period, which it used to predict future performance. This streamlined Citigroup's original nine-month process to three months.[65]

On a broader scale, IBM and Thomson Reuters Regulatory Intelligence offers a RegTech solution for real-time monitoring of financial services data. After acquiring Promontory Financial Group, a 600-staff RegTech start-up, IBM was able to integrate the cognitive capabilities of its AI, IBM Watson, with their regulatory compliance consultancy. Using Promontory's expertise, the RegTech uses NLP to identify obligations and controls required to address regulatory change. Clients create libraries of relevant regulatory requirements, map them to their internal framework and have their impacts assessed. In 2019 Thomson Reuters was brought on board to deliver its 'trusted intelligence' of the global regulatory environment.[66]

Compliance.ai provides a one-stop depository for professionals to keep up with evolving regulations and address emerging compliance risk. It uses 'expert-in-the-loop' machine learning and NLP models to classify regulatory content,

[63] thetalake.ai/.

[64] www.ayasdi.com/.

[65] R Bharadwaj, 'Artificial Intelligence in Regulatory Technology (RegTech) – 5 Current Applications', *Emerj*, 13 August 2019.

[66] 'IBM, Thomson Reuters Introduce Powerful New AI and Data Combination to Simplify How Financial Institutions Tackle Regulatory Compliance Challenges', 1 May 2019, www.thomsonreuters.com/en/press-releases/2019/may/ibm-thomson-reuters-introduce-powerful-new-ai-and-data-combination.html.

identifying high-risk areas of compliance to which it sends suggested responses. A case study with the Bank of Marin shows it was able to automate regulatory tracking which was previously done manually by compliance officers. Compliance.ai automatically identified relevant requirements and provided personalised insights, saving compliance employees the time of tracking changes from the websites or newsletters of regulatory bodies like Federal Deposit Insurance Corporation and California Department of Business Oversight.[67]

Trading

The aftermath of the global financial crisis also saw increased regulation in the field of trading to strengthen financial markets and safeguard investors. The World Economic Forum has identified the following 'pain point':

> Every positive alert in today's market-surveillance engines needs to be validated, classified and documented. This is often a manual process that requires the collation of data from various sources in order to complete paper reports that will be submitted to regulatory bodies and risk groups.[68]

Compliance has also moved beyond just monitoring behaviour and communications of traders for transparency and market conduct, and now imposes comprehensive reporting and record-keeping obligations, specific storage requirements and further stringency on best execution of trades. AI is being adopted to address these requirements more comprehensively and efficiently.

Record Keeping

The *Dodd-Frank Act*, for example, requires swap dealers to keep full, systemic records of all the swaps they execute. Records should include all information necessary to conduct a trade reconstruction, including:

- pre-execution information – records of all oral and written communications provided or received concerning quotes, solicitations, bids, offers, instructions, trading and prices, that lead to the execution of a swap, whether communicated by telephone, voicemail, facsimile, instant messaging, chat rooms, electronic mail, mobile device, or other digital or electronic media;
- execution trade information – trade execution records, including the price and terms of each swap;
- post-execution trade information – an itemised record of all relevant post-trade processing and events.[69]

[67] Bharadwaj (n 65).
[68] World Economic Forum, *The New Physics of Financial Services*, August 2018, 136.
[69] Commodity and Securities Exchanges 17 CFR § 23.202 (Daily Trading Records).

This means that banks and financial institutions must keep all communications prior to a swap, correlate them and add the execution and post-execution information to reconstruct the complete trade.

Similarly, the Markets in Financial Instruments Directive (MiFID II) applies to any businesses operating within the European Economic Area and requires financial organisations to record all communication methods, including voice, email, chat, social media and SMS, and any related documentation and order management system. Not only the communication with the end customer, but also the internal communication must be recorded.[70]

Compliant Storage

The *Dodd-Frank Act* requires that all records must be kept in their original form for five years.[71] Furthermore, records must be preserved exclusively in a non-rewritable, non-erasable format. The quality and accuracy of the storage media recording process must also be verified automatically, meeting WORM (Write Once Read Many) standards as well as having a managed audit trail.

MiFID requires original files to be stored in a durable, unalterable format and to be readily available to clients for five years and up to seven years for regulators. When requested by the regulator or a customer, the complete communication chain must be reconstructed in a timely manner.[72]

Best Execution

Under the *Investment Advisers Act of 1940*,[73] the SEC imposes a federal fiduciary duty on advisors with responsibility to direct client trades to seek 'best execution' in client transactions.[74] An advisor must execute their trades in such a manner that the total costs or proceeds of each transaction are the most favourable under the circumstances.[75]

Likewise, MiFID II RTS 27 requires financial organisations to: Take all sufficient steps to obtain, when executing orders, the best possible result for their

[70] MiFID II arts 16.7, 24.3.

[71] Commodity and Securities Exchanges 17 CFR § 1.31 (Regulatory Records; Retention and Production).

[72] Loesch (n 41) 224.

[73] See, eg, *Transamerica Mortgage Advisors, Inc v Lewis* (1979) 444 US 11, 17 ('[Section] 206 establishes federal fiduciary standards to govern the conduct of investment advisers' (quotation marks omitted)); *SEC v Capital Gains Research Bureau, Inc* (1963) 375 US 180, 191 ('The *Investment Advisers Act of 1940* thus reflects a congressional recognition of the delicate fiduciary nature of an investment advisory relationship' (quotation marks omitted)).

[74] Section 28(e) of the *Securities and Exchange Act of 1934*.

[75] SEC, 'Interpretive Release Concerning the Scope of Section 28(e) of the *Securities Exchange Act of 1934* and Related Matters' (Release No 23170, 28 April 1986); see also SEC, 'Commission Guidance Regarding Client Commission Practices under Section 28(e) of the *Securities Exchange Act of 1934* (Release No 54165, 18 July 2006).

clients taking into account price, costs, speed, likelihood of execution and settlement, size, nature or any other consideration relevant to the execution of the order. This requires financial organisations to report on any transaction and make the details available for the public under the Best Execution requirements.[76]

Shield FC[77] helps financial institutions control communication data to meet regulatory requirements. It operates across a number of forms of regulation by providing a complete view of electronic communications and trade and market data utilising machine learning and NLP. For Dodd-Frank swap transaction reporting requirements the Shield FC record-keeping platform connects to the organisations' communication channels and reconstructs the swap from pre- to post-execution for a compliance officer. Shield FC can also meet MiFID II's requirement to reconstruct a complete communication chain when needed.

Market Misconduct/Insider Trading

Market misconduct involves action aimed at artificially inflating or depressing the price of securities. The Supreme Court of the United States has stated that the term market manipulation 'connotes intentional or willful conduct designed to deceive or defraud investors by controlling or artificially affecting the price of securities'.[78] Manipulative trading techniques are known by a number of colourful descriptions such as 'wash trading' (an investor simultaneously sells and buys the same financial instruments to create the appearance of activity in the marketplace), 'pump and dump' (entering into transactions at successively higher prices so as to give the appearance of real activity by investors then selling at the artificially inflated price) and 'rumourtage' (spreading false or misleading rumours about company value in order to alter the share price).[79]

Perhaps the most well-known form of market manipulation is insider trading. In general, insider trading involves the buying or selling by someone in possession of non-public, price-sensitive information. The classic insider trading example is when a director or company insider in possession of the information engages in the trading. However, insider trading can extend to a person who receives the information from an insider and trades, usually called tipping. It can also apply where a third party, such as a broker, obtains the inside information and trades.[80]

AI-based anomaly detection has been used heavily in surveillance systems to monitor suspicious activities, such as those relating to insider trading or market manipulation. The World Economic Forum compared the traditional and AI-empowered approach to compliance in this area. Traditional 'rules-based approaches' to detect market abuse are based on retrospective flagging of

[76] Loesch (n 41) 218.
[77] www.shieldfc.com/.
[78] *Ernst & Ernst v Hochfelder* (1976) 425 US 185, 199.
[79] P Redmond, *Corporations and Financial Markets Law* (7th edn, Thomson Reuters, 2017) 884.
[80] ibid 897–98; 14 *Fletcher Cyclopedia of the Law of Corporations*, § 6856.

transactions using incomplete transaction histories based exclusively on internal systems.[81] Conversely, machine learning can be used to provide market surveillance by combining providers' 'whole-market' order data and other unstructured data, such as a trader's messages. It can also use insights from transaction patterns across institutions.[82]

Hentsū allows firms to monitor the behaviour of traders over different types of data, including communications, trades and personal data.[83]

Hentsū's machine learning is applied in trade or transaction monitoring by examining the historical trading pattern of an individual and seeing if a particular trade is part of their style or strategy versus 'spoofing'. The pattern recognition and ability to 'learn' over time allows for more accurate alerts rather than traditional tools, which would only create alerts upon hard-coded thresholds being reached.

A firm can train the software for detection scenarios of insider training, exposing hidden relationships. By using natural language processing, Hentsū can identify when a trader is talking to other market participants with whom they have a personal relationship. Any potential collusion triggers an investigation into the other channels of communication. It then detects correlations between communications and trade events, such as if there are any patterns of particular individuals or groups moving their chats to encrypted instant messaging (IM) applications like WhatsApp or WeChat which coincide with trades at key times such as during a benchmark setting.[84] Hentsū Connect captures IM apps' native metadata, ensuring that all content is stored, including emojis, photos and even shared documents that have been deleted. An AI cloud platform collects these types of disparate data and meets the five-year requirement of the *Dodd-Frank Act* as well as the seven-year requirement of MiFID.[85]

Promontory uses IBM's Watson AI to pre-emptively identify potential misconduct by establishing behaviour-based trader profiles. Promontory Watson first performs unsupervised learning by clustering. Clustering is a method of unsupervised learning that finds patterns in the data by identifying 'clusters' of data that have similar underlying characteristics.[86] Promontory then analyses a combination of trade data, electronic and voice communications records to observe emerging patterns of behaviour. By applying this voice surveillance technology to discern trade conversations, banks may prevent wrongdoing before it occurs rather than investigating it after the fact.[87]

[81] World Economic Forum, *The New Physics of Financial Services*, August 2018, 136.
[82] ibid.
[83] hentsu.com/artificial-intelligence-and-compliance-the-regtech-movement/.
[84] ibid.
[85] hentsu.com/mifid-ii-guide-meeting-end-end-requirements/.
[86] See Chapter 5.
[87] IBM, *Insight on Business*, www.ibm.com/blogs/insights-on-business/banking/how-promontory-and-ibm-are-reshaping-financial-services-through-ai/.

Data Privacy

Data protection regulations and privacy laws have been adopted across a number of jurisdictions. Most OECD nations have enacted their own framework of privacy laws off the back of OECD guidelines on privacy and cross-border uses.[88] At a general level, these laws place new limitations and requirements on the collection, transmission and storage of personal data. One of the most far-reaching and developed of these laws is the EU's GDPR.[89]

On 25 May 2018 the EU's GDPR came into force, requiring that any enterprise or business providing services to Europeans, independent of where it is located, that collects personal information must comply with its terms. Failure to do so can result in fines of up to 20 million euros or 4 per cent of global turnover, whichever is higher. The basic requirements are:

- Consent – any personal data collected should be explicitly approved by the customer. General consent is not allowed anymore and an explanation why and how the personal data will be used is mandatory.
- Secure – personal data should be kept in secured storage, available for authorised persons only.
- Access – customers should have access to see, amend and correct their personal data.
- Forget – unless the personal data should be kept to comply with other regulations (such as financial regulations), customers have the right to be forgotten, and the organisation is obligated to delete all their personal data.[90]

Tessian provides an enterprise email security platform.[91] Its Human Layer Security (HLS) platform uses machine learning to identify unsafe emails that may lead to data loss or security threats. It devises security filters by analysing historical email data and finds patterns in employee email behaviour. These filters then monitor outgoing emails and detect anomalies. This personalised monitoring is in contrast to traditional, rule-based solutions to email cybersecurity. Taylor Vinters, a UK law firm, used Tessian to ensure their obligations under the GDPR were met, preventing email breaches proactively or the sending of misaddressed emails which would have led to a GDPR breach.[92]

[88] OECD, 'Guidelines on the Protection of Privacy and Transborder Flows of Personal Data' (July 2013).

[89] The GDPR is supplemented by Directive 2002/58/EC of the European Parliament and of the Council of 12 July 2002 concerning the processing of personal data and the protection of privacy in the electronic communications sector (ePrivacy Directive), which imposes further restrictions on the use of traffic and location data. The GDPR is discussed further in Chapter 11 as a form of regulation for AI.

[90] Loesch (n 41) 187–94.

[91] www.tessian.com/.

[92] Taylor Vinters, 'Tessian Case Study', 5 February 2018, www.youtube.com/watch?v=UgfPLYjYj90.

Text IQ uses machine learning to pre-emptively identify sensitive and compromising information in big data.[93] Its Deep Concept Analysis identifies words and phrases that have similar meanings to known ones, relying on a combination of natural language processing and relationship analytics to flag and narrow down document sets for human review. It is also able to find systemic behaviours in employee work patterns such as the use of embarrassing language or code words that violate internal policies and infringe regulations.[94] In its eDiscovery applications, it can prevent leaking of sensitive documents by auto-redacting or auto-pseudonymising personally identifying information, protected health information and personal data to meet GDPR requirements.[95] Text IQ claims to be able to deduce links between parties that are not apparent on the face of the text, for example combining 10 medical documents to reasonably infer identities or spotting attorney–client privilege just from a lawyer's tone.[96]

Environmental Laws

In the introduction to this chapter it was explained that RegTech is broader than FinTech and can be used in other regulatory contexts. An example of AI's use in another area is in environmental regulation. 'GreenTech' companies have used AI to facilitate 'solar energy remote monitoring to water treatment analytics … [and] to provide energy use optimization'.[97]

Pluto is taking advantage of the sensorification of modern water treatment plants and machine learning to present managers with a dashboard that quantifies the status of all assets at a given water treatment plant. Monitoring and prediction can allow for leaks or anomalies to be detected.[98] A similar company providing AI solutions for water and gas is TaKaDu.[99] Tempus Energy uses AI to control and optimise when flexible assets use energy. By predicting volatility in carbon intensity and market prices the AI tech allows customers to reduce their energy costs – while simultaneously enhancing their use of renewables.[100] Tempus Energy aims to reduce costs and adopt a more environmentally friendly approach to energy usage for customers. While voluntary at present, environmental regulation mandating such action could be complied with using the same technology.

[93] www.textiq.com/.

[94] query.prod.cms.rt.microsoft.com/cms/api/am/binary/RE36LYP.

[95] www.textiq.com/legal.

[96] A Konrad, 'How AI Startup Text IQ Got Profitable by Shaving Millions off Customers' Legal Costs', *Forbes*, 1 February 2017, www.forbes.com/sites/alexkonrad/2017/02/01/ai-startup-textiq-shaves-millions-off-legal-costs/#1fbdb55c6692.

[97] I Amesheva, 'The Potential of RegTech in Improving the Effectiveness of Environmental Regulation' in Barberis et al (eds) (n 34) 272–73.

[98] www.plutoshift.com/.

[99] www.takadu.com/solution.

[100] www.tempusenergy.com/.

General Compliance

Firms today are constantly having to comply with ever-changing regulatory requirements. AI provides the opportunity to address these compliance pressures and centralise regulatory management.[101]

Cognitive+ provides legal and regulatory analytics to enable firms to understand their compliance obligations. It uses machine learning, NLP and rule-based AI to automate repetitive tasks such as contract analysis and provides tailored regulatory intelligence based on the content of a company's policies and contracts. The AI identifies topics of interest and relationships between various events, entities and obligations in unstructured text.[102] It also provides regulatory content feeds and catalogues of relevant laws/regulations, and provides business impact analysis.

Waymark Tech assists clients to integrate new bodies of regulation into their regulatory operations.[103] It uses machine learning and natural language processing to read and interpret the implications of regulatory documentation. Waymark 'ingests' Financial Conduct Authority and Prudential Regulation Authority handbooks and uses NLP to parse and cross-reference the relevant parts. It then tags and collates key terms and informs the client of what obligations have changed and require revision.

CUBE is an end-to-end RegTech platform that extracts regulatory obligations and maps them to internal policies to automate the process of compliance.[104] It uses machine learning and NLP to automatically track global regulatory data and detect real-time changes, visually representing it in a 'heat map' of areas of non-compliance by jurisdiction and line of business. CUBE's 'data lake', or repository of raw data, is claimed to cover regulations for financial services internationally (across 180 countries and in 60 languages). Relying on this system, all relevant obligations to a client's individual policy, procedures, controls and records are mapped. It then provides insight as well as how to meet ongoing regulatory obligations. AI is also used in CUBOT, the platform's chatbot, which leverages CUBE's regulatory intelligence to provide clients with on-demand immediate answers.[105]

SupTech

The adoption of technology to support regulation and enforcement has been under way for some time. However, more recently that technology has been AI.[106]

[101] D Craig, 'The Augmented Compliance Office?' in Barberis et al (eds) (n 34) 224.
[102] www.cognitivplus.com/.
[103] waymark.tech/.
[104] www.cube.global/documents/CUBE_Overview.pdf.
[105] www.cube.global/solution.
[106] D Broeders and J Prenio, 'Innovative Technology in Financial Supervision (Suptech) – The Experience of Early Users', *FSI Insights on Policy Implementation No 9* (Financial Stability Institute, July 2018).

In 2013 the SEC introduced the Market Information Data Analytics System or 'MIDAS' to analyse 'big data' generated by equity markets. MIDAS collects and processes records from the proprietary feeds of the national equity exchanges and the consolidated tape which allows the Division of Trading and Markets to monitor market behaviour and understand market events. Suggested uses for MIDAS, in addition to research, are monitoring and understanding mini-flash crashes, or identifying possibly troublesome or illegal behaviour, 'for example, by noting excessive cancellations of message traffic'.[107]

The use of AI to aid enforcement is illustrated by the SEC's Advanced Relational Trading Enforcement Metric Investigation System (ARTEMIS). ARTEMIS combines historical trading and account holder data with other data sources 'to enable longitudinal, multi-issuer, and multi-trader data analyses'.[108]

Brokers are required to provide Blue Sheet data files containing both trading and account holder information to the SEC. The ARTEMIS program analyses historical patterns and relationships from the Blue Sheet data. For example, in the insider trading context, ARTEMIS flags traders who exhibit an unusual pattern of making judicious trades in advance of the release of company news that affects stock prices.[109] In August 2015 the SEC brought a case against 32 defendants who made more than $100 million in illegal profits by trading based on pre-release corporate earnings announcements stolen from multiple newswire services. Former Chair Mary Jo White stated:

> We now have new technological tools and investigative approaches that allow us not only to pinpoint suspicious trading across multiple securities but also to identify relationships among traders. The SEC's Enforcement Division sorted through literally millions of trades, thousands of earnings announcements and gigabytes of data on IP addresses in order to identify these defendants who went to great lengths to evade detection, often identifying these traders based on their patterns of trading.[110]

The Australian Securities and Investments Commission has similar capability called the Market Analysis and Intelligence system.[111]

The Monetary Authority of Singapore is developing algorithms to scan suspicious transaction reports (STRs) and identify those that warrant further attention, so as to allow supervisors to focus their resources on higher-risk transactions. Supervisors will then be able to look for more data, such as transactions from the entities under suspicion.[112]

[107] E Walter, 'Harnessing Tomorrow's Technology for Today's Investors and Markets', speech delivered at American University School of Law, Washington DC, 19 February 2013.

[108] Piwowar (n 1).

[109] P Murphy, 'SEC Embracing Analytics as Tool to Catch Crooked Traders', *New England Inhouse*, 3 December 2018.

[110] MJ White, 'Remarks at a Press Conference Announcing Enforcement Charges Involving an International Hacking Trading Scheme', 11 August 2015.

[111] Broeders and Prenio (n 106) 10.

[112] ibid 11.

Several supervisory agencies use chatbots to answer consumer complaints automatically. The Bangko Sentral ng Pilipinas (BSP), with support from RegTech for Regulators Accelerator (R2A), is developing a prototype chatbot to answer consumer complaints. The system will be able to triage the concerns received and answer simple questions. The data received will also allow BSP to analyse potential areas of concern. Complaints can signal unlawful behaviour by a supervised entity.[113] The Australian Securities and Investments Commission is developing a chatbot to advise a business whether it needs a financial services or credit licence.[114]

In the environmental area a study using five different machine learning algorithms for classification problems was found to improve the efficiency of environmental monitoring by allocating inspections of facilities at higher risk of non-compliance.[115]

Role of the Lawyer in RegTech

In-house Lawyers

The role of the in-house lawyer is expanding. In many organisations the in-house lawyer does not simply provide legal advice or manage external law firms, but is intimately involved in compliance, corporate governance, and risk and reputation management. This role involves prevention of contraventions as opposed to dealing with allegations of contravention and enforcement actions.[116] It also involves a broad view of legal risk, namely the legal consequence of any compliance failure or breach of the law in relation to the corporation's operations.[117] The law may be private law such as contract or public regulatory law, however the focus in this chapter, as shown by the examples above, is the latter.

The Association of Corporate Counsel has opined that 'the general counsel should be a key ally and partner in establishing a corporate culture that supports corporate performance without compromising ethical behavior, and legal and regulatory compliance'.[118] While the in-house lawyer's 'most basic job' is ensuring adherence to the law, it is also to educate others in the corporation that compliance

[113] ibid 9.

[114] Australian Securities and Investments Commission, 'ASIC's Regtech Initiatives 2018–19 – Report 653' (December 2019) 17–18.

[115] M Hino, E Benami and N Brooks, 'Machine Learning for Environmental Monitoring' (2018) 1 *Nature Sustainability* 583 (examining enforcement of the US *Clean Water Act* by the Environmental Protection Agency).

[116] ZJ Barclift, 'Preventive Law: A Strategy for Internal Corporate Lawyers to Advise Managers of Their Ethical Obligations' (2008) 33 *Journal of the Legal Profession* 31, 32 ('because internal corporate lawyers are employees of the corporation and embedded with the client, they are able to deliver more effectively the proactive legal services advocated by Preventive Law'); Steinberg and Yeager (n 11).

[117] Moorhead, Vaughan and Godinho (n 17) 104–06.

[118] Richardson and Blatch (n 12) 1–2.

'creates value' because integrity is rewarded by stakeholders such as employees and customers.[119] Allen & Overy has opined that the in-house legal function is well positioned to 'drive initiatives that embed, at the heart of their organisations, governance, culture and corporate purpose, … risk controls and smart responses to regulatory change and policy'.[120]

The in-house lawyer is by definition closer to the corporation than an external lawyer, more familiar with its operations, and therefore said to be well placed to identify and prevent corporate misconduct.[121] However, to perform this preventative role the in-house lawyer must be clear on who their client is – the corporation, not management.

In Australia Justice Gzell in the trial judgment of the James Hardie asbestos litigation case stated that 'Guarding against legal risks to [the corporate entity] was at the core of … responsibilities as general counsel'.[122] The High Court of Australia agreed, stating:

> An important element in [the general counsel's] responsibilities was his giving advice about and, where appropriate, taking steps necessary to ensure compliance with all relevant legal requirements, including those that applied to [the corporate entity] as a listed public company. The primary judge and the Court of Appeal described this aspect of [the general counsel's] responsibilities as a duty to protect the company 'from legal risk'.[123]

In summary, the above discussion of in-house lawyers advocates for a gatekeeper model, rather than a 'hired gun or total commitment model',[124] where the lawyer continues to seek to promote the client's interests but does so in a more holistic way by focussing on the longer term where it is the corporation's interests to be law abiding. A gatekeeper serves as an independent evaluator of corporate actions. The gatekeeper inhibits wrongdoing by saying 'no' when company actions will contravene the law. In this role the lawyer's primary responsibilities are to identify, manage and communicate corporate legal risks to the relevant persons.[125]

Another way of configuring the in-house lawyer role is as 'persuasive counselors'. Under the 'persuasive counselor' model, 'lawyers attempt to guide their clients to the right course of action by providing independent advice, backed up

[119] Heineman (n 2) 131.

[120] Brayne (n 15) 19.

[121] Kim (n 13) 199–200.

[122] *Australian Securities and Investments Commission v Macdonald (No 11)* (2009) 71 ACSR 368, [394].

[123] *Shafron v Australian Securities and Investments Commission* (2012) 247 CLR 465, [15].

[124] See J Fisch and K Rosen, 'Is There a Role for Lawyers in Preventing Future Enrons?' (2003) 48 *Villanova Law Review* 1097, 1102 (setting out the two models but also recognising that there are a broader array of models including the problem solver).

[125] R Nelson and LB Nielsen, 'Cops, Counsel, and Entrepreneurs: Constructing the Role of Inside Counsel in Large Corporations' (2000) 34(2) *Law & Society Review* 457, 470; Barclift (n 116) 42; see also American Bar Association, 'Model Rules of Professional Conduct' rr 1.6(b)(2), 1.13.

by the persuasive power of the lawyer's personal courage and influence'.[126] The role may also be looked at from the perspective of what *not* to do:

> the [general counsel] must not succumb to the temptation to 'go along to get along.' She cannot be mere 'window dressing' on corporate decision making, placing her imprimatur of legal approval on tough questions. Instead, she must actively engage in and influence the decision-making process.[127]

Independence is particularly important for the in-house lawyer because their client is the corporation but they are dealing with its officers on a day-to-day basis, and those officers may, or may not, reflect the corporation's best interests.[128] However, in-house lawyers have been criticised, or warned to adopt safeguards, because corporate relationships (being part of the team and seeking to maintain influence), expectations (commerciality and commitment to the business) and incentives (salary, bonuses, promotion) can undermine independence.[129] Independence cannot be taken for granted but must be protected.

So what does this mean for RegTech? Lawyers should be part of the regulatory compliance team that helps design RegTech and then monitors how RegTech is used.[130] The lawyer is meant to be sceptical and willing to test whether the technology does indeed assure compliance with what the law requires.[131] The lawyer may find it necessary to explain to other members of the team that in testing legality they are also looking out for the corporation's interests. Further, once a system is operational the lawyer may be part of the process when a compliance problem is detected so as to ensure that steps are taken to correct the problem rather than have it be overlooked or concealed. This may include designing and operating a whistleblower policy/programme to encourage front-line staff to report acts or omissions that contravene the law or corporate policy. Where the law or corporate policy may have been contravened then the lawyer may need to assume responsibility for an internal investigation.[132]

[126] EN Veasey and CT Di Guglielmo, 'General Counsel Buffeted by Compliance Demands and Client Pressures May Face Personal Peril' (2012) 68 *Business Lawyer* 57, 65–66.

[127] ibid 60.

[128] Barclift (n 116) 43; R Bird and S Kim Park, 'The Domains of Corporate Counsel in an Era of Compliance' (2016) 53 *American Business Law Journal* 203, 219–20 (explaining the issue through agency theory); Moorhead, Vaughan and Godinho (n 17) 214.

[129] Moorhead, Vaughan and Godinho (n 17) 70–74, 132–46. See also Nelson and Nielsen (n 125) 470–73.

[130] Richardson and Blatch (n 12) 5 ('When the general counsel is included in discussions of business strategies before they are implemented, she can help the company assess and avoid legal and business risks'); Heineman (n 2) 144 (summarising in-house counsel's role as to prevent, detect and respond).

[131] R Gruner, 'General Counsel in an Era of Compliance Programs' (1997) 46 *Emory Law Journal* 1113, 1159 ('Because of their familiarity with governing legal standards and past offenses within their companies, general counsel will often be able to make valuable contributions in specifying the criteria and targeting strategies applied in compliance monitoring systems').

[132] Steinberg and Yeager (n 11) 283, citing W McLucas, L Wertheimer and A June, 'Preparing for the Deluge: How to Respond When Employees Speak Up and Report Possible Compliance Violations' (2012) 44 *Securities Regulation & Law Report* 922.

Gartner Inc, a leading research and advisory company, has identified a need 'to prevent AI gone wild' ie, AI that does not function correctly or has unintended consequences leading to legal, financial and reputational risks.[133] One of the concerns identified with RegTech is that the

> programmers who develop automated compliance systems de facto make decisions about how to best understand the law, and how to translate and convert it into code. Once this conversion is over, the law, as applied may be altered in significant ways from the law that lawmakers and regulators created.[134]

In short, the software code or algorithm seeks to give effect to the law. The assumption in the quote above is that the law is changed. But that is not correct. The law remains the same but if the interpretation of it by the RegTech is incorrect, then compliance may not be achieved. Consequently, there is a risk that the technology adopted to achieve compliance actually ensures contravention.

However, ascertaining and complying with the law is not straightforward, as observed by Robert Gordon:

> There's nothing simple or straightforward about complying with framework norms in the modern regulatory state – often just figuring out what they are is a considerable undertaking. Regulatory regimes tend to be appallingly complex and technical, crammed with loopholes and ambiguities, sometimes put there by regulated interests, often inadvertent. Regulatory statutes are often utopian; full compliance is impossible. They are often in part only symbolic – sweeping commands considerably qualified or even retracted in practice by a large discretion or ridiculously low budget for enforcement.[135]

The complexity of the modern regulatory state may be illustrated by the length of some recent statutes – the *Dodd-Frank Act* was almost 1,000 pages long and the original healthcare package called Obamacare was 906 pages. To this must be added the regulations and guidance that various regulators adopt to give effect to legislation. There may also be case law interpreting some provisions.[136] But even sophisticated commercial judges may face difficulties. In a case dealing with misselling of synthetic collateralised debt obligations the judge referred to Australian

[133] J Council, 'Companies Bolster AI Governance Efforts', *Wall Street Journal*, 20 August 2019. See also B Yerak and T Shumsky, 'More Companies Flag a New Risk: Artificial Intelligence' *Wall Street Journal*, 9 January 2019 (discussing the inclusion of AI in the risk-factor section of annual reports, not just due to the effect of AI being adopted by competitors, which can reduce costs and provide new product offerings, but also execution risks for the company in its adoption of AI); K Broughton, 'Risk Managers Grapple with Potential Downsides of AI', *Wall Street Journal*, 2 December 2019.

[134] N Geslevich Packin, 'Regtech, Compliance and Technology Judgment Rule' (2018) 93 *Chicago-Kent Law Review* 193, 216. See also KA Bamberger, 'Technologies of Compliance: Risk and Regulation in a Digital Age' (2009) 88 *Texas Law Review* 669.

[135] R Gordon, 'Why Lawyers Can't Just Be Hired Guns' in D Rhode (ed), *Ethics in Practice – Lawyers' Roles, Responsibilities and Regulation* (Oxford University Press, 2000) 48. See also Moorhead, Vaughan and Godinho (n 17) 129.

[136] G Hadfield, *Rules for a Flat World* (Oxford University Press, 2017) 171–73.

legislation addressing what is a financial product or a financial service as 'legislative porridge'.[137] Complexity does not end with the law – it may also exist in the underlying facts. The agreements that created the financial products at the heart of the Global Financial Crisis are a clear example.[138]

Nonetheless, the lawyer needs to determine how they respond to that complexity and uncertainty. Gordon takes the view that

> in most contexts lawyers can fairly readily tell the difference between making good-faith efforts to comply with plausible interpretation of the purposes of a legal regime, and using every ingenuity of his or her trade to resist or evade compliance.[139]

Similarly, Ben Heinmann, former general counsel for General Electric, states that in-house lawyers must not 'try to interpret away the law's purpose and effect through strained, hyper-technical readings that are obfuscatory and not in the range of credibility if viewed by an independent third party'.[140] There are, however, concerns that where the legal answer is unclear but the commercial answer *is* clear, there may be an expectation or incentive for the lawyer to 'adjust one's view of the legal uncertainties to accommodate the organisational imperatives'.[141] Equally, the answer to whether something is legally permissible may depend on a risk assessment where the seriousness of the ramifications of a contravention, ie civil or criminal, quantum of fines/damages, loss of life/financial loss/reputational harm, impacts whether a lawyer will sign off.[142]

Despite the difficulties of complexity, uncertainty and commercial preferences, in-house lawyers must bring their specialised legal knowledge, understanding of the circumstances and independent judgement to bear in reaching a defensible position. It is this role of the lawyer that is undertaken as part of the team responsible for designing and monitoring RegTech.

Compliance Specialists not Lawyers

An alternative view is that corporate compliance should be the domain of compliance specialists and not lawyers.[143] To some degree this is the result of lawyers

[137] *Wingecarribee Shire Council v Lehmann Brothers Australia Limited (in liq)* [2012] FCA 1028, [948]. See also *The 'Putbus'* [1969] P 136, 152 ('Were bewilderment the legitimate aim of statutes, the *Merchant Shipping (Liability of Shipowners and Others) Act, 1958*, would clearly be entitled to a high award. Indeed, the deep gloom which its tortuousities induced in me has been lifted only by the happy discovery that my attempt to construe them has led me to the same conclusion as my brethren').

[138] Hadfield (n 136) 175. See also *Wingecarribee Shire Council v Lehmann Brothers Australia Limited (in liq)* [2012] FCA 1028, [13] (The 'SCDOs were highly complex financial instruments, underpinned by equally complex, and at points arcane, legal documentation to give them effect') [118]; *Belmont Park Investments PTY Ltd v BNY Corporate Trustee Services Ltd* [2011] UKSC 38, [22].

[139] Gordon (n 135) 48.

[140] Heineman (n 2) 141.

[141] Moorhead, Vaughan and Godinho (n 17) 212–13.

[142] Heineman (n 2) 141 ('How much "legitimate" legal risk does a corporation wish to take?'); Moorhead, Vaughan and Godinho (n 17) 129–32.

[143] Bird and Kim Park (n 128) 205.

typically being more costly than compliance specialists, and where numerous people are needed to undertake the compliance function that cost will be an important consideration, although the rise of RegTech should streamline the compliance function and remove the need for some lower-level roles.

However, there are two responses to this view. First, lawyers stand apart from these other occupations because of their subject-matter expertise, determining what the law requires, which, as explained above, can be a difficult task, and the ethical requirements they are subject to, even as in-house lawyers.[144] If the lawyer is to be limited to advising on legality as a legal technician then the gatekeeper role may be lost.[145] Second, RegTech requires a team approach with diverse skill sets[146] that include in-house lawyers and the compliance function, as well as technology and design expertise. There may be differences of opinion as to how reporting structures should work but the lawyer needs to be in the room.

Private Practice

Law firms have previously established practices to advise their corporate clients on implementing compliance programmes and this is able to extend to RegTech.[147] The external lawyer may be called on to assist the in-house legal function in dealing with the issues discussed above, such as resolving the requirements of the law where there is complexity and uncertainty, but also to provide an independent perspective.

In the RegTech context the law firm may also, like the in-house lawyer, perform a quality assurance role where they evaluate a technology product to assess whether it meets legal requirements. For example, Australian law firm Allens was asked by Westpac Banking Corporation to work with Red Marker[148] to determine if the algorithms used reflected both the corporate law and bank policies.[149]

The report on the development of the chatbot for licensing developed by the Australian Securities and Investments Commission illustrated the role of lawyers as follows:

> The complexity of the licensing regime made mapping the logic of the TAG tool a challenging task. The level of overlap across guidance for products and services, along with associated exemptions, required skilled practitioners with confidence in their

[144] SH Duggin, 'The Pivotal Role of the General Counsel in Promoting Corporate Integrity and Professional Responsibility' (2007) 51 *Saint Louis University Law Journal* 989, 1012; Bird and Kim Park (n 128) 221–22; Heineman (n 2) 171.

[145] M DeStefano, 'Creating a Culture of Compliance: Why Departmentalization May Not Be the Answer' (2014) 10 *Hastings Business Law Journal* 71, 144–54.

[146] D Bundi, 'RegTech – A Mindset for Breakthroughs' in M DeStefano and G Dobrauz (eds), *New Suits: Appetite for Disruption in the Legal World* (Staempfli Verlag, 2019) 414, 426.

[147] Bird and Kim Park (n 128) 215.

[148] www.redmarker.ai/.

[149] J Eyers, 'Allens Taps AI for Compliance Model', *Australian Financial Review*, 14 June 2019, 33.

> understanding of the regulatory landscape. This is doubly important when attempting to balance for user experience by optimising the language of the questions and the number of questions users must answer. Specialised human input does not stop there – with legislation and regulatory guidance being as dynamic as it is, there will be an ongoing need for continual updates to the TAG tool.[150]

However, with the advent of AI the law firm's expertise can also be automated in some respects. To be able to compete with RegTech start-ups, that expertise can be sold as a legal product. In the Red Marker example, Allens also invested in the company and helped to build an inventory of products that clients can license off the platform, with Allens receiving a proportion of Red Marker licence fees. Allens' banking partner, Simun Soljo, explained that this was a shift away from traditional hourly billing and reflected a form of alternative fee arrangement:

> Up until now law firms have made money from hourly rates, lawyers doing work. The idea of this is to create a product that Red Marker can license, that we have an interest in because we helped create it. So there's an upfront investment but an opportunity to generate revenue on an ongoing basis.[151]

Government/Regulator Lawyers

Similar to the in-house lawyer, lawyers employed by a regulator should be part of the team that helps design SupTech and then monitors its use in relation to whether it is accurately giving effect to the legal requirements that it operationalises. While regulated entities want to confirm that RegTech is indeed fostering compliance with the law, regulators want to ensure that tools that detect suspicious activity are designed so that suspicious activity aligns with illegality as defined by the law. It is also important to note that when it comes to acting on the findings of SupTech there is still a need for human and legal judgement, as acknowledged by Rob Gruppetta, Head of the Financial Crime Department with the Financial Conduct Authority:

> Of course, we're mindful that making predictions based solely on machine learning algorithms can be misleading, so we take great care to ensure that these are overlaid with appropriate financial crime and sector expertise. We only ever use them as the first step in a rigorous, multi-layered risk assessment process to help us target the riskiest firms. Simply put, the algorithms improve, rather than replace, supervisory judgment.[152]

The advisory role of lawyers employed by a regulator may also extend the RegTech. In an advisory and educative role the lawyer may engage with regulated entities

[150] Australian Securities and Investments Commission, *ASIC's Regtech Initiatives 2018–19 – Report 653* (December 2019) 18.

[151] Eyers (n 149) 33.

[152] R Gruppetta, 'AI and Financial Crime: Silver Bullet or Red Herring?' (speech delivered London, 19 November 2018).

to communicate the regulator's stance or policy on what particular laws allow or disallow. This is to promote compliance. An important form of support for RegTech from regulators is the regulatory sandbox.[153] The Financial Conduct Authority provides a sandbox that seeks to provide firms with the ability to test products and services in a controlled environment, and support in identifying appropriate consumer protection safeguards to build into new products and services. The sandbox provides access to regulatory expertise and a set of tools to facilitate testing and alter legal requirements if warranted, such as individual guidance, informal steers, waivers and no enforcement action letters.[154] The expertise that the regulator is sharing includes that of its lawyers.

While responsibility for a RegTech product remains with the regulated entity that employs it, the regulator's lawyers can assist in-house lawyers and private practice lawyers in addressing complexity and uncertainty in the law.

Future Developments

RegTech has been described as 'the sleeping giant of the financial services world' as it offers the opportunity of a more efficient and effective way of achieving compliance.[155] RegTech will undoubtedly spread into other areas of regulation and compliance as better and cheaper compliance with the law is desired by all sectors of the economy. Indeed, it is RegTech's link to private enterprise and cost saving that may see it power ahead of other uses of AI considered in this book.

As discussed above, lawyers will be a key part of the team that helps design and monitor RegTech. However, the greater use of RegTech, while desirable, will also require the lawyer to ensure that past lessons are not forgotten but also to recognise new challenges.

In corporations it has been accepted that there is a need to avoid compliance being seen as just a box-ticking exercise and there is a larger, and more difficult, requirement of promoting a corporate culture that is law abiding and ethical. A former Chair of the SEC has noted that 'deficient corporate cultures are often the cause of the most egregious securities law violations'.[156] As the UK Hampel Committee on Corporate Governance observed many years ago, 'The true safeguard for good corporate governance lies in the application of informed and

[153] M Butler, 'Turning Technology against Financial Crime' (speech delivered London, 23 October 2019).

[154] www.fca.org.uk/firms/innovation/regulatory-sandbox. See also J Burnie and A Henderson, 'Legal Guidance for Entering the Sandbox and Taking Advantage of Cross-Border Cooperation Agreements' in Barberis et al (eds) (n 34) 102.

[155] N Cook, 'Meeting the Pace of Technological Change' (speech delivered at Chief Data Officer Exchange Financial Services Conference, London, 6 November 2019).

[156] MJ White, 'A Few Things Directors Should Know About the SEC' (speech delivered at Stanford University Rock Center for Corporate Governance – Twentieth Annual Stanford Directors College, Stanford, California, 23 June 2014).

independent judgement by experienced and qualified individuals'.[157] It is this judgement that is needed in the design, use and review of RegTech.

The concern is that 'It is naïve to assume that RegTech could, by itself, change financial institutions' behavioral culture, ethical approach towards business making and attitude regarding the law and complying with it'.[158] The Enron collapse, although pre-AI, illustrates the problem. Enron had a highly touted Risk Assessment and Control department but the culture of deal making and risk taking meant that deal makers were permitted to set unrealistic assumptions for the models that provided the likelihood of various outcomes for a transaction.[159]

Fast forward to the Global Financial Crisis and Frank Pasquale documents how finance's algorithms contributed to, or did not prevent, corporate greed causing the financial system to collapse. Pasquale refers to the pricing tool INTEXcalc, which provided the return and risks for a particular mortgage-backed security, but such outputs depended on the underlying assumptions. A credit rating agency employed a model known as LEVELS (loan evaluation and estimate of loss system) to rate mortgage-backed securities but did not update the underlying data set with the more risky loans that were being written so that high ratings could continue to be given.[160]

RegTech is only a tool. It automates compliance tasks and facilitates choices based on data-provided insight, but a human is (or should be) still part of the decision making and that human's response will be impacted by the culture in which they operate.

Equally, there will be new regulatory challenges. For example AI needs high-quality, voluminous data but at the same time there may be questions as to where that data is sourced from and legal requirements such as privacy, confidentiality and security that need to be addressed.[161] Previously, the data that needed to be protected was summarised as personally identifiable information, such as names and tax or social security numbers, however, with the expansion of available data many innocuous data points may be collected but when combined they reveal private information.[162]

While the in-house lawyer is the chief source of legal advice and central to ensuring compliance they may also assume the role of corporate guardian or moral compass. The in-house lawyers' ethical and professional duties and responsibilities as lawyers when combined with knowledge of corporate operations is what puts them in the position of being the moral compass for both complying with the law but also acting ethically.[163] Richard Moorhead, Steven Vaughan and

[157] The Committee on Corporate Governance (the Hampel Committee) *Final Report* (Gee Publishing, 1997) [1.14].

[158] Packin (n 134) 212.

[159] B McLean and P Elkind, *The Smartest Guys in the Room* (Penguin Books, 2004) 114–17.

[160] F Pasquale, *The Black Box Society* (Harvard University Press, 2015) 106–07, 110–11.

[161] V Mayer-Schonberger and K Cukier, *Big Data* (Mariner Books, 2014) 152–56.

[162] ibid 192.

[163] See, eg, KPMG, *Restoring Corporate Trust: What It Means for the General Counsel* (2019) 9–10; Brayne (n 15) 19.

Cristina Godinho in their empirical study of in-house lawyers identified that 'The relationship between the role of in-house lawyer as interpreter of legal obligations and as strategic advisor interpreting legal risk may have opened something of a space in which ethical considerations may operate'.[164] Put another way, the lawyer is not just advising on 'can we do it' but 'should we do it'.

The in-house lawyer may have the capacity to advise the corporation's officers as to how to act in an ethical as well as legal manner. Where the law is unclear or establishes minimum requirements the lawyer can factor in reputational risk and advise on an approach that is not just legally defensible but which will also avoid criticism from media, customers, regulators and other 'influencers'. The lawyer is part of creating a culture of not just compliance but acting in the spirit of the law and 'doing the right thing'.

RegTech is both a source of the need for, and a challenge to, ethical or moral action. AI is amoral but its programmers, designers and users are not. The lawyer's general role as moral compass informed by their ethical and professional responsibilities, such as independence, should be applied to RegTech. The areas of uncertainty that need to be navigated to inform the programming and use of the AI require consideration of the legal and the ethical to protect the corporation's interests.

[164] Moorhead, Vaughan and Godinho (n 17) 142.

9

AI and Criminal Lawyers

Introduction

Attempts to profile criminal offenders have a long history, traversing predictions of where crimes might take place, who is likely to commit them, and who is likely to reoffend.[1] Recidivism is a central issue in decisions about criminal sentencing, bail (whether a person is to be detained pending trial) and parole (whether a person is released from custody to serve out a sentence in the community). Meanwhile, attempts to predict the incidence of crime more generally – where, when and the type of crime which may occur – is a preoccupation of policing.

The concepts of risk profiling and the use of crime statistics are therefore not new to criminal lawyers. In many jurisdictions, tools labelled 'actuarial' can be found 'at every stage of the court and correctional system'.[2] Actuarial refers to having a basis in statistical calculation, often contrasted with clinical assessments which focus on individuals and their pathology. Use of technology in this sphere is also not novel: authors have described a lengthy process of 'scientification' of policing, marked out by the use of 'technological tools'.[3]

What may be new is the use of AI – specifically machine learning – to conduct these actuarial analyses. The use of such programs throws up new issues about fairness, transparency (especially in the case of systems which are protected by intellectual property regimes), human oversight and accountability. Long-expressed concerns about the shortcomings of risk assessment have also been reinvigorated: crime and indeed 'risk' itself are socially constructed concepts which attain an aura of scientific neutrality when numericised in a dataset.[4]

[1] See B Harcourt, *Against Prediction: Sentencing, Policing, and Punishing in an Actuarial Age* (University of Chicago, 2007); and J Monahan and JL Skeem, 'Risk Assessment in Criminal Sentencing' (2016) 12 *Annual Review of Clinical Psychology* 489 (for a history of risk assessment tools).

[2] AM Holsinger et al, 'A Rejoinder to Dressel and Farid: New Study Finds Computer Algorithm is More Accurate Than Humans at Predicting Arrest and as Good as a Group of 20 Lay Experts' (2018) 82(2) *Federal Probation* 50, 51.

[3] M Kaufmann, S Egbert and M Leese, 'Predictive Policing and the Politics of Patterns' (2019) 59(3) *British Journal of Criminology* 674, 677, citing RV Ericson and C Shearing, 'The Scientification of Police Work' in G Böhme and N Stehr (eds), *The Knowledge Society: The Growing Impact of Scientific Knowledge on Social Relations* (Reidel, 1986) 129; RV Ericson and KD Haggerty, *Policing the Risk Society* (Clarendon Press, 1997); PK Manning, *The Technology of Policing: Crime Mapping, Information Technology, and the Rationality of Crime Control* (New York University Press, 2008).

[4] Fred Benenson coined the term 'mathwashing': EE Joh, 'Feeding the Machine: Policing, Crime Data, & Algorithms', Symposium: Big Data, National Security, and the Fourth Amendment (2017) 26(2) *William & Mary Bill of Rights Journal* 287, 292 fn 29.

Further, the challenges which inhere in 'disentangling … poverty-correlated factors from individualised factors has opened … risk assessment mechanisms to criticisms of racial and economic bias'.[5] In the last few years, more and more lawyers and legal scholars have begun to scrutinise the use of machine learning in policing and in the criminal justice system.[6] This is unsurprising when the use of AI occurs at those points in time when individuals come up against the coercive powers of the state.[7]

It is argued, though, that sophisticated data analytics can also expose biases in human decision making which would otherwise go undetected or be impossible to prove. Hence, alongside growth in a generally critical literature examining problems with the use of machine learning for risk assessment, there are claims that policing and the criminal justice system could actually be made more fair by the use of data analytics.[8] Part of the debate concerns the meaning of 'fairness', a kaleidoscopic term in this context.

In this chapter, we examine the use of machine learning, including automated facial recognition (AFR) systems, for policing and for decisions about bail, parole and sentencing – areas which are the remit of the criminal lawyer. We begin by setting out the ways that AI is being used in law enforcement, discussing policing and risk assessment. We then move to look at the role of the lawyer when it comes to the use of AI by the state in the criminal justice context. Lawyers must understand the limitations of the AI tools which are being (and look set to continue to be) deployed in this area, so that they may respond effectively to challenge their use – especially where fundamental rights are impacted.

Criminal Law and Lawyers

The realm of criminal law is directly relevant to the protection of fundamental rights as it involves 'the right to liberty of the person … a central feature of most

[5] AG Ferguson, 'Policing Predictive Policing' (2017) 94(5) *Washington University Law Review* 1109, 1119–20, citing SB Starr, 'The New Profiling: Why Punishing Based on Poverty and Identity is Unconstitutional and Wrong' (2015) 27 *Federal Sentencing Reporter* 229, 229.

[6] D Lehr and P Ohm, 'Playing with the Data: What Legal Scholars Should Learn About Machine Learning' (2017) *UC Davis Law Review* 658; J Koepke and DG Robinson, 'Danger Ahead: Risk Assessment and the Future of Bail Reform' (2018) 93 *Washington Law Review* 1725; The Law Society (Law Society Commission on the Use of Algorithms in the Justice System and The Law Society of England and Wales), *Algorithms in the Criminal Justice System* (June 2019) https://www.lawsociety.org.uk/support-services/research-trends/algorithm-use-in-the-criminal-justice-system-report/.

[7] C McKay, 'Predicting Risk in Criminal Procedure: Actuarial Tools, Algorithms, AI and Judicial Decision-Making' (2020) 32 *Current Issues in Criminal Justice* 22, 23, citing JL Zittrain, C Barabas, K Dinakar, J Ito and M Virza, 'Interventions over Predictions: Reframing the Ethical Debate for Actuarial Risk Assessment' (2018) 81 *Proceedings of the 1st Conference on Fairness, Accountability and Transparency in Machine Learning, Proceedings of Machine Learning Research* 62–76, http://proceedings.mlr.press/v81/barabas18a.html; L Eckhouse, K Lum, C Conti-Cook and J Ciccolini, 'Layers of Bias: A Unified Approach for Understanding Problems with Risk Assessment' (2019) 46(2) *Criminal Justice and Behavior* 185; The Law Society (n 6).

[8] S Goel, JM Rao and R Shroff, 'Personalized Risk Assessments in the Criminal Justice System' (2016) 106(5) *The American Economic Review* 119.

statements of human rights or constitutional rights'.[9] It invokes many other fundamental individual rights too – to ensure that people are not subjected to arbitrary search, seizure, arrest or detention; are presumed innocent until proven otherwise; and are found guilty only if a charge is sufficiently proved in accordance with fair procedures, such as improperly obtained evidence being excluded. The criminal law is often expressive of and guided by constitutional principles,[10] reflecting a balancing of individual and state interests.[11]

The goal of the criminal justice system can be summarised as bringing those who offend against the law to account, tempered by considerations related to efficiency, democratic participation and protection of individual rights.[12] Different jurisdictions elect to undertake the balancing act in variable ways. A classic distinction is that between inquisitorial and adversarial systems.[13] While both seek to bring offenders to justice, the inquisitorial model relies upon a neutral fact finder to do so, the adversarial model on a vigorous contest between prosecution and defence.

The criminal justice system has four elements: the substantive law, which sets out what constitutes a criminal offence (criminal law); the process for determining whether a person has committed a crime (criminal procedure); the process for investigating crime (in order to bring people within the system); and the sentencing of persons once convicted.[14] Our focus is on arrest, pre-trial processes, and sentencing – in other words, the elements other than the substantive criminal law being criminal procedure, investigative process and sentencing. The decisions made in relation to these processes differ from many other adjudicative or judicial decisions in that they are forward looking, concerning what a person may do in the future.[15] Though past events and present circumstances inform the decision, it is essentially predictive and our interest is in the use of machine learning tools to inform those predictions.

The lawyer's role is multifaceted. In an inquisitorial model,

> the case (and not the person) is investigated by a judicial inquirer charged with representing not the partisan interest of either prosecution or defence, but with the task of

[9] A Ashworth and L Zedner, *Preventive Justice* (Oxford University Press, 2014) 52, citing Article 5 ECHR. Other relevant statements include the United Nations International Covenant on Civil and Political Rights (ICCPR) (entered into force 23 March 1976) art 9.

[10] A Shytov and P Duff, 'Truth and Procedural Fairness in Chinese Criminal Procedure Law' (2019) 23(3) *The International Journal of Evidence & Proof* 299, 301, citing ICCPR arts 125 and 126.

[11] N Foster and S Sule, *German Legal System and Laws* (4th edn, Oxford University Press, 2010) 379.

[12] J Iontcheva Turner, 'Limits on the Search for Truth in Criminal Procedure: A Comparative View' in JE Ross and SC Thaman (eds), *Comparative Criminal Procedure* (Edward Elgar, 2016) 35, 35.

[13] M Langer explains that while this remains the classic way that analysis of comparative criminal procedure has been undertaken, it may be changing: 'Strength, Weakness, or Both? On the Endurance of the Adversarial–Inquisitorial Systems in Comparative Criminal Procedure' in Ross and Thaman (eds) (n 12) 519.

[14] KJ Arenson and M Bagaric, *Criminal Processes and Investigative Procedures* (4th edn, LexisNexis, 2019) 1–2.

[15] A parallel may be found in decisions about child welfare – and predictive analytics is apparently being deployed in this area too: see M Garrison, 'Taking the Risks Out of Child Protection Risk

> 'searching for the truth'. There is a strong emphasis on the pretrial phase rather than the trial as the locus for resolving factual and evidential issues.[16]

It has been argued, therefore, that the defence lawyer has a narrower role than their counterpart in adversarial proceedings,[17] though one expanded in European countries by decisions of the European Court of Human Rights, which have required defence counsel to be given 'more opportunity to confront and question prosecution witnesses either at trial or as part of the formal pre-trial procedures'.[18] Meanwhile, prosecutors have 'a robust duty to function objectively as they are required to investigate the facts both for and against the defendant'.[19] In adversarial systems prosecutors usually have specific professional duties too and are under an onerous obligation to avoid misuse of state power, for instance by engaging in unethical conduct.

The initial stages of crime investigation are usually conducted by police, whether the system is inquisitorial or adversarial. In France, for example, most criminal cases are investigated by police, supervised by the public prosecutor; some by the *judge d'instruction*, the investigating judge.[20] Following initial investigative stages, it is usually the decision of prosecutors as to whether a case will continue to a trial.[21]

The role of lawyers in relation to police investigation – specifically, the ways that police exercise their power to investigate crime (eg stop and search powers) and their powers of arrest – is primarily in making subsequent challenges to the legitimacy of the exercise of those powers. In many jurisdictions there are strong protections against arbitrary search and arrest, which typically means that police may not search or arrest a person without some basis for suspecting that person of having committed a crime. If police do not have a warrant for search, typically issued by a magistrate or judge, then the search will be unlawful (and any evidence found inadmissible) unless police have the requisite suspicion. The power to arrest is expressed in differing formulations but is usually founded in a 'reasonable suspicion' or 'probable cause' on the part of police (or the concept of flagrancy,[22] in much

Analysis' (2012) 21 *Journal of Law and Policy* 5, 19–20 (describing the use of algorithms to guide child protection policymakers and case workers).

[16] J Hodgson, 'Constructing the Pretrial Role of the Defence in French Criminal Procedure: An Adversarial Outsider in an Inquisitorial Process?' (2002) 6(1) *The International Journal of Evidence & Proof* 1, 2.

[17] But note, expanded somewhat since 2010: J Mazzone, 'Silence, Self-Incrimination and Hazards of Globalization' in Ross and Thaman (eds) (n 12) 308, 326.

[18] Shytov and Duff (n 10) 301.

[19] SM Boyne, 'Procedural Economy in Pre-Trial Procedure: Developments in Germany and the United States' in Ross and Thaman (eds) (n 12) 219, 221.

[20] Hodgson (n 16) 2. In France the investigating magistrate/judge may take the lead on pre-trial investigative processes.

[21] See also M Bohlander, 'Basic Concepts of German Criminal Procedure: An Introduction' (2011) 1 *Durham Law Review* 1, 23–24.

[22] R Vogler and S Fouladvand, 'Standards for Making Factual Determinations in Arrest and Pre-Trial Detention: A Comparative Analysis of Law and Practice' in Ross and Thaman (eds) (n 12) 191, 200–04 (referencing France, Germany, the Netherlands, Spain, Belgium, Greece, but noting that flagrancy is 'giving way' in some jurisdictions to a 'reasonable suspicion' model).

of continental Europe).[23] Without the requisite basis, arrest may constitute an assault or denial of liberty. But Richard Vogler and Shahrzad Fouladvand explain that 'arrest is, by its nature, also the most unobserved and clandestine aspect of decision-making in criminal procedure'.[24]

An absence of reasonable suspicion will also likely lead to any evidence obtained as a result being inadmissible. In Russia, for example:

> The current Criminal Procedure Code … emphasizes the mandatory admissibility of evidence for criminal proceedings. The principle of legality is partially based on the provision that any violation of the [Code] by a court, prosecutor, investigator, inquiry body or investigator during criminal proceedings results in the invalidity of evidence.[25]

To be reasonable, 'the suspicion must have an objective basis in fact, information, or intelligence that links this individual to the kind of article for which the search is made, or may be based on the person's behaviour'.[26] When it comes to the use of AI in policing, key questions devolve around whether machine learning systems' information can satisfy the requirement for reasonable suspicion or corresponding standard that is required. The role of the lawyer is to challenge arrest and policing practices and associated evidence obtained.

Lawyers also play a role in the determination of whether or not a defendant will be detained pending their trial (remanded or held on remand) or be released into the community (pre-trial release or bail). Andrew Ashworth and Lucia Zedner have noted that roughly one-third of all defendants who are committed for trial in the English Crown Courts 'are remanded in custody at some stage'.[27] Pre-trial detention represents a deviation from the presumption of innocence. Ashworth and Zedner consider that there are circumstances in which it is appropriate to override the presumption but argue that 'there must be (predictive) evidence of at least the same level of persuasiveness for pre-trial detention as for conviction'.[28] The granting or not granting of bail is also significant, not just because it determines whether a defendant will remain incarcerated until trial, but because it appears to be linked to the ultimate outcome of the trial. Denial of bail is correlated with an increased likelihood of the defendant being convicted, incarcerated and sentenced

[23] C Steiker, 'Foreword: The Limits of the Preventive State' (1998) 88(3) *Journal of Criminal Law & Criminology* 771; Vogler and Fouladvand (n 22) set out the international conventions' terminology. The latter note, however, that the model for arrest set out in international conventions 'does not reflect the very diverse approaches to arrest standards implemented around the world' at 194.

[24] Vogler and Fouladvand (n 22) 191.

[25] R Kostenko and G Yuriev, 'The Admissibility of Statements Provided by an Accused Person in the Russian Criminal Procedure' (2018) Vol IX 5(35) *Journal of Advanced Research in Law and Economics* 1684, 1685 (citations omitted).

[26] Ashworth and Zedner (n 9) 57, citing Police and Criminal Evidence Act *Code of Practice A* (2011) para 2.2.

[27] ibid 65.

[28] ibid 67, citing RA Duff, 'Pre-Trial Detention and the Presumption of Innocence' in A Ashworth, L Zedner and P Tomlin (eds), *Prevention and the Limits of the Criminal Law* (Oxford University Press, 2013) 115, 120.

to a longer period of time.[29] Thus, it is argued that generally 'pre-trial detention has an impact on the outcome of the proceedings which goes well beyond any predictable correlation between the bail and sentencing decisions'.[30]

Parole or conditional release, a concept recognised in most legal systems, involves ending a convicted offender's physical detention and returning him or her into the community. Parole inevitably has conditions attached which will result in a return to detention if breached (breach of parole). Whether or not an offender receives parole may be determined not just by judges alone, but by specially constituted boards or panels which include lay people.

Finally, sentencing is fundamental to 'life and liberty', perhaps more so than any other point in the criminal justice process.[31] Scrutiny of sentencing practices has resulted in critiques of 'penal populism' and the carceral state.[32] Broadly speaking, there are differing underlying rationales as to what the sentence is intended to achieve: general and specific deterrence, rehabilitation, restorative justice, punishment and retribution. Typically, passing sentence involves a judicial officer weighing a range of different considerations related to both the nature and circumstances of the offence and the offender. Differences exist in the level of judicial discretion to be exercised and how much this may be constrained by legislatures (such as the introduction of 'mandatory' sentencing or minimum sentences). For example, sentencing guidelines in England and Wales set out factors which ought be considered when sentencing, with 'most major offences … covered by definitive guidelines'.[33]

The role of defence lawyers in decisions about pre-trial release, conditional release and sentencing is to present specific arguments based on the guiding criteria or legislation on behalf of their defendant client, which may involve challenging the evidence presented by the state. In the US, where machine learning tools are widely used for risk assessments in this area, defence lawyers have been instrumental in critiquing their use and in running appeals in individual cases.

[29] CE Jones, 'Give Us Free: Addressing Racial Disparities in Bail Determinations' (2013) 16(4) *New York University Journal of Legislation and Public Policy* 919, 936–37, citing M Sacks and AR Ackerman, 'Bail and Sentencing: Does Pretrial Detention Lead to Harsher Punishment?' (2012) 20 *Criminal Justice Policy Review* 1, 1, 11; T Schlesinger, 'The Cumulative Effects of Racial Disparities in Criminal Processing' (2007) 7 *Journal of the Institute of Justice & International Studies* 261, 261, 264, 270–71.

[30] Vogler and Fouladvand (n 22) 192, citing Sacks and Ackerman (n 29); and V Karth, 'Between a Rock and a Hard Place': Bail Decisions in Three South African Courts' (Open Society Foundation for South Africa, 2008).

[31] BD Johnson, 'Sentencing' in M Tonry (ed), *The Oxford Handbook of Crime and Criminal Justice* (Oxford University Press, 2011) 696, 696; see also R Wexler, 'Life, Liberty, and Trade Secrets: Intellectual Property in the Criminal Justice System' (2018) 70 *Stanford Law Review* 1343.

[32] JV Roberts, LJ Stalans, D Indemaur and M Hough, *Penal Populism and Public Opinion: Lessons from Five Countries* (Oxford University Press, 2002) (describing the rise of penal populism in Canada, the UK, the US, Australia and New Zealand).

[33] J Pina-Sánchez, JP Gosling, H-I Chung, E Bourgeois, S Geneletti and ID Marder, 'Have the England and Wales Guidelines Affected Sentencing Severity? An Empirical Analysis Using a Scale of Severity and Time-Series Analyses' (2019) 59(4) *The British Journal of Criminology* 979, 980 ('15 offence-specific guidelines are in operation in England and Wales, structuring the sentencing process of more than 149 offence types').

In some jurisdictions, lawyers for both prosecution and defence may engage in plea negotiations – the process of reaching an agreement on the charges a defendant will plead guilty to, and in some cases agreement on the sentence proposed. On the other hand, as Andrew Boon explains:

> There is no precise definition of a plea bargain. The term might include agreements whereby a defendant agrees to plead guilty to charges if a prosecutor agrees to drop others. This happens in England and Wales, although not as a result of bargaining. Prosecutors are supposed to decide charges objectively, without entering a process of negotiation with the defendant's lawyers.[34]

Boon notes that prosecutors do have some discretion in terms of the offences which will be charged but its exercise is guided by the public interest.[35]

Reportedly, some 90 per cent of all criminal cases in the US are 'plea bargained',[36] though the agreements reached must be sanctioned by the court.[37]

Application of AI in the Criminal Justice System

In 2016 reporters at online news agency ProPublica published a story about a software program being used in the gaols and criminal justice systems of many States of the United States.[38] The software was called Correctional Offender Management Profiling for Alternative Sanctions, or COMPAS. Its purpose was to generate risk scores that were used (along with other indicia) to determine an individual's post-conviction 'rehabilitation needs' and whether they were likely to reoffend. COMPAS had in fact been in existence for years and in use in the criminal justice system since the early 2000s.[39] Yet the ProPublica story, titled 'Machine Bias', catapulted it into international headlines: it was reported on in South Africa, Iran and India, as well as widely in the US.[40] Reporters Julia Angwin, Jeff Larson, Surya Mattu and

[34] A Boon, *The Ethics and Conduct of Lawyers in England and Wales* (3rd edn, Bloomsbury, 2015) 662.

[35] ibid.

[36] C Nestler, 'Sentencing in Germany' (2003) 7(1) *Buffalo Criminal Law Review* 109.

[37] Boon (n 34) 662.

[38] J Angwin, J Larson, S Mattu and L Kirchner, 'Machine Bias', *ProPublica*, 23 May 2016, www.propublica.org/article/machine-bias-risk-assessments-in-criminal-sentencing.

[39] ibid ('New York State, for instance, started using the tool to assess people on probation in a pilot project in 2001'). The *New York Times* reported that in 2010 Pennsylvania's legislature directed the State's sentencing commission to develop a set of algorithms that could be used to inform sentencing judges about a defendant's risk of being arrested again: M Smith, 'In Wisconsin, A Backlash Against Using Data To Foretell Defendants' Futures', *New York Times*, 22 June 2016, www.nytimes.com/2016/06/23/us/backlash-in-wisconsin-against-using-data-to-foretell-defendants-futures.html (quoting M Bergstrom, executive director of the Pennsylvania Commission on Sentencing).

[40] J Naughton, 'Even Algorithms are Biased Against Black Men', *The Observer* (UK) 26 June 2016, 21; 'How Maths Can Get You Locked Up' *Iran Daily*, 17 October 2016; 'Fighting Our Algorithmic

Lauren Kirchner drew attention to the racial inequities in the risk (or recidivism) 'scores' generated by COMPAS. Angwin and colleagues had obtained the scores of 7,000 individuals in Florida and followed up to see how many had actually gone on to be charged with the crimes which the scores suggested they would commit.[41] They reported:

> The score proved remarkably unreliable in forecasting violent crime: Only 20 percent of the people predicted to commit violent crimes actually went on to do so … We also turned up significant racial disparities … The formula was particularly likely to falsely flag black defendants as future criminals, wrongly labeling them this way at almost twice the rate as white defendants.[42]

As explained below, ProPublica's analysis generated much discussion (and critique[43]) among researchers about the different means of modelling something like recidivism, where choices must be made about accuracy, and how disparities – whether false negatives or false positives – might manifest. There are three additional challenges with programs like COMPAS – data, design and opacity.

First, the data. Data is all important in machine learning programs. Yet, as decades of work on the use of crime statistics attests to, the accuracy of the type of data in use is premised on multiple assumptions. Not everyone is convicted for the crimes they commit – they may not be caught at all; they may be arrested but not charged; charged but not convicted; or be convicted wrongly. Elizabeth Joh has explained: 'Crime and disorder are not natural phenomena. These events have to be observed, noticed, acted upon, collected, categorized, and recorded – while other events are not'.[44]

Second, the use they were designed for: initially, much risk assessment was intended to identify those individuals the most suitable for 'alternative' or non-custodial sentences (hence the reference to this in COMPAS's name); and those already incarcerated most likely to engage in misconduct prior to release. In other words, it was used to divert people away from incarceration and into rehabilitative programmes, and by prison officers to manage prisoners. Generally speaking, the use of risk assessment tools to manage populations within prisons and detention facilities (especially for juveniles) is extremely common around the world.[45] There are, accordingly, issues with using such tools for a purpose for which they

Overlords', *The Financial Express* (India) 2 September 2017; S Mckeown, 'Value-Neutral Bots Inherit Our Desire to Tick Prejudiced Boxes', *Business Day* (South Africa) 24 October 2018.

[41] J Larson, S Mattu and L Kirchner and J Angwin, 'How We Analyzed the COMPAS Recidivism Algorithm', *ProPublica* (23 May 2016) www.propublica.org/article/how-we-analyzed-the-compas-recidivism-algorithm.

[42] Angwin et al (n 38). See also Larson et al (n 41).

[43] AW Flores, K Bechtel and CT Lowenkamp, 'False Positives, False Negatives, and False Analyses: A Rejoinder to "Machine Bias"' (2016) 80(2) *Federal Probation* 38, 39 (citations omitted).

[44] Joh (n 4) 289.

[45] Pew Center on the States, 'Risk/Needs Assessment 101: Science Reveals New Tools to Manage Offenders' *Public Safety Performance Project* (Pew Center, September 2011).

were arguably not designed, such as to *increase* the length of a person's custodial sentence.

Third, there are issues around lack of transparency, and whether this should ever be permissible when a person's fundamental rights (to due process and equality in the application of the law, including understanding the basis for conviction and sentence, and being assured that the process was fair) are at stake. Scholars have argued that opacity, even on the basis of intellectual property rights, should not be permitted in such instances, where machine learning programs are being used in state decision making.[46]

In this section, we consider these and other issues in relation to three uses of AI in criminal justice: predictive policing, facial recognition technologies, and individual risk assessments such as COMPAS.

Predictive Policing

Where once policing may have relied on local know-how and the individual and collective experiences of police officers, 'predictive policing' uses large datasets and machine learning analysis to generate predictions about crime.[47] It is sometimes also referred to as 'big data policing'.[48] The data which is used is itself generated by police – as clearly crime statistics reflect those crimes which are identified and policed, rather than all crimes committed.[49] In addition, unlike the individualised risk assessments investigated by ProPublica, the use of statistical analysis in policing had, until quite recently, focussed almost solely on geospatial features (the *where* and *when*) rather than individuals (the *who*) of crime commission.[50]

An early example of geographical profiling is Compstat (referring to 'compare statistics'), a program to analyse police activity in New York City used from the mid-1990s on.[51] Many other large US police departments followed New York in introducing similar programs.[52] By mapping the location of reported crimes, arrests and other police undertakings, Compstat could be used to direct

[46] M Zalnieriute, L Bennett Moses and G Williams, 'The Rule of Law and Automation of Government Decision-Making' (2019) 82(3) *Modern Law Review* 425.

[47] See Joh (n 4) 287–88.

[48] AD Selbst, 'Disparate Impact in Big Data Policing' (2017) 52(1) *Georgia Law Review* 109.

[49] Joh (n 4) 289; L Bennett Moses and J Chan, 'Algorithmic Prediction in Policing: Assumptions, Evaluation, and Accountability' (2016) *Policing and Society* 1, 2.

[50] N Berg, 'Predicting Crime, LAPD-Style', *The Guardian*, 25 June 2014, www.theguardian.com/cities/2014/jun/25/predicting-crime-lapd-los-angeles-police-data-analysis-algorithm-minority-report (quoting P Jeffrey Brantingham, Professor of Anthropology, University of California Los Angeles, who developed PredPol); but *cf* Ferguson (n 5) 1109–90.

[51] JA Eterno and EB Silverman, 'The New York City Police Department's Compstat: Dream or Nightmare' (2006) 8(3) *International Journal of Police Science & Management* 218, 219.

[52] ibid.

policing activity.[53] The idea was to identify the geographic locations which have features associated with increased crime – initially, property crime. Interestingly, this was not Compstat's original intended use. Its genesis lay in simply generating weekly crime statistics for each department (before this, there were delays of several months in reporting stats).[54] While Compstat looks like a statistical application of the 'broken windows theory' of policing[55] this was coincidental rather than by design, as Compstat was not planned or developed for this function.[56]

It is claimed that the application of machine learning programs to the type of data used by Compstat increases the sophistication of the analysis and therefore the accuracy of predictions of crime.[57] As with legal outcome prediction, algorithmic predictive policing has been targeted by a 'growing analytics industry'[58] of partnerships between large technology companies, governments and academics.[59]

A popular program among police forces is PredPol, which is used by many forces in the US and also in the UK;[60] another is Risk Terrain Modeling (RTM), developed by the Rutgers Center for Public Security. HunchLab, which uses RTM, utilises many different variables: 'population density; location of bars, churches, and transportation hubs; and census data',[61] but also 'seasons, time of month, day of week, time, holidays, sporting events, weather'.[62]

There are many more programs and quite a long history of usage in some jurisdictions.[63] Predictive policing is reportedly being used by police forces in

[53] Criticisms include that this results in over-policing of certain communities, notably along racialised lines: see P Hanink, 'Don't Trust the Police: Stop Question Frisk, Compstat, and the High Cost of Statistical Over-Reliance in the NYPD' (2013) 13 *Journal of the Institute of Justice and International Studies* 99–114.

[54] Eterno and Silverman (n 51) 220.

[55] See generally ibid and Hanink (n 53).

[56] Eterno and Silverman (n 51) 220.

[57] Berg (n 50) (quoting P Jeffrey Brantingham).

[58] Ferguson (n 5) 1131 and the references cited therein at fn 134 ('Other academics and large technology players including IBM, Motorola, and Lexis-Nexis now compete in the growing analytics industry').

[59] See, eg, Bennett Moses and Chan (n 49) listing 'IBM® (eg Blue CRUSH in Memphis and Blue PALMS in Miami), Information Builders® (Law Enforcement Analytics), Azavea® (HunchLab), SPADAC® (Signature Analyst®), Accenture®, and Hitachi®'); see also 'UAE: Dubai Police, SAS Harness AI and Analytics for Digital Transformation', *UAE Government News*, 8 October 2019; 'Dubai Police Transforms Investigative Processes and Efficiencies with SAS Analytics & AI Solutions', *Al-Bawaba News*, 15 October 2019 (both reporting on partnership between SAS and Dubai police).

[60] It has been reported that one-third of UK police departments are using some kind of predictive policing program: C Nuttall, 'How Many Speakers It Takes to Fill the Albert Hall', *Financial Times*, 3 April 2019: 'At least 14 police forces across the UK – around a third – are already using what has been coined "predictive policing"'); but see below at n 65.

[61] S Brayne, 'The Criminal Law and Law Enforcement Implications of Big Data' (2018) 14 *Annual Review of Law and Social Science* 293, 297.

[62] Ferguson (n 5) 1136. See also Azavea, *HunchLab: Under the Hood* (Azavea, 2015).

[63] D Wilson, 'Algorithmic Patrol: The Futures of Predictive Policing' in A Završnik (ed), *Big Data, Crime and Social Control* (Routledge, 2018) 108–27. See The Law Society (n 6) 33–34 for some older 'hotspot' systems used in the UK, citing KJ Bowers, SD Johnson and K Pease, 'Prospective Hot-Spotting: The Future of Crime Mapping?' (2004) 44 *British Journal of Criminology* 641 and SD Johnson, DJ Birks, L McLaughlin, KJ Bowers and K Pease, *Prospective Crime Mapping in Operational Context: Final Report* (Home Office Online Report 19/07, 2007) and at 34–35 for current uses.

jurisdictions as disparate as Vietnam, India and the United Arab Emirates.[64] Of the UK, the Law Society of England and Wales noted:

> No central information exists on the number of [police] forces using algorithmic tools, the crimes or other issues these technologies are applied to or the stage of deployment they are at. A freedom of information based study … in 2016 asked all police forces whether they used any sort of computational or algorithmic data analysis or decision making in relation to the analysis of intelligence, and to confirm the nature and purpose of any such algorithms, and 14% of police forces reported affirmatively.[65]

Police forces in Germany and Switzerland are trialling software called 'Precobs' or the Pre-Crime Observation System, though reportedly some forces are resisting its use.[66]

Academics have identified two key shifts in the development of predictive policing.[67] First came the shift from mapping property crimes to mapping of crimes of violence. Andrew Ferguson explains that RTM is used in this way, as it 'develops digitized risk terrain maps identifying particular factors associated with particular crimes. Identified factors are layered on a computer map to highlight the intensity of risk in particular micro-areas'.[68] Still, even with this first shift, the focus remains on the geospatial location where a crime or crimes are likely to take place, rather than the individuals who might be the perpetrators. *That* focus has come with the second shift, which inclines towards individual risk assessment.[69] This approach dovetails with those which are used for risk assessments of individuals who have already been identified from their contact with the criminal justice system – focussed on personal and individual features rather than being place based (discussed below). As well as geographic tools, police are now therefore also using tools which identify specific individuals according to a risk assessment score.[70] It is said that some software can link both: the *Guardian* reports that one

[64] eg, 'Big Expectations for Vietnam in Sustainable Smart City Development', *Vietnam News Summary*, 11 October 2019; S Chatterjee, 'Rules for the Machine', *Indian Express*, 28 February 2019 ('the Maharashtra and Delhi police have taken the lead in adopting predictive policing technologies'); S Egbert, 'Predictive Policing and the Platformization of Police Work' (2019) 17(1/2) *Surveillance and Society* 83; and the references at n 59.

[65] The Law Society (n 6) 33, citing M Oswald and J Grace, 'Intelligence, Policing and the Use of Algorithmic Analysis: A Freedom of Information-Based Study' (2016) 1(1) *Journal of Information Rights, Policy and Practice*, DOI: https://doi.org/10.21039/irpandp.v1i1.16.

[66] A de Vries and S Smit, 'Predictive policing: politiewerk aan de hand van voorspellingen' (2016) 42(3) *Justitiele Verkenningen* 9.

[67] Ferguson (n 5) 1115–16 and 1143 (arguing that these shifts have taken place without sufficient consideration of the different theoretical issues involved); Brayne (n 61) (referring to location-based and person-based predictive policing).

[68] Ferguson (n 5) 1135, citing LW Kennedy, J Caplan and EL Piza, 'Risk Clusters, Hotspots, and Spatial Intelligence: Risk Terrain Modeling as an Algorithm for Police Resource Allocation Strategies' (2011) 27 *Journal of Quantitative Criminology* 339, 345–46; LW Kennedy, J Caplan and E Piza, *Results – Executive Summary: A Multi-Jurisdictional Test of Risk Terrain Modeling and a Place-Based Evaluation of Environmental Risk-Based Patrol Deployment Strategies* (Rutgers Center on Public Security, 2015) 4–6.

[69] Ferguson (n 5) 1137–43.

[70] eg, the Strategic Subject List cited by Joh (n 4).

English police force is 'trialling software called Valcri, aimed at generating plausible ideas about how, when and why a crime was committed as well as who did it'.[71] In this kind of program, geographical maps are overlaid with information about people and their relationships and connections to one another.[72]

Moves toward an individualised focus are significant. In a 2011 interview, Jeffrey Brantingham, one of the developers of PredPol, explained that it was 'definitely not about individuals' behaviour', and pointed to the problems with arresting people who have not yet committed any offence.[73] Several years later, Brantingham was still explaining that the tool 'is about predicting where and when crime is most likely to occur, not who will commit it'.[74] Yet at around the same time, tools to do just that were being developed.

In 2016 the *New York Times* reported on a program used by Chicago police which 'draws … on variables tied to a person's past behavior, particularly arrests and convictions, to predict who is most likely to become a "party to violence"'.[75] Termed the Strategic Subject List (SSL), it is intended to assist police to predict both perpetrators and victims of crimes.[76] A study of the SSL found, however, that it was not necessarily very accurate: 'A quasi-experimental evaluation of the strategy found individuals on the SSL were no more or less likely to become a victim of a homicide or shooting than those in the comparison group, but they were more likely to be arrested for a shooting'.[77] Unsurprisingly then, as a professor of psychology and criminology at Loyola University Chicago commented, it is not clear whether the SSL is actually having any impact on crime reduction.[78]

Researchers in Hamburg, Germany, have argued that predictive policing is unlikely to be of any use there. Their concerns are that the existing police data that would be needed to train a system was both poor quality and too small a dataset to

[71] H Devlin, 'Software "No More Accurate than Untrained Humans" at Judging Reoffending Risk', *The Guardian*, 18 January 2018, www.theguardian.com/us-news/2018/jan/17/software-no-more-accurate-than-untrained-humans-at-judging-reoffending-risk.

[72] Ferguson (n 5) 1136, citing Azavea (n 62); M Thomsen, 'Predictive Policing and the Fantasy of Declining Violence in America', *Forbes*, 30 June 2014.

[73] Australian Broadcasting Corporation (Antony Funnell interviewing Jeff Brantingham), 'The World of Predictive Modelling', *Future Tense*, 24 March 2011.

[74] Berg (n 50).

[75] M Davey, 'Chicago Police Try to Predict Who May Shoot or Be Shot', *New York Times*, 23 May 2016, www.nytimes.com/2016/05/24/us/armed-with-data-chicago-police-try-to-predict-who-may-shoot-or-be-shot.html?_r=0?action=click&module=RelatedCoverage&pgtype=Article&region=Footer. See also J Gorner, 'Chicago Police Use "Heat List" As Strategy to Prevent Violence', *Chicago Tribune*, 21 August 2013.

[76] See J Saunders, P Hunt and JS Hollywood, 'Predictions Put into Practice: A Quasi-Experimental Evaluation of Chicago's Predictive Policing Pilot' (2016) 12 *Journal of Experimental Criminology* 347.

[77] ibid; Brayne (n 61) 298; N Rhee, 'Study Casts Doubt on Chicago Police's Secretive "Heat List"', *Chicago Magazine*, 17 August 2016, www.chicagomag.com/city-life/August-2016/Chicago-Police-Data/.

[78] Davey (n 75) (quoting Arthur J Lurigio).

generate valid results.[79] This raises an interesting question about how police actually make use of such tools, as the Law Society reported:

> While it might be assumed that police officers would be likely to over-rely on systems, in practice, evidence is mixed, with officers in some roles appearing anecdotally to follow decision-support systems closely, and officers in other roles expressing strong dislike of them.[80]

Similarly, Alexander Babuta and Marion Oswald have referred to the 'apparent disinclination' of many police forces in England and Wales to adopt this kind of technology, suggesting that their reluctance 'could be partly due to an absence of authorised professional guidance, leading to a lack of clarity over how to address legal and ethical concerns, as well as concerns regarding public and media opposition'.[81]

Facial Recognition

Police forces have long been able to make use of the footage from closed-circuit television (CCTV) cameras, increasingly placed in both public and private locations. The use of images from CCTV generated privacy concerns in the 2000s.[82] AFR technology arguably takes these concerns to a new level. In 2019 the High Court of England and Wales became the first court to consider whether the use of AFR by police forces breached fundamental rights, finding that it did breach the Article 8(1) right to respect for privacy and family life under the European Convention on Human Rights.[83] The European Union Agency for Fundamental Rights also discussed the issue in a 2019 report, *Facial Recognition Technology: Fundamental Rights Considerations in the Context of Law Enforcement*.[84] The previous year, the American Civil Liberties Union obtained documents through public records requests demonstrating that Amazon had been selling AFR technology to law enforcement agencies.[85]

[79] 'Hamburg Researchers Speak against Predictive Policing', *German Collection*, 23 April 2019 (abstracted from an original article in *Die Welt* ('Verzicht auf Verbrechens-Prognosen)' by Sabrina Winter) ('Researchers from the criminal research centre at the Hamburg State Office of Criminal Investigations, or LKA, have spoken against the use of predictive policing in the city as they see no potential for it there').

[80] The Law Society (n 6) 36, citing M Veale, M Van Kleek and R Binns, 'Fairness and Accountability Design Needs for Algorithmic Support in High-Stakes Public Sector Decision-Making' in *Proceedings of the ACM Conference on Human Factors in Computing Systems, CHI 2018* (ACM Press, 2018) doi:10/ct4s.

[81] A Babuta and M Oswald, 'Machine Learning Predictive Algorithms and the Policing of Future Crimes: Governance and Oversight' in JLM McDaniel and K Pease (eds), *Policing and Artificial Intelligence* (Routledge, forthcoming 2020) ssrn.com/abstract=3479081, 1–2.

[82] eg, *Peck v The United Kingdom* (ECHR Application No 44647/98, 22 January 2003).

[83] *R (Bridges) v CCSWP and SSHD* [2019] EWHC 2341 (Admin) [47]–[52] ('Everyone has the right to respect for his private and family life, his home and his correspondence').

[84] European Union Agency for Fundamental Rights, *Facial Recognition Technology: Fundamental Rights Considerations in the Context of Law Enforcement* (FRA, 2019).

[85] J Greene, 'Amazon's Tool for Facial Recognition Fans Privacy Fears', *The Wall Street Journal*, 23 May 2018, B4.

Associate Professor of computer science Arvind Narayanan has said that face recognition technology gives rise to ethical concerns precisely because of its high accuracy;[86] it has shown rapid improvement over the past decade, with advances in image analysis more generally. In 2012 a group of researchers won the ImageNet Classification competition with a system that used convolutional neural networks.[87] This system demonstrated 85 per cent accuracy in image classification.[88] Subsequently, and 'In less than two years, advancements in the field brought classification in the ImageNet contest to reach an accuracy of 96%, slightly higher than the human one (about 95%)'.[89]

When used in relation to human faces, AFR is classified as a biometric identification system. AFR enables

> the automatic identification of an individual by matching two or more faces from digital images. It does this by detecting and measuring various facial features, extracting these from the image and, in a second step, comparing them with features taken from other faces.[90]

The EU Agency for Fundamental Rights explains that there are three main ways that AFR technology is used in law enforcement: verification; identification; and categorisation or matching of general characteristics.[91] Verification or one-to-one comparison is used to check whether two different images depict the same person, for example at automated border control points. Identification or one-to-many comparison involves searching an image against a database, as Ferguson explains:

> Today, facial recognition software can identify a suspect by comparing the observed suspect's face to a database of stored faces. As sources of photographs proliferate, and law enforcement databases link these sources together, the utility and ease of the technology will expand rapidly.[92]

While, as noted, police have had the ability to examine sources of images such as CCTV footage for some time, AFR enables automated searching of huge

[86] A Narayanan, 'How to Recognize AI Snake Oil' (Presentation, Center for Information Technology Policy, Princeton) www.cs.princeton.edu/~arvindn/talks/MIT-STS-AI-snakeoil.pdf, 7.

[87] A Krizhevsky, I Sutskever and GE Hinton, 'Imagenet Classification with Deep Convolutional Neural Networks' (2012) *Advances in Neural Information Processing Systems*, 1097–1105.

[88] F Corea, 'A Brief History of AI: An Outline of What Happened in the Last 60 Years in AI' (24 March 2017) medium.com/@Francesco_AI/a-brief-history-of-ai-baf0f362f5d6.

[89] ibid, citing Krizhevsky, Sutskever and Hinton (n 87) 1097–105.

[90] European Union Agency for Fundamental Rights (n 84) 2, citing L Introna and H Nissenbaum, 'Facial Recognition Technology: A Survey of Policy and Implementation Issues', Lancaster University Management School Working Paper 2010/030 (2010).

[91] European Union Agency for Fundamental Rights (n 84) 7–8.

[92] AG Ferguson, 'Big Data and Predictive Reasonable Suspicion' (2015) 163(2) *University of Pennsylvania Law Review* 327, citing LK Donohue, 'Technological Leap, Statutory Gap, and Constitutional Abyss: Remote Biometric Identification Comes of Age' (2012) 97 *Minnesota Law Review* 407, 447–48 ('the Interstate Photo System … draws heavily on [facial recognition technology] and data mining technologies – and the database on which it is built is rapidly growing. As of 2009, [the database] included more than 6.75 million photos. By February 2012, this number had increased to more than 114.5 million').

databases, with millions of images.[93] Hence, as Ferguson predicts, 'the technology will complete searches in real time by allowing police to scan multiple faces along a street'.[94] Indeed, this is the way that the technology discussed in the High Court's decision *R (Bridges) v Chief Constable of South Wales Police and Secretary of State for the Home Department* was used. In that case, the Court set out the following stages of AFR:

> (1) *Compiling/using an existing database of images.* AFR requires a database of existing facial images (referred to in this case as 'a watchlist') against which to compare facial images and the biometrics contained therein. In order for such images to be used for AFR, they are processed so that the 'facial features' associated with their subjects are extracted and expressed as numerical values.
> (2) *Facial image acquisition.* A CCTV camera … takes digital pictures of facial images in real time. This may be done by (i) taking a static photograph in a 'controlled' environment …; or (ii) capturing a moving image when a person passes into the camera's field of view, using a live feed. This case is concerned with the latter, *i.e.* the use of AFR cameras in real time, in a 'live' context.
> (3) *Face detection.* Once a CCTV camera used in a live context captures footage, the software (i) detects human faces and then (ii) isolates individual faces.
> (4) *Feature extraction.* Taking the faces identified and isolated through 'face detection', the software automatically extracts unique facial features from the image of each face, the resulting biometric template being unique to that image.
> (5) *Face comparison.* The AFR software compares the extracted facial features with those contained in the facial images held on the watchlist.
> (6) *Matching.* When facial features from two images are compared, the AFR software generates a 'similarity score'. This is a numerical value indicating the likelihood that the faces match, with a higher number indicating a greater likelihood of a positive match between the two faces. A threshold value is fixed to determine when the software will indicate that a match has occurred.[95]

If a match is generated, the usual next step would be a human check, where the human operator decides whether there is indeed a match.

Risk Assessments

In 2016 an otherwise unremarkable criminal case from Wisconsin, US, made international headlines.[96] Eric Loomis, a 34-year-old man, was accused in 2013 of being the driver of a car involved in a drive-by shooting and was charged with seven offences.[97] Loomis entered a guilty plea to the two most minor

[93] Donohue (n 92) reporting on the Interstate Photo System.
[94] Ferguson (n 92) 366.
[95] *R (Bridges) v CCSWP and SSHD* [2019] EWHC 2341, [24]. On the issue of setting a threshold and error rates, see the discussion below about accuracy and fairness and bias.
[96] J Palazzolo, 'Algorithms Face Court Test', *The Wall Street Journal*, 6 June 2016, A7.
[97] *State v Loomis* 881 N.W.2d 749 (Wis 2016) (*Loomis*).

charges: attempting to flee from a traffic officer and operating a motor vehicle without the owner's consent.[98] His plea was accepted by the county Circuit Court.

When Loomis came before the judge for sentencing on this plea, the judge explained to Loomis that the other charges (which related more specifically to the shooting) would be 'dismissed but read-in'.[99] This meant that although Loomis maintained he was innocent of those charges, the Court was entitled to sentence on the assumption that the facts forming the basis of the charges were true – even though Loomis was ostensibly being sentenced only for the two charges to which he had pleaded guilty.[100] In sentencing, the Court also considered a Presentence Investigation Report (PSI Report) prepared about Loomis; attached to this report was a COMPAS risk assessment. The COMPAS report became the focus of attention when Loomis later challenged its use in determining his sentence.

The COMPAS report assessed Loomis as high risk. Judge Horne, the sentencing judge, stated:

> In terms of weighing the various factors, I'm ruling out probation because of the seriousness of the crime and because your history, your history on supervision, and the risk assessment tools that have been utilized, suggest that you're extremely high risk to re-offend.[101]

Ultimately Loomis was sentenced to four years for attempting to flee and seven years for the use of the vehicle, to be served concurrently.

Loomis subsequently petitioned for the Circuit Court to reconsider the sentence imposed on the basis that the Court should not have assumed the factual basis of the read-in charges was true, but also due to the Court's use of COMPAS. An expert witness gave evidence that: COMPAS was not designed for use as a tool to increase a person's sentence; it was likely that risk would be overestimated; and there was almost no information available about how the program generated its scores.[102] Specifically, the source of the data used to train COMPAS was not known – so it could not be known if that population was in any way similar to the Wisconsin population to which it was being applied. The Circuit Court, however, stated that it would have imposed the same sentence even in the absence of the COMPAS risk assessment, and the post-conviction motion was denied. Later, Loomis's appeal to the Court of Appeals in Wisconsin was unsuccessful. His eventual petition to the US Supreme Court was also denied.

Interestingly, in an earlier case heard by the same Wisconsin appellate Court, the Court had denied an appeal on the opposite basis.[103] The defendant,

[98] *Loomis* 754 [12].

[99] *Loomis* 755–56 [20]–[22].

[100] This is similar to the federal issue exemplified in *U.S. v Booker*, 543 US 220 (2005) (regarding relevant conduct); see also Johnson's explanation in 'Sentencing' (n 31) 709–10). Such an approach is not typically permissible under the common law: see, eg, *The Queen v De Simoni* (1981) 147 CLR 383, 389 (Australia).

[101] *Loomis* 755, [19] (quoting transcript of the plea hearing).

[102] *Loomis* 756, [26]–[27].

[103] *State v Samsa*, 2015 WI App 6, 359 Wis.2d 580, 859 N.W.2d 149 (Wis 2015) (*Samsa*).

John Samsa, had argued that the Court erred in failing to give sufficient weight to his PSI report and attached COMPAS report, which suggested that Samsa was a low risk of reoffending. Samsa had been convicted of third-degree sexual assault on a 14-year-old child and sentenced to five years' confinement followed by supervision. In upholding his sentence, the Appeals Court explained: 'Samsa's risk of violent or nonviolent reoffense was determined to be low by the COMPAS assessment. However, the Circuit Court ultimately rejected that conclusion, and it was perfectly within the court's discretion to do so'.[104]

The arguments raised in *Loomis* and in *Samsa* are discussed further in the following section. Though both concerned sentencing, individualised risk assessments are found in different contexts in the criminal justice system: they may be used in pre-trial decision making (bail and plea bargaining) and parole determinations – decisions which are predictive in character. Much recent critical literature has focused (post *Loomis*) on the use of risk assessments in sentencing in the US;[105] however, their use in pre-trial decision making is also highly important. As noted above, bail hearings involve determining whether a person charged with but not yet convicted of a criminal offence will remain in custody pending their trial or be released into the community.[106] If a person is to be released pending trial, then the conditions of their release – usually payment of a monetary sum – must be set. Cynthia Jones describes risk assessments as 'a critical component' of the process of determining bail.[107]

Use of risk assessments is also relevant to plea bargaining, where defence counsel and prosecutors negotiate deals between state and defendant, though plea bargains can be overturned by the court. Indeed, this can occur where judges feel that the plea bargain does not adequately reflect the risk posed by the offender – rather as occurred in *Samsa*.[108]

Risk assessments are also highly relevant to parole determinations[109] and to sentencing. Sentencing is the area perhaps best known for the use of risk assessments generated from machine learning programs. This may be partly due to *Loomis*, or the reporting by ProPublica, which provoked much discussion,[110] as well as the fact that many states of the US either mandate or permit judges to have

[104] *Samsa* 154 [13].

[105] eg ME Donohue, 'Note: A Replacement for Justitia's Scales? Machine Learning's Role in Sentencing' (2019) 32(2) *Harvard Journal of Law & Technology* 657.

[106] In many jurisdictions, these determinations are made by a judge but they can also be made by lay bail commissioners: see Jones (n 29).

[107] ibid 931.

[108] Angwin et al (n 38).

[109] In 2017, for example, R Wexler reported on the denial of parole for an offender held in New York State prison, despite an exemplary record during his time inside, which appeared to be solely a response to his 'high risk' COMPAS score: 'Code of Silence', 49 (6–8) *Washington Monthly*, 1 June 2017, 18. See also R Berk, 'Balancing the Costs of Forecasting Errors in Parole Decisions' (2010–2011) 74 *Albany Law Review* 1071.

[110] IM Beriain, 'Does the Use of Risk Assessments in Sentences Respect the Right to Due Process? A Critical Analysis of the *Wisconsin v Loomis* Ruling' (2018) 17(1) *Law, Probability & Risk* 45.

regard to risk assessments when imposing sentence.[111] It also coalesces with a body of scholarly work (and indeed popular media) which has analysed the process of sentencing by human judges and the broader politics of sentencing.

In some ways, sentencing seems to lend itself to machine analysis – as well as being a predictive or forward-looking decision, a sentence should typically have factored in a number of different elements or circumstances. Kelly Hannah-Moffat has noted: 'Although the laws, policies, and principles of sentencing vary considerably by jurisdiction and country, the introduction of risk into sentencing is a recent and increasing international trend'.[112] She argues that 'American, Asian, Australian, Canadian, British, and European jurisdictions are increasingly mandating or incorporating risk tools into sentencing policy for nonviolent offenders'.[113]

Role of the Lawyer

What, then, is the role of lawyers when it comes to the use of AI tools in the criminal justice system? Regardless of whether they represent a criminal defendant or the state, lawyers have a role to play in questioning the way such tools are being deployed and in ensuring that their use does not transgress fundamental rights and the rule of law. The lawyer's role is therefore quite different, when it comes to AI in the criminal justice system, from the roles described in the other chapters of this part. Lawyers must understand the flaws in machine decision making in order to challenge the use of tools in the criminal justice context – just as they would challenge problematic human reasoning or actions.

Plentiful critiques of the use of machine learning and big data analytics in policing and criminal justice system processes are now emerging.[114] A number of these critiques take as their starting point issues concerning the use of predictive analytics more generally. The way the software has been built and trained may be problematic and therefore result in unreliable or biased outputs. There are also broader questions about exactly how 'fairness' in such systems is being defined. Finally, there are enormous issues related to lack of transparency. The most widely used programs, such as PredPol and COMPAS, are proprietary and there is therefore no transparency as to how they operate.[115] For this reason, it is difficult for

[111] eg, Idaho, Kentucky, Louisiana, Ohio, Oklahoma, Pennsylvania, Virginia: *Loomis* 759 [42], fnn 23 and 24 and the references cited therein.

[112] K Hannah-Moffat, 'Actuarial Sentencing: An "Unsettled" Proposition' (2013) 30(2) *Justice Quarterly* 270, 271.

[113] ibid (citations omitted).

[114] See, eg, R Brownsword and A Harel, 'Law, Liberty and Technology: Criminal Justice in the Context of Smart Machines' (2019) 15(2) *International Journal of Law in Context* 107; S Endo, 'Technological Opacity and Procedural Injustice' (2018) 59(3) *Boston College Law Review* 822; Ferguson (n 5); Wexler (n 31); *cf* N Stobbs, D Hunter and M Bagaric, 'Can Sentencing Be Enhanced by the Use of Artificial Intelligence?' (2018) 41(5) *Criminal Law Journal* 261.

[115] Wexler (n 31).

anyone – defendants, lawyers, journalists, academics, even judges – to independently evaluate whether or not a system's outputs are indeed reliable.

Eric Loomis appealed to the Wisconsin Court of Appeal and his case – that use of the COMPAS risk assessment in sentencing violated his due process rights – was heard by a bench of three judges. Loomis's appeal on this point had three elements. The first was that the workings of COMPAS are opaque and unknowable, and therefore he could not be certain that he had been sentenced according to accurate information. Secondly, Loomis claimed that the use of the tool had violated his right to an individualised sentence. Finally, because one feature utilised by COMPAS is gender, he claimed that this had been improperly considered, in violation of constitutional protections guaranteeing equality before the law.

The Wisconsin Court of Appeal unanimously found that Loomis's due process rights had not been violated by the use of COMPAS. Subsequently, in 2017, the US Supreme Court denied Loomis's petition for certiorari – in other words, declined to hear a further appeal.[116]

Though it rejected Loomis' claims, the Court of Appeal did note that the use of COMPAS for sentencing raises due process concerns.[117] In response, it set out some parameters or guidance as to the future use of comparable risk assessment tools. The separate judgments of Roggensack CJ and Abrahamson J, in particular, stress that COMPAS should be used cautiously and selectively. Evidence suggests that this is probably inadequate, yet risk assessment tools are becoming ubiquitous in the US criminal justice system. In many other jurisdictions it seems likely that the use of such tools would not be permissible – or would be permissible only with safeguards such as demonstrable accuracy and transparency.

This next section is divided into three parts, reflecting three vital elements about the use of machine learning which lawyers must understand in order challenge its use: accuracy; fairness and bias; and opacity.[118] Regardless of the particular criminal justice context, each element has the potential to undermine safeguards related to fundamental rights, including rights to equal treatment without discrimination, to life and liberty, and to not be subjected to arbitrary arrest or detention.

Accuracy

Lawyers must be cognisant of whether an AI system is, in fact, accurate – or more particularly, of the ways in which the system may be inaccurate. Ascertaining this is likely to be challenging both because of the complexity of a system, and due to lack of transparency, an issue discussed in the following section. As explained in Chapter 4, development of a machine learning system requires that many

[116] *Loomis v Wisconsin*, 26 June 2017, Docket no 16-6387.

[117] ibid, 759 [41].

[118] J Kleinberg and S Mullainathan, 'Simplicity Creates Inequity: Implications for Fairness, Stereotypes, and Interpretability' (2019) arxiv.org/pdf/1809.04578.pdf.

choices be made by the humans engineering the system, related to determining what will be measured (the predictive goal); the algorithms that will be deployed; the training data and how it will be used; and how the system will be tested and updated. A familiar method for measuring accuracy, as noted there, is a measure of statistical significance.

All 'data' in the criminal justice context is, however, both crude and fragmentary. Broadly, it cannot be assumed that material available for data collection accurately represents 'reality' (nor indeed that 'reality' has a clear meaning; or that this is even possible). Craig Dalton and Jim Thatcher draw attention to the fact that in 'its production and interpretation, all data – "big" included – are *always* the result of contingent and contested social practices that afford and obfuscate specific understandings of the world'.[119] In relation to policing, reports of criminal activity are highly dependent on a multitude of different elements such as who observed particular behaviour, how that behaviour was interpreted by the observer, whether it was reported, the response of individual police officers, and so on. Thus, while the number of offences an individual has *committed* is likely measured by how many offences they have been *convicted* of, this may or may not be the same thing. (Comparing the prosecutorial systems of Germany and the US, Shawn Marie Boyne notes that 'prosecutors in both systems lack the resources necessary to prosecute all cases in which a suspicion exists that a crime has been committed'[120] – giving an indication of the partiality of the data). Convictions may yet be an acceptable proxy for offences committed, but in still other areas, even finding an adequate proxy may be very challenging.[121]

David Lehr and Paul Ohm's breakdown of the design of a machine learning system, described in Chapter 4, begins with the need to translate a policy goal into a 'predictive' goal. They use the example of reducing violence in a prison. While this may be the overarching policy objective, to convert it into a predictive goal more specificity is needed. The predictive goal could be defined as predicting the likelihood that any one individual will commit an act of violence while in prison.[122] But then, a further translative act must take place in reducing the predictive goal down to a specific outcome variable. Choices must be made as to how to represent this outcome variable, which might be either binary or continuous and could measure different things. Lehr and Ohm explain some options:

> [A] binary variable indicating an individual's involvement in a violent altercation within the first year of incarceration, a continuous variable indicating how many times an individual is involved in a violent altercation during the entirety of his or her incarceration,

[119] C Dalton and J Thatcher, 'What Does a Critical Data Studies Look Like, and Why Do We Care?' (2014) societyandspace.org/2014/05/12/whatdoes-a-critical-data-studies-look-like-and-why-do-we-care-craig-dalton-and-jim-thatcher/ (emphasis added).

[120] Boyne (n 19) 228.

[121] Lehr and Ohm (n 6) 675. An example is how to measure whether a person is a 'good' employee: S Barocas and AD Selbst, 'Big Data's Disparate Impact' (2016) 104 *California Law Review* 671, 679–80.

[122] Lehr and Ohm (n 6).

> a continuous variable indicating the average number of altercations in which a prisoner is involved per year of his or her incarceration, etc.[123]

The nature of the chosen proxy and precise outcome variable is likely important. For example, is a risk assessment measuring the likelihood of arrest or of criminal conviction?

There is also the inescapable fact that the prediction pertains to a group in aggregate, and cannot hold true for all specific individuals.[124] Depending on how accurate or inaccurate a program is, it may hold true for smaller or larger proportions of people – but there will always be degrees of inaccuracy.

Another major issue is whether the data used to train a machine learning system is comparable to the real-world data to which it will be applied. The debate about representativeness of data has been had in many contexts over many years.[125] Writing of social science research generally, Judy Cashmore and Patrick Parkinson have explained:

> Perhaps the most important aspects of the sample in a research study is how representative it is, and to what extent it is possible to generalize from that sample to other groups or a larger population. The questions that need to be asked include: Is there anything particular to the sample that would make generalization problematic or misleading? Are they similar in terms of socioeconomic status, education, ethnicity, and experience? How were the participants in the study selected?[126]

The data used to train a system may be non-representative, may be old, or may be representative of a particular population but one which is different to that from which the defendant in question hails. In the UK it has been noted that most studies of risk assessments originate in the US, calling into question whether they can successfully apply in a different context.[127] This is even leaving aside any issues of bias. While there are methods, carefully described by Lehr and Ohm, by which such limitations may be partially remedied, the results will inevitably be imperfect.

Further, the use of machine learning software to generate predictions in the policing or criminal justice context may, in a sense, create or contribute to a self-fulfilling prophecy. For instance, over-policing of certain communities likely leads to higher arrests and ultimately higher crime rates in certain areas. If a 'predictive policing' system causes more police to be deployed to the neighbourhood this may rise still further.[128] Hence, as an article in the *Huffington Post* reported,

[123] ibid 674–75.

[124] See PM Casey, JK Elek, RK Warren, F Cheesman, M Kleiman and B Ostrom, *Offender Risk & Needs Assessment Instruments: A Primer for Courts* (National Center for State Courts, 2014) 14. This is discussed further below in relation to fairness and bias.

[125] See generally M Maguire and S McVie, 'Crime Data and Criminal Statistics: A Critical Reflection' in M Maguire, R Morgan and R Reiner (eds), *The Oxford Handbook of Criminology* (Oxford University Press, 2017) 163.

[126] J Cashmore and P Parkinson, 'The Use and Abuse of Social Science Research Evidence in Children's Cases' (2014) 20(3) *Psychology, Public Policy, and Law* 239. See also Lehr and Ohm (n 6) 680.

[127] Babuta and Oswald (n 81) 3.

[128] Bennett Moses and Chan (n 49) 810.

'Predictive Policing Software is More Accurate at Predicting Policing Than Predicting Crime'.[129]

Further, if a machine learning system used for individual risk assessment identifies a correlation between past arrests and future crime commission then the individuals within the area will be further disadvantaged by comparison to those who are under-policed. Arguably, 'person-based predictive policing can … generate a feedback loop in which an individual with a high risk score is more likely to be stopped, and *that* police contact further increases the individual's score'.[130] Moreover, treating people who are, in fact, 'low risk' as if they were high risk – which may mean incarceration instead of release, subjection to more intensive supervision or police stops – may paradoxically increase their recidivism risk.[131] At the same time, under-policing is also problematic as it may lead to increased crime and more victimisation. For example, one study found that neighbours are the most likely people to contact police to alert them to domestic violence incidents, so people who live in homes with shared (party) walls such as apartments or terraces are more likely to come to the attention of police for domestic violence offences.[132] A system trained on this data might link dwelling type to likelihood of offending, over-policing those who live in dwellings with shared walls and under-policing those in detached homes.

Part of the ProPublica investigation into COMPAS involved looking at data from a county in Florida where the tool was routinely used by courts. Angwin and her colleagues took the data of defendants from this county who had been arrested in 2013/14 and assessed using COMPAS (after some data trimming, the database had over 10,000 people). Angwin et al then compared the tool's predictions with the actual arrests of those defendants up until March 2016:

> ProPublica obtained a dataset of pretrial defendants and probationers … who had been assessed with the COMPAS screening system between January 1, 2013, and December 31, 2014 … The survey is completed by pre-trial services in cooperation with the defendant after his or her arrest … [and] is typically administered the same day or the day after a person is jailed.[133]

The dataset used by Angwin et al is publicly available and hence has been used by multiple researchers since. Much discussion about COMPAS concerns its fairness or lack thereof. Yet an important part of the story is simply how accurate

[129] E Edwards, 'Predictive Policing Software is More Accurate at Predicting Policing Than Predicting Crime', *Huffington Post*, 31 August 2016, www.huffpost.com/entry/predictive-policing-reform_b_57c6ffe0e4b0e60d31dc9120.

[130] Brayne (n 61) 299 (emphasis added).

[131] Casey et al (n 124) 20.

[132] C Doctorow, 'Garbage In, Garbage Out: Machine Learning Has Not Repealed the Iron Law of Computer Science', *BoingBoing*, 29 May 2018 (quoting Patrick Ball, Director of Research, Human Rights Data Analysis Group, Benetech Initiative, hrdag.org).

[133] The description of M Barenstein, 'ProPublica's COMPAS Data Revisited' (8 July 2019) arxiv.org/pdf/1906.04711.pdf, 3.

predictive tools are to begin with. This is challenging as often such tools are not independently assessed, or if they are, have not been validated on specific local populations.[134] A RAND Corporation evaluation of one predictive policing tool concluded that it was 'no better than traditional "hotspot" policing'[135] – the term used to describe frequent policing monitoring of geographic locations associated with high crime, those locations being determined by a combination of statistics and local knowledge.

A primer for US State courts on offender risk assessments explains that ideally statistical significance would be used in conjunction with another measure of accuracy for offender risk assessment scores, the 'area under the curve' (AUC) value.[136] The AUC value represents

> the computed probability of the number of correct classifications, or 'hits', versus the number of incorrect classifications, or 'false alarms', by the risk assessment tool … An AUC = .5 means that an assessment tool is no better than chance at discriminating between recidivists and non-recidivists. The closer the AUC value is to 1, the more effective the assessment tool is at discriminating between recidivists and non-recidivists.[137]

The primer examined six different instruments,[138] summarising the available information and research evidence on each. In summary, it concludes, COMPAS is 'moderately' accurate.[139]

In an earlier, 2007 evaluation of COMPAS, prepared for California's Department of Corrections and Rehabilitation, Jennifer Skeem and Jennifer Eno Louden found that the tool was not a good predictor of recidivism, noting that many of its scales were created with very small samples and lacked cross-validation.[140] Skeem and Louden concluded: 'Given present limitations in evidence on inter-rater reliability, predictive utility, and construct validity, we cannot recommend the COMPAS for application to individual offenders'.[141] Another assessment published the following year concluded that the predictive validity of COMPAS varied significantly for different ethnic groups.[142] It was most effective for male Caucasians (an AUC of .81) but very poor for male African Americans (AUC of .48: in other words, *less than* random chance).[143] The authors noted that the initial

[134] Casey et al (n 124) 18–19.

[135] P Hunt, J Saunders and JS Hollywood, 'Evaluation of the Shreveport Predictive Policing Experiment' (RAND Corporation, 2014) 33, www.rand.org/pubs/research_reports/RR531.html.

[136] Casey et al (n 124) 14.

[137] ibid 17.

[138] ibid A-1, reviewing: Correctional Assessment and Intervention System; Correctional Offender Management Profile for Alternative Sanctions; Level of Service Assessments; Offender Screening Tool; Ohio Risk Assessment System; and Static Risk and Offender Needs Guide.

[139] ibid A-23.

[140] JL Skeem and JE Loudon, 'Report Prepared for the California Department of Corrections and Rehabilitation' *Assessment of Evidence on the Quality of the Correctional Offender Management Profiling for Alternative Sanctions (COMPAS)* (2007) 28.

[141] ibid.

[142] TL Fass, K Heilbrun, D DeMatteo and R Fretz, 'The LSI-R and the COMPAS: Validation Data on Two Risk-Needs Tools' (2008) 35 *Criminal Justice and Behavior* 1095.

[143] ibid.

validation study performed on COMPAS had used only 241 offenders, and while it reported good predictive ability (AUC of .79), the original analysts themselves had concluded this may have been inflated.[144]

In 2018, researchers Julia Dressel and Hany Farid argued that COMPAS is 'no more accurate or fair than predictions made by people with little or no criminal justice expertise'.[145] They had compared the predictions of participants in their study, which were based upon the participant reading a 'short description of a defendant that included the defendant's sex, age, and previous criminal history, but not their race',[146] to COMPAS scores. Dressel and Farid also found that they could achieve similar accuracy to COMPAS using only seven inputs (the ones read by their study participants) in a 'simple linear regression' model.

Dressel and Farid were taken to task by a group of academics and members of the Administrative Office of US Courts (Alexander Holsinger et al) who pointed out flaws in the way that the human assessors were supported in their decision making.[147] Holsinger et al noted also that

> Dressel and Farid actually found that the COMPAS did outperform laypeople in predicting recidivism – at a statistically significant level. The authors downplay this finding – claiming that laypeople's accuracy is 'just barely' lower than that of COMPAS. For … people who are the subject of recidivism predictions, 'just barely' lower probably matters.[148]

On the other hand, what Dressel and Farid's research does indicate is that COMPAS does not have especially high predictive accuracy – around 65 per cent (the scores referred to were laypeople: 62.8 per cent; COMPAS: 65.2 per cent). Indeed, Dressel and Farid's main point is that if COMPAS and other tools like it are not providing superior accuracy, or are providing a level of accuracy which can be quite easily replicated by people who are given support or guidance, then the use of such a tool (with its expense, and opacity) does not seem particularly worthwhile. The same argument is made by Narayanan, who points out that better accuracy (67 per cent) is achieved through the use of two factors (the person's age, and the number of prior offences of which they have been convicted) in a linear regression than using COMPAS, which ostensibly uses 137 factors.[149]

[144] ibid.

[145] J Dressel and H Farid, 'The Accuracy, Fairness, and Limits of Predicting Recidivism' (2018) 4(1) *Science Advances*, DOI: 10.1126/sciadv.aao5580.

[146] ibid 1.

[147] Holsinger et al (n 2) 52–53, citing S Ægisdóttir et al, 'The Meta-Analysis of Clinical Judgment Project: Fifty-Six Years of Accumulated Research on Clinical Versus Statistical Prediction' (2006) 34 *The Counseling Psychologist* 341; WM Grove, DH Zald, BS Lebow, BE Snitz and C Nelson, 'Clinical versus Mechanical Prediction: A Meta-Analysis' (2000) 12 *Psychological Assessment* 19; and PE Meehl, *Clinical versus Statistical Prediction* (University of Minnesota Press, 1954).

[148] Holsinger et al (n 2) 53.

[149] Narayanan (n 86); and see A Chouldechova and M G'Sell, 'Fairer and More Accurate, But For Whom?' (2017) arXiv:1707.00046.

Holsinger et al, by contrast, argue that actuarial risk assessments have long been used in criminal justice and that there is a large body of research indicating that such assessments are more accurate than humans. Likewise, Anthony Flores, Kristin Bechtel and Christopher Lowenkamp state:

> The issue that is no longer up for debate is that [actuarial risk assessment instruments] predict outcomes more strongly and accurately than professional judgment alone. Several studies and meta-analyses have reached similar conclusions indicating that actuarial risk assessments are superior to unstructured professional judgment in terms of predicting the likelihood of both general recidivism and even specific recidivism outcomes.[150]

Studies of human decision making do often identify inconsistency and bias.[151] Research suggests also that 'structuring' decision making tends to result in more accurate predictions.[152] Hence the use of sentencing guidelines to (among other things) increase the consistency of sentencing among judges.[153] Ferguson makes a similar point in relation to police work, observing that it is possible that 'big data policing' will increase accuracy: 'More information, and more precise information, should make it more likely that police target actual criminals rather than innocent people'.[154] On the other hand, he notes that the availability of a wealth of data could actually generate unwarranted suspicions. In like vein, evaluation of facial recognition technology used by police in South Wales found that 'some of the results delivered by the technology were impressive', though it also had shortcomings, leading the researchers to conclude that 'the technology is more accurately described as affording 'Assisted Facial Recognition', than 'Automated Facial Recognition'.[155]

Fairness and Bias

The focal point of ProPublica's story was racial bias in the operation of the COMPAS tool – its tagline was 'There's software used across the country to predict future criminals. And it's biased against blacks'.[156] In response, the company that sells COMPAS denied this claim, as did Flores, Bechtel and Lowenkamp in their

[150] Flores, Bechtel and Lowenkamp (n 43) 39, citations omitted.

[151] Noting that definitions of 'consistency' and 'inconsistency' are not straightforward: M Tonry, 'Legal and Ethical Issues in the Prediction of Recidivism' (2014) 26 *Federal Sentencing* 167, 168. See further Chapter 4.

[152] JL Skeem and J Monahan, 'Current Directions in Violence Risk Assessment' (2011) 20(1) *Current Directions in Psychological Science* 38.

[153] Johnson (n 31) 699.

[154] Ferguson (n 92) 389.

[155] B Davies, M Innes and A Dawson, 'An Evaluation of South Wales Police's Use of Automated Facial Recognition' (Universities Police Science Institute and Crime & Security Research Institute, Cardiff University, 2018) 42.

[156] Angwin et al (n 38).

analysis of the ProPublica data.[157] As ProPublica made their dataset accessible, many other researchers have now also used it, to differing effect.[158]

Generally, bias in this context can be conceived as occurring in 'circumstances where an algorithm is not as effective for, and/or over-classifies specific demographic groups'.[159] One group of scholars, led by Laurel Eckhouse, has recommended thinking about bias in risk assessments as comprising or occurring in three different layers (Figure 9.1).[160]

Figure 9.1 Layers of bias

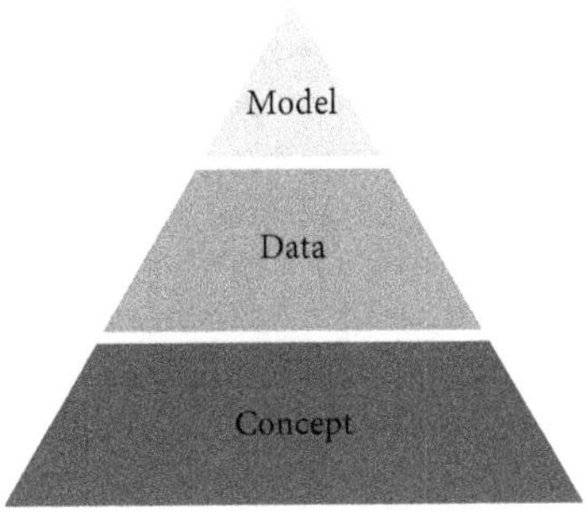

The top layer in Figure 9.1 – Model – involves the algorithmic or statistical models themselves ('types of statistical fairness and the tradeoffs between them').[161] The second layer – Data – comprises the bias which may arise from problematic data (such as data which reflects historic biases in policing). Finally, the bottom layer – Concept – draws out conceptual issues with risk models generally. In other words, this layer signifies queries around the bigger picture of whether it is fair to make decisions about individuals based on aggregate or group data.[162] Eckhouse et al argue that the fairness of each layer depends on fairness in the one/s below.[163]

Much of the debate post 'Machine Bias' has looked at the top layer – the ProPublica story generated an informative debate on exactly how 'fairness' ought to be conceived, and more importantly, how it should be incorporated into a system used to predict the future behaviour of individuals. Several researchers suggested that the ProPublica results were not, in fact, incompatible with the analyses of Northpointe (now equivant[164]). Rather, each used differing methods to

[157] equivant, www.equivant.com; Flores, Bechtel and Lowenkamp (n 43).

[158] eg, S Corbett-Davies, E Pierson, A Feller, S Goel and A Huq, 'Algorithmic Decision Making and the Cost of Fairness' (2017) in Proceedings of the 23rd ACM SIGKDD International Conference on Knowledge Discovery and Data Mining, 797.

[159] Holsinger et al (n 2) 51.

[160] Eckhouse et al (n 7) 185–209.

[161] ibid 189.

[162] ibid.

[163] ibid.

[164] equivant, www.equivant.com.

determine or construct what was 'fair'. Indeed, researchers such as Jon Kleinberg and colleagues have explained that there are 'inherent trade-offs' involved, and it is not possible to satisfy multiple different conceptions of fairness simultaneously.[165]

One decision which must be made when adopting a particular conception of fairness involves choices about rates of false positives and false negatives. A *false positive* is where a defendant is wrongly classified as higher risk than they are (resulting in the corresponding risk that the person receives harsher treatment, which is unwarranted); a *false negative* is where a defendant who is in reality a higher risk is misclassified as lower risk (with the attendant possibility that high-risk individuals are given more lenient treatment).

ProPublica found that COMPAS was more likely to mis-classify African American defendants as high risk – in other words, the rate of false positives for these defendants was higher than the rate for white defendants.[166] Northpointe's response indicated that it was using a different measure of fairness – one in which the risk score allocated to an individual represented the same likelihood of that person reoffending regardless of race.[167] As researchers have since pointed out, if there are differences in recidivism between different racial groups (which is the case, according to US national statistics) then it is not possible to simultaneously have equal predictive validity and equal rates of false positives.[168] We could also think about the false negative rate – whether people who *do* go on to later commit more offences had received similar scores.[169] ProPublica asserted that this was also skewed in that white defendants who went on commit further offences were more likely to have been given lower scores originally.

This is only one example of the analyses which have been done of both COMPAS and of ProPublica's particular investigation. Yet, it demonstrates that the debate stretches beyond the statistical models and provokes broader questions about criminal justice policy and value choices.

The second layer concerns the data used to train machine learning programs and the integrity of that data. Since all machine learning systems are dependent on

[165] J Kleinberg, S Mullainathan and M Raghavan, 'Inherent Trade-Offs in the Fair Determination of Risk Scores' (2016) arxiv.org/pdf/1609.05807.pdf. See also M Spielkamp, 'Inspecting Algorithms for Bias', *MIT Technology Review*, 12 June 2017, www.technologyreview.com/s/607955/inspecting-algorithms-for-bias/, citing K Gummadi, head of the Networked Systems Research Group at the Max Planck Institute for Software Systems in Saarbrücken, Germany ('Gummadi, who has extensively researched fairness in algorithms, says ProPublica's and Northpointe's results don't contradict each other. They differ because they use different measures of fairness'). See further A Chouldechova, 'Fair Prediction with Disparate Impact: A Study of Bias in Recidivism Prediction Instruments' (2016) arXiv:1610.07524.

[166] Angwin et al (n 38).

[167] W Dieterich, C Mendoza and T Brennan, 'COMPAS Risk Scales: Demonstrating Accuracy Equity and Predictive Parity', Technical Report (Northpointe, July 2016) www.northpointeinc.com/northpointe-analysis; A Feller, E Pierson, S Corbett-Davies and S Goel, 'A Computer Program Used for Bail and Sentencing Decisions was Labeled Biased Against Blacks. It's Actually Not that Clear', *Washington Post*, 17 October 2016; Kleinberg, Mullainathan and Raghavan (n 165) 1.

[168] Eckhouse et al (n 7) 192. See also Corbett-Davies et al (n 158); A Chouldechova, 'Fair Prediction with Disparate Impact: A Study of Bias in Recidivism Prediction Instruments' (2016) arXiv:1703.00056.

[169] Eckhouse et al (n 7) 190.

data, the nature of what is available is fundamentally important. In many jurisdictions, the criminal justice system reflects deep social inequities, often on racialised lines. An independent review of Black, Asian and Minority Ethnic individuals in the criminal justice system of England and Wales, conducted by parliamentarian David Lammy, opens by explaining:

> Over the course of this review I visited six countries and 12 cities around the world. In each jurisdiction, I found governments and civil society organisations grappling with how best to reduce racial disparities within their own criminal justice systems. In France, Muslims make up an estimated 8% of the population and between a quarter and a half of the prison population. In America, one in 35 African American men are incarcerated, compared with one in 214 White men. In Canada, indigenous adults make up 3% of the population but 25% of the prison population. In Australia, Aboriginal and Torres Strait Islander [people] make up 2% of the population, but 27% of prisoners. In New Zealand, Maoris make up 15% of the population, but more than 50% of the prisoners.[170]

In addition to the incomplete and partial nature of crime data, described above, it is likely that data reflects historical and existing biases in policing, prosecution and incarceration practices. Further, most risk assessments are based on data from specific populations – such as prisoners – rather than randomly selected members of the general population. Hannah-Moffat comments that this 'raises concerns about the ability of any instrument to generate an unbiased prediction of risk':[171]

> With the advent of computer mapping and geographic information systems, real-time crime hot spot forecasting has become an important interest to policing. Nevertheless, crime hot spot forecasting presents challenges to policing. There is a high volume of crime hot spot misclassifications and a lack of theoretical support for existing forecasting algorithms. Additionally, many algorithms are complex and proprietary. Thus, they require expensive contracts with private vendors, and they do not have the transparency necessary. Transparency is particularly important as police use of stop-question-frisk tactics in hot spots has been linked to racially disparate treatment of non-whites, and excessive interference in the daily lives of people who are not involved in crime.[172]

An example of bias in policing is found in comparisons of marijuana use and arrests for marijuana possession. In the US, marijuana use is (on self-report studies) very similar across black and white populations: indeed, use is more prevalent among whites. Yet black people are over four times more likely to be arrested for marijuana possession in those states where it is not decriminalised.[173] Similar disparities are found in England and Wales where a black person is six times

[170] UK Government, *The Lammy Review: An Independent Review into the Treatment of, and Outcomes for, Black, Asian and Minority Ethnic Individuals in the Criminal Justice System* (8 September 2017).

[171] Hannah-Moffat (n 112) 277.

[172] YJ Lee, SH O and JE Eck, 'A Theory-Driven Algorithm for Real-Time Crime Hot Spot Forecasting' (2019) *Police Quarterly*, doi.org/10.1177/1098611119887809.

[173] The effect is strongest in areas with high or middle incomes: see American Civil Liberties Union, *The War on Marijuana in Black and White* (ACLU, June 2013) 17, 21.

more likely to be arrested for drug offences than a white person, figures not borne out in the conviction rates.[174] Hence, as one professor of criminology explained, 'Predictive policing is at the cutting edge of policing today. The problem is that, historically, the cutting edge of policing is dull'.[175] These same issues arise in terms of AFR, too, as systems typically are better at identifying Caucasian males and poorer at identification of females and non-Caucasian ethnicities.[176]

A now well-known story about statistical analysis, reported by the *New York Times* in 2012, concerns the US chain store Target sending promotional material (such as coupons for baby clothes) to prospective mothers. In some cases, this occurred before the women in question had informed those close to them of the pregnancy, or indeed perhaps before they even knew of the pregnancy themselves.[177] Rather, Target worked out how to predict when a woman was pregnant by analysing its own customer data. Initially the company based its analysis on the history of purchasing by female customers who later used Target's gift registry for their baby shower. It found that certain patterns of product buying correlated with pregnancy. Importantly, customers were not buying anything so obvious as baby toys or clothing, but items such as unscented skin lotion and cotton balls. In other words, a change in shopping habits and purchase of particular items among female customers of a certain age, was a proxy for (correlated highly with) pregnancy, even though the customers were not purchasing specific 'baby' or 'pregnancy' items.

Even Target realised that pregnant women might find it unnerving that the store could learn of their pregnancy without having been explicitly informed.[178] In the criminal justice context, concerns about proxy variables are amped up much further. While COMPAS reportedly does not include race as an input, the response is that it does not need to. A person's race or ethnic background can be readily inferred from other data that it does utilise, like postcode and occupation.[179] These factors themselves are proxies for socioeconomic status, which, in the US, is in turn highly correlated with race.[180]

There is much investigation within machine learning about how best to deal with biases which exist in data. Indeed, it may be better to leave undesirable or

[174] Vogler and Fouladvand (n 22) 195–96, citing Ministry of Justice, *Statistics on Race and the Criminal Justice System 2012* (HMSO, 2013) 37; see also Press Release, www.release.org.uk/press-release-racial-disparities-drug-policing.

[175] Berg (n 50) (quoting Professor J Eck, University of Cincinnati).

[176] R Yu and GS Ali, 'What's Inside the Black Box? AI Challenges for Lawyers and Researchers' (2019) *Legal Informational Management* 2, 3–4.

[177] C Duhigg, 'How Companies Learn Your Secrets', *New York Times*, 16 February 2012, www.nytimes.com/2012/02/19/magazine/shopping-habits.html.

[178] ibid, see also E Siegel, *Predictive Analytics: The Power to Predict Who Will Click, Buy, Lie, or Die* (John Wiley & Sons, 2013).

[179] M Leese, 'The New Profiling: Algorithms, Black Boxes and the Failure of Anti-Discriminatory Safeguards in the European Union' (2014) 45(5) *Security Dialogue* 494.

[180] C Robertson, S Baradaran Baughman and MS Wright, 'Race and Class: A Randomized Experiment with Prosecutors' (2019) 16(4) *Journal of Empirical Legal Studies* 807.

discriminatory factors (things like gender, race, age or disability) *in* so that their impact can be actively counteracted or mitigated against.[181] In Loomis's case, the Wisconsin Court of Appeal found that it was appropriate to consider his gender as part of the risk assessment score, as a failure to do so would diminish its accuracy.

Then again, the process of 'cleaning up' data also involves many human decisions. The Partnership on AI has noted that 'what data to use, how to handle missing data, what objectives to optimize, and what thresholds to set all have significant implications on the accuracy, validity, and bias of these tools' too.[182] For facial recognition technology, the setting of 'similarity scores' will affect how many false alarms are generated – if too high a level of similarity is required, the system will miss identifying persons of interest, while if set too low, it risks misidentifying people who are not of interest.

More broadly, Julia Powles and Helen Nissenbaum have argued that the focus on trying to make AI fair, or rectifying the problem of bias, hides the fact that bias is largely a problem of social inequity.[183] Moreover, they suggest, it distracts from more important issues, such as scrutinising and regulating how personal data is used and controlled. This segues to the bottom or base layer described by Eckhouse and colleagues, which concerns the very idea of using group characteristics to make decisions about individuals. In its June 2019 report, *Algorithms in the Criminal Justice System*, the Law Society of England and Wales summarised this topic succinctly under the heading: 'Individuals Not Treated as Such'.[184]

This is not a new critique. In 1988, Jonathan Simon (now Professor of Law at the University of California, Berkeley) wrote of actuarial practices:

> Because they operate on the basis of aggregate data, they conflict with the strongly held value that people be considered primarily as individuals. Because they operate in terms of predicted future outcomes, they conflict with the related value that those aspects of a person that reflect her intentional efforts be privileged over those aspects that are involuntary. Finally, because they demoralize – treat as morally neutral – differences that carry highly-charged political and social significance (such as race and gender), they threaten to obscure the historical effects of domination and conflict with modern efforts to remedy discrimination.[185]

[181] J Kleinberg, J Ludwig, S Mullainathan and CR Sunstein, 'Discrimination in the Age of Algorithms' (2018) 10 *Journal of Legal Analysis* 113, 119. See further Chapter 10.

[182] Partnership on AI, *Report on Algorithmic Risk Assessment Tools in the U.S. Criminal Justice System* (26 April 2019).

[183] J Powles and H Nissenbaum, 'The Seductive Diversion of "Solving" Bias in Artificial Intelligence', *Medium* (8 December 2018) onezero.medium.com/the-seductive-diversion-of-solving-bias-in-artificial-intelligence-890df5e5ef53.

[184] The Law Society (n 6) 19.

[185] J Simon, 'The Ideological Effects of Actuarial Practices' (1988) 22(4) *Law & Society Review* 771, 776. See also K Hannah-Moffat, 'Criminogenic Needs and the Transformative Risk Subject: Hybridizations of Risk/Need in Penalty' (2004) 7(1) *Punishment and Society* 29.

In failing to distinguish between static (immutable) factors such as race, and dynamic factors such as education, the assumption is that offenders cannot reform.[186]

Opacity and Interpretability

Perhaps the most significant problem for lawyers, defendants or anyone subjected to some form of assessment (for example, for credit scoring, or when applying for a job) undertaken by machine learning is the opacity of the software used to perform the assessment. There is an ongoing debate about transparency, interpretability and explainability in machine learning. Matthias Spielkamp, executive director of advocacy group AlgorithmWatch,[187] has described the problem as follows:

> [O]ften we don't know enough about how [automated decision making] systems work to know whether they are fairer than humans would be on their own. In part because the systems make choices on the basis of underlying assumptions that are not clear even to the systems' designers, it's not necessarily possible to determine which algorithms are biased and which ones are not.[188]

Spielkamp points out that algorithmic assessments *may* be more accurate and less biased than people – but if they are not transparent, no one can be sure whether that is the case. Ironically, too, Kleinberg and Sendhil Mullainathan have noted that pursuing interpretability may mean sacrificing accuracy.[189] However, opacity in areas such as bail, parole and sentencing is not only problematic for the individuals subject to the decision, but is likely to generate wider, public mistrust in the administration of justice.

In the US context, Rebecca Wexler has argued that trade secrets, including the functioning of risk assessment software, should not be privileged in criminal proceedings.[190] Wexler also points to the increasingly privatised nature of criminal justice, with some jurisdictions having privatised prisons and even privatised police.[191] While some State organisations are developing machine learning tools 'in-house', many more are developed by private industry, who license their use to State bodies.[192]

[186] DS Sidhu, 'Moneyball Sentencing' (2015) 56 *Boston College Law Review* 671, 675.

[187] algorithmwatch.org/en/.

[188] Spielkamp (n 165).

[189] Kleinberg and Mullainathan (n 118) 2.

[190] Wexler (n 31).

[191] ibid 1349, citing J Jouvenal, 'Private Police Carry Guns and Make Arrests, and Their Ranks are Swelling', *Washington Post* (28 February 2015).

[192] Lehr and Ohm (n 6) 662; D Robinson and L Koepke, 'Stuck in a Pattern: Early Evidence on "Predictive Policing" and Civil Rights' (Upturn, 2016), www.upturn.org/static/reports/2016/stuck-in-a-pattern/files/Upturn_-_Stuck_In_a_Pattern_v.1.01.pdf, 3 tbl 1 (identifying nine leading predictive policing systems that were developed either solely by private industry or through a collaboration between academics and private industry).

Challenging the Use of AI Tools

Lawyers must understand these shortcomings in order to appropriately challenge their use in criminal proceedings. Specifically, lawyers must challenge inappropriate use by police and in the courts, as discussed in this section. But lawyers also have a broader responsibility to uphold the rule of law, and to protect and promote the rights of all without discrimination. Likewise, the consequences of individual rights transgressions are that broader structures may be impugned: 'Secrecy in the specifics of risk assessment algorithms also undermines the general trust of the public in the integrity of the judicial system'.[193] In *Algorithms in the Criminal Justice System*, the Law Society emphasised the lawyer's broader role, noting:[194]

> Many of the heavily individualised, legal safeguards proposed to algorithmic systems in commercial domains, such as individual explanation rights, are unlikely to be very helpful in criminal justice, where imbalances of power can be extreme and are exacerbated by dwindling levels of legal aid. Societal, systemic oversight must be placed at the forefront of algorithmic systems in this sector.[195]

Lawyers have joined the chorus of concerned voices querying the use of AI in the criminal justice system, and lawyers and legal scholars have argued that people should not be the subject of criminal processes whose workings are opaque and whose accuracy cannot be guaranteed.[196]

For individuals subjected to police interventions, key questions concern whether the outputs of machine learning systems are sufficient to justify the generation of suspicion.[197] In the US context, Ferguson has discussed this in detail,[198] querying whether the Fourth Amendment to the US Constitution (the prohibition on unreasonable search and seizure) permits a police stop based on aggregated information which is specific to an individual but not in and of itself criminal; or whether a search which would otherwise be impermissible can be justified in light of such aggregated information in conjunction with the person's observed actions.[199] Ferguson suggests that

> [w]ithout the requirement of some observable activity, the odds increase that predictive stops will target innocent people, criminalize by association, and negatively impact individuals based on little more than a hunch supported by non-criminal facts. On the other hand, many judges might find this totality of suspicions – even if focused on a particular suspect and not a crime – sufficient to justify an investigatory stop.

[193] A Rizer and C Watney, 'Artificial Intelligence Can Make Our Jail System More Efficient, Equitable, and Just' (2018) 23(1) *Texas Review of Law & Politics* 181, 213.

[194] The Law Society (n 6).

[195] ibid 5.

[196] Wexler (n 31); Eckhouse et al (n 7).

[197] Searches without such suspicion are likely unlawful, eg *Case of Gillan and Quinton v United Kingdom* [2010] ECHR 28; *Terry v Ohio*, 392 US 1 (1967).

[198] Ferguson, 'Predictive Policing and Reasonable Suspicion' (2012) 62(2) *Emory Law Journal* 259; Ferguson (n 92).

[199] Ferguson (n 92) 330.

> Reasonable suspicion is a low threshold. Thus, in practice, aggregated reasonable suspicion would likely justify a stop in many courtrooms.[200]

Police contact with individuals without a basis in observed activity would seem to be a step towards policing people based on who they are rather than on their observed actions – a similar criticism to that levelled at the use of risk assessments. One academic has referred to the propagation of a 'categorical suspicion' against people, based on, for instance, their location in a particular geographic area.[201] Ferguson does identify several arguments as to why the use of predictive analytics could be useful in policing, among them that it could result in greater accuracy both in terms of individuals who are stopped and those who are bypassed (in other words, police might discover exculpatory information which prevents them from making contact with a person).[202] Against this, however, must be balanced the issues discussed above such as a lack of accuracy and lack of transparency. For facial recognition systems, it is likely that a 'human in the loop' will remain to confirm or reject a 'match' generated by an AFR system.[203] In other words, the match may generate an investigative lead but this must be followed up with human intervention. The High Court explained that

> [i]f during a deployment of AFR Locate the software identifies a possible match between a face captured on the CCTV and an image on the watchlist, the two images are reviewed by an AFR operator ('the system operator', who is a police officer) to establish whether he believes that a match has in fact been made. In our view, the fact that human eye is used to ensure that an intervention is justified, is an important safeguard.[204]

In response to Eric Loomis's claim that he could not understand (and therefore could not challenge) the way that the COMPAS risk assessment had been generated, the Appeals Court held that giving a defendant access to the *results* of the risk assessment was sufficient.[205] Justice Bradley explained: 'Although Loomis cannot review and challenge how the COMPAS algorithm calculates risk, he can at least review and challenge the resulting risk scores set forth in the report'.[206] It is unclear, however, on what basis Loomis could possibly challenge the risk score without access to the information which the model had determined to be relevant, or a sense of how different pieces of information were weighted.[207]

[200] ibid 387.

[201] G Marx quoted in N Berg, 'Predicting Crime, LAPD-Style', *The Guardian*, 25 June 2014, www.theguardian.com/cities/2014/jun/25/predicting-crime-lapd-los-angeles-police-data-analysis-algorithm-minority-report ('predictive policing creates "categorical suspicion" of people in predicted crime areas, which can lead to unnecessary questioning or excessive stopping-and-searching').

[202] Ferguson (n 92) (he also cites as benefits increased documentation of the investigative process; efficiency; generation of unexpected insights).

[203] C Garvie, A Bedoya and J Frankle, Georgetown Law Center on Privacy & Technology, 'The Perpetual Line-Up: Unregulated Police Face Recognition in America' (2016) 46–47, 121, 128, 138.

[204] *R (Bridges) v CCSWP and SSHD* [2019] EWHC 2341 [33].

[205] *Loomis* 761.

[206] ibid.

[207] See also J Turner, *Robot Rules: Regulating Artificial Intelligence* (Palgrave Macmillan, 2019) 343.

The logical corollary should be that while a court could use the raw inputs, it should not be able to use the conclusions of someone else (in this case, software) as to their meaning.

At the very least, the tool should be verified through rigorous validation studies. Justice Abrahamson said:

> I would hold that a circuit court, in considering COMPAS (or another risk assessment tool) in sentencing, must evaluate on the record the strengths, weaknesses, and relevance to the individualized sentence being rendered of the evidence-based tool (or, more precisely, the research-based or data-based tool).[208]

Her Honour noted further that prosecution and defence counsel had both been questioned extensively by the Court about COMPAS's functioning but were able to provide little assistance.[209]

The Court in *Loomis* set out the limitations of COMPAS which, it concluded, courts should be informed about: it cannot be known how different factors are weighted by the software; there is presently no study of whether the scores are actually valid for a local population; in any event, it is necessary to continually update the program with current data; and there are 'questions' as to whether minority offenders are disproportionately likely to be mistakenly classified as high risk.[210] What is perhaps surprising is that the Court nevertheless concluded that the use of COMPAS in sentencing did not transgress due process protections. It noted that the Circuit Court judge had stated that he would have imposed the same sentence even without the input of the COMPAS report. Loomis's claims were probably hindered by the congruence between the other findings of the sentencing judge (such as a history of prior offending) and the risk assessment. Roggensack CJ emphasised that it was permissible to *consider* but not to *rely* on COMPAS.[211]

Loomis's claim that he had not been sentenced as an individual was also rejected by the Court, which held that 'consideration of a COMPAS risk assessment at sentencing along with other supporting factors is helpful in providing the sentencing court with as much information as possible in order to arrive at an individualized sentence'.[212] The Court noted that the assessment 'does not predict the specific likelihood that an individual offender will reoffend. Instead, it provides a prediction based on a comparison of information about the individual to a similar data group'.[213] Yet in the very next sentence, the Court stated 'Loomis's COMPAS risk scores indicated that he presented a high risk of recidivism …'.[214] In fact, by the Court's own description, the COMPAS scores indicated rather that Loomis had

[208] *Loomis* 775.
[209] *Loomis* 774.
[210] *Loomis* 763–64 [66].
[211] *Loomis* 772 [123].
[212] *Loomis* 765.
[213] *Loomis* 754.
[214] *Loomis* 755.

been deemed to be very similar to (share many characteristics with) other individuals who had a high risk of recidivism. In this vein, Dawinder Sidhu has argued strongly (and similarly to Simon) that risk assessment tools are incompatible with principles of sentencing:

> [R]isk-assessment tools identify risk on the basis of an offender's group membership or group identity, assign the same monolithic risk profile to everyone in the group, and premise punishment on group characteristics which the individual possesses by accident of birth or cannot otherwise meaningfully change. In doing so, risk-assessment tools sever the link between punishment and individual conduct, and between punishment and individual control.[215]

This is, arguably, a deviation from the very underpinnings of the criminal justice system, which is premised on individual responsibility (and accordingly, individualised sentencing). A further corollary is that risk assessment tools cannot factor in positive or protective individualised factors ('intentional efforts') either – such as volunteering or helping others; obtaining qualifications or studying; or developing religious faith. However important these activities may be to the individual concerned, they will not alter the person's score, which (it seems) is devised from largely immutable characteristics.

A guide for judicial officers on pre-trial risk assessment tools advises judges to be aware of certain issues, advising that they check things such as:[216]

- What exactly is the 'risk' that the tool purports to measure?
- What statistical probability do labels such as 'high risk' or 'medium risk' correlate to in the tool's scoring system?
- What types of inputs have gone into the tool?

For the last question, the guide advises caution around the use of 'imperfect' measures such as previous criminal history, and age. Noting that age is heavily weighted in (for example) COMPAS scores, the authors say:

> Imagine you have two defendants in front of you, and both are labeled 'high risk.' One has this label because she has an extensive record of convictions for serious crimes. The other has this label because she is 19 years old and has a prior marijuana arrest. Statistically speaking, the two defendants actually may have the same level of risk – but their circumstances and histories are very different. Teenagers and young adults are in a different developmental stage than older adults; they may be more susceptible to peer influence, have limited ability to appreciate long-run consequences, and may have higher capacity to rehabilitate. Thus, the appropriate pretrial decision for the teenager may be different from the appropriate decision for the serial offender, even where their risk numbers are the same.[217]

[215] Sidhu (n 186) 675.

[216] DG Robinson, HJ Sassaman and M Stevenson, 'Pretrial Risk Assessments: A Practical Guide for Judges' (2018) 57(3) *The Judges' Journal* 8.

[217] ibid, citing C Slobogin and M Stevenson, 'Algorithmic Risk Assessment and the Double-Edged Sword of Youth' (Unpublished Working Paper, 2018) 14.

In jurisdictions where such tools are used, lawyers have an important role in drawing these types of shortcomings to the attention of decision makers. A 2019 story published in *The Atlantic*, reporting on the case of a juvenile defendant, 'D', in Washington, District of Columbia, is illustrative:

> As the case approached sentencing, the prosecutor agreed that probation would be a fair punishment. But at the last minute, the parties received some troubling news: D had been deemed a 'high risk' for criminal activity. The report came from … an algorithm that uses data about a defendant to estimate his or her likelihood of committing a future crime. When prosecutors saw the report, they took probation off the table, insisting instead that D be placed in juvenile detention.
>
> [The defendant's lawyer] issued a challenge to see the underlying methodology of the report … D's heightened risk assessment was based on several factors that seemed racially biased, including the fact that he lived in government-subsidized housing and had expressed negative attitudes toward the police … When [she] and her team looked more closely at the assessment technology, they discovered that it hadn't been properly validated by any scientific group or judicial organization. Its previous review had come from an unpublished graduate-student thesis. [The defendant's lawyer] realized that for more than a decade, juvenile defendants in Washington, DC, had been judged, and even committed to detention facilities, because the courts had relied on a tool whose only validation in the previous 20 years had come from a college paper.[218]

In this case, *The Atlantic* reported, the judge had 'thrown out' the risk assessment.

Future Developments

In many jurisdictions, it seems likely that the use of risk assessments and other uses of AI systems for policing and criminal justice processes will continued to be viewed as impermissible transgressions on individual rights. However, these tools are routinely used in many places, and use of AFR software is also growing.

In the High Court of England and Wales' decision in *Bridges* the Court found that the use of AFR did breach the Claimant's Article 8 rights, even though there was no long-term storage of the data, namely his image. However, the Court concluded that, nevertheless, the use of AFR in public spaces 'struck a fair balance and was not disproportionate'.[219] The Court went on:

> Nobody was wrongly arrested. Nobody complained as to their treatment (save for the Claimant on a point of principle). Any interference with the Claimant's Article 8 rights would have been very limited. The interference would be limited to the near instantaneous algorithmic processing and discarding of the Claimant's biometric data. No personal information relating to the Claimant would have been available to any

[218] D Thompson, 'Should We Be Afraid of AI in the Criminal-Justice System?' *The Atlantic*, 20 June 2019, quoting Rachel Cicurel, attorney at the Public Defender Service for the District of Columbia.

[219] *R (Bridges) v CCSWP and SSHD* [2019] EWHC 2341 [101].

> police officer, or to any human agent. No data would be retained. There was no attempt to identify the Claimant. He was not spoken to by any police officer.[220]

However, noting a seeming drive towards uptake of AFR systems, Joe Purshouse and Liz Campbell have commented that, in the UK,

> [a]lthough [facial recognition technology] is becoming more pervasive in the force areas that have trialled it, we still do not have much published data with which to evaluate its accuracy, and the positive contribution it can make towards policing objectives. Each trialling police force claims to have made numerous arrests after successful identifications. However, these arrests appear to be far outweighed by the number of false positive matches, presenting a risk that any crime prevention successes will come at the expense of the rights of innocent people who may be subject to stops and other coercive policing measures.[221]

Even if the technology is sufficiently advanced to result in 'significant crime prevention benefits', these authors argue that there are still reasons to restrict AFR use in public spaces to times when it is necessary to respond 'to documented, credible and serious threats to public safety'.[222]

The EU's General Data Protection Regulation (GDPR), which came into effect in 2018, has the effect of prohibiting automated processing or profiling unless there are appropriate measures in place to protect individual rights, freedoms and legitimate interests.[223] Kleinberg and Mullainathan noted that this is premised on 'interpretable decisions' being a 'component of fair outcomes'.[224] The GDPR is of wide scope and substantial fines have already been imposed for its transgression.[225] In France, algorithms used for government decision making must be publicly available, meaning that they can be tested and checked;[226] and Germany's Data Ethics Commission has reportedly recommended:

> Systems with considerable potential harm, such as companies that have quasi-monopolies in credit scoring, should publish the details of their algorithms, including

[220] ibid.

[221] J Purshouse and L Campbell, 'Privacy, Crime Control and Police Use of Automated Facial Recognition Technology' (2019) (3) *Criminal Law Review* 188, 191.

[222] ibid 203.

[223] EU Regulation 2016/679 on the Protection of Natural Persons with regard to the Processing of Personal Data and on the Free Movement of Such Data, and repealing Directive 95/46/EC, [2016] OJ L119/1, art 22 – Automated individual decision making, including profiling.

[224] Kleinberg and Mullainathan (n 118) 2, citing B Goodman and SR Flaxman, 'European Union Regulations on Algorithmic Decision-Making and a "Right to Explanation"' (2018) 38(5) *AI Magazine* 50; and ZC Lipton, 'The Mythos of Model Interpretability' (2018) 61(10) *Communications of the ACM* 36.

[225] For example, Sweden's Data Protection Authority fined Google an amount equivalent to 7 million Euros: 'The Swedish Data Protection Authority Imposes Administrative Fine on Google', *Datainspektionen* (11 March 2020) www.datainspektionen.se/nyheter/the-swedish-data-protection-authority-imposes-administrative-fine-on-google/.

[226] Editorial, 'AI in Law Enforcement Needs Clear Oversight', *The Financial Times*, 7 May 2019; Nicolas Kayser-Bril, 'Automating Society: France', Report, Algorithm Watch, 29 January 2019, https://algorithmwatch.org/en/automating-society-france/ citing Article L311-3-1 of the 'Code of relations between the public and the administration'.

> the factors used in the calculations and their weights, the data processed and an explanation of their inner logic. Controls should be possible via a real-time interface.[227]

On the other hand, in jurisdictions such as the US, risk-scoring tools are already used routinely. The Partnership on AI, an American non-profit organisation, has called for transparency in risk assessment tools, including in both data and methods; and disclosure to defendants.[228] In March 2019 Idaho became the first State to act, enacting laws 'specifically promoting transparency, accountability, and explainability in pre-trial risk assessment tools'.[229] The Law Society of England and Wales called for similar protections to be legislated:

> The Government should take stock of the practices surrounding the development of risk assessment tools used in sentencing and offender management, and enshrine at least the current best practices – such as regular analysis, reviewing and reporting – as statutory responsibilities.[230]

It noted further that 'value-laden decisions around the design of systems in criminal justice should never be outsourced' or privatised.[231]

A desire for cost savings seems to be a primary motivation for the use of AI tools in criminal justice[232] though the Law Society identifies other factors too – such as the availability of data resources, changes to the 'nature of crime', themselves brought about by technology, and 'belief in the efficacy of computational prediction'.[233] As Solon Barocas, Sophie Hood and Malte Ziewitz have commented:

> Seemingly, algorithms could be a boon to due process because they formalize decision-making procedures. Consistently rendered decisions, on the basis of articulable and fixed criteria, are the hallmark of the kind of fairness that due process attempts to ensure. And even where the move to algorithms fails to purge bias from the decision-making procedure, it may at least have the salutary effect of making bias more evident. At the same time, algorithms may involve rules of such complexity that they defy attempts to trace their reasoning. Is this the perfect perversion of due process: the uniform application of an inarticulable rule?[234]

[227] AlgorithmWatch summary of German report: algorithmwatch.org/en/germanys-data-ethics-commission-releases-75-recommendations-with-eu-wide-application-in-mind/.

[228] Partnership on AI, 27.

[229] Electronic Privacy Information Center, Algorithms in the Criminal Justice System: Pre-Trial Risk Assessment Tools, https://epic.org/algorithmic-transparency/crim-justice/.

[230] The Law Society (n 6) 8 and 55; Sub-Recommendation 6.1 Formalise Governance of Risk Scoring.

[231] ibid 62.

[232] J Monahan and JL Skeem, 'Risk Redux: The Resurgence of Risk Assessment in Criminal Sanctioning' (2014) 26 *Federal Sentencing Reporter* 158, 158; The Law Society (n 6) 13.

[233] The Law Society (n 6) 14–15.

[234] S Barocas, S Hood and M Ziewitz, 'Governing Algorithms: A Provocation Piece', New York University (29 March 2013) governingalgorithms.org/resources/provocation-piece/.

PART III

The Future of Lawyers and the Legal Profession

10

Limitations of AI

Introduction

In most areas, AI is not a panacea: its successful use is presently limited to narrow fields and endeavours. With AI successes have come egregious failures.[1] Yet concerns about AI stem from both its successes (such as its increasing capacity for facial recognition) and its failures (pedestrians killed by self-driving cars). Other shortcomings are less egregious but nevertheless important: we may be unaware of AI's limitations, or we may rely on AI despite those limitations, because we lack sufficient understanding of them. As Ryan Calo has pointed out, just like AI, these concerns are also not new:

> [L]ooking back twenty, forty, or even a hundred years, one encounters similar hopes and concerns around Al systems and the robots they inhabit. Batya Friedman and Helen Nissenbaum wrote *Bias in Computer Systems*, a framework for evaluating and responding to machines that discriminate unfairly, in 1996. The 1980 New York Times headline 'A Robot Is After Your Job' could as easily appear in September 2017.[2]

Here, we focus, as we have in earlier chapters, on those limits which are salient for AI's legal applications.[3]

In Chapter 2 we referred to the categorisation of legal AI systems as pragmatic (operational) and purist (theoretical).[4] The limitations of AI could also be classified in this way. We might think of practical or technical limitations or inaccuracies, and 'purist' limitations as concerning more fundamental issues – not only about AI, but about law as a social system, its functions and purposes. This chapter deals

[1] T Friend, 'How Frightened Should We Be of AI?' *The New Yorker*, 14 May 2018.

[2] R Calo, 'Artificial Intelligence Policy: A Primer and a Roadmap' (2017) 51(2) *UC Davis Law Review* 399, 401 (citations omitted).

[3] More generalised discussion of AI's limitations is found in E Broad, *Made by Humans: The AI Condition* (Melbourne University Press, 2018); J Kaplan, *Artificial Intelligence, What Everyone Needs to Know* (Oxford University Press, 2016); and A Husain, *The Sentient Machine: The Coming Age of Artificial Intelligence* (Scribner, 2017).

[4] R Susskind, 'Pragmatism and Purism in Artificial Intelligence and Legal Reasoning' in A Narayanan and M Bennun (eds), *Law, Computer Science and Artificial Intelligence* (Ablex, 1991) 33.

with both, as we emphasise how AI's technical implications are relevant to its legal applications, for example the challenges of using machine learning analytics when only small datasets are available, such as in jurisdictions or areas without extensive bodies of case law. In Chapter 2 we also discussed the limitations of earlier 'waves' of AI. Different kinds of AI have different advantages and limitations, especially when it comes to their interpretability or explainability (Table 10.1).

Table 10.1 Explainability of Different Types of AI

	Expert systems	Machine learning	Deep learning
Description	Manually programmed system which can guide user through a series of steps to reach predetermined outcomes	Mathematical analysis of training data which is used to extrapolate to new data	Sophisticated analysis of data, involving complex calculations and 'weighting' of many features
Autonomy	Low, as the program is dependent on human programming	Medium, humans usually guide the program, eg by cleaning up data	High, the program decides on feature selection and weighting
Explainability	High	Medium	Low

Source: M Legg and F Bell, *Artificial Intelligence and the Legal Profession: A Primer* (Law Society of NSW, 2019) 9 (Table 1).

In this chapter we concentrate on the limitations of machine learning. As Table 10.1 indicates, a strength of expert systems is that they have high explainability. Other of AI's limitations or deficits we might conceptualise, on the flipside, as human strengths – things like empathy; the ability to compare seemingly incommensurable things such as experiencing emotional distress versus receiving a monetary sum;[5] common sense or generalised, tacit knowledge. We do not explore this here in detail, save to note the argument that a fundamental difference between AI systems and humans when it comes to the practice of law is that the lawyer has the capacity to exercise moral agency. We come back to the idea of human strengths in the final chapter of this book, Chapter 12.

Here, we consider limitations in data and design, in transparency, and in accountability. We also consider whether these limitations can be overcome. We then turn to issues of cost and sustainability.

[5] A McCay, 'The Value of Consciousness and Free Will in a Technological Dystopia' (2018) 28(1) *Journal of Evolution and Technology* 18 (describing the 'plausible reasoning' of David Hodgson).

Data and Design

It is important to conceptualise AI systems as just that – systems, invariably comprising different interlocking steps or stages. In a 2019 report, *Algorithms in Society*, the OECD describes the 'AI system lifecycle' as follows:

1. *Design, data and modelling* includes several activities, whose order may vary for different AI systems:
   - *Planning and design* of the AI system involves articulating the system's concept and objectives, underlying assumptions, context and requirements, and potentially building a prototype.
   - *Data collection and processing* includes gathering and cleaning data, performing checks for completeness and quality, and documenting the metadata and characteristics of the dataset. Dataset metadata include information on how a dataset was created, its composition, its intended uses and how it has been maintained over time.
   - *Model building and interpretation* involves the creation or selection of models or algorithms, their calibration and/or training and interpretation.
2. *Verification and validation* involves executing and tuning models, with tests to assess performance across various dimensions and considerations.
3. *Deployment* into live production involves piloting, checking compatibility with legacy systems, ensuring regulatory compliance, managing organisational change and evaluating user experience.
4. *Operation and monitoring* of an AI system involves operating the AI system and continuously assessing its recommendations and impacts (both intended and unintended) in light of objectives and ethical considerations. This phase identifies problems and adjusts by reverting to other phases or, if necessary, retiring an AI system from production.[6]

AI's limitations are therefore found at a number of points. We first consider the initial stages identified by the OECD: design, data and modelling.

Data

A story recounted about a machine learning system involves a hospital which trialled machine learning in an effort to predict which patients admitted with pneumonia would develop severe complications.[7] In a test, two different systems

[6] Organisation for Economic Co-operation and Development, *Artificial Intelligence in Society* (OECD Publishing, 2019) ch 1: 'The Technical Landscape'.

[7] R Caruana et al, 'Intelligible Models for Healthcare: Predicting Pneumonia Risk and Hospital 30-day Readmission', Proceedings of the 21st ACM SIGKDD International Conference on Knowledge Discovery and Data Mining (2015) 1721 cited in AM Bornstein, 'Is Artificial Intelligence Permanently Inscrutable?', *Nautilus*, 1 September 2016, nautil.us/issue/40/learning/is-artificial-intelligence-permanently-inscrutable.

were used, to see which was the more accurate at making such predictions. This meant that both a neural network and a more readable system were trained on the hospital's existing data. When the 'human readable rules' of the more interpretable system were checked an odd discovery was made: 'One of the rules instructed doctors to send home pneumonia patients who already had asthma, despite the fact that asthma sufferers are known to be extremely vulnerable to complications'.[8] The rule discovered by the system in the data was that patients presenting with both asthma and pneumonia were at a low risk of developing complications.

While this goes against all accepted medical knowledge, it emerged that it was, in fact, what the data showed. Hospital policy was to always send patients presenting with both pneumonia and asthma to the hospital's intensive care department due to their high-risk status, and as a result they almost never developed severe complications. To the system, then, asthma was correlated with a *decreased* likelihood of developing bad complications. While even a layperson could hazard a guess that this is unlikely to be the case in the real world, the system had no way of knowing this.

Machine learning systems can identify patterns of which humans would be otherwise unaware. The corollary is, though, that they cannot know which patterns exist nowhere outside of training data; or in this instance, where the correlation has been generated by human (medical) intervention. The data was not 'garbage'.[9] It was not poor quality, incomplete or too small a sample – it just lacked the context in which it had been generated and which made it different to the 'real world'.

Much real-world data is not, however, of sufficient quality to meet the requisite high standards. In an article titled 'If Your Data is Bad, Your Machine Learning Tools Are Useless', Thomas Redman explains:

> To properly train a predictive model, historical data must meet exceptionally broad and high quality standards. First, the data must be right: It must be correct, properly labeled, de-deduped, and so forth. But you must also have the *right* data – lots of unbiased data, over the entire range of inputs for which one aims to develop the predictive model.[10]

In other words, the data must be correct, and it must also be the appropriate data for the task, which is not tainted by partiality or selection bias. Considering these two issues in turn, there are, first, a number of ways that data may not be correct. It may be poorly labelled or misclassified. There may be 'borderline' cases which present a choice as to how they should be labelled, or missing information, both of which require the interpolation of human judgement to decide how they should be dealt with.[11]

[8] Bornstein (n 7).

[9] TC Redman, 'If Your Data is Bad, Your Machine Learning Tools Are Useless', *Harvard Business Review*, 2 April 2018, hbr.org/2018/04/if-your-data-is-bad-your-machine-learning-tools-are-useless?autocomplete=true.

[10] ibid (emphasis in original).

[11] S Barocas and AD Selbst, 'Big Data's Disparate Impact' (2016) 104 *California Law Review* 671, 681.

Shlomit Yanisky-Ravid and Sean Hallisey have said that there are four qualities which are key to a dataset being useful – volume, velocity, variety and veracity:

> Volume indicates its size; velocity indicates its 'freshness,' that is, whether or not the datapoints have become outdated; variety refers to the sources of data (for example, some datasets combine information from various sources, often making them more valuable); and veracity refers to the data's accuracy.[12]

In terms of veracity, limitations also arise depending on how much the data deviates from the real world. If there is selection bias, training will not adequately represent actual conditions due to sampling problems, such as inaccurate measurements or non-standardised self-reporting. Some groups might be over-represented, or the sample size might be too small, generating patterns which are anomalous. One issue with the use of risk assessment tools in the criminal justice system is that they need to be validated on local populations to check that the population being subjected to the risk assessment is the same as that on which the tool was trained.[13] But most US States using such risk assessment tools have never conducted any validation studies.[14]

If certain types of data are under-represented, the system will also produce less accurate results for those data as greatest accuracy is usually attained through volume. When building a facial recognition system, selection bias might come from an over-supply of images of Caucasian people, leading to poorer capacity to recognise people of other ethnicities:

> Algorithms learn by being fed certain images, often chosen by engineers, and the system builds a model of the world based on those images. If a system is trained on photos of people who are overwhelmingly white, it will have a harder time recognizing nonwhite faces.[15]

If facial recognition systems are used in social control or criminal justice settings such lack of accuracy is highly problematic, especially if false positives occur more frequently among certain groups.[16]

[12] S Yanisky-Ravid and SK Hallisey, 'Equality and Privacy by Design: A New Model of Artificial Intelligence Data Transparency via Auditing, Certification, and Safe Harbor Regimes' (2019) 46(2) *Fordham Urban Law Journal* 428, 440.

[13] PM Casey, RK Warren and JK Elek, *Using Offender Risk and Needs Assessment Information at Sentencing: Guidance for Courts from a National Working Group* (National Center for State Courts, 2011) 29–30; see generally Chapter 9.

[14] Electronic Privacy Information Center, 'Algorithms in the Criminal Justice System', epic.org/algorithmic-transparency/crimjustice; J Angwin, J Larson, S Mattu and L Kirchner, 'Machine Bias', *ProPublica*, 23 May 2016, www.propublica.org/article/machine-bias-risk-assessments-in-criminal-sentencing.

[15] K Crawford, 'Artificial Intelligence's White Guy Problem', Opinion, *The New York Times*, 26 June 2016, 11.

[16] J Snow, 'Amazon's Face Recognition Falsely Matched 28 Members of Congress with Mugshots', *American Civil Liberties Union Blog*, 26 July 2018, www.aclu.org/blog/privacy-technology/surveillance-technologies/amazonsface-recognition-falsely-matched-28 ('Nearly 40 percent of Rekognition's false matches in our test were of people of color, even though they make up only 20 percent of Congress').

AI for legal outcome prediction is also limited by available data.[17] In a sense, all cases that have proceeded to a determination are unusual in that they represent the apex of a pyramid of disputes.[18] Most disagreements are resolved without even necessarily rising to the level of 'dispute'; many are resolved without recourse to law; and of those which do engage with legal systems, most are resolved prior to hearing and judgment. Those cases proceeding to judgment are already incongruent. Arguably, privatised dispute resolution services, such as those offered by eBay, therefore have an advantage over courts as they have expansive data capturing all outcomes. In contrast, settled matters lack a judgment; depending on the basis on which they have settled, there may also be a lack of information about the facts and issues in dispute and the terms of settlement (though class actions and regulatory litigation may be exceptions). Usually, though, there is little to no general access to this type of information.

An example of limited data in action is the concept of lawyer rating systems, such as that provided by Premonition™.[19] Premonition's analytics enables scrutiny of metrics such as lawyers' 'win rates' and the average length of time cases have taken to resolve. Yet, without the context for these metrics, their meaning is diminished. For example, if lawyers can choose their cases, some may choose carefully, others less so. Some may take cases which they seem less likely to win, in a fight for the underdog or because the lawyer is less risk averse. Lawyers working in firms may feel unable to refuse a case, even if its prospects do not seem good. Different predilections are also relevant to relations with judicial officers – judges may know those lawyers whom they trust to only bring claims that do have merit, as well as those they mistrust. Premonition emphasises the volumes of data that it uses but it is also unclear what types of matters are being 'won' – are they interlocutory steps, or only final trials? Did the party 'win' the case but have their compensation overshadowed by legal costs? When the length of time to resolve a case is examined is its complexity considered? If a lawyer specialises in complex, challenging cases of a particular kind, prefers not to go to court (and hence litigates very few cases) and charges high fees, it seems likely that this person will appear in Premonition's system with a red flag, even if their clients would do no better with a different lawyer. Premonition's data crunching of the 'win rates' of barristers appearing in the Court of Appeal of England and Wales[20] likewise found 'a slight negative correlation … between win rate and hiring popularity'.[21] Although Premonition noted the existence of the cab-rank rule – the principle that a barrister cannot turn down

[17] MK Osbeck, 'Lawyer as a Soothsayer: Exploring the Important Role of Outcome Prediction in the Practice of Law' (2018) 123(1) *Penn State Law Review* 41.

[18] WLF Felstiner, RL Abel and A Sarat, 'The Emergence and Transformation of Disputes: Naming, Blaming, Claiming …' (1980) 15(3/4) *Law & Society Review* 631.

[19] Premonition, *Everything You Know About Lawyer Selection Is Wrong: Big Data Analyzes Litigation*, undated, premonition.ai/everything-know-lawyer-selection-wrong/.

[20] Presumably: Premonition refers to the 'UK Court of Appeals': ibid 16.

[21] ibid 16.

a client[22] – no attempt was made to consider how this might affect 'win rates'. For instance, a barrister might have a reputation as a person who is capable at handling difficult cases, for instance by minimising the damages awarded, rather than 'winning'.

Finally, if training data reflects existing patterns of inequality, discrimination or prejudice, then these patterns will be replicated in the system's findings.[23] Hence the claim that the limitations of machine learning are, in part, the limitations and biases of the social world, for which no 'quick fixes' are available.[24] By contrast, board games such as chess and Go, at which machine learning programs excel, have 'no bad data to analyze'.[25] As Daniel Shapiro explains, 'Games are a nice constrained problem set, but in most real world data, there is bias'.[26] It is therefore fallacious to claim that because AI can seemingly exercise creativity and originality ('teach itself to play') in the world of games, that it can do so with the same success in regard to a messy social system such as law. When it comes to law, the data available is not the pure application of rules but the partial and flawed application of those rules by people and their institutions. And, in machine learning, most 'patterns are merely correlations amongst vast reams of data, rather than causative truths or natural laws governing our world'.[27]

Design

One (perhaps welcome) limitation of AI is that human input is still crucial to the functioning of AI systems. This may seem obvious since humans create AI systems.[28] But it may also be limiting in that human biases may be present from the beginning.[29] Kate Crawford used the phrase 'white guy problem' to describe AI.[30] By this, Crawford was not just referring to partial data (data that might skew in certain ways, such as over-representing particular groups). She was talking

[22] See *Rondel v Worsley* [1967] 3 All ER 993.

[23] D Lehr and P Ohm, 'Playing with the Data: What Legal Scholars Should Learn About Machine Learning' (2017) *UC Davis Law Review* 658, 665; W Knight, 'Forget Killer Robots – Bias is the Real AI Danger', *MIT Technology Review*, 3 October 2017.

[24] PT Kim, 'Auditing Algorithms for Discrimination' (2017) 166(1) *University of Pennsylvania Law Review Online* 189, 196; J Kleinberg, J Ludwig, S Mullainathan, CR Sunstein, 'Discrimination in the Age of Algorithms' (2018) 10 *Journal of Legal Analysis* 113; H Nissenbaum and J Powles, 'The Seductive Diversion of "Solving" Bias in Artificial Intelligence', *Medium*, 8 December 2018, onezero.medium.com/the-seductive-diversion-of-solving-bias-in-artificial-intelligence-890df5e5ef53.

[25] D Shapiro, 'Artificial Intelligence and Bad Data', *Towards Data Science*, 6 November 2017.

[26] ibid.

[27] K Leetaru, 'A Reminder That Machine Learning Is About Correlations Not Causation', *Forbes*, 15 January 2019, www.forbes.com/sites/kalevleetaru/2019/01/15/a-reminder-that-machine-learning-is-about-correlations-not-causation/#32fa84e26161.

[28] DC Vladeck, 'Machines without Principals: Liability Rules and Artificial Intelligence' (2014) 89 *Washington Law Review* 117, 120.

[29] Kleinberg et al (n 24) 117.

[30] Crawford (n 15) 11.

about the 'tech' industry as a whole skewing too: its creators, creatives, designers, engineers and so on. Crawford wrote:

> Like all technologies before it, artificial intelligence will reflect the values of its creators. So inclusivity matters – from who designs it to who sits on the company boards and which ethical perspectives are included. Otherwise, we risk constructing machine intelligence that mirrors a narrow and privileged vision of society, with its old, familiar biases and stereotypes.[31]

The significance of this is that problems, whether of commission or omission, may be overlooked (such as Apple's notorious failure to include a menstrual cycle tracking function within its health tracker app, widely interpreted as a sign of a male focus[32]). Women and minority groups are under-represented in the tech world, which also risks embedding, whether consciously or not, a particular, privileged view.[33] In the case of legal services, this also likely affects the type of systems which are funded and built. While there is optimism about the power of tech to increase access to justice, many developments have been in the commercial and corporate spheres, powered by large firms, as we discuss below in relation to cost.

All the human choices made in the building of AI systems are sources of potential error, bias or simply differing outputs. David Lehr and Paul Ohm note that 'some of the … harms of machine learning … are brought about when algorithms are chosen and developed, not when data are collected or variables are specified'.[34] Likewise, Jon Kleinberg, Jens Ludwig, Sendhil Mullainathan and Cass Sunstein have explained that 'given the important role that human decisions play in the construction of algorithms, it would be irresponsible – even dangerous – to confuse "data-driven" with "nondiscriminatory," "unbiased," or "objective"'.[35] These authors identify three design choices which can lead to algorithms operating in a discriminatory manner: the choice of output variable; the choice of input variables (candidate predictors); and the choice of training procedure.[36] We expand on these below. Note that Kleinberg et al focus on discrimination in '*screening decisions*, where a person is chosen from a pool of candidates to accomplish a particular goal'.[37] They explain that systems like this involve two algorithms: the *screener* 'scores' each individual candidate; while the *trainer* uses data to create the screener, thereby optimising some function. Creating the trainer involves

[31] ibid.

[32] A Griffin, 'Apple's Health Data App Gets Period Tracking', *Independent Online*, 9 June 2015, www.independent.co.uk.

[33] See K Crawford and R Calo, 'There is a Blind Spot in AI Research' (2016) 538(7625) *Nature* 311; C Whittfield, 'The Ethics of Artificial Intelligence in Law', *PWC Digital Pulse*, 28 March 2017, www.digitalpulse.pwc.com.au/artificial-intelligence-ethics-law-panel-pwc/ (quoting Chris Vein).

[34] Lehr and Ohm (n 23) 668.

[35] Kleinberg et al (n 24) 138, citing S Goel et al, 'The Accuracy, Equity, and Jurisprudence of Criminal Risk Assessment' (2019) https://papers.ssrn.com/sol3/papers.cfm?abstract_id¼3306723

[36] ibid 139-43.

[37] ibid 115.

'deciding which past cases to assemble to use in predicting outcomes for some set of current cases, which outcome to predict, and what candidate predictors to consider'.[38]

Returning to Kleinberg et al's three design choices – first, problems may be generated by the very setting up of the problem to be addressed by an AI system, the choice of output variable. If the goal is to map or predict something which is to any degree amorphous or non-mathematical, such as 'creditworthiness', then proxies for the attribute must be found.[39] This end goal, or what is to be estimated or predicted, is referred to as the output or target variable. In this initial definition stage, bias can be introduced because the process is necessarily subjective.[40] There are different possible answers to the question of what measurable qualities add up to the target variable of, for example, a good or not good lawyer. Is a good lawyer one who wins the highest proportion of cases, who litigates frequently or who settles?

The measurable qualities selected may also be proxies for personal attributes, resulting in discriminatory decision making. Eliminating 'protected characteristics' – those which anti-discrimination law prohibits consideration of – such as gender, ethnicity and age, may be insufficient to prevent biased outcomes as there are too many proxy variables that correlate to such characteristics.[41] Suppose we decide that a 'good' advocate is one who speaks more than average in court. If women are briefed in particular kinds of cases, and spend less time speaking in court,[42] then this measure may well be a proxy for gender, leading to gender discrimination in its application.[43] Kleinberg et al explain that in such situations it may actually be preferable to retain these characteristics. Using their example of referee letters written by high school teachers, they say:

> Suppose, for example, that college applications require recommendations from high school teachers. Any racial bias by teachers could lead to differences in average letter quality across race groups. Interestingly, in some cases, the best way to mitigate the discriminatory effects of biased data is to authorize the algorithm to have access to information about race. To see why, note that only an algorithm that sees race can detect that someone from a given group has better college grades than their letters would suggest, and then adjust predicted performance to address this disparity.[44]

[38] ibid 132.

[39] Barocas and Selbst (n 11) 678; Lehr and Ohm (n 23).

[40] Barocas and Selbst (n 11) 678.

[41] Kim (n 24) 193; see also Angwin et al (n 14).

[42] Studies of the Australian Bar suggest that this is, indeed, the case: K Eastman, *Visible Targets: The Case for Equitable Briefing* (June 2016) 2.

[43] J Kroll, J Huey, S Barocas, EW Felten, JR Reidenberg, DG Robinson and H Yu, 'Accountable Algorithms' (2017) 165(3) *University of Pennsylvania Law Review* 633, 681.

[44] Kleinberg et al (n 24) 119, citing J Kleinberg, J Ludwig, S Mullainathan and A Rambachan, 'Algorithmic Fairness' (2018) 108 *American Economic Association Papers and Proceedings* 22–27; T Gillis and J Spiess, 'Big Data and Discrimination' (2019) 86(2) *University of Chicago Law Review* 459.

They note that this is somewhat counter-intuitive, in terms of anti-discrimination law, as usually consideration of protected features is precisely what it 'seeks to prevent'.[45]

Second, in relation to input variables, problems can again arise in relation to choices about the information which should be given to a system to 'consider for possible inclusion in the final statistical model'.[46] This may come about through the provision of information which favours particular groups, through having too little information, or through collecting information which is itself the result of human judgement and therefore subjective (such as including teachers' letters of recommendations in college admissions procedures).[47] Mullainathan has written about a study of one algorithm used to make healthcare decisions across the US (for around 70 million people).[48] He and his co-investigators found that the algorithm has a disturbing bias: 'At similar levels of sickness, black patients were deemed to be at lower risk than white patients'.[49] The reason for this 'lay in a subtle engineering choice' of how the gravity of a person's sickness would be measured. Mullainathan explains that for this measure, the designers chose the most accessible data, which was expenditure on health care. 'But because society spends less on black patients than equally sick white ones, the algorithm understated the black patients' true needs'.[50] Black patients were not less sick but less money was being spent on their care.

Third, in terms of the training procedure, biases can be introduced through the way that the person training the system responds to its mistakes. Kleinberg et al explain:

> [O]nce the designers of an algorithm have chosen an outcome measure and a set of input variables, they need to run a training procedure based on past data in order to produce the screener. Discrimination can easily be introduced in this phase … Perhaps most simply, the designers could under-optimize in the training phase and produce a screener that helps some groups and hurts others while only poorly approximating the intended outcome measure.[51]

Yanisky-Ravid and Hallisey also note that the way the trainer operates can result in overfitting to the data, 'forcing the AI system to create arbitrary connections that result from the randomness of the feedback it received'.[52]

[45] ibid.

[46] Kleinberg et al (n 24) 140.

[47] ibid.

[48] S Mullainathan, 'Biased Algorithms Are Easier to Fix Than Biased People', *New York Times*, 6 December 2019, www.nytimes.com/2019/12/06/business/algorithm-bias-fix.html.

[49] ibid, citing Z Obermeyer et al, 'Dissecting Racial Bias in an Algorithm Used to Manage the Health of Populations' (2019) 366(6464) *Science* 447.

[50] Mullainathan (n 48).

[51] Kleinberg et al (n 24) 141.

[52] Yanisky-Ravid and Hallisey (n 12) 450.

Can Data and Design Problems be Overcome?

Mullainathan writes that, compared to human biases, 'Discrimination by algorithm can be more readily discovered and more easily fixed'.[53] In the case of the healthcare study mentioned above, he explained, identifying bias 'was a statistical exercise – the equivalent of asking the algorithm "what would you do with this patient?" hundreds of thousands of times, and mapping out the racial differences'.[54] Moreover, it is also argued that if well designed, the use of algorithmic systems can expose the 'trade-offs' which are frequently being made among competing social values in any kind of decision making.[55]

There is now much literature concerning ways to avoid or correct incorrect, biased or discriminatory outcomes when using AI systems, especially in decision making. IBM's 'AI Fairness 360' tool claims to be able both to identify bias in AI systems, and provide explanation of decision making.[56] The fairness tool involves checking both data (the training data and the results of deployment) and the model, by testing its operation (see Figure 10.1).

Figure 10.1

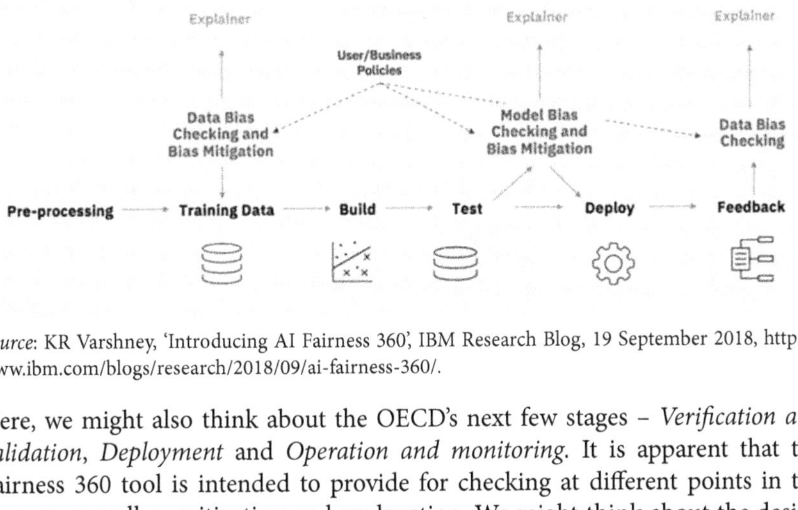

Source: KR Varshney, 'Introducing AI Fairness 360', IBM Research Blog, 19 September 2018, https://www.ibm.com/blogs/research/2018/09/ai-fairness-360/.

Here, we might also think about the OECD's next few stages – *Verification and validation*, *Deployment* and *Operation and monitoring*. It is apparent that the Fairness 360 tool is intended to provide for checking at different points in the process, as well as mitigation and explanation. We might think about the design choices that were made in setting up the problem to be addressed in the first place;

[53] Mullainathan (n 48).

[54] ibid.

[55] CR Sunstein, 'Algorithms, Correcting Biases' (2019) 86(2) *Social Research: An International Quarterly* 499, 499–500, citing Kleinberg et al (n 24).

[56] T Lockwood, 'Artificial Intelligence Can Now Explain Its Own Decision-Making', *IoT For All*, 8 January 2019, www.iotforall.com/artificial-intelligence-can-explain-own-decision-making/.

and then of the measurable things about the system which we can check, test or audit.[57] These latter need to be ongoing, if the AI system is engaged in a continuous process:

> Regular measurement helps to manage the twin phenomena of *concept drift* – changes in the world that can invalidate assumptions baked into collected data or data collection and normalization methodology – and *modelling error* – choices which cause the assumptions of a computer system to diverge from the reality of the world.[58]

Ensuring validity is therefore tied up with some degree of transparency, as calls for (variously) transparency, explainability, interpretability and legibility[59] indicate. Without any windows into the system's operations, it will be difficult to check or validate its functioning. Transparency is therefore important, but alone is insufficient.[60] In this section, we first discuss the concepts of transparency, explainability and interpretability before turning to briefly describe some of the ways that systems may be verified. We then discuss the limitations of accountability.

Transparency, Explainability and Interpretability

Transparency is often thought to be key when it comes to AI.[61] The 'black box' problem – that AI cannot be fully known or understood by people, and certainly not by laypeople or those unversed in the technology – has been well documented.[62] The black box refers to the inability of a human to see inside and identify how the software is functioning:

> The algorithms in question operate on data. Using this data as input, they produce an output; specifically, a classification … They are opaque in the sense that if one is a recipient of the output of the algorithm (the classification decision), rarely does one have any concrete sense of how or why a particular classification has been arrived at from inputs. Additionally, the inputs themselves may be entirely unknown or known only partially.[63]

Many legal scholars have made criticisms along these lines about the use of AI in areas such as finance, social welfare, health, and policing and the criminal justice

[57] JA Kroll, 'The Fallacy of Inscrutability' (2018) *Philosophical Transactions of the Royal Society, A* 376: 20180084 dx.doi.org/10.1098/rsta.2018.0084.

[58] ibid 8.

[59] G Malgieri and G Comandé, 'Why a Right to Legibility of Automated Decision-Making Exists in the General Data Protection Regulation' (2017) 7(4) *International Data Privacy Law* 243.

[60] AD Selbst and S Barocas, 'The Intuitive Appeal of Explainable Machines' (2018) 87(3) *Fordham Law Review* 1085, 1094.

[61] OECD (n 6) 'Transparency about the Use of AI and as to How AI Systems Operate Is Key'.

[62] See the examples given by DR Desai and JA Kroll, 'Trust But Verify: A Guide to Algorithms and the Law' (2017) 31(1) *Harvard Journal of Law & Technology* 1; F Pasquale, *The Black Box Society: The Secret Algorithms That Control Money and Information* (Cambridge University Press, 2015).

[63] J Burrell, 'How the Machine "Thinks": Understanding Opacity in Machine Learning Algorithms' (2016) 3(1) *Big Data and Society* 1.

system.[64] Others have responded that in fact, the problem is not that algorithms are incapable of being understood, but that most people, including lawyers and legal scholars, have a poor understanding of how AI processes work. For this reason, 'transparency' is not all that useful if we cannot understand what we see.[65] Critics might also miss opportunities to challenge or investigate the operation of AI processes if they lack a detailed or nuanced understanding.[66]

As the OECD has noted, transparency can mean different things:[67] it may be around how humans are using AI (for example, how it fits into or is being used in a lawyer's decision making); or it may mean enabling humans to understand how an AI system itself is functioning.[68] There are also different sub-issues relating to transparency. First, as most providers of AI software are commercial entities, they may not desire, and likely are not required, to disclose precisely how the software operates as it may comprise a trade secret.[69] As well as the statistical model itself, it may not be possible or advisable to disclose all the inputs, for reasons of privacy and to prevent misuse of the system.[70] Secondly, even if disclosure is available, the machine learning process itself might be unknowable, or too complex for humans to grasp. This could be due to a lack of specialised knowledge, such as the inability to read code; or it may be to do with the nature of complex machine learning systems,[71] as 'black-box functions may be extremely complex and have an internal state composed of millions of interdependent values'.[72] Kalev Leetaru argues that even data scientists may not have such understanding:[73]

> [T]he ease with which modern machine learning pipelines can transform a pile of data into a predictive model without requiring an understanding of statistics or even programming has been a key driving force in its rapid expansion into industry. At the same time, it has eroded the distinction between correlation and causation as the new

[64] See, eg, D Keats Citron and FA Pasquale, 'The Scored Society: Due Process for Automated Predictions' (2014) 89(1) *Washington Law Review* 1; Barocas and Selbst (n 11); J Tashea, 'Risk-Assessment Algorithms Challenged in Bail, Sentencing and Parole Decisions', *American Bar Association Journal*, 1 March 2017, www.abajournal.com/magazine/article/algorithm_bail_sentencing_parole; T Wang, C Rudin, D Wagner and R Sevieri, 'Learning to Detect Patterns of Crime' in H Blockeel, K Kersting, S Nijssen and F Železný (eds), *Machine Learning and Knowledge Discovery in Databases* (Springer, 2013) 515.

[65] Desai and Kroll (n 62) 4; Selbst and Barocas (n 60) 1094.

[66] Lehr and Ohm (n 23) 668.

[67] Burrell (n 63) also notes that opacity has different meanings, too.

[68] OECD (n 6).

[69] Lehr and Ohm (n 23) 662; AM Carlson, 'The Need for Transparency in the Age of Predictive Sentencing Algorithms' (2017) 103 *Iowa Law Review* 303; B Sheppard, 'Warming Up to Inscrutability: How Technology Could Challenge Our Concept of Law' (2018) 68(Supp 1) *University of Toronto Law Journal* 36.

[70] D Hogan-Doran, 'Computer Says "No": Automation, Algorithms and Artificial Intelligence in Government Decision-Making' (2017) 13 *The Judicial Review* 345, 346.

[71] Burrell (n 63).

[72] B Mittelstadt, C Russell and S Wachter, 'Explaining Explanations in AI', Proceedings of the 2019 Conference on Fairness, Accountability, and Transparency (Atlanta, 29–31 January 2019) 279, 279.

[73] See also Kroll (n 57).

> generation of data scientists building and deploying these models conflate their predictive prowess with explanatory power.[74]

Identifying the factor which carried the most weight in a particular decision will not necessarily be helpful or increase understanding, as there may be thousands of different variables which contributed to the decision, so even the most significant factor might still only be a miniscule contributor to the output.[75] This has been referred to as 'inscrutability'.[76]

Calls for transparency in AI systems have to some extent been overshadowed by interest in a different concept – explainability. Explanation can mean both a statement or account that gives clarification, and a reason or justification. IBM's tool includes points at which explanations would be generated. Yet despite the centrality of explanation (especially to law, for example) there is little consensus about what adequate explanation comprises.[77] In part, it is suggested, different understandings of explanation stem from transposing the concept from the humanities (philosophical, psychological) into a technical discipline[78] – Explainable AI (XAI):[79]

> Briefly, the [Explainable AI] community investigates interpretability (or explainability) and ways of providing explanations of algorithmic models and decisions. 'Interpretability' refers to the degree of human comprehensibility of a given 'black-box' model or decision … In contrast, 'explanation' refers to numerous ways of exchanging information about a phenomenon, in this case the functionality of a model or the rationale and criteria for a decision, to different stakeholders.[80]

The importance of explainability in this domain is well recognised.[81] Andrew Selbst and Solon Barocas suggest, though, that technical interpretability is narrower than a more legalistic concept of explanation. Moreover, the lack of consensus about explanation is also unsurprising in that it may need to fulfil many different purposes:[82]

> Explanations can be necessary to comply with relevant legislation, verify and improve the functionality of a system (i.e. as a type of 'debugging') and help developers and humans working with a system learn from it, and enhance the trust between individuals subject to a decision and the system itself.[83]

[74] Leetaru (n 27).
[75] Sheppard (n 69) 50.
[76] Burrell (n 63); Selbst and Barocas (n 60).
[77] Selbst and Barocas (n 60); Mittelstadt, Russell and Wachter (n 72).
[78] Mittelstadt, Russell and Wachter (n 72) 279–80.
[79] A Adadi and M Berrada, 'Peeking Inside the Black-Box: A Survey on Explainable Artificial Intelligence (XAI)' (2018) 6 *IEEE Access* 52138, 17 September 2018, DOI: 10.1109/ACCESS.2018.2870052.
[80] Mittelstadt, Russell and Wachter (n 72) 280 (citations omitted).
[81] For instance, the US Defense Advanced Research Projects Agency launched an XAI program in 2017: Adadi and Berrada (n 79) 52138.
[82] ibid 52142–43, identifying as reasons for XAI justification, control, improvement, and discovery.
[83] Mittelstadt, Russell and Wachter (n 72) 280.

Selbst and Barocas identify, in the literature, two kinds of explanation: those accounting for outcomes ('how particular inputs lead to a particular output') but also those concerning the logic of decision making ('full or partial descriptions of the rules of the system').[84] Likewise, Riccardo Guidotti et al have said that 'explanation is at the heart of a responsible, open data science, across multiple industry sectors and scientific disciplines'.[85] Yet they pose a series of questions to which, they suggest, there are few consensus answers:

> What does it mean that a model is interpretable or transparent? What is an explanation? When a model or an explanation is comprehensible? Which is the best way to provide an explanation? Which are the problems requiring interpretable models/predictions? What kind of decision data are affected? Which type of data records is more comprehensible? How much are we willing to lose in prediction accuracy to gain any form of interpretability?[86]

Finale Doshi-Velez and Mason Kortz, lead authors for a group of legal academics, computer scientists and others based at the Berkman Klein Center, Harvard University, say that explanation 'should permit an observer to determine the extent to which a particular input was determinative or influential on the output'.[87] Therefore explanation might relate to identifying which factor or factors impacted significantly on an outcome. We might also want an explanation to tell us whether changing some particular factor would have altered the outcome, or why seemingly similar cases were decided differently.[88] This leaves us with three types of explanation which might be desirable:

- explanation of the main factor/s
- explanation of the determining factor/s
- explanation of why two similar cases were treated differently.[89]

There is, then, a subset of issues about how explanation should be enabled and whether this should be contemporaneous or after the fact. Doshi-Velez and Kortz suggest that there are two main technical requirements for explanation of AI processes: local explanation (an explanation of how a specific result was arrived at, rather than of how the entire process or system works) and counterfactual faithfulness (an explanation is causally linked to the outcome – so 'if a person was told that their income was the determining factor for their loan denial, and then their income increases, they might reasonably expect that the system would now deem

[84] Selbst and Barocas (n 60) 1099.

[85] R Guidotti, A Monreale, S Ruggieri, F Turini, D Pedreschi and F Giannotti, 'A Survey of Methods for Explaining Black Box Models' (2018) 51(5) *ACM Computing Surveys 1*.

[86] ibid 3.

[87] F Doshi-Velez and M Kortz, 'Accountability of AI Under the Law: The Role of Explanation' Berkman Klein Center Working Group on Explanation and the Law, Berkman Klein Center for Internet & Society working paper, 2017, 3.

[88] ibid 3.

[89] ibid, see also OECD (n 6).

them worthy of getting a loan').[90] They claim that both can be implemented without the need to actually disclose the intricacies of how the AI system functions.[91] Accordingly, they argue for separate 'explanation systems' to be implemented along with AI systems.

Design Safeguards

There are differing views expressed about the utility of different methods for overcoming bias in machine learning and enabling explanation.[92] What seems clear is that there is no single solution, but rather an assortment of design options, testing or auditing mechanisms, and 'explanation systems' – all of which must be considered by reference to the point made above, that bias permeates the human world. In light of this, the initial step in overcoming limitations of explainability lies in a rigorous design process by which goals and choices are responsibly documented.[93] This is about being explicit regarding the way that policies are driving design. Selbst and Barocas give the example of credit scoring, where a policy of minimising risk in lending will lead to different design choices when compared with a policy of maximising profit.[94] Joshua Kroll has said that when it comes to 'transparency' in machine learning systems, the initial design process is important:

> [H]ow were requirements determined? By whom were requirements determined? Were alternatives considered? Which ones? Why were they rejected? Was a particular negative outcome under scrutiny a property of only some alternatives, or was it a necessary consequence of the system however it was designed? How do we know that the system in practice satisfies the requirements that were established for it?[95]

There are also ways of ensuring that the technical construction of a system allows checking and interpretability. Selbst and Barocas explain, first, that there are various ways of building AI models which are more susceptible to interpretation, including:

- Choosing to consider a more limited set of variables;
- Using a method whose outputs can be parsed (such as a decision tree);
- Setting the parameters of the learning process so that the resulting model is not too complex;
- Using simplicity as an optimising criterion (in other words, assigning a cost to excess complexity);

[90] Doshi-Velez and Kortz (n 87) 7.
[91] ibid.
[92] See, eg, Kroll et al (n 43) and the response of Kim (n 24).
[93] Kroll (n 57) 6.
[94] Selbst and Barocas (n 60) 1131.
[95] Kroll (n 57) 6.

- Constraining the learning process so that all features exhibit monotonicity (where the relationship between variables 'is either always positive or always negative'). This simplifies the process of reasoning about how variables will change.[96]

Kroll et al argue that building in safeguards is usually preferable to methods developed or added later as the 'tools available during the design and construction of a computer system are far more powerful and expressive than those that can be bolted on to an existing system after one has been built'.[97] They describe four additional methods by which, they suggest, verification methods can be built in to machine learning systems: software verification, cryptographic commitments, zero-knowledge proofs, and fair random choices.[98] Software verification refers to 'a set of techniques for proving mathematically that software has certain properties'.[99] Essentially this means being able to demonstrate that some characteristics of the model are unchanging. Cryptographic commitments are 'the digital equivalent of a sealed document held by a third party'.[100] Both of these enable a degree of checking to be performed on how the software is operating. In the case of a cryptographic commitment, the entity responsible for the decision can use the commitment to later prove that the software was implemented in a certain way at a fixed time (for instance, without being influenced by subsequent events). Another aspect of a cryptographic commitment is a 'zero-knowledge proof', which enables the software user to show that a particular property is present but without having to show how the property is known or what the guiding decision policy is.[101]

Kroll et al suggest that these methods are preferable to an examination of source code,[102] or post hoc auditing.[103] In response, though, Kim argues that auditing, in particular, is a useful way of establishing discrimination:[104]

> Auditing is another method for promoting transparency. When the goal is nondiscrimination, auditing could involve techniques to ensure that an algorithm follows a specified rule – for example, sorting must not occur based on race or sex. Alternatively, auditing for discrimination could take the form of examining inputs and outputs to detect when a decision process systematically disadvantages particular groups.[105]

[96] Selbst and Barocas (n 60) 1112.
[97] Kroll et al (n 43) 637.
[98] ibid 662.
[99] ibid.
[100] ibid 665.
[101] ibid 668.
[102] Kroll et al (n 43) 647.
[103] ibid 661.
[104] Kim (n 24) 190.
[105] ibid.

Selbst and Barocas also describe 'post-hoc' means of interpreting a machine learning system, such as by building a simpler model of the more complex model;[106] or creating a model which can give some (limited) explanation about the relative importance of different features to the first model.

These mechanisms are not complete solutions, however. Brent Mittelstadt et al from the Alan Turing Institute have explained:

> It is not enough to simply offer a human interpretable model as an explanation. For an individual to be able to trust such a model as an approximation, they must know over which domain a model is reliable and accurate, where it breaks down, and where its behaviour is uncertain. If the recipient of a local approximation does not understand its limitations, at best it is not comprehensible, and at worst misleading.[107]

Accountability

Related to transparency, explainability and interpretability are questions around accountability and regulatory strategy.[108] Explanation, in particular, is relevant to accountability because being accountable may require that justification be provided:

> Lawyers use explanation as their primary tradecraft: judges write opinions, administrators respond to comments, litigators write briefs, and everyone writes memos. Explanations are the difference between a system that vests authority in lawful process and one that vests it in an unaccountable person.[109]

Accountability is, however, a social and legal construct and can be distinguished from technical accountability, 'a technical concept about making sure that software produces evidence allowing oversight and verification of whether it is operating within agreed-upon rules'.[110] Rather, 'legal-political' accountability 'enables holding political and private actors responsible'.[111] We cannot necessarily speak of a lack of accountability as a limitation of AI – it is perhaps better characterised as a limitation of systems of governance. The requirements for 'accountability' will depend on the context of the AI system and relevant laws of the jurisdiction (for example, anti-discrimination law). Within the EU, the combination of various different sections of the General Data Protection Regulation (GDPR), which came into operation on 25 May 2018,[112] is sometimes

[106] See Mittelstadt, Russell and Wachter (n 72).
[107] ibid 281.
[108] Desai and Kroll (n 62) 8–9.
[109] Selbst and S Barocas (n 60) 1088.
[110] Desai and Kroll (n 62) 10.
[111] ibid 9.
[112] EU Regulation 2016/679 on the Protection of Natural Persons with regard to the Processing of Personal Data and on the Free Movement of Such Data, and repealing Directive 95/46/EC, [2016] OJ L119/1.

referred to as providing for a 'right to explanation' of how decisions are being made, including automated decision making.[113] It may be though that in fact the sections provide for something rather less than fully fledged explanation, 'a more limited right to be informed'.[114] We discuss these issues further in the next chapter in relation to regulation.

Nevertheless, technical and legal accountability are related: technical accountability may provide insights into political-legal accountability. Desai and Kroll argue that technical accountability would require AI systems to create 'evidence' as they go which can be used to check that they are working properly.[115] Ed Felton has also argued that if AI is to be more commonly used in lieu of human decision making, then systems must be made more technically accountable.[116] However, as Selbst and Barocas note, the types of explanation available from machine learning systems may not be capable of functioning as justificatory. For instance, they may be correlative rather than causal.[117]

Accountability can be both after the fact ('providing an account of certain decisions or conduct') or before ('mechanisms that act as "checks on decision-making"').[118] The OECD describes accountability as follows:

> *Accountability* focuses on being able to place the onus on the appropriate organisations or individuals for the proper functioning of AI systems. Criteria for accountability include respect for principles of human values and fairness, transparency, robustness and safety … For policy makers, accountability depends on mechanisms that perform several functions. The mechanisms identify the party responsible for a specific recommendation or decision. They correct the recommendation or decision before it is acted on. They could also challenge or appeal the decision after the fact, or even challenge the system responsible for making the decision.[119]

The OECD has also set out different ways that technical accountability might support a broader political-legal accountability. Just as with transparency and explanation, the context of the AI system is crucial to the type of accountability which is needed. Thus, as Table 10.2 illustrates, some means may be well suited to some situations but not to others. In some situations, showing that the system has

[113] B Goodman and S Flaxman, 'EU Regulations on Algorithmic Decision-Making and a "Right to Explanation"' (ICML Workshop on Human Interpretability in Machine Learning, New York, WHI, 2016arxiv. org/abs/1606.08813 v1, 2016; Malgieri and Comandé (n 59) 2.

[114] Malgieri and Comandé (n 59) 2; S Wachter, B Mittelstadt and L Floridi, 'Why a Right to Explanation of Automated Decision-Making Does Not Exist in the General Data Protection Regulation' (2017) *International Data Privacy Law* (2017) 7(2) *International Data Privacy Law* 76, 89–90.

[115] Desai and Kroll (n 62) 10; Mullainathan (n 48) also advocates this.

[116] E Felten, 'Accountable Algorithms', *Freedom to Tinker*, 12 September 2012, freedom-to-tinker.com/2012/09/12/accountable-algorithms/.

[117] Selbst and Barocas (n 60) 1123–26.

[118] J Loughrey, 'Accountability and the Regulation of the Large Law Firm Lawyer' (2014) 77(5) *Modern Law Review* 732, 735.

[119] OECD (n 6) citing S Helgason, *Towards Performance-Based Accountability: Issues for Discussion, Public Management Service* (OECD Publishing, 1997) www.oecd.org/governance/budgeting/1902720.pdf.

been designed such that it can be shown to only operate within certain parameters (a theoretical guarantee) may be sufficient. In others, statistical evidence about overall functioning might be enough[120] – as in the US healthcare example discussed above. An analogy may be our acceptance of the efficacy of some medicinal drugs based on statistical analyses, even though we do not know precisely how they work.[121]

Table 10.2 Approaches to improve the transparency and accountability of AI systems

Approach	Description	Well-suited contexts	Poorly suited contexts
Theoretical guarantees	In some situations, it is possible to give theoretical guarantees about an AI system backed by proof.	The environment is fully observable (eg the game of Go) and both the problem and solution can be formalised.	The situation cannot be clearly specified (most real-world settings).
Statistical evidence/ probability	Empirical evidence measures a system's overall performance, demonstrating the value or harm of the system, without explaining specific decisions.	Outcomes can be fully formalised; it is acceptable to wait to see negative outcomes to measure them; issues may only be visible in aggregate.	The objective cannot be fully formalised; blame or innocence can be assigned for a particular decision.
Explanation	Humans can interpret information about the logic by which a system took a particular set of inputs and reached a particular conclusion.	Problems are incompletely specified, objectives are not clear and inputs could be erroneous.	Other forms of accountability are possible.

Source: Organisation for Economic Cooperation and Development, *Artificial Intelligence in Society* (OECD Publishing, 2019) Table 4.1, citing F Doshi-Velez and M Kortz, 'Accountability of AI Under the Law: The Role of Explanation' Berkman Klein Center Working Group on Explanation and the Law, Berkman Klein Center for Internet & Society working paper, 2017, 3.

Finally, the OECD notes that explanation is particularly needed for accountability when 'fault needs to be determined in a specific instance'.[122]

As we discuss in the next chapter, methods for ensuring accountability may occur at a regulatory level: thus Yanisky-Ravid and Hallisey propose auditing of data; certification regimes; or a 'safe harbour' approach, where legal liability could be limited if particular circumstances are complied with.[123]

[120] OECD (n 6) citing Barocas and Selbst (n 11); and Crawford (n 15).
[121] CEA Karnow, 'The Opinion of Machines' (2017) 19 *Colombia Science and Technology Law Review* 136, 171.
[122] OECD (n 6).
[123] Yanisky-Ravid and Hallisey (n 12) 438.

It is also argued that in the case of 'harmful or coercive decisions', existing design safeguards are still insufficient to allow machine learning to be used.[124] This is most evident in the use of algorithmic risk assessments in the criminal justice system. It is difficult, if not impossible, for a defendant to challenge the assessment if he or she is not able to access, nor understand, how it was generated. This is problematic because the assessment might be wrong in some way, but for other reasons too – the requirement for an explanation, and to know that rule of law values are being upheld.[125] Karen Yeung has noted:

> [I]t is widely accepted that human decision-making processes and outcomes are far from perfect and often deeply flawed. But contemporary legal systems have a wealth of experience in confronting flaws in human decision-making, at least in the context of decisions by governmental authorities, and it is the task of identifying, responding to, and remedying these flaws that has become the staple diet of modern administrative law.[126]

After all, judges remain accountable for their decisions, and for explaining their decisions.[127] For this reason, the OECD notes that in certain areas, it is vitally important to keep a 'human in the loop' – and this is also required by the GDPR. The OECD says, also, that an outcome generated purely by AI should not be the sole factor on which a decision is premised:

> In high-stakes situations, formal accountability mechanisms are often required. For example, a judge using AI for criminal sentencing is a 'human-in-the-loop'. However, other accountability mechanisms – including a traditional judicial appeals process – help ensure that judges consider AI recommendations as just one element in a prediction.[128]

Cost and Sustainability

Many legal AI systems are expensive to build and train, probably needing ongoing maintenance and attention, which likely exerts pressure towards a commercial orientation. In an echo of the 'white guy problem', Mireille Hildebrandt comments that 'If IBM's robolawyer … is trained by top lawyers from major corporate law firms, it will reduplicate their concerns and those of their clients'.[129]

[124] Sheppard (n 69) 47.

[125] See K Brennan-Marquez, 'Plausible Cause: Explanatory Standards in the Age of Powerful Machines' (2017) 70 *Vanderbilt Law Review* 1249.

[126] K Yeung, 'Why Worry about Decision-Making by Machine?' in K Yeung and M Lodge (eds), *Algorithmic Regulation* (Oxford University Press, 2019) 21, 23.

[127] F Pasquale and G Cashwell, 'Prediction, Persuasion, and the Jurisprudence of Behaviourism' (2018) 68(Supp 1) *University of Toronto Law Journal* 63.

[128] OECD (n 6) citing S Wachter, B Mittelstadt and L Floridi, 'Transparent, Explainable and Accountable AI for Robotics', *Science Robotics*, 31 May 2017, robotics.sciencemag.org/content/2/6/eaan6080.

[129] M Hildebrandt, 'Law as Computation in the Era of Artificial Legal Intelligence: Speaking Law to the Power of Statistics' (2018) 68(Supp 1) *University of Toronto Law Journal* 12, 31.

Very large law firms are better placed to make the investment in technology which might be required. This is supported by, for example, Vicki Waye et al's survey, wherein respondents reported that the primary barrier to innovation was the cost of projects – 35 per cent of respondents rated this as a critical or very significant barrier.[130] Yet, small firms may be more adaptable and better able to effect change.

There is a much larger question here about 'how … we ensure that the risks and benefits of artificial intelligence are evenly distributed across society?'[131] Noting the growing divide between those who are in the position of collecting data and those who provide it, Sora Park and Justine Humphrey have written:

> Some of the public risks of this divide foreshadowed include limiting research to only those who can afford expensive access to commercially restricted datasets and to the experts to analyse these. This in turn leads to uneven distribution of data and knowledge, particularly when algorithmically processed.[132]

Though the 'divide' is not quite so clear cut when it comes to legal AI, it remains salient. Valuable datasets include those of legal publishers and law libraries, as well as data on disputes held by, for instance, insurance companies.[133] In 2015 it was announced that Ravel Law (later acquired by LexisNexis[134]) was partnering with Harvard Law School to digitise the Langdell Library's entire collection of Federal and State US case law, amounting to 40 million pages.[135] So far, collections pertaining to several states have been completely digitised.[136] Ravel's intention is 'to make American caselaw open and free'.[137] However, the analytics performed by Ravel will likely remain subscription only. As Kate Crawford and Vladan Joler have noted, 'A dataset may still be publicly owned, but the meta-value of the data – the model created by it – is privately owned'.[138]

In general, academia also cannot keep pace with industry when it comes to AI due to the investment needed, which skews the types of projects which are investigated. The biggest investments in LegalTech are (unsurprisingly) in its commercial applications: the growth of LegalTech has been championed as attracting huge

[130] V Waye, ML Verreynne and J Knowler, 'Innovation in the Australian Legal Profession' (2018) 25(2) *International Journal of the Legal Profession* 213, 231.

[131] Calo (n 2) 413.

[132] S Park and J Humphry, 'Exclusion by Design: Intersections of Social, Digital and Data Exclusion' (2019) 22(7) *Information, Communication & Society* 934, 937, citing D Boyd and K Crawford, 'Critical Questions for Big Data: Provocations for a Cultural, Technological, and Scholarly Phenomenon' (2012) 15(5) *Information, Communication & Society* 662; T Gillespie, 'The Relevance of Algorithms' in T Gillespie, PJ Boczkowski and K Foot (eds), *Media Technologies: Essays on Communication, Materiality, and Society (Vol 6)* (MIT Press, 2014) 167; and MT McCarthy, 'The Big Data Divide and Its Consequences' (2016) 10(12) *Sociology Compass* 1131.

[133] MK Osbeck, 'Lawyer as a Soothsayer: Exploring the Important Role of Outcome Prediction in the Practice of Law' (2018) 123(1) *Penn State Law Review* 41.

[134] Ravel Home, home.ravellaw.com/.

[135] A Ziegler, 'Continued Support for the Caselaw Access Project', *Et Seq: The Blog of the Harvard Law School Library*, 8 June 2017, www.etseq.law.harvard.edu/category/caselaw-access-project/.

[136] ibid.

[137] Ravel Home, home.ravellaw.com/.

[138] K Crawford and V Joler, 'Anatomy of an AI System', anatomyof.ai/.

investment. Investment on this scale is needed to make viable products: LawGeex's contract review software reportedly took three years to train to reach an acceptable standard.[139] With high research and design costs, high-volume usage will be needed for the project to be worthwhile. For subscription-type services like LawGeex, benefits come through having many clients. There are also costs attached to accountability mechanisms: as described above, this may mean constant monitoring and evaluation.[140]

The benefits for firms themselves are somewhat harder to track. Deloitte has observed:

> Small firms may face greater margin pressures as the cost of investments will be higher relative to turnover. However, they may also be more nimble and adapt to change more easily. Small firms are likely to feel the impact last. Larger firms will require change programmes to shift culture and behaviours that have become entrenched in the organisation … Pressure on the mid-sized law firms will increase …[141]

There is a broader issue around the way that lawyers have traditionally charged for their time, a model which does not necessarily reward lawyers or law firms for their productivity. Software is a product and therefore should be sold at volume to increase profits, as opposed to the service provided by lawyers to individual clients.[142] To a large extent, this depends on how much pressure lawyers are under to pass on cost savings to clients, or how they will choose to do this. Arguably, small firm and solo lawyers are in some ways better placed to take advantage of time-saving AI tools such as document automation to make their services more efficient and thereby help more clients. Large firms traditionally might have leveraged from this kind of routinised work as part of offering a bespoke service but sophisticated clients are now less willing to pay these costs.

One in-house counsel has noted that 'While some e-billing and management matter programs have shown cost savings, the monetary benefit of using artificial intelligence is not as easily proven'.[143] Legal service entity QuisLex undertook an examination of 10 different AI tools developed for text abstraction,[144] finding that

> [t]ime savings and accuracy had a high degree of variance, not just from tool to tool but within tools, from one agreement to the next and from one provision to the next – including some instances where using the tool took more time than manual review. The usefulness of each tool is dependent on the tool/project fit and the process built to support the workflow. Cost savings and [return on investment] will also vary depending on the cost of the resource whose time is being saved.[145]

[139] Z Abramowitz, 'LawGeex Free Contract Review Could Be a Gamechanger', *Above the Law*, 21 April 2016.

[140] OECD (n 6) noting that 'As with all metrics, monitoring and evaluation can be costly'.

[141] *Developing Legal Talent: Stepping into the Future Law Firm* (Deloitte, February 2016) 13.

[142] ibid.

[143] S Reisinger, 'Experts Disagree on Who Leads the Way on Legal Tech – Law Firms or In-House Counsel' (2019) 225(8) *New Jersey Law Journal* 25.

[144] C D'Agostino, *Project Johnny 5: A Case Study on Evaluating AI Abstraction Tools* (QuisLex, 2019).

[145] C D'Agostino, 'AI Abstraction Tools Driving Real Savings, But Not Yet a Magic Button' (2019) 227(7) *New Jersey Law Journal* 28.

In other words, cost savings were dependent on exactly who was being replaced, or whose time was being saved, through the use of the tools, as well as how they were being applied in a given instance.

There is hope that legal AI can improve access to justice. There are opportunities to capitalise on, for example, widespread smart phone ownership combined with simple apps which can provide legal information that would previously have been inaccessible.[146] In the United States, free programs such as A2J Author enable legal services to assist many clients with simple matters by offering form-filling-type services. The story is more complex, however, when it comes to vulnerable members of society with multiple interconnected problems.[147] In looking more broadly at non-lawyer ownership in legal services markets, Nick Robinson has noted that technology (including AI technology) is often associated with new methods of offering legal services. Interestingly, Robinson found that while there was a scale impact, it was less clear that these developments did actually improve access to justice:

> The country studies provide support to the argument that non-lawyer ownership can, and in some circumstances does, lead to new innovation in legal services, larger economies of scale and scope, and new compensation structures. Yet, perhaps counter-intuitively, there is little evidence indicating that these changes have substantially improved access to civil legal services for poor to moderate-income populations.[148]

Moreover, there are concerns that in increasing instances, marginalised populations are being subjected to the use of AI,[149] rather than AI being enabling and assistive. As Calo notes, responsible design of AI systems, building in explainability and other safeguards, with the costs this brings, are not extended to all.[150] While police may use proprietary technology to target geographic areas or even people for investigation, 'investment firms [don't] initiate transactions on the basis of machine learning that they cannot explain to wealthy, sophisticated investors'.[151]

Finally, the environmental and human labour costs of making AI systems are considerable: 'producer and consumer practices in the context of AI technologies may in themselves contradict sustainability goals'.[152] *New Scientist* reported that training a large neural network generates up to five times' the lifetime carbon dioxide emissions of an average car, due to the energy needed.[153] As well as energy

[146] See, eg, Barefootlaw, barefootlaw.org/.

[147] F Bell, 'Family Law, Access to Justice, and Automation' (2019) 19 *Macquarie Law Journal* 103.

[148] N Robinson, 'When Lawyers Don't Get All the Profits: Non-Lawyer Ownership, Access, and Professionalism' (2016) 29(1) *Georgetown Journal of Legal Ethics* 1, 44.

[149] Calo (n 2) 412; see generally Chapter 9.

[150] Calo (n 2) 412.

[151] ibid.

[152] T Hagendorff, 'The Ethics of AI Ethics: An Evaluation of Guidelines' (2020) 30(1) *Minds and Machines* 99 (citations omitted).

[153] D Lu, 'Creating an AI Can Be Five Times Worse for the Planet than a Car', *New Scientist*, 6 June 2019, www.newscientist.com/article/2205779-creating-an-ai-can-be-five-times-worse-for-the-planet-than-a-car/#ixzz6FgMZTTtU, reporting on E Strubell, A Ganesh and A McCallum, 'Energy and Policy Considerations for Deep Learning in NLP' (paper presented at the 57th Annual Meeting of the Association for Computational Linguistics (ACL), Florence, Italy, July 2019).

consumption, Thilo Hagendorff identifies 'lithium mining, e-waste, the one-way use of rare earth minerals … low-wage "clickworkers" creating labels for data sets or doing content moderation'.[154] Crawford and Joler produced 'Anatomy of an AI System' in which they mapped the Amazon Echo (a 'home assistant' tool) in terms of 'human labor, data and planetary resources'.[155] The map and accompanying essay document the damage inflicted:

> The scope is overwhelming: from indentured labor in mines for extracting the minerals that form the physical basis of information technologies; to the work of strictly controlled and sometimes dangerous hardware manufacturing and assembly processes in Chinese factories; to exploited outsourced cognitive workers in developing countries labelling AI training data sets; to the informal physical workers cleaning up toxic waste dumps.[156]

Not being Human

It is argued that machines are presently incapable of legal reasoning, and indeed much higher-order legal work.[157] For example, it is generally thought that AI is not able to engage in reasoning by analogy,[158] a hallmark of legal reasoning, which also requires a degree of creativity of thought. Although creativity and imagination are not necessarily skills traditionally valued by lawyers, these are important points of differentiation. In the mid-nineteenth century, Ada Lovelace commented on the 'Analytical Engine' (widely credited as the first computer program),[159] saying:

> The Analytical Engine has no pretensions whatever to originate any thing. It can do whatever we know how to order it to perform. It can follow analysis, but it has no power of anticipating any analytical relations or truths. Its province is to assist us in making available what we are already acquainted with.[160]

In other words, a computer cannot 'think' originally, or engage in acts of creativity. While it can appear that this is what some programs are doing – viz, AlphaGo's style of game playing – this is not the same as human creativity.

[154] Hagendorff (n 152).
[155] Crawford and Joler (n 138).
[156] ibid.
[157] JC Smith, 'Machine Intelligence and Legal Reasoning' (1998) 73 *Chicago-Kent Law Review* 277, 311.
[158] Katz argues that 'we are still far away from a machine that can engage in "hard" analogical reasoning' but considers we might be able to develop a 'soft' version: DM Katz, 'Quantitative Legal Prediction, or – how I learned to stop worrying and start preparing for the data-driven future of the legal services industry' (2013) 62(4) *Emory Law Journal* 909, 956.
[159] See www.computerhistory.org/babbage/engines/.
[160] A Lovelace, 'Notes' in R Taylor (ed), *Scientific Memoirs, Selections From the Transactions of Foreign Academies and Learned Societies and From Foreign Journals, Vol III* (R and JE Taylor, 1843) 772 cited by P Sanderson and H Sommerlad, 'Exploring the Limits to the Standardization of the Expert Knowledge of Lawyers: Quality and Legal Aid Reforms in the United Kingdom' (2002) 52 *Syracuse Law Review* 987, 989.

It would similarly be very difficult to program AI to take account of policy and social factors which are also integral to the development of the law:

> Legal analysis requires an understanding of existing policy, the recognition of how a policy argument can win a case, awareness of the real-life implications of a decision, and insight into the constantly changing landscape of politics. In short, it requires cognizance of human factors.[161]

AI can be programmed to know what the law is, but not *why* it is what it is.[162] It is also sometimes said that being a lawyer is about knowing the questions to ask, rather than the answers. In any event, legal questions tend to have more than one answer or no single correct answer.[163] It is argued that without the experience of emotions, or empathy,[164] AI lacks moral standing and does not currently have the ability to 'talk a client around'.

A recent UK survey found that a majority of those surveyed would prefer to have a human rather than a robot lawyer.[165] This perhaps supports the claim that 'affective, psycho-social skills must be regarded as just as important as technical skills in professional service work'.[166] Arguably, providing the correct legal answer is not all that consumers of legal services want: they want to be listened to, they want reassurance, they want 'a guide, a coach, a friend, and an ally'.[167] Two American academics suggest that there will accordingly continue to be a need for lawyers who can form 'emotional bonds with clients':[168] people seek an emotionally intelligent fellow human being to guide them through their legal problem.

[161] SD Becerra, 'The Rise of Artificial Intelligence in the Legal Field: Where We Are and Where We Are Going' (2018) 11 *Journal of Business, Entrepreneurship & Law* 27, 50–51.

[162] Thomson Reuters, 'Video: Will Artificial Intelligence Have a Radical Impact on the Legal Profession', Legal Executive Institute, 1 August 2016, legalexecutiveinstitute.com/-video-will-ai-impact-legal-profession/.

[163] Becerra (n 160) 50.

[164] S Delacroix, 'Computer Systems Fit for the Legal Profession?' (2018) 21(2) *Legal Ethics* 119–35.

[165] www.legalcheek.com/2018/04/fall-of-the-robots-86-of-brits-prefer-legal-advice-from-humans/; see also patentlawyermagazine.com/14-of-brits-would-take-legal-advice-from-a-robot/.

[166] Sanderson and Sommerlad (n 160) 998, citing I Macneil, 'The Many Futures of Contracts' (1974) 47 *Southern California Law Review* 691, 712; D Rosenthal, 'Evaluating the Competence of Lawyers' (1976) 1 *Law and Society Review* 257; GD Doherty, 'Quality Standards, the Consumer Paradigm and Developments in Higher Education' (1997) 5 *Quality Assurance in Education* 239, 241; M Trow, 'The Business of Learning', *Times Higher Education Supplement*, 8 October 1993, 20; R Laughlin and J Broadbent, 'The Managerial Reform of Health and Education in the UK: Value for Money or a Devaluing Process?' (1994) 65 *Political Quarterly* 152; J Walker, A Brooksby, J McInerny and A Taylor, 'Patient Perceptions of Hospital Care: Building Confidence, Faith and Trust' (1998) 6(4) *Journal of Nursing Management* 193; H Waitzkin, *The Politics of Medical Encounters: How Patients and Doctors Deal with Social Problems* (Yale University Press, 1991).

[167] B Tarascio, 'Hacking the Future of Lawyering', *Law Practice Today (ABA Law Practice Division)*, 14 May 2018.

[168] JO McGinnis and RG Pearce, 'The Great Disruption: How Machine Intelligence Will Transform the Role of Lawyers in the Delivery of Legal Services' (2014) 82(6) *Fordham Law Review* 3041, 3042.

Conclusion

'Any sufficiently advanced technology is indistinguishable from magic', wrote Arthur C Clarke.[169] There are long-expressed concerns that people tend to attribute to AI a kind of infallibility. Yet as its use becomes ever more pervasive, it is increasingly important for lawyers to understand its shortcomings, not just in strictly 'legal' applications but more generally. AI lacks what is referred to as 'common sense'[170] (generalised or tacit knowledge), creativity and imagination.[171] A good example of lacking common sense is that above, where asthma was associated with a decreased risk of severe complications in pneumonia. AI systems are confined to the data which they are presented with, and are generally poor at extracting answers from incomplete data, in comparison with humans:

> The human mind can draw correct inferences from very limited information, allowing a human lawyer to use context, analogies, and common sense to identify [an unanticipated problem]. By contrast, current machine learning software will identify the reference as problematic only if something related to the problematic language was anticipated and included in the training data.[172]

AI systems are constrained by the data which is available. As explained, for legal applications, these limitations may be very significant. This is due to the nature of the data itself (partial, messy) but also to cost and other restrictions on large databases.

The design of systems is also very important. An AI process cannot be liable for its outputs as machines are not legal persons.[173] Kroll et al, however, reject the idea that people should also not be held responsible for the operation of AI systems. This attribution of responsibility flows on from their views (described above) about the importance of responsible design in algorithmic systems.[174] Thus:

> Viewing computer system behaviours as though they are uncontrollable ignores the fact that these systems are human artefacts, built to a purpose by some human agency that must be accountable for the behaviours of those artefacts. Such a view defers too strongly to the power dynamics at play, placing actions with human agency beyond governance, control and accountability. Even when the specifics of how a system will interact with the world are not directly foreseeable, they can be reviewed, managed and constrained.[175]

[169] AC Clarke, *Profiles of the Future: An Inquiry into the Limits of the Possible* (2nd edn, Pan Books, 1973).

[170] Doshi-Velez and Kortz (n 87) 2. For a discussion of common sense, see GK Hadfield, *Rules for a Flat World* (Oxford University Press, 2017) 25.

[171] TC Redman, 'Algorithms Make Better Predictions – Except When They Don't', *Harvard Business Review*, 17 September 2014.

[172] D Remus and F Levy, 'Can Robots Be Lawyers: Computers, Lawyers, and the Practice of Law' (2017) 30(3) *Georgetown Journal of Legal Ethics* 501, 517–18.

[173] Vladeck (n 28) 121; J Turner, *Robot Rules: Regulating Artificial Intelligence* (Palgrave Macmillan, 2019) ch 5: 'Legal Personality for AI?'.

[174] Kroll et al (n 43).

[175] Kroll (n 57) 7.

In the absence of regulation, however, lawyers will also have a role in questioning whether design best practice has been adhered to. Kleinberg et al suggest that if properly designed and used, algorithmic systems can be used to effectively demonstrate bias in human endeavours and therefore be 'a positive force for equity'.[176] For example, anti-discrimination lawyers may need to understand the ways that a machine learning system may have resulted in discriminatory outputs. However, as Mullainathan said: 'with proper regulation, algorithms can help to reduce discrimination. But the key phrase here is "proper regulation," which we do not currently have'.[177] Indeed, Kroll suggests that 'inscrutable' systems are a choice of the designer, 'perhaps one born of laziness', which should be treated as 'malpractice'.[178]

At present, however, most lawyers will be dependent on that designer or software provider as they will lack the knowledge to independently evaluate a system's design or performance.[179] For example, in Technology Assisted Review it is usually necessary for lawyers to work closely with the software provider to train the software appropriately and to troubleshoot problems. Yet, it is lawyers who retain the ultimate professional responsibility for the outcomes generated by the software, as we discuss in the next chapter. Brian Sheppard writes of trade secrecy in the area of AI tools:

> Secrecy makes it harder for consumers to realize the full benefits of a competitive marketplace. Lawyers will struggle to make educated choices between programs, stifling their ability to choose the best product for themselves and for their clients. Making matters worse, their lack of understanding will stifle the improvement of the algorithms, themselves.[180]

For this reason, any additional regulation around the development of AI systems would likely benefit lawyers by ensuring that software is appropriately designed and developed, and enabling them to share the burden of responsibility with others.

[176] Kleinberg et al (n 24).
[177] Mullainathan (n 48).
[178] Kroll (n 57) 4.
[179] See Hildebrandt (n 129).
[180] B Sheppard, 'Does Machine Learning Powered Software Make Good Research Decisions? Lawyers Can't Know For Sure', *ABA Journal*, 22 November 2016, https://www.abajournal.com/legalrebels/article/does_machine-learning-powered_software_make_good_research_decisions_lawyers.

11

Legal Ethics, Liability and Regulation in an AI World

Introduction

Advances in AI create significant challenges for law and regulation. Debate has begun over issues of control, responsibility and liability when it comes to automated systems, such as self-driving cars.[1] If AI is not to have legal personality,[2] then decisions have to be made about who will take legal responsibility for it – whether this is the creators or developers of a product, owners or users.[3] The legal profession will naturally take a role in addressing legal responsibility as obligations are set out in agreements, disputes arise and need to be quelled, and regulators and government seek to develop new laws. However, AI will also impact on the law of lawyering[4] – how the legal profession functions and the responsibilities of lawyers. This is the focus of this chapter.

At present AI provides various tools that have legal applications and can perform some aspects of a lawyer's role, but lawyers are frequently still part of the process.[5] Nevertheless, change is occurring rapidly, and fundamental tenets of professionalism need to adapt to the presence of AI. This includes the need for lawyers to effectively deploy technology in keeping with their professional and

[1] European Parliament Committee on Legal Affairs Working Group, 'Civil Law Rules on Robotics', 27 January 2017.

[2] L Solum, 'Legal Personhood for Artificial Intelligences' (1992) 70 *North Carolina Law Review* 1231; Institute of Electrical and Electronics Engineers Global Initiative on Ethics of Autonomous and Intelligent Systems, *Ethically Aligned Design – A Vision for Prioritizing Human Well-being with Autonomous and Intelligent Systems* (Institute of Electrical and Electronics Engineers, 2017) 149 ('the technology has not yet developed to the point where it would be legally or morally appropriate to generally accord [AI] the rights and responsibilities inherent in the legal definition of personhood'); House of Lords Select Committee on Artificial Intelligence, 'AI in the UK: Ready, Willing and Able?' HL Paper 100 ch 8, 16 April 2018.

[3] S Morley and D Lawrence quoted in House of Lords Select Committee on Artificial Intelligence (n 2) 97 [315].

[4] Lawyers' professional responsibilities are derived from the general law, statute and professional/ethical rules.

[5] S Semmler and Z Rose, 'Artificial Intelligence: Application Today and Implications Tomorrow' (2017–18) 16 *Duke Law & Technology Review* 85, 86; M McKamey, 'Legal Technology: Artificial Intelligence and the Future of Law Practice' (2017) 22 *Appeal: Review of Current Law and Law Reform* 45, 50.

ethical responsibilities, while also avoiding liability where AI does not function as expected, resulting in some form of harm.

However, AI applications may also have the ability to remove the lawyer from the provision of legal services, which raises questions for consumers/users and regulators. If there is no lawyer to take responsibility for the use of the AI, assuming that they could be responsible, then how is the consumer protected? This in turn then raises for consideration whether it would be prudent for a consumer to still retain a lawyer so as to access additional legal protections, such as claims against the lawyer and their insurance. Indeed a feature of a profession is that 'caveat emptor cannot be allowed to prevail'.[6] Related to these questions is the issue of the provision of legal services by non-lawyers. In some jurisdictions non-lawyers are prohibited from providing legal services, while in others only some legal services may not be provided. However, the scope of the prohibition may require reassessment as AI develops. These are complex policy questions without easy answers.

Legal Ethics in an AI World

Legal Professional Standards

Self-regulation has traditionally been viewed as a hallmark of a profession. For lawyers, the traditional self-regulatory model was focused on the point of entry to the profession. Provided that the individual was 'fit and proper' and committed to serving the public (another of the indicia of a profession), there was little further regulation in the absence of poor conduct. Acting in service of the public involves a duty to the administration of justice, duties to the client and exercising independent professional judgement. Now, however, due to a range of factors, the regulatory model has changed in some jurisdictions, and under rubrics of competition and consumer protection, lawyers may be regulated in co-regulatory arrangements.[7] In addition to professional obligations, the lawyer is subject to the general law, including contract, tort and statutory protections for consumers.

The justifications for regulating legal services provision and granting monopoly protections, meaning that only lawyers may provide the service, may be summarised as:

- there is a public interest in ensuring that people with legal issues are provided with competent and ethical services;
- the layperson often lacks sufficient information to adequately evaluate the legal services being provided to them so that regulation ensures a minimum level of quality and provides remedies for any harm;

[6] MS Larson, *The Rise of Professionalism* (University of California Press, 1977) 9.

[7] See Chapter 3 for a detailed discussion of the regulation of the legal profession and how it has changed over time and across jurisdictions.

- there is a need to promote the rigorous study and development of expertise and competency in law to achieve social goals, such as the protection of rights and facilitation of commerce; and
- lawyers play critical roles in the administration of justice and in the maintenance of a free and democratic society, which requires specialised knowledge and skill.[8]

Put another way, the idea of a professional calling has been said to involve a cluster of beliefs and attitudes:

> [A] belief that the field of work has special importance to the public welfare; a belief that those engaged in this work can, for better or worse, affect the public good, and that therefore it is important that they consider themselves to be engaged in a form of public service; a belief that the work is complex and performing it well is not easy, and that it is important that those performing it be competent and dedicated to performing at a high level; and a belief that through continuous and collective improvement the profession can make increasingly valuable contributions to the public good.[9]

Professions 'strike a bargain with society' which commits them to serving the interests of the client and community above themselves, acting with competence and integrity, and protecting and advancing professional expertise and institutions.[10] For lawyers, this is embodied in their ultimate fidelity to the law and the administration of justice and the duty to serve the client's interests. It also manifests itself in requirements such as the lawyer being obliged to act in a way that upholds the integrity of, and trust in, the legal profession.[11] The lawyer has a duty to carry on the practice of law and discharge all responsibilities to clients, tribunals, the public and other members of the profession honourably and with integrity.[12]

This chapter examines the legal profession's main ethical requirements from the perspective of how the existence of AI impacts these obligations.

Competence

Competence may be defined as having knowledge of the law and being able to use the law (both in terms of substance and procedure) with skill to solve problems. It refers to technical proficiency. It involves effectiveness and efficiency – achieving

[8] Larson (n 6) 226; E Friedson, 'The Theory of Professions: State of the Art' in R Dingwall and P Lewis (eds), *The Sociology of the Professions* (St Martin's Press, 1983) 19; Law Society of Ontario, Technology Task Force, 'Update Report', 29 November 2019, 28.

[9] CT Bogus, 'The Death of an Honorable Profession' (1996) 71 *Indiana Law Journal* 911, 937–38.

[10] D Rueschemeyer, 'Professional Autonomy and the Social Control of Expertise' in Dingwall and Lewis (eds) (n 8) 41.

[11] Solicitors Regulation Authority (England and Wales), Principles, principle 2.

[12] Federation of Law Societies (FLSC) of Canada's Model Code of Professional Conduct, 14 March 2017, Preface.

an outcome in a timely and cost-effective manner. It may also be interpreted to mean the ethical application of knowledge or skills as the lawyer is a professional.[13]

The American Bar Association's Model Rules of Professional Conduct include Rule 1.1, which states: 'A lawyer shall provide competent representation to a client' and further that 'competent representation requires the legal knowledge, skill, thoroughness and preparation reasonably necessary for the representation'. The impact of technology on the functioning of law and the legal profession was highlighted by the American Bar Association when it approved changes to the Model Rules of Professional Conduct. Rule 1.1, Comment 8 was added to make clear that lawyers have a duty to be competent not only in the law and its practice, but also in technology.[14] Comment 8 provides:

> To maintain the requisite knowledge and skill, a lawyer should keep abreast of changes in the law and its practice, including the benefits and risks associated with relevant technology, engage in continuing study and education and comply with all continuing legal education requirements to which the lawyer is subject.

In England and Wales, competence is dealt with by the Code of Conduct for Solicitors, Registered European Lawyers and Registered Foreign Lawyers, as follows:

> You ensure that the service you provide to clients is competent and delivered in a timely manner.
>
> You maintain your competence to carry out your role and keep your professional knowledge and skills up to date.[15]

Similar ethics rules exist in Australia, Canada, Singapore and Hong Kong.[16]

In jurisdictions outside the US where there is no specific rule or commentary addressing technology, the general requirement of competence may nonetheless be viewed as including competence with technology.[17] This argument can be made on the basis that it is not possible to carry out legal representation without being able to use technology. The law, the various commentaries on the law, and the base materials for court filings and agreements all require the use of technology.

[13] See generally GE Dal Pont, *Lawyers' Professional Responsibility* (6th edn, Thomson Reuters, 2017) 115–16; J Littrich and K Murray, *Lawyers in Australia* (4th edn, Federation Press, 2019) 249–52.

[14] R Ambrogi, 'Make That 30 States, As Another Adopts Ethical Duty of Technology Competence' LawSites, 14 March 2018, www.lawsitesblog.com/2018/03/make-30-states-another-adopts-ethical-duty-technology-competence.html.

[15] Solicitors Regulation Authority (England and Wales), Code of Conduct for Solicitors, Registered European Lawyers and Registered Foreign Lawyers, rr 3.2, 3.3. The rules came into effect on 25 November 2019.

[16] Legal Profession Uniform Law Australian Solicitors' Conduct Rules 2015, r 4.1.3; Federation of Law Societies (FLSC) of Canada's Model Code of Professional Conduct, 14 March 2017, r 3.1–2; The Hong Kong Solicitors' Guide to Professional Conduct, r 6.01; Legal Profession (Professional Conduct) Rules 2015 (Singapore), r 5.

[17] F Bell and M Legg, 'Lawyers and the Black Box of Technology' (2020) 94 *Australian Law Journal* 107; Australian Law Reform Commission, Technology – What It Means for Federal Dispute Resolution, Issues Paper 23 (1998) [8.10], citing C Lanctot and JE Amule, 'The Internet – Hip or Hype? Legal Ethics and the Internet' in *The Internet for Lawyers* (Pennsylvania Bar Institute, 1995), opining that lawyers who are unable to use the internet may be regarded as not possessing the necessary competence.

However, it may also be argued that thinking like a lawyer now incorporates using technology.[18] This is because technology changes how lawyering is undertaken.[19] A straightforward example is legal research before and after the rise of electronic databases, the internet and various forms of search – keywords, connectors (ie AND, OR) and natural language. The way a lawyer finds the law has changed and with it the way a lawyer must think about finding the law. The lawyer who only relies on the textbooks, legislation and case law physically in their office cannot be as comprehensive as the lawyer with access to online databases. However, the effectiveness of using those online databases requires knowledge of how to search. The technology changes how the lawyer practises. This is not to say that the lawyer who consults a text or recalls a case from past experience does not have something valuable to add, only that alone it may not produce a competent rendering of the relevant law.

If technological competence is a requirement for lawyers, then a further question which arises is whether the use of specific technologies that employ AI is required. American legal ethics professor Roy Simon has opined:

> A lawyer is not required to stay current with every new app and every new form of technology – that would be impossible – but to the extent a lawyer actually uses or should use technology in her law practice, the lawyer must understand how to use that technology and keep up with changes in that technology.[20]

Where the lawyer is using AI then that will obviously require an adequate degree of understanding in order to be able to properly and effectively use that AI. Lawyers need to ensure that the process will work. For example, it is argued that some methods of conducting Technology Assisted Review (TAR) for discovery are more effective than others,[21] and if lawyers are to agree to a TAR protocol in conjunction with their opponents, they need to comprehend what is being agreed.[22] In other words: 'it is the lawyer's duty to remain competent in using these sophisticated tools correctly and interpreting their results correctly when providing legal advice to clients'.[23]

The availability and use of AI in legal practice is currently uneven, which points to the more difficult question of when the lawyer *should* use AI.[24] The depth

[18] A McPeak, 'Disruptive Technology and the Ethical Lawyer' (2019) 50 *University of Toledo Law Review* 457, 471.

[19] N Miller and D Witte, 'Helping Law Firm Luddites Cross the Digital Divide – Arguments for Mastering Law Practice Technology' (2009) 12 *SMU Science and Technology Law Review* 113, 118–20.

[20] R Simon, *Simon's New York Rules of Professional Conduct Annotated* §1.1:9. See also GC Hazard Jr, WW Hodes and PR Jarvis, *The Law of Lawyering* (4th edn, CCH, 2019) §4.02.

[21] See Chapter 5.

[22] JL Brickell and PJ Pizzi, 'Towards a Synthesis of Judicial Perspectives on Technology-Assisted Review' (2015) 82 *Defense Counsel Journal* 309, 313.

[23] K Medianik, 'Artificially Intelligent Lawyers: Updating the Model Rules of Professional Conduct in Accordance with the New Technological Era' (2018) 39 *Cardozo Law Review* 1497, 1516.

[24] J Rogers and F Bell, 'The Ethical AI Lawyer: What Is Required of Lawyers When They Use Automated Systems?' (2019) 1(1) *Law, Technology and Humans* 80; JQ Walker, 'What's Artificial About Intelligence? The Ethical and Practical Considerations When Lawyers Use AI Technology', *Bloomberg Law* (2018).

of knowledge required depends to an extent on the nature of the lawyer's firm or practice. Some lawyers may say that they do not use AI and do not need to. It may be suggested that a lawyer is unlikely to be retained in a matter with an enormous volume of discovery to undertake unless their firm is big enough to take the case on, so that something like TAR may be less of an issue for small or sole practitioner firms.[25] However, plaintiffs that sue large corporations or government may be represented by small law firms and need to be able to effectively engage with discovery from large defendants. Perhaps more significantly, it is the more routine consumer-oriented tasks, such as conveyancing, traffic offences, standard contracts and wills, that AI start-ups will target. Lawyers in smaller firms will need to combine AI with their legal expertise to be able to compete. In sales speak the lawyer will try and 'upsell'[26] the client from the standard tech-based service to the more tailored lawyer-provided service. Of course the lawyer has to be able to add value that the client wants.

More generally, for lawyers to remain successful in the future they are going to need the assistance of AI to be able to deliver quality and cost-effective legal services.[27] Increasingly sophisticated legal technology is a baseline expectation for clients who have technology in every other aspect of their lives.[28] The use of AI to assemble contracts and automate due diligence and discovery will increase the speed, quality and accuracy of the lawyer's work product and lead to better outcomes. Outcome prediction can add to the lawyer's evaluation of prospects of success and aid in choosing forums, motion strategy and evaluation of potential settlements.[29] A lawyer who undertakes legal work without these technologies when they verifiably improve the lawyer's service – quality and/or efficiency – and therefore aid the client may not be acting with competence. Equally if the AI tool is employed without due regard to its effectiveness then this may illustrate incompetence.

Competence may also be required so as to enable a lawyer to challenge or interrogate AI tools. A particular concern for civil liberties and the administration of justice is the use of algorithmic risk assessments in the criminal justice system as discussed in Chapter 9. Such risk assessments have been used in the US to assess

[25] Legal Services Board, 'Technology and Innovation in Legal Services – Main Report', November 2018, 14.

[26] Upselling is a sales technique used to get a customer to spend more by buying an upgraded or premium version of what is being purchased. Examples include airlines asking passengers if they want to upgrade from economy to business or a telephone/streaming service that offers different packages of services.

[27] M Lauritsen, 'Toward a Phenomenology of Machine-Assisted Legal Work' (2018) 1 *Journal of Robotics, Artificial Intelligence and Law* 67, 78–79.

[28] D Clarke and R Kinghorn, 'Experience Is Everything: Here's How to Get It Right' (PriceWaterhouseCooper, undated) 3, 7.

[29] E Walters, 'The Model Rules of Autonomous Conduct: Ethical Responsibilities of Lawyers and Artificial Intelligence' (2019) 35 *Georgia State University Law Review* 1073, 1077; H Surden, 'Artificial Intelligence and Law: An Overview' (2019) 35 *Georgia State University Law Review* 1305, 1331–32; Chapters 4–9 in this text.

a person's likelihood of reoffending if bailed or paroled; for the purpose of managing the individual while they are incarcerated; or when determining a sentence. They may also be used in police work.[30] Though risk assessment tools themselves have a lengthy history, AI provides the option of eliminating human involvement in both the design of criteria and the way that the criteria are considered in the decision-making matrix. Provided with data, AI software can teach itself about the likelihood that individuals will skip bail, cause trouble while incarcerated or breach parole, and so on. Concerns have been voiced about the use of AI software to make such predictions, including whether it can potentially amount to a denial of due process/procedural fairness.[31] There is also the problem that the data used to train the algorithm may reflect historic inequalities and discriminatory patterns of policing, prosecution and incarceration. For a lawyer to be able to challenge the use of algorithmic risk assessment in relation to a client they need to comprehend how such tools function.

The concern to understand and challenge AI may also arise in more mundane settings. The order in which search results are presented has not been subject to a great deal of scepticism or evaluation for relevance or accuracy.[32] However, an algorithm for listing hotels was found to breach consumer protection legislation because its operation was not consistent with the representations made as to how it operated.[33] For a lawyer undertaking research it can create problems if the lawyer becomes too reliant on AI producing the most authoritative cases or commentary when they do not understand how results are generated and cannot independently assess the results.[34]

While it may be accepted that competence with technology may mean understanding AI, there remains an issue of what level of competence or understanding is needed. Michael Mills from Neota Logic explains that lawyers do not need to understand AI at the level of an engineer nor to be able to build the tool. Rather, Mills uses the analogy of being able to cross-examine the engineer, ie to be able to elicit what the engineer knows and what they can defend or not defend about the tool. This means being able to ask intelligent questions, evaluate the answers and then make a judgement about whether the tool is appropriate.[35] But, as we

[30] J Jouvenal, 'Police Are Using Software to Predict Crime. Is It a "Holy Grail" or Biased Against Minorities?', *Washington Post*, 17 November 2016.

[31] L Barrett, 'Reasonably Suspicious Algorithms: Predictive Policing at the United States Border' (2017) 41(3) *New York University Review of Law & Social Change* 327–66; Recent Cases, 'Wisconsin Supreme Court Requires Warning before Use of Algorithmic Risk Assessments in Sentencing' (2017) 130 *Harvard Law Review* 1530.

[32] J Baker, 'Beyond the Information Age: The Duty of Technology Competence in the Algorithmic Society' (2018) 69 *South Carolina Law Review* 557, 571.

[33] *Australian Competition and Consumer Commission v Trivago NV* [2020] FCA 16, where statements on a website that the best price hotels would be found for users was misleading as the algorithm had been programmed to give priority to hotels that advertised with the website.

[34] Baker (n 32) 571–73.

[35] Legal Talk Network, 'The Intersection of Ethics and Artificial Intelligence', *Digital Detectives Podcast*, 30 January 2020.

discuss below in relation to independence and regulation, some forms of AI are more transparent and easier to explain and understand than others.

So how then does a lawyer ensure technological competence? In 2015 the State Bar of California Standing Committee on Professional Responsibility and Conduct issued Formal Opinion 2015-193, in which it considered the ethical obligations of a lawyer in handling discovery of electronically stored information. That Committee concluded that a lawyer's obligations under California's rules governing competence 'evolve as new technologies develop and become integrated with the practice of law'. Specifically, the Committee stated that competence in the practice of litigation 'requires, among other things, and at a minimum, a basic understanding of, and facility with, issues related to e-discovery, including the discovery of electronically stored information'. The Committee concluded that a lawyer lacking the required competence for e-discovery has three options: (1) acquire sufficient learning and skill themselves; (2) associate with or consult technical consultants or other competent lawyers; or (3) decline the representation.[36]

Turning to the first suggestion of the California Bar, obtain learning and skill, one US federal court, the Northern District of Illinois, in addressing discovery of electronically stored information advised lawyers not to 'freak out' and to review available educational materials.[37] The Court pointed out that consulting materials on TAR was the same as consulting a medical dictionary for a personal injury case. One of the goals of this book is to provide lawyers with greater understanding of how AI works in a range of different contexts. Lawyers who are looking at using an AI tool should ask the vendor for a demonstration and supporting documentation (often called a white paper) that explains how the tool works. The lawyer must be comfortable that they understand the capabilities and limitations of the tool so they can determine, first, if the tool is suitable and, second, if it is working as intended.

The second option recognises that lawyers may need to seek the assistance of experts in AI. The Canadian and Hong Kong rules on professional conduct advise that a lawyer should recognise that competence for a particular task may require seeking advice from or collaborating with experts in scientific, accounting or other non-legal fields.[38]

Lawyers routinely use both non-lawyer employees and outside independent contractors to assist in providing legal services to clients. In the US this practice,

[36] The State Bar of California Standing Committee on Professional Responsibility and Conduct, Formal Opinion 2015-193. See also Federation of Law Societies (FLSC) of Canada's Model Code of Professional Conduct, 14 March 2017, r 3.1-2, commentary [6].

[37] *City of Rockford v Mallinckrodt ARD Inc*, 326 FRD 489, 492 n2 (ND Ill 2018) referring to the Grossman-Cormack Glossary of Technology-Assisted Review (2013) 7 *Federal Courts Law Review* 1; The Sedona Conference Glossary: E-Discovery & Digital Information Management, (2014) 15 *Sedona Conference Journal* 305.

[38] Federation of Law Societies (FLSC) of Canada's Model Code of Professional Conduct, 14 March 2017, r 3.1-2, commentary [7]; The Hong Kong Solicitors' Guide to Professional Conduct, r 6.01, commentary [5].

which is described as 'outsourcing', is permissible under the Model Rules as long as one or more lawyers sufficiently control the work being performed and also exercise reasonable care in the selection and, where necessary, training of the non-lawyers.[39] As noted, for example, in ABA Formal Opinion 08-451:

> A lawyer may outsource legal or nonlegal support services provided the lawyer remains ultimately responsible for rendering competent legal services to the client under Model Rule 1.1. In complying with her Rule 1.1 obligations, a lawyer who engages lawyers or nonlawyers to provide outsourced legal or nonlegal services is required to comply with Rules 5.1 and 5.3.[40] She should make reasonable efforts to ensure that the conduct of the lawyers or nonlawyers to whom tasks are outsourced is compatible with her own professional obligations as a lawyer with 'direct supervisory authority' over them.

The use of AI may be considered to amount to 'outsourcing' work to the third-party AI vendor.[41] In relation to electronic discovery utilising a third-party vendor, a US court held that the lawyers were responsible for the vendor's errors.[42] Similarly in other jurisdictions expert assistance can help a lawyer in gaining understanding and proficiency but it is still the lawyer's competence that is the focus in relation to professional obligations. The lawyer cannot delegate their own competence.

Central to competence is knowledge. We focus on education for lawyers in Chapter 12.

Duty to Client

The duty to the client is typically characterised by requirements of loyalty, partisanship and acting in the client's best interests.[43] The lawyer is required to put the client's interests before their own, although the lawyer is permitted to charge a fee for the services they provide. The lawyer must also retain independence and take account of their duty to the court and the administration of justice, which are discussed below.

The Preamble to the ABA Model Rules recognises a 'lawyer's obligation zealously to protect and pursue a client's legitimate interests, within the bounds of the law'.[44] The Restatement of the Law Governing Lawyers requires a lawyer to 'proceed in a manner reasonably calculated to advance a client's lawful objectives'.[45]

[39] Hazard, Hodes and Jarvis (n 20) §49.04.

[40] Rule 5.3 requires supervision by a lawyer where there is non-lawyer assistance. In 2012 the title of the rule was changed from 'Nonlawyer Assistants' to 'Nonlawyer Assistance' to 'encompass nonlawyers whether human or not': American Bar Association, Report on Resolution 112, August 2019, 6.

[41] T Spahn, 'Legal Ethics and Artificial Intelligence: Final Frontier or Today's Reality?' in *The American Law Institute Continuing Legal Education Course Materials*, 22 February 2018, 52.

[42] *In re Seroquel Prod. Liability Litigation*, 244 FRD 650, 664 (MD Fla 2007).

[43] A Boon, *The Ethics and Conduct of Lawyers in England and Wales* (3rd edn, Hart Publishing, 2015) 333; Dal Pont (n 13) 113–14.

[44] American Bar Association Model Rules of Professional Conduct, Preamble [9].

[45] Restatement (Third) of Law Governing Lawyers (2000) §16.

It also draws the link between the lawyer's competence and protection of client confidentiality as aspects of the duty to the client. The Restatement then links the duty to the client with the lawyer's role as a fiduciary where the lawyer is entrusted with another person's affairs but the other person cannot supervise performance, meaning special safeguards are needed – namely the imposition of the ethical duty to the client but also general law protections, which are discussed below.[46] Acting in the client's best interests includes ascertaining the client's goals and consulting as to the course of action to be pursued.[47]

In England and Wales the Solicitors Regulation Authority Principles mandate that solicitors 'act … in the best interests of each client'.[48] The Code of Conduct for Solicitors, Registered European Lawyers and Registered Foreign Lawyers then requires that 'You give clients information in a way they can understand. You ensure they are in a position to make informed decisions about the services they need, how their matter will be handled and the options available to them'.[49]

In Australia a solicitor must 'act in the best interests of a client in any matter in which the solicitor represents the client'.[50] In Canada the duty to the client is at its zenith in relation to advocacy where 'the lawyer has a duty to the client to raise fearlessly every issue, advance every argument and ask every question, however distasteful, that the lawyer thinks will help the client's case and to endeavour to obtain for the client the benefit of every remedy and defence authorized by law'.[51] Outside of the advocacy context '[a] lawyer has a duty to provide courteous, thorough and prompt service to clients. The quality of service required of a lawyer is service that is competent, timely, conscientious, diligent, efficient and civil'.[52] Singapore and Hong Kong also impose similar duties to the client.[53]

As discussed in relation to competence, AI may improve the quality and/or efficiency of the lawyer's work. This can mean a better result for the client. AI can assist the lawyer in promoting the client's interests by bringing about the outcome the client seeks – winning at litigation (which can include a settlement) or bringing a transaction to successful completion. For example, if machine learning aids in finding the key documents in litigation or as part of due diligence then acting in the client's best interests requires the use of the AI tool.

[46] Restatement (Third) of Law Governing Lawyers (2000) §16 comment b.

[47] American Bar Association's Model Rules of Professional Conduct, r 1.4; Restatement (Third) of Law Governing Lawyers (2000) §16 comment c.

[48] Solicitors Regulation Authority (England and Wales), Principles, principle 7.

[49] Solicitors Regulation Authority (England and Wales), Code of Conduct for Solicitors, Registered European Lawyers and Registered Foreign Lawyers, r 8.6.

[50] Legal Profession Uniform Law Australian Solicitors' Conduct Rules 2015, r 4.1.1.

[51] Federation of Law Societies (FLSC) of Canada's Model Code of Professional Conduct, 14 March 2017, r 5.1-1 and commentary [1].

[52] Federation of Law Societies (FLSC) of Canada's Model Code of Professional Conduct, 14 March 2017, r 3.2-1.

[53] The Hong Kong Solicitors' Guide to Professional Conduct, r 7.01; Legal Profession (Professional Conduct) Rules 2015 (Singapore) r 5.

This argument has also been made in medicine, where AI is used as a diagnostic tool. Machine learning programs may already be more accurate than human experts at, for example, analysing visual data such as X-rays, Magnetic Resonance Imaging (MRI) and Computed Tomography (CT) scans.[54] As within the legal services industry, partnerships are arising between (for example) IBM Watson and various hospitals and providers of medical imaging programs, seeking to utilise vast amounts of patient data. Implications for human doctors are also somewhat similar; their expertise will still be needed, but they will have new and powerful tools to use as well. Would a doctor fail to act in the patient's best interests if they performed a diagnosis without using available AI technology?

The charging of fees is also part of professional responsibility. The American Bar Association Model Rules provide that a lawyer 'shall not make an agreement for, charge, or collect an unreasonable fee or an unreasonable amount for expenses'.[55] The Code of Conduct for Solicitors, Registered European Lawyers and Registered Foreign Lawyers requires that

> [y]ou ensure that clients receive the best possible information about how their matter will be priced and, both at the time of engagement and when appropriate as their matter progresses, about the likely overall cost of the matter and any costs incurred.[56]

In Canada '[a] lawyer must not charge or accept a fee or disbursement, including interest, unless it is fair and reasonable and has been disclosed in a timely fashion'.[57] In Australia legal fees must be fair, reasonable and proportionate.[58]

Andrew Arruda, the CEO of ROSS Intelligence (an AI legal research tool), has argued that lawyers have an ethical obligation *to use* AI in their work so as to not charge excessive fees.[59] Arruda's argument is that AI can save so much time that it would be unethical for lawyers to bill for doing these tasks manually or using (for example) inferior technology. The American Bar Association's Science and Technology Section appears to accept this argument. It states in its report in support of Resolution 112, which urges courts and lawyers to address the ethical issues arising from the use of AI, that 'Failing to use AI technology that materially reduces

[54] C Garling, 'A Startup Hopes to Teach Computers to Spot Tumors in Medical Scans', *MIT Technology Review*, 22 August 2014, www.technologyreview.com/s/530261/a-startup-hopes-to-teach-computers-to-spot-tumors-in-medical-scans/.

[55] American Bar Association Model Rules of Professional Conduct, r 1.5.

[56] Solicitors Regulation Authority (England and Wales), Code of Conduct for Solicitors, Registered European Lawyers and Registered Foreign Lawyers, r 8.7.

[57] Federation of Law Societies (FLSC) of Canada's Model Code of Professional Conduct, 14 March 2017, r 3.6-1.

[58] *Legal Profession Uniform Law 2014* (NSW) s 172.

[59] A Arruda, 'An Ethical Obligation to Use Artificial Intelligence: An Examination of the Use of Artificial Intelligence in Law and the Model Rules of Professional Responsibility' (2017) 40(3) *American Journal of Trial Advocacy* 443, 455–56. See also R Simon, 'Artificial Intelligence, Real Ethics', *New York State Bar Association Journal*, April 2018; A Bernstein, 'Minding the Gaps in Lawyers' Rules of Professional Conduct' (2019) 72 *Oklahoma Law Review* 125, 131.

the costs of providing legal services arguably could result in a lawyer charging an unreasonable fee to a client'.[60]

Confidentiality and Legal Professional Privilege

The American Bar Association Model Rules of Professional Conduct Rule 1.6 states that 'a lawyer shall not reveal information relating to the representation of a client unless the client gives informed consent, the disclosure is impliedly authorized in order to carry out the representation' or the disclosure is permitted by certain exceptions such as to prevent the client from committing a crime or fraud, for the lawyer to obtain ethics advice, or to comply with another law or a court order.[61] US lawyers also have a duty to protect that information and it is set forth in Rule 1.6(c), which states: 'A lawyer shall make reasonable efforts to prevent the inadvertent or unauthorized disclosure of, or unauthorized access to, information relating to the representation of a client'.[62]

Similarly, in England and Wales the lawyer must 'keep the affairs of current and former clients confidential unless disclosure is required or permitted by law or the client consents'.[63] Australia, Canada, Singapore and Hong Kong impose confidentiality requirements on lawyers in relation to past and present clients as well.[64] The commentary to the Canadian rules explains that

> [a] lawyer cannot render effective professional service to a client unless there is full and unreserved communication between them. At the same time, the client must feel completely secure and entitled to proceed on the basis that, without any express request or stipulation on the client's part, matters disclosed to or discussed with the lawyer will be held in strict confidence.[65]

Legal professional privilege, also called attorney–client privilege, protects from disclosure communications between a client and their lawyer, made for the purpose of giving or obtaining legal advice or the provision of legal services, including representation in legal proceedings.[66] The rationale for the privilege is 'that it promotes the public interest because it assists and enhances the administration of

[60] American Bar Association, Report in Support of Resolution 112, August 2019, 6.

[61] American Bar Association Model Rules of Professional Conduct, r 1.6.

[62] ibid r 1.6(c).

[63] Solicitors Regulation Authority (England and Wales), Code of Conduct for Solicitors, Registered European Lawyers and Registered Foreign Lawyers, r 6.3.

[64] Legal Profession Uniform Law Australian Solicitors' Conduct Rules 2015, r 9; Federation of Law Societies (FLSC) of Canada's Model Code of Professional Conduct, 14 March 2017, rr 3.3-1–3.3-7; The Hong Kong Solicitors' Guide to Professional Conduct, r 8.01; Legal Profession (Professional Conduct) Rules 2015 (Singapore) r 6.

[65] Commentary to Federation of Law Societies of Canada's Model Code of Professional Conduct, October 2019.

[66] *Daniels Corporation International Pty Ltd v Australian Competition and Consumer Commission* (2002) 213 CLR 543 at [9] (dominant purpose in Australia); Restatement (Third) of Law Governing Lawyers (2000) §68.

justice by facilitating the representation of clients by legal advisers'. Legal professional privilege achieves this by maintaining secrecy over communications, which in turn induces the client 'to make a full and frank disclosure of the relevant circumstances to the solicitor'.[67] The UK House of Lords summarised the effect of the privilege as the lawyer's 'mouth is shut for ever'.[68]

The issue of technology and confidentiality has previously been considered in a number of contexts, namely the use of mobile phones, email, wireless technologies (such as public Wi-Fi) and data storage in the 'cloud'. In each case concerns over loss of confidentiality and privilege were raised. US bar associations addressed these concerns through alerting lawyers to the need for caution and inquiry as to how the communications are or can be protected.[69] The California Bar provided a useful list of issues for the lawyer to consider in evaluating an expectation of confidentiality and the ramifications of confidentiality being lost when determining whether to use a particular technology:

> 1) the level of security attendant to the use of that technology, including whether reasonable precautions may be taken when using the technology to increase the level of security; 2) the legal ramifications to a third party who intercepts, accesses or exceeds authorized use of the electronic information; 3) the degree of sensitivity of the information; 4) the possible impact on the client of an inadvertent disclosure of privileged or confidential information or work product; 5) the urgency of the situation; and 6) the client's instructions and circumstances, such as access by others to the client's devices and communications.[70]

It should be noted that while a key concern is cybersecurity, and law firms have been 'hacked', meaning that complacency as to security is unwise,[71] lawyers also need to focus on human error and inadvertent disclosure.[72]

The issue in relation to AI is that client (or law firm) communications, including electronic versions of documents, may need to be analysed by the AI as part of its use. Machine learning applications generally require a volume of data in order to be trained, so the status of this data must be clarified in order to maintain its confidentiality. For example, an AI product can be used to cite check a memorandum of law or court submissions to ensure that cases have not been overruled or questioned, and to suggest additional cases. However, to perform this function the draft and confidential memo/submission must be accessed by the AI product.[73]

[67] *Grant v Downs* (1976) 135 CLR 674 at 685. See also *R v Derby Magistrates' Court* [1995] UKHL 18; Restatement (Third) of Law Governing Lawyers (2000) §68 comment e.

[68] *R v Derby Magistrates' Court* [1995] UKHL 18, [48], citing *Wilson v Rastall* (1792) 4 Term Rep 753.

[69] Spahn (n 41) 34–41. See also Littrich and Murray (n 13) 278–79 for the similar Australian position.

[70] State Bar of California Standing Committee on Professional Responsibility and Conduct, Formal Opinion 2010-179 (2010).

[71] C Simmons, X Dong and B Hancock, 'More Than 100 Law Firms Have Reported Data Breaches. And the Problem Is Getting Worse', *Law.com*, 15 October 2019.

[72] Littrich and Murray (n 13) 278–79.

[73] Simon (n 59).

Another example would be the use of natural language processing in relation to speech. The AI will need to be given the recorded speech to convert it to written text. This then raises a number of questions: Are the recordings being saved? If so, who owns them or has access to them? Are the recordings being used for AI improvement? What security measures are in place?[74] If the recording contains confidential or privileged information the lawyer needs to obtain assurances that the recording will remain confidential and not be disseminated. Indeed, it would be prudent to go further and require that the recording be deleted after it has been converted to text.

Independence

Professional independence is typically discussed in relation to different pressures upon lawyers – commercial interests, pressure from more senior colleagues or employers and from demanding clients.[75] The definition of independence is the ability to act and to exercise judgement free from external pressure. The meaning of independence, however, can be ambiguous. As Bruce Green has noted, 'professional independence means independence from clients. This can be either a state of mind, eg, detachment or objectivity, or something more tangible'; however, at other times it 'implies independence from the pressures and influences of others who might compromise lawyers' loyalty to clients'.[76]

The first definition is important as it reinforces the duty to the administration of justice, one of the lawyer's fundamental duties. The second places the emphasis on the importance of the lawyer's loyalty to the client.[77]

The American Bar Association Model Rule 2.1 provides:

> In representing a client, a lawyer shall exercise independent professional judgment and render candid advice. In rendering advice, a lawyer may refer not only to law but to other considerations such as moral, economic, social and political factors that may be relevant to the client's situation.

In England and Wales the Solicitors Regulation Authority Principles mandate that 'you act … with independence'.[78] In Australia the Uniform Solicitors Rules specify that solicitors must 'avoid any compromise to their integrity and professional

[74] S Teicher, 'Tech Tock, Tech Tock: The Countdown to Your Ethical Demise' (2019) 31 *Journal of the American Academy of Matrimonial Lawyers* 481, 507; American Bar Association, Report in Support of Resolution 112, August 2019, 6.

[75] IBA Presidential Task Force on the Independence of the Legal Profession, 'The Independence of the Legal Profession: Threats to the Bastion of a Free and Democratic Society' (2016); G Dal Pont, 'Independence Rules' (2018) 92(4) *Law Institute Journal* 60.

[76] B Green, 'Lawyers' Professional Independence: Overrated or Undervalued?' (2013) 46 *Akron Law Review* 599, 608.

[77] M Regan Jr, Z Hutchinson and J Aiken, 'Lawyer Independence in Context: Lessons from Four Practice Settings' (2016) 29 *Georgetown Journal of Legal Ethics* 153, 204.

[78] Solicitors Regulation Authority (England and Wales), Principles, principle 3.

independence'.[79] Moreover in relation to advocacy, the lawyer 'must not act as the mere mouthpiece of the client'.[80]

The first challenge of regulating lawyers' use of AI is whether such 'outsourcing', even if on a small scale, could compromise a lawyer's independent judgement.[81] It is argued that if a lawyer is relying on software outputs (whether about the most relevant precedent case, most important contractual clauses, or likely outcome of proposed litigation), they are not exercising independent professional judgement.[82]

Accordingly, it is suggested that lawyers should treat AI 'like a junior associate' and carry out their usual supervisory role.[83] Indeed, this is the approach in the US in relation to complying with the competence requirement as discussed above. Yet this is complicated by the fact that lawyers may not be able to independently evaluate the functioning of the software due to their own lack of technical knowledge, which is quite different to supervising a junior lawyer.[84] There is also the lack of transparency in a system's functioning, or the fact that no one (even its developers) may fully understand how its conclusions were reached. The Organisation for Economic Co-operation and Development Working Party on Competition and Regulation has referred to this as the creation of new information asymmetries, wherein those reliant upon technology are unable to assess its quality.[85] This is discussed further below in relation to regulation. However, not all AI is unable to be tested. The supervised machine learning used in TAR for discovery is able to be tested using statistical sampling as explained in Chapter 5.[86]

Nonetheless, the lawyer will still retain professional responsibility and liability (as discussed below) for decisions made in the course of the retainer, even if AI has had input into them. Accordingly, one argument is that rules of professional conduct should be clarified to ensure that lawyers verify the results generated by AI software and use it only as an 'assisting tool' rather than 'an autonomous agent'.[87] However, this may impact upon the efficiency of using the tool in the first place.

Duty to the Administration of Justice – Rule of Law

As discussed in Chapter 6, lawyers have a duty to the court, or the administration of justice. While the duty is enforced by the court it is 'owed to the larger

[79] Legal Profession Uniform Law Australian Solicitors' Conduct Rules 2015, r 4.1.4.

[80] ibid r 17.1.

[81] Bernstein (n 59) 132.

[82] Medianik (n 23) 1518.

[83] ibid.

[84] D Remus, 'The Uncertain Promise of Predictive Coding' (2014) 99 *Iowa Law Review* 1691.

[85] OECD Directorate for Financial and Enterprise Affairs Competition Committee, Working Party No 2 on Competition and Regulation, *Protecting and Promoting Competition in Response to 'Disruptive' Innovations in Legal Services*, 13 June 2016, [63].

[86] Walker (n 24).

[87] Medianik (n 23) 1527–28.

community which has a vital public interest in the proper administration of justice'.[88] In England and Wales the Solicitors Regulation Authority principles commence with the statement that 'You act … in a way that upholds the constitutional principle of the rule of law, and the proper administration of justice'.[89] In England, Lord Reid stated how the duty to the court interacted with the duty to the client in *Rondel v Worsley*:

> Every counsel has a duty to his client fearlessly to raise every issue, advance every argument, and ask every question, however distasteful, which he thinks will help his client's case. But, as an officer of the court concerned in the administration of justice, he has an overriding duty to the court, to the standards of his profession, and to the public, which may and often does lead to a conflict with his client's wishes or with what the client thinks are his personal interests. Counsel must not mislead the court, he must not lend himself to casting aspersions on the other party or witnesses for which there is no sufficient basis in the information in his possession, he must not withhold authorities or documents which may tell against his clients but which the law or the standards of his profession require him to produce.[90]

However, as Lord Hobhouse explained in *Medcalf v Mardell*, the duty to 'represent his lay client and promote and protect fearlessly and by all proper and lawful means his lay client's best interests' is also in the public interest because it allows for 'rights, obligations and liabilities [to] be recognised and given effect to in accordance with the law and disputes be justly (and efficiently) resolved'.[91]

In Australia the position is stated succinctly: 'A solicitor's duty to the court and the administration of justice is paramount and prevails to the extent of inconsistency with any other duty'.[92] Singapore's Professional Conduct rules provide that a legal practitioner has 'a duty to assist in the administration of justice, and must act honourably in the interests of the administration of justice'.[93] Further a legal practitioner must conduct cases 'in a manner which maintains the fairness, integrity and efficiency of those proceedings and which is consistent with due process'.[94] In Canada the duty to the client is circumscribed by the lawyer needing to act legally and not mislead the court or abuse its processes.[95] The Canadian lawyer's zeal in furthering the interests of their client is tempered by a need to take into account that 'she is not simply a servant of her client; that she has a responsibility to further the administration of justice'.[96] The US recognises a duty to the court but

[88] D Ipp, 'Lawyers' Duties to the Court' (1998) 114 *Law Quarterly Review* 63, 63.
[89] Solicitors Regulation Authority (England and Wales), Principles, principle 1.
[90] *Rondel v Worsley* [1969] 1 AC 191, 227. See also Boon (n 43) 684.
[91] *Medcalf v Mardell* [2002] UKHL 27; [2003] 1 AC 120, [51].
[92] Legal Profession Uniform Law Australian Solicitors' Conduct Rules 2015, r 3.
[93] Legal Profession (Professional Conduct) Rules 2015 (Singapore) r 9(1)(a).
[94] ibid r 9(1)(e).
[95] Federation of Law Societies of Canada's Model Code of Professional Conduct, 14 March 2017, r 5.1-2
[96] A Woolley, 'Integrity in Zealousness: Comparing the Standard Conceptions of the Canadian and American Lawyer' (1996) 9 *Canadian Journal of Law and Jurisprudence* 61, 92.

its interaction with the duty to the client appears to have varied over time. The duty to the client is expressed as the lawyer's first duty but it is subject to the need to stay within the law. Zealous representation therefore justified pushing to the very limits of permissible conduct.[97] However, this extreme level of engagement seems to have lost favour more recently.[98]

While a lawyer undoubtedly has a duty to the court, especially as admission to practice results in the lawyer being an officer of the court,[99] the position taken here is that the duty to the administration of justice is broader than the duty to the court. It extends beyond obligations to not break the law or mislead the court as part of representing a client.[100] The duty to the administration of justice includes upholding the rule of law. The position is eloquently stated by Lon Fuller and John Randall:

> The lawyer's highest loyalty is at the same time the most intangible. It is a loyalty that runs, not to persons, but to procedures and institutions. The lawyer's role imposes on him a trustee ship for the integrity of those fundamental processes of government and self-government upon which the successful functioning of our society depends.[101]

The duty to the administration of justice, to uphold the rule of law, speaks to the lawyer's role in a democratic or civil society. The lawyer as a professional must act in the service of the public and seek to promote the elements of the rule of law, such as equality and fairness. Anthony Kronman argues that for a lawyer to lead a responsible professional life the lawyer must concern themselves with the 'integrity of the rules and institutions that form the framework' of society.[102] Further the lawyer must actively seek to better those arrangements lest the law 'loses its status as a calling and degenerates into a tool with no more inherent dignity than a hammer or a gun'.[103] While this view may be applied to the structures and balances needed for a democratic or civil society, the aim here is to turn that professional-ethical obligation towards technology, and AI in particular.

Technology is frequently assumed to be mechanistic, value free or morally neutral. Big Data analytics, in particular, is portrayed as enabling an accurate reflection of the world due to the capacity to process vast amounts of data with speed and accuracy. The insights generated come from maths and statistics on a grand scale. This also enables not just a look at the past, but the generation of predictions. Machine learning finds relationships or patterns in data through using various algorithms. Yet the effects of technology are not always benign. In the case

[97] Y Ross, *Ethics in Law* (5th edn, LexisNexis, 2010) 498–99.

[98] Boon (n 43) 322–25.

[99] Ipp (n 88) 66.

[100] See Boon (n 43) 327.

[101] L Fuller and J Randall, 'Professional Responsibility: Report of the Joint Conference' (1958) 44 (12) *American Bar Association Journal* 1159, 1162.

[102] A Kronman, *The Lost Lawyer: Failing Ideals of the Legal Profession* (Harvard University Press, 1993) 364.

[103] ibid.

of machine learning, quality is dependent on the data with which the system is provided, as well as the design of the system itself, including the cleaning of data and choice of algorithm. If data with latent social biases is used, outputs may also be biased, disadvantaging particular societal groups based on gender, race, age or other protected characteristics. In the justice system, those biases may find their way into processes such as applications for bail, with serious consequences for the rule of law.[104]

Lawyers must understand the technology that they use not just to ensure compliance with their professional conduct rules, but as part of the larger role that they play in society of upholding the rule of law. The use of black box technology could change the legal system in fundamental ways.[105] In the past the duty to the administration of justice may have meant representing unpopular persons. Today it may mean questioning (un)popular technology, especially where it interfaces with the justice system.

Access to Justice

A lawyer has an ethical duty to facilitate access to justice. As the main possessors of legal knowledge and skills, and with typically a monopoly on exercising these, lawyers have a key role to play in ensuring access to the justice system. Indeed, providing access is in keeping with the duty to the administration of justice and upholding the rule of law because equality before the law is only possible if all citizens can access the law.[106]

In the US the American Bar Association Model Rules provide that 'Every lawyer has a professional responsibility to provide legal services to those unable to pay'; moreover 'a lawyer should aspire to render at least (50) hours of pro bono publico[107] legal services per year'.[108] In Canada, in relation to integrity, lawyers are encouraged to enhance the profession through activities such as 'participating in legal aid and community legal services programs or providing legal services on a pro bono basis'.[109] Other jurisdictions, such as England and Wales, and Australia, do not specify the undertaking of legal work for free or pro bono as an ethical

[104] See, eg, L Bennett Moses and J Chan, 'Using Big Data for Legal and Law Enforcement Decisions: Testing the New Tools' (2014) 37(2) *University of New South Wales Law Journal* 643.

[105] A Paliwala, 'Rediscovering Artificial Intelligence and Law: An Inadequate Jurisprudence?' (2016) 30(3) *International Review of Law, Computers & Technology* 107–14.

[106] D Rhode, 'Pro Bono in Principle and in Practice' (2003) 53 *Journal of Legal Education* 413, 431.

[107] Pro bono publico means for the public good. In the legal context it generally means the provision of legal services on a free or significantly reduced fee basis, with no expectation of a commercial return. See Australian Pro Bono Centre, *The Australian Pro Bono Manual* (Lexis Nexis, 2016) ch 1.2, setting out definitions from a number of jurisdictions.

[108] American Bar Association Model Rules of Professional Conduct, r 6.1.

[109] Federation of Law Societies (FLSC) of Canada's Model Code of Professional Conduct, 14 March 2017, commentary to r 2.1-2.

requirement in their rules, but it is accepted to be so.[110] In the UK in 2006, the slogan 'It's part of being a lawyer' was adopted to promote pro bono work.[111] The former Chief Justice of the Australian High Court, AM Gleeson, has explained that

> [t]he legal profession is a profession and not only a business … its members have a duty to temper their pursuit of individual self-interest; and … they have a collective obligation to do their best to make legal services available to needy people. Collectively, this is a matter of duty, not generosity.[112]

The duty to facilitate access to justice may be met through AI. At the individual lawyer level and at the profession level there is scope for AI to be used to assist those that cannot afford legal services to obtain advice, the drafting of documents and dispute resolution services.[113] AI may 'lower the barriers (financial, psychological, informational, and even physical) that people face in accessing the law and the legal system'.[114] In some cases the lawyer may be able to fulfil their duty through providing or directing the person to the AI-provided service or product. The delivery model of 'one-to-many', as opposed to 'one-to-one', offers the opportunity to serve unmet legal needs as the AI product once created can be used repeatedly without additional cost or effort.[115] However, it is also likely that the lawyer will still have a role to play in supporting the person during or after the use of the AI-provided service or product, depending on the complexity of the problem or what is at stake.

Before leaving the ethical obligation of the lawyer to facilitate access to justice, it is worth noting that the commercialisation of law and the concomitant inability of citizens to access justice has been one driver of AI. Disruption comes from new entrants who provide services to the under-served, or unserved, people in the market.[116]

[110] Boon (n 43) ch 15; P Baron and L Corbin, *Ethics and Legal Professionalism in Australia* (2nd edn, Oxford University Press, 2017) 249–53; Australian Pro Bono Centre, Statements of Principles for the National Pro Bono Target, www.probonocentre.org.au/provide-pro-bono/target/statement-of-principles/.

[111] J Corker, 'Pro Bono Assistance for Resolving Civil Disputes' in M Legg (ed), *Resolving Civil Disputes* (LexisNexis, 2016) 272 (first used during the fifth National Pro Bono Week in the UK (2006)).

[112] AM Gleeson, 'Opening Speech' (speech delivered at National Access to Justice and Pro Bono Conference, Melbourne, 11 August 2006) 5. See also *Re Foster* (1950) 50 SR (NSW) 149, 151 ('in a profession pecuniary success is not the only goal. Service is the ideal, and the earning of remuneration must always be subservient to this main purpose').

[113] See Supreme Court State of Arizona Task Force on the Delivery of Legal Services, 'Report and Recommendations', 4 October 2019, 9 (noting that AI platforms had stepped in to serve clients unserved by lawyers).

[114] Law Society of Ontario (n 8) 15. See also C Coumarelos et al, *Legal Australia-Wide Survey: Legal Need in Australia* (Law and Justice Foundation of NSW, 2012) 37–38 (discussing barriers to accessing legal advice).

[115] W Henderson, 'Legal Market Landscape Report: Commissioned by the State Bar of California' (2018) 11; Law Society of Ontario (n 8) 15.

[116] CM Christensen, M Raynor and R McDonald, 'What Is Disruptive Innovation?', *Harvard Business Review*, December 2015, 52. For an example see P Holley, '"Swipe Right to Sue": Now You Can File Lawsuits the Same Way You Find Hookups on Tinder', *Washington Post*, 16 October 2018 (describing Joshua Browder's Do Not Pay app); though there are notes of scepticism too: see, eg, EST Poppe, 'The Future is ~~Bright~~ Complicated: AI, Apps & Access to Justice' (2019) 72(1) *Oklahoma Law Review* 185.

Liability for AI

Using and implementing AI from a technical perspective means using and implementing software and computer systems. However, both software and hardware may not function correctly, resulting in various kinds of errors.[117] This then raises for consideration when the lawyer or the AI may be liable when the AI does not operate as expected.

The lawyer–client relationship is typically contractual but overlaid with tort and fiduciary duties. The law of legal malpractice provides an important further standard by which lawyers' behaviour may be judged. Tort and contract claims overlap with professional requirements of competence, and breach of fiduciary duty claims overlap with the duty to the client. Lawyers may also owe additional obligations to clients or third parties as a result of legislation or regulations. The most common example would be consumer protection legislation aimed at such matters as misleading conduct, unfair contract terms and unconscionability.

In each jurisdiction the standards for liability may vary from what is required in relation to lawyers' ethical responsibilities, however of main concern here is that the general law rather than codes of professional responsibility provide clients with a remedy – some form of compensation or possibly a court order stopping particular conduct, such as an injunction. Consequently the lawyer needs to be clear on the extent to which they are responsible for the actions or omissions of AI. As a result we now sketch the possible causes of action in relation to AI liability.

As the focus of liability regimes is to provide a remedy, a useful starting point is consideration of what the harm may be that requires a remedy. Typically the harm will be financial or, as expressed in some jurisdictions, pure economic loss. The AI fails to perform as expected, which causes loss to the client. Some examples can illustrate the possible harms. The risk for the lawyer is that they employ AI as part of due diligence or discovery and it fails to identify a relevant clause or document. In due diligence this has the effect that a risk, such as a warranty or inability to assign a contract, is not identified, causing the client loss. In discovery this could mean failing to comply with court orders which give rise to an order or sanction, such as costs, that impacts the client. Alternatively, documents that do not need to be discovered, or are subject to privilege, are provided to an opponent, which causes a case to be lost. Similarly, if AI is used for predicting litigation outcomes or whether regulatory laws such as anti-money laundering are complied with, and the AI gets it wrong so that litigation is lost or the client breaches the law, the client suffers loss. Some of these losses may be small but there is a risk that if a faulty review of a key document prevents a lucrative transaction or a failure to prevent a legal contravention results in a hefty fine, the loss could be significant. The client may sue the lawyer for these types of loss.

[117] World Economic Forum, 'AI Governance: A Holistic Approach to Implement Ethics into AI' (January 2019) 7.

The lawyer's liability commences with the terms of the retainer. There may also be concurrent liability in tort or statute. Generally speaking, the allegation will be that the lawyer was required to, but failed to, exercise reasonable care and skill.[118] The care and skill required may include choosing an appropriate AI product/service for the required task and monitoring the system's functioning and performance. The lawyer may include a term stating who would be legally responsible for the failure of the AI, or limiting liability to a particular quantum, or simply excluding the lawyer's liability. The limitation or exclusion of liability may extend to claims in tort. However, legislation may prohibit such terms, including on the basis that they are unfair contractual terms in relation to consumers, or require special attention be drawn to particularly onerous terms.[119]

If the lawyer is sued by the client then the lawyer may seek to recover from the AI product/service or to join them to any litigation. The AI product/service, absent recognition of AI as a legal person or a specifically crafted regime (which are discussed below in relation to regulation), is most likely to be subject to liability regimes based on contract, tort and product liability.[120] The lawyer may also need to determine who to claim against – the 'manufacturer' or owner of the AI program, or the third-party supplier that the lawyer obtained the AI product from (assuming that the two are different entities).

In relation to a contract or tort claim the question is what was the content or scope of the duty agreed or imposed by law on the AI provider, and did the AI perform in accordance with that duty? Under a product liability regime the question will typically be whether the product is defective, ie was there a design or manufacturing defect, or a failure to instruct or warn on the appropriate use of the AI?[121] Typically product liability regimes employ strict liability so that once a defect is found the manufacturer or supplier is liable regardless of fault or wrongdoing.[122] Other forms of product liability, such as implied terms of fitness for purpose, may also be applicable.

However, a number of uncertainties may arise. Causation is usually required under each cause of action. Proving cause and effect may be difficult if the operation of the AI is not readily explicable. This is more likely to be a problem with forms of machine learning such as deep learning where the AI finds correlations in

[118] See *Lanphier v Phipos* (1838) 173 English Rep 581, 583 ('Every person who enters into a learned profession under-takes to bring to it the exercise of it a reasonable degree of care and skill'); Restatement (Third) of Law Governing Lawyers (2000) §48 comment c; Hazard, Hodes and Jarvis (n 20); S Walmsley, B Zipser, A Abadee and G Sirtes, *Professional Liability in Australia* (3rd edn, Thomson Reuters, 2016) ch 3.

[119] J Turner, *Robot Rules* (Palgrave Macmillan, 2019) 106, 111–12.

[120] Expert Group on Liability and New Technologies – New Technologies Formation, *Liability for Artificial Intelligence* (European Union, 2019) 17; European Commission, On Artificial Intelligence – A European Approach to Excellence and Trust, 19 February 2020, 16 ('existing provisions of EU law will continue to apply in relation to AI').

[121] D Vladeck, 'Machines Without Principles: Liability Rules for Artificial Intelligence' (2014) 89 *Washington Law Review* 117, 127.

[122] Expert Group on Liability and New Technologies (n 120) 27.

data without explicit human programming so that unpicking the workings of the AI is more difficult, if not impossible.[123] The opacity of AI can become even more problematic when other causes of loss potentially exist. There is a question as to whether liability can be found when the AI requires user input or training, such as when the lawyer teaches the AI, as in relation to TAR for discovery.

In relation to product liability there may be difficulties in demonstrating a defect, or if a defect is found, the state-of-the-art defence may apply.[124] As for causation, a manufacturing or design defect necessitates understanding how the AI operates, which may be difficult. Moreover, the state-of-the-art defence shields an entity from liability if the state of scientific or technical knowledge at the time the good was supplied was such as to make the defect not discoverable. AI's difficulties with transparency and explainability may mean the defect could not be detected. Another defence is that the defect did not exist at the time of supply.[125] This may be applicable where a machine learning algorithm after supply subsequently adopts biases based on its operation and learning. Although these are principles of law, their application will turn on the particular factual circumstances surrounding the AI product.

To the extent that AI is used to produce advice or an output in response to individualised input from a user, 'it may be said to more closely resemble the paradigm of a service rather than a product'.[126] This may render a product liability regime inapplicable. However, laws for services may then apply, such as under the Australian Consumer Law, which states that in the supply of services to a consumer, there is a guarantee that the services will be rendered with due care and skill and the service will be fit for purpose.[127]

The above challenges also apply in relation to other professions such as medicine. Some have argued that medical liability regimes need to be amended to provide for the situation where an AI system is incorrect or leads to a patient suffering harm.[128] The same argument may be made in relation to lawyers, given the growing impact of AI systems. However, absent such a change the lawyer needs to take available steps consistent with their duty to the client to ensure that they choose appropriate AI products, that the AI is functioning correctly, or at least, that there is no indication of malfunctioning. The lawyer may need to retain an AI expert to assist them in discharging their duty.[129] The 'lawyer in the loop' may also be a way in which to prevent the above harms from AI. Indeed the lawyer may be

[123] ibid 20. See also Chapter 2 explaining the difference between expert systems and machine learning.
[124] Expert Group on Liability and New Technologies (n 120) 28.
[125] Turner (n 119) 98.
[126] ibid 96.
[127] *Competition and Consumer Act 2010* (Cth) Schedule 2 ss 60, 61.
[128] JS Allain, 'From Jeopardy to Jaundice: The Medical Liability Implications of Dr Watson and Other Artificial Intelligence Systems' (2013) 73 *Louisiana Law Review* 1049.
[129] P Hacker, R Krestel, S Grundmann and F Naumamm, 'Explainable AI under Contract and Tort Law: Legal Incentives and Technical Challenges' (2020) *Artificial Intelligence and Law*, doi.org/10.1007/s10506-020-09260-6.

expected to conduct a risk assessment of the AI outputs and determine to question particular recommendations or have human review of key documents or laws. For example, if the value of a business acquisition turns on particular contracts being capable of assignment then the lawyer will assess those herself. Further, the lawyer must have sufficient understanding of the AI to be able to assess the risks and when reliance on the AI alone is not reasonable. The downside of this approach is that the lawyer's preventative steps, if unsuccessful, may mean that the AI cannot be seen to be the cause of any harm or loss. While this is cold comfort for the lawyer, the positive side is that it provides a very good reason for a client to engage a lawyer rather than to rely on AI alone. Only the most novice of lawyers would not appreciate that clients may retain a lawyer not just to access their expertise, but also to be able to access their insurance coverage.

Regulation

The concept and reason for regulation may be summarised as follows:

> The act of regulating has been defined as controlling or directing by rule, principle or method. Rules and principles enable regulators to prohibit or allow certain conduct, communicate expectations and provide guidance as to what is required or allowed. Regulation seeks to govern, direct or alter human behaviour in particular areas of endeavour … Regulation may be embodied not just in legislation and regulations, but also in standards, policy statements, rulings, codes of conduct and the like.[130]

Regulation may be undertaken to achieve a range of goals, such as promoting or protecting competition. Another goal is to give effect to social policy. This involves advancing some conception of the public welfare and meeting human needs for such things as education, health, safety and a clean environment. Regulation aimed at social policy tends to cut across industry or sectors of the economy as a society-wide outcome is desired. The regulation may seek to directly intervene in societal affairs or indirectly shape social behaviour. Examples include occupational, health and safety legislation, anti-discrimination legislation and consumer protection legislation.[131] Consumer protection is an important strand of social regulation because of the existence of information asymmetry, which exposes the consumer to various risks, such as receiving a defective or unsuitable product. Social regulation has therefore been described as 'an essential element of a just and humane society, protecting those most vulnerable to the depredations inevitable in an industrial setting'.[132] Today we may say it is to protect all persons, including the vulnerable, in an informational or data-centric setting.

[130] M Legg, 'Regulatory Theory, Litigation and Enforcement' in M Legg (ed), *Regulation, Litigation and Enforcement* (Thomson Reuters, 2011) 1.
[131] ibid 4–5; G Bryner, 'Trends in Social Regulation' in D Rosenbloom and R Schwartz (eds), *Handbook of Regulation and Administrative Law* (CRC Press, 1994) 73–74.
[132] P Schuck, 'Book Review – The Politics of Regulation' (1981) 90 *Yale Law Journal* 702, 709.

The regulation of AI has largely been put forward to achieve various social policies, including preventing bias or discrimination in their operation, loss of privacy, lack of transparency and/or explainability, and lack of accountability.[133] These were discussed in Chapter 10 as limitations of AI and are briefly reiterated here.

Bias is a prejudice for or against something or somebody that may result in unfair decisions. Bias and discrimination arise because humans are biased and humans create and train AI. The data used to train machine learning reflects the human prejudice in the data used. The data may lack demographic or racial diversity so that biased patterns are identified. For example, the AI for image recognition may learn that CEOs or computer programmers are white men because the pool of images labelled 'CEO' and 'programmer' were skewed that way.[134]

AI requires data to be able to learn and function. Typically the more data the better, and much of that data includes sensitive personal information.[135] Even when data is anonymised the vast amount of data available can result in re-identification of a person.[136] AI when combined with the digitalisation of many domains, such as banking, shopping and even finding friends and partners, means that there are many more opportunities for 'generating, capturing and exploiting information that previously were essentially inaccessible'.[137] AI may impinge on a right to privacy, if otherwise recognised by law.

AI systems are often criticised for their lack of transparency.[138] The UK Information Commissioner's Office states: 'The complexity of the processing of data through such massive networks creates a "black box" effect. This causes an inevitable opacity that makes it very difficult to understand the reasons for decisions made as a result of deep learning'.[139] The Institute of Electrical and Electronics Engineers (IEEE) has identified that transparency is important for users of AI because it provides a simple way for them to understand what the system is doing and why.[140] However, the owners of an AI product may be unwilling to provide transparency because it can undermine the proprietary nature of the AI – if competitors can see how the AI functions they may be able to duplicate it.

Accountability generally refers to giving account of one's actions to some other person or body. Giving account means to explain or justify actions.[141] It also

[133] MU Scherer, 'Regulating Artificial Intelligence Systems: Risks, Challenges, Competencies, and Strategies' (2016) 29 *Harvard Journal of Law and Technology* 353.

[134] W Knight, 'AI Is Biased. Here's How Scientists Are Trying to Fix It', *Wired*, 19 December 2019; CS Smith, 'Dealing With Bias in Artificial Intelligence', *The New York Times*, 3 January 2020.

[135] V Mayer-Schoenberger and K Cukier, *Big Data* (First Mariner, 2013) 152.

[136] ibid 154–56.

[137] W Hoffmann-Riem, 'Artificial Intelligence as a Challenge for Law and Regulation' in T Wischmeyer and T Rademacher (eds), *Regulating Artificial Intelligence* (Springer, 2020) 17.

[138] World Economic Forum (n 117) 6.

[139] UK Government Office for Science, 'Artificial Intelligence: Opportunities and Implications for the Future of Decision Making' (2015) 16.

[140] IEEE Global Initiative on Ethics of Autonomous and Intelligent Systems (n 2) 29.

[141] C Scott, 'Accountability in the Regulatory State' (2000) 27 *Journal of Law and Society* 38, 40.

involves holding a person responsible for those actions.[142] In relation to AI the concern is that a lack of transparency makes it difficult to ascertain who or what is responsible for AI's actions.

Each of these concerns or risks may be addressed through a number of regulatory tools or approaches. The aim of the discussion here is not to consider or critique that regulation in depth. Rather it is to outline the types of regulations or protections that have been or may be formulated because if AI is regulated then that may assist the lawyer in meeting their ethical and legal obligations. If AI is well regulated than the lawyer will find it easier (not necessarily easy) to ascertain how a particular AI product functions so as to be able to assess whether it should be employed, including whether it will maintain confidences and not breach other laws. Equally, well-regulated AI will protect the consumer.

Principles

A common form of soft law or self-regulation is the adoption of AI ethics principles or guidelines. Indeed studies have identified at least 84 such initiatives,[143] leading to the observation that AI is being subject to 'principle proliferation'.[144] The frequency with which a principle appears in one of the 84 AI guideline documents is set out in Table 11.1. Another study of 22 guidelines sets out the issues covered by each guideline. The top five issues were: (1) privacy protection, (2) fairness, non-discrimination, justice, (3) accountability, (4) transparency, openness, and (5) safety, cybersecurity.[145] Yet another study set out five core principles derived from six AI ethics initiatives: (1) beneficence (promoting well-being, preserving dignity, and sustaining the planet), (2) non-maleficence (privacy, security and 'capability caution'), (3) autonomy (the power to decide), (4) justice (promoting prosperity, preserving solidarity, avoiding unfairness), and (5) explicability (enabling the other principles through intelligibility and accountability).[146]

These guidelines may provide direction for companies that produce AI products to adopt guidelines that operate within the company.[147] However, there is also a concern that principles may be 'mere virtue-signalling' aimed at forestalling government regulation or a focus on technical solutions.[148]

[142] P May, 'Regulatory Regimes and Accountability' (2007) 1 *Regulation & Governance* 8, 9; M Bovens, 'Analysing and Assessing Accountability: A Conceptual Framework' (2007) 13 *European Law Journal* 447, 450.

[143] A Jobin, M Ienca and E Vayena, 'The Global Landscape of AI Ethics Guidelines' (2019) 1 *Nature Machine Intelligence* 389; B Mittelstadt, 'Principles Alone Cannot Guarantee Ethical AI' (2019) 1 *Nature Machine Intelligence* 501.

[144] L Floridi and J Cowls, 'A Unified Framework of Five Principles for AI in Society' (2019) 1 *Harvard Data Science Review* 1, 2.

[145] T Hagendorff, 'The Ethics of AI Ethics: An Evaluation of Guidelines', *Minds and Machines* (Springer, 2020).

[146] Floridi and Cowls (n 144) 1.

[147] Hoffmann-Riem (n 137) 19.

[148] Mittelstadt (n 143) 501.

From the perspective of the lawyer utilising AI in legal practice the chief principle that would aid in ethical practice and limitation of liability, if adhered to, is explicability or transparency. This would also be central to a lawyer's role in challenging AI. In addition, preventing unfairness through discrimination or bias would be necessary from two perspectives: the accuracy or reliability of the AI outputs and avoiding contraventions of laws that prohibit discrimination, although in relation to the latter, lawyers do not typically use AI in a way that impacts individuals; rather it is to find documents or predict case outcomes. However, lawyers are likely to interact with AI that impacts their clients in the areas of civil dispute resolution and the criminal justice system. The acceptance of AI outcomes in both fields will turn on acceptance that they are fair, including not biased or discriminatory in their operation. The lawyer's obligations in relation to confidentiality will mean that privacy and security are key concerns in relation to client information.

Table 11.1 Ethical principles identified in AI guidelines

Ethical principle	Number of documents	Included codes
Transparency	73/84	Transparency, explainability, explicability, understandability, interpretability, communication, disclosure, showing
Justice and fairness	68/84	Justice, fairness, consistency, inclusion, equality, equity, (non-)bias, (non-)discrimination, diversity, plurality, accessibility, reversibility, remedy, redress, challenge, access and distribution
Non-maleficence	60/84	Non-maleficence, security, safety, harm, protection, precaution, prevention, integrity (bodily or mental), non-subversion
Responsibility	60/84	Responsibility, accountability, liability, acting with integrity
Privacy	47/84	Privacy, personal or private information
Beneficence	41/84	Benefits, beneficence, well-being, peace, social good, common good
Freedom and autonomy	34/84	Freedom, autonomy, consent, choice, self-determination, liberty, empowerment
Trust	28/84	Trust
Sustainability	14/84	Sustainability, environment (nature), energy, resources (energy)
Dignity	13/84	Dignity
Solidarity	6/84	Solidarity, social security, cohesion

Source: A Jobin, M Ienca and E Vayena, 'The Global Landscape of AI Ethics Guidelines' (2019) 1 *Nature Machine Intelligence* 389, 395, Table 3.

Technical Instructions, Standards and Design

Specification or design standards seek to prevent adverse outcomes by setting out how a product or process is to be created or undertaken so as to demonstrate a particular quality.[149] Instructions are typically more specific than standards and set out step-by-step requirements. The standards or instructions may be developed privately, by an industry association, by government or through some combination of the above.

The IEEE launched an initiative in December 2015 to ensure that technologists are educated, trained and empowered to prioritise ethical considerations in the design and development of autonomous and intelligent systems.[150] To this end, the IEEE Global Initiative issued the document, 'Ethically Aligned Design – A Vision for Prioritizing Human Well-being with Autonomous and Intelligent Systems'.[151] A second and more substantial version followed.[152] Of significance here is that the IEEE went a step beyond principles and also created working groups to develop standards, the IEEE P7000™ series, for AI and autonomous system designers. The standards include: Model Process for Addressing Ethical Concerns During System Design; Transparency of Autonomous Systems; Data Privacy Processes and Algorithmic Bias Considerations.[153] The purpose of the Standards is 'to allow organizations to demonstrate that their products conform to a high level of ethics'.[154]

While instructions and standards may be developed in the private sector they may have legal consequences when they are used to evaluate the standard of care in connection with claims in negligence.[155] Standards may also be evidence of the state of scientific or technical knowledge which is relevant to product liability laws.

Certification

In terms of regulating AI systems, one suggestion from the US is the creation of a government agency to certify AI systems for safety.[156] Under this proposal, the agency would not actually ban unsafe systems (as the US Food and Drug

[149] R Baldwin, M Cave and M Lodge, *Understanding Regulation* (2nd edn, Oxford University Press, 2012) 297; A Freiberg, *Regulation in Australia* (Federation Press, 2017) 211.

[150] R Chatila, K Firth-Butterfield, JC Havens and K Karachalios, 'IEEE Global Initiative Aims to Advance Ethical Design of AI and Autonomous Systems', 29 March 2017, spectrum.ieee.org/automaton/robotics/artificial-intelligence/ieee-global-initiative-ethical-design-ai-and-autonomous-systems.

[151] IEEE Global Initiative for Ethical Considerations in Artificial Intelligence and Autonomous Systems, *Ethically Aligned Design: A Vision for Prioritizing Wellbeing With Artificial Intelligence And Autonomous Systems* (IEEE, 2016).

[152] IEEE, 'New IEEE Standards for Artificial Intelligence Affecting Human Well-being', 8 August 2017.

[153] IEEE Global Initiative on Ethics of Autonomous and Intelligent Systems (n 2) 3–4.

[154] IEEE (n 152).

[155] Expert Group on Liability and New Technologies – New Technologies Formation, *Liability for Artificial Intelligence* (European Union, 2019) 23; Hoffmann-Riem (n 137) 21 (providing the example of IT security standards developed by a Bitkom working group).

[156] Scherer (n 133) 393.

Administration does) but would administer a liability system. Put simply, if the program was certified by the agency, its liability would be limited, while non-certified programs would be subject to a strict liability regime.[157] Another commentator has, however, identified issues with this proposal: first, that certification would require extensive knowledge of the technology, which may be difficult for a federal agency; secondly, that there are many types of AI system, so maintaining expertise across all of them would also be difficult; thirdly, that it will be hard for regulators to keep up with change; and finally, that even strict liability may not be a sufficient deterrent if the potential profits from the AI system are very considerable.[158]

Additional problems are that corporations might be updating their models so frequently as to make a certification requirement impractical or too expensive. There will also be difficulties related to setting appropriate review standards, finding qualified reviewers and operating the scheme. These could prove a significant challenge given that they would require expertise in both legal and technical fields. A last problematic factor would be keeping the review criteria secret, with a view to preventing vendors or other parties from manipulating the results.[159]

The EU has similarly raised the idea of prior conformity assessment and the use of procedures for testing, inspection or certification.[160] Indeed the EU's General Data Protection Regulation (GDPR), which is discussed further below, provides for accreditation by appropriate bodies and data protections seals and trademarks that indicate that a particular AI product is 'compliant' with specified standards or laws.[161] The *European Ethical Charter on the Use of Artificial Intelligence in Judicial Systems and their Environment* also endorsed a certification model as a way to ensure transparency and impartiality in the use of AI in the judicial system.[162]

These approaches apply equally well to the regulation of AI systems which are being used in the delivery of legal services. That is, while the expertise (both in-depth and broad – about many types of system) required would be considerable, and keeping up with change could also be challenging, it could be undertaken. Lawyers or their professional bodies could determine that only an AI product that was certified as meeting the requirements for data security, data confidentiality, anti-discrimination requirements and so on, could be employed.

Disclosure

Disclosure seeks to make private information public to overcome the problem of information asymmetry. Information asymmetry involves one party to a

[157] ibid 393.

[158] Medianik (n 23) 1500.

[159] R Yu and G Spina Ali, 'What's Inside the Black Box? AI Challenges for Lawyers and Researchers' (2019) *Legal Information Management* 2, 6.

[160] European Commission, 'On Artificial Intelligence – A European Approach to Excellence and Trust', 19 February 2020, 23

[161] Hoffmann-Riem (n 137) 21.

[162] European Commission for the Efficiency of Justice (CEPEJ), *European Ethical Charter on the Use of Artificial Intelligence (AI) in Judicial Systems and their Environment* (2018) 9.

transaction knowing more than the other party, which puts the less knowledgeable party at a disadvantage in terms of accurately determining price or other qualities of the good such as risk.[163] In the field of AI a range of disclosures are possible, from a warning that the person is interacting with a product that employs AI, to disclosure of the certifications or preventative measures undertaken, to adopting a requirement of explainability and setting out how the AI reaches a decision.

However, the recipient of the information is left to make their own assessment of the product and whether they wish to use/purchase it.[164] The deficiencies in this type of regulation are that users of the information disclosed need to have the necessary education, resources and incentives to be able to employ the information accurately in their decision making.[165]

These concerns may be particularly relevant to advanced AI and any attempt at explainability. Eric Siegal explained that 'decision trees [expert systems] are often considered the most user friendly … they consist of rules you can read like a long (if cumbersome) English sentence, while other methods are more mathy'.[166] Of course the user needs to have sufficient capability to engage with that long sentence. AI using neural networks may never be truly explainable because the calculations undertaken by the AI are far too numerous and complex for the human brain to be able to process so that any explanation will be a simplified version of what the AI is actually undertaking. As Cassie Kozyrkov, Chief Decision Intelligence Engineer, Google explains: 'AI is all about automating the ineffable, but don't expect the ineffable to be easy to wrap your head around'.[167]

Audit Trails

A further approach is the idea of an audit rating service to validate and certify the quality and accuracy of AI systems. The IEEE has recommended that AI systems used in law should generate audit trails recording the facts and law supporting decisions and such systems should be amenable to third-party verification to show that the trails reflect what the system in fact did.[168] Auditing when compared to certification may be seen as operating ex post rather than ex ante. Certification examines how the AI is intended to operate and whether it complies with the necessary requirements. Auditing looks at how the AI actually operated and whether compliance was achieved.[169] The two can be combined, rather than operating as

[163] S Breyer, 'Analyzing Regulatory Failure: Mismatches, Less Restrictive Alternatives and Reform' (1979) 92(3) *Harvard Law Review* 548, 556; Legg (n 130) 18.

[164] Breyer (n 163) 579.

[165] Legg (n 130) 18–19.

[166] E Siegel, *Predictive Analytics* (Wiley, 2016) 171.

[167] C Kozyrkov, 'Explainable AI Won't Deliver. Here's Why', *Hackernoon*, 17 November 2018, hackernoon.com/explainable-ai-wont-deliver-here-s-why-6738f54216be.

[168] IEEE Global Initiative on Ethics of Autonomous and Intelligent Systems (n 2) 153.

[169] M Favaretto, E De Clercq and BS Elger, 'Big Data and Discrimination: Perils, Promises and Solutions: A Systematic Review' (2019) *Journal of Big Data* 6, 15–16.

alternatives.[170] Auditing suffers from many of the drawbacks discussed above: the need for auditors with the relevant expertise, setting appropriate review standards, and ensuring sufficient demand and payment for such a service.

Legislation

Legislation may be principles based or rules based. The former is more open ended, while the latter is more prescriptive. Principles-based regulation is advantageous as it can remain applicable even as technological advancements or changes occur. However, a principles-based approach can create uncertainty, including not being interpreted by regulators or courts as expected.[171]

An example of a legislative approach is the GDPR agreed upon by the European Parliament and Council in April 2016, with effect from 25 May 2018, which regulates how companies protect EU citizens' personal data. It provides an example of a legislative response to the regulation of AI, albeit operating indirectly through its application to data.[172] The GDPR is enforceable in each Member State by its Data Protection Authority.

Article 5 of the GDPR sets out a number of principles applicable to personal data, including that it 'shall be … processed lawfully, fairly and in a transparent manner in relation to the data subject'[173] and 'processed in a manner that ensures appropriate security of the personal data'.

Article 9 contains a prohibition on the processing of personal data linked to fundamental rights and freedoms, including racial or ethnic origin, political opinions, religious beliefs, genetic data, and data concerning health. However, exceptions apply, including where there is consent to the processing of the personal data for one or more specified purposes, unless the law provides that the prohibition may not be lifted by the data subject.

Chapter 3 of the GDPR contains a number of rights for the data subject. This includes Article 13, which deals with the provision of information when personal data is collected from a data subject. Article 13(2)(f) provides that

> the controller shall, at the time when personal data are obtained, provide the data subject with the following further information necessary to ensure fair and transparent processing: …
>
> (f) the existence of automated decision-making, including profiling, referred to in Article 22(1) and (4) and, at least in those cases, *meaningful information about the logic involved*, as well as the significance and the envisaged consequences of such processing for the data subject (emphasis added).

[170] European Commission for the Efficiency of Justice (CEPEJ) (n 162) 9.
[171] C Diver, 'The Optimal Precision of Administrative Rules' (1983) 93 *Yale Law Journal* 65.
[172] O Rogynskyy, 'What GDPR Means for Businesses With an AI Strategy', *Forbes*, 6 September 2019.
[173] Data subject means an identified or identifiable natural person according to art 4.

The italicised text is also in Article 14(2)(g) (information to be provided where personal data have not been obtained from the data subject) and Article 15(1)(h) (the right to obtain from the controller confirmation as to whether or not personal data concerning him or her are being processed, and if so certain details about that personal data including the purposes of the processing; the categories of personal data concerned and meaningful information about the logic involved where there is automated decision-making).

Article 22(1) states that 'The data subject shall have the right not to be subject to a decision based solely on automated processing, including profiling, which produces legal effects concerning him or her or similarly significantly affects him or her'. Article 22 then goes on to set out exceptions, such as consent, and protections, such as implementing 'suitable measures to safeguard the data subject's rights and freedoms and legitimate interests, at least the right to obtain human intervention on the part of the controller, to express his or her point of view and to contest the decision'.

Scholars are divided over whether the above provisions create a 'right to an explanation'. Sandra Wachter, Brent Mittelstadt and Luciano Floridi argue that there is no explicit right to an explanation, with that language only appearing in non-binding recital 71 of the Preamble to the GDPR.[174] Rather there is only a right to be informed of system functionality, ie the general structure and architecture of the processing model, but not about individual decisions or concrete weights and features of the model.[175]

In response, Andrew Selbst and Julia Powles argue that the italicised text above relates to the rights of the data subject so that meaningful information means meaningful to the data subject, which is a human without technical expertise. Further, to be meaningful it must facilitate the date subject's exercise of their rights.[176]

The goal here is not to enter the statutory construction debate. However, it can be agreed that the utility of such a protection is low if the consumer is only handed 'a description of the particular deep learning algorithm used to train the classifier that made the decision'.[177] Similarly, if the requirement might be satisfied by a data dump of millions of lines of code it does not assist with explicability.[178] Equally, legislation can be an effective way of regulating AI if the requirements imposed by the legislation are both meaningful and clear. In relation to the GDPR it has been

[174] Recital 71 of the Preamble to the GDPR, in discussing art 22(3) GDPR, states that the safeguards should, inter alia, include 'the right … to obtain an explanation of the decision reached after such assessment'.

[175] S Wachter, B Mittelstadt and L Floridi, 'Why a Right to Explanation of Automated Decision-Making Does Not Exist in the General Data Protection Regulation' (2017) 7(2) *International Data Privacy Law* 76.

[176] AD Selbst and J Powles, 'Meaningful Information and the Right to Explanation' (2017) 7(4) *International Data Privacy Law* 233.

[177] S Russell, *Human Compatible: Artificial Intelligence and the Problem of Control* (Viking, 2019) 129.

[178] Turner (n 119) 329.

said that the regulation can 'encourage companies to build privacy standards into their products from the start – known as "privacy by design"'.[179] This sentiment applied more broadly suggests that the providers of AI products can be incentivised to adopt the legislative requirements as design norms and facilitate the core AI principle discussed above – transparency.

Legislation that provides meaningful enforceable rights and a private right of action can give comfort to lawyers who employ AI products as part of their provision of legal services to clients that the AI conforms with the legislative requirements, or at least that some form of relief will be available if it does not. Equally, for a person who chooses not to use a lawyer, meaningful enforceable rights and a private right of action will assist and protect them.

Litigation

The enforcement of the law, whether it be contract, tort or a statute dealing with product liability, consumer protection or privacy can develop standards of conduct. Court judgments are able to explicate legal requirements, especially when set out in broad terms, such as principles. Judgments can also disapprove of undesirable actions and through statements of conduct as being illegal and the imposition of penalties, finding of civil contraventions and awarding of compensation, deter misconduct and change behaviour. Indeed, if regulation of AI remains at the level of principles and self-regulation then resort to existing laws will be necessary. However, it would clearly be better if AI complied with desirable principles or laws rather than having to bring legal action against non-compliance. Prevention is better than a cure. However, experience shows that enforcement of laws to hold persons or corporations accountable is often necessary to ensure compliance.[180]

Legal Practice by Non-Lawyers

There is a long-running critique of the professions, including law, as state-sanctioned monopolies that advance the interest of members over that of society.[181] Regulation allowed professions to maintain high barriers to entry and keep their expertise 'pure' or free from other forms of expertise and non-professional forms of work. The critique favours the breaking down of barriers to entry. Professions originally obtained their status through renouncing the market and the profit

[179] Rogynskyy (n 172) 9.

[180] See, eg, International Organization of Securities Commissions, 'Credible Deterrence in the Enforcement of Securities Regulation' (June 2015) 6.

[181] See, eg, R Abel, 'The Decline of Professionalism?' (1986) 49(1) *Modern Law Review* 1, 15–16; D Rhode, 'Ethics in Practice' in D Rhode (ed), *Ethics in Practice* (Oxford University Press, 2000) 12–14 ('the self-regarding tendencies of self-regulating processes').

motive in favour of public service. However, that trade-off has altered in relation to legal practice in some areas as law has become more businesslike, leading to claims that lawyers should forego their monopoly and accept competition. Equally, around the world an inability for people to afford lawyers to obtain assistance with legal problems has grown.

The advent of AI in relation to low-cost legal services has seen it put forward as a source of competition for lawyers and a way to make many forms of legal service cheaper and more accessible. LegalTech providers like LegalZoom, Nolo, Rocket Lawyer and LegalVision have emerged to offer fast, cheap and accurate legal services in areas where the law is routine and where there are lots of potential consumers: think property transactions, will drafting and probate matters, family law and divorce, and much of criminal law.[182] Other LegalTech providers, such as HighQ, Neota Logic, OPA, Xakia and Josef, provide simple-to-use expert system shells, chatbot authoring tools and business logic workflow tools to law firms and lawyers, seeking to help them automate their practices and reap efficiency gains from computerisation.[183] However, these tools may also be used to compete with lawyers.

The debate about whether technology such as AI can be used to provide legal products/services is usually considered through the frame of the prohibition of non-lawyers from engaging in legal practice, or as the US refers to it, the unauthorised practice of law (UPL). The reason for a prohibition on non-lawyers practising law is explained by Geoffrey Hazard Jr, William Hodes and Peter Jarvis as follows:

> UPL rules prevent clients from entrusting their affairs to people who have not endured the intellectual rigors of law school, the quality check of a bar examination, and the personal check of a character and fitness inquiry. It also protects clients from the incompetence of out-of-state lawyers, who may not be well versed in local practice. This is consumer protection at its best, because the average person – especially a one-off user of legal services – has essentially no ability to judge even what basic skills and qualities are necessary to ensure that money spent to secure legal advice is not totally wasted. Moreover, just as society would prohibit heart transplant patients from utilizing 'cut rate' services provided by a medical school dropout who has set up an operating theatre in his garage, protection of the public demands that some legal tasks be performed by licensed personnel only.[184]

As explained above and revisited in Chapter 12, the lawyer's ethical duties and legal liability provide significant protection for the client and the public in general. Restricting legal work to legal professionals and ensuring that legal professionals make their own judgements and do not rely improperly on technology are regarded as ways of ensuring the protection of consumers of legal services. As

[182] *LegalZoom*, www.legalzoom.com; *Nolo*, www.nolo.com/; *RocketLawyer*, www.rocketlawyer.com/; *LegalVision*, legalvision.com.au/.

[183] *HighQ*, highq.com; *Neota Logic*, www.neotalogic.com/; 'Oracle Policy Automation', *Wikipedia*, en.wikipedia.org/wiki/Oracle_Policy_Automation; Xakia, xakiatech.com; *Josef*, joseflegal.com/;.

[184] Hazard, Hodes and Jarvis (n 20). See also *Legal Profession Uniform Law 2014* (NSW) s 9.

well as quality control safeguards, clients have access to professional indemnity insurance in the event that loss flows from the improper actions of their lawyer. In terms of receiving legal advice from a non-lawyer or via an automated system, the OECD Working Party has noted that the absence of such a scheme may mean that consumers will not have access to the same protections and means of redress as they would if consulting a lawyer.[185] Those who are not sophisticated may not realise that the services which they are accessing are not being provided by a lawyer; or may not realise the implications of this. In the absence of a lawyer–client relationship, they will not have the associated protections of a fiduciary relationship, confidentiality, legal professional privilege and all the other duties of a lawyer. There might be problems with misleading information being given, forms being inappropriate or out of date – and of course there is no follow up, or guarantee, that a legal problem has actually been resolved correctly.[186]

However, those same rules prohibiting non-lawyers from engaging in legal practice reduce competition and increase prices. People cannot find a lawyer who will advise or represent them at a price the person can afford. The goal of protecting clients rings hollow if an AI system can provide a legal product/service as effectively as a lawyer, but at considerably lower cost.[187]

While the UPL debate has frequently been heated, the way forward is to find an approach that reconciles the need, on the one hand, for enabling the administration of justice and consumer protection with, on the other hand, access to affordable legal services.

One way of looking at the issue is through the scope of what is legal practice, or how broadly the term 'practice of law' is defined. The broader the scope the greater the exclusion of non-lawyers.[188] Prohibitions exist in the US, Australia and Canada, though they have been somewhat relaxed in England and Wales.[189] For example, in the Australian States of New South Wales and Victoria, the legislation prohibits, with certain exceptions,[190] non-lawyers from 'engaging in legal practice'.[191] Penalties can be monetary or up to two years' imprisonment.[192] In contrast, in England and Wales, regulators have reserved six specific types of legal

[185] OECD Directorate for Financial and Enterprise Affairs Competition Committee (n 85) 25–26, [82].

[186] CJ Lanctot, 'Regulating Legal Advice in Cyberspace' (2002) 16 *St. John's Journal of Legal Commentary* 569, 583.

[187] V Waye, ML Verreynne and J Knowler, 'Innovation in the Australian Legal Profession' (2018) 25(2) *International Journal of the Legal Profession* 213, 217.

[188] Hazard, Hodes and Jarvis (n 20) §49.04.

[189] See LS Terry, S Mark and T Gordon, 'Trends and Challenges in Lawyer Regulation: The Impact of Globalization and Technology' (2012) 80 *Fordham Law Review* 2661, 2676; J Bennett, T Miller, J Webb, R Bosua, A Lodders and S Chamberlain, 'Current State of Automated Legal Advice Tools – Discussion Paper 1' (Networked Society Institute, University of Melbourne, 2018) 19.

[190] For example, in Victoria non-lawyers may carry on a conveyancing business provided they are licensed by the Business Licensing Authority and comply with the requirements in the *Conveyancers Act 2006* (Vic).

[191] *Legal Profession Uniform Law 2014* (NSW) s 10; *Legal Profession Uniform Law 2014* (Vic) s 10.

[192] ibid.

work to those with a professional legal title – the exercise of a right of audience, the preparation and conduct of litigation, preparation of a contract for the sale or transfer of land, probate and notarial activities, and the administration of oaths – and have left the remainder to other market actors.[193] Consequently, one approach would be to determine that non-lawyers could undertake some areas of legal practice and to impose regulatory arrangements, such as licences and insurance requirements, depending on the particular area. Where AI operated in those areas then it would need to be subject to regulation such as that discussed above.

As explained in Chapter 3, even without reference to AI, technology such as the internet and smart phone apps make legislation, case law and commentary readily available so that the line between practising law and simply providing information about the law is blurred.[194] In the US, a particular target of UPL claims in the early 2000s were services which assist clients to prepare legal documents.[195] The same claims can be directed at any form of tailored advice, for example via a chatbot or online expert system. For example, in Florida the Bar alleged that TIKD Services LLC was engaged in UPL. TIKD allows a person who has received a traffic ticket to upload a picture of the ticket which an algorithm processes to determine whether TIKD will provide its services to the driver. If TIKD accepts the matter the driver is charged a percentage of the face amount of the ticket and TIKD retains a lawyer to defend the matter and pays that person a flat fee. The Bar's Petition was referred to a referee by the Supreme Court of Florida. The referee issued a report recommending dismissal of the claim but the matter was then argued before the Court.[196] Trying to specify what activities are or are not legal practice may be difficult. However, efforts could be devoted to seeking to clarify the scope of what is considered to be 'the practice of law'. This could carve out areas from legal practice but it could also prevent AI applications from operating without lawyer oversight in areas where the involvement of a lawyer was thought to be necessary.

Another approach is to allow lawyers and non-lawyers to associate so as to draw on their combined skill set for the provision of automated legal services. The US has traditionally maintained strict laws about multidisciplinary partnerships (MDPs) and incorporated legal practices, which prevent lawyers and non-lawyers sharing fees.[197] In comparison, the Australian State of New South Wales has permitted these alternative practice structures since 2001.[198] Today the governing legalisation provides that 'legal services may be provided under any business structure'.[199] As a result the largest and best-known providers of online legal services in Australia – LawPath, LegalVision and Lexvoco – are all incorporated

[193] *Legal Services Act 2007* (UK) s 12.

[194] Hazard, Hodes and Jarvis (n 20) §49.04.

[195] See Chapter 3.

[196] MH Stanzione, 'Florida Ticket App Case Arguments Spotlight Access to Justice', *Bloomberg Law*, 5 March 2020.

[197] American Bar Association's Model Rules of Professional Conduct, r 5.4.

[198] See Chapter 3; Dal Pont (n 13) 665–71.

[199] *Legal Profession Uniform Law 2014* (NSW) s 32; *Legal Profession Uniform Law 2014* (Vic) s 32.

legal practices. Thus, even if giving legal advice, they are unlikely to be engaging in unauthorised practice. We see this as a positive way in which to facilitate accessible legal services while also maintaining the protections that the lawyer's ethical duties and legal liability provide.

Regardless of the above adopted approach there is a need to achieve a balance between promoting accessible legal services and avoiding a compromise of consumer protections. AI holds out the prospect of making law more accessible but it may weaken the protections available to users as compared to a lawyer-provided service. There may need to be a trade-off between opening up the legal services market to competition from AI providers and preventing the provision of legal services that are not fit for purpose.[200] Although legal applications of AI have the potential to increase access to justice, this should not occur in an unregulated context.[201]

Conclusion

The practice of law is a highly regulated area in aid of requiring lawyers to put their clients' and the public's interest before their own self-interests. Consequently lawyers are subject to stringent ethical and legal requirements. The advent of AI does not change this. Lawyers retain professional responsibility (and liability) for their work, regardless of whether it is supplemented or enhanced by AI tools. Equally, not utilising AI may give rise to contraventions in some circumstances. The lawyer must therefore be aware of their obligations in an AI world.

From a client's perspective, the ethical and legal requirements imposed on lawyers provide greater protection than an AI-only legal solution. This state of affairs provides strong reasons for a client to continue to retain a lawyer. However, the cost of those legal services will also be a crucial factor in client choice.

Both the lawyer's ability to discharge their responsibilities, and the client's ability to utilise AI alone, will depend significantly on how AI is regulated in the future. This chapter has demonstrated that a number of regulatory approaches are possible, with varying forms of rights and enforceability. However, it is unlikely that even a well-regulated AI system will provide the same level of protections that exist when a client retains a lawyer. We continue this discussion in Chapter 12.

The cost of legal services and citizens' inability to afford legal services has seen the regulation of legal practice as exclusionary and more in the interests of lawyers than the public. This has resulted in questions about the scope of legal practice and whether it should be rolled back to facilitate AI solutions. However, a better approach based on the protections that the client receives when utilising a lawyer would be to permit the combination of lawyers and non-lawyers so as to facilitate AI's adoption in legal practice.

[200] Law Society of Ontario (n 8) 27.

[201] D Remus and F Levy, 'Can Robots Be Lawyers: Computers, Lawyers, and the Practice of Law' (2017) 30(3) *Georgetown Journal of Legal Ethics* 501, 551.

12

Future of the Legal Profession

Introduction

Life-threatening experiences can lead to an existential crisis in which individuals question whether their lives have meaning, purpose or value. The rise of legal AI and the joy taken by commentators in predicting the demise of lawyers could be that existential moment for the legal profession. Lawyers are accustomed to criticism but AI requires deeper reflection. It has been said that in the future lawyers will only be used where 'they can bring value that no alternative people, processes, or systems can offer'.[1] Many commentators see value in only financial terms – how legal services can be made cheaper or more efficient. Cost and efficiency are central concerns, which lawyers must address, but they are not the only concerns. Value is much broader and includes principles or behaviours that are beneficial or important. Here, we refer to three kinds of 'value' – of expertise, of ethics, and of human-specific characteristics or skills.

This broader context of the profession is key. Anthony Kronman said that law is not an autonomous discipline.[2] By this he meant, in sentiments echoed by others, that professions are social institutions and part of the social structure. Lawyers serve a variety of clients in a range of practice settings, with a range of needs but in accordance with a consistent ethical framework. Lawyers also perform an institutional role in the administration of justice and the maintenance of a democratic society.

We conclude by first summarising the threats and opportunities that AI poses for lawyers. We then turn to the values just described that lawyers must both embrace and provide. Finally, we discuss how lawyers can learn to utilise AI and develop other complementary skills so as to respond to the new conditions of legal practice.

Threats and Opportunities in the Use of AI for Lawyers

For the legal profession in the twenty-first century, AI will change the practice of law by automating parts of the lawyering process and lawyers will need to be able

[1] R Susskind, *Online Courts and the Future of Justice* (Oxford University Press, 2019) 237.

[2] A Kronman, *The Lost Lawyer: Failing Ideals of the Legal Profession* (Harvard University Press, 1993) 356.

to use those new tools to enhance their professional offering, but also to supervise, question and interpret AI. AI will remove the need for human lawyers to undertake some steps in the lawyering process, whether that be litigation, transactions or advice, but AI will not replace lawyers wholesale.

At present, the overarching message about the growing use of AI in the law is that lawyers are still needed and not in immediate danger of replacement. That said, it is worth remembering that we tend to overestimate the effect of a technology in the short run and underestimate the effect in the long run. In 2019 the American Bar Association reported that only 10 per cent of law firms were using AI.[3] Nonetheless, legal practice has clearly been impacted with AI being adopted in a range of practice areas, as we have detailed in Part II of this book. In its report *Developing Legal Talent*, Deloitte observed that in the UK to date, 'Lower skilled jobs, such as legal secretary, have been lost while new high-skilled roles have been created to develop and manage new technologies'.[4] This theme is likely to reflect future developments. Innovation is essential for lawyers 'to adapt to changes in technology and to changes in client expectations to remain competitive'.[5]

AI also brings exciting opportunities for lawyers. AI will remove routine or repetitive legal work and enable it to be undertaken more efficiently. The combination of machine learning and big data can provide insights that were not previously possible. Lawyers may be able to gain a deeper understanding of problems through new forms of analysis, which in turn can lead to novel solutions. In this way AI will augment lawyers' capabilities. Expertise, meanwhile, can be directed towards work that requires uniquely human and professional skills such as judgement, creativity and empathy.

It is also argued that efficiency gains will enable lawyers to take on more clients and that smaller firms and conglomerations of lawyers at online sites will be able to make use of technology to deliver 'leaner', more competitive services. Equally it has been observed that the cost and knowledge needed to obtain and support AI products means that only larger firms, in-house legal departments and entities built on technology platforms from their beginnings will be able to make extensive use of AI.

However, as our analysis in Part II demonstrates, it is challenging to make wide generalisations about AI's impact on the legal profession. Rather, a closer look at the role of the lawyer in a particular area, and the AI technologies being used, grounded in the specificities of legal practice, is needed. There appears to be less need for junior lawyers to conduct legal research and review documents due

[3] V Hudgins, 'ABA Survey: Only 10 Percent of Law Firms Are Currently Using AI', Law.com (11 January 2019) www.law.com/legaltechnews/2019/01/11/aba-survey-only-10-percent-of-law-firms-are-currently-using-ai/?slreturn=20200209183338.

[4] *Developing Legal Talent: Stepping into the future law firm* (Deloitte, February 2016) 4, citing *Transformers: How machines are changing every sector of the UK economy* (Deloitte LLP, February 2016).

[5] V Waye, ML Verreynne and J Knowler, 'Innovation in the Australian Legal Profession' (2018) 25(2) *International Journal of the Legal Profession* 213, 224 (reporting on survey findings).

to advances in outcome prediction and document review, both in litigation and for due diligence in transactions. Yet lawyers who can train the AI systems and interpret their outputs are essential. In the area of dispute resolution AI can facilitate the resolution of small claims, including those for which it would never have been economical to obtain traditional legal assistance. Yet in more high-stakes, sensitive or complex disputes the human advocate, strategic-thinker, creative and compassionate lawyer will be needed for all or parts of the process. The use of AI in regulatory compliance will cause the continued expansion of the in-house lawyer's role through safeguarding the corporation and questioning whether the AI system does indeed achieve compliance with the law. However, through this analysis, we can also see commonalities across what aspects of lawyering lawyers will continue to be needed, and the skills that they will need for those roles.

We now turn to the three kinds of 'value' mentioned – of expertise, of ethics, and of human-specific characteristics or skills – that lawyers, with the necessary skills and approach, are uniquely placed to provide in an AI world.

The Expertise Value

Specialised knowledge and skill among members has long been fundamental to the delineation of a profession. In many instances, professional controls restrict entry to those who have demonstrably attained such knowledge. The need for specialised knowledge means that law functions as a credence good, where the purchaser of the service is not able to evaluate the quality of what they are receiving. Rebecca Sandefur writes: 'Expertise exists when possessing knowledge and skills necessary to perform certain tasks involves a degree of specialization and devoted training that generates unequally distributed understanding'.[6] Professional controls in the form of regulatory strictures therefore reassure that this evaluation is being conducted by those who are capable of evaluating quality. Further, lawyers' expertise seems to matter.[7]

Defining expertise is, however, not especially straightforward. Micha-Manuel Bues and Emilio Matthaei give a helpful description, contrasting the work of lawyers with the tasks which may be automated:

> Lawyers need to process convoluted sets of facts and circumstances, consider applicable legal rights and obligations and render reasoned opinions and guidance on the best course of action based on all of that information. A lawyer (ideally) has the ability to understand the background and context of events, general knowledge of how the world

[6] R Sandefur, 'Elements of Professional Expertise: Understanding Relational and Substantive Expertise through Lawyers' Impact' (2015) 80(5) *American Sociological Review* 909, 911.

[7] J Szmer and M Humphries Ginn, 'Examining the Effects of Information, Attorney Capability, and Amicus Participation on US Supreme Court Decision Making' (2014) 42(3) *American Politics Research* 441, 443–44.

> works, and knowledge of the law and its application. The work of lawyers involves a lot of automatic filtering out of irrelevant noise and focusing in on the signal. For computers it is generally highly challenging to perform these tasks. To completely replicate a (human) lawyer would mean to re-engineer a process that could produce creative, imaginative and innovative ideas and results, whilst drawing on a comprehensive set of legal information and an 'experience database' comparable to an experienced lawyer.[8]

Good lawyers, then, have the capacity to distil information down but also retain a broad and contextualised knowledge base to work with. In contrast, AI is superior when it comes to analysing a vast quantity of data, both in terms of the volume it can manage, and the objectivity it can bring to the analysis.[9]

Expertise is also needed because the law is complex, and only growing more so, as Gillian Hadfield has described.[10] In a review of the Susskinds' *The Future of the Professions*, Frank Pasquale comments:

> Situations involving conflicting rights, unusual fact patterns, and open-ended laws will remain excessively difficult to automate for the foreseeable future. … *The Future of the Professions* argues that standardization of legal filings, briefs, and judgments is the way of the future, bringing the logic of interchangeable parts to the work of the mind. But, as Trachimovsky counters, 'given modern trends in legislative and regulatory drafting, in particular the use of "creative ambiguity" […] demand for custom services will only increase.' Note, too, that much of this legal complexity is not simply a question of redundant, easily simplified legal verbiage. It reflects, instead, deep-seated social tensions that are unlikely to be resolved any time soon.[11]

Pasquale goes on to explain that legislating is a messy process of addressing a multiplicity of different interests, often resulting in untidy political compromises, and not easily 'solved' or simplified.

Expertise also has a relational aspect. In a meta-analysis of different studies comparing how litigants fared both with lawyers and without, Sandefur drew attention to two different aspects of professional expertise: 'one reflecting knowledge of professional theories, concepts, and tools, and the other reflecting skill at navigating the social contexts of professional work'.[12] Sandefur refers to these as substantive expertise and relational expertise, respectively. Her analysis found that, somewhat counter-intuitively, lawyers had a significant impact on the outcome

[8] M Bues and E Matthaei, 'LegalTech on the Rise: Technology Changes Legal Work Behaviours, But Does Not Replace Its Profession' in K Jacob, D Schindler and R Strathausen (eds), *Liquid Legal* (Springer 2017) 94.

[9] DM Katz, 'Quantitative Legal Prediction – Or – How I Learned to Stop Worrying and Start Preparing for the Data-Driven Future of the Legal Services Industry' (2012) 62(4) *Emory Law Journal* 909, 928.

[10] GK Hadfield, *Rules for a Flat World: Why Humans Invented Law and How to Reinvent It for a Complex Global Economy* (Oxford University Press, 2017).

[11] F Pasquale, 'Automating the Professions: Utopian Pipe Dream or Dystopian Nightmare?' *Los Angeles Review of Books* (15 March 2016) lareviewofbooks.org/article/automating-the-professions-utopian-pipe-dream-or-dystopian-nightmare/ (citing Seymour Trachimovsky).

[12] Sandefur (n 6) 911 (citations omitted).

of cases in matters involving more complex procedures (rather than complex substantive law). Sandefur posited that this could be due to the importance of relational expertise: what 'being represented' signified to other parties and to courts.[13]

Expert lawyering requires the exercise of judgement, and in turn the making of value choices, and the weighing up of incommensurables. Pasquale argues that professional roles are not solely about delivery of information as they can involve complex value choices, which society deems should be made by people.[14] Howard Gardner and Lee Shulman referred to the need for professionals to make complex judgements under conditions of uncertainty:

> [T]he hallmark of all professions, even beyond the prototypical practices of each, is the ubiquitous condition of uncertainty, novelty, and unpredictability that characterizes professional work. While much of professional practice is routine, the essential challenges of professional work center on the need to make complex judgments and decisions leading to skilled actions under conditions of uncertainty. This means that professional practice is frequently pursued at or beyond the margins of previously learned performances.[15]

It is said that the traditional professional ideal of the lawyer is fundamentally about good judgement. Good judgement 'represents … practical wisdom … that cannot be captured in formulas or mechanical rules. Sound judgment … responds in a particularistic way to particularized situations'.[16] Judgement represents a capacity which AI is unable to emulate. Likewise Joshua Davis has argued that even if AI can become better than humans at describing the law and predicting how people will apply it, AI will not be able to address value judgements about what the law *should* be.[17] In one example, Davis refers to Ronald Dworkin's concepts of *fit* (how closely a case matches precedent) and *justification*.[18] While a computer may be able to do the former, he suggests it will struggle to persuasively do the latter – even assuming that the concepts can be successfully disentangled.

The Ethics Value

Ethical and legal standards applicable to lawyers are designed to protect clients and the administration of justice so as to promote the public interest. The Canadian

[13] ibid 924–25. This was likely more significant in the studies Sandefur surveyed as many of them involved poverty law scholarship where clients were suffering not just lack of legal knowledge but stigma and other disadvantage.

[14] Pasquale (n 11).

[15] H Gardner and LS Shulman, 'The Professions in America Today: Crucial but Fragile' (2005) 134(3) *Dædalus* 13.

[16] D Luban and M Millemann, 'Good Judgment: Ethics Teaching in Dark Times' (1995) 9(1) *Georgetown Journal of Legal Ethics* 31, 34.

[17] JP Davis, 'Artificial Wisdom? A Potential Limit on AI in Law (and Elsewhere)' (2019) 72(1) *Oklahoma Law Review* 51, 54–55.

[18] ibid, citing R Dworkin, *Law's Empire* (1986).

Model Code of Professional Conduct observes that 'While lawyers are consulted for their knowledge and abilities, more is expected of them than forensic acumen. A special ethical responsibility comes with membership in the legal profession'.[19] At the first Conference of Australia's Legal Societies in 1933, Sir John Latham, who would later be appointed as Chief Justice of the High Court of Australia, said that 'the independence of the profession is one of the strongest safeguards that any community has'.[20] Justice Frankfurter of the Supreme Court of the United States, in speaking of what is required for a lawyer to be of moral character, pointed to 'those qualities of truth-speaking, of a high sense of honour, of granite discretion, [and] of the strictest observance of fiduciary responsibility'.[21]

While lawyers' ethical responsibilities are commonly referred to as rules, they are far from being well-defined, clear-cut statements that can be mechanically applied. Indeed almost all ethical duties involve the resolution of some uncertainty or conflict. The ethical practice of law also involves lawyers deciding 'on a personal level … what the rules mean, how to obey them [and] what to do when there are gaps or conflicts in the rules'.[22] One component of 'good judgement' is therefore good ethical judgement.

The Chief Justice of the High Court of Australia has observed that

> [a]n ethical lawyer is not just one who has an awareness of a Code of Conduct and what may constitute a breach of that Code. A guide to right conduct is provided by an understanding of the place of the profession in the legal system and therefore in society.[23]

The lawyer needs to develop the reflective judgement necessary to assess the demands made upon them by clients or colleagues at a particular time within the larger framework of being a member of the legal profession, which requires integrity, honesty, loyalty and maintenance of the standing of the profession in the eyes of the community.

When a client consults a lawyer that relationship is clothed with protections and responsibilities that a purely commercial relationship cannot mirror. The lawyer must be competent and put the client's interest first. This is most evident in the content of the fiduciary duties owed by lawyer to client. In one word, the obligation is loyalty. As Cardozo CJ said, it is 'stricter than the morals of the marketplace. Not honesty alone, but the punctilio of an honor the most sensitive' and that 'the level of conduct for fiduciaries [is] at a level higher than that trodden by the crowd'.[24] The result is that 'the law takes a hard line against faithless fiduciaries'.[25]

[19] Federation of Law Societies (FLSC) of Canada's Model Code of Professional Conduct, 14 March 2017, Preface.

[20] JG Latham, 'Duties and Opportunities of the Legal Profession in Australia' (1933) 7 *Australian Law Journal* 15, 18.

[21] *Schware v Board of Bar Examiners of the State of New Mexico* 353 US 232, 247 (1957).

[22] C Parker and A Evans, *Inside Lawyers' Ethics* (3rd edn, Cambridge University Press, 2018) 14.

[23] S Kiefel, 'Ethics and the Profession of the Lawyer', Queensland Law Society, The Vincents' 48th Annual Symposium 2010, 26 March 2010, 6.

[24] *Meinhard v Salmon* 249 NY 458, 464 (1928).

[25] *Cadbury Schweppes Inc v FBI Foods Ltd* [1999] 1 SCR 142, [29].

The ethical and legal obligations of lawyers to promote the public interest is what sets the legal profession apart from businesses and commercial interests: 'the world of commerce has different imperatives'.[26] The standards of conduct required of a lawyer are professional standards. However, as Roscoe Pound said in describing a profession as 'a group … pursuing a common calling as a learned art and as a public service – no less a public service because it may incidentally be a means of livelihood'.[27] However, the making of money is 'incidental'[28] or 'a very secondary thing'.[29]

Legal fees cannot be unfair or unreasonable yet we see large law firms with multi-million-dollar profits per partner and class actions lawyers receiving multi-million-dollar fees per case. John Flood argues that major law firms have 'shifted away from traditional logics based around notions of public interest … to the logic of the market'.[30] Similarly, Robert Gordon points out that the lawyers' public service role has been substantially diminished as 'elite lawyers have mostly dropped the rhetoric of professional public-serving ideals'.[31] These observations applied before the rise of AI. But if law is equated with a business seeking profit then the question arises as to why it should not face the same competitive pressures as business does. The market should decide who has the better legal service offering.

The loss of professionalism and the undervaluing of ethical obligations invites deregulation. At present lawyers are 'supported by a superstructure of regulatory and legal protections that no other guild in history has had'.[32] These protections follow from the lawyer's public service obligations. If lawyers recognise and honour the value of ethics in the way that they practise, not just as lip service, then AI may be argued to act as an adjunct to the lawyer, rather than as a replacement, because society needs ethical lawyers for the law to function. The combination of lawyer and AI could be a powerful step to realising equality in access to the law, protection of the rule of law, and client protections. Some may think 'this boat has sailed', but we are more optimistic and believe that the legal profession can reaffirm its foundational role.[33]

Alternatively, it may be argued that if lawyers do not honour their side of the 'regulatory bargain', namely serving the public interest, including the duty to the administration of justice and facilitating access to justice, then the superstructure should be relaxed (some might go further and say removed). As we noted

[26] Kiefel (n 23) 6.

[27] R Pound, 'What is a Profession – the Rise of the Legal Profession in Antiquity' (1944) 19 *Notre Dame Law Review* 203, 203.

[28] ibid 204.

[29] J Wigmore, 'Introduction' to O Carter, *Ethics of the Legal Profession* (Northwestern University Press, 1915) xxii.

[30] J Flood, 'The Re-Landscaping of the Legal Profession: Large Law Firms and Professional Re-Regulation' (2011) 59 *Current Sociology* 507, 522.

[31] R Gordon, 'Portrait of a Profession in Paralysis' (2002) 54 *Stanford Law Review* 1427, 1443.

[32] P Kirgis, 'The Knowledge Guild: The Legal Profession in an Age of Technological Change' (2010) 11 *Nevada Law Journal* 184, 191.

[33] See also DA Remus, 'Reconstructing Professionalism' (2017) 51(3) *Georgia Law Review* 807.

in Chapter 11, in discussing legal practice by non-lawyers, the scope of what is legal practice, or from the obverse, who is a 'lawyer', could be redefined to allow non-lawyer service providers greater scope to operate in traditional areas of legal practice. Service providers who do not have to comply with ethical obligations of a lawyer, but would be subject to some form of regulation, could be permitted to operate. In this situation, we still see lawyers' ethical values as a point of difference that needs to be leveraged.

When a consumer utilises an AI legal product or service without a lawyer they enter a commercial relationship. Even with the added consumer protections provided in some jurisdictions that may prevent the AI purveyor from taking advantage of the consumer, it remains a business transaction. The AI provider looks out for themselves first. While they may not mislead or be dishonest, they do not have to positively assist the consumer in seeking to achieve their objective. Lawyers, in contrast, must put all of their knowledge and skills towards achieving the client's goal. As a consequence the innovative AI legal product is not risk free.[34] The consumer and society exchange lower protections in search of lower costs.

The lawyer's duty to the court and the administration of justice are to the benefit of society more generally as they provide institutional protections that support the rule of law and a democratic society. In basic terms we strive for a society that applies the law fairly and equally – nobody is above the law and nobody is without law.[35] The aim is justice and the avoidance of tyranny. The lawyer is part of the justice structure because of the needs for checks and balances. The lawyer enables the lay person to obtain legal advice and put their case in the best possible manner. The lawyer stands between the state and the individual. This is not to say that the system operates perfectly, as explained above. However, in contrast, AI products/services or their vendors do not have an obligation of public service, and public interests are not granted primacy over commercial interests.[36]

A lawyer's duties to both the administration of justice and to their client may conflict and require the lawyer to determine how to address that conflict. The High Court of Singapore has emphasised the very human aspects of how this conundrum is to be addressed:

> [A] solicitor's abiding and unerring guide must be his very own conscience combined with the collective conscience of the profession – not that of his client's. …
>
> Solicitors must exercise practical and deliberative wisdom and restraint in striking a prudent and pragmatic balance between ethics and expediency. Ethical rules and conventions can never exhaustively prescribe or proscribe standards of professional

[34] N Semple, 'Tending the Flame: Technological Innovation and the Legal Services Act Regime', Paper prepared for the Legal Services Board, 6 August 2019, 5 ('The flame of technological innovation can also be dangerous. It can scorch consumers with new kinds of deficient, exploitative, or monopolistic legal services').

[35] T Bingham, *The Rule of Law* (Penguin, 2011) 8.

[36] B Mittelstadt, 'Principles Alone Cannot Guarantee Ethical AI' (2019) 1 *Nature Machine Intelligence* 501, 502, 505.

> conduct. Using established standards as basic guides, solicitors must draw on their own internalised moral compasses to guide them through the myriad of conflicting priorities they have to regularly address and make in practice. …
>
> Within the boundaries of ethical permissibility, the client's interests should be accorded supremacy. Beyond these boundaries, the priority to be accorded to the client's interests evanesces. Granting that this entails neither a cut-and-dried nor mechanical approach, it must be pointed out that solicitors grapple with these conflicting priorities regularly and without too much trial or tribulation. Their own internalised moral compasses provide the surest touchstone in resolving these tensions appropriately.[37]

The nebulous nature of ethics and the need for judgement, morality and conscience are raised here to both remind the lawyer of what is required, but also to distinguish the human lawyer from AI. AI may be seen as reflecting the moral choices of its designer, even though such choices may not have been explicitly made. However, such choices are static rather than capable of deliberation and change. AI follows the programming of the algorithm, which is typically aimed at achieving an objective, such as predictive accuracy.[38] It lacks the ability to decide that such ends should not be pursued or to grapple with competing moral or ethical choices. Indeed the problem or limitation of AI may be said to be that defining true human goals completely and correctly is highly problematic. If the goal is uncertain then it is not possible to accurately align AI's objective with the lawyer's objective.[39] However, the lawyer as professional is bound not just to be able to operate the machinery, but also to not misuse the machinery.[40]

Some lawyers see their ethical obligations, and corresponding limits on how they are permitted to practise as giving the LegalTech start-ups and new entrants an advantage through an uneven playing field. We take the position that lawyers and non-lawyer technology competitors do offer different things and that the lawyer must differentiate themselves from the AI-only offering. We argue that the lawyer can acquire the know-how to be able to 'do' technology (as explained below) while also being true to the values of the profession.

The Human Value

AI will also increase the relative value of exclusively 'human' skills, including emotional intelligence, empathy, trust, cooperation, creativity and

[37] *Public Trustee v By Products Traders Pte Ltd* [2005] 3 SLR(R) 449, [54]–[55], [57].

[38] S Russell, *Human Compatible: Artificial Intelligence and the Problem of Control* (Viking, 2019) 49, 59.

[39] ibid 137. Russell goes on to explain how this problem can see virtuous objectives like curing cancer or countering the acidification of the oceans result in harm to humanity because AI pursues the goal absolutely.

[40] Pound (n 27) 208.

communication.[41] The lawyer is not just a technician producing answers to legal questions but must interact with other humans.

Emotional Intelligence and Empathy

Emotional intelligence is a combination of skills, including psychology, collaboration, group dynamics and organisational behaviour. The need for this skill set is well described in a report to the Canadian Bar Association: 'Clients need our empathy, perspective and personal commitment in order to feel that we really understand and appreciate what they're going through'.[42] The significance of emotional intelligence derives directly from the changes wrought by technology. AI lacks empathy or emotions of its own[43] although research is progressing into AI which can recognise human emotions (from facial expression or tone of voice) and respond accordingly.[44] Sylvie Delacroix has written:

> Given the rapid progress of affective computing, it is only a matter of time before we are able to converse with 'embodied conversational agents' who are able to pick up on subtle, non-verbal behaviour cues to learn about our emotional states and themselves use both verbal and non-verbal cues to signify empathy far better than most professionals would.[45]

Delacroix explains, though, that there remains 'a world of difference between *signifying* and *experiencing* empathy'.[46] In the context of algorithmic decision making, Karen Yeung has written of the importance for individuals of being 'listened to' by decision makers, and

> their subjective experience has been properly acknowledged: this requires recognition of the emotional cost and *meaning* of the events in question for which empathy and compassion is the morally appropriate response … While AI systems are increasingly capable of simulating human emotions and responses, they are artificial and inferior

[41] P Brest and L Hamilton Krieger, 'Lawyers as Problem Solvers' (1999) 72(4) *Temple Law Review* 811, 811–12; M Legg, 'Embrace Robotic Disruption But Don't Lose Your Human Skills', *The Australian*, 16 June 2017, 26; P Daugherty and HJ Wilson, *Human + Machine: Reimagining Work in the Age of AI* (Harvard Business Review Press, 2018) 138, Figure 6–1 (Daugherty and Wilson identify certain areas of activity – leading, empathising, creating and judging – as 'human only').

[42] J Furlong, *Do Law Differently – Futures for Young Lawyers* (Canadian Bar Association, 2016) 18. See also R Susskind, *Tomorrow's Lawyers: An Introduction to Your Future* (2nd edn, Oxford University Press, 2017) 75.

[43] M Lauritsen, 'Liberty, Justice and Legal Automata' (2013) 88 *Chicago-Kent Law Review* 945, 953.

[44] See, eg, Daugherty and Wilson (n 41) 117–18; Affectiva: www.affectiva.com; R Feloni, 'Consumer Goods Giant Unilever has been Hiring Employees Using Brain Games and Artificial Intelligence', *Business Insider Australia*, 29 June 2017, www.businessinsider.com.au/unilever-artificial-intelligence-hiring-process-2017-6?r=US&IR=T.

[45] S Delacroix, 'Drawing a Non-Consequentialist Line: Augmenting v Replacing the Professions with Computer Systems', SSRN, https://ssrn.com/abstract=2840864, 33.

[46] ibid (emphasis added).

> substitutes for authentic empathy, compassion, and concern of those with whom we share the common bonds of human experience.[47]

This applies, also, to clients being listened to by their lawyers.

Chalen Westaby and Emma Jones have written on the value of empathy in legal practice.[48] While noting that traditionally lawyers were expected to bury emotional responses in the quest for rationality, they argue that in fact empathy can increase the effectiveness of legal practice.[49] AI does not currently have the ability to 'talk a client around'. Hence, it is argued, 'the crucial difference between the human and the machine is very simple: the human [lawyer] can talk back. She can offer counter-reasons and moral suasion to the client's reasons'.[50] Because AI can only simulate empathy, it lacks the moral authority to reason with a client.

Humans want to deal with humans, especially on important matters that affect their well-being. As Geoff Colvin has explained, 'We want to hear our diagnosis from a doctor … because we want to talk to the doctor about it … and know we're being heard by a human being'.[51] It has been identified that there are many experts who, while excellent technicians, lack emotional intelligence.[52] There are therefore skills to be learnt.

No matter how sophisticated AI may get, it will never be human.

Trust

When clients deal with human lawyers in a face-to-face relationship they develop trust and understanding.[53] This is reinforced by the duty to the client, including the restrictions on conflicts of interest, and duties of confidentiality and legal professional privilege. The significance of trust should not be underestimated. Yet it does not arise in every dealing or relationship. We noted in Chapter 3 that lawyers perform work at different 'levels', from task-based and technical to holistic advising.[54] It is one thing to engage with AI for small, simple, task-based claims and transactions, but quite another to entrust one's economic or personal well-being to a machine.[55] A significant challenge for an AI-only product or service is gaining the trust of the user. However, lawyers also need to ensure that they are not 'just another self-interested participant in the market economy, [who] does right

[47] K Yeung, 'Why Worry about Decision-Making by Machine?' in K Yeung and M Lodge (eds), *Algorithmic Regulation* (Oxford University Press, 2019) 21.

[48] C Westaby and E Jones, 'Empathy: An Essential Element of Legal Practice or "Never the Twain Shall Meet"?' (2018) 25(1) *International Journal of the Legal Profession* 107.

[49] ibid.

[50] D Luban, 'Optimism, Skepticism, and Access to Justice' (2016) 3 *Texas A&M Law Review* 495, 507.

[51] G Colvin, 'Humans are Underrated', *Fortune*, 23 July 2015, 106.

[52] R Susskind and D Susskind, *The Future of the Professions* (Oxford University Press, 2015) 251.

[53] Kirgis (n 32) 195.

[54] DH Maister, CH Green and RM Galford, *The Trusted Advisor* (Free Press, 2000) 7.

[55] Pasquale (n 11).

by her customers because it makes for good business'.[56] Most vendors comply with their legal obligations so as to avoid costs such as fines, damages claims and reputational harm. But trust may also be seen as relational – a client trusts in a particular person and the relationship itself, not just the legal framework supporting the relationship.[57] Thus, while the value of ethics is clear, the human relationship is the essence that makes those ethical requirements come to life in a specific relationship. It has been argued that achieving trust can be more difficult when legal services are being broken up into their component parts and outsourced to various low-cost providers. In that situation the client may rely on a lawyer episodically, 'rather than for the wisdom and perspective that comes through the combination of legal knowledge, breadth of experience, and a close confidential relationship over time'.[58] It might be suggested that this is the client's loss. However, the client may not be prepared to invest, in a financial sense, in trust. For the lawyer though, relational trust is something that they can offer that AI cannot. It is an attribute of the lawyer–client relationship that distinguishes the lawyer from others.

Collaboration and Teamwork

If legal services are being deconstructed or unbundled then that gives rise to a need to be able to work with others who are contributing to the service being provided, requiring skills in teamwork and collaboration.[59] Unbundling of legal services requires lawyers to collaborate not only with the client or other lawyers, but also with technologists, project managers and other professionals.[60] Globalisation means that 'lawyers will also collaborate across geographies, cultures, and in different political and regulatory environments'.[61] Especially in larger law firms or for lawyers working as in-house counsel, there is a need to develop teamwork skills. The practice of law involves one-on-one interactions but as law firms and clients become larger and more complex the lawyer needs to be able to work in an environment with multiple contributors to the legal service.

Creativity

Human history is a story of humans coming up with novel, creative ideas. Creative thinking is the generation of ideas (a) that are unusual, or original, and (b) that

[56] R Vischer, 'Big Law and the Marginalization of Trust' (2012) 25(1) *Georgetown Journal of Legal Ethics* 165, 170.
[57] ibid 170–73.
[58] ibid 188.
[59] Colvin (n 51) 108.
[60] M Cohen, 'The Future Lawyer', *Forbes*, 30 May 2017.
[61] ibid.

satisfy some standard of value.[62] Creative thinking can mean 'forward' thinking or invention to come up with new alternatives. It can mean resolving conflicts in actions or ideas. It may include 'lateral thinking', as developed by Edward de Bono,[63] which to is to take approaches different to the thinking process with which we are most comfortable. Another approach is 'divergent thinking', which requires consideration of factors that might not have seemed relevant in a traditional problem-solving exercise. And yet another is to recognise multiple intelligences[64] so that the lawyer who is comfortable with logic in their area of expertise draws on other forms of intelligence, emotional intelligence being an example.[65]

Creative thinking is essential to problem solving and can be used to address legal problems such as devising a theory of liability to ground the commencement of litigation, or structuring a transaction to achieve some end, such as avoiding breach of competition law restrictions. It can involve considering a number of interpretations of a statute, or considering potential resolutions to a dispute.

Creativity is also a process that may offer benefits. Preet Bharara, former US Attorney for the Southern District of New York and criminal prosecutor, in describing the investigation process into criminal misconduct drew parallels with the artist, writer and entrepreneur, whose 'painstaking, backbreaking, stop-and-go labor is not necessarily evident in the elegance of the brushstrokes, the clarity of the prose, or the simplicity of the business model'.[66] The lay person focuses on the end product – they see the destination but not the journey. In doing so the lay person misses the 'false starts, dead ends and winding detours'.[67] But they also miss the creativity, the serendipity, the making of obscure connections. Bharara's observations apply to many areas of law, including structuring transactions and developing litigation strategy.[68] The developers of AI promote their innovations as removing the cost and delay of the mis-steps and detours. However, they also remove the opportunity for the creativity and the happenstance that comes from labouring through the process.

Communication

Lawyers must be able to articulate clear, actionable advice for a client. They must be able to *read the room* or *read the client* to ensure that the advice they provide

[62] J Weinstein and L Morton, 'Stuck in a Rut: The Role of Creative Thinking in Problem Solving and Legal Education' (2003) 9 *Clinical Law Review* 835, 837–38.

[63] E de Bono, *Serious Creativity: Using the Power of Lateral Thinking to Create New Ideas* (HarperBusiness, 1992).

[64] H Gardner, *Intelligence Reframed: Multiple Intelligences for the 21st Century* (Basic Books, 1999).

[65] Weinstein and Morton (n 62) 838–43.

[66] P Bharara, *Doing Justice: A Prosecutor's Thoughts on Crime, Punishment, and the Rule of Law* (Bloomsbury, 2019) 3.

[67] ibid.

[68] See Chapters 6 and 7.

is user friendly, 'friendly' meaning that it takes account of the characteristics of the client, including education, proficiency with the language of the jurisdiction and age.[69] The need to read the client applies equally to sophisticated corporate clients and to the individual dealing with personal matters. The corporate client may have business constraints and objectives that affect the workability of a legal solution. The individual may have relationship, cultural or religious factors that need to be considered.[70] AI programs can adopt user interfaces aimed at being accessible, but they cannot adapt with the same flexibility as the human lawyer who sees that the client does not understand, or that the proffered solution does not satisfy their needs. David Luban says that this communication is important because lawyers must talk to their clients about serious and personal matters, in a dialogic process.[71] Even the 'simple' (and readily automatable) task of preparing a will involves discussions about mortality and property:

> Part of the reason is that human beings can have moral authority, and machines have none … Moral sense is not quite the same as emotional intelligence, but it is an indispens[a]ble piece of legal judgment and legal advice.[72]

The lawyer may also need to explain AI outputs to a client, including putting the outputs in context or in terms of actionable steps.[73]

Constraints

While all the above human-specific or human-centred characteristics are highly desirable and would undoubtedly give the client a better experience when needed, they come at a price. And, of course, not all lawyers possess them.[74] If the client cannot afford the price then they are forced to do without the benefits of humanity. The legal profession needs to develop ways to alleviate this constraint in accordance with its public service obligation. Pro bono has been one approach. Government funding through legal aid programmes may be another. Both have a stake in having citizens receive personal assistance where it is needed because both need the support of the public.

Further, while emotional intelligence, teamwork, collaboration and trust are undoubtedly important, lawyers must also be cognisant of their ethical obligations. Lawyers must act in the best interests of clients but also avoid any compromise to

[69] The Law Society of New South Wales, *The Future of Law and Innovation in the Profession* (2017) 15.

[70] A Carrel, 'Legal Intelligence Through Artificial Intelligence Requires Emotional Intelligence: A New Competency Model for the 21st Century Legal Professional' (2019) 35(4) *Georgia State University Law* Review 1153, 1160.

[71] Luban (n 50) 505.

[72] ibid 505.

[73] Carrel (n 70) 1174.

[74] Luban writes: 'We all know lawyers with less empathy and emotional intelligence than the average housecat; they're called "partners"' (n 50) 505.

their integrity and professional independence. Empathy and personal commitment cannot be at the expense of independence. As explained above in relation to operationalising ethics, these are difficult judgements, but also ones that lawyers are trained and experienced in addressing.

Education

In Chapter 3 we used five activities – transacting, advising, negotiating, representing and structuring – to give an overview of what it is that lawyers do. In the chapters which followed, we looked in more detail at what different, and more specific, lawyer roles require, and where AI might augment or even replace elements of those roles. Here, we think more specifically about the skills that lawyers need in this process.

Lawyers are using AI-powered legal products today and will likely use them more in the future. Legal education needs to reflect this fact. Lawyers need to be able to competently engage with technology which requires a number of skills. At the same time, lawyers need to retain, and likely enhance, many other more traditional lawyering skills.

Skill Sets Lawyers Need to Work With AI

Professor Mireille Hildebrandt proposes lawyers should ask three questions before adopting new technologies: what problem does this technology solve, what problems are not solved, and what problems does it create?[75]

Engaging with and using AI involves a number of elements. Lawyers need to be able to identify technology that should be employed because it is the more efficient way to proceed: it will achieve the client's objective or obligation in a cost-effective manner. To do this the lawyer must understand what the technology does and be able to deploy it in appropriate circumstances. But lawyers must understand the limitations of the technology, too – both technically and in terms of whether it can meet client needs. It has been argued that this is really a basic business skill, which lawyers are coming to somewhat later than those in other industries.[76]

How much of a technology skill set does a lawyer need? It has been argued that 'You'll be paid in the future based on how well you work with robots'[77] – in

[75] M Hildebrand, 'The Magic of Data Driven Regulation', The Allens Hub for Technology, Law and Innovation Annual Lecture, University of New South Wales, Sydney (13 December 2018) https://newsroom.unsw.edu.au/news/business-law/ai-law-how-lawyers-and-scientists-can-avoid-automated-injustice.

[76] K Hume, 'How to Spot a Machine Learning Opportunity, Even if You Aren't a Data Scientist', *Harvard Business Review*, 20 October 2017, https://hbr.org/2017/10/how-to-spot-a-machine-learning-opportunity-even-if-you-arent-a-data-scientist.

[77] K Kelly, 'Better than Human: Why Robots – and Must – Take Our Jobs', *Wired*, 24 December 2012.

other words, that technological skills will be fundamental. The answer to this question is also sometimes framed in terms of whether future lawyers need to be taught to code.[78] One answer is that lawyers do not need to create the technological solution, or have the skills to create it, rather they need to be able to use it. As one commentator has explained, 'Lawyers do not need to know how to code any more than aspiring doctors need to know how to build lasers or fabricate surgical instruments'.[79] Other responses are that lawyers will never code as well as computer scientists as this is not their primary skill set and therefore not where their competitive advantage lies. Yet another response is that coding will be the blue collar work of the future because everyone will do it and it will be outsourced to the cheapest provider.[80]

But learning to code for the lawyer is not about being a coder, it is about being able to understand code, comprehend how an AI system functions and communicate with computer scientists and engineers. As Steve Jobs said in a 1995 interview: 'But much more importantly, [creating computer programs] had nothing to do with using them for anything practical. It had to do with using them to be a mirror of your thought process. To actually learn how to think'.[81] Coding involves expressing ideas and concepts in a different manner to oral or written language. The lawyer needs to be able to make the connection between what law requires or allows and how the AI system will function. It may be possible to do this without learning to code, but understanding coding will certainly assist.

To be able to use the technology the lawyer also needs to comprehend the output of the technology. For example, TAR requires statistical literacy and quantitative skills:[82] the ability to understand, apply and infer from data. These skills will also be crucial to interpreting outcome prediction software.[83] Lawyers will also need to be able to challenge or critique the results of the technology, such as looking for biases or reliance on incomplete data.[84] Pasquale explains that expert humans will play a key role in identifying when data is 'bad' and its limitations in a given context – so humans must be able to engage with such data.[85] Of course, the lawyer may be able to obtain assistance in comprehending and critiquing from legal data scientists, but to effectively seek this assistance, must have an initial understanding of the right questions to ask.

[78] Examples of coding courses for law students include Georgetown Law School's 'Computer Programming for Lawyers: An Introduction' and Harvard Law School's 'Programming for Lawyers'.

[79] C Denvir, 'The Rise of the Multi-Disciplinary Lawyer: A Challenge for Legal Education', *Legal Futures*, 26 May 2017.

[80] It should be noted that the secondary education system is changing so that coding may be taught in schools along with 'reading, writing and arithmetic' as it becomes a life skill, which in turn may impact the need for teaching coding in law schools.

[81] C Forsman, 'Steve Jobs on Programming, Craftsmanship, Software, and the Web', *Ars Technica*, 7 August 2012. The quote comes from *Steve Jobs: The Lost Interview*, conducted on 20 April 1995.

[82] See Chapter 5.

[83] See Chapter 4.

[84] See, eg, A Caliskan, J Bryson and A Narayanan, 'Semantics Derived Automatically From Language Corpora Contain Human-Like Biases' (2017) 356(6334) *Science* 183.

[85] Pasquale (n 11).

While ethical and legal rules require competence with technology, those rules need to be put into action through education. This can be through courses in the university law degree, extra-curricular activities (eg hackathons), as part of the requirements for admission to practise and/or as continuing professional development requirements.[86] The main decision is whether this subject matter is provided as an opportunity for interested lawyers and students, or as a compulsory requirement. Is it delivered through law school extra-curricular activities, electives or compulsory courses? Is it examined as part of Bar exams? Are there available professional development options, or compulsory units? Further, is this technical knowledge taught in a stand-alone manner or as it applies to, and is shaped by, law and its underlying tenets? At present lawyers and students are typically left to seek out this knowledge based on their own interest. However, if AI is going to have as profound an effect as is predicted, then a more obligatory approach, where technical elements become ingrained in the law curriculum, seems prudent.

It is also important that focussing on these technical skills does not push out the so-called 'soft' skills discussed above: emotional intelligence, communication and collaboration.[87] Some people will naturally excel at these skills compared to others. However, they can be learnt and ideally are part of the law school curriculum. Many law schools, especially with the advent of clinical teaching, provide the opportunity for students to engage with 'real people' as clients and to then reflect on that engagement and learn from their experience and their instructors.[88] Additional approaches to acquiring these skills include adopting more structured forms of collaboration and communications such as drawing on legal project management and design theory. Methodologies from other disciplines may also be fruitfully employed.[89] A further approach is to provide inter-disciplinary experiences where law students engage with students and practitioners in other areas of expertise. For example, in start-up law clinics, law students may be given the opportunity to work with budding entrepreneurs from a range of backgrounds, including computer science and business, as well as experienced lawyers to advise on corporate structures, tax, employment and intellectual property issues relevant

[86] A Arruda, 'An Ethical Obligation to Use Artificial Intelligence: An Examination of the Use of Artificial Intelligence in Law and the Model Rules of Professional Responsibility' (2017) 40(3) *American Journal of Trial Advocacy* 443; M Legg, 'New Skills for New Lawyers: Responding to Technology and Practice Developments' in K Lindgren, F Kunc and M Coper (eds), *The Future of Australian Legal Education* (Thomson Reuters, 2018); T Schaefer, 'The Ethical Implications of Artificial Intelligence in the Law' (2019) 55 *Gonzaga Law Review* 221, 231; J Council, 'Top Law Schools Add AI Courses, *Wall Street Journal*, 22 April 2019.

[87] Carrel (n 70) 1160; D Susskind, *A World Without Work* (Allen Lane, 2020) 155 ('teach people skills that will make them better at whatever machines are bad at').

[88] A Cody and F Gibson, 'Dispute Resolution and Experiential Learning' in M Legg (ed), *The Future of Dispute Resolution* (LexisNexis, 2013) 272.

[89] This is not a novel suggestion as law has engaged with areas such as economics, criminology, history and psychology previously.

to new businesses.[90] Indeed such clinics can be collaborations with computer science and business schools.

Lawyers as Innovators?

Several commentators have argued that law firms and lawyers in general are not capitalising as they might on the new legal applications of AI.[91] Richard Susskind has commented that 'In 10 years' time if you were to look at the top 20 legal providers by revenue, half will be non-lawyers'.[92] Using the example of TAR, Daniel Katz argues that law firms were slow to see the potential of machine learning for discovery, and as a result a number of external providers have sprung up to serve this market.[93] Others say that there is still opportunity for lawyers to develop and control these kinds of software systems, if they are able to leverage it:

> If the legal services industry relies exclusively on venture-backed software companies to innovate in the next generation of legal services, they should not be surprised when the path of legal tech routes around them … if lawyers and their firms innovate with AI tools, create their own supervised learning tools, and harness the intelligence tied up in their people and systems, there is great potential …[94]

Thus, there are calls for lawyers to be at the forefront of innovation when it comes to the legal applications of AI: 'Lawyers have to discern whether and to what degree each task should be computerized, standardized or automated or really needs a handcrafted solution'.[95]

Views about whether lawyers are up to the task of engaging with new technologies are mixed. On one hand, it is claimed that the personalities of lawyers, and the nature of legal culture, tend to militate against such innovation.[96] Others suggest that this view may be somewhat dated.[97] An Australian survey of the receptiveness of lawyers to innovation found more positive results,[98] suggesting that the profession is more open to adapting than perhaps it is given credit for. One US lawyer explains: 'I'm optimistic that AI will soon permeate law firm cultures, which will

[90] See, eg, Technology Startup Clinic at University of California – Hastings; Tech Startup Clinic at Cardozo Law School; Start Up Ventures Clinic at Duke Law School; and Entrepreneurship Clinic at University of Michigan Law School.

[91] JA Sherer and E Walters, 'Transitioning from Consumer Tech to Legal Intelligence Engineering' (2018) *Law Practice* 33, 35; M McKamey, 'Legal Technology: Artificial Intelligence and the Future of Law Practice' (2017) 22 *Appeal: Review of Current Law and Law Reform* 45.

[92] Quoted in J Croft, 'Artificial Intelligence Disrupting the Business of Law', *Financial Times*, 6 October 2016, www.ft.com/content/5d96dd72-83eb-11e6-8897-2359a58ac7a5.

[93] Katz (n 9) 944–45.

[94] Sherer and Walters (n 91) 35.

[95] Bues and Matthaei (n 8) 106.

[96] McKamey (n 91) 55–57; J Rogers and F Bell, *Change Leadership for Lawyers* (Law Society of NSW, 2019).

[97] Rogers and Bell (n 96).

[98] Waye, Verreynne and Knowler (n 5).

in turn provoke new companies and new investments to improve and increase law firm AI solutions so that every lawyer in every law firm will use and benefit from AI'.[99]

Lawyers are Still Lawyers

Traditional black-letter law areas of knowledge and lawyer skill sets need to be maintained. This is for at least three reasons. First for lawyers to be able to perform the role of providing competent and ethical legal services to clients, they must know the law. Similarly, legal knowledge and values are needed to perform the specialised roles that form part of the administration of justice. Knowledge of the law is far more complicated and nuanced than many computer programmers and entrepreneurs comprehend. There are some simple areas of law, provided they are being applied to simple fact patterns,[100] but much of the law is complex and requires expertise, as discussed above.

Second, the critical thinking, problem solving, communication and self-learning skills that are part of the current law degree are still crucial to success as a lawyer.[101] There will be clients that will need or want to access a lawyer with those traditional areas of knowledge and skills, bespoke lawyering, where the law is applied to a specific client's particular problem.[102]

Third, traditional legal skills and law school courses may also be argued to be necessary to undertake the innovation discussed above.[103] To identify existing problems in legal services (ie failure to provide access to justice) and appreciate the advantages of new legal services one needs to have studied the current system of law and legal services.

Deskilling

Some argue that without a need to retain the skills replaced by AI, human experts will eventually lose them.[104] For example, if contract review software can identify

[99] N Ismail, 'Artificial Intelligence in the Legal Industry: Adoption and Strategy – Part 1', *Information Age*, 6 August 2018, www.information-age.com/artificial-intelligence-in-the-legal-industry-123473948/ (quoting Geoffrey Vance).

[100] Pound (n 27) 206.

[101] Law Society of New South Wales, *The Future of Law and Innovation in the Profession* (2017) 77.

[102] R Susskind, *The End of Lawyers? Rethinking the Nature of Legal Services* (Oxford University Press, 2008) 39; J Garon, 'Legal Education in Disruption: The Headwinds and Tailwinds of Technology' (2013) 45 *Connecticut Law Review* 1165, 1205. However, in Susskind, *Tomorrow's Lawyers* (n 42) 25–26 it is stated that 'much less legal work requires bespoke treatment than many lawyers would have their clients believe'.

[103] Susskind (n 42) 145.

[104] See N Carr, *The Glass Cage: Automation and Us* (WW Norton, 2014).

the problematic clauses in seconds, how will new lawyers learn how to spot issues on their own? No longer having to do dull, tedious tasks such as discovery 'appears to liberate lawyers' – but it may also be that this was how 'junior lawyers learnt the craft of lawyering … [which could] be lost in the future'.[105] In general terms, the World Economic Forum summarises the concern as follows:

> While the development of intelligent assistants may be convenient and help to manage administrative and other daily tasks, in certain respects the rise of intelligence and autonomy in machines and software tools may also decrease the intelligence and autonomy of the human user. Digital dementia is a phenomenon described by psychologists as a possible consequence of overusing digital technology, which could result in the deterioration or breakdown of cognitive abilities. Overuse of digital technology may also have an impact on personal autonomy, depending on the degree of digital assistance that is increasingly relied upon to complete even trivial tasks, such as watering indoor plants. As a consequence of the growing reliance on digital assistance, basic human capabilities could be lost. Indeed the self-determination theory suggests that humans need autonomy to function properly in life.[106]

On the other hand, it has been argued that the type of repetitive tasks which are susceptible to automation, such as document review and discovery, are only a small part of what lawyers do.[107]

The use of machines in areas once exclusively the province of human experts has other unpredictable ramifications too, such as how people will react when confronted by a system which can generate results as accurate as an expert's.[108] Discussing radiology and the use of machine learning systems to interpret scans, Federico Cabitza has speculated about the effect of the software on the medical professionals whose work it supplements – will it undermine the self-confidence of senior radiologists, or perhaps make newer ones 'more lazy and dependent on its recommendations'?[109]

This also impacts on questions of liability – at what point will medical professionals be expected to question the decision of a machine?[110] We can see parallels

[105] B Simpson, 'Algorithms or Advocacy: Does the Legal Profession Have a Future in a Digital World?' (2016) 25(1) *Information & Communications Technology Law* 50, 52.

[106] World Economic Forum, *AI Governance: A Holistic Approach to Implement Ethics into AI* (January 2019) 7.

[107] D Remus and F Levy, 'Can Robots Be Lawyers: Computers, Lawyers, and the Practice of Law' (2017) 30(3) *Georgetown Journal of Legal Ethics* 501.

[108] F Cabitza, 'Breeding Electric Zebras in the Fields of Medicine', arXiv:1701.04077; M Hildebrandt, 'Law as Computation in the Era of Artificial Legal Intelligence: Speaking Law to the Power of Statistics' (2018) 68(1) *University of Toronto Law Journal* 12, 32.

[109] ibid.

[110] See MU Scherer, 'Regulating Artificial Intelligence Systems: Risks, Challenges, Competencies, and Strategies' (2016) 29(2) *Harvard Journal of Law and Technology* 353, 356.

here with lawyers. The risk for the legal profession is that humans relinquish their critical thinking skills and rely too heavily on machine predictions:

> Even where the goal and purpose of involving AI in legal decision-making is to increase consistency, there are still risks that it will lead to standardization, which in automated legal decision-making processes can have a regulatory effect on the people involved.[111]

This is a type of 'herd effect'. Decision makers might feel obliged to make decisions within a particular range or in conformity with others. At earlier stages, such an approach may hinder access to justice. At later stages, it is argued that 'reliance on computer programs … may further complicate public deliberation about administrative decisions, because few if any observers will be entirely capable of understanding how a given decision was reached'.[112]

Limits to Education

Education and retraining are the way in which modern economies have met the challenge of technological unemployment. However, Daniel Susskind has argued that education cannot indefinitely solve the problem of unemployment due to technological progress as 'the best existing education systems cannot provide the literacy, numeracy, and problem-solving skills that are required to … compete with today's machines',[113] the argument being that computers are more proficient at those skills than most humans. This leads on to a dystopic future where there is a class of 'economically useless people'.[114] Rather than retraining there is an acceptance that there is not enough meaningful work to go around and the State must respond through changes such as a universal basic income and taxation policy.[115]

Daniel Susskind does not really give up on education but rather suggests it needs to be redirected. This redirection is towards the skills that AI cannot replicate,[116] or if people are unemployable, to teach people how to live fulfilling lives without work – character and life skills.[117] The discussion above on the value of expertise, ethics and human skills identifies the skills that AI cannot replicate, or the tasks humans will not want to be undertaken by machines because they prefer human

[111] M Guihot, AF Matthew and NP Suzor, 'Nudging Robots: Innovative Solutions to Regulate Artificial Intelligence' (2017) 20(2) *Vanderbilt Journal of Entertainment and Technology Law* 385, 410.

[112] MF Cuellar, 'A Simpler World: On Pruning Risks and Harvesting Fruits in an Orchard of Whispering Algorithms' (2017) 51 *UC Davis Law Review* 27, 37.

[113] Susskind (n 87) 153, 165.

[114] ibid 166, citing Yuval Harari, *Homo Deus: A Brief History of Tomorrow* (Harvill Secker, 2015) 269.

[115] T Walsh, *It's Alive – Artificial Intelligence from the Logic Piano to Killer Robots* (La Trobe University Press, 2017) 269. The state could, however, accept growing inequality and division between the wealthy and the unemployable.

[116] Susskind (n 87) 155.

[117] ibid 226–27.

interaction. However, it is also not clear that AI performs better than humans on literacy and problem-solving skills in general. As explained in Chapter 11, AI's advantage is only in very defined circumstances. Education must respond to the development of AI but it is unlikely to be able to address the effects of technological progress on employment alone.

A less extreme but important concern raised above in relation to deskilling is how new members of the profession obtain the experience and socialisation to develop the needed skills and ethics to be lawyers if AI has removed the entry-level work of the past.[118] One approach is to suggest that junior lawyers could undertake 'samples' of such work,[119] even if the bulk of it is outsourced to an AI system. Indeed, law firms are more and more looking to law schools to teach this experience. Experiential learning is one way in which this might be done. Experiential learning is learning by doing. It involves undertaking a practical experience, critical reflection or evaluation of that experience, determining what is useful from the experience, and using that learning to perform the activity again but with greater skill.[120] The experience may be more or less a facsimile of actual practice. It follows that law firms and proficient legal practitioners need to actively and continually expose the new lawyer to the experiences they will need to develop expertise, ethics and human skills for legal practice.

Supporting AI-Enabled Legal Practice

The rise of AI has resulted in the observation that 'the market will most likely no longer tolerate the inefficiencies of the traditional law firm models and lawyering', including the prevailing pricing model – the billable hour.[121] While market demand is important, regulatory requirements and lawyer choices also impact whether and how AI may be adopted by lawyers.

Law Firm Structures

The provision of legal services by lawyers through structures such as corporations or multi-disciplinary partnerships that permit lawyers to join with non-lawyers, such as computer scientists, statisticians and business people, and which enable investment from outside sources, allow lawyers to access two key ingredients for adopting AI in their practice: expertise and financing. Moreover, such legal

[118] B Simpson, 'Algorithms or Advocacy: Does the Legal Profession Have A Future in a Digital World?' (2016) 25(1) *Information & Communications Technology Law* 50.
[119] Susskind (n 42) 170.
[120] Cody and Gibson (n 88) 269.
[121] Bues and Matthaei (n 8) 106.

practices can obtain the benefits of scale and specialisation.[122] US Supreme Court Justice Neil Gorsuch, in discussing access to justice, has observed that 'market participants with greater access to capital can increase output and lower price'.[123] In contrast, traditional law firm models have 'a restricted capital base (limited to equity and debt of individual partners), [with the result that] the output of legal services is restricted, and the price raised above competitive levels'.[124] The concern with permitting business structures beyond the traditional law firm and the sharing of legal fees with non-lawyers is the loss of professional and ethical values.

The adoption of non-traditional (or alternative) structures so as to reap the above benefits which support AI and lawyer viability, while maintaining the ethics value, is achievable. This can be done by (1) including lawyers as part of the body that manages/controls the entity; (2) limiting the undertaking of legal services to lawyers, with the lawyers still subject to their ethical duties; and (3) requiring through regulation that non-lawyers in the organisation refrain from acting in way that could cause the organisation or the lawyers to contravene their ethical obligations.[125] This approach draws on the regulatory environment in England and Wales but does not go so far as to alter how the practice of law is defined. This is to make the point that adopting law firm structures that support AI-enabled legal practice does not have to equate with alterations to what is defined as legal practice or the unauthorised practice of law. This approach is more lawyer friendly than the English approach, but our objective is not to reshape legal practice wholesale but rather to promote change that responds to the advent of AI. Nonetheless, we see value, as explained above, in having lawyers, with their attendant professional and ethical obligations, being the practitioners of law, rather than those who do not have those obligations.

Alternative Fee Arrangements

Legal fees have been charged in a number of ways throughout history, including scales or schedules of fees, task-based billing and annual retainers.[126] However, time-based billing or the billable hour became the most used fee arrangement because research demonstrated that 'The lawyer who records time is consistently a higher earner than the non-timekeeper'.[127] The advent of AI that allows legal work

[122] GK Hadfield and DL Rhode, 'How to Regulate Legal Services to Promote Access, Innovation, and the Quality of Lawyering' (2016) 67 *Hastings Law Journal* 1191, 1194.

[123] N Gorsuch, 'Access to Affordable Justice' (2016) 100(3) *Judicature* 47, 49.

[124] ibid 49.

[125] Hadfield and Rhode (n 122) 1209.

[126] H Leblebici, 'Your Income' in L Empson, *Managing the Modern Law Firm – New Challenges, New Perspectives* (Oxford University Press, 2007) 121–26; M Trotter, *Profit and the Practice of Law* (University of Georgia Press, 1997) 150–54.

[127] M Miller, 'A Systemic Approach to Time Control' in *Law Office Efficiency* (American and Canadian Bar Associations, 1972) 157.

to be conducted more efficiently is of most benefit when the legal work is charged for on a basis that is not linked to time. For lawyers who bill by the hour the efficiencies achieved by AI so that a task can be completed more quickly will reduce income.[128] Indeed the billable hour is inherently in conflict with maximising efficiency and fostering innovation in law firms. Consequently, lawyers need to find a way of billing that provides a return on the lawyer's skill and the investment in the technology but which also provides an attractive fee proposition to the client who may choose from a number of law firms.

The fee arrangement that has been most commonly adopted to support AI-provided legal work is a flat or fixed fee. In a fixed-fee arrangement, the lawyer agrees to provide legal services in exchange for a specified fee, regardless of the time needed to perform the service. The fee can be structured so that the fee is paid for some parts of a matter, an entire matter or multiple matters.[129] Alternatively, the fee may be structured as a retainer, or subscription fee, where a fixed fee is paid for a particular time period, a month or a year, which allows the client to use the AI-provided legal work as much or as little as it desires during that time period. Other alternatives, such as value-based billing, which sets fees by reference to the perceived or estimated value of the service to the client,[130] will develop.

AI may also assist the lawyer to develop profitable fee arrangements by data mining past matters and monitoring ongoing matters to determine how costs are incurred. This can then let the lawyer set a fee from an informed base.

Conclusion

Technology has been painted as the extinction-level event for the lawyer species. As one commentator observed:[131]

> Perhaps one day, self-driving-car accident disputes will be resolved with checks of the vehicle's logs and programming. Your grievance against the local pizza joint's guarantee of a hot delivery in 10 minutes will be checked by a GPS sensor and a smart thermometer. Divorce papers will be prepared when your iPhone detects, through location tracking and text-message scanning, that you've been unfaithful. Your will could be executed as soon as your Fitbit detects that you're dead.

Much will depend on the future capabilities of technology, especially AI, which are currently unclear but continue to develop.

An alternative view is that only human lawyers can practise law, albeit with the aid of AI. Three reasons can be given for this. From a regulatory perspective it may

[128] W Ross, *The Honest Hour* (Carolina Academic Press, 1996) 69–70; A Krikorian, 'Billing Outside the Box' (2014) 27(3) *Georgetown Journal of Legal Ethics* 655, 663.

[129] Association of Corporation Counsel and Crowell Moring, *Handbook for Value-Based Billing Engagements* (2015) 3; Krikorian (n 128) 664.

[130] M Friston (ed), *Friston on Costs* (3rd edn, Oxford University Press, 2018) ch 42.

[131] J Koebler, 'Rise of the Robolawyers', *The Atlantic*, April 2017.

be argued that a human who has been admitted as a legal practitioner is necessary to protect clients from the unqualified and unethical, ie to promote competence and integrity in the public interest. The lawyer is a fiduciary required to act in the client's best interests. The lawyer is different from the taxi driver, the travel agent or hotelier that has experienced disruption from the likes of Uber, Expedia and AirBnB because the lawyer–client relationship is not just commercial, but professional and fiduciary. A second reason is that legal practice requires a lawyer who can provide judgement, discretion, creativity, empathy and understanding to a client, characteristics that are very much human. Lastly, lawyers, in their many roles, are essential to civil society, liberty and the rule of law: goals or conditions that humans value and seek to protect.

Lawyers should not think that they are immune from change. While there are interpersonal and institutional reasons that the lawyer role will continue, it will be with an enhanced skill set that needs to be actively acquired. Equally, even if the advent of AI does not sound the death knell of the legal profession, it should be a wake-up call to reflect on why society needs lawyers – what is the public interest that lawyers serve? Professions exist to advance the public interest. If they cease to do so then society will abandon them.

INDEX

Note: Alphabetical arrangement is word-by-word, where a group of letters followed by a space is filed before the same group of letters followed by a letter, eg 'legal practice' will appear before 'legality testing'. In determining alphabetical arrangement, initial articles and prepositions are ignored.

à law carte legal services, 153–55
ABA, *see* **American Bar Association**
ABS (alternative business structures), 61–64
ACC (Association of Corporate Counsel), 193, 210
access to justice:
- costs, 150
- crisis, 40
- delivery model, 307
- dispute resolution services, 307
- drafting of documents, 307
- ethical duties to facilitate, 306
- facilitation through AI, 307
- human right, 150
- improvement by legal AI, 284
- legal ethics in an AI world, 306–307
- legal services, 307
- pro bono, 306–307
- unbundling assisting with, 154
  - unmet legal needs, serving, 307

access to law, equality in, 331
accessibility, courts, 156
accountability:
- AI ethics principles, 313
- lack as governance system limitation, 278
- limitations of AI data and design, 278–81
- mechanisms, costs attached to, 283
- regulation, 312–13
- regulatory strategy, 278
- accreditation, GDPR, 316

accuracy:
- AI ethics principles, 314
- interpretability pursuit may sacrifice, 250
- of AI systems, ascertaining:
  - criminal lawyers' roles, 238–44
  - policy goals translated into predictive goals, 239
  - statistical significance measures, 239
- predictive, 241–43

acquisition of knowledge, *see* **knowledge**
acquisitions and mergers, 47, 170
activation functions, neural networks, 31
active learning, TAR, 111–12, 125
actuarial analyses:
- machine learning, 220–21

actuarial risk assessments, 244
administration of justice, viii
- advocates' duty to, 135
- dispute resolution lawyers' duty to, 135
- duty to, 302–306
- fidelity to, profession of lawyers, 291
- lawyers, Canada, 304
- lawyers' duties to, 10, 332
- legal ethics in an AI world duty to, 303–306
- legal knowledge and values needed for special roles, 343
- legal practitioners assist in, 304
- protection, ethics, 329
- Solicitors Regulation Authority upholding, 304

administrative law:
- regulatory lawyers challenging laws and regulations through, 194

admission requirements:
- education part of, 341

ADR, *see* **alternative dispute resolution**
Advanced Relational Trading Enforcement Metric Investigation System (ARTEMIS), 209
advent of artificial intelligence:
- lawyers and, into the unknown, 5–8

advice:
- AI use in, 10
- of lawyers, 97
- provided, user-friendly, 337–338
- production, AI liabilities, 310

advisory roles, regulator lawyers, 194

advocacy, 133–35
  human skills, 158
  oral, 51
  Uniform Solicitors Rules, Australia, 303
  work, 51
advocates, 44
  duty to administration of justice, 135
  duty to clients, 134–35
  duty to court, 134–35
  duty to uphold rule of law, 135
  human skills, use to interact with other humans, 158
  independence, 158
  roles, 133–37
  specific requirements, 135
  work, 52
affective form of trust, 186
AFR, *see* **automated facial recognition**
African American defendants:
  mis-classified, COMPAS, 246
after-the-fact accountability, 279
age, weighted, COMPAS, 254
algorithmic assessments, transparency, 250
algorithmic decision-making, 334
algorithmic models, bias, 245–246, 250, 257
algorithmic predictive policing, 229
algorithmic risk assessments, 294–95
algorithms, 14
  design, 268, 281
  discrimination:
    reduction with proper regulation, 288
  discriminatory manner, operating in:
    bias introduced, 269
    discovery, 271
    fixing, 271
    input variables (candidate predictors) choice, 268, 270
    output variables choice, 268, 269–70
    screening decisions, 268
    training procedures choice, 168
  explanations, 274
  government decision-making, 256
  healthcare decisions, 270
  human biases, 271
  human decisions in construction of, 268
  machine learning, 306
  opacity, 272
  pre-trial processes, 113–14
  risk assessments, 251, 281, 294–95
  screeners, 268
  TAR, 113, 127–28
  trade-offs exposed, 271
  trainers, 268–69
  training, bias, 270
***Algorithms in the Criminal Justice System* report, Law Society of England and Wales,** 249, 251
Alibaba, 141–42, 148, 161, 164
Alipay, 148
AlphaGo, 14, 285
AlphaGo Zero, 15
alternative business structures (ABS), 61–64
alternative dispute resolution (ADR), 131
  arbitration, 132
  avoiding disputes, 164
  British Columbia Civil Resolution Tribunal, 145, 153
  China's Internet Courts, 148
  complex and high-stakes disputes, 162
  England and Wales Online Court, 146
  future developments, 160–64
  mediation, 132
  more disputes, 163–64
  more technology, but will it be AI?, 160–62
  online, *see* online alternative dispute resolution
  simplified process – simplified law, 163
alternative firms, 69
alternative practice structures, 323, 347
alternative fee arrangements, 347–48
Amazon Echo, 285
American Bar Association (ABA), 65
  Commission of the Future of Legal Services, 3
  law firms using AI, 326
  Model Rules of Professional Conduct, 292, 297, 299, 300, 302, 306
  Restatement of the Law Governing Lawyers, 297–98
AML (anti-money laundering), 191, 195, 197–99
amplification, expertise, 7
analogy, reasoning by, 158
analysis:
  broad-scope, 174
  in-depth, 173
  merger agreements, 174
  stage, EDRM, 122
  transactional law, 172–75
analytics:
  data, *see* data
  industry, 229
anchoring susceptibility, humans, 96
anomalous information:
  contract review, 177
anomaly detection in surveillance systems, 204

anti-bribery regulation, 194
anti-discrimination legislation, 311
anti-fraud screening and protection, RegTech, 195
anti-money laundering (AML), 191, 195, 197–99
arbitrary search and arrest, 223
arbitration:
ADR, 132
electronically stored information, 125
information gathering, 104, 108–109
area under the curve (AUC), 242
argument retrieval, 27, 35, 36
argumentation approach, 21
argumentation mining, 36
arrest, 223–24
Artificial General Intelligence, 16
Ashley, Kevin, 21–22, 23, 36, 89, 90–91, 101
ASIC, *see* **Australian Securities and Investments Commission**
assembly, documents, transactional law, 179
assisted facial recognition, *see* **automated facial recognition**
Association of Corporate Counsel (ACC), 193, 210
attorney–client privilege, *see* **legal professional privilege**
AUC (area under the curve), 242
audience, exercise of right of, 323
audit trails, 317–18
auditing, 277
augmenting tools, 181
Australia:
Anti-Money Laundering and Counter-Terrorism Financing Act 2006 (Cth), 197
barristers, unbundling and direct briefing, 154
clients:
best interests, solicitors acting in, 298
confidentiality, 300
Consumer Law, 310
document categories, 124
Federal Court of Australia:
direct relevance, 106
standard discovery, 106
in-house lawyers, 60
incorporated legal practices, 62
large corporate law firms, 57
Law Society of New South Wales, vii, 4
lawyers' receptiveness to innovation, survey, 342
legal practice by non-lawyers prohibited, 322
legal work pro bono, 306–307
number of lawyers, 54, 56
pre-trial information gathering, 106
small law firms, 57
solicitors' duties to court and administration of justice, 304
Uniform Solicitors Rules, 302–303
women, 66
see also New South Wales; Victoria
Australian Securities and Investments Commission (ASIC), 209, 210, 215–16
authoring tools, 321
auto pseudonymising, 207
auto-redacting, 207
automated contract management, 178
automated decision-making, 279
automated facial recognition (AFR), 232–34, 244, 248, 252, 256
see also facial recognition
automated legal advice tools, 37
automated processing and profiling, GDPR, 319
automated processing prohibition, GDPR, 256
automated profiling prohibition, GDPR, 256
automated reviews:
non-disclosure agreements, 175
automatic analysis:
of textual description of facts, outcome prediction, 90
automation:
bias, 7–8
discovery subject to, 344
documents, 6, 165, 179–80, 183, 344
impact on work of lawyers, 40
systems, drafting contracts, 178–80, 184
autonomy:
AI ethics principles, 314
deep learning, 262
expert systems, 262
machine learning, 262
personal, 344
availability constraining:
limitations of AI data, 287
avoiding disputes, 164
Axcelerate, 116–17
Axiom, 178
Ayasdi, banking, 201

backpropagation, 32, 33
bail, 224–25, 236, 250
banking, 195, 199–202

Bar of California, 296, 301
barristers, 44, 54
  solicitors and, 52
  unbundling and, 154
  win rates, 266–67
  work, 52
BASEL II, 200
Bayesian algorithms, 30
before-the-fact accountability, 279
behaviour, organisational, 334
behavioural sciences, 79
beneficence, 313, 314
benefit of society:
  lawyers' duties for, 332
benefits:
  of AI, 282
  distribution from predictive analytics, 95
  of scale, 345
  specialisation, 347
BEPP, eBay, 141
best practice:
  limitations of AI design, 288
best execution, trading, 203–204
best interests of clients, 298, 304, 338
bias:
  algorithmic models, 245–246, 250, 257
  automated facial recognition, 248
  cognitive, 95, 96
  concept layer, 245, 249
  criminal lawyers' roles, 244–50
  in data, 248
  data layer, 245, 246–47
  decision-making, 257
  drug offences arrests, 247–48
  effects susceptibility, humans, 96
  human decision-making, 244
  human, 271
  human world permeation by, 276
  introduced:
    algorithms operating in discriminatory manner, 269
  layers, 245
  machine bias, 245
  machine learning, *see* machine learning
  model layer, 245–46
  neural networks, 31
  outputs, machine learning:
    rule of law consequences, 306
  in policing, 247–48
  problematic data, 245
  racial, 244–45
  rectifying problem, 249
  regulation, 312
  in risk assessments, 245, 247
  risk models, conceptual issues, 245
  selection, 265
  social, 306
  as social inequality problem, 249
  social world, 267
  statistical models, 245
  training, algorithms, 270
  see also fairness
big data:
  AI tools application, 78–79
  analytics, 205, 237
  data analytics using machine learning, 78
  growth rate, 78
  machine learning and, combination of, 326
  outcome prediction using deep learning techniques, 79
  policing, 228, 237, 244
  SEC Market Information Data Analytics System (MIDAS), 209
  sensitive and compromising information identification, Text IQ, 207
  transactional law, 165
  use in legal analytics, 98
Big Law, 59, 70, 168–69, 181, 187
billable hour, fees, 347–48
billing, *see* **fees; legal fees**
biological neurons, 30–31
biometrics, 199, 233
black box:
  problem, 272
  technology, 306
blind-bidding systems, 160
blockchain technology, 132
boilerplate contract terms, 166, 172
Boolean keywords, 26
box-ticking exercise, 217
branches of Artificial Intelligence, 16–17
Brazil:
  foreign legal services markets, 57
  local legal services markets, 57
  organisational forms of lawyers, 54
  solo legal practice, 56
breach of fiduciary duty, 308
breach of law, 210
bridging program, 90–91
Briggs Lord Justice, 145, 147, 152
Britain, *see* **England and Wales; Scotland, United Kingdom**
British Columbia Civil Resolution Tribunal, 144–45, 153
broad-scope analysis, 174
'broken windows theory' of policing, 229

Browder, Joshua, 37
business agreements:
translating into legal agreements, 186
business goals:
transactional lawyers' clients, 170
business lawyers, *see* **transactional lawyers**
business logic workflow tools, 321
Business Purchase Protection (BEPP), eBay, 141
business structures, alternative (ABS), 61–64
business transactions:
consumers utilising AI legal products or services, 332
business interests, 331

California:
Bar, 296, 301
legal practice by non-lawyers prohibited, 322
Canada:
alternative business structures recommended by Canadian Bar Association, 63
barristers and solicitors, 52
British Columbia Civil Resolution Tribunal, 145, 153
Canadian Bar Association:
emotional intelligence, 334
Futures: Transforming the Delivery of Legal Services in Canada, 3
clients:
confidentiality, 300
duties to, 298, 304
fees, 299
lawyers:
administration of justice, 304
legal aid, 306
legal service on pro bono basis, 306
Model Code of Professional Conduct, 329–30
number of lawyers, 54
organisational forms of lawyers, 54
professional conduct rules, 296
candidate predictors:
choice, algorithms operating in discriminatory manner, 268, 270
capital:
base restricted:
traditional law firms, 347
minimum, banking, 200
non-lawyer, 70
reputational, 70, 168–69, 187
Capital Requirements Directive IV, EU, 200
carceral state:
sentencing critiques, 225
care and skill:
failure to exercise, 309
case-based reasoning (CBR), 21–25, 27, 76
case management:
England and Wales Online Court, 146
case law:
internet, readily available, 323
smart phones, readily available, 323
CaseCrunch, 93
categorical suspicion against people, policing, 252
causal reasoning, 18–19
causal explanations:
machine learning, 279
causation, AI liabilities, 309, 310
cause and effect:
proving, AI liabilities, 309
CBR (case-based reasoning), 21–25, 27, 76
CCAR (Comprehensive Capital Analysis and Review), US, 200, 201
CCTV (closed-circuit television), 232, 233
CEPEJ, *see* **European Commission for the Efficiency of Justice**
certification:
audit trails compared, 317–18
regimes, accountability, 280
regulation, 315–16
challenging use of AI Tools, 251–55
change of control transactions, 174
changing circumstances:
lawyers adapting to, 6
character-based requirements for entry, 65
character skills, 345
charges:
lawyers, traditionally, 283
see also costs; fees
chat communications, 201
chatbots:
Australian Securities and Investments Commission, *see* Australian Securities and Investments Commission
authoring tools, LegalTech providers, 321
Bangko Sentral ng Pilipinas (BSP), 210
know your customer, 199
China:
Alibaba, 148, 161, 164
Alipay, 148
foreign legal services markets, 57
Hainan, non-lawyers as partners in law firms, 62
Hangzhou, 148–49
Hubao, litigation guiding robot, 149

Intelligent Complaint Machine, 148–49
Internet Courts, 147–49
Jilin, 147–48
lawyers, 39
local legal services markets, 57
number of lawyers, 56
online litigation platforms, 148
Supreme People's Court (SPC), 147–48
Zhejiang, 147–48, 161

citizens:
roles of lawyers after online dispute resolution, 149–51

civil dispute resolution, AI use in, 10

civil law jurisdictions:
judiciary appointments, civil service model, 66–67
litigation lawyers, gathering information and evidence, 107–108
pre-trial information gathering, 107–108
regulation of lawyers, 66

Civil Procedures Rules (CPR), England and Wales, 106–107

class actions, 53, 83

classification, 17
probabilistic approach to, 174
classifier creation, TAR, 111

cleaning data:
machine learning, 29, 306

cleaning up data, 249

Clearwell system provided by Symantec, 119

clients, 45
advocates' duty to, 134–35
Australia, *see* Australia
best interests, 298, 304, 338
collaboration with, 336
confidences, lawyers, 9
confidentiality:
Canada, 300
England and Wales, 300
information, 300, 301
protection, 298
Singapore, 300
corporate, 338
dispute resolution lawyers' duty to, 134–35
duty to, viii, 332
acting in best interests, 297–98
AI liabilities, 308
Canada, 298, 304
ethical, 298
fiduciary, 330
lawful objectives, advancing, 297–98
legal ethics in an AI world, 297–300
legitimate interests, pursuing, 297–29
loyalty, 297
partisanship, 297
Singapore, 298
generating options for, 49
Hong Kong, 298, 300
identification companies, RegTech, 196
independence from, professional independence as, 302
information confidentiality, 300, 301
interests, 49, 291, 330
lawyers:
defenders of after online dispute resolution, 155–58
emotional bonds with, 286
legal practice by non-lawyers, 320–22
loyalty to, independence, 302
negotiation with, 51
organisational, 45
pressures from, independence, 302
professional indemnity insurance, access to, 322
professional independence as independence from, 302
protection, 331
ethics, 321, 329
lawyers, 10
legal liabilities, 321
reading, 337–338
reasoning with, 100
representation facilitating:
legal professional privilege, 301
roles:
EDRM, 123
suing, AI liabilities, 309
transactional lawyers, *see* transactional lawyers
trust, 335–36
lawyers, 9
unable to afford price, 338

clinical teaching, 341

CLOC (Corporate Legal Operations Consortium), 61

closed-circuit television (CCTV), 232, 233

clustering:
algorithms, 30
market misconduct, 205
pre-trial processes, 113–14
unsupervised learning by, market misconduct, 205

co-ordination of steps, EDRM, 123

co-regulatory arrangements, 64, 290

Code of Civil proceedings, Japan, 108

coding, education, 340

cognitive biases, 95, 96
cognitive form of trust, 186
cognitive limitations, expert systems, 24
cognitive technologies, 14
Cognitive+, 208
collaboration, 49, 334, 336, 338, 341
collection stage, EDRM, 122
commercial interests, 302, 331
commercial leases, 175
commercial relationships, 332
commission, errors of, 181
Commission of the Future of Legal Services, ABA, 3
commoditisation of law, 40
commodity legal documents, 180–81
common law jurisdictions:
costs, 152
judiciary appointments from senior practising lawyers, 66
litigation lawyers, gathering information and evidence, 105–107
pre-trial information gathering, 105–107
regulation of lawyers, 66
common sense, AI lacking, 287
communication:
advice provided, user-friendly, 337–38
corporate clients, 338
human value, 334, 337–38
law degrees, 343
reading the client, 337–38
reading the room, 337
secrecy, legal professional privilege, 301
skill sets lawyers need, maintaining, 343
skills, technical skills not to push out, 341
technology use, OADR, 161
work, 51
COMPAS, 226–28, 235–36, 238, 241–46, 248, 252–54
compassion, authentic, 335
compassionate lawyers, 327
competence:
algorithmic risk assessments, 294–95
challenging AI tools, 294
client confidentiality protection, 298
e-discovery, 296
effectiveness involved, 291–92
efficiency involved, 291–92
electronically stored information handling, 296
ethical application of knowledge or skills, 292
interrogating AI tools, 294
legal ethics in an AI world, 291–97
outcome prediction, 294
outsourcing, 297
professional requirements, AI liabilities, 308
seeking assistance of experts in AI, 296–97
technical proficiency, 291
technology, 292–93, 296
competent legal services, 343
competition regulation, 194, 311
competitive-consumerist paradigm, 64
competitive marketplace for TAR, 127
competitive services, 326
complex disputes, ADR and ODR, 162
complex judgements, 329
complexity:
in-house lawyers' response to, 214
of law, needing expertise, 343
compliance:
as box-ticking exercise, need to avoid, 217
failures, in-house lawyers, 210
general:
AI application to regulation, 208
companies, RegTech, 196
government lawyer roles, 194
in-house lawyers dealing with, 193
integration of new bodies of regulation, Waymark Tech, 208
machine learning, 208
management, in-house counsel and, 60
market misconduct, 204–205
natural language processing, 208
RegTech, 195, 214–15
regulatory analytics provision, Cognitive+, 208
regulatory obligations mapped to internal policies, CUBE, 208
requirements, Law Society of England and Wales, 191
rule-based AI, 208
specialists not lawyers, 214–15
trading, 202
World Economic Forum on, 204–205
Compliance.ai, banking, 201–202
compliant storage, trading, 203
Comprehensive Capital Analysis and Review (CCAR), US, 200, 201
compromise to integrity, avoidance, 338–39
compromising information identification, Text IQ, 207
Compstat, 228–29
computers:
codes, TAR, 125
creative acts incapable of engaging in, 285
power, TAR, 127
programs, pre-trial processes, 110

thinking, incapable of, 285
vision, 16–17
concept layer, bias, 245, 249
concept drift, 272
conceptualising work of lawyers, 48
concern, authentic, 335
conditional fees, 150
conditional release, 225–26
condominium property disputes:
British Columbia Civil Resolution Tribunal, 144–45
conduct, misleading, AI liabilities, 308
confidence, TAR, 112
confidentiality, viii
ABA Model Rules of Professional Conduct, 300
California Bar, 301
client information, 300, 301
cybersecurity, 301
documents, pre-trial information gathering, 126–27
human error, 301
inadvertent, 301
legal professional privilege and, 300–302
protection, clients, 298
recorded speech conversion to text, 302
regulatory challenges, 218
technology and, 301
transparency or, TAR, 126
trust, 335
conflicts of interest, 9, 335
connectionists, 30
conscience, need for, 333
consensus positions, 75
consent, data privacy, 206
consistency with law, ODR, 152
constitutional law, 194
constitutional rights, 221–22
constitutional principles, 222
constraints, 338–39
Consumer Law, Australia, 310
consumers:
commercial relationships as business transactions, 332
exchange lower protections for lower costs, 332
protection legislation, 308, 311
content extraction, 17
Context, 93
contextualising, 130
contingency fees, 150
continuing role of courts, 156
continuous active learning, TAR, 111–12, 125
continuous review:
anti-money laundering, 198
contracts:
automated management, 178
data points, 178
discrete, 185
drafting, 166, 173, 178–80, 184
enforcement costs, 166
form completion services, free, 188
liabilities for AI, 308, 309
machine analysis of, 173
machine learning, 175–76
management products, transactional lawyers' roles, 181
one-off, 185
precedent agreements, 167
predictive contracting, 173, 180
relational theories, 166, 185
review, 165, 175, 176–78
terms, 166, 167, 172, 184, 185
transaction costs, 166
transactional, 185
unfair terms, 308, 309
work, 47
contravention prevention:
in-house lawyers, 210
control:
personal data scrutinising and regulating, 249
profession of lawyers, 43–44
sets, TAR, 112
controls, professional, 327
conversational agents, embodied, 334
conveyancing, 47, 48, 67
cooperation, 158, 333
core activities, lawyers, 6
corporate clients, 338
corporate cultures, 217
corporate governance, 217–18
corporate greed, 218
corporate guardians, 218
'corporate hemisphere', 45
corporate lawyers, *see* **transactional lawyers**
corporate legal departments, 181
Corporate Legal Operations Consortium (CLOC), 61
corporate legal risks, 211
corporate legal service, 59
corporate misconduct prevention, 211
corporate opportunity waivers, 76, 174
corporate reorganisation work, 53

corporations:
interests looking after, role of lawyers in RegTech, 212
law firms as, 345–47
Correctional Offender Management Profiling for Alternative Sanctions, *see* **COMPAS**
costs:
access to justice, 150
accountability mechanisms, attached to, 283
common law jurisdictions, 152
enforcement, contracts, 166
environmental, 284–85
governance, risk and compliance, 195
human labour, 284–85
limitations of AI, 281–85
lower, 332
needed for obtaining and supporting AI products, 326
recovery, 151–52
saving links, RegTech, 217
savings, 284
shifting, 152
transactions, 166, 173
see also fees; legal fees
counselling work, 169
counter terrorism financing (CTF), 197–96
counterfactual faithfulness, 275–76
counterparty identification companies, RegTech, 196
County Court Money Claims Centre (CCMCC), England and Wales, 147
County Court Online Pilot, England and Wales, 147
courts:
accessibility, 156
advocates' duty to, 134–35
continuing role, 156
dispute resolution lawyers' duty to, 134–35
fairness, procedures for ensuring, 164
humanity, extending to disputants, 164
inappropriate use of AI tools, 251
justice, procedures for ensuring, 164
lawyers' duty to, 303, 304–305, 332
legal representation, 156
non-lawyers, designed for, 163
online, *see* online courts
procedural fairness, 156
proceedings commencement steps, ODR, 138
rule of law, 155
self-representation as anomaly, 163
simplification of process, ODR, 163
system links, ODR, 138
COVID-19 pandemic, 160
CPR (Civil Procedures Rules), England and Wales, 106–107
Crawford, Kate, 267–68, 282, 285
creative problem-solving, 159
creative thinking, 159, 336–37
creative lawyers, 327
creativity, 159, 333
AI lacking, 287
computers incapable of engaging in acts of, 285
divergent thinking, 337
emotional intelligence, 337, 338
forward thinking, 337
human skills, 158
human value, 333, 336–37
invention, 337
lateral thinking, 337
multiple intelligences, 337
problem-solving, 337
requiring expertise, 326
see also entries beginning with creative
credit scoring, 276
credit risks, banking, 200–202
crime:
police investigations, 223
prevention, automated facial recognition benefits, 256
statistics, 220
criminal justice:
actuarial risk assessments, 244
adversarial systems, 222
prosecutors, 223
algorithms risk assessments, 281
application of AI:
data, 227
design, 227–28
COMPAS, 226–28
facial recognition, 232–34
opacity, 228
predictive policing, 228–32
risk assessments, 227–28, 234–37
big data analytics, 237
criminal procedure, 222
facial recognition systems use, 265
individualised sentencing, 254
inquisitorial systems, 222
investigative process, 222, 223
post-conviction rehabilitation needs, 226
predictions, machine learning generating, 240
privatised nature, US, 250
proxy variables, 248

racial inequities reflecting, 247
sentencing, *see* sentencing
social inequities reflecting, 247
value choices, 246
value-laden decisions not to be outsourced or privatised, 257

criminal law, 221–2
AI use in, 10
conditional release, 225
constitutional principles, 222
individual interests:
state interests and, balancing, 222
innocence presumptions, 224
parole, 225
pre-trial detention, 224–25
sentencing, *see* sentencing
state interests:
individual interests and, balancing, 222

criminal lawyers, 220–26
defence, 223, 225–26
plea bargaining, 226
prosecution:
plea negotiations, 226
roles, 237–38
accuracy of AI systems, ascertaining, 238–44
bias, 244–50
challenging use of AI tools, 251–55
defendants' bail, 224
defendants' pre-trial detention, 224
defendants' remand, 224
fairness, 244–50
inaccuracy of AI systems, ascertaining, 238–44
inquisitorial systems, 222–23
interpretability and opacity, 250
machine learning flaws, understanding, 237
opacity and interpretability, 250
police investigations and, 223

criminal misconduct, 335

criminal status:
investors with, anti-money laundering restriction of, 198

critical thinking, 343

cryptographic commitments, 277

CTF (counter terrorism financing), 197–99

CUBE, 208

CUBOT, 208

cultures:
collaboration across, 336
corporate, 217

customisation, drafting contracts, 166

cut-off points, TAR, 115

cybersecurity, 301, 313

Da Silva Moore v Publicis Groupe, 116–17, 130

data:
accessible, transactional lawyers, 183
analytics, 78, 94, 102, 196, 221
auditing, 280
availability limitation, outcome prediction, 266
bias in, 248
cleaning, 86, 249
collection, 85–86
COMPAS, 227
criminal justice application of AI, 227
financial, historical hidden patterns, banking, 201
hard, 42
labelling, 36
layer, bias, 245, 246–47
limitations of AI, 263–81, 287
machine learning, *see* machine learning
order, 205
partitioning and statistics review, 86–87
personal, 249
see also General Data Protection Regulation
points, 178, 218
privacy, 206–207
protection:
companies, RegTech, 196
legislation, personal data, GDPR, 318–20
seals, GDPR, 316
real world:
machine learning training data used, 240
relationships characterisation, 80
scans, anti-money laundering, Quantexa, 199
storage, 301
subject rights, personal data, GDPR, 318–19
textual, 90
unstructured, 196, 205

data-driven approaches, 7

data-driven knowledge, 18–19

data-driven techniques, 18

Data Ethics Commission, Germany, 256–57

Data Privacy Processes and Algorithmic Bias Considerations, IEEE, 315

databases:
AFR automated searching of, 233–34

datasets:
predictive policing, 228
variables, 79

de Bono, Edward, 337

deal facilitating, 47
deal making:
transactional lawyers' work, 165, 169, 170, 171
decision analysis, patents, 92
decision fatigue, judges, 96
decision-makers:
algorithmic decision-making, importance of being listened to by, 334
decision-making:
algorithmic, 334
automated, 279
bias, 257
human, *see* human decision-making
in-house lawyers engaging in and influencing, 212
judicial, 79–80
skills not necessarily improved by experience, 95
structuring, 244
Supreme Court, United States, 82–83
trade-offs in competing social values, 271
decision support systems, 27
decision trees, 317
AI and Law history, 27–28
decision support systems, 27
disclosure, 317
expert systems, 28
machine learning, 27, 28, 30
nodes, 27
ODR, 137
rule-based, 28
statistical modelling, 27
Supreme Court Forecasting Project, 81–82
deconstructed legal services, 336
deductive reasoning, 20, 24–25, 158
Deep Blue, 14–15
deep concept analysis, TextIQ, 207
deep learning, 3, 17
AI liabilities, 309–10
autonomy, 262
description, 262
explainability, 262
image recognition, 33
machine learning, 30, 33–35
natural language processing, 33
OECD, 33
outputs cannot be intelligibly explained, 38
techniques, 38, 79
unsupervised learning, 34–35
deep neural networks, 31, 33–34
default probability, 200
defeasible logic, 21
defects, AI liabilities, 310
defence:
counsel, ECtHR, 223
criminal lawyers, 223, 225–26
defendants, 224, 246
deficient corporate cultures, 217
definitions of Artificial Intelligence, 14
delawyering after online dispute resolution, 151–53
Deloitte, 6, 70, 195, 283, 326
dementia, digital, 344
'Der Rechtsdienstleistungsmarkt 2030' (German Bar Association), 3
deregulation, 64, 68, 70–71, 331
design:
algorithms, 268, 281
COMPAS, 227–28
criminal justice application of AI, 227–28
human-centred, 152
legal, 152
limitations of AI, 263, 267–81, 288
machine learning, *see* machine learning
privacy by, 320
role of lawyers in RegTech, 212
safeguards, data, limitations of AI, 276–78
standards regulation, 315
theory, 341
deskilling, 343–45
detention, pre-trial, 224–25
determining factors, explanations of, 275
deterrence, sentencing, 225
***Developing Legal Talent* (Deloitte),** 326
development of AI, 13, 346
diagram, EDRM, 121
digital dementia, 344
digital technology overuse, 344
dignity, AI ethics principles, 314
direct briefing, barristers, 154
disaggregation, 40, 153
disagreements:
resolved without becoming disputes, 266
disclosure:
AI use in, 10
decision trees, 317
documents, *see* documents
information asymmetry, 316–17
neural networks, 317
orders in relation to, England and Wales, 106–107
prevention, client information, 300
regulation, 316–17
standard, 106–107
transactional lawyers' work, 169, 171

discovery:
AI use in, 10, 308
algorithms operating in discriminatory manner, 271
arbitration information, 108–109
Australian Law Reform Commission review in Federal Court, 123
disputes, TAR, 126
Federal Rules of Procedure, USA, 107
junior lawyers, less need for, 129
machine learning unsupervised methods used in, 113
pre-trial information gathering, 124–25
pre-trial processes, 109–10
process, ESI challenges during, 129
standard, 106
subject to automation, 344
technology-assisted review in, 9, 124, 126, 303
discrete task representation, 153–55
discretion:
technology difficulty in replicating, 8
discrimination:
algorithms, *see* algorithms
machine learning, auditing establishing, 277
outputs, machine learning, 288
patterns, machine learning training data reflecting, 267
regulation, 312
dispute resolution, 50, 51
fair, society's interest in, 157
lawyers, 133–37, 153–55
privatised services, 266
services, access to justice, 307
voluntary, machine learning, 138
disputes:
avoidance, 164
complex, 162
disagreements resolved without becoming, 266
discovery, TAR, 126
high-stakes, 162
more, ADR, 163–64
resolution, *see* dispute resolution
disruption, 2–5
disruptive innovation, 150, 188
distributed ledger technology (DLT), 192
divergent thinking, 337
divorce or separation matters, 47
divorce or separation matters:
online dispute resolution, 143
DLT (distributed ledger technology), 192
documents:
analysis, outcome prediction features, 90
automation, *see* automation
categories, Australia, 124
computer-coded reviewed, TAR, 125
confidential, 126–27
conversion to readable electronic format, 123
court-related, 160
disclosure:
arbitration information, 108–109
for discovery:
pre-trial processes, 109–10
drafting, *see* drafting
exchange of, France, 108
generation, ODR, 138
indexing, 124
introducing into evidence, France, 108
legal, *see* legal documents
machine learning training to review, 175–77
non-responsive, TAR, 125
pre-trial processes:
for discovery, 109–10
information gathering, civil law jurisdictions, 108
privileged, 126–27
privileged, 126–27
production:
by court order, Japan, 108
regulatory investigations, USA, 109
relevant, identifying:
pre-trial information gathering, common law jurisdictions, 105
retrieval:
information retrieval distinguished, 26
review:
advances in, 327
junior lawyers, less need for, 326–27
subject to automation, 344
sensitive, 207
transactional law, 165, 179–80
transactional lawyers, 183
Domingos, Pedro, 14, 15, 28, 29, 37, 38
DoNotPay chatbot, 37
drafting:
access to justice, 307
contracts *see* contracts
merger agreements, 174
transactional law, 173, 178–80
transactional lawyers' work, 169, 171, 172, 182, 186
work, 48

due diligence, 6
AI employed for, 308
anti-money laundering, 198
contract review, 176–78
counter terrorism financing, 198
document review advances in, 327
large-scale, 176–78
in merger and acquisition context, 171–72
outcome prediction advances in, 327
products, transactional lawyers' roles, 181
technology-assisted review in, 9
transactional lawyers' work, 171–72
unstructured aspect, 177
due process:
fundamental rights, 228
duty to administration of justice, 303–306
duty to clients, *see* **clients**
duty to courts, 303, 304–305
duty to uphold rule of law, 305
dynamic factors:
static factors and, failing to distinguish between, 250
dynamics, group, 334

e-commerce, 140–43, 161
e-discovery, 123, 296
e-waste, 285
eBay, 164, 140–41, 266
eBrevia, 185
Ecertic, Spain, 199
ECHR, *see* **European Convention on Human Rights**
economic loss, pure, 308
Economides, Kim, 46–47, 48, 49, 50–51, 53, 99
ECtHR, *see* **European Court of Human Rights**
EDGAR, public database, 183–84
eDiscovery, Text IQ, 207
EDRM (Electronic Discovery Reference Model), 107, 121–25
education, 194, 250, 339–46
effectiveness, 291–92
efficiency:
engendered by artificial intelligence, 6
gains, 7, 190, 326
involved, competence, 291–92
transactional lawyers' roles, 181–82
Electronic Discovery Reference Model (EDRM), 107, 121–25
electronically stored information (ESI):
challenges during discovery process, 129
EDRM, 121, 122–23
handling, competence, 296
pre-trial processes, 110
roles of lawyers, arbitration, 125
email, 131, 132, 160, 301
embodied conversational agents, 334
emotional bonds:
clients and lawyers, 286
emotional intelligence, 337, 338
Canadian Bar Association, 334
collaboration, 334
group dynamics, 334
human skills, 158
human value, 333, 334–35
organisational behaviour, 334
psychology, 334
emotions, 286
empathy, 51
human skills, 158, 159
human value, 333, 334–35
independence and, 339
lawyers, 8
in legal practice, 335
requiring expertise, 326
work of lawyers and, 40
enforcement costs, contracts, 166
enforcement roles, regulator lawyers, 194
England and Wales:
alternative business structures (ABS), 63
barristers, unbundling and, 154
Civil Procedures Rules, 106–107
client confidentiality, 300
Code of Conduct for Solicitors, *see* Solicitors Regulation Authority
County Court Money Claims Centre (CCMCC), 147
County Court Online Pilot, 147
lawyers, 39
Legal Services Act 2007 (LSA), 63
legal work:
pro bono, 306–307
types reserved to those with professional legal titles, 322–23
Online Civil Money Claims Pilot, 147
Online Court, 145–47, 151–52
orders in relation to disclosure, 106–107
plea bargaining, 226
pre-trial information gathering, 106–107
public access scheme, 154
Solicitors Regulation Authority, *see* Solicitors Regulation Authority
standard disclosure, 106–107
see also United Kingdom
Enron, 62, 218

ensemble algorithms, 30
enterprise email security platform, Tessian, 206
enterprise formation and operations, 47
entities built on technology platforms:
extensive use of AI, 326
entry, restricting, 327
environmental costs, 284–85
environmental laws, 207
environmental regulation, 194
equality:
application of law, fundamental rights, 228
rule of law, 305
equivant, 245
Equivio's Relevance software, 117–18
error, margins of, TAR, 112
ESI, *see* **electronically stored information**
'Ethically Aligned Design – A Vision for Prioritizing Human Well-being with Autonomous and Intelligent Systems' (document), IEEE, 315
ethics, viii
administration of justice protection, 329
client protection, 329
corporate cultures, promotion, 217
duties:
access to justice facilitation, 306
client protection, 321
to clients, 298
in-house lawyers, 218, 219
lawyers still subject to, 347
frameworks, lawyers operating in, 10
judgements:
discovery, pre-trial information gathering, 124
good ethical, 330
lawyers' obligations, 1, 9, 10
legal ethics in an AI world, 289–306
obligations, 305, 331, 338
principles of AI ethics, 313–14
professional, 95
public interest promotion, 329, 331
requirements, unbundling and, 155
responsibilities:
AI liabilities, 308
in-house lawyers, 218, 219
roles of transactional lawyers, 185–87
rules:
requiring competence with technology, 341
skills application, 292
teaching, law schools, 346
value, 329–33, 36
European Commission for the Efficiency of Justice (CEPEJ):
European Ethical Charter on the use of AI in judicial systems and their environment, 157, 316
European Convention on Human Rights (ECHR):
automated facial recognition and, 232
CEPEJ drawing on, 157
European Court of Human Rights (ECtHR):
defence counsel, 223
outcome prediction, 91–92, 94
European Ethical Charter on the use of AI in judicial systems and their environment, 157
European Market Structure Regulation, EU, 200
European Union:
Capital Requirements Directive IV, 200
European Market Structure Regulation, 200
General Data Protection Regulation, *see* General Data Protection Regulation
Markets in Financial Instruments Directive (MiFID II), 191
Money Laundering, Fourth Directive on (4MLD), 197–98
prior conformity assessment, 316
European Union Agency for Fundamental Rights (FRA), 232–33
experience:
empathy, 334
predictive judgement not necessarily improved by, 95
transactional lawyers, 182–83
expert-in-the-loop:
machine learning, 201–202
expert lawyering, 329
expert systems, 17, 20–21
autonomy, 262
decision support systems, 27
decision trees, 28
England and Wales Online Court, 145
explainability, 262
factor against adoption, 161
high value claims, 162
human decision-making support, 38
information provision, 138
interpretability, 37
knowledge acquisition bottleneck, 161
limitations, 23–25, 161
ODR, 137–38, 161
simple-to-use shells, LegalTech providers, 321

Solution Explorer, British Columbia Civil Resolution Tribunal, 144–45, 160–61
tailored information and direction provision, 161
transparency, 37
user interfaces, 161
expertise:
amplification, 7
complexity of law needing, 343
creativity requiring, 326
defining, 327–28
knowledge, 327, 328
lawyers, 8, 9, 10
professional skills requirements, 326
relational, 328–29
skills, 327, 328
value, 327–29
experts:
human, *see* human experts
see also entries beginning with expert
explainability:
accountability related to, 278
deep learning, 262
difficulties, AI liabilities, 310
expert systems, 262
Explainable AI (XAI), 274–275
limitations of AI data and design, 272–76
machine learning, 262
regulation, 312
validity, 272
see also explanations; interpretability
Explainable AI (XAI), 274–275
explaining, lawyers' roles in, 130
explanations, 274–75
accountability, relevance, 278
algorithms, 274
of automated decision-making, 279
counterfactual faithfulness, 275–76
of determining factors, 275
local, 275–76
machine learning, 279
rights, personal data, GDPR, 319
see also explainability
explicability:
AI ethics principles, 313, 314
see also explainability; explanations
external lawyers, RegTech, 215–16

face biometrics, 199
facial recognition:
criminal justice application of AI, 232–34
systems, 265
technology, 249, 252, 256
see also automated facial recognition
fact investigation, 53
factors:
outcome prediction, 90
reasoning, 22, 23
facts:
outcome prediction, 89, 90
proving, 108
fair operation, ODR, 152
fair outcomes, 256
fair processing:
personal data, GDPR, 318
fair random choices:
machine learning, 277
fairness, 221
AI ethics principles, 313, 314
conception of, 245
courts, procedures for ensuring, 164
criminal lawyers' roles, 244–50
crucial, OADR, 157
false negative rates, 246
false positive rates, 246
focus on achieving, 249
inherent trade-offs, 246
or lack of, COMPAS, 241
predictive validity, 246
procedural, 156
rule of law, 305
statistical, 245
see also bias
faithfulness, counterfactual, 275–76
false negative rates, 246
false positive rates, 246
fault determinations, 280
FCA, *see* **Financial Conduct Authority**
Federal Court of Australia, *see* **Australia**
Federal Reserve Comprehensive Capital Analysis and Review (CCAR), US, 200, 201
Federal Rules of Evidence, USA, 127
Federal Rules of Procedure (FRCP), USA, 107
feed-forward networks, 32, 33
fees:
ABA Model Rules of Professional Conduct, 299
alternative fee arrangements, 347–48
billable hour, 347–48
Canada, 299
conditional, 150
contingency, 150
fixed fee, 348
flat fee, 348

lawyers sharing with non-lawyers, prohibitions on, 61
legal ethics in an AI world, 299
profitable arrangements, 348
as retainers, 348
scales of, 347
schedules of, 347
SRA Code of Conduct for Solicitors, Registered European Lawyers and Registered Foreign Lawyers, 299
subscription, 348
task-based billing, 347
value-based billing, 348

fiduciary duties, 308, 330
Financial Conduct Authority (FCA):
Financial Crime Department, 216–17
regulatory sandbox, 217
Waymark Tech ingests handbooks, 208
financial data, 201
financial harm, 308
financial services, 201
financial system collapse, 218
financial technology (FinTech), 192, 195
financing, access to, 346
financing work, 47
fingerprint biometrics, 199
FinTech (financial technology), 192, 195
fitness for purpose, 309
fixed fees, 348
flat fees, 348
formal dispute resolution, ODR, 138
forms:
completion free services, 188
generation, ODR, 138
forward thinking, 337
FRA (European Union Agency for Fundamental Rights), 232–33
France:
alternative business structures resisted, 63
Conseil National des Barreaux, 65
criminal cases, 223
documents, 108, 109
facts, proving, 108
government decision-making algorithms, public availability, 256
judge analytics prohibition, 77–78
Justice Reform Act, 77–78
pre-trial information gathering, 108
regulatory investigations, 109
FRCP (Federal Rules of Procedure), USA, 107
freedom:
AI ethics principles, 314

fundamental rights:
due process, 228
equality in application of law, 228
liberty of the person, 221–22
respect for, CEPEJ first principle, 157
funding litigation, 150
future for lawyers, 10, 69–71
Future of Law and Innovation in the Profession (FLIP) Commission of Inquiry, vii, 4
future of legal profession, 325–49
Future of Legal Services Report:
Law Society of England and Wales, 3
***Futures: Transforming the Delivery of Legal Services in Canada* (Canadian Bar Association),** 3

gaming regulation, 194
'garbage in, garbage out', machine learning, 29
gas and oil work, 47
gatekeeper model, 211
Gavelytics, 93
GDPR, *see* **General Data Protection Regulation, EU**
general Artificial Intelligence, 16
general compliance, 196, 208
general counsel, 193, 210
General Data Protection Regulation (GDPR), EU, 206–207
accreditation, 316
automated processing or profiling prohibition, 256
data protection seals, 316
explanation, rights to, 278–79
'human in the loop' importance, 281
personal data, 318–20
trademarks, 316
geographies, collaboration across, 336
Germany:
alternative business structures resisted, 63
attorneys with special admission, 52
Bar Association, 3
'Der Rechtsdienstleistungsmarkt 2030', 3
Data Ethics Commission, 256–57
evidence taking, 108
in-house counsel, 60
local legal firms, mergers with large Anglo-American firms, 57–59
pre-trial information gathering, 108
predictive policing, 230, 231–32
regulation, 67–68
***Getting to Yes* (Fisher, Ury and Patton),** 158–59

Global Financial Crisis, 218
Global Initiative, IEEE, 315
global law firms, 57–58
global RegTech market, 195
Global Social Network Analytics Platform, HSBC, 199
good judgement, 329, 330
governance:
accountability lack as, 278
governance, risk and compliance (GRC), 195
government agencies, USA, *see* **United States**
government decision-making algorithms, 256
government lawyers, 54, 55, 194–95, 216–17
GRC (governance, risk and compliance), 195

Hadfield, Gillian, 45, 54, 63, 65, 328
hackathons, 341
Hampel Committee on Corporate Governance, UK, 217
Hangzhou, China, 148–49
harms:
AI liabilities, 308–11
financial, 308
machine learning, 268
Harvard Negotiation Programme, 158
health and safety, occupational, 311
healthcare decisions, 270
healthcare regulation, 194
hearings, online, 160, 161
Henderson, William, 45, 48, 59, 61, 70, 168–69, 187
Hentsū, 205
herd effect, 345
heuristics, 95, 96
high-level reasoning, 16
high-stakes disputes, 162
high value claims, 162
HighQ, 321
Hildebrandt, Mireille, 99, 102, 281, 339
historical financial data hidden patterns, banking, 201
history of AI and Law, 17–28, 32
HLS (human layer security), 206
honesty, legal profession members, 330
Hong Kong:
Anti-Money Laundering and Counter-Terrorist Financing Ordinance, 197
clients, 298, 300
professional conduct rules, 296
Hubao, litigation guiding robot, China, 149
human advocates, 327
human, AI not being, 285–86
human-centred design, 152
human choices, 268
human decision-making:
in algorithms construction, 268
bias, 221, 244
emotional upsets affecting, 97
expert systems support, 38
flawed, 96
inconsistency, 244
human error, 181, 301
human experts:
identifying outcome prediction features, 89–90
machine use in areas once exclusive to, 344
simple statistical formulae more accurate than, 98
human goals, 333
human input, 267
human intelligence clarification, 18
human labour costs, 284–85
human layer security (HLS), 206
human removal, e-commerce, 161
human review, TAR, 112
human rights:
access to justice, 150
liberty of the person, 221–22
human skills, 8, 10, 158–60, 326
human value, 333, 334–39, 341
humanity:
courts, extending to disputants, 164
human skills, 159
lawyers, 8, 10
humans, 96, 252, 345
see also entries beginning with human
HunchLab, 229

IBA, *see* **International Bar Association**
IBM Watson, 201
IBM AI Fairness 360 tool, 271, 274
ICO (Information Commissioner's Office), UK, 312
identification of issues:
England and Wales Online Court, 145
identification stage, EDRM, 122, 123, 124
identity management and control, RegTech, 195
Idmission, US, 199
IEEE, *see* **Institute of Electrical and Electronics Engineers**
IM (instant messaging), 132, 160, 205
image recognition, 17, 33
ImageNet Classification, 233
in-court work, 52

in-house counsel, 55, 60–61, 193
in-house lawyers:
as corporate guardians, 218
empirical study of, 219
ethical duties and responsibilities, 218, 219
as moral compass, 218–19
professional duties and responsibilities, 218
RegTech, 210–15
regulatory lawyers, 192–93
reputational risk, factoring in, 219
roles, 210–14, 219
transactional lawyers, 170
in-house legal departments, 326
inadvertent confidentiality, 301
incorporated legal practices:
Australia, 62
New South Wales, 323–24
North America, 62
United States, 323
independence:
administration of justice, duty to, 302
advocates, 158
clients, 302
commercial interests and, 302
definitions, 302
empathy and, 339
in-house lawyers, 212
legal ethics in an AI world, 302–303
of legal profession, 330
outsourcing and, 303
personal commitment and, 339
professional, 302–303
SRA Code of Conduct for Solicitors, 302
independent regulators, 54
indexing documents, 124
India:
foreign law firms bar, 68
hemispheres theory, 45
in-house lawyers, 60
lawyers, 39
legal process outsourcing, 56
number of lawyers, 56
individual rights, 255
individualised sentencing, 254
individually negotiated contract terms, 167
information:
asymmetry, 311, 316–17
clients, confidentiality, 300, 301
extraction, 36
gathering:
AI use in, 10
arbitration, 104, 108–109
machine learning unsupervised methods used in, 113
pre-trial, *see* pre-trial information gathering
governance stage, EDRM, 122
incomplete, 24
intake mechanism, ODR, 139
legal, *see* legal information
missing, 264
personally identifiable, 218
provision, 137, 138
retrieval (IR), 26–27
Information Commissioner's Office (ICO), UK, 312
information technology (IT), 131–32, 161
innovation, 326
barriers, 7
disruptive, 150, 188
firms, 69
lawyers' receptiveness to, 342–43
input variables, 268, 270
inquisitorial systems, 222–23
insider trading, 204–205
instant messaging (IM), 132, 160, 205
Institute of Electrical and Electronics Engineers (IEEE):
audit trails recommendations, 317
Data Privacy Processes and Algorithmic Bias Considerations, 315
'Ethically Aligned Design – A Vision for Prioritizing Human Well-being with Autonomous and Intelligent Systems' (document), 315
Global Initiative, 315
Model Process for Addressing Ethical Concerns During System Design, 315
transparency important for AI users, 312
Transparency of Autonomous Systems, 315
insurance:
legal costs, 150
regulation, 194
integration of new bodies of regulation, Waymark Tech, 208
integrity, viii
compromise to, avoidance, 338–39
legal profession members, 330
Uniform Solicitors Rules, Australia, 302–303
intelligence:
automation, 6
definitions, 14
emotional, *see* emotional intelligence
Intelligent Complaint Machine, China, 148–49

interests:
best, of clients, 298, 304, 338
business, 331
clients, 49, 330
commercial, 331
conflicts of, 9, 335
public, *see* public interest
internal investigations, 212
internal outcome prediction features, 88
International Bar Association (IBA):
Rules on the Taking Evidence in International Commercial Arbitrations (2010), 109, 125
International Commercial Arbitrations:
internet, 131, 323
portals, 150–51, 160
Internet Courts, China, 148
Internet of Things, 110
interpersonal interactions, 50–51
interpretability:
accountability related to, 278
decisions as fair outcomes component, 256
expert systems, 37
Explainable AI (XAI), 274–275
limitations of AI data and design, 272–76
machine learning, 250, 276
pursuit may sacrifice accuracy, 250
technical, 274–75
validity, 272
see also explainability
INTEXcalc pricing tool, 218
investigations:
internal, 212
regulatory, 109
transactional law, 173, 174
investigative process, criminal justice, 222, 223
IR (information retrieval), 26–27
Irish Bank Resolution Corporation Limited v Quinn, 118–19, 120, 125
IT (information technology), 131–32, 161

Japan:
Code of Civil proceedings, 108
documents, production by court order, 108
evidence supporting allegations, 108
inquiry by parties, 108
pre-trial information gathering, 108
preservation of evidence, 108
Jilin, China, 147–48
judge analytics:
prohibition, France, 77–78
tool of Ravel Law, 93
judgement, viii
complex, 329
ethical, 99, 124
exercise of, expert lawyering, 329
legal, 99, 124
moral quality, 99
need for, 333
prediction and, difference between, 99
reflective, 330
requiring expertise, 326
technology difficulty in replicating, 8
judges, 44
cognitive biases, 96
decision fatigue, 96
decision-making, 79–80
ODR assistance, 153
resolution by, England and Wales Online Court, 146
judgments, statistical analysis of, 101
Judicata, 93
judiciary, 66–67
see also judges
junior lawyers:
discovery, less need for, 129
document review, less need for, 326–27
ethics development by, 346
experiential learning, 346
legal research, less need for, 326–27
skills development by, 346
juror-arbiters, 132
justice:
access, *see* access to justice
administration, *see* administration of justice
AI ethics principles, 313, 314
courts, procedures for ensuring, 164
provision, technology assistance, 156
restorative, 225
system, technology interfacing with, 306
Justice Reform Act, France, 77–78

k-Means, 114
k-Nearest Neighbours, 114
keywords:
Boolean, 26
searches, pre-trial processes, 110
Kira Systems, 176–77, 181
know-how acquisition, 333
know your customer (KYC), 195, 197–99
knowledge:
acquisition:
bottleneck, 24, 36, 161
expert systems limitations, 24

of artificial intelligence, among legal profession, 9
data-driven, 18–19
engineering, 20, 37
expertise, 327, 328
hand-coded, 18–19
legal, 343
needed for obtaining and supporting AI products, 326
systems, 19, 21
see also expert systems
utilisation, expert systems limitations, 24–25
Korean Bar Association, South Korea, 68
KYC (know your customer), 195 197–99

labelling:
data, 36
machine learning data, 264
Langdell Library, 282
language processing, 190
large law firms, 57–58, 331
large-scale due diligence, 176–78
latent semantic analysis, 26
latent semantic indexing, 26
law:
access, equality in, 331
commoditisation, 40
complexity, needing expertise, 343
consistency with, ODR, 152
criminal, *see* criminal law
equality in application of, fundamental rights, 228
incorrect interpretation, RegTech, 213
without lawyers, 151
open textured nature, 24, 32
predictability in, 171
as programmed system of rules, 19
routine, LegalTech providers, 321
rule of, *see* rule of law
transactional, *see* transactional law
unauthorised practice, *see* unauthorised practice of law
law curriculum, education, 341
law degrees, 343
law firms:
corporations, 345–47
global, 57–58
large, 57–58, 331
looking to law schools to teach skills and ethics, 346
multi-disciplinary partnerships, 345–47
new lawyers' experiences development, 346
non-traditional, 347
role in transactional law as supporting structures, 171
structures, 346–47
traditional, 347
using AI, ABA, 326
law schools, 343, 346
Law Society of England and Wales:
Algorithms in the Criminal Justice System report, 249, 251
Future of Legal Services Report, 3
regulatory and compliance requirements, 191
risk assessment tools, legislation called for, 257
Law Society of New South Wales, vii, 4
lawful objectives, 297–98
lawful processing:
personal data, GDPR, 318
LawGeex, 175, 181, 187–88, 190, 283
laws of lawyering, 49–50
lawyer-client relationships, 41
lawyer-free online courts, 152
'lawyer in the loop', 310–11
leaner services, 326
learning:
continuous active, TAR, 111–112, 125
deep, *see* deep learning
experiential, 346
neural networks, 32
process, machine learning, 276
reinforcement, 15
self-learning, 343
simple active, TAR, 111, 112, 125
simple passive, TAR, 111, 112, 125
styles, 29
supervised, *see* supervised learning
unsupervised, *see* unsupervised learning
legal advice:
applications, 179
giving reasons, about, 103
lawyers, 6
legal information and, distinction between, 69
regulation of lawyers, 69
legal aid, 150, 306, 338
legal analysis:
companies, RegTech, 196
human factors cognisance required, 286
strategy work and, 53
legal analytics:
Big Data use in, 98
provision, Cognitive+, 208
legal costs insurance, 150
legal data scientists, 340

legal decision texts, 36
legal design, 152
legal documents:
commodity, 180–81
preparation, US, 323
legal-engineering, 163
legal ethics in an AI world, 289–306
legal fees:
large law firms, 331
opponents', 152
own, 152
see also costs; fees
legal information:
accessibility, 37–38
legal advice and, distinction between, 69
regulation of lawyers, 69
retrieval, 25–27, 35
legal liabilities, 321
legal malpractice, 308
legal obligations:
interpreters, in-house lawyers, 219
public interest promotion, 331
legal practice:
incorporated, *see* incorporated legal practices, 69
low-cost legal services, 321
by non-lawyers, 320–22
'practice of law' defining, 322
professional indemnity insurance absence, 322
rules preventing, 322
scope of, 322
use of AI, 73–74
alternative dispute resolution, *see* alternative dispute resolution
criminal lawyers, *see* criminal lawyers
online courts, *see* online courts
outcome prediction, *see* outcome prediction
pre-trial information gathering, *see* pre-trial information gathering
regulatory lawyers, *see* regulatory lawyers
transactional lawyers, *see* transactional lawyers
legal professional privilege, viii
client representation facilitating, 301
communications secrecy, 301
confidentiality and:
legal ethics in an AI world, 300–302
lawyers, 9
pre-trial information gathering, roles of lawyers, 126
public interest promotion, 300–301
recorded speech conversion to text, 302
trust, 335
legal professionals:
legal work restriction to, 321–22
standards, 290–91
legal project management, 341
legal protections, 331
legal reasoning, 158
clarification, AI and Law endeavours, 18
machines incapable of, 285
reasoning by analogy hallmark of, 285
legal representation:
courts, 156
no longer needed, 151
precluded, 151
legal risks:
broad view, in-house lawyers, 210
corporate, 211
interpreters, in-house lawyers, 219
legal rules:
requiring competence with technology, 341
legal services:
à law carte, 153–55
access to justice, 307
assistants, 153
competent, 343
deconstructed, 336
disaggregated, 153
ethical, 343
limited to lawyers:
non-traditional law firms, 347
non-lawyer provision, 188
providers, 41
regulation justifications, 290–91
software-driven, 6–7
for those unable to pay, 306
unbundling, 336
Legal Services Act 2007 (LSA), England and Wales, 63
legal technologists, 129–30
legal text summarisation, 25–26
legal work, 40
AI, proportion undertaking, 42
computer programs for, 189
England and Wales, *see* England and Wales
restriction to legal professionals, 188–89, 321–22
see also work of lawyers
Legalist, 75
LegalTech, 165, 282–83, 321
LegalVision, 321, 323
LegalZoom, 188, 321
legibility, validity, 272

legislation:
GDPR, 318–19
internet, readily available, 323
principles-based, 318
regulation, 318–20
rules-based, 318
see also regulation
legitimate interests:
duty to clients pursuing, 297–29
Lex Machina, 92, 93, 94, 95
LexisNexis, 92, 282
LexPredict, 180
Lexvoco, 323
liabilities:
for AI, 289–90, 308–11
exclusion, 309
legal, 321
machine decisions, questioning, 344–45
strict, 309
licences, procuring, 47
life skills, 345
limitations:
of AI, 161–62, 261–88, 333
artificial intelligence, 5–6, 9, 10
expert systems, 23–25, 161
jurisprudential, expert systems, 24
machine learning, 262
data, 265, 267
natural language processing, overcoming, 25
neural networks, 25
overcoming, explainability, 276
limited liability partnerships (LLP):
North America, 62
limited scope services, 152–55, 189–90
limits to education, 345–46
liquidity, banking requirements, 200
literacy:
skills required to compete with machines, 345–46
statistical, TAR, 340
litigation:
document review advances in, 327
funding, 150
guiding robot, Hubao, China, 149
hold notices, EDRM, 122–23
initiation as voluntary act, 156
lawyers, gathering information and evidence, *see* pre-trial information gathering
outcome prediction advances in, 327
preparation and conduct of:
legal work, England and Wales, 323
regulation, 320
rule of law, 156–58
transactional law contrasted with, 165
LLP, *see* **limited liability partnerships**
local explanations, 275–76
local legal services markets, 57
logic:
reasoning models, 30
rule-based reasoning and, 19–25
Logistic Regression algorithm, TAR, 113
Loomis, 234–35, 238, 249, 252–53
loyalty:
to clients, 297, 302
legal profession members, 330
LSA (Legal Services Act 2007), England and Wales, 63
machine bias, 245
machine decisions, 344–45
machine learning (ML), 14, 17
actuarial analyses, 220–21
algorithms, 306
auditing, 277
automated process of discovering correlations between dataset variables, 79
autonomy, 262
banking, 200–202
Bayesian algorithms, 30
biases, 246–47, 248
design, 268
outputs, 306
overcoming, 276
rule of law consequences, 306
clustering algorithms, 30
compliance, 208
critiques, 25
cryptographic commitments, 277
data:
cleaning, quality dependence on, 306
limitations of AI, 263–67
privacy, 206, 207
quality, 29, 306
quantity, 29
deep learning, 30, 33–35
design:
bias, 268
human choices as potential error sources, 268
human input, 267
output differences, 268
quality dependence on, 306
safeguards, 276–78, 281
discriminatory outputs, 288
Ecertic, Spain, 199
expert-in-the-loop, 201–202

high value claims, 162
human layer security platform, 206
Idmission, US, 199
interpretability, 250, 276
know your customer, 199
learning style, 29
limitations, 262
market misconduct, 205
natural language processing, *see* natural language processing
neural networks, 30–33
Onfido, UK, 199
outcome prediction use, 75–76, 82–84
deployment, 88
model selection and training, 87–88
overfitting, 87
outliers elimination, 86–87
problem definition, 84–85
running models, 88
statistics review and data partitioning, 86–87
outputs:
discriminatory, 288
parsing, 276
predictive policing, 228, 229, 240
regression algorithms, 29–30
risk assessments, 241, 265
supervised, 17, 29, 110–12
techniques, RegTech, 196–97
Technology Assisted Review, *see* Technology Assisted Review
training, 80, 175–77, 240, 301
unsupervised learning, 17, 29, 113–14

machines:
incapable of legal reasoning, 285
literacy / numeracy skills required to compete with, 345–46
superintelligence, 16
translation, 17, 35
use in areas once exclusive to human experts, 344
vision, 17
see also machine learning
management:
lawyers as part of, non-traditional law firms, 347
transactional law, 173, 175–78
manual contract review, 177–78
manufacturers, claims against, 309
margins of error, TAR, 112
Market Abuse Unit Analysis and Detection Center, SEC, 191–92
Market Analysis and Intelligence system:
Australian Securities and Investments Commission, 209
market for ODR, 163
market logics, 331
market manipulation / misconduct, 204
market surveillance, 205
marketplace, competitive, 191–92
Markets in Financial Instruments Directive (MiFID II), 191
McConnell Dowell Constructors v Santam, 120, 126
MDP, *see* **multi-disciplinary partnerships**
mediation:
ADR, 132
carried out remotely, British Columbia Civil Resolution Tribunal, 144–45
human skills, using, 158
module, Modria, 141
ODR, 138
roles of lawyers in, 135–37, 154
medicine:
liability regimes, AI liabilities, 310
machine learning use in, 299, 344
Merlon Intelligence, 198
Microsoft Teams, 160
MiFID, 203, 205
MiFID II, 191
minimum capital:
banking requirements, 200
misleading conduct, AI liabilities, 308
missing information, 264
ML, *see* **machine learning**
Model Code of Professional Conduct, Canada, 329–30
Model Process for Addressing Ethical Concerns During System Design, IEEE, 315
Model Rules of Professional Conduct, *see* **American Bar Association**
modelling error, 272
Modria, 141
Monetary Authority of Singapore, *see* **Singapore**
money laundering, 195, 197–99
Money Laundering, Fourth Directive on (4MLD), EU, 197–98
monitoring companies, RegTech, 196
monitoring of steps, EDRM, 123
monopoly protections, 67
monotonous tasks, 6
moral character of lawyers, 330
moral compass, in-house lawyers, 218–19

moral quality, judgement, 99
morally neutral assumptions, 305
multi-disciplinary partnerships (MDP), 62
  law firms, 345–47
  United States, not permitted, 63, 323
multivariate algorithms, 160

Naïve Bayesian Classifier algorithm, TAR, 113, 174
named entity recognition, 35
nat-arb.com, 142
natural language processing (NLP), 17, 35
  argument retrieval, 35
  banking, 200, 201–202
  compliance, 208
  data privacy, 207
  deep learning, 33
  information retrieval and, 27
  limitations overcoming, 25
  machine translation, 35
  market misconduct, 205
    outcome prediction, 88–91
    recorded speech conversion to text, 302
  RegTech, 196–97
  regulatory technology (RegTech), 35
  ROSS Intelligence, 36
  security measures, 302
  semantic analysis, 26, 35
  speech recognition, 35
  syntactic analysis, 35
  technology assisted review, 35
near neighbour approach:
  outcome prediction, 90
negative rates, false, 246
negotiation:
  with clients, 51
  gradual process of, contract terms, 185
  human skills, using, 158
  module, Modria, 141
  between parties, ODR, 138
    transactional lawyers' roles, 169, 182, 186, 187
  work, 48, 50–51
Neota Logic, 179, 321
Networked Society Institute, 18–19, 37
neural networks:
  activation functions, 31
  biases, 31
  computational, 31
  deep, 31, 33–34
    learning, 32
  limitations overcoming, 25
  machine learning, 30–33
  OECD, 33
  perceptrons, 30
  prediction accuracy, but inability to explain basis, 101
  predictive purposes use, 76–77
  recursive, 79
neurons, 30–31
New Law, 69
NLP, *see* **natural language processing**
Nolo, 321
non-discrimination:
  AI ethics principles, 313
non-lawyers:
  capital, 70
  courts designed for, 163
  lawyers joining with, 346
  legal practice by, 320–22
  legal services provision, 188
  service providers, 332
non-legal skills, 51
non-maleficence, 313, 314
non-responsive documents, TAR, 125
non-traditional law firms, 347
non-verbal communication, 51
numeracy skills, 345

OADR, *see* **online alternative dispute resolution**
obligations:
  pre-trial information gathering, discovery, 124–25
  undervaluing, 331
OCR (optical character recognition), 199
ODR, *see* **online dispute resolution**
OECD, *see* **Organisation for Economic Co-operation and Development**
OFAC (Office of Foreign Assets Control), US, 198
omissions:
  of AI, lawyers' responsibilities, 308
  errors of, 181
  use of transactional lawyers, 188
onboarding, anti-money laundering, 198
'one to many' delivery model, 307
'one to one' delivery model, 307
Onfido, UK, 199
online alternative dispute resolution (OADR), 131, 139
  British Columbia Civil Resolution Tribunal, 145, 153
  fairness crucial, 157
  information and communications technology use, 161

Online Civil Money Claims Pilot, England and Wales, 147
online courts, 131, 139
email, 132
England and Wales Online Court, 145–47, 151–52
instant messaging, 132
lawyer-free, 152
virtual hearings, 132
online dispute resolution (ODR), 131
AI-driven, 161, 164
Alibaba, 141–42
avoiding disputes, 164
blind-bidding systems, 160
blockchain technology, 132
China's Internet Courts, 147–49
complex and high-stakes disputes, 162
consistency with law, 152
courts, 138, 163
decision tree analysis, 137
documents generation, 138
e-commerce example, 140–43
eBay Resolution Centre, 140–41
examples, 139–140
expert systems, 137, 138, 161
fair operation, 152
formal resolution, 138
forms generation, 138
future developments, 160–64
high value claims, 162
human skills, foregoing access to, 159–60
information:
intake mechanism, 139
provision, 137, 138
market for, 163
mediation, 138
Modria, 141
negotiation between parties, 138
nat-arb.com, 142
judges' assistance, 153
juror-arbiters, 132
preparation for formal dispute resolution, 138
problem identification, 137
process, 137–39
Rechtwijzer, 143
roles of lawyers after, *see* roles of lawyers
self-resolution, 138
SettleToday.com, 142
Smartsettle, 142
technology use in, 139
telephone conferencing, 138
text messaging, 138
third-party-facilitated ADR, 138
tribunal system links, 138
uitelkaar.nl, 143
underserved latent legal market, 163
video conferencing, 138
VirtualCourthouse.com, 142
voluntary resolution, 137–38
online hearings, 160, 161
online litigation platforms, 148
online trials, 160
online tribunals, 139
opacity:
of AI, 310
algorithms, 272
criminal justice application of AI, 228
machine learning software, 250
openness, AI ethics principles, 313
opportunities and threats:
in use of AI for lawyers, 325–27
optical character recognition (OCR), 199
order data, 205
Organisation for Economic Co-operation and Development (OECD):
accountability, 279–81
Algorithms in Society, 263
competition and Regulation Working Party, 189
new information symmetries creation, 303
professional indemnity insurance not available, 322
'human in the loop' importance, 281
privacy and cross-border uses guidelines, 206
transparency, 273
organisational behaviour, 334
organisational clients, 45
organisational forms of lawyers, 54–55
alternative business structures, 61–64
firms, *see* partnerships *below*
global law firms, 57–58
global professional services firms, 57
government, employed in, 54, 55
in-house counsels, 55, 60–61
large law firms, 57–58
multi-disciplinary partnerships, 62
partnerships, 55–60
outcome prediction, 75–78
advances in, 327
AI use, 78–103, 161
competence, 294
data availability limitation, 266
ECtHR cases, 91–92, 94

factors, labelling, 90
facts, 89, 90
features, 88–91
future developments, 101–103
Lex Machina, 92
machine learning, *see* machine learning
near neighbour approach, 90
Ravel Law, 92–93
regression analysis, 89
role of lawyers, 94–101
social concerns, 102–103
statistical modelling, 79–82
as supplemental tool, 94
technical concerns, 101–102
text analysis and natural language processing, 88–91
using deep learning techniques, Big Data, 79

outliers:
elimination, 86–87

outputs:
biases, machine learning, 306
discriminatory, 288
explanation lacking, 25
explanations for, 18
machine learning, *see* machine learning
parsing, machine learning, 276
scripted, 20
variables choice, algorithms operating in discriminatory manner, 268, 269–70

outsourcing:
competence, 297
independence and, 303

overfitting, 87
overturns, TAR, 125
owners, claims against, AI liabilities, 309

parole:
criminal law, 225
determination relevance, 236
opacity, 250

parsing, 26
partisanship, duty to clients, 297
Partnership on AI, 249, 257
Pasquale, Frank, 6–7, 91–92, 103, 126, 218, 328–29, 340
passive learning, simple, TAR, 111, 112, 125

patents:
attorneys, 44
decision analysis, 92
lawyers, 44

Patriot Act, US, 197

patterns:
through algorithm use, machine learning data, 305
discrimination, 267
historical financial data hidden patterns, banking, 201
inequality, 267
machine learning, *see* machine learning
recognition, market misconduct, 205
statistical in machine learning data, 29
statistical modelling, judicial decision-making, 79–80
transaction, insights, market misconduct, 205

PD (probability of default), 200
PEP status, 198
perceptrons, neural networks, 30
personal autonomy, 344
personal commitment, independence and, 339
personal data, 249
GDPR, 318–20

'personal-plight hemisphere', 45
personally identifiable information, 218

persuasive counsellors:
in-house lawyers as, 211–12

pharmaceuticals regulation, 194

Philippines:
Bangko Sentral ng Pilipinas (BSP) chatbots, 210

Planet Compliance RegTech Directory, 196
planning, 17, 169, 123
platform models, 69
plea negotiations, 226

police:
arrest, 223–24
automated facial recognition use, 232–34
contact with individuals without basis, 252
inappropriate use of AI tools, 251
investigations, criminal lawyers' roles and, 223
machine learning systems, 224
privatised, US, 250
see also predictive policing

policing:
bias in, 247
big data, 237, 244
hot spot forecasting, 247
predictive, *see* predictive policing

political compromises, 328
political environments, 336
political-legal accountability, 278, 279
politically exposed person (PEP) status, 198
positive rates, false, 246

post hoc auditing, 277–78
post-execution trade information, 202
PRA, *see* **Prudential Regulation Authority**
practice of law:
clarifying scope of what is, 323
future for lawyers, 69–71
introduction, 39–43
legal practice, defining, 322
organisational forms, *see* organisational forms of lawyers
profession of lawyers, 43–45
regulation of lawyers, 64–69
work of lawyers, *see* work of lawyers
pre-execution information, 202
pre-trial detention, 224–25
pre-trial information gathering, 104
arbitration, 108–109
Australia, 106
civil law jurisdictions, 107–108
common law jurisdictions, 105–107
discovery, 124–25
England and Wales, 106–107
France, 108
future developments, 127–28, 130
Germany, 108
human element remaining important, 130
Japan, 108
litigation lawyers, gathering information and evidence, 104–109
processes, *see* pre-trial processes
regulatory investigations, 109
roles of lawyers, *see* roles of lawyers
Technology Assisted Review, 125–26
United States, 107
pre-trial processes:
algorithms, 113–14
computer programs, 110
clustering, 113–14
documents, 109–10, 126–27
electronically stored information (ESI), 110
examples, 116–21
human element remaining important, 130
Internet of Things, 110
keyword searches, 110
precision, 114–15
recall, 114–15
relevance, 115
social media, 110
supervised machine learning, 110–12
unsupervised machine learning, 113–14
validation, 112
pre-trial release, 224–26
pre-trial risk assessment tools, 254, 257
precision, pre-trial processes, 114–15
Precobs (Pre-Crime Observation System), 230
predictions:
judgement and, difference between, 99
machine learning, 76
predictive analytics, 76–78
association, machine learning, 79
critiques, 237
distribution of benefits from, 95
legal practices based on, adjustment by lawyers, 103
policing and, 252
predictive contracting, 173, 180
predictive policing:
algorithmic, 229
bias, 248
big data policing, 228, 237
'broken windows theory' of policing, 229
Compstat, 228–29
countries used in, 229–250
criminal justice application of AI, 228–32
datasets, 228
HunchLab, 229
machine learning analysis, 228, 229
PredPol, 229, 231
risk assessments, 230
Risk Terrain Modelling (RTM), 229, 230
Strategic Subject List (SSL), 231
Valcri, 231
PredPol, 229, 231
Premonition, 93, 266–67
pricing tool, INTEXcalc, 218
principles:
of AI ethics, 313–14
regulation, 313–14
principles-based legislation, 163, 318
prior conformity assessment, EU, 316
prisons:
populations managing, risk assessments, 227–28
privatised, US, 250
privacy:
data, 206–207
by design, 320
protection, AI ethics principles, 313, 314
regulatory challenges, 218
rights to, 312
and family life, police AFR use breaching, 232
private enterprise links, RegTech, 217
private information:
data points, revealed by, 218
privatised dispute resolution services, 266

privilege:
limitations in relation to, TAR, 127
pre-trial information gathering, roles of lawyers, 126–27
professional, *see* legal professional privilege
United States, 127
privileged information:
recorded speech conversion to text, 302
privileged views:
technology industry embedding, 268
pro bono legal work, 306–307, 338
probabilistic approach to classification, 174
problem-solving:
collaborative work with, 49
creative, 159
creativity, 337
evaluative work with, 49
facilitative work with, 49
law degrees, 343
maintaining skill sets lawyers need, 343
skills required to compete with machines, 345–46
work, 49
problems:
created by new technology, 339
definition, machine learning, 84–85
identification, ODR, 137
legal, 337
not solved by new technology, 339
solved by new technology, 339
solving, *see* problem-solving
procedural fairness, 156, 295
see also due process
processes, pre-trial, *see* **pre-trial processes**
processing stage, EDRM, 122, 123, 124
product liability:
AI liabilities, 309, 310
production stage, EDRM, 122
profession of lawyers, 43–45
branches, 44
clients:
interests of, serving, 291
co-regulatory arrangements, 290
control, 43–44
fidelity to law and administration of justice, 291
legal work, 44
regulation, 43–44, 290–91
self-regulation, 290
professional controls, 327
professional duties, in-house lawyers, 218
professional-ethical obligations:
towards technology, 305
professional ethics, 95, 289–306
professional indemnity insurance, 189, 322
professional independence, 302–303
professional privilege, *see* **legal professional privilege**
professional responsibilities:
in-house lawyers, 218
machine learning and, balancing, 95
transactional law, 190
unbundling and, 155
professional skills, 326
professional standards, legal, 290–91
professionalism, viii, 41–42
impacts on, 70
loss of inviting deregulation, 331
meaning altered, 58
regulation of professionals, 64
professions:
specialised knowledge and skill fundamental to delineation of, 327
profitable arrangements for fees:
AI assisting by data mining past matters and monitoring ongoing matters, 348
profits maximisation, lending, 276
programming:
algorithms, AI following, 333
expert systems, required, 161
machine learning inverse of, 28
project management, legal, 341
project management model, EDRM, 123
project managers, collaboration with, 336
PROLOG (programming in logic), 20
Promontory Financial Group, 201
Promontory Watson, 205
proportionality:
discovery, pre-trial information gathering, 124
Federal Rules of Procedure, USA, 107
pre-trial information gathering, common law jurisdictions, 105
ProPublica, 226–27, 236, 241, 244–46
prosecution, 226
prosecutors, 44
protections, 331
protocols, TAR, to apply, 126
proxy variables, criminal justice, 248
Prudential Regulation Authority (PRA):
Waymark Tech ingests handbooks, 208
psycho-social skills, 286
psychology:
emotional intelligence, 334
public access scheme, England and Wales, 154

public interest:
immunity, pre-trial information gathering, roles of lawyers, 126
litigation work, 53
promotion, 300–301, 329, 331
regulator lawyers, 195
pure economic loss, AI liabilities, 308
Pyrrho Investments Ltd v MWB Property Ltd, 120

qualifications:
jurisdictional differences, 65
qualities, machine learning data, 265
quality:
dependence on data provided, machine learning, 306
design, machine learning, dependence on, 306
in drafting contracts, 184
technology, unable to be tested, 303
Quantexa, 199
quantitative skills needed, TAR, 340
question and answer programs:
transactional law, documents, 179
question answering, 17, 35
Quintilian, 1
QuisLex, 283

R (Bridges) v Chief Constable of South Wales Police and Secretary of State for the Home Department, 234, 255–56
R2A (RegTech for Regulators Accelerator), 210
race:
education and, failing to distinguish between, 250
not included as input, inferred from other data, COMPAS, 248
socioeconomic status correlated with, US, 248
racial bias, 244–45
racial inequities:
criminal justice, reflecting, 247
random sampling, TAR, 112
RAR (Relativity Assisted Review), 119
rating systems for lawyers, 266–67
Ravel Law, 92–93, 282
RAVN System, 177
real-time transcripts, trials, 132
real-world data, machine learning, 265
reasonable search:
conducting, pre-trial information gathering, discovery, 124
reasonable suspicion, arrest, 223, 224
reasoning:
advice of lawyers, weakness in, 97
by analogy, 158, 285
case-based (CBR), 21–25, 27, 76
causal, 18–19
deductive, 20, 24–25, 158
by example, 158
factor-based, 22, 23
high-level, 16
inductive, 25, 158
judges, weakness in, 97
legal, *see* legal reasoning
rule-based, 19–25
statistical, 18–19
teleological, 23
with values, 23
reasons:
giving, legal advising about, 103
for regulation, 311
see also reasoning
recall:
point estimates, TAR, 112
pre-trial processes, 114–15
TAR, 114–15
Rechtwijzer, 143
recidivism, 220, 227, 242, 244, 246
record keeping, trading, 202
recorded speech:
conversion to text, 302
recovery of costs, 151–52
rectifying bias problem, 249
recurrent networks, 32
recursive neural networks, 79
Red Marker, 215–16
reflective judgement, 330
regression algorithms, 29–30
regression analysis, 89, 90
RegTech (regulatory technology), 35, 191
anti-fraud screening and protection, 195
anti-money laundering, 195, 197–99
banking, requirements, 200–202
client and counterparty identification companies, 196
compliance, 195, 214–15
cost saving links, 217
counter terrorism financing, 197–99
data protection companies, 196
data warehousing and analytics companies, 196
examples, 197–210
external lawyers, 215–16
future developments, 217–19

general compliance companies, 196
global market, 195
identity management and control, 195
in-house lawyers, 210–15
know your customer procedures, 195, 197–99
law, incorrect interpretation, 213
legal and regulatory analysis companies, 196
machine learning techniques, 196–97
money laundering, 197–99
monitoring companies, 196
natural language processing (NLP), 196–97
Planet Compliance RegTech Directory, 196
private enterprise links, 217
private practice law firms, 215–16
regulator lawyers, 216–17
regulatory and legal analysis companies, 196
regulatory reporting, 195
regulatory sandbox, 217
reporting companies, 196
risk management, 195
role of lawyers in, 210–17
as 'sleeping giant of financial services world', 217
team approach requirements, 215
as tool only, 218
training companies, 196
transaction monitoring, 196

RegTech for Regulators Accelerator (R2A), 210

regulation:
accountability, 312–13
anti-discrimination legislation, 311
application of AI to, 195–97
anti-money laundering and know your customer, 197–99
banking requirements, 200–202
data privacy, 206–207
environmental laws, 207
examples, 197–210
general compliance, 208
know your customer and anti-money laundering, 197–99
market misconduct/insider trading, 204–205
SupTech, 208–10
trading, 202–204
see also RegTech
areas of, regulatory lawyers, 194
audit trails, 317–18
bias, 312
certification, 315–16
competition promotion or protection, 311
compliance, 208
concept of, 311
consumer protection legislation, 311
design standards, 315
disclosure, 316–17
discrimination, 312
explainability, 312
information asymmetry, 311
justifications, legal services, 290–91
lawyers, *see* regulation of lawyers
legislation, 318–20
litigation, 320
occupational health and safety legislation, 311
principle-bases, 163
principles, 313–14
profession of lawyers, 43–44, 290–91
reason for, 311
social policies, 311, 312
specifications, 315
standards, 315
technical instructions, 315
transparency, 312, 313, 320
see also legislation; self-regulation

regulation of lawyers, 64–69
character-based requirements for entry, 65
civil law jurisdictions, 66
co-regulatory arrangements, 64
common law jurisdictions, 66
competitive-consumerist paradigm, 64
controlling entry to profession, 65–66
deregulation, 64, 68, 70–71
independent regulators, 54
judiciary, 66–67
legal advice, 69
legal information, 69
monopoly protections, 67
professionalist-independent mode, 64–65
qualifications, jurisdictional differences, 65
re-regulation, 64
self-regulation, 64–65
women, 66

regulation technology, *see* **RegTech**

regulator lawyers, 194–95, 216–17

regulators, independent, 54

regulatory agencies:
regulatory lawyers dealing with, 194

regulatory analysis companies, RegTech, 196

regulatory analytics:
provision, Cognitive+, 208

regulatory challenges, 218

regulatory compliance, 53, 327

regulatory environments, 336

regulatory frameworks:
lawyers operating in, 10
regulatory investigations, 109
regulatory lawyers, 192–95, 217–19
role in RegTech, *see* RegTech
regulatory obligations:
mapped to internal policies, CUBE, 208
regulatory practice:
AI use in, 10
regulatory protections, 331
regulatory provisions:
regulatory lawyers interpreting, 194
regulatory reporting, RegTech, 195
regulatory requirements:
Law Society of England and Wales, 191
regulatory sandbox, 217
regulatory smoothing:
government lawyers, 194–95
regulatory strategy:
accountability, 278
regulatory strictures:
professional controls, 327
regulatory technology, *see* **RegTech**
rehabilitation:
post-conviction needs, 226
sentencing, 225
reinforcement learning, 15
relational expertise, 328–29
relational roles:
transactional lawyers, 185–87
relational theories, contracts, 166, 185
relational trust, 336
relationships:
through algorithm use, machine learning data, 305
analytics, data privacy, 207
Relativity Assisted Review (RAR), 119
release:
conditional, 225–26
pre-trial, 224–26
relevance:
direct, 106
pre-trial processes, 115
reliability:
AI ethics principles, 314
reliance on technology, 303
Remus, Dana, 23, 46, 48, 50, 51, 53, 58, 102, 129, 176, 177, 190
renaissance of artificial intelligence, 2–3
repetitious tasks:
transactional lawyers' roles, 180
reporting companies, RegTech, 196
representation of knowledge, 24
representing work, 50, 51–53
reputational capital, 70, 168–69, 187
reputational intermediaries, 168
reputational risk:
in-house lawyers factoring in, 219
reputational roles:
transactional lawyers, 185–87
resolution of disputes:
formal, 138
voluntary, 137–38
responsibility:
AI ethics principles, 314
attribution, limitations of AI, 287
individual, 254
Restatement of the Law Governing Lawyers:
American Bar Association, 297–98
restorative justice, 225
restricting entry, 327
retainers:
fees as, 348
terms, AI liabilities, 309
retraining:
technological unemployment challenge, meeting, 345
retrieval:
argument, 27, 35, 36
conceptual, 26
information (IR), 26–27
legal information, 25–27, 35
review:
automated:
documents, transactional lawyers, 183
non-disclosure agreements, 175
continuous:
anti-money laundering, 198
contracts, 165, 175, 176–78
stage, EDRM, 122
transactional law, 175–78, 181
Revolut, 199
richness, TAR, 112
right to be forgotten:
data privacy, 206
rights:
constitutional, 221–22
fundamental, *see* fundamental rights
human, *see* human rights
to privacy, 312
risk assessments, 220, 234
actuarial, 244
AI outputs, 311
algorithms, 251, 281, 294–95
area under the curve (AUC) value, 242
bail determination process, 236

bias in, 245, 247
COMPAS, 227–28, 235–36, 252–53
criminal justice:
algorithms, 281
application of AI, 227–28, 234–37
data from specific populations, 247
as impermissible transgressions on individual rights, 255
Loomis, 234–35, 238
machine learning, 241
offenders, 242
parole determination relevance, 236
pre-trial tools, 254, 257
predictive policing, 230
prison populations managing, 227–28
prisoners, data from, 247
Samsa, 236
sentencing relevance, 236–237
tools:
incompatible with sentencing principles, 254–55
legislation called for, Law Society of England and Wales, 257
verification, machine learning, 265
transparency, 247, 257
in US criminal justice system, 238
risk management:
in-house counsel and, 60
RegTech, 195
transactional lawyers' roles, 171
risk models:
conceptual issues, bias, 245
risk profiling, 220
risk-scoring tools, US, 257
risk screening:
anti-money laundering, Merlon Intelligence, 198
Risk Terrain Modelling (RTM), 229, 230
risks:
of AI, 282
credit, banking, 200–202
innovative AI products not free of, 332
legal, *see* legal risks
minimisation, lending, 276
reputational, 219
see also entries beginning with risk
robotics, 16–17
robots, 14, 149
Rocket Lawyer, 321
roles of lawyers, 94–96
arbitration, 125
chatbots, 215–16
contexts, 45
in contextualising, 130
criminal lawyers, *see* criminal lawyers
EDRM, 123
in explaining, 130
government lawyers:
compliance roles, 194
regulatory smoothing, 194–95
hard to define, 39–40
in-house:
legal obligations interpreters, 219
legal risks interpreters, 219
transactional law, 165–66
in mediation, 135–37, 154
after online dispute resolution, 149–60
outcome prediction, 96–101
pre-trial information gathering, 121–27
in RegTech, 210–17
regulator lawyers, 194
TAR, 125–26
technology use challenging if not consistent with rule of law, 156
transactional lawyers, *see* transactional lawyers
see also work of lawyers
rooms:
reading, 337
ROSS Intelligence, 36, 299
RTM (Risk Terrain Modelling), 229, 230
rule-based AI, compliance, 208
rule-based approaches:
market misconduct, 204–205
rule-based decision trees, 28
rule-based legislation, 318
rule-based reasoning, 19–25
rule-based systems, 21, 27
rule of law:
advocates' duty to uphold, 135
courts, 155
dispute resolution lawyers' duty to uphold, 135
duty to uphold, 305
equality, 305
fairness, 305
lawyers defenders of after online dispute resolution, 155–58
legal ethics in an AI world duty to, 303–306
litigation, 156–58
machine learning biases, consequences, 306
procedural fairness, 156
protection, 331
Solicitors Regulation Authority upholding, 304
technology, 156
upholding:
lawyers' societal or structural role in, 9, 10

rules:
ethical, 341
ethics responsibilities commonly referred to as, 330
legal, 341
preventing legal practice by non-lawyers, 322
professional conduct, *see* professional conduct
rumourtage, 204
running models, 88
Russia:
Criminal Procedure Code, 224
notaries (*notaryusi*), 45
private sector lawyers unregulated, 65
regulation, 67

safe harbour approach:
accountability, 280
safeguards:
algorithms design, 281
limitations of AI design, 276–78, 281
machine learning design, 276–78, 281
safety, AI ethics principles, 313
sampling, random, TAR, 112
SAR (suspicious activity reports), 198, 199
savings, costs, 284
scale benefits, 345
scales of fees, 347
scaling, expert systems limitations, 24
scans, data, anti-money laundering, Quantexa, 199
schedules of fees, 347
Science and Technology Section, ABA, 299
scientification of policing, 220
Scotland:
alternative business structures (ABS), 63
solicitor-advocates, 52
see also United Kingdom
screeners, algorithms, 268
scripted outputs, 20
scrutiny, strict, 10
search:
arbitrary, 223
legal, 25
terms, 26
unreasonable, 251
SEC (Securities and Exchange Commission), *see* **United States**
secrecy:
trade, *see* trade secrecy
secured storage, data privacy, 206
Securities and Exchange Commission (SEC), *see* **United States**
securities:
fraud, class actions prediction model, United States, 83
regulation, 194
work, 47
security:
cybersecurity, 301, 313
measures, NLP, 302
personal data, GDPR, 318
regulatory challenges, 218
seed sets:
TAR, 110–12, 125
segmentation, 26
seizure, unreasonable, 251
selection bias, 265
self-incrimination, 126
self-learning, 343
self-regulation, 64–65, 290, 313
self-representation, 163
self-resolution, ODR, 138
semantics:
analysis, 26, 35
net presentations, 26
sensitive documents, 207
sensitive information identification, Text IQ, 207
sentencing, 222
COMPAS use for, 238
decisions, criminal defence lawyers, 225–26
deterrence, general and specific, 225
disparities in following upset losses, 97
fundamental to life or liberty, 225
guidelines, 225, 244
individualised, 254
judges' disparities in, 97
mandatory, 225
minimum sentences, 225
opacity, 250
penal populism critiques, 225
principles, risk assessments tools incompatible with, 254–55
punishment, 225
rehabilitation, 225
relevance, risk assessments, 236–237
restorative justice, 225
retribution, 225
separation or divorce matters, 47, 143
service agreements, 176
service paradigm, AI liabilities, 310
services, law for, AI liabilities, 310
settlement negotiations, unsuccessful, 97
SettleToday.com, 142
shallow neural networks, 33

shifting costs, 152
similarity scores, 249
simple active learning, TAR, 111, 112, 125
simple passive learning, TAR, 111, 112, 125
simple statistical formulae, 98
simplification, court process, ODR, 163
simplified law, 163
Singapore:
clients, 298, 300
discipline of domestic and foreign lawyers, 68
High Court:
ethics and expediency, prudent and pragmatic balance between, 332–33
Monetary Authority of Singapore:
suspicious transaction reports (STR), 209
Professional Conduct rules, 304
singularity, 16
skill and care:
failure to exercise, 309
skill sets lawyers need:
maintaining, 343
to work with AI, 339–42
skills:
character, 345
collaboration, 341
communication, 341, 343
development by junior lawyers, 346
emotional intelligence, technical skills not to push out, 341
ethical application of, competence, 292
expertise, 327, 328
human, 158–60, 326
knowledge and, specialised:
fundamental to delineation of professions, 327
legal, traditional, 343
life, 345
literacy, required to compete with machines, 345–46
at navigating social contexts of professional work, expertise, 328
numeracy, 345
possession, expertise, 327
problem-solving, required to compete with machines, 345–46
professional, 326
psycho-social, 286
quantitative, needed, TAR, 340
sets lawyers need, 339–42, 343
teaching, law schools, 346
teamwork, 336
technical, 286, 341
technological, 340–42
that AI cannot replace, 345–46
***Skills for the 21st Century General Counsel* (Association of Corporate Counsel) survey,** 193
Skype, 132
small claims:
resolution facilitated by AI, 327
smart phones:
apps, 150–51
case law readily available, 323
commentary readily available, 323
legislation readily available, 323
ownership, access to justice, 284
Smartsettle, 142
social biases, 306
social concerns, 102–103
social construct, 278
social constructions, 185
social contexts of professional work, 328
social control:
facial recognition systems use, 265
social factors:
AI difficult to program to take account of, 286
social inequality, 249
social inequities, 247
social media, 110, 131, 132
social policies, regulation, 311, 312
social values, competing, 271
social world biases and limitation, 267
society:
fair dispute resolution, interest in, 157
lawyers and, trust between, 9
socioeconomic status, COMPAS proxies, 248
soft AI, 16
soft law, 313
software:
contract review, 175
outputs, reliance on, independence, 303
as product for sale, 283
verification, machine learning, 277
software-driven legal services, 6–7
solar energy remote monitoring, 207
solicitors, 44
barristers and, 52
clients' best interests, acting in, Australia, 298
duties to court and administration of justice, Australia, 304
work, 52

Solicitors Regulation Authority (SRA):
Code of Conduct for Solicitors, Registered European Lawyers and Registered Foreign Lawyers, 292, 298
fees, 299
independence, 302
administration of justice upholding, 304
rule of law upholding, 304
solidarity, AI ethics principles, 314
Solution Explorer, British Columbia Civil Resolution Tribunal, 144–45, 160–61
source code:
examination, machine learning, 277
South Korea:
foreign legal services markets, 57
Korean Bar Association, 68
legal service sector opening up, 68
local legal services markets, 57
Spain:
advocates (*abogados*), 44–45, 52
legal arms of multinational audit firms, 62
notaries, 44
solicitors (*procuradores*), 45, 52
SPC (Supreme People's Court), China, 147–48
specialisation:
involved, expertise, 327
benefits, 347
specialised knowledge and skill:
fundamental to delineation of professions, 327
specific populations, data from, 247
specifications, regulation, 315
speech functions, 16–17
speech recognition:
natural language processing, 35
speech to text, 17
spokespersons, mediation, 136
SRA, *see* **Solicitors Regulation Authority**
SSL (Strategic Subject List), 231
stabilising:
transactional lawyers' roles, 171
standard disclosure:
England and Wales, 106–107
standard discovery:
Federal Court of Australia, 106
standard forms, contract terms, 166
standardisation, drafting contracts, 166
standards, regulation, 315
state-of-the-art defence:
AI liabilities, 310
state organisations:
machine learning tools, developing in-house, 250
static factors:
dynamic factors and, failing to distinguish between, 250
statistical analysis:
of judgments, 101
predictive policing, 228
statistical evidence, accountability, 280
statistical fairness, 245
statistical literacy, TAR, 340
statistical modelling, 27, 76, 79–82, 102, 245
statistical patterns, 29
statistical reasoning, 18–19
statistical significance, 80, 239
statistical thinking, 38
statistics review and data partitioning, 86–87
statute liabilities for AI, 309
stemming, 26
storage, secured, data privacy, 206
STR (suspicious transaction reports), 209
Strategic Subject List (SSL), 231
strategic-thinkers, 327
stress tests, 200
strict liability, 309
strict scrutiny, 10
strong AI, 16
structuring:
decision-making, 244
law, 53
transactional lawyers' work, 169, 171
work, 48, 53
subject-matter expertise, 215
subscription fees, 348
substantive expertise, 328
subsymbolic reasoners, 32
supervised learning:
deep learning, 34–35
machine learning, 17, 29, 110–12
supervisory roles of AI, 303
supervisory technology, *see* **SupTech**
supplemental tools, 94
Support Vector Machine (SVM), 113, 119–20
supportive professional participants, 136
Supreme Court, US, *see* **United States**
Supreme People's Court (SPC), China, 147–48
SupTech (supervisory technology), 191
brokers' provision of Blue Sheet data files to SEC, 209
regulation, application of AI to, 208–10
regulator lawyers, 216

SEC Advanced Relational Trading Enforcement Metric Investigation System (ARTEMIS), 209
SEC Market Information Data Analytics System (MIDAS), 209
surveillance systems, 204
suspicious activity monitoring, 199
suspicious activity reports (SAR), 198, 199
suspicious transaction reports (STR), 209
Susskind, Richard, 4, 18, 24, 25, 40, 153, 179, 328, 342, 345
sustainability:
ethics principles, AI, 314
limitations of AI, 281–85
SVM (Support Vector Machine), 113, 119–20
Switzerland:
predictive policing, 230
symbolic reasoning systems, 19
see also knowledge: systems
symbolists, 30
syntactic analysis, 26, 35
syntax, 26
system lifecycle of AI, 263
system links:
courts, ODR, 138

tacit knowledge:
lacking, limitations of AI, 287
tailored information and direction provision, 161
TaKaDu, 207
TAR, *see* **Technology Assisted Review**
Target, 248
task-based billing, 347
task representation, discrete, 153–55
tax planning work, 53
tax work, 47, 53
TAXMAN system, 20
taxonomic approach:
transactional law investigations, 173
teaching, clinical, 341
team approach:
RegTech requirements, 215
teamwork, 336, 338
technical accountability, 278, 279
technical concerns, outcome prediction, 101–102
technical instructions, regulation, 315
technical interpretability, 274–75
technical limitations, expert systems, 23–25
technical proficiency, competence, 291
technical roles, transactional lawyers, 182–85
technical skills, 286, 341
technological skills, 340–42
technological tools, 220
technological unemployment, 3, 345
technologists:
collaboration with, 336
legal, 129–30
technology:
assisted review, 6, 9
audio-visual, 160
black box, 306
blockchain, 132
communications, OADR, 161
competence, 292–293, 296
confidentiality and, 301
contributing to reputational capital shift, 169
digital, overuse, 344
discretion, difficulty in replicating, 8
ethical obligations towards, 305
ethical rules requiring competence with, 341
facial recognition, 249, 252, 256
information, 131–32, 161
investment in, 282
judgement, difficulty in replicating, 8
justice provision assistance, 156
justice system, interfacing with, 306
know-how acquisition, 333
lawyers' embracing, 9
legal rules requiring competence with, 341
mechanistic assumption, 305
morally neutral assumption, 305
more, but will it be AI?, 160–62
new, questions before adopting, 339
ODR, use in, 139
output, understanding, 340
professional-ethical obligations towards, 305
promises, 8
quality unable to be tested, 303
regulatory, *see* RegTech
reliance on, 303
rule of law, 156
solving access to justice crisis, 40
transactional law use, 190
use:
challenging by lawyers if not consistent with rule of law, 156
to deliver leaner, more competitive services, 326
transactional law, 190
value free assumption, 305
voice surveillance, 205
Technology Assisted Review (TAR), 109
algorithms, 113, 127–28
better, adding, 127–28

Bolch Judicial Institute guidelines for, 112
classifier creation, 111
coding approval:
investigations, government agencies, USA, 125
competitive marketplace for, 127
computer codes, 125
computing power, 127
confidence intervals, 112
confidence levels, 112
confidentiality or transparency, 126
continuous active learning, 111–12, 125
control sets, 112
cut-off points, 115
discovery, 124, 126, 303
documents computer-coded reviewed, 125
easy intelligibility lacking, 129
EDRM role, 122
examples, 116–21
human review, 112
lawyer competence, 293
Logistic Regression algorithm, 113
margins of error, 112
model creation, 111
Naïve Bayesian Classifier algorithm, 113
natural language processing, 35
non-responsive documents, 125
overturns, 125
pre-trial information gathering, roles of lawyers, 125–26
precision, 114–15
privilege, limitations in relation to, 127
protocols to apply, 126
quantitative skills needed, 340
ramifications for lawyers of employing, 129–30
random sampling, 112
recall, 114–15
recall point estimates, 112
relevance, 115
richness, 112
role of lawyers, 125–26
seed sets, 110–12, 125
simple active learning, 111, 112, 125
simple passive learning, 111, 112, 125
statistical literacy needed, 340
successful use, 124
supervised machine learning, 112
Support Vector Machine (SVM) algorithm, 113, 119–20
training:
lawyers working closely with software providers, 288
sets, 110–12, 125
transparency or confidentiality, 126
uncertainty sampling, 111
validation, 112
technology industry, 268
telephone conferencing, 132, 138
templates:
contract review, 176
drafting, transactional law, 179
Tempus Energy, 207
terms of contracts, ***see*** **contracts**
Tessian, 206
test cases, 53
text:
analysis:
machine learning, 27
outcome prediction, 88–91
classification:
Naïve Bayesian Classifier algorithm use, 174
natural language processing, 35
generation, 17
messaging, ODR, 138
recorded speech conversion to, confidentiality, 302
to speech, 17
summarisation:
legal text, 25–26
natural language processing, 35
Text IQ, 207
textual data, 90
theoretical guarantees, 280
thinking:
computers incapable of, 285
critical, 343
deterministic, 38
humanly, tests, 14
rationally, tests, 14
third-party data providers:
transactional lawyers and, 183
third-party-facilitated ADR, 138
third-party suppliers:
claims against, AI liabilities, 309
Thomson Reuters Regulatory Intelligence, 201
threats and opportunities:
in use of AI for lawyers, 325–27
TIKD Service LLC engaged in UPL, 323
time of supply:
defects not existing at, AI liabilities, 310
time-saving products:
transactional lawyers' roles, 181
tipping, 204
tool, RegTech as only, 218
topic modelling, 90

tort:
AI liabilities, 308, 309
tournaments of influence, 58
trade-offs:
algorithm exposed, 271
inherent, 246
trade secrecy:
limitations of AI, 288
misappropriation, 22
trademarks, GDPR, 316
traders' messages, market misconduct, 205
trading, 202–204
traditional legal skills, 343
trainers:
algorithms, 268–69
training:
bias, algorithms, 270
companies, RegTech, 196
expertise, 327
identifying outcome prediction features after, 90–91
machine learning, 80, 175–77, 240, 301
procedures choice, algorithms operating in discriminatory manner, 168
sets, TAR, 110–12, 125
Technology Assisted Review, *see* Technology Assisted Review
transacting work, 47–48, 50, 51
transaction cost engineers, 167
transaction costs, 166, 173
transaction monitoring, RegTech, 196
transaction negotiations, 170–71
transaction patterns, 205
transaction reporting, 204
transactional contracts, 185
transactional engineers, 169
transactional law:
analysis, 172–75
application of AI to, 172–180
big data, 165
broad-scope analysis with machine learning, 174
contract commoditisation and lawyers, 166–72
contract review, 165
documents, 165, 179–80
drafting, 173, 178–80
form completion services, free, 188
in-house lawyer role, 165–66
investigations, 173, 174
LegalTech applications, 165
litigation, contrasted with, 165
machine learning, 165
management, 173, 175–78
negotiation and, 167
non-lawyer software providers affecting, 188
professional responsibility obligations, 190
reputation, 168
review, 175–78, 181
as supporting structures, law firms role in, 171
technology use, 190
transactional lawyers, 165–66
application of AI to transactional law, 172–80
category breadth, 169
clients:
business goals translation into terms agreed by parties, 170
professional indemnity insurance access, 189
quality control safeguards, 189
trust, 186–87, 189
corporate legal departments, 181
data, accessible, 183
documents, 183
ethical credibility, 187
experience, 182–83
external, 170
facilitating, 182
future developments, 189–90
review and management, 175–78
human errors reduction, 181
human interaction importance, 185–86
in-house, 170
insider knowledge, 170
large firm, value added by, 170
omitting use of, 188
prestigious firms, 182–83
private deals, knowledge of terms of, 170
reputation, 168, 187
reputational capital, 187, 169
roles of:
advising, 182, 186
augmenting tools, 181
business agreements, translating into legal agreements, 186
commodity legal documents production, 180–81
contract management products, 181
deal making, 165
drafting, 182, 186
due diligence products, 181
efficiency, 181–82
enhancing tools, 181
ethical, 185–87
front-end work, 165

large firms, 181
legal agreements, business agreements translating into, 186
negotiation, 182, 186, 187
no role at all, 187–89
presentational aspects, 186
relational, 185–87
repetitious tasks, 180
reputational, 185–87
risk management, 171
social constructions, 185
stabilising, 171
technical, 182–85
technology contributing to reputational capital shift, 169
time-saving products, 181
third-party data providers and, 183
as transaction cost engineers, 167
as transactional engineers, 169
transactional law, contract commoditisation and lawyers, 166–72
trust, 186–87, 189
value, 182–83
value added by, 170
value division, 167
work of:
acquisitions and mergers, 170
advising, 169
counselling, 169
deal making, 169, 170, 171
disclosure, 169, 171
drafting documents, 169, 171, 172
due diligence, 171–72
mergers and acquisitions, 170
negotiating, 169
planning, 169
predictability in law, maintaining level of, 171
structuring, 169, 171
transaction negotiations, 170–71
verifying skills, 171

transcripts, real-time, trials, 132

translation:
machine, 17, 35
work, 47

transnational legal practice, 57

transparency:
accountability related to, 278
AI ethics principles, 313, 314
algorithmic assessments, 250
confidentiality or, TAR, 126
difficulties, AI liabilities, 310
expert systems, 37
important for AI users, IEEE, 312
improvement approaches, 280
as key, 272–74
lack of *see* opacity
limitations of AI data and design, 272–76
machine learning, 250, 276
manner of processing personal data in relation to data subject, GDPR, 318
pre-trial risk assessment tool, 257
regulation, 312, 313, 320
risk assessments, 247, 257
validity, 272

Transparency of Autonomous Systems, IEEE, 315

transport regulation, 194

trials:
information technology impact, 132
online, 160
real-time transcripts, 132
telephone conferencing, 132
video conferencing, 132

tribunals:
online, 139
system links, ODR, 138

trust, 338
clients, *see* clients
confidentiality, 335
conflicts of interests restrictions, 335
ethics, AI principles, 314
human skills, 158
human value, 333, 335–36
lawyers, 8, 9
legal professional privilege, 335
relational, 336
society and lawyers, between, 9
transactional lawyers, *see* transactional lawyers

trusted advisers, 41

truth-speaking, 330

Turing Test, 13, 14

tweets, 132

tyranny avoidance, 332

uitelkaar.nl, 143

UK, *see* **United Kingdom**

unauthorised practice of law (UPL), 69, 189, 321–22, 323, 347

unbundling:
access to justice, assisting with, 154
AI use with concept of, 189–90
barristers and, 154
dispute resolution lawyers and, 153–55
ethics requirements and, 155

legal expertise and, 155
legal services, 336
professional requirements and, 155
roles of lawyers after online dispute resolution, 153–55
uncertainty:
evaluation, humans' heuristics use, 96
in-house lawyers' response to, 214
sampling, TAR, 111
unconscionability, 308
under-policing, 241
underlying purposes and values, 23
underserved latent legal market, ODR, 163
understanding, 8, 335
undervaluing of obligations, 331
unexpected information, contract review, 177
unfair contractual terms, 308, 309
Uniform Solicitors Rules, Australia, 302–303
United Kingdom:
facial recognition technology, 256
Financial Conduct Authority, *see* Financial Conduct Authority
Hampel Committee on Corporate Governance, 217
Information Commissioner's Office (ICO), 312
Institute of Electrical and Electronics Engineers, *see* Institute of Electrical and Electronics Engineers
Money Laundering Regulations 2017, 197
number of lawyers, 54, 56
organisational forms of lawyers, 54
Prudential Regulation Authority, *see* Prudential Regulation Authority
small partnerships, 56
see also England and Wales; Scotland
United States:
A2J Author, 284
alternative business structures not permitted, 63
Am Law 100, 59
American Bar Association, *see* American Bar Association
attorneys, 52
Big Law, 59
California, *see* California
clients, duties to, 305
corporate legal service, flattening of demand for, 59
Correctional Offender Management Profiling for Alternative Sanctions, *see* COMPAS
courts, duties to, 304
documents production, 109
Dodd-Frank Act, 191, 200, 203, 203, 205, 213
Federal Reserve Comprehensive Capital Analysis and Review (CCAR), 200, 201
Federal Rules of Evidence, 127
Federal Rules of Procedure (FRCP), 107
Florida:
TIKD Service LLC engaged in UPL, 323
government agencies:
certification by, suggestion, 315–16
Technology Assisted Review coding approval, investigations, 125
Idaho:
pre-trial risk assessment tools, 257
in-house counsel, 60
incorporated legal practices, 323
large firm groups, 58–60
lawyers, 39
fee sharing with non-lawyers, 61
movement between firms, 59
number of, 54, 56
receptiveness to innovation, 342–43
legal documents preparation, 323
legal infrastructure, 65
multi-disciplinary partnerships (MDP), 63, 323
Office of Foreign Assets Control (OFAC), 198
organisational forms of lawyers, 54
Patriot Act, 197
pre-trial information gathering, 107
privilege, 127
prohibition of unreasonable search and seizure, 251
race, socioeconomic status correlated with, 248
regulatory investigations, 109
representative associations, 65
risk-scoring tools, 257
Securities and Exchange Commission (SEC), 76
Advanced Relational Trading Enforcement Metric Investigation System (ARTEMIS), 209
Division of Trading and Markets, 209
EDGAR, public database, 183–84
Market Abuse Unit Analysis and Detection Center, 191–92
under Investment Advisers Act of 1940, best execution, trading, 203
securities fraud class actions prediction model, 83
small partnerships, 56

socioeconomic status correlated with race, 248
solo legal practice, 55
Supreme Court:
Database, 81
decision-making, 82–83
Forecasting Project, 81–82
on market manipulation, 204
trial attorneys, 52
unauthorised practice of law (UPL), 69, 321, 322, 323
university law degrees, 341
unmet legal needs, 307
unreasonable search and seizure, 251
unstructured communication, 190
unstructured data, 205
unsuccessful settlement negotiations, 97
unsupervised learning:
by clustering, market misconduct, 205
deep learning, 34–35
machine learning, 17, 29, 113–14
UPL, *see* **unauthorised practice of law**
USA, *see* **United States**
user-friendly advice provided, 337–338
utilisation of knowledge, 24–25

Valcri, 231
validation, TAR, 112
validity:
explainability, 272
interpretability, 272
legibility, 272
predictive, 242, 246
transparency, 272
value:
ethics, 329–33, 36
expertise, 327–29
lawyers, 8–9
transactional lawyers, 170, 182–83
value-based billing, 348
value choices:
criminal justice, 246
making, expert lawyering, 329
value free assumptions, technology, 305
values:
legal, 343
reasoning with, 23
transactional lawyers' reputation, 168
underlying, 23
variables, limited set of:
machine learning, 276
variety, machine learning data, 265
Vehicle Purchase Protection (VPP), eBay, 141
velocity:
machine learning data, 265
veracity:
machine learning data, 265
verification:
machine learning, methods built in, 277
rather than trust, transactional lawyers, 189
skills, transactional lawyers' work, 171
very large law firms, 57–58
video communications, banking, 201
video conferencing, 132, 138, 160
virtual firms, 69
virtual hearings, online courts, 132
VirtualCourthouse.com, 142
virtue-signalling, 313
voice biometrics, 199
voice surveillance technology, 205
volume, machine learning data, 265
voluntary acts:
litigation initiation as, 156
voluntary dispute resolution, 137–38
VPP (Vehicle Purchase Protection), eBay, 141

wash trading, 204
watchlists, anti-money laundering, 198
water treatment analytics, 207
Waymark Tech, 208
weak Artificial Intelligence, 16
WeChat, 205
WEF, *see* **World Economic Forum**
WhatsApp, 132, 205
whistleblower policies:
designing, role of lawyers in RegTech, 212
white guy problem, 267, 281
'whole-market' order data, 205
Wi-Fi confidentiality, 301
wills work, 47
wireless technologies, confidentiality, 301
wisdom:
human skills, 158
without-prejudice-privilege, 126
women:
regulation of lawyers, 66
under-represented in technology industry, 268
words:
sense disambiguation, natural language processing, 35
as surrogates for facts, outcome prediction, 89
work of lawyers, 46–47
acquisitions and mergers, 47
advising, 48–50, 51

advocacy, 51
advocates, 52
areas of law, 45
automation impact, 40
barristers, 52
class actions, 53
clients, 45, 49, 51
collaborative with problem solving, 49
communication, 51
conceptualising, 48
context, 45
contracts, 47
conveyancing, 47, 48
'corporate hemisphere', 45
corporate reorganisation, 53
deals, facilitating, 47
dispute resolution, 50, 51
divorce or separation matters, 47
drafting, 48
empathy, 51
enterprise formation and operations, 47
evaluative with problem solving, 49
executing, 48
facilitating deals, 47
facilitative with problem solving, 49
fact investigation, 53
financing, 47
gas and oil, 47
hard data, 42
in-court, 52
individuals, work done for, 47
interpersonal interactions, negotiating, 50–51
lawyer–client relationships, 41
legal analysis and strategy, 53
legal service providers, 41
legal writing, 53
legislative change, assisting clients' efforts, 53
licences, 47
mergers and acquisitions, 47
negotiating, 48, 50–51
non-legal skills, 51
non-verbal communication, 51
oil and gas, 47
oral advocacy, 51
ordering or structuring of law, 53
organisational clients, 45
'personal-plight hemisphere', 45
policy goals, 53
policy implementation, legislative or public service lawyers' activities, 53
probate, 47
problem solving, 49
procuring licences, 47
public interest litigation, 53
real estate transactions, 47
regulatory compliance, 53
representing, 50, 51–53
roles, *see* roles of lawyers
securities, 47
separation or divorce matters, 47
solicitors, 52
structuring, 48, 53
tax, 47
  planning, 53
test cases, 53
transacting, 47–48, 50, 51
transactional lawyers, *see* transactional lawyers
translation, 47
trusted advisers, 41
'two hemispheres' of legal work, 45
varies, 42
vendor level, 41
wills, 47
work done for individuals, 47

work with AI:
  skill sets lawyers need, 339–42

workflow tools:
  business logic, LegalTech providers, 321

World Economic Forum (WEF):
  on compliance, 204–205
  deskilling summary, 344
  trading, 202

WORM (Write Once Read Many), 203

XAI (Explainable AI), 274–75
Xakia, 321

zero-knowledge proofs:
  machine learning, 277
Zhejiang, China, 147–48, 161
Zoom, 132